I0529896

It's Me, The Early Years:
Letters To My Daughter

The extraordinary life of an ordinary individual

By
Walter P. Benesch

Copyright © 2025 by Walter P. Benesch

All rights reserved. No part of this publication may be reproduced, distributed, or transmitted in any form or by any means, including photocopying, recording, or other electronic or mechanical methods, without the prior written permission of the author, except in the case of brief quotations embodied in critical reviews and certain other noncommercial uses permitted by copyright law.

978-1-965552-32-2 (Paperback)

BOOKWRIGHTS
HOUSE

admin@bookwrightshouse.com
☎ (213) 286 6700

Contents

Preface v

Introduction vii

Chapter 1   Brooklyn Beginnings 1

Chapter 2   Out of New York—Out of This World 16

Chapter 3   Normal Routine for a Youngster? 25

Chapter 4   Old Memories, Real Old Memories! 39

Chapter 5   Flora, Fauna and Masonry 46

Chapter 6   The Flood and Changes 56

Chapter 7   More About Mom, Her Friends, and Me 66

Chapter 8   The Last Straw and Race to Safety 76

Chapter 9   Floridian Parental Visits and Challenges 92

Chapter 10   The Trio Plus and Remarkable Dogs 122

Chapter 11   Connecticut Racism 135

Chapter 12   Off to the Bay State 150

Chapter 13   Would You Believe Deutschland Bound? 190

Chapter 14   Home Again, Home Again, Jiggity Jig 219

Chapter 15   Back to The Hill 240

Chapter 16   High School, More Protests and the Admiral 254

Chapter 17   College(s)?!? 280

Chapter 18   Franconia and An Unknown Future 312

Photos 333

Acknowledgements 345

Preface

AFTER A FEW MONTHS in college my freshman daughter was settling down to academic life. During a phone call I asked if she would be interested in a series of letters about my life. Having heard a variety of stories, some quite remarkable, many totally out of the norm, she thought it would be fun to read. She expressed a desire to learn more about her Dad. Thus began a series of letters, originally to be sent weekly, then monthly, and ultimately becoming irregular. The letters sent through her undergraduate years at Washington University St. Louis and beyond are presented here in book form. They have been edited for clarification and with elaboration on specific details.

As is typical of any child relating to her parent, she did request that anything of a sexual nature not be included. Sexuality is a key to the growth of any young boy, but out of respect for my daughter, most of the sexually explicit experiences were omitted in the letters. There are a few exceptions.

After my daughter graduated from college, I wrote and sent the letters only sporadically, but they continue for years. My involvement in South Bronx's Fort Apache, adventures working in Washington, DC for the DC government and the federal government at the Pentagon, and my retirement after years in the Department of Homeland Security have yet to be written, likely that will happen in book form.

Presented here are my recollections from my first memories to the end of my college years. Are they all completely accurate? Perhaps not, but I am confident that most are. Many recollections were from when I was a small child. Then again, what history is perfectly accurate? While alive my mother would tell stories from many of these early years, helping me recall many of the incidents related here.

I have attempted to avoid self-promotion. It's important to realize this volume is an individual's point of view and time tends to alter memories. I do have one advantage in the recollection of memories: being trained in a variety of meditation techniques from an early age. It is safe to say my childhood recollections are far more accurate than most as a result of this training.

Interspersed throughout the book are some of my mother's recollections she related to me from an early age. There are some which challenge history, some that are horrific, and a lot that are amusing. They all convey a strong feminist position concerning issues she faced in her life. Many of these same issues continue today.

The WWII memories have been with me from an early age and remain today. The UFO memories were often discussed with my mother before her death, when she was living with the family in an "in-law" apartment. These were subjects of many conversations. They are written here as a joint recollection. Accept them or not. Hopefully they will keep you entertained.

Introduction

It was December 1944. Before I joined the Army. Belgium was only something shown on a map of Europe in school. Now here we were in a forested area called the Ardennes. Most of the troops were looking forward to Christmas. The Armed Forces Radio was constantly playing Christmas music, at least when we were near enough to a radio to hear the tunes. Most of us were thinking the Germans were in retreat. The war would be won in a short time. How wrong we were.

It was cold and cloudy most of the time. Snow had fallen, making marching slippery and difficult. Unexpectedly, the Germans broke through our lines. Chaos ensued. Lines shifted. One did not know where the Germans were and where Allied forces still held.

Overnight, some of the panzers pushed through on a ridge near our lines and the horrors of war became apparent once again. Our platoon suffered a severe number of casualties. My sergeant was hit in the head and didn't last through to morning. What was left of our platoon was trying to hold what was thought to be a good defensive position. But there was one problem. The ridge nearby. What we didn't realize at first was the Germans had placed a machine-gun on top of the ridge overnight to prevent any counter attack.

The officers behind our lines decided that was where a counter attack should take place. Word was passed down the lines that an attack would take place in the early morning. The first attempt failed. Our lieutenant was killed. Soon it was evident I was the highest ranking member of the platoon. A corporal! Shit! I didn't want to be in charge. But there was no choice.

Word was sent asking for mortar support if we were to take the machine-gun nest. The charge was set for 9 a.m. We watched the seconds tick by. Then, at the precise time our whole platoon charged up the hill. The Germans saw us coming and opened fire. Several of my buddies were immediately cut down. Torn to shreds. Faces blown apart by the bullets raining down on us. Then I heard a round of mortar shells coming. My first thought was that if they hit near the machine-gun we might have a chance. The first shell hit to my left and slightly behind me. Running through my mind:

"Oh no, they are falling short. They are killing their own men."

Then I felt a sudden pain in my left buttocks and everything went black.

Chapter 1

Brooklyn Beginnings

Hi T:

I have been sending you letters about what is happening at home. DULL! So, it is time to start on my history, beginning from early youth. Who knows, by the time you finish graduate school we may have covered my complete autobiography, one letter at a time. So much has happened during my lifetime, I may not reach my senior year in high school by the time you reach your senior year in college. But we must start with your grandmother.

I was born in Lenox Hill Hospital in New York City. Yes, the hospital on Park Avenue. A true New Yorker! Though known for its sports celebrities and wealthy 5th Avenue patients, it did accept the lower classes on occasion. In the case of our family, we were the latter. My parents were lower middle class. But the circumstances surrounding my birth justified your grandma's admittance, which must be disclosed before the focus shifts to your father.

Your grandma had lost my brother the year before. He lived for two days. Being premature he was too small to survive in 1947. His birth certificate simply says "Baby B as he was not expected to live. Weighing less than three pounds at birth, he struggled for a while. Then he lost weight. Too weak and small to survive in those times. Funny, with today's medicine and techniques he probably would have lived. At the time it was a great loss to your grandparents. It was devastating to your grandmother. Your grandfather was hit by the loss of a son which in his machismo world proved a man's worth. Both were determined to try to have another child. But you must learn of your grandmother's background first.

When your grandmother became pregnant with me she knew she needed help. She went to a well-known specialist to receive the best care. She believed carrying a fetus for a full nine months was unlikely for her. Her first two husbands did not want children; her first husband forced her to have multiple illegal abortions whenever she became pregnant—this was before she was aware of any kind of birth control—and her second husband didn't want children either, although by that time she was using a diaphragm.

Sarsfield W., husband number one, was a large man over six feet tall. Your grandmother was She was 16 at the time of their marriage (the reason for this marriage will be made clear later). At 5'2", with red hair and sexy as anything, you could understand Sarsfield had the hots for your grandmother. After all, he was in his mid-50s and already had three sons, all fully grown and older than his new wife. He refused to have more children. But he enjoyed fucking the hell out of her and she was apparently very fertile. So, she ended up knocked up several times a year. Each time, with no thoughts about her health or feelings, Sarsfield would drag your grandma off to an illegal abortion clinic. They were usually down a back alley, or in a country doctor's back office. There, Grandma received less than quality care at exceptionally high prices. She told me she once bled for over a week and almost died.

Sarsfield was acting as what today would be considered a secretary. His major income was from his creation of a variation of shorthand. It was not the standard later adopted by most industry but one which a few companies used likely those who were familiar with Sarsfield's variation. Few people know what shorthand is in this age of computers. Shorthand was an abbreviated writing method which used symbols to denote groups of letters. It was used by secretaries who were take dictation from their bosses. There were several types of shorthand. The advantage was one could use it as a speedy way to capture what was being dictated. Pitman shorthand was the most popular and the one your grandmother used when she started out as a secretary. This was before the use of recording devices.

Your grandmother told me she made Sarsfield rich, but in a most unorthodox way. She was 17 when this occurred. Sarsfield's brother had struck it rich by being one of the very early wildcat oil drillers in Texas. Sarsfield was jealous and wanted some of the wealth. One evening in a speakeasy (Prohibition was still in place), Sarsfield, Grandma and his brother were part of a larger crowd having a party. Everyone was drunk. An idea popped into Sarsfield's head. He knew his bother wanted to screw your grandmother. He whispered into her ear: "If you let my brother fuck you we can both be richer for it." She was a little shocked but looked at him with a "Really?" expression. He simply nodded. Being neither religious nor coming from a "moral" family, if that's what her husband wanted it must be OK.

At the time she was a very toothsome young woman, wearing a typical 1920s flapper dress, which didn't even cover her knees. She started to make eyes at the brother. Then excused herself to go to the bathroom, which was on the opposite side of the establishment. She walked in a most inviting way past the brother. He let her get ahead a few yards, then followed. Just as she was finished in the bathroom, there was the brother. He pushed her down over the sink and sunk in cock deep within her. It was evident this was something he had long desired. She said after the fourth or fifth shove, he came. It was over in less than a minute. Upon returning to the table, Sarsfield asked:

"Did he fuck you?"

She nodded. Sarsfield smiled and didn't say another word.

The object of letting his brother sleep with your grandmother was to propitiate a favor, if not his machinations, by exposing what had taken place, which would have created an imbroglio in the family, shaming his brother. A few days later, Sarsfield obtained the rights to several oil fields that were owned by his brother. Grandma left Sarsfield shortly thereafter. Under Texas law back then, since she divorced him and not the other way around, she received nothing.

After she left him, and while contemplating moving to California, she called Sarsfield. He had taken most of his earnings from the oil fields and had invested them in stocks. This was the summer of 1929. She had begun to read the financial pages to get a better understanding of the stock market and particularly the oil industry. She didn't like what she felt was over-speculation. She called up Sarsfield to warn him about the possibility of a stock market pull-back. That was her last conversation with him until after the Crash.

By September she was in California tying to get into the movie business. But not having much luck, she got a job in a candy store where they made all the candy on site. She once showed me the receipt book, which has since been lost. Then the stock market crash occurred. She got a letter from her sister after the crash. Sarsfield had lost almost everything and having been heavily in margin, had to sell many of the oil rights. He was broke!

While in Hollywood she tried to attract individuals who were in the movies. The 'Talkies' were really taking off by 1930. One of the people emerging as a possible star was a tall, thin actor by the name of John Carradine, who had a magnificent baritone voice. She had several dates with John and seemed to be getting along with him. One night he asked if she would like to go to a Hollywood party. She didn't know it was one of those parties where nice girls wouldn't be get caught dead attending.

Off they went. When they arrived there were many famous and soon-to-be-famous actors and actresses, although she only mentioned Barbara Stanwyck by name. There were other women there who were willing to do anything to get into the business. After a few drinks, the clothes started coming off. Barbara teamed up with one of the gentlemen and was enjoying a passionate session on one of the sofas. John, the very example of a sophist, told her this was how a girl gets into the movies. Soon your grandmother was nude, as was John. He gently pulled her down on top of him and had her mount him, cowgirl style. She looked over at an actress who was doing the same with a famous director. Soon another actor got on top of them both and started to fuck this future star in the ass. She didn't seem to mind a bit. Another man came up to them with a huge erection. She simply took it in her mouth and sucked him dry. This woman had a reputation which indicated her enjoyment of triple penetration. Though never naming this actress, in the late 1950's Loretta Young had her TV show. Mom would always snicker when she came on the screen. Once she said:

"Remember the party I told you about?"

I nodded. She then nodded towards the TV. While watching all that was going on, still astride John, his distinct voice boomed: "C wants to be a star. Let's show her how."

The next thing she knew some man was penetrating her anally causing intense pain. Then after he came, another took his place. John came, rolling her off, only to be replaced by another. She estimated as many as twenty men raped her that night. She felt humiliated. Once home she sat crying in the shower for an hour. She gave up the idea of bing a star. She even considered becoming a nun to escape what had happened. She was just thankful having the candy store job, which paid $15 a week. Enough to bring her younger sister and later younger brother to join her in Hollywood.

During the height of the Depression, one day a man who looked like he was in his late 30s or early 40s came into the candy store. Mom had a strange feeling about him. He gazed malignantly around the shop, not at the display but to see if anyone was in sight. She felt a malevolent aura was surrounding him Mom turned to him and said:

"You know, if you try to rob me you will be running for the rest of you life. You and your family will never have peace."

He started to cry. His family had not had a decent meal for a week. He couldn't find work and was desperate. Mom opened the cash register and gave him $15.

"You repay me when you get a job. Now go get something for your family to eat."

He thanked her over and over before leaving the store. She never really expected to see him again, but about three weeks later he came back to the store.

"Thank you, you saved by life. I found a job a few days after you helped me. Here is the $15 you gave me. I'll never forget what you did for me."

It was about this time she met a handsome intelligent man who soon introduced her to a totally different life style. They were soon married. Grandma's second husband, Bernard M., allowed her to use a diaphragm, which eliminated the need for abortions. It allowed some time for her body to heal from all the bad experiences in her first marriage. But, like Sarsfield, Bernard had neither the time nor the money for a child. She never told me if she had ever become pregnant by Bernard. She may have. But it was the horrid experiences with hubby number one, that she talked about the most.

While still married to Bernard, Grandma had worked for Alice A. Bailey, the founder of the Arcane School, which was then in New York. As a matter of fact, that is what brought your grandma to New York. Bernard had worked closely with Alice for years out on the West Coast—that is where he met Grandma. After her experience with actors, the idea of acting was null and void. She was also looking for something more than a casual relationship. A relationship that provided more intellectually stimulation, a new view of spirituality, and a non-violent relationship. Besides Bernard was very good looking and filled all her requirements. They married shortly after meeting.

Alice was tired of the West Coast and wanted to move East. She was also told to do so by an individual called "DK". DK dictated the books to Alice, which were published under her name. Alice was convinced moving to New York was the right thing to do. She felt the vibrations generated by the Arcane School and her prized students would be a positive factor in determining the direction of the war. After WWII, the proximity of the school to the UN was thought, though not proven, to have helped generate a positive spiritual force.

Grandma had moved to Los Angles during the Depression. She divorced Sarsfield on the grounds of physical cruelty. Whenever he got drunk, he would hit her for the slightest reasons. Finally one evening when he was hitting her, she got up the courage, and likely a lot of chi energy, picked up her abusive husband and threw him across the room. Amazing considering the size differential. The next day she moved out.

Needing to get away from Texas and Sarsfiled she moved to LA. She was fortunate in having a job in a candy store throughout the hard times. There will be additional flashbacks to her story in these letters. By the mid 1930s she was looking for a spiritual school. The Arcane School fit perfectly. She moved quickly through the meditation training and met Bernard. When Alice wanted to move to NYC, Bernard and Grandma came along. Grandma became one of Alice's secretaries and worked closely with her for years.

Shortly after WWII started Mom felt she needed a change. She also wanted to become a mother and Bernard was not going to let that happen. She divorced Bernard and in 1944 joined the Women's Army Corps, the WACs. It was after the War she met my father.

Love,
Papa

Hey T:

Here is a little background on my Dad. Your grandfather had always hated his brother Milton, blaming him for preventing him from getting an education. Milton had contracted polio when he was young, which required expensive medical care and so Walter was forced to drop out of school after the 8th grade to get a job to support the family. The hatred built up over the years. In Walter's view, it would have been better if the "weakling" had died and left the family alone.

Walter was considered by those around him as very intelligent. Being the oldest, he was therefore looked upon by the family as the one who should succeed. That never happened. The failure to get a good education left him very bitter. He ended up as a salesman in various department stores in NYC. I don't know which ones. He specialized in carpets. He was a good salesman, at least by his own telling.

One evening, Milton brought his date home—your grandmother. Walter made every effort to endear himself to her. After a few meetings they started secretly dating. Eventually he succeeded in convincing Grandma to leave Milton and marry him. But the marriage was rocky from the beginning.

It wasn't until I sat down to write this letter that I considered they were married around 1947. Baby B was born that same year. Theirs may have been a shotgun wedding. But that is pure speculation on my part since the marriage date has been lost over time. When your grandmother became pregnant with me by your grandfather, she sought out the best prenatal care possible; she knew she needed help and believed carrying a fetus for a full nine months was unlikely for her. She got lucky. There was one who practiced out of Lenox Hill who was considered one of the most outstanding physicians in New York City. She informed the doctor of her history, the abortions, the loss of her first child a year before. It was evident special care would have to be taken if this pregnancy was to produce a healthy newborn.

With close monitoring from an excellent physician and limitations on activity, Grandma gave birth to a preemie—ME. I was born two months premature and weighed just over three pounds. Then, I dropped a few ounces under that. At just over two pounds, many of the doctors didn't have an optimistic prognosis. Small, weak and not allowed to feed at my mother's breast, I could have been another Baby B. But the results are evident, as this letter shows. I was on what was equal to life support in an incubator for some time before I was allowed to go home. When I did go home, according to Mom, I was a very frail, small infant.

What was interesting was that my aunt was having a girl in the same hospital at the same time. She was married to my Dad's brother, Milton. I think the girl was born the week before me, at the end of August. There remains a small but constant regret for not keeping in touch with her. I did have some communications with her younger sister, Kim, but when I replied to her last emails she never responded.

My father always wanted a boy. Maybe it was validation of his manhood. Maybe it was the tradition of carrying on the family name. Maybe it was a reflection of the times. A boy was more prized than a girl. We will never know his thoughts. However, this was a rare time when he was truly happy. His first wife had died—cause unknown—but she became ill and died in her late 30s, I guess, based upon photos seen of her. She was beautiful, but even in the photos, looked frail. For some reason she was never able to have any children. I feel Dad always loved her and not Mom.

Theirs was a vengeful marriage, not one of love. Walter A. married your grandma after she had been casually dating his brother. It appeared his brother Milton and Grandma were getting quite close. Walter A. made every effort to steal Grandma away. He was 5'11" with dark black hair and brown eyes. Physically he was strong, having been a former semi-pro wrestler and life guard on Jones Beach in New York. He also had a very smooth delivery line.

There were many questions surrounding my birth. Would I develop normally? Was my brain damaged by the premature birth? Could I ever possibly achieve anything, physically or academically? These were the questions that faced all parents of preemies back then. Would the unknown effects of being born premature contribute to compromised development? There was little doubt this little surviver was not the norm. Just how far from the norm would be evidenced over the years. But then, I was not born to a "normal" mother. Thank the gods for that!

When I was about six months old, Mom took me to see Alice. She missed being at the school. Even during the war she would drop by in her WAC (Women's Army Corp) uniform while on leave from the Army to join the meditations and more importantly to participate in the new Masonic group, which had been formed by Alice at the Arcane School, called Ancient Universal Mysteries (AUM). In 1949, according to Mom, Alice was very pleased to meet the newborn who had taken one of her favorite secretaries away. I was told Alice blessed me and hugged Mom good-bye. That was the last time the two saw each other as Alice died a few months later.

Love,
Papa

Hi T:

Early youth: maybe I should call it "Brooklyn Youth 1".

My first home was at 90 Lafayette Avenue, Brooklyn. I remember little of the apartment, much less of the building. There were steps outside leading to the foyer, I think there was an elevator to the second and third floors—if not an elevator it would have been a stairwell. What I do remember is a door which separated the floors. When we got off the elevator/stairwell, we would turn left.

Our apartment was the first door on the right. The apartment front door was large, at least to a small child, dark in color, with a peephole. The door opened to the dining/living room. The small galley-type kitchen was to the right as you entered. Two bedrooms were to the left, past the living room, down a little hall which led to the only bathroom. A corner of the living room had my playpen and some toys. It was close to the window—the single source of natural light.

One of the first memories was of the Christmas tree It was placed by the radio near the playpen. By the time of my second birthday, I listened to radio programs and music every day. Both your grandparents loved classical music, one common interest they shared. We were fortunate living in New York City as there were a number of classical radio stations in the late 1940s and right on through the time I returned to live in NYC as an adult after college. What was wonderful about the radio then is that it was not limited to music. There were great radio dramas, variety and comedy shows. Broadcasts would cause families to stop everything, cluster around and just stare at the radio speakers, mentally envisioning all that was happening over the airwaves.

Next door to us was another couple. They became very critical in my early development. They were refereed to as Aunt Margaret and Uncle Bill, though there was no biological connection between the families. Uncle Bill was very similar to my father in size and shape. He was stocky but not fat, tall but then at two years of age, everyone seems tall! Uncle Bill was likely around the same height as Dad, maybe an inch shorter. He had dark brown hair. The major difference was his jolly personality. Rarely did he get angry or raise his voice, while at my home, raised voices and arguments were part of the evening's entertainment. The experience for a young child being surrounded by verbal fighting was a horror story. But this was live and not over the radio.

This was the time of the House Un-American Activities Committee. Though created in the 1930s, the Committee really gained traction in the late 1940s and into the 1950s. Dad, being very conservative and poorly educated, supported the work of the Committee. Mom, having been exposed to California and considerably more educated than he, was left-leaning. It was even possible she may have met some of the actors and writers being called before the Committee while she was in LA. You can imagine the arguments. The fights only got worse as the McCarthy hearings evolved into a side show in the House in the 1950s.

At Uncle Bill's home, things were quiet and peaceful No shouting. No arguments. Just a tranquil setting. This may have been due to Margaret, Bill's wife. She was tall and thin. She appeared to be of Eastern European background, indicated by her dark hair and the clothes she wore. She was definitely not into fashion! Not attractive, but not unattractive. Her personality was such that she would never contradict her spouse. Arguments of any kind would have been unthinkable.

Margaret was my babysitter. She would take care of me during the day while Mom was at work. I remember her pushing my stroller before I could walk. Later she would walk with me to the local stores for food. When I was over two and could barely walk, she would take my hand and help. It was slow going. She had patience and never rushed me, except for this one time.

It is stuck in my memory for reasons which may come out later. We were crossing a dead-end street. At the street's end was a stone wall. The buildings on either side were apartment buildings, most without windows facing the alley. A fence on top of the stone wall divided the park on the other side from the pavement. I saw a man with a scared look on his face staring at a man in a coat standing between him and us. The man in the dark coat had his back to us. He didn't know we were there. Margaret took a quick look, grabbed my hand and pulled me FAST across the street and down the block. Never before had she reacted this way. The rapid pulling may have been the reason this incident remained in my memory.

As we crossed the intersection around the side of the next building, I heard a sharp noise. I didn't pay any attention. Margaret continued to the local grocery store as if nothing had happened. But there was a strange look on her face. She was shaking. As we shopped in the store the fear subsided in her. When we left the store, I remember Margaret was carrying a shopping bag. As we approached the street she had so swiftly pulled me across earlier, I saw police cars all around and there, at the end of the street, was a sheet with a hump underneath. Later I understood that I had (or had almost) witnessed a "hit" by one of the crime families of NYC. The hump under the sheet was the corpse of the man with the frightened expression. That was my first experience of death. It was not to be my last, and most would occur from unnatural causes.

My father would occasionally take me to the park. This did not happen often but it was wonderful in a child's mind to have his father take him out. I would play in the sandbox or on the merry-go-round. There is a picture that stands out in my mind to this day. It was most likely remembered from a photograph taken by my mother. My father is seen from behind in his heavy gray winter overcoat. He has a scarf on, too and is looking at me in front of him. We are both smiling. In the background is a children's merry-go-round. Not the electric kind, with animals and music, this was one you would find in a child's section of a playground where someone would grab on the handles and spin it around.

What is most interesting in the photo is the grey coat, which later provided me years of warmth after his death. I used it on winter days until it fell apart. The photo must have been taken in late autumn or early winter. As for me, I am wearing a winter jacket with mittens attached to each other by a long string going from one arm of my winter coat to the other—a common solution back then so mittens would not get lost. The memory of Dad being in the park with me is one of the few times I pictured a smile on my father's face. I remember an oval picture of him (later confirmed it was actually his brother) that was once in the basement. If you saw this picture it resembles what your grandfather looked like when he was young.

Another fond early memory was when my father took me to a Brooklyn Dodgers baseball game at Ebbetts Field. I know Jackie Robinson must have been playing because I heard the "N word" for the first time. At least it was not 1947, when it was shouted loudly. This was likely 1951, when the word was no longer shouted but quietly spoken among some.

I can't visualize the outside of the stadium, it was just another strange building in Brooklyn. I do remember after we went through the gates, there was a long climb up to our seats and that while seated, there seemed a rush of excitement. I didn't really know why. Perhaps because I had heard games on the radio with no understanding of what was happening and now I was witnessing a game in person. Remember, I was very small. As much as my father was trying to explain baseball to me, I only remember the players hitting the ball up in the air to the outfield. I thought each hit was a home-run—whatever that was! I remembered how green the grass was. Little attention was paid to the pitcher, or the men standing around the infield. The focus of everyone's attention were the men with the bats in their hands swinging at the little balls. The image of the men running all over the place with no clear reason why was funny to a child's mind. The game seemed chaotic. All the players looked small, which might tell you how high up in the stands we were sitting. You could compare our seats with the Weasley family seat in the *Harry Potter and the Goblet of Fire* film. This was my first baseball memory. To this day I can claim that I saw Jackie Robinson play, though I do not remember him individually.

Something must have sunk in at the game. I took a deeper interest in listening to the radio broadcasts of other games—these were the great baseball years in New York. My father was a huge Giants fan and my mother loved underdogs, the Dodgers. Robinson may have added to that attraction for her. As for me, never fully understanding why, I became a Yankee fan, maybe a prognostication of times to come. In the distant future the Yankees and Yankee Stadium would play another important, if only brief, part in my professional life as a social worker.

Love,
Papa

It's Me:

The phrase "It's Me" arose out of the apartment years. When Dad and Uncle Bill came home, I would immediately run down the hall to the Uncle Bill's apartment and knock on the door. Of course, I was too short for anyone to see me through the spy hole in the door, so Aunt Margaret would call out:

"Who's there?"

My response was always: "It's me!"

She would then let me in and Uncle Bill would join me once he had finished changing from work clothes.

I loved going down there because they had a TV. We did not. That is where I watched all those early shows. Uncle Bill would often hold me in his lap as we watched. My favorite was *The Andy Divine Show*. Andy was the fat shotgun rider in John Wayne's first popular movie, *Stage Coach*. More on Andy later. *The Howdy Doody* show was another love. Howdy was a marionette with Buffalo Bob Smith as host. Bob Keeshan was Clarabell the Clown until 1953 when he became another childhood TV show host as Captain Kangaroo. The other character I was most interested in was Princess Summerfall Winterspring, an American Indian character that fascinated me. It was the first positively portrayed American Indian character seen on TV, which was very positive for those times. In the movies and many of the Westerns on TV, American Indians were still portrayed negatively, and Princess Summerfall Winterspring was a counter to the stereotype.

As often as I could get away with it, I would ask to stay for dinner so I could avoid the problems at home. Then I'd stay and watch *Howdy Doody*. Staying at Uncle Bill's would cause more fights at home between Dad and Mom, which in turn made me want to stay away more (avoidance!). It was a true catch 22. Dad ended up hating TV and hating Mom for giving me permission to stay. As for me, I just wanted to escape the bellicose exchanges.

When home, Dad would sit and listen to the radio programs on the air at that time. Occasionally I would sit in his lap in the big chair. Never as at ease as with Uncle Bill, yet he was my father when home, and he did his best to be a good father.

What was fun about the radio were the pictures it created in our minds; TV and movies could not compete with the images we envisioned from those radio programs—the heroes and villains could be pictured in any way you could imagine them. Dramatic scenes would be enhanced with active imaginations even beyond what the movies could provide at that time. Until computer generated images and action nothing could compare to the radio shows. Still, TV was fun.

If you ever have a chance to download old radio shows, do so. By listening to them you will say: "Oh yeah, Dad listened to it when he was a small boy."

Mom, who grew up in Texas, always liked the Westerns. We would listen to *Wild Bill Hitchcock*. I loved Andy Devine as Jingles. Funny there is little or no real memory of Guy Madison who played Wild Bill until seeing him on TV years later. Andy's graveled voice is still clear in my head. Of course, the sound of his voice would be reinforced later by all his old movies, from *Stage Coach*, to *The Man Who Shot Liberty Valance*, one of the really great westerns. Early on at Uncle Bill's, I saw Andy on TV. It may have been the TV version of *Wild Bill* in addition to his own children's show. From that point on the sounds from the radio invoked a picture of him on a horse, rocking back and forth, almost like Humpty Dumpy on a wall. That's the western I have the strongest memory of in Brooklyn, though there were others.

My father liked *The Shadow*. The opening phrase: "What evil lurks in the hearts of man? The Shadow knows." It held little attention for a small boy. It is interesting to note that Orson Welles starred as Lamont Cranston in the early shows of *The Shadow*. I think we listened to *The Whistler* because I have a recollection of the opening of the show (someone whistling—what else?). That would make sense as *The Whistler* was a spin off from *The Shadow*. There were a variety of shows on that attracted a child's attention.

I have a clearer memory of more shows once we moved to Connecticut. But in New York it seems I would listen to *Fibber Magee and Molly* regularly. Years later I gave a cassette tape of four of their old shows to your sister. We may have listened to *Abbott and Costello*. My Dad liked *Amos and Andy*. Mom liked *Blondie* also the futuristic science fiction's *Buck Rogers in the 25th Century* and *Flash Gordon*. *Edgar Bergen and Charlie McCarthy* were very popular though much of the humor was in the form of innuendo, for adults not children. Yet Charlie McCarthy would play a fun roll when I was living in a graduate dorm at Boston University years later. More on old radio when I get to Connecticut.

During the summer we would go to the family's Connecticut home across the Housatonic River from Falls Village. The Hill was jointly owned by the whole family. When I first went up there, my paternal grandmother and grandfather would be there. By the second summer, my grandfather died. I have is no memory of him. My mother told me how my grandmother was very cold, even hostile. This anger was directed towards her, but also me.

Mom told me years later, she didn't dare leave me alone with my grandmother. My grandmother was so jealous of my stealing away my father's devotion towards her, that Mom felt Grandma would have caused an "accident" resulting in my death. One time, she saw my grandmother standing over my crib with a pillow in her hand.

"Is Wally OK?" she asked.

This made the old woman aware she was being watched. She jumped back. A spurious smile came across her face. Mom felt she was about to smother me. By immediately asking the question it defused the temptation of a woman who felt a child had stolen her son's affections.

We moved out of New York, to the extended family home in northwestern Connecticut shortly before I turned four years old. This was way out in the country. The Connecticut house, off Sugar Hill Road, was referred to by all as "The Hill". The driveway to the house was on the left and the Appalachian Trail on the right. It was a summer retreat for everyone, but Dad wanted sole ownership and bought out his brother and parents while still living in NYC.

There was no TV stations nearby and a limited number of radio stations, mostly to the stations from Hartford; we would only get the New York radio stations irregularity, depending on the weather conditions. The Hill was to become my longest lasting home until moving to Virginia after graduate school. It was a two-story house. Mom told me the deeds went back to the 1600s. The original building was a log cabin, which became the kitchen. This is where Mom and I spent many hours talking, eating and living. The kitchen had two stoves: a typical gas stove for cooking and an old cast iron wood stove to help keep the house warm in winter when we didn't have fuel for the furnace. The cast iron allowed heat rise to the bathroom above through a vent in the ceiling and the water pipes ran along the ceiling in the kitchen to prevent freezing in winter. There was a walk-in pantry where food could be kept on multiple shelves. In winter it acted as a secondary refrigerator as it faced north and was the coldest place in the house. Off the kitchen was the dining room with a china closet behind the door to the kitchen. Dad preferred to eat in the dining room, so we usually are dinner there.

The front door opened to a hall and staircase. The hall led to the dining room and the stairs to the bedrooms were slightly on the right, before you entered the kitchen. To the left of the entrance was the living room. This was where there was another source of heat: a beautiful large fireplace dominated the room. Easily four feet wide and just under four feet high, it was made from stones taken from the area. The mantel was made of cement about nine inches wide and extended beyond the opening to the stone wings which were on either side of the fireplace.

The wings extended out a little over three feet. We used one for storing wood and the other we could sit on and warm ourselves on cold evenings. On winter nights it was delightful to toast marshmallows on a special fork, roast hot dogs, or simply warm your hands, feet and rear-end when you stood in front of it with your back towards the flames.

Upstairs were three bedrooms. My bedroom was at the top of the stairs to the right. It was the most pleasant room, filled with light during the day as it faced southwest. The walls were covered in an off-white wallpaper with rose buds. Not exactly what many would consider appropriate for a boy's room, but the design was soothing. The guest room was opposite my room. It was long and narrow with two twin beds and a dressing table. The master bedroom was large with a narrow walk-in closet. Rarely did I go in there as it was associated with Dad—something I wanted to avoid. The bathroom was down the hall next to the stairs. On the wall was an antique map of Long Island opposite the railing over the staircase The hall ran almost the length of the house. Then you would turn left. Immediately above the stairs was a door to the attic stairs. Past that door was the bathroom. It was large with what would be considered antique plumbing and a cast iron tub. There were two large closets used for linens and storage, later a darkroom.

The attic was a child's make-believe adventure. It was all cider wood and had a nice smell. On the sides, under the slanting roof, there were three closets, perfect for storage or, in the mind of a child, hidden treasures. With no light in the closets it was hard to tell what was inside them without using a flashlight. The rest of the attic was lit by a single light bulb hanging from the center of the ceiling. Despite not being insulated, with the chimneys on either end and and the westerly facing window above my bedroom, the attic kept surprising warm most of the year, even in winter.

Aunt Margaret and Uncle Bill would try to come up to The Hill for the weekend as often as possible. The guest room, being closest to mine, had a warm, comforting feel for the child who missed these adults. They were always welcomed as it would give Mom and Dad an evening break. Aunt Margaret always seemed happy to renew her role as sitter.

One summer night when they were visiting, I had just been put to bed. It must have been approaching 9 p.m. in June—I remember because the last rays of the sun were still shining through my west-facing window. I looked up at my ceiling. A spider was trying to jump across part of the ceiling to the wall but missed. He swung down on his thread, straight towards me! I screamed—there was a flying spider attacking me! Aunt Margaret came running in and killed the spider, but I was terrified for an hour or more, fearful the spider's relatives would seek revenge. She sat down and held me until I went to sleep. My parents must have been at the movies, or out to dinner with Bill, as only Margaret and I were in the house.

I think it was the same visit, that I was playing outside and jumped off the small stone wall at the eastern side of the house. All of a sudden, a bumblebee stung me. I yelled out in pain. Uncle Bill came running. He picked me up, took me inside and removed the stinger, then put baking soda and a Band-Aid on the wound, drying my tears as he did so.

Then he took me back to where I was stung. I asked why the bee had stung me. He sat me down on the wall where I had jumped off. He pointed to the bee and the partly destroyed nest. I must have jumped on it. The bumblebee was trying to repair the damage. Bill explained the bee was just trying to protect his home. My jump destroyed where he lived.

"How would you feel if some giant came by and stepped on your house? You would be mad, wouldn't you? Well, that is what the bee was feeling about you when you stepped on his house."

I loved Uncle Bill for giving me this insight. The incident that day led to a great respect for all animals. Even today I will make every effort I can to carefully put honeybees and bumblebees, when in the house, outside without hurting them. Not so for yellow jackets! I will explain why later.

Uncle Bill was the loving and kind father I wanted. As I got older Dad became colder and often appeared to be angry. I felt close to Uncle Bill. Years later, Mom told me that Uncle Bill had told her that I would be taken care of if anything happened to him. I don't know exactly what that meant. It was assumed he had left me a considerable amount of money in a will or insurance policy.

A few months after the bee adventure, Mom came to tell me that Uncle Bill had died. I cried for a long time, quietly to myself. I sat on the wall where we had watched the bee. It took years for me to recover from Uncle Bill's untimely death. Aunt Margaret never processed the will; I never got anything.

How did Uncle Bill die? He had a vice. He loved the horses. Whenever he had a chance he would go to the New York race tracks and bet on the ponies. One day he hit the trifecta (naming the top three finishers—win, place and show). It must have been a very large payoff. He was coming home, excited with the winnings, but perhaps too excited as he had a heart attack and dropped dead with his winnings in his pocket.

He always said when Aunt Margaret turned 50 he was going to trade her in for two 25-year olds. He never got the chance to test out the joke.

Love,
Papa—a little sadder after composing this letter.

Hi T: – Miss you already (back flash):

Still in Brooklyn. By the time I was three the radio became more important to me. I mention this because of the influence they have on the development of a young child. These were the shows which helped mold me into who I am today.

Usually I would listen to the kid radio programs and once Uncle Bill got a TV, I couldn't wait to see *Howdy Doody*, or *The Andy Devine Show*. I loved Froggy, though Andy was getting on in age and must have weighed over 400 lbs. One episode I can remember after all these years was when Andy was lifting a barbell. Froggy kept on magically increasing the amount of weight on the bar until either Andy or the floor gave way. As a child, I thought that skit was very funny. Howdy Doody the marionette with Buffalo Bob as the straight man for Howdy.

Jumping years ahead, there is another strong TV memory. There was a special on with Patty McCormick (the child star of *The Bad Seed*) and Harpo Marx of the Marx Brothers fame. Harpo was the silent one in the movies, but he spoke in this special. I don't remember what he said, but I remember being overwhelmed by his love and wisdom. As he spoke on TV it felt as if all the children, including myself, were being overwhelmed with a gift of his blessings. It was understandable why his brothers, Zeppo, Chico and Groucho, kept his mouth shut in the movies. But this memory alone, even without knowing what he said, still brings a little tear to my eyes when I see him play his harp in films. I love the music, but every time I hear it, to this day, the feeling of his warm blessings cascades all over me.

Few remember 1950s TV sets—perhaps best remembered now in the movie *Back to the Future*. They were a tiny picture in a huge cabinet. The screen was rarely more than 21 inches diagonally, if that! All were black and white and there were only three network channels: ABC, NBC, and CBS! Years later and very slowly, PBS started broadcasting, but not while we remained in NYC. Independent channels would offer re-run movies. Most could best be described as lame. They offered movies from the 1930s and occasionally earlier.

Of course, there would be "rabbit ears" on top of the set if you did not have a large antenna on the roof. You know about antennas, don't you? They were those strange metal constructions, which were curved aluminum tubing, usually shaped roughly in the form of different oblong squares, attached to a chimney, helping catch the signals from station transmitters. Sometimes they worked. Sometimes they didn't. In the latter case, and especially with rabbit ears, someone would watch the scrambled picture as another member of the family fiddled with the direction the tubes were pointing in an attempt to obtain a better picture.

I think Uncle Bill and my father worked together or at least near each other because they came home together. Mom came home first. She would pick me up from Aunt Margaret. I don't remember watching TV while I was with Aunt Margaret. Mom would take me back down the hall to our apartment and then start to cook. About an hour later Dad came home. I would rush out the door running down the hall to visit Uncle Bill to watch the TV shows, usually without even acknowledging my father. That's how I got my first scar. Mom said I was running down the hall in the apartment building without saying anything except:

"Uncle Bill's home!"

I rushed out the door but half way to Uncle Bill's I tripped and fell face first. My chin hit the hard floor. I started to cry. Mom rushed out. She put some Band-Aids on my chin, which could have used stitches. But who wants to put a traumatized child through more pain? That was my only major scar until Nim and I used to play tickle games where his chimpanzee fingernails would dig deep into the hands excited by being tickled.

Margaret could not have children so they "adopted" me as the son they never had. They were much more affectionate than my parents. What may have been more important was there were no arguments in their apartment, unlike mine. When I had to go home for dinner, Dad would still be fuming and Mom would be argumentative. Dinner would be tense—most of the time. This kept up until we left Brooklyn in 1953.

It was about this time that another problem had to be solved. I was slow to be toilet trained. Mom told Dad he should take me into the bathroom to show how a man urinates. Dad absolutely refused. He thought the idea was disgusting. Mom asked how else would I learn to use the toilet? He remained unmoved. Thus Mom started taking me in to show how she urinated. I caught on, but in a seated position. What is funny is that to this day it remains my favorite way to pee. Perhaps there is a bit of laziness involved—it's just easier to sit down and take care of either bodily function which require the toilet. Not that I can't use a urinal, which when out to the theatre or dinner is the preferred solution, but while home—let me be seated.

It is important to note since there was no TV in the house, my attention towards Dad increased. The three of us would usually have a more peaceful time when together. At least until other memories started to come to the surface. The fact that Brooklyn was becoming more dangerous, led to my father buying out the other family interests in the Connecticut house and plans were made to move there in the future. The biggest problem was where my father would find a job.

I'll talk about the move latter—it changed my life.

Love,
Papa

Hi T:

This is a recap of the earlier letter to reinforce the information about Brooklyn. Call it early youth, maybe Brooklyn Youth 2. One year, Dad set up his Lionel train tracks. I must have been three years old. They were placed on a standard size piece of plywood. It was a nice small collection, with an antique engine, cars and tiny electric street lights which were placed around the buildings on the set. That little set would be worth a fortune today.

Down the hall to the left was my bedroom. My only memory of the actual room where the play pen was located was a small children's lamp with a lamp shade that slowly rotated. It would cast light images from met cutouts on the walls as it moved. The heat of the bulb rotated blades attached to part of the lamp shade which would turn. The memory of this revolving light remains, but the images have been forgotten. Knowing my mother, it was likely a cowboy/ Indian motif. An image of horse does emerge from deep recesses of the mind, but the other shapes are lost in the fog called time.

Your grandma went back to work as soon as she could after I was born, to help support the family. She also became active in Marie Derasimes Co-Masonic Lodge #352. Many in the United States are not familiar with Co-Masonry. That is unfortunate. The Co-Masonry was a part of Le Droit Human. Headquartered in France, it has been accepting men and women into Masonic Lodges since 1880s. Previous to joining 352 your grandma was part of "The Ancient Universal Mysteries (AUM)", a Masonic group associated with Alice Bailey, which started in the 1930s, after her split with Le Droit Human. The object of AUM was to bring into existence an esoteric Masonic Lodge. It was dedicated to advanced meditation and enlightenment using the rituals of

Masonry. Membership consisted of an inner circle of the Arcane School. Starting off strong with three lodges by 1940, it failed to reconvene after WWII. After the war, Grandma was the youngest AUM Fellow Craft (2o) with nowhere to go to obtain her Master Mason's (3o) Degree.

Later the equipment and jewels of AUM passed on to your grandmother through some of the older AUM members after Alice died. She kept them for a long time. After she turned 75 she was no longer able to endure the Connecticut winders. I found her a nice apartment near me in Arlington, Virginia, just outside Washington, D.C. When she moved to Virginia, the trunk which contained all the valuable silver jewels of two of the old lodges was broken into and the jewels stolen. Only some of the cloths and gavels remained.

Several of the older members of AUM suggested she join Marie Derasimes Lodge #352. Since AUM was not recognized, your grandma had to proceed through the first two degrees again. The new affiliation allowed her to eventually obtain the degree of Master Mason. During that time, she became an active officer. All of this occurred before I was born. Knowing the progression through the line in #352, I have estimated that she must have been either the Junior or Senior Deacon while pregnant with me. It allows me to say I was active in Masonry even before I was born. The picture of her walking around the Lodge with a protruding pregnant belly is comical, yet it must have left some kind of prenatal impression on me.

Love,
Papa.

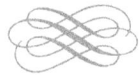

Hello Daughter (have to vary this sometimes):

In Brooklyn there were times when it was good to be outside. Warm, sunny days were ideal. The sun would be beating down on the steps and sidewalks. The park would be bright and green. Spring and Fall offered the most ideal weather for a young child to be outside.

On these occasions Margaret would take me out onto the apartment house's front steps to get fresh air. If Mom was home she would do the same. It was on one of these occasions, I must have been about three, that I remember watching a workman who was replacing the cement sidewalk in front of our building. He asked me my name.

"Wally," was the excited response from a child who was getting attention.

It is also the name I was called when little. I remember he wrote my name in the wet concrete. "W A L L Y". I thought that was great. It was my first introduction to the alphabet. It was a recognition that letters could refer to me. Every time I went outside I would look at my name, even though I couldn't read.

Years later, Jean, my steady at the time, and I took the subway out to Brooklyn to look at the old apartment. I wanted to check to see if Aunt Margaret was still there. As we approached the apartment building, there was a workman replacing the old cement. I went over and talked to him.

"Damn, this old sidewalk must be 30 years old or more. About time it was replaced."

I realized that he had just broken up the "Wally" that had been there for so many years. There was not a single visible letter remaining. I looked at the buttons in the entrance way. There was no "H" on the list of residents. Aunt Margaret had moved. Possibly deceased. Thus she moved into the section of my memories without any hope of renewal or ability to bring her back into current consciousness.

Once when I was outside with Mom—possibly at same park where Dad had taken me or the one on Fulton Avenue—she let me pet and play with the dogs of the neighborhood. I remember a long-haired English Spaniel I made friends with. Mom taught me how to read dogs' moods, to watch their tails' expressions, and to know when they should be approached. On this occasion, Mom took a photo of me and the dog. I think it's still around the house somewhere. My joyful expression of making an animal friend is evident. To this day, that same joy comes whenever an animal and I greet each other, without fear, as one living being towards another. I must have had a Buddhist tendency at this early age.

I don't remember going into the city itself; we mostly stayed around Brooklyn. But the neighborhood was becoming more populated with Black families at this time and Dad became concerned that the neighborhood was on the decline. He felt the schools would not be the best environment to raise a child.

I do remember a conversation in the apartment when I had returned from the park one day, a vague recollection of some neighborhood kids picking on me. Mom had her back to me, likely talking to a neighbor. The kids started to push me and called me names, most of which I didn't comprehend. She had to confront the kids to stop them from pushing me. I was still small for my age. This was my first confrontation with another child. It wouldn't be the last.

Although I ate well, my premature birth was still affected my growth. Significant weight gain didn't occur until we moved to Connecticut. I don't think I was hurt in the incident but it was the beginning of Dad's concerns. The episode reinforced Dad's racist views of Black people in general. Was he a hardcore racist? Or was it a reflection of the general attitudes at the time towards Black people? Hard to say. He had to work with and wait upon Black people as a salesman. But there was always an undercurrent of dislike and distrust when he spoke about them. The change in the demographics of the area was a major contributor to the decision to move out of New York. We became part of the "white flight" from the city.

As for the move, there is not much to recall. I do remember boxes and other things being moved around the apartment in preparation for our departure, an overwhelming sadness sweeping over me knowing that I would no longer be near Uncle Bill, although he had promised to visit me up in Connecticut when he could, as you learned in previous letters. Through the tears, I knew he would not be there for me as he had been.

Then the day arrived. The furniture and boxes were moved. When the apartment was cleared out. Mom, Dad, and I walked out of the apartment, down to the street. The car's back seat was packed with boxes with barely enough space for one child in the back. The suitcases stored in the trunk. I was placed into the car. Dad moved in behind the wheel, Mom slipped into the passenger seat in front of me. The car started to move slowly away from the curb. Away from the only home I had known.

We drove into the evening. It was truly the nightfall of one era of my life and the beginning of a new. I had no way of knowing the drive would key in memories. Memories which had not entered into my young mind up to that point. Yet the flood of these memories would have after effects that had a real impact, on me, on Mom and on Dad. None positive.

Love,
Papa.

Chapter 2

Out of New York—Out of This World

Hi T – the move to Connecticut.

Another note as we left Brooklyn—Mom said I had a favorite toy, a "doll baby". My father objected to me playing with it.

"Wally is a boy and should not be playing with dolls," he said.

I know this kind of opinion is no longer accepted but he apparently got quite mad. Still, I clung to the doll for a few years. I still had it when I was five and so it had to make the move with me. I would not settle down in my seat until the doll was in my arms. This just made Dad even angrier, but Mom gently put it into my arms to quiet me down. It worked.

Now back to the move.

Dad and Mom were in the front seat of the car when we left the city. We traveled up the NY side of the Hudson River, a direction we rarely took. The Connecticut state line was on the east side of the Hudson River. This was the long way around. We must have been on the Palisades Parkway. Usually we went up the NY/Conn border on the east side of the Hudson using the Sawmill Parkway. That evening we didn't.

I slept most of the trip in the back seat, holding tight to "doll baby". I remember one large turn that looped around a mountain, possibly Bear Mountain (?), and descended towards the Hudson; we were heading for the river crossing at Peekskill. It was that descent, that curve, that section of the road, that triggered something. Something beyond any five-year-old child's understanding.

I had been on that road before—but not as Wally. Yes, we had taken it before when we went to The Hill for holidays. But that evening was different. With the darkness of night beginning to envelope the countryside, house and street lights shone in the valley, and as the car rounded a curve in the road, it triggered something in the deep recesses of my subconscious.

I had been taken on that road before, but in the opposite direction! An image appeared where I was in a uniform. How could that be? Yet, the memory flashed clearly in my mind. Then a realization came with the vision. I was not with Mom and Dad but with others whose names I had forgotten. The image of a truck suddenly became vivid. I was sitting on a bench in the back of the truck, a truck with a group of other soldiers. We were coming back from upstate New York, going back to the city.

It was clear that this occurred just before we were to take a ship to go across the ocean. Then more images came clearly to my mind, most of which I didn't have names for. It was not a long, continuous memory but bits and pieces of many associated memories. Of me! But *not* me! Of a life, but NOT this life!

Later, when I was older, I realized that truck was coming from a training exercise prior to the soldiers being shipped overseas. We were to join the rest of the US Army in England prior to D-Day. Somehow, we were not involved in D-Day but were the reinforcements that came later. Those flashbacks were my first clear images of another life. A life before this life. In a different body. From a different time. What may have been most strange was that it was a self-image as an adult man, not a boy. Not as a child, but as a soldier.

Those flashbacks triggered more memories in the days to come. I was that life. But I was this five-year-old too. At that stage I had no understanding of which life was current and which was the past. It was as if the two lives were living in parallel with one another. The more critical problem was that the memory opened up a channel to those of my "buddies" still on the other side. This became a problem later, once we settled in The Hill. One that would begin to haunt me.

I don't really remember when we actually arrived at our new home. Mom carried me up to my bed. I went fast to sleep. When I woke up I realized I was in my little room that faced west-southwest. The view was the most unobstructed in the house (very important later). Depending on the window I could view the old garden to the south. Beyond that one could see the fence that separated our property from our neighbor's. The barn and berry patch were visible from western facing window. Everywhere else in the house trees were close to the windows and blocked any clear view; one could only see part of the view of the Housatonic River Valley to the east through the trees as you looked from the master bedroom.

I had the best view! It had the most sun during the day and beautiful sunsets. I could see the yard below, the breezeway roof to the right, and the garage/barn beyond. Out the other window was a very beautiful place, in the quiet part of the country, which I would call home for a long time. More later.

Love,
Papa

Hello T:

Maybe in two parts. Let the fun begin!!

After Alice Bailey died, (remember she was the founder of the Arcane School) there was a struggle within the inner circle of the Arcane School. Foster Bailey (Alice's widower) had taken over the school but was not a good manager. Even with the help of Bernard M., your grandma's second husband who was still active in the school and other newer members like Norman Artist, it was more than Foster could handle.

Soon a younger attractive follower attached herself to Foster. They were soon married and the new Mrs. Bailey (Mary) took over the school. Although dedicated to Alice's books, she wanted nothing to do with the direction of the inner circle, or to continue with the unfinished work. To say nothing of the fact she, like Annie Besant of the Theosophical Society (TS) so many years before, was not capable of taking the DK's dictations.

You likely need a little history about the TS and The Arcane School. DK is one of the masters identified by the TS, also known as "the Tibetan". In theory DK helped Helena P. Blavatsky (HPB) in composing her books such as *The Secret Doctrine*. HPB went on to found the TS, which in the latter part of the 19th century became a very popular philosophical society. Annie Besant took over the TS, and also promoted Co-Masonry in England where it became very popular. But Annie was not approached by DK to continue HPB's work. Instead Alice Bailey was asked to continue the work. Annie became furious. This ultimately forced Alice to leave the TS and found the Arcane School. Was history about to repeat itself when Alice died?

In some ways Mary Bailey's new leadership in the Arcane School now Lucius Trust, created a split within the members. What Mary did not want to recognize was the special, hand-selected group of students, which Alice had kept close. Your grandma was among that group. For the most part they did not agree in the direction Mary Bailey was taking the Arcane School. The Walters, Homer C, Marcia M, Wei T, Grandma and others began a separate meditation group of their own. This inner circle struggled. Who would be in charge to carry on the work planned by Alice but never completed?

My godmother, Marion Walter, was one of the few in contact with DK. But she was not strong enough to resist attacks from the forces from the "dark side", to borrow from *Star Wars* terminology. She had to discontinue to prevent serious physical illnesses. Marion was instructed by D.K. *never* to do this work again! The problem was once you opened yourself to the other planes of existence, where dangerous spirits and downright malevolent beings would try to influence you. They could be very threatening and evil. No one else wanted to (and/or could) take over. Some because they were too busy trying to rebuild their corners of the world after WWII. Others because they didn't have the time or resources to continue the work. Yet the group kept up a correspondence course.

Grandma was the secretary for the group and distributed the lessons, minutes of meetings, and the newsletters. This group was involved in very advanced meditations. By the way, one of the members of the group was Homer Carnegie, related to Dale Carnegie. Maybe I will tell you a secret about Homer and Dale in another letter. Still, Homer is someone to remember for future letters of these memoirs.

The solitude of The Hill was ideal for meditation. It is also important to realize that in the early 1950s there was a rash of UFO sightings and reports. On July 19, 1952 a number of UFOs "buzzed" the White House, Capitol and the Pentagon. They were picked up on radar. Bystanders were able to take photos. Those photos were never adequately explained. A second account of UFOs over Washington, DC was reported on the 26th, just a few days later. There were reports of other sightings around the country. A meditation put an idea in my Mom's head. If there are intelligent beings from other planets what would show them that there is intelligent life here on Earth?

As I mentioned earlier, she was a member of Marie Deraismes Lodge #352 in New York and around this time she was its Right Worshipful Master (head). It came to her that the symbols of Freemasonry would be universal. It even says so in part of the ritual where, after the dimensions of the lodge, it asks "Of what does it form?" The reply is: "Universal Masonry.". Intelligent life would depend upon the symbols as a means to construct and build. The working tools of Freemasonry are the basic tools from which intelligent beings construct buildings, machinery and modern scientific instruments. Why not use the symbols of Freemasonry as a signal to other intelligent life forms? The fairly flat field behind the barn would be a perfect place to conduct a little experiment. Especially since we had just purchased our first power lawnmower!

One week, Mom told me we would have a little adventure. She would mow a pattern in the field behind the barn with the new mower. I would follow, putting down extra-long sheets of white paper behind her. The paper was 8 1/2 x 14", left over from a secretarial job she had completed. To earn extra money, she had a secretarial service, which you will hear more about later.

We quickly realized we would have to weigh down the paper with small stones to prevent the wind from blowing it away. After all, The Hill was just that, on a hill. The collection of hills which surrounded us are often referred to as the foothills of the Berkshires. The Berkshires is the mountain range that extends from northern Connecticut through Massachusetts, and merges with the Green Mountains of Vermont.

Off I went to gathering stones. I had no idea of the size or shape of the "paths" we were making. All I knew was that there were long straight lines in the tall grass. It was actually fun finding and putting stones on the paper. It gave 5-year-old me a sense of purpose. I took pride in helping my mother. By Sunday afternoon, we were finished. Mom told me we might get some visitors in the future. The year was 1954 (maybe '55). Sure enough, all sorts of unusual things started happening.

The first unusual thing was high in the sky—a star **in the daytime**! Then, some days there were two or three. My Dad insisted they were stars.

Me: "But how come I can't see more stars, Daddy?"

Dad: "Because these are especially bright stars."

He told me that if I dug a hole in the ground deep enough, I would be able to see more stars in the day. Another funny thing about them, was that there was never more than three. And as the afternoon progressed, the stars didn't move.

Suddenly, there was a huge noise. A squadron of four Saber Jets (F86s—the same as were being used in the Korean War) flew very low over the house. I could tell they were low because the pilot was clearly visible. Mom and I waved at them as they flew over. But when the jets came, the stars disappeared.

As the jets came over the house they separated into groups of two flying in different directions—but all going up! Soon they disappeared too. About 15 minutes after the Saber jets took off, the stars came back in exactly the same position. Mom thought the whole thing funny. It was an effort for her to keep the laughter to herself.

Dad was mad as hell! I couldn't figure out why. For a young boy this was a great game, lots of fun. There were stars glowing in the day. Jets were flying over the house, so close you could make out the helmets of the pilots, and as the jets appeared the stars disappeared. Then, once the jets likely went back to base or wherever, the stars came out again. Being in the country with not many other activities to do, this was a great afternoon.

Mom was getting more excited each day the stars appeared in the sky. Each time they appeared, the jets would come over within 30 minutes to an hour. Occasionally it was a single jet that flew over the house. Sometimes they would break the sound barrier right over the house! The **boom** just added to the excitement. The plates and cans on the pantry shelves would rattle when the sonic boom hit the house. Mom would love to see the jets fly over but would laugh when the formations would breakup. Mom told me they were trying to catch something. Could it be the stars??? She would sit in one of the rocking chairs on the breezeway with a huge smile, if not a quiet little laugh, as all this was happening.

About a week after these activities started, Mom gave me a very special instruction. We were going to receive some visitors soon. She was going to prepare a welcome basket for our guests. She put a small table under the pine trees to the north side of the barn. This is where there were a number of pine trees just before a gentle slope down to the same level of the patterns we had placed. From the trees the patterns and the field were clearly visible.

My instructions were that if anyone came behind the barn, I should go out and greet them, offering the basket if she was not around. The basket was kept full of fresh fruit and bread. I never actually saw her change what was there. I think she did it in the night after doing the dishes when Dad was reading or listening to the radio. I'm not sure if he even realized the table was out there with the basket on it (at least not until later).

How's that for the lead in to the next letter—wager you can't wait!!! coming!!!!!!

Love,
Papa

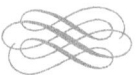

Hi T – ready for patterns in the grass

Let's call it Out of This World!

Bet you know who's

The hide and seek between the jets and the "stars" kept up for a couple of weeks. Dad still insisted upon the lights being stars. But now they would move in patterns. First to the south of the house, then more to the west over the pattern. They were also growing bigger!!!

If I asked any questions about this change in the behavior of the "stars" Dad would just get furious and storm off into the house. Best not to ask him any questions! Where once they were the size of one of the stars in Orion's belt, they then became were the size of Jupiter, then twice that size. Soon it was apparent that they could not be stars. But they were still a mystery to a small boy who was enjoying the excitement. Mom had an almost constant smile on her face.

I was just taking everything in my stride with no idea what was going on. It was just fun to watch the stars and the jets and the stars again. One time there was a different kind of plane (with propellers on it) that flew over. Slower and bigger. I could swear there was someone in it taking pictures of the property and especially Mom's pattern. Mom told me maybe the stars where flying saucers (UFOs). She explained the stars were really visitors from another planet. That caught my interest. It helped explain what was going on in the sky. She told me not to talk to Dad about it because he would just get mad and say that:

"There are no such things as flying saucers!" A phrase he would use repeatedly until his death.

It was a summer Saturday. Dad and I were "working" in the barn. It was a small barn if one considers it associated with an actual farm. But The Hill was not a farm. Even so, the barn was much bigger than a normal car garage. Two cars could easily fit, back to back, in the parking area. Then to the southwestern side of the interior there was ample space for a spacious workshop or anything else that was needed (a space of approximately 10 x 15 feet). That is where the mower and a large pile of junk were stored. Much of the implements were from the previous owners were still there. To the southeastern side was a slightly larger space, with antique tools and a old wooden wheelbarrows, much larger than those used today. The wheels of these alone were close to three feet in diameter. Then there were the gardening tools, old wooden boxes, and a lot of odds and ends from when The Hill was an experimental gardening center of the former owner.

A child could play with these things, imagining building all sorts of fantastic structures (at least within his or her own mind). In the center of the barn there were two four-foot walls made of very old lumber, dividing the area for the cars, the junk area and workshop space. The back of the barn was where Dad kept most of his actual tools—saws, scythes, snowshoes and a host of other items. In the center of the barn was a major support pillar with a "T" section, about 12 feet off the floor, spanning from one side to the other.

I loved to watch was on top of the T. It was where the annual nest of barn swallows was located. A broken window pane above the large door allowed them to dart in and out and it was such a joy watching them flying in and out through the broken window, and once the eggs hatched feeding the young swallows.

On this particular day Dad was working with some tools at the workbench in a corner of the interior. Mom was out visiting someone or maybe at the store. This was an absence she would regret for the rest of her life.

Dad said he couldn't find a special screwdriver and thought it might be in the house. I was playing with the junk on the storage side. He told me to stay where I was.

"I'll be back in a minute."

I continued to "build" something out of the junk. Then I heard the strangest whirring sound. It was like an engine if you could muffle the noise. Yet it was unlike anything I ever heard before or since. I went outside and down the little drive to the yard east of the barn. I didn't see anything, but the sound had been very close. It had sounded as if it was almost right on top of me.

I decided to walk to the side of the barn. I went to the southeast side, just above the stone wall that separated the upper lawn from the lower section of the barn. There was the beginning of the path to the level behind the barn. I turned to look towards the back of the barn, where the pattern was. I froze!!!!!

In back of the barn, below where I was standing, was a giant flying saucer sitting in the middle of the pattern, which was below me, past the slope that ran down from the south side of the barn (see the map in a later letter). I was scared shitless. It was bright silver. It looked like the classic vision from the comic books. No seam, rivet or bump could be seen. There were no lights or other visible markings. The edges were gently curved. It was beautiful. Perhaps the most beautiful thing I had ever seen, at least of any item made by intelligent life. I couldn't say "human" because it was not of anything made on Earth.

Then I remembered what Mom had once told me:

"They are our friends and you have to greet them."

I TRIED AND TRIED TO MOVE—BUT MY FEET WOULDN'T BUDGE! I told myself over and over:

"I have to go down and say hello."

Somehow, although I could see no windows, I knew I was being watched. Watched by who or whatever was inside.

Then it came to me. If I go into the barn and count to 10, maybe then I would be able to go down to the back and greet them as I should. I went back in the barn and started to count (out loud) 1, 2, 3, 4, 5, 6, (I remember reaching 6) then I heard the whir again. I ran out. There, above the trees and quickly disappearing, was the flying saucer.

I shouted: "Come back! I'm sorry. I was scared."

But it was too late. Its rate of climb was amazing—almost straight up and incredibly fast. Then it started in a southwesterly direction, quickly turned 90o and was gone in seconds. It had to have been traveling at hundreds of miles per hour or more to disappear so quickly. Again, beyond anything humans could have done at that time. Come to think of it, we still don't. At least not within the Earth's atmosphere.

I think I shed a tear. But then the excitement of being that close to a UFO hit me. Years later, when I saw the movie *Close Encounters* I thought to myself: "If only I had been about three, the age of the kid in the movie, I might have been too young to be so scared. I might have even gotten a ride like he did." Remember the little boy in the movie was wearing a Boston University sweatshirt—funny. I would later receive one of my graduate degrees from BU! I have that connection with the movie too. But many years in the future.

I went running into the house and shouted through the kitchen door:

"Daddy, Daddy, did you see it?" No answer. "Daddy, where are you? Did you see it?"

Then I heard a noise coming from my room. Remember this was the only room which had a perfect view of the barn. I ran up the stairs. There was Dad crawling out from under my bed.

"Daddy did you see..."

A response came from a deep but shaking voice: "**I didn't see anything!**"

"But a flying saucer was in our yard right there."

I pointed to the barn where my window faced. There I could see the partly flattened berry vines and a depression which looked round in one small spot.

"**I didn't see anything!**" was all I could get out of him.

Then it hit me: "Daddy, what were you doing under my bed?"

"Oh, um, I dropped one of my tools behind your bed. I was crawling under to get it."

I looked out the window. He had a perfect view of everything from above. The top of the UFO would have been clearly visible, along with at least half of the ship itself.

I thought to myself, "Where is it?" The tool he was looking for. It wasn't in his hand. Nor was it on the bed or the chest of drawers. I decided it best not to push it. I could see a mixture of great fear and now an expression of anger building on his face. I started to go out again.

"I want you to stay in the house and play!"

That was a command not to be challenged. So, I stayed. Fun! Ah well. But there would be hell to pay shortly.

Love,
Papa

Now for the aftermath:

When Mom came home, Dad met her outside. Instinct told me this was not a good sign. I didn't want to watch, but something inside me said I should. Maybe a concern for Mom's safety. It might have been a fear that Dad would lose control and start beating her. Slowly moving the curtains slightly, I watched from the living room window.

Dad was yelling at the top of his lungs. In between the rants one thing was made clear. He wanted all the paper to be taken up in the back. "Right now!!!" Mom later told me that she went back there to pick up the strips of paper, in the midst of the pattern she saw three indications in the ground forming a perfect equilateral triangle. The grass between the depressions had the tops broken or bent. There was no sign of any burning or heat that may have emanated from the craft's landing pods. After a closer look, there was no burned grass in the center but rather the tops of the stalks were brown and bent over. By the end of that afternoon, all the paper was gone from the field.

Dad commanded her not to take any photos of the holes, the grass, or anything back there. This must have been hard for Mom, who did a lot of photography, a hobby she learned from her second husband. It may have been while Mom was picking up the paper or perhaps when Dad walked to the barn, but whenever it was, he discovered the table and the picnic basket. Then a real explosion occurred. Knowing his temper, it was surprising he did not strike Mom.

Later I was allowed outside.

"Daddy, where did these holes come from?"

"Those were made by a fox for a den. If not foxes, then some deer has slept there. This is why the holes were so deep."

No other questions were asked. Dad did not want any further questions. Interesting, the soil was hard and the holes were perfect circles, about four feet in diameter. The impressions in the ground were about 18 to 24 inches deep. When I was older, I mused the foxes must have had a set of compasses to draw such perfect circles. These intelligent foxes must also have used some strange tool to make the perfect triangular patter in the three depressions. Somewhere in the old files, or perhaps lost, was a drawing Mom did with the exact dimensions, which she measured later.

Years later, while playing canasta with Mom, I asked why there were no photos when she could have taken them when Dad was not around. She said she didn't think of it. I do not believe this to be true. However, I believe she was very afraid of what he might do if the photos were ever discovered. He was bigger and stronger than most men. Her fear was well justified.

When Dad was not around, Mom and I would talk about what I saw. Every detail was given, more than once. The sound, the color, the shape, the lack of windows or markings—everything was described. Yet I had the feeling that at all times I was being watched by whatever was inside. She was feeling very guilty not being there since it was her message and pattern that brought them. The next day we ate the fruit and bread from the basket.

"You remember I told you they were our friends. You should have greeted them."

"But Mom, my legs wouldn't move. I tried, I really tried, but I couldn't."

She forgave me for being so scared. The trouble is that to this day I have never forgiven myself!

Mom continued her meditations. About a week later as she was descending the stairs from her bedroom she said to me:

"They told me never to use that pattern again, unless it was a dire emergency."

Maybe one day she would tell me what the pattern was. For a number of years, I was curious about what pattern she used. After I was 18, the pattern became so obvious she didn't have to tell me. That was right after I became a member of Marie Deraismes #352 Masonic Lodge. You can guess the connection.

One of the most interesting outcomes of this whole episode was the change in the U.S. Geological Survey (USGS) topographical map for the area. The earlier maps (I believe the previous map was 1948) showed very clearly the driveway, the house and the barn. Yet only a year or two after this occurred, the next map released, in around 1956, only showed the driveway up to the second turn. The upper driveway disappears into the field. There is no indication of the existence of a house or barn. All such indications that a house with a barn on top of The Hill were removed from the maps.

Remember the slower aircraft flying over the house taking pictures? Well it appears that Project Blue Book, the Air Force UFO investigation group, must have classified our house and grounds as Top Secret, or higher, as it forced the change in the US Geological Survey topographical maps. When I asked someone at the USGS what happened to the house and barn the response I got was:

"Well, the trees must have been obscuring the buildings."

Interesting in that the trees had been there in the '40s and the house and barn were shown on all the previous maps. I never bought into the explanation given.

Dad never again wanted to talk about what happened.

He lost most, if not all, of my respect for three reasons. First, because he was never willing to admit what he had seen that Saturday afternoon. Second, because he was so scared that he hid under my bed! And finally, because he was so mad. From that moment on he made Mom's life even more miserable.

Years later, when I visited him in Florida, I asked if he remembered the UFO. He got red in the face and snapped back:

"UFOs aren't real!"

Funny, he got a lot closer to one than most people who do believe in them ever get. Yet they believe and he refused to believe their existence even after being so close to one.

There will be more about UFOs later. But now you can see why my interest is so great, although I am hardly obsessed about them. For years I liked to keep abreast of what research was finding out about them.

Whenever Mom or I heard a UFO cover-up story we would look at each other. She would wink or we would nod our heads in unison.

Love,
Papa

Chapter 3

Normal Routine for a Youngster?

Poor T – all the excitement is over.

Mom was working more and more in a secretarial service she had created. She found our neighbor, Lorraine B, would be willing to babysit me after school. Lorraine had two children, Susan (a year older than I), and Johnnie (one and a half years younger). You met Johnnie on our trip to Connecticut; he was with his father working on clearing some of the forest at the end of Sugar Hill Road. He was actually bulldozing part of the Appalachian Trail. I'm sure without a permit.

Lorraine and her husband were country folk in the most classic, stereotypical way. Their parents had been farmers and laborers. They lived across the street from the Clarks, her parents, whose properties surrounded The Hill. The Clarks still used their land for their limited dairy farm. At no time do I think they had more than two dozen cows producing milk. But they did have plenty of fields where the cows could graze, on three sides of our house and property. At one time, so the story goes, the farmhouse where Lorraine's parents lived was the chief farmhouse in the community. Diagonally across the street was the second farmhouse which originally was built for the heirs of the original farmer who owned the whole area around the house.

It appeared that over the years, parcels of the land were sold to raise money for the family. This permitted them to live on in the original farmhouse and the additional house near the cow's barn. Down the hill from the main house a number of homes had been built over the past thirty years, ever decreasing the size of the overall farm. The "farmer's" chief house and yard, though not as nice as ours, it was the largest on Sugar Hill Road's flat strip, stretching from Lorraine's property to our driveway.

"The Hill" had been the home of the original farm owner. He chose the house overseeing the farm and river valley and most likely expanded it. The original house was reportedly a log cabin dating back to the 1600s. The rumor was he would only spend a third of his time in that house before tending a similar farm elsewhere in Connecticut. He spent another third of his time on another farm somewhere in southwestern Massachusetts. According to the stories, each farm had a wife and children. The children would take over the farms in the houses built by their father, usually down the road(s) from the master house. When he died, no one dared to probate a will, as neither of the three "wives" knew who was the first, second, or third. The fear of not having a clear title resulted in each of the three families pretending to ignore the existence of the other two. Lorraine and her children had a one in three chance of being descended from bastard stock. This is a term which would not be used today but was still quite common in the 1950s.

This is how the Clark's came into possession of the property on Sugar Hill and the farm. The farm never paid for itself. The worse blow to their pride was when the founder of the farm sold The Hill and its seven acres to the horticulturalist in the 1920s. That was originally the principal house and the pride of the family. As a result, all the subsequent owners were hated by Lorraine's mother, Mrs. Clark. Old lady Clark would actually make every effort to make whoever lived in The Hill as miserable as possible. More on her later.

John, Lorraine's husband had little interest in farming. He focused on doing construction work. He had a bulldozer and would be hired to clear areas for private driveways, or new construction. After he married Lorraine, he built a new modern house across the street from the Clark's home which is where I would be taken in the mornings.

Lorraine was a typical housewife who did a little babysitting on the side to bring in a little extra cash for the family. Neither she nor John were particularly friendly, at least not beyond what one would call necessary. Nor did either of them provided any indication of having education beyond the basic high school level, if that.

The days with the Lorraine were scheduled around Mom's work hours in her Lakeville Letter Shop. Lorraine's house was down from The Hill, about 120 yards down Sugar Hill Road from my driveway. In many ways it was a different world. John's aunt and uncle lived next door in the second house on the block, diagonally across from Mrs. Clark. This is what I referred to as the 'farmer's' house, the largest on the street. Old lady Clark's red house was next to the barn, housing the cows and later a horse.

I was beginning to get used to being away from Mom. I do remember one day when Susan and Johnnie were running all around the house. Lorraine was hanging the laundry on the clothesline in the yard after taking them from the clothes washer. The next load of clothes had been put in the machine, which was rolled out into the kitchen floor from its usual storage area in a mini pantry. I was in the kitchen watching everything going on around me. The old fashion wringer washing machine was chugging away with the next load of laundry. The plug from the washing machine stretched a few feet from the sink to the socket to the left of the sink. The hose in similar fashion was placed in the sink with the help of a 'J' connector at its end, to allow the dirty water to drain into the sink.

Johnnie and Susan had been playing in another part of the house. As usual without my participation. I was in the kitchen trying to find something to do, with little success. Susan ran through the kitchen and right into the electric wire. She fell, got up, and ran out the kitchen door. I noticed the plug had been pulled most of the way out of the wall, but not completely. Suddenly sparks started to fly out of the socket. A flame caught the wall and started to burn. I ran out of the house and call to Lorraine:

"There is a fire in the house!"

She ran back in and saw the fire. She grabbed the washing machine plug, pulling it out completely. She then grabbed a pot of water and threw it on the fire. She was lucky. The fire was out. All that was left was a section of burnt wall about one inch wide and two and half inches high, with smoke stains reaching up to the ceiling.

Lorraine thanked me. She later told my mother that I saved the house. I was very proud. I also thought Johnnie and Susan were neither smart nor observant. Although we continued seeing each other as we attended the same schools and lived near each other, I was never very friendly with them, nor they with me. Most likely influenced by their grandmother across the street.

Finally, the day came when I had to be taken to kindergarten. Mom and Dad were having their usual fights. I clung to Mom as a result. I'm sure she must have been telling me I was about to start school. But little, if anything, sunk in.

Then came the day. Mom drove me to school in Lakeville / Salisbury. The newly completed elementary school was a modern structure for the early 1950s: a single floor, with the lower grades close to the entrance and next to the playground. The classrooms were well lit. It was new and exciting—the halls and classrooms even smelled new with a hint of fresh paint. It was called the "upper school", in that K-6 grades were there. The "lower" school had what others would call Middle School or Junior High School (grades 7 and 8). The prior school was the K through 8 grade building down the hill from the new structure. It was old and poorly lit, smelly and anything but inviting. It was likely built in the 1920s with few renovations since.

Mom took me to the door of the kindergarten and said goodbye.

It hit me. I was to be left there alone…*with strangers*. With kids I had never seen before. With Dad and Mom fighting all the time. What if something happened while I was away? What if Dad did something to Mom? What would happen to me?

I had a fit and ran after her towards the car. I grabbed on her leg for all my life! The teacher, who was younger than most at the school, came to reassure me. A lot of good that did—what was this stranger telling me?

"It will be alright. Come on in, there are other children who want to meet you. Your mother will be back to pick you up," etc.

She may as well have been talking to a wild chimpanzee for all the good those words were doing. It didn't matter what she said! She was trying to get me away from my mother! I don't remember how it happened, but long after the bell rang for the start of class, I was sitting at a small desk, still crying, but no longer out loud.

Looking all around I saw other kids. Some were staring at me. WHY? It may have been because they were scared like me. Or could my tantrum have influenced them? It likely made them even more scared than when they first arrived. But I was in school. Sitting in a little chair, looking all around the kindergarten room, but not really caring what was around me.

How I survived that first day I do not know. Mom picked me up that day but that was the last time. From then on, she would drop me off before going to her letter shop. The next challenge was taking the "bus" back home.

Amesville was across the Housatonic River from Falls Village, which was only a mile away, being on the west side of the river it was a part of Salisbury township, not Canaan township where the Falls Village children attended school. Yet there were not many young children living in Amesville. So, the "bus" with the 6-plus kids, was a station wagon driven by Jimmy.

Jimmy was a mechanic employed at a local gas station. He was a person of short stature what is now referred to as a 'little person.' He was just a little bit taller than six-year-old me. In the mornings and afternoons he was the Amesville driver for the school bus. As long as I went to the upper school he was the one who would pick me up each day. Jimmy would stop the other kids from teasing me about taking a nap in the car. He would see to it the other kids did not pick on me during the rides. Throughout my school career (including HS), whenever I drove through Lakeville, I would shout a "Hi Jimmy!" when passing the gas station where he worked.

To this day I remember him very fondly, a great little man with a big heart. I would meet another little person years later; another man with a big heart that was broken by a city that didn't value people over politics.

The problem was I got car sick very easily if it was the wrong "smelling" car. At home, Mom's '38 Pontiac was fun to be in. I loved to take rides in it. I would climb all over that car (my personal jungle gym) when parked in the yard. I'd sit on the roof, climb up the fender to the hood and slide down. But the second I got into Dad's Oldsmobile. Instantaneous car sickness upon entering the back seat. Well, the "bus" smelled like the Olds. I threw up all over the back on that first trip home! This did not sit well with the others on the bus. But Jimmy felt sorry for me and didn't complain.

Jimmy began to watch me. I think I would tell him *if* I felt sick. He would stop and let me out where I would dump my "cookies" on the side of the road. Sometimes he would have me sit next to an open window to get fresh air. That helped. But in the cold weather, an open window would freeze the others. Soon I learned if I took a nap during the ride, I would not lose my lunch. Sitting in the back, resting my head against the window, I would fall asleep as quickly as possible all the way to Amesville. Jimmy would then quietly give me a little shake and wake me up telling me it was time to walk home. Actually, Lorraine's house—over the crest of the hill—about 25 yards from the bus stop. Susan was on the same bus, and a year later Johnnie joined the bus ride.

So, Susan, Johnnie and I would walk that short distance to their house. I would wait for Mom to get off work. She was now doing the Lakeville Letter Shop thing almost full time. She actually had a small office in town, underneath a lawyer's office with its own separate entrance. Her hours were flexible as necessary since this was a one-woman operation. If necessary, a sign would be hung in the window stating when there might be an expected return when she was not in.

Love,
Papa

Dear T – let's call this "the sandbox and a haunted house":

More about the Lorraine's place. When Susie, Johnnie and I were out walking northwest from their house. I climbed up a hill and onto some rocks. There are a lot of limestone formations in Amesville. Remember the quarries we visited when you drove through the old areas I grew up in? Most of the area was either metamorphic rocks or limestone (gypsum). The little hill behind Lorraine's house had an outcropping from a limestone up thrust. The limestone was surrounded by the gneiss and schist complexes, most Precambrian.

There, in the middle of this limestone formation was a little rounded out section with a slight depression. The limestone around it had been worn down by rain and snow. The water flow washed the granular limestone into this little hollow creating a perfect play area. This was area of about 15 square feet. When the limestone was dry, it was a natural sand box, but with limestone not silicate.

We rarely went up there as it was out of sight of the house. Lorraine would not want any of us to be out of sight, at least not for long. But whenever I had the chance I would go up to this little natural limestone box. What I loved most was on early spring days, I would go to this sheltered spot where the sun would warm the rocks and sand. I could lay down in the limestone sand being warmed by the radiant heat generated from the sand, the white rocks, and the sun above. It was nice to be in the sun, under the protection of the larger rocks, with the warm sandy surface. On hot summer days, the sandy surface, once stirred up, offered a cool respite from the sun's heat as the sand underneath the shallow surface was cool and refreshing.

Sometimes when I was to go *directly* home, and not to Lorraine's house, I would sneak past the house, climb the mound and "play" in the "sand". I was never interested in building sandcastles.

I did love to draw in it and look for patterns in the rock. It was about that time I found my first Indian arrowhead up on that hill. I was constantly looking for anything unusual. Never found another arrowhead, but did find pyrite and other minerals.

That it was a quiet, hidden space added to its endearment. I think I would return to it a number of times over the next few years. Once my relations with the Clark's took an ugly turn, I never visited it again, at least from the south or east. However, just over the rise to the east was my friend Peter's house—more on him later. I didn't know him yet. Years later, Peter and I would climb up the hill and enter the hollow from the west side, out of sight from the Clarks. But those visits were seldom.

Of interest in the neighborhood was the old house on the corner where the bus stop was. This was a very small house, surrounded by pine trees and perpetually in the shade. There could not have been more than three rooms, a kitchen, and the little screened-in porch facing the street. The paint was old and peeling. The shutters were falling apart. The roof was in need of repairs and there was even a hole in the roof over the little screened porch on the south side. Some of the windows had boards over them. You could see where the glass had been broken and not replaced. A couple of the older kids in the neighborhood likely threw stones at the window on the side of the house. Whoever lived there restricted himself to the front and back, not the south-east side. The windows were perfect targets for mischievous teens. The front door was painted in a dark color—maybe green, but with the moss and age you could not be sure which color it was. It did match the decay of the wood door and siding.

An old hermit lived there. Few of us ever saw him. As typical of kids our age, rumors were rampant about "Barney". Some said he had killed his wife and children and buried them in the back of the house. Others said he once kidnapped children to eat them. These were youthful imaginative minds. After all, few if any ever saw him go out shopping for food or anything else. There was a mailbox by the road, but there was hardly anything delivered to it that we could tell. Still, some just thought he was an imaginary ghost, a spirit who haunted Sugar Hill. It was about a year after I started to hear the rumors that I finally saw Barney. I must have been in second grade.

He was coming out of the house. He was small and stooped, maybe about 5'4" and no more than 120 lbs. He wore a dark, almost black plaid shirt and dark pants. His whiskers were salt and peppered with age. It was evident that he had not shaved for several days, if not weeks. He stared blankly at me for a moment and then went back into his house after picking up some mail, the first time I had seen him getting any letters. He was the "Boo Radley" of Amesville (reference to the character in *To Kill a Mocking Bird*). That was the only time I ever saw him. To me, he looked like all the rumors could be true and wrapped into his tiny frame.

Sometime later, Barney died, or at least that is what I was told. The house became totally abandoned. It was the source of even more ghost stories and tall tales. The ghosts of his former victims had killed him and taken away the body. A monster had eaten him. It now lived in a tunnel that went back into the hill behind the house towards Lorraine's and under the limestone outcropping. Maybe one of his sons came back and took revenge on their absent father by slitting his throat. Of course, we didn't even know if he had a son.

What made it worse was the elementary school bus stop was right in front of the old house. Most of the time we tried not to pay any attention to it. If a slight noise came from the house, a squirrel jumped on the roof, a twig fell on the gutter, or a rabbit jumped on a stick, we all jumped with fear that the monster would come out and eat us. Years later it was explained to me that he was an alcoholic and had drank himself to death (liver failure). That was a disease I would become more intimately aware of in future years.

Across Sugar Hill Road, at the same intersection, was a very nice house. It was owned by one of the families that could afford to send their two boys to the private schools, not the most expensive, but a decent one. The father was going deaf. Every Saturday he would be working in the garage or doing minor repairs on his car in the driveway, with the radio on very loud. I knew it was Saturday. The Saturday broadcast of the Metropolitan Opera Company's live performance could be heard throughout the neighborhood.

That was my first introduction to opera; I was six or seven. Unlike the other kids who made fun of it, I found it moving and was interested in knowing more. But being shy I never talked to him. Sometime when listening I could hear the voice of Milton Cross describe the plot of the opera. On those days, I would walk very very slowly by the house. I would *drop* something in the grass diagonally across and spend minutes looking for the non-existent item. As I advanced in age, eventually we would talk briefly about the operas and his love of classical music. Knowing both Mom and Dad liked classical music helped me approach this neighbor. We never had long conversations, just spoke briefly, but it almost always was about the music. Later in high school, I made polite inquiries about his sons. They were older and in colleges out of the area. I never got to meet them. His wife kept to herself and rarely emerged from the house.

They also had a lame dog, a terrier, similar to your dog Frankie, but with a hind leg that had been broken and had never healed properly. It would point forward like a stick never touching the ground when he moved. He would hobble around on his other three legs all over the neighborhood. He was attached to his master, the opera lover and when the owner was outside, the dog would stay close by.

More later—Love,
Papa

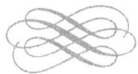

Hi T – one of the forgotten:

I'm not sure how much you remember of my old house attempting to take you and your sister on a visit to all the old places where your papa grew up.

We only had a single visit. Do you remember that Sugar Hill Road followed the Appalachian Trail up the mountain? The last 100 yards of paved road had a cluster of houses (more built since I lived there). Where the road ended, the Appalachian Trail continued over the mountain, towards Salisbury. Most of the houses at the end of the road were on a little flat area of the mountain before the Trail began to rise again, going deeper in the woods.

The first house on the right as you drove up to the top of Sugar Hill Road was a nice large (but run down) old house where Mrs. Wooden, a widow, lived. She was one of the more interesting characters in Amesville.

The house was heated by a wood stove and a fireplace. Mrs. Wooden would chop wood or hire some boy to do it for her. There were stacks of several cords of cut wood next to the house. A little field in the back is where horses once roamed, but no longer. That was evident by the small barn with stalls visible inside. An old log fence showed where the "pasture" for the horse must have been. There was no running water. An old well with a hand crank for a bucket was on the side of the house. A hand pump was visible through the kitchen window. Old Mrs. Wooden was only about five feet tall. She must have been in her late 70s, maybe older, when I got to know her. I would often see her walking past our mailbox. She had no car—she didn't believe she had a need for one. Mom would give her a lift whenever we passed her on the road. That is how I got to know about her, sitting the back seat asking her questions, or more often just listening to her converse with Mom.

Mrs. Wooden would walk down the mountain all the way to Falls Village to get food at the local general store then walk all the way back carrying the groceries. This was about a five-or six-mile round-trip walk, that is if she could not get a lift.

All year round she would wear this old, dark trench coat when she walked. I have to admit sometimes she did not smell very nice. However, as with so many elderly people she had a rather unusual history. Perhaps if we would give other elderly people a chance to tell their stories, they would prove as interesting as she was. If Mrs. Wooden wanted to do more extensive shopping, she would literally walk up to one of the neighbors she knew. If they were home, they would hear:

"I need to go shopping in Canaan, get your car keys and let's go."

There were a number of elderly residents on Sugar Hill Road who did not take offense to her behavior, including my nearest neighbors up the road, the Ciminos (who deserve a letter by themselves). They would give her a ride on the excuse they had to go to the larger stores in Canaan, too.

I knew if she had to go to the city, she would pull the same routine on the railroad.

In the early 1950s Falls Village had a "flag stop" railway station. We had about two trains traveling south in the morning and the same coming back in the evening. If someone wanted to get on the train, they would raise the red triangular signal flag on the station's pole. The train engineer would spot the flag as he came around the bend from the Housatonic River's falls and slow down to pick up the passengers. The train was a commuter train ending at Grand Central Station in NYC. Mom and I would occasionally take it on Saturdays, rather than drive, when we could afford it, which was seldom.

Well, Mrs. Wooden would raise the flag and rather than get in the passenger section of the train, which would require a ticket that cost money, she would hop into the engine car. She would tell the engineer where she wanted to be dropped off—and avoided paying for a ticket. I don't know who or what she knew, but she got away with it.

When the conductor(s) saw who had raised the flag they would just climb back on the steps and ignore who got on. I think once a year she would go all the way to NYC and back for a major shopping trip (returning with two bags of items rather than one) and the returning train would drop her off in the evening. I do know sometimes she would use the train to go to visit friends in West Cornwall (another flag stop) and stay overnight there.

What was interesting about Mrs. Wooden was she was a circus widow. Her late husband had been the "giant" in the Barnum and Bailey Circus (before it joined Ringling Brothers). She described him as 7′ 4″ tall. She had known General Tom Thumb, P.T. Barnum himself and a host of other famous circus personalities from the turn of the century (that is the turn of 1900). She fell in love with this BIG, lovable man.

When he left the circus, they moved to Amesville. Their goal was to build a small farm and grow unusual crops and fruit trees. There had been a small apple orchard and some pear trees. Corn took up the corner of one field and could still be seen. You could still see some of the trees in the back of the house, but the old crops had been overgrown by the encroaching forest. Few of the trees produced fruit anymore. The reason for the property's decay was simple. Like most oversized giants, he died in his late 40s, leaving her a widow.

She had tried to keep up farming but eventually gave up. But, she refused to leave the old house. We often asked her if she needed any money, but she always answered: "No."

It was no wonder, with all the freebies she got in transportation! Somehow, she lived on Social Security and perhaps some retirement savings from her husband. It was a marginal existence, surviving on only the bare minimum. A special treat would be a chocolate bar my mother would sometimes give her if she saw her and had one in the car. There was a suspicion that Mom would keep a chocolate bar or two in the car just for Mrs. Wooden.

She died when I was about eight. I don't know exactly when, but Mom just mentioned that we would not be seeing her anymore.

I tell you this to remind you that everyone has a story to tell. No life is so unworthy as to be ignored. Mrs. Wooden is just one of those unknown individuals who cross your path. If you take time to explore their life story, just a little, you may find out interesting things from them. Like my life, it may not be one that would ever make the newspapers, nor anything newsworthy, but it is a life, good or bad. No matter what, lessons can always be learned from what can be shared.

Love,
Papa

Hi T:

Your grandma had learned to read by the time she was three, thanks to her father (her mother was marginally literate). Like so many of the children in the old West, she first learned to read from the Bible. Then, once she started going to school, she had access to books, just not many, because back then there were rarely school libraries. This was unlike most schools today.

It was during my experience in kindergarten that Mom noticed I was not picking up on learning to read. She consulted the teachers and was assured they knew the latest and best techniques for teaching reading. She was *not* to teach me at home. Mom thought this was bad advice. Yet, to her regret she followed it, totally against her gut feeling—the "professionals" knew best. So, I would look at pictures and have her read to me. I was not learning the alphabet. I was not learning how to sound out the letters. Phonics was totally unknown then.

Kindergarten came and went. Most of the time, the teacher was reading to the class and not having the class read back. In 1st grade it quickly became apparent that I was having reading problems. The teachers "diagnosed" me as having a learning disability. Mom related it to my premature birth; the key—I was not learning how to read! I couldn't read at the level expected. Back then there were not as many expectations as there are today. What is expected of kindergarteners today is about what was expected for a 1st grader in the 1950s. So I was really much further behind if you apply current standards to my capabilities at the time.

Math was difficult, but with a little help I began to improve. I remember the 1st grade teacher, a recent college graduate, was much younger than most teachers at Salisbury Central Elementary School. She really tried to help me. Finally, there was a conference with Mom, the teacher and me. She was very nice but it was really depressing. I was being discussed as an inferior student, not on par with the others in the class. Because of my lack of reading skills other things were more difficult. I had trouble understanding written instructions. I tested poorly. Social study lessons and homework were negatively impacted. The only thing I could do was math. There was little chance of ever getting into college or having any kind of education beyond high school I was passed to the 2nd grade without mastering the reading skills necessary to succeed, as a result of Mom's pleading for me not to repeat the 1st grade. This might be called an early case of social promotion. It didn't help.

All of this was impacting the environment at home. Dad did not want a failing child. Mom regretted not teaching me to read earlier. She felt the schools had failed. But 2nd grade was even more of a disaster. I could not read the harder materials. All my grades slipped. I was feeling less and less confident. The school was going to hold me back. Mom, even more desperately than before, wanted to avoid me being held back.

During this time she was working at Hotchkiss School, as a secretary in the infirmary, as the Lakeville Lettershop did not bring in enough money to support the family. Hotchkiss provided a steady income, even if low. Nearby was a very small private elementary school that would accept me as a 3rd-grader and promised to give me the additional attention I needed. So, off I went. I remember having a lot fun in my one year there. We staged little plays acting out historical events and engaged in a lot more group activities. The children there were mostly upper-class. The school was far more intellectually stimulating than Salisbury Central. But the reading problem persisted.

The school itself was right across from the Hotchkiss golf course. There was a small clearing in the woods to the west of Hotchkiss where they had carved out a little space for a small school. What was nice was there were no bus rides. Mom would be able to take me and pick me up immediately after school. If she had more work, I went up to the infirmary where she worked or walked around the school. If not, we would sometimes go home early.

But by the end of that school year, my reading had not improved, at least not enough. So, I went back to the Salisbury Elementary and repeated 3rd grade there. We just couldn't afford to continue at the private school.

Now, be aware this letter has taken you forward a little fast. There are still tales from kindergarten and my early years to come. But this is important background information. It is also a good place to stop as your first year in college comes to an end.

Love,
Papa

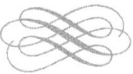

T – now, on to Connecticut's plants. You need the map for this, and the next letters.

On The Hill there were a lot of interesting plants and trees in the yard and around the property. The owner before my father's family (my grandfather bought the house in the late '20s) was a gardener, who traveled around the world collecting plants and trees. He wanted to see if they would grow in his little corner of Connecticut. This was long before any restrictions on importing plants for fear of invasive species, so it was a lot easier to get plants into the country back then. Thank goodness none of the gardener's plants were invasive species; in fact, many were very interesting.

We had a large pine right at the southeast corner of the house, which rose far above the roof. As a child I thought it was protecting us from any lightning coming from that corner of the house. On the northeast side was a line of sugar maples—about 10 on each side—that lined the driveway. Sugar Hill Road got its name from those trees on our property. Three other sugar maples were in the front yard. They protected the house on that side from lightning coming from the north. One year I did try to tap them, but didn't collect the sap as regularly as I should have, so we didn't have enough to make syrup. Still, it was a nice sweet, clear drink. I was about 10 at the time.

To the south, outside the windows by my bed, were many strange flowers and pretty plants. I never knew most of their names. When we first moved to The Hill, there was a fenced-in area where the old rows of plants could be seen. Some may have been edible; most were flowers. But they were already beginning to become overgrown by the weeds by the time we arrived. My family were never gardeners and they slowly let the old exotic plants die out. I do remember a stone path to the fence surrounding what was once a beautiful garden. There were only hints of the old plants remaining. The original garden would have been a full acre in size. The total property was about 7.5 acres.

One of the most unusual trees was an acacia tree in the southeast corner of the house, very close to the giant pine. The original acacia had died, but a sprig was saved and transplanted nearby. The stump of the old tree was still there, slowly decaying. The new acacia was thin, but strong, and growing fast. What was interesting was that the original acacia was a sprig taken from the same acacia grove from which Jesus' crown of thorns and the Cross were made—at least that was the story that was passed down to the family, although it may have just been a story told to a curious little boy.

The acacia is a hardwood commonly used for special purposes throughout the Middle East. The Ark of the Covenant in the Bible was made of acacia wood, as was the Cross on which Jesus was nailed, as I have said. Jesus' crown of thorns was made from an interwoven series of small branches of acacia. Acacia trees (actually a genus of trees—as I think there may be over 600 species) all have "leaves" which are actually clusters of small leaves, looking a little like miniature ferns. The tree in our yard was typical of most acacias. Sharp needle-like thorns grew to be three to four inches long along the trunk, branches, and everywhere.

Though not my favorite tree, it was certainly the most unusual as it was descended from the trees used in the Bible. That made it very special to me. When I was older, I would try to climb it to the first branch, quite a way off the ground, without being stabbed by the thorns. I rarely (make that never) succeeded. And you never walked barefoot around that tree, although the leaves and little flowers were very beautiful in the spring.

What may help visualize the property is the little map below that I made of The Hill. One of my favorite trees was a Bosc pear tree in the corner of the yard just before reaching the lower field. I could see it out my bedroom window facing southwest. It was a small tree and never grew any larger. Each summer it would give some fruit. The first year it gave about a dozen pears, the next year only eight, then five, etc. I would love to pick and eat them. It was a sickly little tree. I believe my love kept it alive for another five years. I remember the year it only gave one pear. I would hug the tree and say that I still loved it anyway. When it did finally die, I was very sad. That is why Bosc pears have always been my favorite.

Near the acacia was one of the three kinds of mulberry tree, one had light purple berries. The one in the field was a dark-berry producer and the one on the other side of the big pine (in the fenced in garden mentioned above) was a white mulberry tree. Mom and I would go out to pick as many as we could reach on the lower branches. In the spring I had all the berries I could eat. Another love I still have.

Love
Papa

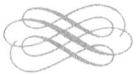

Hi T – more plant talk:

Another interesting plant was in the backyard, down the slope, on top of the septic tank! Rhubarb thrived on this swampy fecal-fertile bog. The leaves were giants! Some would be over 18 inches in diameter and almost a yard long. The stalks were huge, some as big as a woman's wrist, even bigger. I have never seen anything to match those plants. They spread beyond the septic tank and at one time there were at least three or more clusters of these giant rhubarb plants.

   We never picked all the rhubarb, there was just too much. I don't think my Dad was interested and Mom didn't have enough time to cook it. Remember my rhubarb pie in the contest at Wolf Trap? There are many ways to prepare rhubarb, not just in a pie garnished with candied cicadas! When the back field, where the rhubarb thrived, went fallow, the blackberry vines took over. Eventually all rhubarb was killed off—another great loss. We just weren't up to keeping control of the garden with Mom working and Dad wanting to relax as much as possible, especially after a week of his long commute. Besides, he had no interest in plants.

   Dad had found a job in Hartford. The problem with the job was it was about an hour's drive from Falls Village, but it was the closest store that sold carpets, his specialty. With the little income from the Lakeville Letter Shop, plus the salary from the department store, we were able to survive on what would be considered a standard lower middle income.

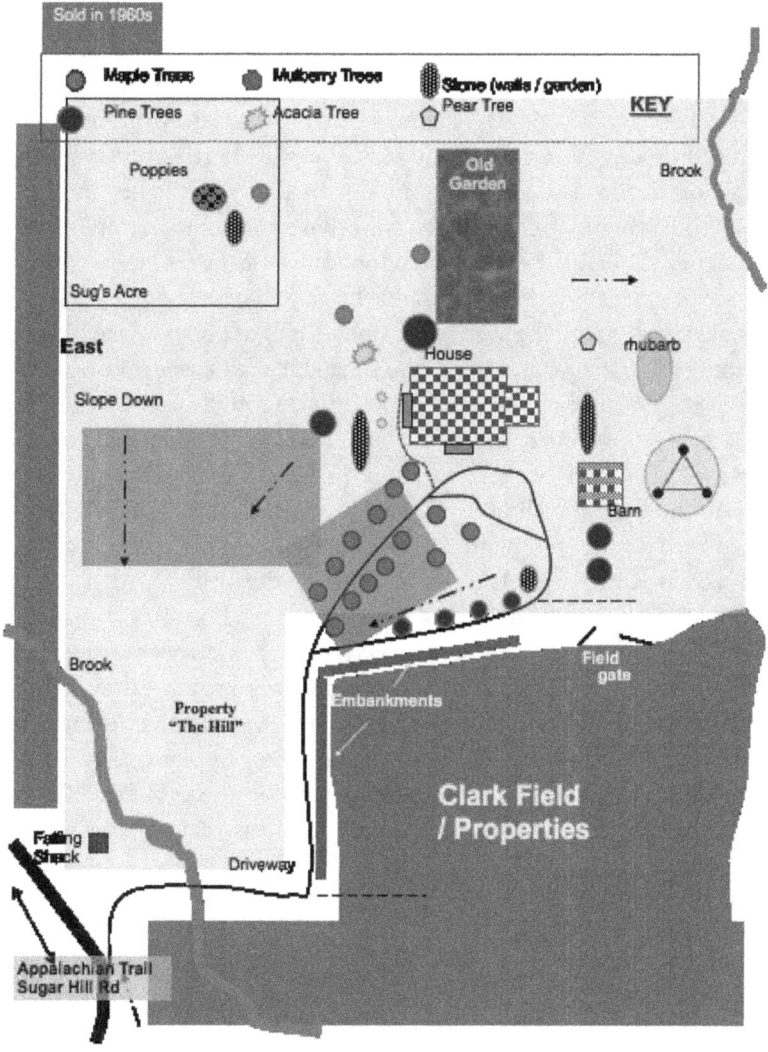

During the summer, Mom and I would go out to the mulberry tree in the south-east field, where it overlooked the Housatonic Valley. When the Housatonic Falls were rushing after prolonged rain, the sound would be clear up at the house, especially in this part of the property.

The dark purple mulberry tree was at the top of The Hill. It had a small cluster of rocks and shrubs nearby. One spring morning when I was about six, Mom and I went out to pick berries. When we arrived, a timber rattlesnake threatened us by the usual shaking of its tail rattle. The snake was curled up on the rocks and watching us closely. Since this was the first time we had encountered each other, it didn't know if we were friend or foe. Mom told me to ignore it but keep away. She said when a rattlesnake was scared it would curl up and shake its tail as a warning not to come any closer. She explained its bite was dangerous but if we just minded our own business, it would eventually relax.

The snake watched us pick berries for some time. It soon realized we were not a threat and relaxed, slightly; at least the rattling stopped and it was no longer in a striking position. When we left, Mom approached the snake and left a few berries to show it what we had done. The next time we went there, it coiled but didn't rattle. The next day, it didn't even coil. Mom found a mouse or something the snake would be interested in eating and knelt down at its level. It slowly came over and put out its little forked tongue to smell. Then, ever so slowly, it took the food from Mom's hand.

After feeding it twice more over a few weeks, Mom held out the food in her right hand but put her left hand between the snake and the food. As it crossed over her left hand, she slowly picked it up. This continued for a number of days. At times in the early morning, I think it was more interested in the warmth of our bodies than any food. Eventually when it felt our footsteps it would come out of its hole, almost as if greeting us. When there were no more mulberries, we visited the stony area just to see how the rattler was doing. It was well-fed, thanks to Mom.

After a while I was feeding it, too. By the end of the summer, Mom and I would pick it up and drape it over my shoulders. It watched me pick the blackberries by this time and seemed to be enjoying our walking over the field. It became our little pet. Thus began my love and respect for snakes and mulberries. By the way, I've been told that timber rattlers are more poisonous than the famous sidewinder in the Southwest desert. More on rattlesnakes later—years later. The key is they never pose a threat, at least if you understand them. Just give them space.

Very near the stones where the snake lived was a small patch of poppies, like the ones in *The Wizard of Oz*. There were mostly bright red ones, a few white, or at least a different color. I was never sure if these were the opium variety or not. They were tall and beautiful, another plant brought in by the previous owner. These only lasted a few summers before the fields and berry vines took over, killing them. What I remember most is the "fuzzy" stalk of the flower and the beautiful red color with the black center.

This patch was on the opposite slide of the rocks where the snake lived. You could tell it was once a boxed-in area with a variety of plants. By the time our family moved to The Hill, almost all the plants in the boxed area had died. It must have been a beautiful garden of esoteric flowers in the '20s, but now only the poppies remained and even they died out a few years later.

Somewhere near there, maybe in the same overgrown garden were lilies, daises, Black-eyed Susans, lilacs, and some other flowers. What was missing were roses—they didn't grow anywhere on The Hill. I'll talk about the lilacs in a future letter (they were by the breezeway—see the map).

The Hill remained a place of great beauty offering a variety of plants and trees. It is too bad the subsequent owners had no appreciation of the flora found on the property. Most were destroyed, including the acacia and lilac after the sale of The Hill and the move by my mother to Virginia.

Enough of plants for now.

Love,
Papa

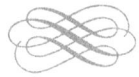

It's Me again. Now for the animals and neighborhood around The Hill:

Shortly after we moved to The Hill I was playing outside in the driveway; near the house (see the diagram) it was mostly grass, compacted earth and a few tire tracks. The driveway formed a big loop. Then it split into a double oval path toward the front of the house. It proceeded down through the sugar maples where it met the gravel road at the bottom.

One morning Mom was working in the kitchen with the breezeway doors to the driveway open. She heard me saying "Doggie" and was curious to see if one of the Clarks' dogs had come up to our yard, even though they were usually very well-trained and stayed on their property. When she came out she saw a large red fox eyeing me. She watched for a short time. He began to approach me. Not knowing if he thought "Wally" was food or friend, she ran out and chased him away. That fox would return later when we tried to have some chickens.

When we first moved to The Hill, the barn swallows had a nest in the barn, right in the center of the ceiling, as mentioned before. They would fly in and out of the window above the huge door, but Dad never bothered to fix it. So, the swallows raised their young in the barn. This continued for a couple of summers. I loved to watch them and they didn't seem to be bothered by being watched.

There were always a number of bats circling the house in the evenings. I loved to watch them fly around the back yard where there were fewer trees to block my view. I would watch either from my window or sitting on the breezeway. One summer, the swallows' nest in the barn fell. I think it was during a very bad storm. The baby birds died and the swallows disappeared for the remainder of the season. I was very happy to see them back the next summer, when two males and one female built a new nest in the breezeway. It was fairly close to the exterior wall of the kitchen, well protected.

At first, when we came out there they would charge at us in an attempt to chase us away. After a while, they relaxed, especially if we sat in the rocking chairs on the breezeway. Sitting made us appear shorter and not quite able to reach their nest. One swallow would stay on the nest while the other two were off feeding on insects. When the babies were born, they became defensive again, at least for the first few days. Mom and I spent hours watching the parents gather bugs and fly in to feed the babies (usually three). When the babies began to fly, they had no fear of us. After all, they had seen us since they first stuck their heads out of the nest.

Between the bats and the swallows I was rarely bitten my mosquitoes. Currently, the decline in the bat population is becoming a threat to humans. I would rather not spray for insects and let the bats and swallows take care of them, an optimal solution rather than spreading insecticides all over neighborhoods.

The next year the swallows rarely buzzed us at all unless we were sitting on the step to the backyard, which blocked their entrance to the nest. Then, one summer they failed to come back. We waited and hoped but they were never seen again. I had grown to love the swallows. I longed to watch them dart in and out of the breezeway. Another loss. Buddha is right—life is suffering.

One night (late fall, I think) we heard a racket on the breezeway. Dad went out to see what was making the noise. In a minute he came back in and put on his heavy leather work gloves. I saw him hopping around the corner of the breezeway near the old well. Suddenly he darted down, then up he came with an opossum by the tail. The opossum was not happy, but as usual played dead. The confused marsupial couldn't find the tiny opening in the breezeway where he'd been gaining access. Usually in late fall, several planks of siding would be placed on the open side to keep the winter's cold from getting in the kitchen. Since we had not closed off the opening entirely, the opossum got in. But he panicked and couldn't get out. His running around tipping over a small table and chairs made the racket which got our attention. My Dad chasing him added to his panic. Dad held him up and brought the terrified animal close for me to see. Then he let him down, just outside the steps. I don't think I ever saw him again, but it was the first of many nocturnal creatures I would become familiar with on The Hill. We would have numerous other four-footed visitors over the years.

When I was about four or five, before the "patterns" letter, Mom thought it would be fun to have a chicken coop in the ground floor of the barn. The barn had once had a small stable for two horses (back before cars). The Hill was originally a log cabin, but was expanded many times. The barn was one of the additions. Not for cows, but likely for a few draft horses and a carriage or two. The lower section of the barn was perfect for chickens: a dirt floor and a low ceiling, with little ledges for them to roost on.

The chickens had easy access in and out through the broken door. The stone wall and a small fence to kept them out of the back field. It made a perfect area for them roam in. We got miniature Bantam chickens, about eight of them. I loved feeding them, especially when they learned to come up the little path to the backyard and they looked forward to me coming out to feed them. One or two were friendly enough to pick up and pet. But most were not. I loved watching them as they hunted for bugs, worms, and seeds. So did a fox—but not for worms and seeds. His first appearance was as if he was casing the joint prior to executing his plans.

One afternoon Mom saw the fox come into the yard. At first the chickens ran away, but the fox pretended to be sniffing something on the ground and not paying attention to them. The hickens were curious and approached the fox. Snap—he gobbled one up whole! Once his stomach settled down a little, he got up and resumed his little dance.

Other chickens started to follow him again. Same thing happened. Snap! Munch, munch ... Soon three chickens were dead. Mom grabbed the shotgun and ran outside shouting a warning to the fox. He started his routine again. Mom raised the shotgun and aimed. Bam! Right through the nose. Dead on the first shot! Not hard with a shotgun, but still a good shot.

Mom hung him up by the tail at the corner of the breezeway. From tail to nose he was about six feet long. Mom said she cried for an hour after, for killing anything that beautiful. However, she said:

"I couldn't let him keep eating Wally's chickens."

I was away with Dad that afternoon and saw the fox hanging up when I returned. I don't remember any emotions, just curiosity about him and why some of the chickens were missing—especially my favorite rooster.

Love
Papa

P.S. I have included a diagram of the house for you to get a better picture of its layout and where things were oriented in the house. It should help.

Chapter 4

Old Memories, Real Old Memories!

T: I'm calling this letter "Visiting the Past". By the way, the fox episode takes place around this timeframe, but before the UFO visit.

Shortly after the move to The Hill I started to have bad dreams. It was as if the move during the night in the car triggered something in my mind. Or, rather, opened up something in my subconscious. I would wake up screaming. Sometimes I would be holding the back of my left thigh saying it hurt. Mom would hear me talking in my sleep.

I kept saying my "buddies" were visiting me at night. She had no idea who the buddies were, or where they came from. All she knew was they were disturbing her child. Another problem was they would sometimes bring the nightmares with them, visions a young child could not have had any knowledge of; many of these visions were beyond a young child's vocabulary not to mention his experiences.

As the dreams became more frequent, more and more details

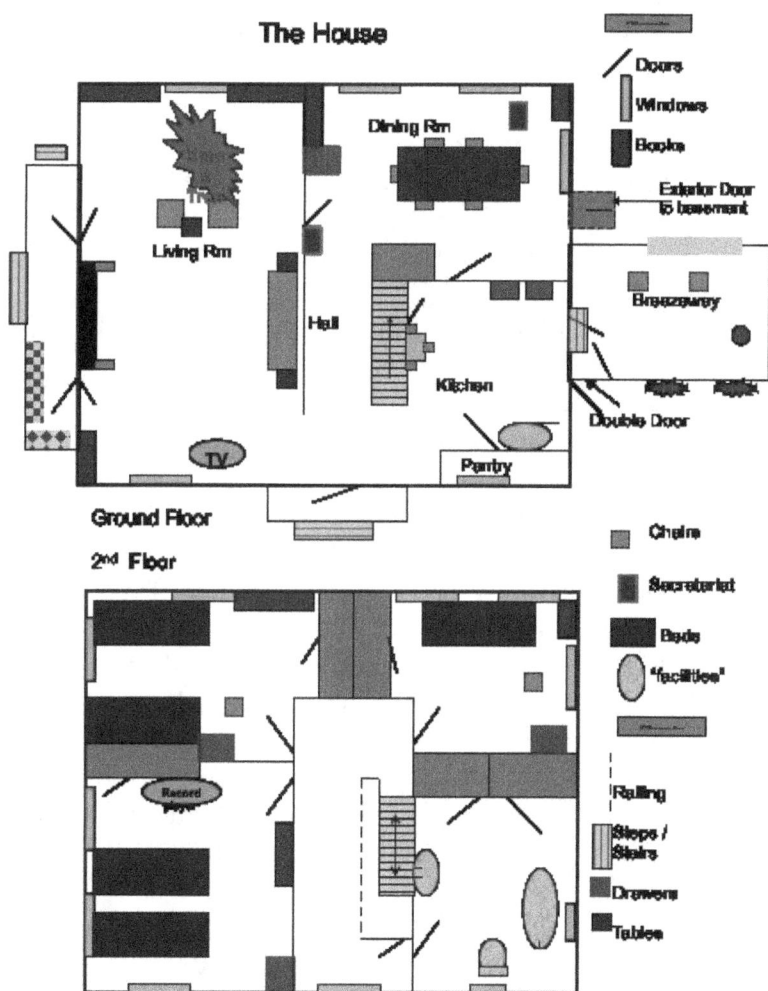

The House

Doors
Windows
Books

Dining Rm

Exterior Door to basement

Living Rm

Breezeway

Hall

Kitchen

Double Door

TV

Pantry

Ground Floor

2ⁿᵈ Floor

Record Player

Chairs

Secretariat

Beds

"facilities"

Railing

Steps / Stairs

Drawers

Tables

arose. Yet there were no experiences in my life that could account for such memories. Some visions were very simple. Cold. Snow. Mud. Noise. Brief visions of guns. But such images were impossible as I had no experience with these items, particularly guns. When I relayed these nightmares to my parents, Dad became upset. One day, I was playing just off the breezeway with some sticks, moving them back and forth. My Dad came up to me and asked what I was doing. Without thinking:

"My M1 needs cleaning" was my response.

Dad got furious. He slapped me on the back of my head saying: "You can't know anything about that."

The dreams only intensified. And I was cold—always in the cold. Crouching in mud with a helmet on. Darkness of night. Wishing I was somewhere else. Sometimes having a brief thought that it was Christmas time. More visions of snow mixed with mud and blood. More and more guns. Running. Shots. Screams. Seeing things like a head being torn apart by bullets. Not normal images for a child of four or five years old.

Of course, such visions would wake me up with a scream. Slowly, a full picture was emerging. There was an existing group of men I was part of. More than that, I had become their leader.

Attempting to understand what was happening, Mom spent more time trying to interpret the dreams. She was able to pull out some of the details. It was a war. As a former WAC (Women's Army Corp) who served in WWII, she was able to draw little sketches to help determine what the images were. After several months a more complete picture evolved. Mom took notes. These would be the discussion points for many years later. This is what she was able to piece together.

The second lieutenant and sergeant were dead. I became head of the platoon. There was no one else. It appeared I was in charge due to the decimation within the ranks.

There was a tremendous battle. The lines were constantly changing. The enemy had captured some high ground less than a hundred yards from our dug-in position. A machine gun placement pointed at us from on top of a hill. Orders came down. We had to take the hill and disable the machine gun nest. There was a confusing description of my calling on a "funny phone" asking for support. Something with a crank on the side of a box, nothing that would have been seen in my short life.

A group of men started running up a hill in the early daylight. I had to join them. I heard a whooshing overhead and thought:

"Good, we have cover."

Then an explosion to my left. Another in front, then on the right, striking our men as they charged.

Then thinking: "There short, they're short, they are killing their own men."

This dream always ended with a sharp pain in the back of my left leg near my buttock. I would then wake up with a scream, sweating and trembling in fear. Sometimes my platoon buddies would be calling me back to them.

Mom would come and hold me until I drifted off to sleep. I didn't understand what I was dreaming or what it all meant; my young mind could not comprehend all that was being presented in the dreams.

It wasn't until years later that I was able to understand all the images that were there. I was a corporal in the United States Army's 93rd or 101st Division, deployed in Belgium. It was December 1944. The Germans were launching a counterattack. It was the beginning of the Battle of the Bulge. During the night the Germans had set up a machine gun nest overlooking our position. To the north (I think it was north), less than a quarter mile away, the German panzer tanks were roaring through. I was part of a platoon of solders caught in the middle of a major battle. My lieutenant went to see the major. On his was back he was killed. The sergeant had been killed earlier in the battle. As a corporal, I was now the highest rank in the platoon.

Early, an hour or more before dawn, the major came by.

"I want your platoon to take that hill at dawn and hold it. We have to get a better view of what Gerry is doing."

At dawn, we started to move up the hill. But the machine gun fire was intense. We pulled back briefly. I called, asking for mortar support, and waited. I heard the first rockets flying, the whole platoon started to charge, on my orders! As we ran up the hill I looked to my left. I saw one of the men buckle over as the bullets tore into his midsection. Then one of the men to my immediate left had his head shot apart. The first of the mortar shells hit and two of my men fell dead. Another shell exploded to my right and just in front of me. They were falling short of the target.

I thought: "My God, they're killing their own men."

Today that is called "friendly fire". Well, it was not very friendly. That was the last thought that ran through that mind. I felt a great pain in my left leg and was thrown off my feet. Everything went black. There was no more memory, only of what happened later.

I was floating above this horrifying scene of a battlefield filled with dead bodies. I saw two men walking around turning the dead over and marking down names. The U.S. Army soldiers (a staff sergeant and a private) were collecting dog tags from the dead. They came upon this one body covered in a blood-red snow cone of death.

I thought to myself: "Boy, this guy really bought it."

They turned him over. It was me! Only then did I realize I was dead.

Love,
Papa

Now for the other side:

I looked around. It was as if I could see two worlds at the same time overlaying each other. The view resembled a window of an aquarium. I was looking both above the water level and below. Below was the blood, mud and snow of the battle. Frozen bodies were scattered all over the fields. Death was all around. In the far distance I could see troop movement. The battle was still raging on. I could see the Germans gathering prisoners. Somehow the tank advancement had stopped. I could see our army fighting back in various places. Yet the area around me was quiet. The battle here had moved to other areas nearby.

Parallel but slightly above the world of war was a group of my men all floating above the scene. My platoon. They were whole again. The man whose face had been torn off was restored, as was the one blown up by the shell. For that fact, so was I. They turned to me:

"What's happening Paul?" (Years later someone thought my name had been Paul in that life—this was later confirmed).

They were all looking to me as their leader. Looking around on this new plane of existence where there was nothing but beauty. There was no snow. It was warm and inviting. It was full of fresh fields and wildflowers, with beautiful gardens.

Suddenly faint memories came to me as if in a dream. I knew I was dead. We all were. What was more important, I knew what had to be done next. Images of a life as a Hindu monk came to me, just long enough to remember what needed to be done. The realization we could not stay here came into my thoughts. I turned to my men and told them:

"We're dead, but I know where we have to go. Come on guys, together!"

My confidence was enough to bring the troops together. My thoughts were conveyed up and down the line of what had once been my platoon. Mentally, a command went out. We all hooked arms, about five or six on either side of me. Again, I was taking the lead. It appeared that all those who were with me that fateful morning had been killed. We formed a "V" shape like a flock of geese.

Then we started moving through the air in a gradual ascent. As our movement continued upward, a white light appeared and became brighter. The images of war and thoughts of the carnage were being left behind. The world of what we knew as the earthly realm began to fade. My target was to move towards the "white sun", which was unlike anything I had ever seen in the physical world. It was brighter than any natural light I had seen. It was warm, not hot, and inviting, as if it were a door to another world flooded with this unmistakably bright light.

One of the men, who had come from a very conservative or fundamentalist Christian Church started to panic.

"You are leading us into the fires of HELL!" he yelled.

Mentally I told him: "Don't be silly—you are coming with us."

He tried to break away. I sent a mental message down the line to the ones next to him to grab on tighter and not let him go. It worked; his will was not strong enough to escape the hold. His fears remained but his resistance subsided. If the commanding thoughts were not holding him in formation, he might have tried to bolt from the group. This I could not allow.

As we started to get closer to the white light, the whole platoon began to change form. Our G.I. uniforms melted off. Not in a negative way, they just started to dissolve. At first it seemed as if the uniforms were being replaced by white robes. Then as we progressed it seemed the robes and we were one.

As the white etheric sun got closer, other images started to appear. Some men thought they saw Jesus. Another saw Moses. Others saw relatives long dead. They were coming to greet us. I no longer feared any of the men would break away. We were approaching where we were meant to be. I was not distracted by the figures but continued straight toward the innermost part of the light. All memory of what happened next disappeared. It was as if the closer I went into the light, the less memory could be retained of what had been in the physical world.

Years later, while in graduate school, I wrote a possible first chapter of *It's Me* for a thanatology (study of death and dying) class. It was the past few letters and about my tragic death as experienced during WWII. I included a number of references, including "Ike" Eisenhower's description of the G.I.s on the frontlines at the Battle of the Bulge. I was able to compose it after a long period of meditation where these memories from early childhood were brought back into the conscious mind.

Back to the dreams and The Hill. The problem with all this happening was I was only four or five years old and so it was very scary. The dream of the battle was terrifying. The bullets, blood, bodies and death all in a place called "The Bulge" scared the hell out of me. That's why I would wake up with a scream or start to cry.

This put Mom on edge, night after night. Not every night, but once a week or more, she had to come to me in the middle of the night to sooth my panic, holding me until I fell back into sleep. My Dad was furious about the disruptions. He felt I should get over the dreams by myself. He never understood what they were, nor did he want to. Mom was not only losing sleep but was becoming very concerned. What was this doing to my mental health? Would the sleep disruptions lead to physical problems? She knew something had to be done but there was no clue as to what or how.

As the dreams continued, my play activities during the day emulated the dreams more and more. I was not shown the gun in the house. There was only one, my father's old Ithaca shotgun. At that time, I had never touched it. But I continued to pretend to shoot and charge up the little hill in the backyard. I imagined that the external cellar door was the machine gun nest I was trying to capture and I would charge up the slope in the backyard towards the cellar door. But I would always collapse short, grabbing my left thigh as I fell.

This would be a game that would be repeated for many years to come, even after my buddies ceased to visit my dreams.

But the worst was yet to come.

Love
Papa

T – now for the "Visitors from the Past":

Of course, with all of these visions, I was beginning to be scared of going to sleep. Once on the other side of sleep, my buddies would come to me in my "dreams".

"Paul, come back with us!"

"We are your platoon, why did you leave us?"

"We want you back with us."

"What are you doing down there, come back, come back, come back!" It was as if I was being torn between two worlds.

Thank goodness some nights I had no dreams. But those peaceful nights were becoming fewer and fewer. Mom knew something was terribly wrong. Dad was getting madder every day as more and more memories were acted out in my play activities. Moving stones in formation up a little mound, saying they were my men and that we had been "ordered" to take a hill. Pretending to call for help on a walky-talky even though I didn't know what one was or what it was called. I would hold a small box up to my ear and pretend to pull on an antenna. Then I would pretend to talk into the box.

Dad would blow up!!

At night, the appeals from my old platoon members for me to come back became a constant struggle. I would start to cry, knowing I should be with them but not knowing how to get back. I would tell Mom about their demands for me to join them. She was afraid that I would do something to get back to them.

As for my father, I quickly learned I couldn't say anything about my dreams.

Somehow, Mom knew they were from my past life, and that my buddies wanted me to return to them. They didn't want me in this silly little boy's body. They wanted their old buddy back with them. There was only one way to get back—death.

I think she started to contact her old friends from the Arcane School to get their advice.

As I said before, the Arcane School was a school for meditation and esoteric studies founded by Alice A. Bailey after she was dismissed from the Theosophical Society by Annie Besant. Alice was told to carry on the sayings of the Master called The Tibetan (a.k.a. DK). Mom used to be one of her secretaries. Most think Alice was in some kind of a trance when she transcribed DK's words. But Mom would watch Alice typing away on her typewriter, then suddenly stop, look up and say:

"I don't agree with that! …Well yes, it is your book but are you sure you want to say that? Oh alright, I will put it down as you want."

No one except Alice could see DK. Yet she spoke to him as if he was standing right in front of her and the two of them were carrying on a normal session of dictation.

Alice died shortly after Mom saw her for the last time, never completing her autobiography (which was finished by her husband, Foster Bailey). There was to be a second series of books, but they were never written—more on them much later.

The one good thing about this group was that the circle of influence and friends was rather extensive. Sure enough, Mom found a source of possible help.

Love,
Papa

Getting help with my dreams:

Someone in the Arcane School, or possibly a friend responded to her queries, suggesting that a noted astrophysicist and a professor of astronomy in New Jersey may be able to help Mom understand what was happening to me. Everyone knew him as a professor, but to an inner circle, he was also one of the best astrologists in the country. Mom went to visit him. I think I was there too, though only a very vague memory exists. She told him of my bad dreams and the types of play activities she didn't think were normal for my age. He got the information on my date and time of birth and said he had an idea. He would work my horoscope backward. It had worked for some others he knew who were having problems with past lives influencing their current lives. He would work mine backward and forward to get a full view.

A few weeks later, he either came up to The Hill or called Mom. He had worked my horoscope chart backward and this is some of what he told her, which she related to me years later.

The professor said that something had to be done to get rid of my "buddies", as they were a threat to my current existence. He also worked my horoscope forward. Mom forgot most of the predictions, but it showed I would have trouble in college (Rockford?). An early career would be dedicated to helping others (social work!). What was most unusual was that I would be doing something for the Pentagon—working with them towards the turn of the century. The work would be critical to the country and the military. He didn't know what the work would entail. He didn't think it would be as a member of the military but as a civilian—see why I do not dismiss serious astrologers! This one had a profound capacity for seeing both the past and the future.

The key to this session was that Mom had to get me to tell my "buddies" to go away. She carefully explained to me they needed to go away and not come back. I was to order them! Not give them any choice. I was stronger than they because I was alive and they were spirits from my past. They belonged in another place. They should not be visiting me at night. If they went away, they would proceed with their own growth, perhaps reincarnate themselves. Only then would they find places in their future and not remain stuck in the past, which was what was happening.

When they came to me I followed her instructions. In a strong commanding voice I shouted:

"You are not wanted here. You are to go away and not come back."

Somehow it worked. I think I was crying as I told them. They departed and I never saw or heard from them again, at least not in the same way. In future years, as an adult, I would occasionally bump into a child and I would swear to myself:

"I know you from somewhere."

When in meditation or alone thinking about it, the memories of the platoon would return and I would realize that I had just seen one of my old buddies in his new reincarnation. This only happened about three times, so it was rare. I never pursued contact with any of those children. All these later contacts occurred during and after my high school years.

So much for breaking contact with my buddies, but not with other spirits.

One night I woke up suddenly. I saw someone walking down the hall in the house. I thought it was Mom in a white nightgown, but she didn't owned a white nightgown. I called softly. No response. Then I looked more closely, the image had no feet and was floating down the hall about six inches above the floor. I was shocked, but only a little scared. For some reason I felt no threat.

I asked Mom the next day if she or Dad had gone to the bathroom in the night.

"No."

I told her what I saw. She said she would take care of it. The "ghost" was never seen again. Now, do you see why I'm so weird?

See you REAL SOON.

Love,
Papa

Chapter 5

Flora, Fauna and Masonry

Hi T. A little side letter called: When is Freemasonry not Freemasonry? Let's find out (it's important for what follows).

As you know your grandma was a Freemason. Not Eastern Star, as some mistakenly think, but not part of the usual Masonic organizations universally recognized, like the ones I currently belong to. Here's a little Masonic history and how it plays into your family.

Your grandma was a member of La Droit Humain, (Of Human Rights) which has its headquarters in France. What is unique about the La Droit Humain's Grand Lodge is it admits men and women in the same Lodge. Thus, it is called Co-Masonry. You might remember we visited its old U.S. headquarters when traveling to the West Coast.

The beginnings of Co-Masonry go back to the 1880s when Marie Desraismes, a French philosopher, became a champion for modern education and equal rights for women. Some in France saw her as a major positive force for change. A Lodge under the Grand Orient of France (a "Grand" Lodge in France **not** recognized by U.S. Masons) decided to see if Desraismes would like to become a Mason. She said if it was ever open to women she would. They suggested that she should try. She submitted a petition to become a Mason to the Lodge, which was called appropriately Les Libres Penseurs (The Free Thinkers). Soon she was initiated.

The Grand Orient came down hard on the Lodge Les Libres Penseurs and threatened to take away their charter (the tradition is that without a charter a Lodge cannot meet). The head of the Lodge, rather than caving in, proceeded to give Marie Desraismes her 2o and 3o as quickly as possible, something very unusual in France and the European traditions. The Grand Orient notified them that the charter would be taken but their response was to form their own Grand Lodge. In 1893, Dr. Georges Martin, a French Senator, Marie Martin (no relation, but an advocate of equal rights for women), joined Marie Deraismes and other male Masons in founding in Paris La Respectable Loge, Le Droit Humain, Maconnerie Mixte (Worshipful Lodge, Le Droit Humain, Co-Masonry).

They initiated, passed and raised sixteen prominent French women on March 14, 1893. "Sister" Desraismes initiated these ladies in the presence of Dr. Martin. On April 4th of the same year, La Grande Loge Symbolique Ecossaise de France, Le Droit Humain, came into being. Louis Martin (not sure if he was related to Dr. George Martin) was made the Worshipful Master / Grand Master. He quickly initiated, passed and raised others; they became the founding officers in the new Grand Lodge.

This, plus the fact that the altar and Bible are not mandatory under the Grand Orient of France, is why both Co-Masonry and the Grand Orient are not recognized by U.S. Grand Lodges.

Co-Masonry was introduced in the United States by Louis Goaziou, a French immigrant living in a coal mining town in Pennsylvania in 1880. He contacted Antoine Muzzarelli (a professor at Columbia U), a representative of the International Order's Supreme Council. Muzzarelli began organizing lodges here in 1903. On August 7, 1907, the American Federation of Human Rights (Le Droit Humain) was incorporated in the District of Columbia.

Louis Goaziou was elected the Federation's first president. A year later he was appointed Representative of the Supreme Council of the International Order. A Certificate of Re-Incorporation was registered by the Federation on May 26, 1909:

"The particular business and objects of this society are to demand equal rights for both sexes before the law, to labor according to the Constitution and General By-Laws to be made and adopted by the society for the mutual improvement of its members by combating ignorance under all its forms, the building up of human character, the practice of solidarity, the upholding of high standards of honor, and of social justice with a kindly feeling towards all, and a ceaseless endeavor to promote the moral and material welfare of the human race, and to that end, to organize and to conduct throughout the United States of America, branches or Lodges of Co-Masonry under the authority or jurisdiction of the Supreme Council of universal Co-Masonry with headquarters in Paris, France."

Mom had joined another clandestine Masonic order (truly clandestine, as it was not chartered from a Grand Lodge) Ancient Universal Mysteries (AUM) around 1940. This was one of the inner workings of the Arcane School, and Lillian Pepper and Alice Bailey led this group. But WWII broke out, disrupting the meetings. While on leave back in New York, Mom became the last one of AUM to get her 2nd Degree; she never got her 3rd Degree. After the war, both the inner group and AUM members were dispersed around the world and AUM would never meet again. Mom was concerned about completing her "Masonic" education. Lillian suggested she should join Marie Desraismes Lodge #352. She did, but had to re-take all of her degrees since they did not recognize AUM.

Shortly after she received her degrees she got in line to become an officer. During those intervening years, she had divorced Bernard, married your grandfather and had me! She did return to active participation in the Lodge soon after I was born.

Papa

A little more on Freemasonry, T:

While your grandmother was in line to advance in Marie Desraismes Lodge #352, she would attend meetings regularly. The meetings were held monthly on Saturday afternoons. I think she was pregnant with me while she was an officer. Of course, that was before we moved to Connecticut. After the move, she would make the two-and-a-half-hour drive down from Connecticut, attend the meetings and return in the evening.

Needless to say, my Dad was not at all pleased with this. He never cared for Freemasonry in general and vented considerable dislike of Co-Masonry since Mom was so active.

At less than a year old I became associated with Freemasonry, despite this being considered irregular. Being composed of men and women, Co-Masonry offers a ceremony of baptism which had rarely been performed in the Lodge, but when I was very small Mom had me baptized in the Lodge. Elsie Bruce was the Right Worshipful Master of the Lodge at the time; Mom was either the Junior or Senior Deacon. I know that Marion and Rowe Walter attended as my official godparents. Myron and Jane Kataf were also there. Another member was Grace Petrel, a Past Master who developed great affection towards me, as did most of the older women of the Lodge.

After being baptized in the Lodge, Dad insisted that I also be baptized in the Presbyterian Church. His favorite minister from NYC had moved to the church in Salisbury, Connecticut, which was convenient as The Hill was in the Salisbury Township. So, I was baptized as a Presbyterian. I was told Dad's mother was present, as well as a few of the church members, but none of them ever played a role in my life after that day. To be completely honest, Dad may have taken me to a Sunday session a few times, but we never attended that church after those brief visits.

There were many times when Mom was busy with the Co-Masonic ceremonies inside the Lodge and the monthly drive became a routine, but Dad was not willing to babysit me on the days of the meetings. As a young child was not permitted in the lodge room, during those times Gladys Hunger would take care of me in the anteroom. Over the years she became my "Aunt Gladys." She was one of the senior members of the Lodge. Gladys was a fighter. She and another old member, Harriet Flint, knew the founder of Le Droit Humain in America, Louis Goaziou. In 1903, the first Co-Masonic Lodge Alpha Lodge #301 was formed by Louis and he used a modified translation of the French "Scottish Rite" ritual when Co-Masonry was founded in the 1880's.

The Theosophical Society (TS) attempted to take over Co-Masonry in America by insisting on the adoption of the "British Craft" ritual, which had been created in England by the President of the TS, Annie Besant. Many traditional Co-Masons thought the British Craft ritual was a diversion from traditional Scottish Rite Masonry.

After Louis' death, the Theosophical Society members were pushing hard to force the British Craft ritual on all Co-Masons in America. It was a member of the TS who took over as head of American Federation. This began a fight that continued through the turn of the 21st century, ending in a disastrous major court battle. Harriet and Gladys led the fight to resist the elimination of Louis Goaziou's "North American Ritual", especially in New York. Many of the Co-Masonic lodges in America converted over to the other ritual. Those in NY that switched did not last long. Marie Desraismes Lodge was the last New York holdout. Elsie Bruce, who baptized me in the Lodge, Gladys, Harriet and Grace Petral, another close friend of Mom's, were the ones leading the fight against the TS. It was critical that Marie Deraismes continue to exist. Mom had to attend the meetings. But what about me? Aunt Gladys would look after me in the anteroom, while Mom and Marie Deraismes Lodge were holding firm to the ideal of Co-Masonry and Louis Goaziou's vision. It was this ritual that Mom was dedicated to and loved.

Several years later Mom become the Right Worshipful Master (RWM) of Marie Desraismes and had to be at every meeting. I would play in the outer anteroom, where Aunt Gladys would come up with something to keep me occupied. I was always curious as to why she always sat with her back to the door and with a sword in her lap, a white sash draping from her shoulder and hat with a "33" on it. Occasionally, she would get up and return knocks on the door, but always stayed with me.

Her duties did not prevent her from reading to me or playing simple games. She would bring coloring books and all sorts of activities for a child my age. Sometimes Gladys told me stories. Occasionally read to me. I never remembered being bored when I went down to the Lodge. When Aunt Gladys was not there, Elise would be. Elsie was the one to actually baptize me in the ceremony years before, and never objected to taking care of me during the meetings. Elsie and Gladys were very close friends and lived very near each other in Queens. They were both part of my extended Masonic family until their deaths.

Dad was angry about anything to do with Co-Masonry. It was the center of a lot of shouting matches in the home. I would hide in my room and pull the pillow over my head during these sessions. Now you know why I avoid the shouting at home today. It became one of the several "straws" that lead to the break-up of the marriage of your grandparents. More straws were added soon after.

This letter tells you why the attraction to Freemasonry is so strong within me. I was literally born into it, but unlike many men in America, it was through my mother, not my dad.

Later, I found out that my Uncle Lavern (Mom's brother) was a Mason. He never recognized Mom as a Mason, but he certainly respected her more for that reason. Mom would constantly challenge him on the symbols and meaning of the rituals. She saw it as something far more meaningful than most regular Masons (often called "Old Line Masons") understand. She really believed that part of the catechism (an exchange with the Right Worshipful Master you must memorize to get to the next degree) stated that: "…the length of a Lodge was from East to West, it's width from North to South, it's height—from the highest heights to the center. As such it represents 'Universal Masonry.'" It was a phrase she took quite literally and which she would prove correct (as you learned from the UFO letters).

Slowly, Mom became the spiritual lead for her side of the family, a mantel I would take on once I graduated from college.

Love,
Papa

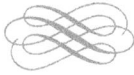

Hi T – Serious again (then, most of my life has been):

There were times when my relationship with my parents started to go downhill. It occurred more often with Dad. But Mom too. Sometimes it was my fault, other times a result of circumstances.

The arguments between Mom and Dad were getting worse all the time. The UFO incident certainly had its impact. As did my slow rate of learning and other problems.

You have to realize the anger between parents can rub off on the child. Underneath, there was a slow burning fury in me. I began to hate Dad because he refused to accept what had happened with the UFO; he saw the UFO but denied it. He would fly into a fury about my past life memories as well. But Mom did not lessen the tensions. Often her anger towards him left me with a cold feeling that there was no love in our house. Certainly none for me.

To make matters worse, I can remember two very bad incidents with my parents—not sure of the order but both had an impact on what was to follow.

The first is what I call a snowball in the dark.

It was wintertime. The nearly mile-long driveway would get snow early and usually by late December it was snowed in. Often we could not drive up to the house again 'til April. There would be breaks in the weather where we would get a private snowplow to dig us out. This would enable the coal to be delivered. The house was heated by an old coal furnace. One time we ran out of coal. A small plow couldn't make the 90o turn up The Hill and got stuck. A bulldozer came in to pull it out and then attempted to plow the rest of the way to the house. Most likely it was our neighbor Johnny Bates who drove the dozer. It made it partly around the turn and then this oversized bulldozer got stuck. Eventually it was dug out. Both it and the plow retreated down the driveway. We used the wood stove and the fireplace to keep the house warm for over a month.

When it was not possible to drive up to the house, the car would be parked just off Sugar Hill Road. The whole family would walk the rest of the way. Usually it was dark when we got out of the car from school, work, babysitters, etc. On one particular day, it had been snowing heavily all day—there was at least a foot of new snow. It was perfect for packing, not too dry and not slushy. I was picked up from the Bates' house. We drove the whole 100 yards to the driveway and down a little hill to a flat area before the turn towards the brook, near the falling down shack at the lower corner of the property. We started walking.

I was just learning how to make and throw snowballs. I thought it would be fun to make a snowball and throw it at my father. I did. It hit him right in the glasses, much harder than even I thought was possible. One look at the fury in his face scared me. I started to run, as fast as I could.

Unfortunately, I was running towards the house—don't know why I thought that would be safe; it was more instinctual. As I got to the infamous turn, I thought I had lost him. It was almost completely dark, with no lights, no stars, not even the moon.

I said out loud: "I don't see him."

Then I heard the response: "But I see you!"

Suddenly a huge black shape came upon me and starting to beat me with his fists. Mom eventually caught up and got him to stop hitting me. I was crying loudly.

He told her: "Leave him there until he stops."

I was sitting in the snow, hurt, with a bleeding lip and crying my heart out. I cried and cried. It seemed like hours, yet it was probably no more than 20 minutes. Finally, Dad popped his head out of the front door and shouted the nearly 50 yards down The Hill:

"If you don't come up there this minute, I will give you something more to cry about."

I slowly trudged up The Hill between the maple trees and was sent to bed without dinner.

The next day Johnny Bates (the husband of my babysitter) said:

"We heard someone crying last night for a long time. Was that you?"

I was too embarrassed to tell the truth so responded with a, "No."

In reality, me, Johnny (Jr.) and Susan were the only small children on that stretch of the road. I knew and they knew it was a lie.

Another incident was in the springtime. Not sure, but I think it followed the snowball.

It was a Sunday afternoon and Mom was fixing a fancy dinner. The table was nicely set. Dad was sitting in his place. I don't remember what caused the argument that had just occurred. I was forbidden to do something; it may have been a radio show I wanted to listen to or an activity that had caught my attention. No matter what it was, to me as a five-year-old it was very important. Both Dad and Mom ganged up on me on this issue. I was to cease the activity immediately. I was furious.

The kitchen/dining room door was right by the china closet. When the kitchen door swung open, it concealed anyone by the closet. I had been pouting by the china closet and decided to get even. When Mom came out of the kitchen carrying a serving dish, I decided to trip her. I did. The food went flying. I started to laugh; it was a funny sight—the dishes flying from the door to the table, Mom trying to catch herself, the food and everything going all over the place.

But the laugh was short-lived. Both Mom and Dad hit me. Hard! I had never seen Mom so mad. She matched Dad in her fury. I didn't get dinner that night, either.

Love,
Papa

Hi T – the artistic neighbor:

This letter could be dated later, but I thought I would throw it in here to have a change of pace. Besides, I just ate a Dove chocolate and the wrapper said: "Write a letter, not just an email", so....

Just past our driveway on Sugar Hill Road, the road had a steep incline with a turn sharply to the right. Less than 50 feet past the turn there was a little driveway which was like a short, elongated inclining "Y" entering Sugar Hill Road. The upper and lower branches of the Y entered the property. The driveway turned to the right toward a very nice house elevated above the main road. Once you entered the driveway, there was a garage on the left with the main house on the right.

That was the home of Harry Cimino. He and his wife were quietly retired and had been together for years. At the time I first became aware of them, they must have been in their late '70s. Their daughter lived in Falls Village with her husband and three children (two boys and a girl, I think—more about them next time). We do have a small pencil drawing of his daughter's in a frame in the powder room.

I remember there were a lot of pictures and paintings on the walls of the house. All the rooms were very neat but filled with all sorts of art objects. I don't have a very clear memory of the interior. I think I was inside less than five times in all before I turned seven. I do know there was an easel and art supplies somewhere. Mr. Cimino had a small shack which, to all outward appearances, looked like a common garage to the left of the house. It may have been used as garage at one time in its history, but like our barn, was used for other purposes. In this case it was an art studio. I only saw the contents through the windows, never went inside. Yet easels, tables, paint brushes, jars and paints were clearly visible; it was Harry Cimino's sanctum sanatorium.

What is both engrossing and fascinating about Harry was that he was a professional artist, now retired, but still producing small pieces for his family and friends. I was later told that he had illustrated over 500 books and magazine articles (we have some of the original illustrations). Most of his illustrations were woodcuts, many for books, adding his artistic interpretation of the story with black and white woodcuts.

Harry was truly an all-around artist. He had designed fabric patterns, wallpaper, calendars, book covers, everything you can possibly imagine an illustrator doing. More on how I got parts of his collection much later, but you know some of his pieces: woodcuts of Pegasus, female nudes. The framed color pencil drawing of a tree is his as well. I have a huge collection of his "stuff" inside a large art valise.

Included in the collection are what I was told are the wallpaper designs once used in Franklin D. Roosevelt's Hyde Park home which is now the FDR Presidential Library in upstate New York. Of course, to someone from NYC "upstate" is any place north of Yonkers—that's a joke—but only to New York City New Yorkers! For book and calendar illustrations you could tell his work by the small "HC" in the lower right corner. I do remember wandering around the house and picking up all sorts of little items and finding them fascinating. There were little pictures in frames on the tables, all sorts of little sculptural objects, and photos (which I didn't touch).

Mrs. Cimino was always very warm and would be happy to give any little boy (I certainly qualified as that back then) a hug. I remember she liked to wear very casual tent dresses with nothing underneath. Her breasts were very large and would sway under the dress. It was only recently when I was looking at Harry's two woodcuts we have with the female figures that it suddenly dawned on me—that was Mrs. Cimino! As a male I can understand why he married her, as the old lady in the movie *Titanic* said: "I was quite a looker back then."

The one thing I most remember about Harry was his joking about his investments. He had become very well off. Not sure if you would call it wealthy by today's definition, but back then he would have probably qualified. I didn't know much about the investments at the time but he would joke with Mom about investing since he knew she once worked for Merrill Lynch. Remember, this was the 1950s.

Harry would joke: "I bought AT&T before the War!"

AT&T (American Telephone and Telegraph) back then held a monopoly for telephones in America.

Harry would wait for someone to say: That was very smart of you to buy it back before World War II."

He was always ready with his favorite comeback: I'm not talking about the Second World War! I bought AT&T before WWI."

I later understood why he never had to work to supplement his art profession / avocation. He was loaded due to the AT&T stock! So here was a non-famous but highly successful and wealthy artist who gained his riches from something other than art.

A lesson I learned early. If you are going to be an artist, make your real money elsewhere!

Love,
Papa

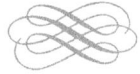

T:

Harry Cimino's daughter was a good friend of your grandmother. She was born the same year, maybe the same month; that is what got them together as friends. I know that she and her husband had three kids. The oldest was high school age, a daughter was the middle child, and the youngest boy was still in grade school. As I mentioned before, I was still a kindergardner at the time.

I remember them because they lived only a block away from the town's milkman (yes, there were still milkmen around who delivered milk in glass bottles to your door every day). But since we lived out of the town proper, we would have to go into town and pick up the milk.

On Sunday mornings, the milkman also provided copies of the Sunday *New York Times* newspaper. People from all around the area came to pick up the Sunday paper and a couple bottles of milk as there was no Sunday delivery. Mom and I would do the same. We would then stop by the younger Cimino's house on the way home (or sometime on the way to the milkman). Mom and the daughter would share information and ideas for an hour or two. The youngest child would sometimes play with me but most of my time was spent with the oldest boy who was around 17 years old.

The husband had a minor job, and although a white-collar job it did not pay well. Back in the 1950s there were essay contests where the best essay on a particular product or company could win you a possible cash award, bikes, cars, appliances, etc. The whole family would work on contests. The family's duty was to find every contest entry form they could from magazines (there were no copy machines back then) and they would sit down in the evenings and work on the entry forms to write the essays. As a family, they were so successful that their winnings supplemented their low income. Their car had been won. Their TV had been another prize. They had a year's supply of multiple products. Their oldest boy's bike was a prize, but it came with a horrible consequence.

Since it was an adult bike it was perfect for the oldest boy as he was a large boy. He was about 6 foot and very strong, well-built but not fat. A week after getting the bike he was riding it down one of the hills in the town and was struck by a car. The accident caused considerable head trauma. He was in the hospital for months. When he came out his personality changed. He was prone to fits of temper and could no longer read or write as he had before the accident. I do remember he could do one thing exceptionally well: make mind puzzles. The object of the puzzles was for you to recreate a design he had made. The trick was to draw it without letting the pencil leave the paper, or re-trace or cross over any line. He had simple ones. But they progressed to more complex designs.

Since he could no longer attend high school, the puzzles were how he made a little money for himself. Soon, his puzzles were published in magazines and provided him with a small income. I liked him and the puzzles were fun, but I was never left alone with him for fear he would burst into a temper tantrum and become exceptionally dangerous. Mom noted it was an interesting example of karma. Here the family was getting all these prizes which were not "earned" in the traditional sense. They paid their karmic debt through the permanent handicapping of their oldest boy on one of the prizes.

The family moved away when I was about six and I never saw them, as a family, again. Sometimes, when the daughter would visit her father, Mr. Cimino, she would drop by the house for a few minutes to talk to Mom. But those visits became fewer and fewer as the years progressed.

Harry and his wife continued to live as our neighbors, but we saw them less and less. After Harry died, his wife stayed there for many years. I think she was in her 90s when she died. I was living in NYC at the time.

The daughter came back to take care of the estate. She and her family had no interest in the art left behind by her parents. So, they gave almost the complete collection to the local church in Limerock—the church she used to attend when she was young.

Mom called me to tell me that the church had had a special "yard sale" of Harry Cimino's art collection. Unfortunately, the call came a few days after the sale occurred. I told Mom that I would be up the following weekend. When I arrived, Mom and I went directly to the church. I asked if they had sold everything from Harry's collection.

"Oh, of course not—there are some boxes in the kitchen."

We asked how much had been sold the weekend before. There had been several tables of art just scattered in no particular order. The minister said that hundreds of Harry's works had been sold, but few people bought more than a dozen pieces. The best went fast. He didn't know if there were any pieces of quality left but invited me to take a look.

The boxes of art were stored under the sink in the rectory. One had water dripping slowly into it. I pulled them out and spent half a day going through everything. The pieces that were wet went back under the sink, but not under the dripping pipe. This was a loss as there were several examples of his illustrations which had been published. The other boxes were in good shape. I pulled out anything of interest. Wallpaper designs included several series of strawberry designs and a few floral patterns, in a very art nouveau style.

There were some calendar illustrations and some signed individual pieces. There were pencil drawings of his children, trees and the neighborhood. I selected a couple of his book woodcuts. There were two versions of a Pegasus in different colors. Part of a calendar which had been published.

Two particularly lovely wood cuts were of a voluptuous woman. Her breasts were very large, her legs shapely. Overall, she would have given Marilyn Monroe a run for her money. My favorite of the two was of her looking into space. It was as if she was being inspired by the vision of the stars in the night sky. There was an impression of divinity within that piece and a sensuousness that was unmistakable. In some ways it might be described as the Western version of the Lakshaman Temple in Khajuraho, India with its erotic sculptures on the outer walls. The lesson is to look beyond the sex acts of the outer temple to contemplate the spirituality within.

In the same way this starry vision of this sensual woman is showing you how to move beyond the sexuality that exudes from her naked form to spiritual planes above. The other piece is a multi-colored woodcut of her emerging from a flower as if she were the stamen. It was an American version of the birth of Venus, not emerging from the sea, but from a flower. For years I just looked at these two works of Harry's as wonderful examples of his 1920s style of art. Years later I remembered the hug Mrs. Cimino would give me when we visited. It was one night while living in Falls Church I looked at the woodcut shown here and realize the woman was Mrs. Cimino.

By the time I was finished picking through the three boxes, I had collected one box worth of materials I thought would be worth saving. Mom asked the minister how much he wanted.

Without even looking at the material I collected (well over a 100 pieces), he and Mom agreed to something less than $100.

I returned to NYC with perhaps the largest collection of Harry Cimino's art assembled by any one collector. This letter is the last and perhaps the only written memory of a very good artist. If you look Harry up on the internet, there are many examples of his works, many selling for several hundred dollars. But there is no information on the man, my neighbor. He only exists in the works of art he left behind.

Love,
Papa

Chapter 6

The Flood and Changes

Guess what T? All things change, even small things.

It was 1955. Remember the Clapps?

Roger Clapp was into weight lifting. Back then there were no sporting goods stores selling weights that a family like the Clapps could afford. So Roger made his own. He would take odd metal poles he found, fill two large tin cans with cement and place them on the ends of the poles. Once the cement hardened he created a barbell. He had done the same with different sized cans. In addition, there were smaller wooden handles to make dumbbells of various weights. For a bench he used a Charlie Horse and a couple of boards and, with all this, created a nice little gym in a little corner of the barn.

I became fond of Roger. When Mom and Dad went out, he became my regular babysitter at home. Roger was the only one in the family aspiring to go to college. Roger was smart—at least to a six year old—strong, friendly and a good role model. His two younger brothers were bullies (not to me—but to other kids in school), loud and always fighting.

I don't remember his mother very well. I know she was the one who took care of me during the day or after school when I no longer went to the neighbor's house, a place which was always a little uncomfortable. The Clapps needed all the extra money they could find. I do remember she was always cooking for the large family (five kids, two grandparents, herself and her husband). She loved to make pies. I think Mr. Clapp was working in one of the factories in Canaan or possibly in the quarry. They like to hunt, as guns were on display in the otherwise sparsely decorated the house.

As with most kids around a farm there comes a shocking moment in the preparation of a meal—getting the chickens ready! The grandfather caught a chicken, put its head on the end of a smooth cut piece of a tree trunk, and then WAMP! Down came the hatchet. He would then throw the body of the chicken aside. Headless it would start running around the yard until the heart caught on that it was actually dead. Once the killing stopped (at least two to three chickens per session), the grandfather would then dunk them in hot water and start plucking off the feathers. After that, he would turn them over to Mrs. Clapp who would gut and clean them for dinner.

You can imagine the horror of being chased by a headless chicken at the age of six. Susan and I would run screaming away from the headless fowl. If anything taught me not to be a farmer or chicken rancher that did. I could not imagine the pain the body of the headless chicken was experiencing, if you can call it pain without a brain. Nor could I imagine the head without its body. Years later I learned that Madam Tussaud, famous for her wax figures, reported seeing the eyes of decapitated heads continue to look in the direction of whoever called their names for several minutes after the guillotine had come down with a thud. As a result, there is a strong feeling those chickens experienced some of the same suffering and awareness of imminent death before it actually came.

One more member of the Clapp family should be mentioned: Rex. Rex was the family's huge collie. He was very friendly and very furry! He shed everywhere. I loved Rex, mostly because he was almost large enough to ride. Susan actually did. He would always come bounding up to people with a wagging tail and a happy expression in his movements. But if he sensed any kind of danger, his whole demeanor changed. He was the protective guard dog and of such a size that no one would want to mess with him. He was the first dog I grew close to and loved to play with.

Can't say what lasting impression the Clapps had on me, but I was much happier staying with them, than the neighbors.

Love,
Papa

Back to a little excitement. Headlines:

"On August 13 (1955) Hurricane Connie dropped four to six inches of rain on Connecticut." Five days later, another hurricane, Diane, dropped an additional fourteen inches of rain in a thirty-hour period between Thursday morning and Friday noon. The floods came on the 19th. The greatest loss of life and destruction to property occurred along the Mad and Still Rivers in Winsted, the Naugatuck, the Farmington, and the Quinebaug... Governor Abraham Ribicoff personally visited the scenes of destruction. President Dwight Eisenhower declared Connecticut a disaster area. It was reported that: "Connecticut was the hardest hit victim of the worst flood in the history of the eastern United States." 91 persons dead and 12 others missing and presumed dead; 86,000 persons unemployed, more than 1,100 families left homeless. Another 2,300 families were at least temporarily without shelter. Nearly 20,000 families suffered flood damage. Sixty-seven of Connecticut's 169 towns were affected by the floods. The damage to individual property, to business, to industry, and to State and municipal facilities has been estimated at almost half a billion dollars.

Downtown Winsted was totally destroyed, never to recover. It had been a factory town, with most of the plants built right on or next to the river. No one would ever think this small "Mad" stream could become a killer. It rose out of its banks and up to the second, even third, floors of buildings. All the factories seemed like children's sand houses with the waves coming in and destroying their creations while they were unable to do anything to save them. Most of the factories were never rebuilt. Ralph Nadar likely watched the flood from a hill near his home. He must have been in his late teens. Nadar later became famous for this attack on the automotive industry and his book Unsafe at Any Speed.

Remember, I lived within walking distance of the Housatonic River. Mom and I would often go fishing in the river. It was in the shadow of the bridge where I was introduced to copperheads. Mom and I used to drive down to a parking lot next to the sandy beach across from the power plant. We would walk across the road just before the entrance to the bridge. There were several small pools of water under the bridge and slightly upstream.

Mom always hoped to catch a trout; most days we settled for blue gills. We moved from one spot to another, creeping every closer under the bridge, which is where we found the copperheads (to be described later).

But on that August day the storms prevented any fishing. The first storm, Connie, did little damage except "the Falls" started going over. These were the great falls of the Housatonic River, "the largest falls east of the Niagara". The same falls could be heard all the way up to our house. They were always very impressive when going over. Most storms rarely reached northwestern Connecticut, but Diane, the second one, was coming towards us.

When she hit, all hell broke loose. Amesville had three roads out of the community. The most commonly used one was over the river across the bridge. This was just above the power plant leading to Falls Village. Another turned right before the bridge and followed the river downstream. The last was about half a mile from the bridge and upstream from the Falls. It became a gravel road just a short distance away from the turnoff to the parking lot near the Falls. The turn-off was a favorite place for fishermen to park and walk to the water's edge and a perfect place for teens wanting to find a place to park at night. A trail led to the dam above the Falls and to the rock overlook which gave you a magnificent view of the Falls when going over.

When hurricane Diane came, Amesville was completely cut off. The Housatonic by the power plant was rising within inches of the only bridge to Falls Village. The power plant was flooded and the road by the sandy area was already covered with rushing water cutting off the road just a downstream from the bridge.

Roger Clapp had a part-time job in Falls Village. He rode his bicycle across the bridge about 6:30 a.m. that day. The river's waves were beginning to crash onto the wood planks that made up the bridge. Seconds after he crossed, a tree limb or some other debris hit the wooden planks of the bridge and a section of the bridge roadway disappeared. I was told he turned around and saw a car coming to a halt and the driver getting out, watching as the hole appeared.

Roger was the last to make it out of Amesville for weeks! The road back to Canaan, which was dirt, was behind the dam. The dirt road led to an Angus cattle ranch and Canaan. But it was covered with over four feet of water for almost a mile. Houses all around the riverbanks had water up to the ceilings of the first floor starting about 25 yards downstream. At the fork, a half mile down from the bridge, the stop sign was covered! The only way in or out of Amesville was across the mountain on the Appalachian Trail by foot. It was too difficult to carry food or water due to the steep and rocky climb where Sugar Hill Road ended. No one was getting out or in.

Almost all the residents of Amesville went down to view the bridge. I remember clearly watching the river batter the bridge, which was usually 15 feet or more above the river. An occasional wave would take out another wooden plank. The highest level of water had occurred just after Roger crossed. The road had been undercut by the river just as you approached the bridge. There was a mini tunnel carved under the road. Susan Clapp and I thought it great fun to walk under the road. When Mom realized where we were, she yelled at us to get out of there. The whole thing could collapse any second. She yelled not because she was mad, but because the sound of the river was deafening. The road Susan and I were under *did* collapse the next day!

Up on The Hill we had a pantry with a lot of canned food. Our old well was in the breezeway if the electric pump was out, and it was an option. All that had to be done was to open the old cover hatch on the breezeway and use buckets to get the water. We didn't suffer. But without power we had no way to tell what was happening.

It was a long time before we could finally get out, possibly two weeks. Despite being only six years old, I remember the flood well. I can still envision the waves crashing over the bridge and more and more of it being taken away. Never again would I hear the sound of cars crossing the wooden planks, rattling with the weight of each vehicle. The larger the vehicle, the louder the rumbling. And only one car at a time, as the bridge was much too narrow for any more than a single car or truck. The Falls Village Bridge was rebuilt with asphalt pavement. No more sounds of the wooden planks as you drove over it!

The old Cornwall covered bridge, 10 miles downriver was almost carried away; its floor and windows were destroyed, and the foundation was moved several feet, so one end no longer aligned with the road or what was left of it. The Historical Society came up with the funds to rebuild this historic bridge.

But the Falls were magnificent! At the height of the flood, they almost resembled Niagara, just narrower, not as tall, but over 100 yards of flume followed by a quarter-mile of rapids to the bridge. That was my first hurricane.

Love,
Papa

T, it is time to learn about early TV so when you visit a museum with displays TV you can say:

"My Dad watched that old program."

It was sometime in early 1955 when we finally got our first TV. I remember Dad placing it by the living room window and plugging it in. Then a special wire had to be run to an antenna on the top of the house. Since the old antenna wires were thin and flat, with two copper wires running through them, they could be placed through a window or door, in this case the window. The antenna itself was attached to the old stone chimney made from the rocks found on the property. It was a beautiful masterpiece of craftsmanship. After the antenna was finally attached, the first TV in The Hill's history was turned on.

Now you must remember this was 1955. No cable. No satellite. We could only get NBC's Channel 6 from Poughkeepsie, NY, and badly. That was the only station. The one good thing they had was an after-school show. It was sponsored by a local bakery with a cartoon character called Freddie Fryhoffer (the bakery sponsor's rabbit mascot). The host would turn children's scribbles into recognizable drawings, usually characters already a part of the show; they would show *Felix the Cat* cartoons and some others. But not being part of the major studios, only old or less popular toons were broadcast. In a lot of ways, it reminds me of the cartoon show that was portrayed in the *Mrs. Doubtfire* movie.

I loved the *Freddie Fryhoffer* show because it was the only children's program I could see. It was a very low-budget program, but one to watch every day after school. I remember one day when the reception was so poor that, in pure anger and frustration, I cut the TV electrical cord with scissors. I was lucky I wasn't killed; Dad got justifiably mad! Mom's favorite scissors had a nick in them which is still there today. Of course, I refused to admit I had done it, but it had to be me. I did get into trouble, but felt the trouble was less than if I confessed. Funny how you fear your parents more for telling the truth than a lie; even when the lie is so evident.

Sometimes we could get (depending on the weather) the ABC affiliate from New Haven. But the really big day arrived when a Hartford CBS station began to broadcast. It was the first station that came in clearly. The whole family tuned in for the opening night celebrations. I don't remember what shows were on but all the politicians and personalities from the Hartford area where there. Those who would become the newscasters, weathermen, etc. all were introduced. Everyone was excited.

What I enjoyed the most were the kids shows I could now watch clearly. Mom loved *Kukla, Fran and Ollie*, a husband and wife team. Fran worked the hand puppets, Kukla and Ollie, much like Mr. Rogers later. I was able to watch *Howdy Doody* again, which I used to watch at Uncle Bill's in NYC but now could in Connecticut. Everyone watched *The Ed Sullivan Show* on Sundays—after all, it was the most watched show in America. The Broadway musical *Bye, Bye, Birdie* gives you an idea of its importance, where the song called *Ed Sullivan* is transformed into a church hymn.

Other shows I remember enjoying were *The Voice of Firestone*, a classical variety show. This was a broadcast of an orchestra and guest talents. Other favorite shows available on either NBC or CBS included the comedies *The George Burns and Gracie Allen Show* and *The Jack Benny Show*. One of my favorite guests on Jack's show was Mel Blanc. Mel was the voice of Bugs Bunny and all the characters on Warner Brothers cartoons. He was a regular guest of Jack Benny's and had some of the greatest routines in the history of TV. If you ever want to see the wonderful timing of Jack and Mel, look up the routine where Mel plays a Mexican called Sal, with a sister called Sue.

Quiz shows were very popular from the early years of TV. *Truth or Consequences* gave Bob Barker's career a start; he later hosted *The Price is Right* for over 30 years. Panel shows like *What's My Line?* got famous personalities as guests. John Charles Daly was the host and it featured Bennett Surf of Random House, actress Arlene Francis, columnist Dorothy Kilgallen, and had Steve Allen and Jayne Meadows (Steve's wife) as backups should one of the regular panelists be out. This is where I was first introduced to Salvador Dali. The panel was blindfolded and had to guess who the guest was and what he did. It was fun seeing these personalities being themselves on TV while still doing a quiz program. I know Kitty Carlisle Hart was on some of the panels, she is the soprano in the Marx Brothers' *Night at the Opera*. Between the movie and her appearances on the quiz shows, I became a big fan. It is interesting to note that she came out with an exercise video for seniors when she was in her 90s.

There was a local Hartford show *Around the World* that was an adult version of *Where in the world is Carmen Sandiego?* That came on right after the news on Mondays and I sat in front of the TV and watched it religiously. The show was an early introduction of geography and culture. By today's standards it would seem unsophisticated but to a very young child, it was fascinating. What was not being taught about in geography at school was being learned through this weekly program. I can still whistle the theme song they used.

The Adventures of Ozzie and Harriet was a must. Ozzie had been a band leader in the 1940s. When TV was introduced they became one of the first TV families. It was the ideal WASP household. A father and mother happily married with two boys, David and Ricky. It was the classic 1950s family. The whole country watched as Ricky Nelson grow up and became a rock star of the 1960s only to die in a plane crash as a young adult.

Even bigger was *Walt Disney's Wonderful World of Disney* show which brought Tinkerbell into our homes every week. Walt was quite a personality in his own right and he hosted the show for years. I still get a little tear in my eyes when I hear *When You Wish Upon a Star*, remembering the show I loved. *The Mickey Mouse Club* was not as interesting, except for Annette. She was every young boy's heart throb. That included me before I turned 10 years old. She became a popular rock and roll singer and made a number of the beach party movies.

Special attention should be given the westerns. I would sometimes watch *Wild Bill Hickok*. Remember that was my favorite western to watch on Uncle Bill's TV or when listening over the radio. Mom of course grew up in Texas and strongly identified with the Western heroes. She liked *Tales of the Texas Rangers* since her great uncle was part of the original Texas Rangers. She learned to shoot using his old Colt 44.

I really liked *The Cisco Kid*, especially Leo Carillo as Poncho the comic sidekick. Mom encouraged watching *Annie Oakley* since two of her relatives worked in *Buffalo Bill's Wild West Show* and knew the real Annie. I would turn on the singing cowboy Gene Autry when I could. But my early favorites were *The Lone Ranger* and *Hopalong Cassidy*, both with big white hats. It was interesting, both would have gun fights where the bad guys were disarmed, but never killed. Big difference from today's shows.

Davy Crockett and *Zorro* were Disney productions I liked. I still find myself singing the theme to Davy once in a while. I remember the theme song from *Wyatt Earp*. It was a compact half an hour show usually with a simple plot. Of course, Wyatt had to show off his Buntline Special. This was modeled after a real gun created for Wyatt Earp by gun manufacturer Ned Bunt. What made this Colt special was the 12-inch barrel. The extra length barrel would have provided more accuracy. It may have been fiction and never really existed for everyday use, but the gun was sure evident on the show every week.

Sky King was about a modern flying cowboy with his niece Penny and showed on Saturday mornings. It was not the old cowboy style program but used what was then modern technology to catch the bad men. Mom being a former pilot liked it because Sky flew his own plane. I was also fond of *Broken Arrow* as it portrayed the Indians in a more positive light than many of the others. But it should be noted at no time did Roy Rogers ever show Indians in a negative light in any of his TV shows or movies. This is a great credit to Roy who claimed to have some Indian blood in his family roots.

Later still there were *Cheyenne*, one of my big favorites, *Sugarfoot*, which Mom loved; we both liked *Maverick*. I grouped those three together because the network would alternate between them in the same time slot. Moving closer to 1960, I watched *Wagon Train* with Ward Bond, an old B-movie actor, and *Rawhide*, where Clint Eastwood got his start. *Bat Masterson*, *The Lawman*, and the best western in TV history, *Have Gun Will Travel* (short, concise and well-thought-out plots) were watched, sometimes while playing canasta with Mom. The shows were her way of passing on her Western heritage since we were in Connecticut far from her roots.

Why all this time on TV? Because it helped me escape the realities of a crumbling home. I could turn off the fighting between Mom and Dad by turning on the set. Later they helped me escape. The shows would transport me into another world. Now maybe you can see why I still have a tendency to turn on TV when all else around is going bad. This continued after Mom and Dad divorced and Mom took up drinking. TV was a way to help me ignore her drunken incoherence.

There were still some radio shows, but they quickly receded into the past.

Love,
Papa

Hi T – let's go fishing.

There is no logical sequence to what is here, just a collection of fish stories about Mom's love of fishing. Fishing was an escape! Often, she would bring me along. I remember fishing in the Housatonic. When we had the chance, we would hit the lakes, Lakeville Lake and Twin Lakes. We had to rent a rowboat or canoe at Lakeville Lake.

Our favorite fishing place was on the river near the bridge mentioned in the last letter about the '55 flood. There were two places. South, across from the power plant, a large bend in the river with a sand bar was perfect to cast a line into the river. It was very popular; sometimes 15 or more people would be fishing at one time. Usually you could catch sunnies (bluegills), occasionally a perch, or a catfish. On rare occasions, if you let your line drift down the river to the rapids about 50 yards downstream, you had a chance at a trout. The first time we went down there, the old wooden planks were still on the bridge because I could hear all the cars rumbling across it.

The second spot we liked was a little to the north under the bridge. There as a large flat rock perfect for sitting and dropping the line into a swirling pool where bluegill liked to congregate. Occasionally, a perch would be caught in the same pool.

One day we had just cast our lines into the pool when we heard a hissing behind us. Mom told me to freeze. Obeying, she told me to walk towards her very slowly. When I had walked about six feet from where I had been she told me to look under the rocks where I had been standing. I turned around and there were two large copperheads with a batch of just hatched little ones. I don't know if snake experts acknowledge "snake families" or not, but there was the male and female watching both their young and us very carefully!

Mom told me to be aware of where they were but pay no attention. Just keep fishing.

Mom caught several fish quickly. I caught a little one. The copperheads were very curious about what we were doing now! The snakes, who at first seemed to be tense and ready to strike, watched intently our every action. Seeing we were after fish, they started to relax, still keeping an eye on our movements.

After about thirty minutes, there were four or five fish in our basket, all small but enough for a serving for the two of us and Dad.

Mom pulled out the smallest of the blue gills from the fishing basket. She told me to look at the snakes and slowly went near the snake den. Very slowly she extended her hand with the small fish just out of striking distance. The snakes just watched and did not appear to be threatened. Mom dropped the fish within easy reach of the larger (male?) snake. We went back to fishing. Although we didn't see everything, when we turned back the fish had been moved into the den and torn apart. Each of the little snakes had eaten a piece.

As we left, Mom left two more of the little sunnies, this time not even being as cautious but still moving slowly so as not to appear threatening. The next week, we returned to the same spot. The snakes seemed to recognize us and actually came out the den to watch us more closely. Again, we dropped off two more fish for their dinner.

Lakeville Lake was good for bass and lake trout, which were annually stocked. Sometimes, Mom would go fishing in a rented boat. While she was fishing, I went in the swim area and out to the raft with the diving boards, about 25 yards from shore. There was one incident which may be considered a "close call." I must have been about eight or nine and was swimming out to the raft.

On the raft were several bullies I'd seen before. As I attempted to climb up the ladder on the raft, one of the older boys grabbed my head and pushed me under. I struggled to get up but his hand held tight. I was running out of air, yet I could not get near the surface with his grip still on my head. Then, the idea came to me: *don't fight against him, swim down and under the raft*. It worked. I broke free of his grip, coming up for air just as it felt that my lungs would burst, between the barrels that kept the raft afloat. Having freed myself, I stayed under the raft between the barrels until the three teens swam back to shore. Only then did I emerged and climb up the ladder with success.

Twin Lakes had more fish and was heavily wooded, with only an occasional house. A narrow dirt road went between the two lakes. Mom would either go to the public beach, off the paved road and rent a boat, or go to friends' houses nearby and park the car off the gravel road in their driveways.

One of the best places to park was the driveway of our TV repair man, who had installed our second antenna and occasionally fixed the set. He was an older gentleman with a belly much like mine now, and white hair. We could walk from this house to a little spot on the shore across and around the bend from the public area. There you could cast a line and have a good chance of getting a big mouth bass, decent size bluegills or other fish.

I remember one day when we had just arrived, I started to walk towards the spot where we liked to fish. I was about 20 yards away from Mom when I heard a crashing noise in the woods. I turned towards the noise and a huge buck, an eight-to ten-pointer, was coming out of the forest. He took one look at me, lowered his head and began to charge.

The TV man and Mom saw this happen. The TV man gave a tremendous yell and started to run towards the buck. The distraction diverted the deer as it ran to my left, just feet from me. I was shaken but none the worse for the incident. Lesson: never be around huge bucks during mating season!

It was about this time that we often visited another friend who lived in another part of that same road. Ruth Sorrell was a photographer at *The Lakeville Journal*. Mom met Ruth when she went looking for work at *The Journal*. She and Ruth hit it off and became close friends until Ruth died about a year after Mom moved to Virginia.

Ruth wasn't that close to the lakes, but she was on the way to the fishing areas, so we would stop by on the way back "for a drink." Once or twice, Ruth joined us for fishing if we were going out in a boat.

Most interesting about Ruth was her house and her three Siamese cats. One cat, the mother of the others, was friendly towards me, the offspring not so much. They were every bit as mischievous as the cats in the movie *Lady and the Tramp*. Ruth had to keep all plants in bird cages to prevent the cats from tearing them up.

The house itself was an adventure. There were no flat floors. They were made of large, roughly sawn logs, which were warped and bent from years of moisture and use and as a result none of the floors slanted in the same direction. One step would have you leaning to the right. The next step the floor would have you leaning to the left. It would be as if climbing a hill. Every room was like this. It was truly a challenge to walk across any of the floors. But, the cats loved it. They could chase balls, or anything that would roll, in totally unpredictable directions and one tap on one part of the floor would send the ball rolling all over with the younger cats chasing it.

Ruth stayed in that house only a few years. I think she got tired of the floors.

Love,
Papa

63

Hi,

One of my favorite memories during this time in Connecticut with my father is of our visits to the Catskill Game Farm in upstate New York. It was about three hours from The Hill. The drive was almost all country and hills, very much like Skyline Drive in Virginia. I remember the signs as we got closer, "Catskill Game Farm 15 miles", "Catskill Game Farm five miles", etc. The Catskill Game Farm had a lot of kiddy rides and lots of animals. I used to go on all the rides appropriate for a five or six year old, and loved them. The key attraction was a merry-go-round. There may have been a spinning cup ride, something like the one in Disney World, but much smaller. Don't remember any roller coaster.

To give you a better idea about the Farm, in 1958 the United States Department of Agriculture recognized Catskill Game Farm as a zoo. It became the first privately-owned venture to achieve zoo status. The zoo spanned more than 914 acres, most of which were used to breed animals for other zoos worldwide. Only around 130 acres were available for public viewing, and then only in the summer and autumn. I think we went up there two years in a row, most likely 1953 and 1954. There may have been another visit, but no clear separate memory of when they may have occurred.

As a zoo, the Catskill Game Farm had a variety of animals. For the public areas they had donkeys, deer, goats, peacocks and other small animals. Many were loose on the grounds. I learned not to get too close to peacocks, especially the males who would peck at you if you bothered them. They also let out one loud scream usually just before they fanned out their feathers in a mating display. The prize of a visit would be finding one of the male feathers on the ground to take home.

The bigger or more dangerous animals were behind enclosures. Still, they would let you feed the elephants and the giraffes. The lions and other African and typical zoo animals were safely behind cages. I think I *carefully* petted an African porcupine brought out to the audience by a game keeper, but I'm not 100 percent sure. The zookeepers would bring animals for a public demonstration/lecture. I do think I was told to pet his chin and watch out for the quills.

What was the most fun at the Catskill Game Farm was the free-roaming petting zoo—it was basically a large barnyard. There were ducks, chickens, donkeys, goats, Shetland ponies and other small animals. You could put a quarter in dispensing machines and get food for the animals. Another option was to purchase a cone filled with animal feed, like an ice cream cone. Available at one of the animal food stands, the cone provided more food for the guests than the dispensers.

The funniest memory I have was when Dad bought me a cone. I began to feed some goats and Dad purchased some crackers for the animals from the dispenser while a donkey nearby watched the whole thing. Dad fed a deer part of one of the crackers and put the rest in his back pocket. The donkey came up to him begging for some, but Dad pushed it away and then turned his back to it. The donkey didn't like being treated like that. He followed closely, his eyes on Dad's back pocket. It got close enough to smell the food, then *chomp!* The donkey got the crackers out of the pocket and took some of Dad's pants with it. He didn't get the underpants, but Dad jumped and gave one hell of a shout.

I laughed my head off. I thought the donkey was smarter than Dad. I was particularly fond of that donkey and fed him most of the cone food I had. I think the staff took Dad to one of the enclosures to fix his pants, while Mom and I remained in the petting zoo area until he returned. He was not in a good mood. That was the year we left earlier than we had on other visits.

On August 2, 2006, the Catskill Game Farm announced it would be closing on Columbus Day. It had been allowed to grow more exotic over the years and had around 2,000 animals from over 150 species imported from around the world.

There went another part of my past. I felt a little like I did when we went to visit the Delafield properties where I lived with Nim years later. I just sat there on the ruins of the old house and relived my memories with Nim. That was how the closing of the Catskill Game Farm hit me. A fond memory from my childhood.

Love,
Papa

Chapter 7

More About Mom, Her Friends, and Me

Mom's Friends – Part 1

One of the things I most remember about going to and from New York City was the number of Mom's elderly friends. Most were the members of Co-Masonry—Gladys Hunger, Elsie Bruce, Grace Petrel, Evelyn Eaton, Myron and Jane Kitaif, a wonderful elderly couple. And Demetria Taylor, a new member, who will come into play when I move to NYC.

One acquaintance who didn't fit with the others was one Violet Dale Cavelle (I think that's how she spelled her last name). She lived in a small apartment in Manhattan. All around her room was memorabilia and pictures of herself some 40-plus (more likely 60) years earlier. She had been a Ziegfeld Follies girl in the 1910s. Florenz Ziegfeld put on musical shows famous for the glamorous girls in elaborate and revealing costumes. Many of the girls would become famous after they made their mark in the Follies. Sophie Tucker was a big name in the 1930s but started in Ziegfeld's 1909 show. The Jardin de Paris show of 1910 had a new performer named Fanny Brice. W.C. Fields, Will Rogers, Eddie Cantor joined Ziegfeld doing comedy. The songs of Victor Herbert and Erving Berlin were part of Ziegfeld's many composers. Ziegfeld was big!

Violet knew all these people and talked endlessly about them. She claimed to have been a member of the Follies and other Vaudeville productions. She worked with the Marx Brothers, Bert Larr and possibly Billie Berke, both from *The Wizard of Oz*. I have searched for her name with no results on the internet—just one of the many forgotten people.

I do remember all the clippings, scrap books and other memorabilia in her house. All the clippings had the dates blacked out—she didn't want anyone to know her real age! Some of the costumes in the pictures were very skimpy. I suspect she was a stripper or a topless dancer in some of the shows. She likely had been in the very early Ziegfeld productions. I remember she had that "old people smell" which may come from a lack of bathing. Besides, it was not a very clean apartment. Still, Mom visited Violet as often as she could.

Of Violet herself, all I remember is a small, very old woman who seldom got out of her easy chair and stayed very close to the first-floor window. There was an old radio on the table next to the chair and I think there was a Tiffany lamp on the table. I do remember there were lace curtains and heavy drapes around the windows. No relatives were ever mentioned; she may have been totally alone in the world. I'm uncertain when she died. It would have been shortly after these visits. My guess would be sometime in the mid to late 1950's. There were many elderly people who end up in such rooms and die uncared for totally forgotten.

One individual I did enjoy visiting was Margaret Hubbard Cobb, most likely in her late 60s when I got to know her. "Cobbie" had a very lively personality. She had been a very active intellect in 1930s and 1940s, likely very political. Now in the 1950s she was semi-retired and traveling around a lot. She may have been part of the Arcane School but not the inner circle. I think she may have been friends with Mom's second husband, Bernard Morrow. I remember she was well-read and could discuss a host of topics at various levels. Mom and Cobbie talked meditation and metaphysics for hours.

If I wanted to join in, Cobbie would change the topic to either something I was interested in or something she knew I could understand and appreciate. One of the more interesting facts was when she was in her 20s, she came into contact with Helen Keller. She learned sign language so the two could talk. She may have meet Helen when both were in college. Cobbie felt Helen Keller's beliefs were being ignored and suppressed in the current state of the world.

Remember, this was the 1950s and McCarthy along with the House Un-American Activities Committee hearings were ongoing; Edward R. Morrow had not challenged them yet. Cobbie stated that Helen was a socialist. Helen felt our economy was not fair to the poor and working class. This may have been my first introduction to politics and social theory. I don't remember the details, but I do remember that Cobbie was very mad at how people were being silenced. What was interesting was that Dad supported McCarthy, while Mom was always had socialist leanings. Another topic that would trigger arguments.

Love,
Papa

Mom's Friends – Part 2

Mom had a lot of more serious friends as well. One whom I remember visiting on the way to or from the Marie Deraismes Lodge meetings was Lillian Morris.

Lillian was a wonderful old woman who had been placed in a high-class nursing home by her children. She lived in a very spacious room with a window overlooking the circular drive up to the nursing home and out over the vast garden estate.

Lillian had been a part of the Alice Bailey inner circle of advanced mediators. She once had a brilliant mind, according to Mom. But she had been put in the home due to declining physical health and mental capacities. She was well into her 90s when I knew her. Mom told me she had done a lot of personal work for Alice Bailey and led several of the study groups for the mediations that continued after Alice died. Mom had been the group's secretary. I remember how Lillian always greeted me, a small boy, with a warm smile and gentle hug. She always had a cookie or some other snack for me. We visited her more than her own family, usually before or after the Co-Masonic meetings in NYC.

The nursing home staff had little time to actually sit and talk to the patients—this was before TV's were common in nursing homes—so what kept Lillian active was using her abilities to communicate with creatures of the unseen worlds. She had fantastic plants growing in the room and on the little balcony, all growing better than any other room in the home. She told me she could communicate with the fairies and gnomes that cared for the plants. They were quite amusing and would talk with her for hours on end when no one else was about. Every now and then one of the plants would move unexpectedly and she would tell me the name of the fairy who was dancing on that leaf or stem. I couldn't see them, but the plants did react when she talked to them in ways that couldn't be accounted for by a breeze or other types of air disturbance.

When Mom and Lillian wanted to discuss more serious issues, I would go outside and walk around the grounds. There were many trees and flowers, with lots of squirrels and rabbits to observe. I knew the conversations between Mom and Lillian were important to both And I tried hard not to be impatient or troublesome. Lillian died when I was about six. She had given most of her important books to Mom, some of which I still have.

Mom was friends with two other women, Lilia and Lenore. Lenore was from South America and a member of a Spanish speaking Co-Masonic Lodge there. When she moved to New York, she joined Marie Deraismes Lodge and she and Mom became friends. Lenore introduced Lilia as her "companion", which was how lesbian couples would describe their partners back then. Lenore was a petite and fairly attractive who was very soft-spoken. She was into meditation and Masonry, just not as much as Mom.

Lilia had no interest in Co-Masonry but she did work in publishing. I'm not sure if she was an editor, screener, or had another role. In middle school, I remember that she gave me *Siddartha* by Hermann Hesse; her publisher was putting out a new edition of Hesse's works. I was also required to read *Demian* and loved it. Lilia promised to get me the whole set as they came out. We have *The Glass Bead Game* and *Steppenwolf,* which came from her. I identified with _Demian_ when I read it in junior high school. Then as a young adult I identified with _Steppenwolf._ She never got around to giving me the whole set. Lenore got cancer and died. We lost contact with Lilia.

Trudy was another friend of Mom's whom she met through Co-Masonry. When they first met, Trudy was a single Greek Orthodox lady. However, she had just left the Church after the breakup of an engagement to a priest of her church (lower-level Greek Orthodox priests could get married). The reason was an interesting story within itself.

Trudy had grown up in a very religious environment and believed everything the Church taught her. To the joy of her family, she had become engaged to a priest. According to what Trudy told Mom, during a conversation with her fiancé he said something she thought was not very positive about someone. She asked her fiancé if that person was going to go to hell. His response was one of wonder:

"Do you really still believe in that folktale?"

He then explained reincarnation and the cycle of the soul after death. He told her the Church keeps up the heaven and hell myth to keep control over its members. She was horrified; so much so that she broke off the engagement and joined Co-Masonry. It was not long after that she left the Church altogether.

Later she married Morris Davinsky, a nice Jewish man from Queens. Trudy and Morris would come to visit us up on The Hill over the years. I attended their oldest son's bar mitzvah when I was in high school. The boys were friendly and we liked to play simple games. They were two and four years younger than me. One weekend I remember we stayed at a local motel near their apartment. When we were about to leave the next morning, our car would not start. Our battery had been stolen! We had to get a new one and have it installed before we could leave. Morris was helpful in getting a garage to come over.

Mom and I would then go down to Queens to see them. I always remember Morris's response to his sons' question: "Where are we going, Daddy?"

His response: "Crazy. Want to come?"

He was a good Dad. He reminded me of a big lovable bear, so warm and friendly towards me and his boys. I liked his extrovert personality; his eyes and expressions were always amusing. It was always a good visit.

On one of the times Trudy and Morris were visiting The Hill, I got a strange initiation with fire. It was after dinner and we were all sitting around the fireplace as it was the best source of heat in the house. The coal furnace was not very efficient.

Years later when talking with their son Philip, he related Trudy's escaping the Nazi taking over her country. How the German troops would take Jewish and other infants, throw them into the air and catch them on their bayonets. She first went to France before the actual war with France and England started. It was there she joined La Droit Humain. When the Nazi's threatened France she moved to England and eventually to the States where after dating the Greek Orthodox priest she met and married Morris. Unfortunately both Trudy and Morris died before I renewed my acquantance with their older son.

I usually sat on one side of the fire and looked for salamanders in the flames. These were not the amphibians in the streams. Salamanders are the elementals of fire. Mom had told me about them. Years later, I would visit the town of Sarlat in France, which has salamanders as its town symbol. When I asked about the symbols, I found out the town was a center of alchemy in the 16th century.

Back to the fire. In winter, when the fireplace was roaring, I would talk to the flames—they were a major source of entertainment before TV invaded the house. Often the flames would dance in an unusual manner and I could almost swear I could see the outline of a funny little creature of flame smiling at me. I never saw this in gas fireplaces; they had to be wood burning fireplaces. We always had plenty of wood as there were several cords stacked on the porch outside the living room. Each night several armfuls were brought into the living room, carefully stacked on the left of the fireplace. This large stack of wood for the evening fires lasting late into the night.

On this evening, I was sitting on the right side of the fireplace roasting marshmallows. Mom and Dad were seated on the opposite side of the fireplace talking with our visitors. I have no idea what they were talking about; my focus was on letting the marshmallow brown and then catch on fire, at which point I would blow out the fire. That was the perfect marshmallow—soft and sticky in the middle, nicely browned on most sides, and slightly burnt on one side. Since we had extendable forks, the marshmallow could be placed right under the andirons where the hottest coals were located.

I was just having fun. The marshmallows were my desert for the evening. One was pulled out of the fire. Somehow, the flame on the marshmallow jumped from the gooey desert to my face. Within an instant the whole left side of my face was on fire. I remember seeing Mom and Dad through the flames. There was no pain, just shock. Dad froze in terror. Trudy let out a gasp of fear. Mom jumped up and blew out the flame on my cheek. She put an ice pack on the area that should have been burned. After the ice pack she put a little butter (which we now know should not be done) on the area. I don't know if it was the ice, the butter or the fast action that worked, but there was no indication of my face having been burned. After, seeing no visible damage, Mom told me it was the salamander's way of giving me a kiss. To this day, I feel fire will not injure me if the source is natural and I have a need to work with it.

After one of Trudy and Morris' visits to The Hill, before they had children, Dad turned to Mom and said:

Out of the blue Dad blurted out: "Thank God those dirty Jews are leaving. I never want to see those kikes up here again."

They never came up again, at least not while Dad was home.

Another Long Island family had a daughter about seven years older than me. She was slightly overweight, wore glasses, and walked funny, at least to a young boy my age. Sometimes she used crutches, yet to me she was attractive. The reason she had a hard time walking was because she was a victim of polio. But she could roller skate. She would spend hours on skates and wanted to be a competitor in skating dance competitions. On skates she was straight and graceful; it was amazing the transformation that occurred once she put on those skates. It was as if the forward momentum created by skating enabled her to be more upright, moving with ease and grace. It allowed her to forget the crippling effects of polio.

People forget how devastating polio was. It was still a major threat in the early 1950s before Dr. Salk's vaccine was widely given. Thousands of children were struck down by the disease each year. It was a major focus of The March of Dimes, which would raise money to support research for childhood illnesses, polio being their primary concern. Here was a brave young teen who was overcoming it. She couldn't walk or run as most children could, but she could roller skate beautifully. It took a great deal of courage to accomplish all she had, along with a lot of pain and effort. This was my first introduction to a serious disease and the courage and strength it takes to rise above it. I did have a little childhood crush on her. I am so sorry her name has slipped from me over these years. I do hope she has had a happy successful life. She deserved it.

Coincidentally, I would meet Dr. Salk and have luncheon with his wife, Francoise Gilot, years later. Francoise was a member of the Feminine Grand Lodge of France and visited the Marie Deraismes Lodge several times. Le Droit Humain and the Feminine Grand Lodge do recognize each other, allowing for visitations in both directions (at least for the women). One time after the meeting, she invited the members to have lunch in their Greenwich Village apartment. It was a large apartment and filled with artwork, many by Picasso—after all, Picasso had been her lover for years and she was Paloma Picasso's mother. Paloma was famous for her own clothing style and a brand of perfume around this time. Francis was intelligent and an excellent conversationalist. Dr. Salk stayed largely in the background, letting his wife be the center of attention. It was an exceptionally enjoyable afternoon surrounded by two of the 20th century's most remarkable personalities.

Love,
Dad

Christmas Time in Falls Village:

We always had a big Christmas tree in the corner of living room at The Hill. I looked forward to Christmas.

I loved when Dad would break out the old Lionel train set he had as a child in early 1920s. I described it once in the Brooklyn apartment. At The Hill we would set up the tracks to the left of the tree. Although not a huge set, it filled up a sheet of plywood. It was fun; I liked to watch the big heavy engine pull the cars around the tracks. It had a smokestack that actually gave off fake puffs of smoke as it went around. There were also some buildings in Dad's set and old fashioned streetlights that lit up. I remember one Christmas getting a bumper car which would race around the tracks. Whenever it hit the engine or caboose, it would reverse direction.

One year, Santa gave me a second modern engine and more tracks. We set up a dual track system so both trains, with their cars attached, could go at the same time without bumping into each other. I remember there was a switching track to make them change their paths.

After Christmas, Dad would sometimes move the set to my room so I could continue to play with it. I kept it under my bed. Years later Mom moved it to the barn when we rented the house and it was nearly destroyed by the elements. When I was in junior high school my Uncle Forest found it. We lent it to him for his grandson. Forest had always been able to fix almost anything mechanical. During WWII he worked on repairing airplanes for the Air Force. I don't remember how he avoided being drafted into the Army during the war. He may have had a physical disability, not serious enough to show in his outward appearance, but enough to keep him out of the Army. He fully restored the train set and I saw it up and running in his house in Texas a few years later. I just wish it had been on "loan" since that set would be worth over $10,000 today.

It was around this time that we purchased a record player with an automatic record changer. In Christmas 1953 Dad bought a record that had two important Dickens stories, which had originally recorded on 78s in 1941 from two radio dramas. It was now on a LP (long playing) 33 RPM (revolutions per minute) record. On the first side was *A Christmas Carol* with the voice of Ronald Colman as Scrooge. Ronald Coleman had been in many radio shows including *The Halls of Ivy* and a major actor in the 1930s and early 1950s. I loved his voice. Hans Conried and Gale Gordon were on the recording too. They were famous in TV long after this recording was made. Hans was Uncle Tenoose on the Danny Thomas show *Make Room for Daddy* (1953-1964). Gale Gordon was Theodore J. Mooney on *I love Lucy,* starring Lucille Ball, throughout the 1960s.

The other side of the record was *Mr. Pickwick's Christmas*, read by Charles Laughton, the great British actor who was in so many fine movies. My favorite movie of his is *Witness for the Prosecution* with Tyrone Power and Marlene Dietrich. And his nurse in the movie was his real wife, Elsa Lancaster. Their marriage was interesting, both were gay and disguised it through their marriage. Both would bring home "friends" and go to their separate bedrooms to "entertain" their guests, yet they were very devoted to each other.

Back to the record, as the years progressed and the fights between Mom and Dad got worse, especially around Christmas, I would turn up the volume on the record player and lose myself in these stories. On the really bad years, the record was the only joy I had during Christmas. You have heard it many times. I was so happy to find it again on a CD. Even to this day, if I don't hear it at least once, I feel it is not really Christmas.

The next Christmas, Dad's principal present was a copy of the Bible. He told me to read it! Of course, I was still having problems with reading in school, but I kept it and by the time I was in junior high school I had finished reading it. It served as my bedtime reading. I would go through several chapters each night. This was the start of my religious self-education.

Before I finished the Bible, long after Mom's separation from Dad, she gave me a copy of the Torah. I read it looking for differences between it and the Bible's first books. I wondered, if they were the books of Moses, how could he have written after his own death? This was one of many inconsistencies in the Bible and Torah I questioned during this period. Soon I started to view the Bible as a book of historical fiction with little to do with what may have actually happened.

The Bhagavad Gita became my favorite holy book. For Buddhism I read some of Sutras, and then back to Hinduism, the Vedanta and the parts of the Upanishad, much later the Ramayana and other Hindu myths. I still keep up my study of comparative religion. I must give credit to the Bible given to me by Dad as the start of my religious readings, which led to me eventually questioning it and other faiths.

At the same time your grandma was teaching me elementary forms of meditation. One was to walk into a room, look around for 30 seconds, then close your eyes and try to place everything you saw. Then open your eyes to see what you got right and what you missed. It was a good way to train the mind to remember things. I just wished it applied to reading comprehension which was poor.

Still, I read as many of the holy books as I could. I did pass on the Koran, just felt it was too much like the Bible and Torah. You can tell which Bible I read by Dad's inscription "To Wally."

Eventually this led to Mom taking me to many churches and other religious services; she was introducing me to as many of the faiths as possible. This created a strong foundation for my involvement in The Temple of Understanding years later.

By the time I was 13, Mom asked me what religion I considered being a part of. You must realize she was a mystical Christian. She even had a vision later in life of Mary and Jesus walking in our back yard. But she totally rejected most of the Christian Churches. Realizing that if I was to choose Judaism, I would need Hebrew lessons, Mom felt it was time for me to declare allegiance to one faith or another. With memories of a past life and all the books I had been exposed to, it was an easy decision.

"I'll call myself a Buddhist/Christian. I believe in the Four Noble Truths and the Eight-Fold Path, but because Buddhism doesn't care if you consider yourself a member of another faith, I can be both Buddhist and Christian. That will keep you happy, Mom."

I have considered myself a Buddhist/Christian ever since. It turned out to be a wise decision, especially later in life when joining the Christian orders of Masonry.

See you soon—after all, Christmas is swiftly approaching once again.

Love,
Papa

T, Summer camp experience—a little out of order but hopefully interesting:

Mom and Dad decided I should go to a week-long summer camp when I was six. They didn't plan this with me. It was sprung it on me rather quickly. I was not excited. I knew things at home were not going well, but I would rather be home watching the disaster than away not knowing what was happening.

The day arrived. Off I went. Mentally I was a disaster. The name and location of the camp escapes me. Most likely in New York somewhere near the mountains, maybe near Saratoga. The drive seemed to last forever. Mom and Dad were both present and the tension was unbearable. To my mind, I felt if I left home even for a week it was an eternity. At age six a week seems like an eternity. There may well be no home to go back to. I was not far from wrong, just a few months premature.

When we arrived, Mom introduced me to my camp counselor. Rather than a young person from college, this was a grown man about my parents' age. His name was Leslie Ottersen. He assured me I would have fun and have a great time. But I wanted no part of it. I clung onto Mom as if I was drowning and she was the life preserver. I cried, screamed and yelled. I didn't want to stay! Dad was getting mad. Mom was worried about him losing his temper. Leslie picked up on the family difficulties. He kept it in the back of his mind, for purposes you cannot imagine.

Finally, Mom tore herself away from me. Leslie was holding on to me. Mom told me she would be back next Saturday to pick me up. Mom and Dad both got into the car. Mom was crying. I was crying. Dad was furious. Leslie busy trying to hold back a kid attempting to run after a car! Great start to summer camp!

After the car was out of sight Mr. Ottersen led me to our "tent." It was a tent on a platform which housed about six kids and him. All the bunks were double-decked, except the counselor's. I was given one on the bottom, near Ottersen.

Leslie made a sincere attempt to make my stay pleasant, along with the rest of the kids. He would check all the boys to see if they "had washed behind their ears"—strange, but that was part of who he was—and he led us to meals.

This was my first experience with Cool Aid and camp food, which was served in the main building. The dining room also doubled as the movie night room. I don't remember what movies were shown; I do remember there were lots of cartoons.

One of the activities was walking the wooded trails around the camp. Our tent was one group. We were told to keep an eye out for unusual rocks and possible Indian arrow heads. It seems strange now, but I actually found one the first day on the trail by myself. That was my first fossil / archeological discovery outside of the one I found behind Lorraine's house. I have been looking at rocks closely ever since.

One of the first things Leslie did was to try to teach me how to swim. Apparently, Mom had asked that I be given swimming lessons. But I was not learning in the class, so he took me aside and taught me personally. I just couldn't coordinate my arms, little less the breathing. There I was in two-and-a-half feet of water, looking as if I would drown any second. After about three days of more than an hour a day, with many struggles, I could propel myself through the water. I looked like a drowning cat, but before the end of the week, I was comfortable in the lake and actually swimming without help. Mostly dog paddle!

The next big thing was shooting—remember this was the 1950s when shooting was common. I was just one month short of the required age limit (seven). Leslie talked the camp counselors into letting me try to shoot. These were 22 caliber rifles at a distance of about 50 feet. We were each given five bullets. The head of the shooting range carefully instructed us how to aim the rifle. How to release the safety catch. How to load the gun. And the precautions necessary before you pull a trigger. I tried to follow the instructions as closely as possible. I took careful aim. Bang. Load the next bullet. Bang. Again bang. Then the final two shots. Two other kids where shooting at the same time.

The instructor went to retrieve the three targets. When the instructor came to give me my target, he was scratching his head:

"How did you do that?"

"Do what?" I asked.

He showed me the target. There were clearly two holes in the bullseye and a third about half an inch outside the immediate center. The other two shots were nowhere to be seen. Everyone was amazed a first-time shooter would hit the bullseye. Even more, how I could hit the target so precisely on three shots and totally miss the other two. I was very proud of the three that hit. I did show them to Mom when she picked me up. She smiled.

Yes, Mom did pick me up, alone. It was a much nicer drive back. She started telling me about how she learned to shoot with an old fashioned six gun. One day she pulled out one of her pistols, which I had not seen before. She set up a target, likely a piece of paper on a box, with a couple of circles, and pointed the gun from her hip. All seven shots were pulled off in quick succession. There was no "aiming", just shooting from her hip. All seven shots were within the two-inch circle. She told me she had learned to shoot as if the gun was a finger and she was pointing at the target. She never aimed in the traditional sense. The pistol was treated as an extension of her hand. Point—shoot!

Dad didn't dare to teach me anything about guns—not after he found out what a good marksman Mom was. It was just another point of jealousy between the two of them. He had a shotgun but I never saw him shoot it more than three times up on The Hill. I don't remember if he even shot at a target.

Dad must have had rifle training when in the Army boot camp, but guns were just not his thing. Mom being raised mostly in Texas, she had a gun in her hand from the age of seven. As a result, she could outshoot most—at least those who were not using a scope.

As for a pistol, she would have come close to her heroine Annie Oakley! By the end of the week, I was actually glad I had stayed at camp. I learned to how to swim, how to shoot a rifle, and a little about Indian arrowheads. After the panic attack which lasted the first two days, I actually started to have fun. I was also very proud that Mom was impressed with my first target.

Love,
Papa

Hi T, a camp follow-on:

There was a direct result of what happened at camp and something I forgot to talk about in last year's letters.

Remember the two holes in the bullseye and one about half an inch outside the immediate center? Mom was very proud of the fact I did so well on my first attempt at shooting and she also took it to indicate I needed a gun of my own. You have to remember back then in the country most boys did have guns. The BB guns were popular for boys in rural towns. If you lived by the fields or woods you had a .22 rifle. If you were out west in the hunting sections of America, it was a 30-30 but usually after you had your .22 or other target guns to prove you could aim straight and hit your target. It was just accepted back in the 1950s that young men had a guns.

In fact, BB guns were advertised in comic books. 22s in many of the magazines orientated towards slightly older boys. Boy Scouts had a shooting badge. Back in Amesville, most of my friends had 22s. Dad being a good Republican agreed a boy needs a gun. He had his Ithaca, 16-gauge double barrel shot gun (the one you have seen and I used when you took me out for skeet shooting).

Mom had grown up with guns. Dad talked about using the shotgun for game birds. I don't think he hunted more than two or three times in his life. Mom had grown up with a six-gun strapped to her side as a kid, was comfortable with guns. She grew up shooting crows out of the corn fields—that will be another letter when I start talk more about her life.

My seventh birthday was coming up. Mom and Dad agreed that I could get a gun. On my birthday I received my 22 caliber, single shot, bolt action, target rifle. The gun came with a cleaning outfit, a variety of targets—circle targets, others with the silhouette of different animals—raccoon, squirrel, rabbit, fox, etc.

The rules were I could only shoot with them present, and only shoot towards the back field. We would set up the target towards the rear of the barn and then shooting from the front side the angle would be downward towards the field, where the UFO landed. The downward direction allowed the bullets to hit the ground and never fly off. They would be buried safely in the mud.

We immediately set up three targets. One for each of us. I was still getting use to the new kind of sight, different than the one used in the camp, but at least I hit the target on the box. Dad hit the target but barely. Mom was close to the bullseye, repeatedly! Dad quickly declared we had other things to do that day and stormed off. Mom and I kept shooting. Target practice over for the day, I had to learn how to clean my gun.

Next Dad insisted it was the father's duty to teaching his son how to shoot. Mom was not allowed to use my rifle! From that day on, which were less than a handful of shooting days, I could practice with him present and only him. He never could accept that Mom was a better shot. But remember the fox she shot with the shotgun? One shot, dead on the nose and head. She did better than him with his gun. However, Mom and I did slip out every now and then, especially on weekdays when we knew Dad would not be home for at least a couple of hours.

The first time your Mom and I took you and your sister to Kings Dominion in Virginia, there was a shooting range over by the flume ride. They still had .22 rifles for the targets. Those types of shooting booths would soon disappear, unfortunately for me, but fortunately for Kings Dominion as there are just too many crazies out there now. But I remember the first time I stood up to that range. There were simple stationary targets close up, then little target bunnies bobbing up and down, and further black bears moving back and forth on a little pivot from behind trees or rocks. Then in the back were the smallest targets, ducks moving across the background pond, and an occasional bird in flight across the sky. All the targets were steel cut-outs, painted to look like the object they represented. When you hit a target it would fall backwards and then pop up again. Great fun!

I stepped up to the shooting line. A man next to me was jerking when he pulled the trigger and not aiming correctly. Turning to him I attempted to point out all he was doing wrong. It was in the most polite voice possible. Still, he took offense.

"Let's see if you can do any better," was his response.

I aimed and pulled off all dozen shots in less than a minute. The first was one of the bobbing targets. Then the rest on the faster moving targets in the back. No misses. All direct hits. The man turned to me and said that was the most remarkable shooting he had ever seen. Then I repeated to him what he had done wrong. I helped him in holding and aiming the .22 and his next shot hit the stationary target. He thanked me for the help.

Back to the past. When we moved to Lakeville (next letter) the rifle stayed up on The Hill. It would be years before I would start shooting again. By that time there was a group of us who would go out in the woods to shoot.

Love,
Papa

Chapter 8

The Last Straw and Race to Safety

T:

One day Dad and Mom had been fighting over something; I was getting irritated with Dad, too. To escape, I went playing outside. Both cars were in the driveway. Since Mom didn't mind my climbing on her old Pontiac I thought it would be alright to climb on Dad's Oldsmobile, but he came out and saw me on his car and blew up. How dare I climb all over his car, and get scratches all over the paint. He grabbed me and pulled me off and started to yell at me. I got upset and called him a bastard.

He was very fond of his mother, who had died less than five years before, and the word made him explode! He started yelling at me for using it. Then he started to hit me. Not with open hands but with his fists. This just made me angrier. I started to cry. Despite his fists hitting me all over my head and shoulders, the only word that could be heard above his yelling was the repeat of the word that set him off, over and over again. My pushing that button made him lose control. The blows were terrible. The more he hit me the more I cried. But instead of crying out loud, the only thing that came out was:

"Bastard, bastard, bastard …"

Mom came out and saw the commotion. She tried to grab Dad and pull him away, but his fists were still flying towards my bruised head. She finally jerked him away and told him he shouldn't ever hit a child like that. Dad threatened her, but stopped short of hitting her. He stormed into the house. Mom checked me all over and put ice on my bruises. Neither of us said anything to Dad for the rest of the day. Although I don't remember him leaving, sometime during the confusion he climbed into the Olds and drove off.

About two weeks later Mom picked me up from the babysitter early and we went home. There were a number of suitcases packed. A box or two were filled with my toys and favorite possessions. All these were piled into the car as quickly as possible. Then she started down the driveway between the maple trees and down Sugar Hill Road. We started to drive quickly towards Lakeville. She had found an apartment to rent. As we drove she told me we were leaving The Hill and Dad.

I started to cry: "What about Kitty Poo? We have to have Kitty Poo."

Mom, in order to find some pet for me to have an affectionate relationship with had found a kitten. We called it Kitty Poo. Funny, I do not remember the cat now, but Mom told me what happened next.

The further we were from The Hill the more desperate were my cries for Kitty Poo. She knew that Dad would be driving back from Hartford would be home any minute. She also knew how fond I was of the kitten. She made a quick U turn and headed back to The Hill. She often told me those were the more terrifying minutes of her life.

We could not have been more than five minutes away but the timing was critical. According to her, she drove like a demon. When we reached the house, she ran in and got the kitten, its bed and some food, then she jumped back into the car and raced down the maple lane again. All the way down Sugar Hill she was fearful Dad would be driving home and see us. We reached the bridge and turned right onto Dugway Road, which ran by the river, and Mom floored the gas until we were out of sight. Turning on to Briton Hill Road, up the steep hill she realized we were out of Dad's grasp, out of his fury, out of reach of his fists! Only then did she begin to breathe normally.

Over Briton Hill, we drove, now a little slower. I was holding tight to the kitten. Down the other side, we made the sharp turn and reached Salmon Kill Road driving past the Folkes' house, a delightful couple Mom was friends with. We made a left turn on Farnum Road, just past the Belter's Farm. Now we were safely on the way to Lakeville. We made a right turn on Main Street and crossing the little stone bridge. Another right on Bostwick Street. There was a house on the corner and a little field with a hill toward Lakeview Avenue which was halfway up the hill. Mom turned into the driveway at the second house on the left.

"This is our new home, Wally. Help me move some of the boxes inside."

I was confused and yet relieved. Dad would not be a threat here—at least that was what we hoped. She had rented the second floor. Downstairs lived a widow who needed extra money to keep the house. At the same time, if necessary, she could watch the seven-year-old who was now moving in. The apartment was long and narrow. There was a room facing the front of the house, which was almost never used. My room was the one on the left. Mom's was on the right. The bathroom was at the end of the hall, with a nice size kitchen on the right at the rear of the apartment. A small table and chairs were set up in a corner of the kitchen. We ate most meals on that table for the next two years. Mom had already made my bed. After a quick bite she put me to bed. Kitty Poo was upstairs too. Her food and bed were placed in the kitchen. She was mostly an outdoor cat and when we moved to Lakeville and a town environment, it was not what she was used to. She was struck and killed by a car within the first few months.

All the sudden changes, the race back to the house for the rescue of Kitty Poo, and the race to get out of Amesville before Dad crossed the bridge from Falls Village, had exhausted both of us. I fell asleep quickly.

Love,
Papa

Hi T:

Lakeville was a new environment. Instead of fields and woods I was now in the center of a thriving little town. It was a long way from the trails and animal paths that I followed around The Hill. This new residence was a block from Main Street, easily within walking distance of everything in town.

There was a vacant lot next door. It was about an acre lot that was narrow but deep, extending from the street to a hill behind, maybe 50 yards from the street. Although vacant, there could have been a house on the lot based on the size of the property. Or, it could have been a part of the extensive property of the house I was now living in. This much I can say, it provided a perfect place to play and build snowmen.

Another house on the other side of lot caught my interest, but for a different reason. I never got to know who lived there. Across the street was a house and a smaller vacant lot which led to the tiny Burton Brook that bisected Lakeville. I quickly discovered it was easily crossed. I would descend the four-foot bank, proceed over a series of stepping stones, and onto the path that led to Walton Street. The various houses there were more closely packed. Most of the houses on Walton were smaller than on Bostwick.

Walton street was occupied by working class and blue-collar families. It seemed Burton Brook divided Lakeville's working class from the middle class. Up the hill on Main Street, closer to the road and to my school, were the finer houses of the upper middle class, which were around Lakeville Lake on Elm Street. There were a number of wealthy individuals on that street. Perhaps the most famous was Artie Shaw, the famous clarinet player and band leader from the 1940s. At the time, he was still popular and making frequent appearances on TV variety shows.

Bostwick Street itself was one long block before turning to the left and up the hill. On top of the hill, it became Prospect Street and led back to Main Street. No more than a dozen houses could be seen prior to turning up the hill. My house was one of the largest on the street. Most of the others were smaller, but similar in style.

At the end of Bostwick was a swampy area. If you followed a little trail to the right, where the road turned left, you would cross Walton Street and the brook. The trail led to the town's park and the old Penn Central Railroad tracks which were on an elevated embankment. The little league baseball diamond was the first thing you saw. There were also two tennis courts in the same general area. The courts were actually closer than the baseball field but were hidden by a tall patch of high grass and weeds growing in the swampy area. A little playground and a softball field for the adult teams were at the far end of the park.

There was a small set of bleachers for both the baseball and softball fields. A gazebo was near a drinking fountain. The gazebo was the place where small bands played and the town had little celebrations and speeches. It was right out of an Andy Hardy film. Andy Hardy films, with Mickey Rooney as the star, were popular in the 1930s. In other words, a Normal Rockwell town painting. Rockwell was the illustrator for *The Saturday Evening Post* magazine, popular back then, along with *Life*.

If you crossed both ball fields you would reach the road which led out of town towards Sharon and Amesville. On the extreme left was a very steep embankment about 15 feet high where the railroad tracks once were. On these tracks the Fourth of July fireworks would be set off. The tracks being elevated above the playground area made the fireworks look more impressive than they actually were. Due to the tracks' elevation, the fireworks were able to display a number of wonderful stationary wooden designed shapes of different sizes. Each year would be different. Almost always, there would a train in fireworks with the wheels going around, animal shapes were popular. A rocket shape would then lead to actual rocket bursts of fireworks high into the sky. It always ended with the American Flag displayed. For a little town, the fireworks were quite impressive and drew a fairly large crowd each Fourth.

Following the track bed, it led to a bridge support where the train station still stood on the other side of the street. Across from the train station was the movie theater. Beyond the theater and the station building was the road to the lake.

The real name of the lake was Wononskopomuc, the name the Native American tribe called it before they were driven off. By the time I moved to Lakeville, the RR Station had been abandoned and the bridge was more a memory than any real identifiable structure. You could see that about 10 yards of tracks still existed by the old station, which were heavily overgrown and very rusty.

Opposite the old station was the only movie theatre in Salisbury Township. It was small but still carried the now forgotten tradition of Saturday matinees for kids. Those were the days when you would buy a ticket for 25 cents and spend an entire rainy-day afternoon at the movies. There was a main feature and a host of shorts, cartoons and maybe a serial or two. Serials were less than 30 minutes flicks, which were like TV shows today. The story would continue from week to week. I don't remember which ones I saw, mostly because we couldn't afford me going weekly! The *Perils of Pauline* was one. Mom's favorite was *Buck Rogers in the 21st Century*. Gee, we are in the 21st century now... *Flash Gordon* was also popular. The Westerns shorts included Roy Rogers, Hopalong Cassidy, others, mostly from Republic Pictures, where John Wayne got his start. Many of these were carry overs from the 1940s. By the mid 1950s the shorts were in their decline. What I really liked were the Warner Brothers cartoons—still in fresh release and almost always accompanying any WB picture! This was during the years that Tweety Bird and Bugs got their Oscars.

In the mid '50s there were enough children in Lakeville to support a movie house, at least for a few more years. In recent times the old farts have pretty much rid their town of small children. Those remaining are mostly hidden behind closed doors and rarely seen. Remember when we drove through Lakeville on Labor Day Weekend in 2004? We stopped by Lake Wononskopomuc. When I was growing up, Labor Day Weekend was a major celebration at the lake. The parking lot would be filled. There were cookouts and loads of people, not just by the lake, but in the park area behind the main building. The swimming area would be full of swimmers and everyone trying to get the last swim in of the summer. Small children would be running, screaming, tossing beach balls on the sand, while the teens would get the last suntan of the season.

When we got there on Sunday, the raft and docks had already been put away for the winter. What was left of the staff was shutting down the dressing rooms and snack bar. There were no other people on sunny Labor Day Sunday! To me, with the memories of what it used to be like, this was depressing. It supports the theory that Lakeville no longer welcomes children, especially of the working classes who would spend their time at this retreat.

Love
Papa

Hi.

As you can figure—Dad found us...

What else! It took only a day or two before he found out where we were. I don't know how Mom found out about him finding us. She quickly called Charles Rodriguez, the minister from Sharon, asking him come over ASAP. Mom and Dad both enjoyed Charles' sermons, which were much more bearable than ones given by Dad's old minister at the Presbyterian Church in Salisbury. Charles was a wonderful individual and someone I would become close to as the years progressed. He had a very attractive wife, blonde, shapely and stylish; it was surprising she became a minister's wife. Unfortunately, they couldn't have children. Not sure whose fault it was, but it caused some friction in the marriage, that and her high aspirations led to a divorce some years later.

Mom loved to test Charles after services on religious interpretation of Christian theology. If lunch was offered, we would go to his church service (Dad enjoyed free food). Mom talked to Charles, challenging most of the traditional interpretations of the Bible using passages and especially the hymnal to support her arguments. Reincarnation was one of her favorite topics. Was Moses really Jewish? Or, just an Egyptian who was sympathetic towards the Hebrews? Did the Jews make him a Hebrew to justify him to their own people? Who were the real authors of the Gospels, the Old Testament? With scientific evidence for evolution and the age of the Earth, how could anyone still believe in the silly idea that the universe was created in seven days. Many points Charles certainly agreed on. Others he questioned himself. Charles greatly respected Mom's intelligence and capacity to have an intelligent debate. She enjoyed these discussions.

On this occasion Mom was scared Charles would not make it to our house before Dad. She was almost in a panic and didn't know how to handle the situation. This is why the second Mom found out that Dad might be coming she called Charles, hoping he would be able to keep Dad in check. Dad did respect Charles. It was a good strategy. They arrived almost together. With Charles there as a witness, Dad had to control his temper.

I remember the feeling in the room was exceptionally tense but strangely polite. I was told to go to my room. I could hear the voices coming from the kitchen, where the three of them were discussing the situation. What was unusual was there was no shouting. I don't remember having any emotions about the situation. I was glad to be away from Dad and his unpredictable temper.

Looking at family histories, Dad's anger follows a rather typical pattern. His father likely struck him when he was a boy. I thought I had broken the pattern. I knew I had the potential. Dad first came out of me when I got mad at Nim the chimpanzee one time. I tried really hard to conquer that anger. I almost did. But it did break out once. Thank goodness a chimp can take a beating better than a human child.

The conversation lasted for over an hour. I was tired and spent the time drawing in my room. It was night. I don't think I had dinner. Since there were no restaurants in Lakeville that Mom and I could afford, I knew that dinner was going to be really late, if we had one. I wanted to snack on something but was too fearful to go into the kitchen. After some time, Dad left. On his way out, he said something to me. The words escape me now, but it was a put-down on Mom and me. Charles stayed a little longer, talking with Mom, but now I felt it was safe to go into the kitchen.

When Mom saw me she remembered we had not had dinner. Charles stayed at the table and Mom began to fix a quick dinner on the stove. Most likely hamburgers, potatoes and frozen peas, my favorite vegetable. That and TV dinners became a common meal over the next few years.

Charles had me sit on his lap. He talked about how sometimes parents have to move away from each other. But not to worry. Mom still loved me and would take care of me. He offered me his help should I ever need to see him. I felt very comfortable with Charles. In a small way, during the next two years he became a quasi second father. Mom and I would go to his church in Sharon more often, then he was given orders to move to another parish and I lost track of him for some years, but Mom kept in touch. Charles, taking Mom's lead, divorced his wife during his absence from Connecticut. I think he was reassigned to a church in New Jersey. He tried to pick up more graduate work at Columbia University in NYC, but his proposed Ph.D. dissertation was on a topic so specifically narrow he couldn't find an advisor. They offered him a position teaching instead. But he didn't want to become a theological professor, so he dropped the idea of obtaining the degree and any connection to Columbia U.

As for Dad, he would visit regularly and kept control of himself. questions:
"Don't you miss your room on The Hill?"

"Don't you miss the woods and the animals on The Hill?"

"Why would you want to live in this town? There is nothing here."

He kept plying me with

That last statement was not entirely true. I did have an escape. Saturday afternoon movies, for one. It was during this time that I started going to the movies regularly.

Love,
Papa

Hi T – a letter out of sequence, with some history.

Tomorrow your Mom and I are going to NYC. She is tired of Times Square and midtown so we are staying further uptown, on the Upper East Side. 70th Street was the old Czech / Bohemia section of Manhattan where your great grandfather worked for Tammy Hall in 1910s through the 1930s. Now all of that is gone. What were once middle-class working family homes have now been replaced with multi-million-dollar condos and apartments. In the '80s, the East Side was the old German section of town. I remember the Gieger Café and the Bohemian Inn almost next to each other. Great food, dramatic differences in price. I don't know if either still exist.

All of this talk of NYC and seeing a PBS show on Pete Seeger on TV reminded me of when I met him, briefly. It was many years ago at the New Port Folk Festival in Rhodes Island. This was the late 1960s when folk music was on the up. Vietnam was getting worse. Protest music was on the rise.

I remember talking with a group of people at the festival. We had just left William F. Buckley, who was doing his usually elitist, extreme right-wing dialogue with someone. As individuals presented opposing views, he would proceed to cut down their positions. If he couldn't destroy their argument he would insult them with erudite language. Many times they did not know they were being insulted.

I had been invited to go to the festival by a group of Baha'is and was talking with one of the girls in the group when I felt a huge push from behind. It was the strangest push I had ever felt. It was not a physical push but a psychic one. I literally had to take a step forward to prevent myself from falling.

I asked the girl: "Who is that behind me?"

She took my shoulder and turned me around. There was Pete Seeger. He was strolling through the crowds with a horde of followers around him. He was enjoying himself as he always did when he was in a crowd. I looked and felt as if there was a giant golden aura surrounding him and those near him. The "push" had been the impact of being contacted by that aura. The pure spirituality of Pete's soul was unmistakable. Never before or since, not even when I have seen him in concert, was this feeling so strong. Not even with the Dalai Lama or Lama Govinda years later. Here was a living bodhisattva (a Buddha in the making), and in the body of a pure and acknowledged atheist! My friend and I followed along.

Between actual shows at the festival there were odd groups with guitars and banjos that would hold impromptu jam sessions scattered around the festival grounds. Pete would go to a group, not attracting much attention. He asked if he could join in, then start playing a song that everyone knew. In between songs he would give pointers on how they could improve playing. When he noticed an improvement in both the crowd and music, and in the middle of a song, he would quietly get up, while singing, bow and leave the group. By that time enough people became interested in that particular group a good number would stay to listen.

Pete would then go to the next group, not getting much attention, and do exactly the same thing. We watched him go to three groups and I realized this was a remarkable individual. This was during the years he was still blacklisted by the House Unamerican Activities Committee and could not appear on TV or radio.

It was around that time Pete Seeger and his friends launched the sloop *Clearwater* in the Hudson River. He was combining a lifelong love of the outdoors and a longstanding desire to do something to clean up the environment, polluted by irresponsible corporate and public usage. More than anyone else, Pete was responsible for the cleaning up of the Hudson River. His songs and sailing the *Clearwater* up and down the river raised so much awareness that action was eventually taken in Albany and new laws were set in place to crack down on polluters. To this day I feel he is one of the greatest individuals I have ever seen or am likely to see in my life.

Love,
Papa

Hi T, back to Lakeville.

After Dad found us and realized what has happened, he tried to calm down. Mom wanted him to do things with me on the weekends. Living in a town with a movie theater, the cinema was obvious choice. Dad agreed he would take me to the movies on some weekends. It was an easy thing to do. Other visits he promised to take me to the ball park and play catch or watch the little league teams play. Looking back on these months, often he never showed up and rarely interacted with me. When he did come over he would continue the old arguments with Mom. We may have made it to the park less than half a dozen times and to the movies maybe twice.

But Dad taking me was important in Mom's eyes. She wasn't very keen on me going to the movies by myself. There were some bullies who hung around the movie house and Mom was aware of them. Since at the age of seven I was still small, she was a little worried. Later I made friends in the neighborhood who would accompany me to the movies, when we could all afford it. That was OK.

Lakeville was an interesting mix of the very wealthy, who would go to live theatre in NYC for entertainment or the Sharon Playhouse, a summer stock theatre a few miles away. They never went to the lower-class movie theater across from the old railroad station, which was left to the working class and their children. Most of the "movie" families were the tradesmen and servants, but as might be expected, the lower-class kids were not examples of best behavior. Fights were common, both outside the theater and inside. Occasionally even among the parents! As for police, there were none anywhere in the area. If trouble did start, they were 20 minutes away and by the time they arrived, the troublemakers would be gone.

We couldn't afford to go to a movie more than once a month, even at 25 cents for me and $1 for Dad. In 1956 the biggest draw for kids was the Dean Martin and Jerry Lewis movies. The films were silly slapstick. Jerry was always the comedian while Dean played the straight man, much like Lou and Bud in the Abbott and Costello films I watched on TV. Dean would usually throw in a song or two to a beautiful female co-star.

I saw the movie *Pardners*, which came out earlier in the year; they announced that another film would be coming out later in the same year. That film was called *Hollywood or Bust*. I was very anxious to see it, which brings up another fact about movies from back then.

There was only one screen in a movie theater and movies ran only one week. There was a constant turnover of films at the theaters to accommodate Hollywood. It was exceedingly rare more than one major film was ever released in a single week. It seemed the major studios alternated between who would release what film and when. It was common to see a Universal film one week, followed by an MGM, a 20th Century Fox, or a Columbia Pictures movie the next. As for the minor studios such as RKO and Republic, they were delegated to the Saturday afternoon kid marathons, rarely running over 90 minutes with the shorts and serials between features.

So, *Hollywood or Bust* had come to Lakeville. Dad had promised me he would take me to the next Martin and Lewis film. On the day I was ready to go, but he informed me that he couldn't take me because he had to take care of other issues. Later I found out it he was planning to move. I burst out crying. Mom was mad. She reminded him that he had promised! He said he would make it up. The next week, it was announced that Martin and Lewis had split up. I was heartbroken—I never saw their last film in a theater!

Dad never did make it up to me. Deep inside I never forgave him for breaking his promise. At that moment any lasting trust in him was killed. From that day and for the rest of his life, he never regained my confidence that any promise would be kept. The relationship between us remained strained until his death. Being physically abused by him was nothing compared to him letting me down on a promise, particularly this one promise that, at the time, meant so much to me. After all it was something as a child I was looking forward to so much.

Now you understand why I love the fairy tales about promises like *The Princess and the Frog*. I have always tried to keep my promises. Not all have been, unfortunately. The one I most regret is not fulfilling the promise about paying for your undergrad or graduate school. But the former was a free ride. Then you began teaching and returned to med school after I had retired. I just couldn't support you as promised, sorry. At least I contributed something each month.

Love,
Papa

Hello there,

During the summer after the separation, Mom wanted to take my mind away from the traumatic break up and move from The Hill. She planned a trip to Maine and Nova Scotia, Canada. We drove up in the old car to Bar Harbor, Maine, and stayed a few days in various motels, then we took a ferry boat to Yarmouth, Nova Scotia, where we stayed a few nights in The Lakeshore Inn.

It's funny, I remember almost nothing of getting to Bar Harbor except the docks. To get there we had to travel through the same territory where you broke your tooth. I do remember taking the boat to Nova Scotia. My first ocean (?) trip! Then taxi drive up to the Lakeshore Inn. From a distance it was an impressive sight. It looked very plush. It was a beautiful resort hotel on the shores of a lake, what else! I had never stayed in a resort hotel before. This was certainly a new experience. The Inn looked massive. The driveway was impressive. The grounds were impressive. The lake was impressive. The whole place was beautiful. Of course, this is the first time I had ever been in a quality hotel so at that age anything would have looked grand.

I was looking for a place to swim. After my summer camp experience I had become an avid swimmer. I could swim in the lake, provided I was okay with cold water. They directed me to the boathouse. Mom had several activities planned but I wanted to swim first. I got into my swimsuit, grabbed a towel and when down to the dock at the lake, actually the inlet of this large lake. Some men were there talking. They said it was okay to swim but it was really cold.

I dove in. Their warning was an understatement. It felt like I had just jumped off the *Titanic*. I started to move fast. Suddenly something jumped over my head. I looked back; the men were laughing. Then they shouted:

"Don't worry, he's harmless."

I looked again and there right in front of me was a freshwater otter. He saw I was looking at him and off he went. I chased after him and then he circled back and darted around me, and even gently bumped me to tease me. I forgot how cold the water was—I had found a playmate.

We chased each other. I would splash him. He would jump over, around and in front of me. It was great fun. He apparently lived under the dock and would usually beg for fish, but he seldom had playmates so this was a special day for both of us. Finally, Mom came down and called me out of the water. She said my whole body had turned bluish from the cold, then she saw the otter and thought it was great I played with him. I was given a warm bath to get my body temperature back to normal. She said my body felt like it had just been pulled out of the arctic. I was not allowed to swim in the lake again it was just too cold.

The next day Mom arranged for one of the hotel dock workers to take us out fishing. I was in the middle of the boat. He took us over to a larger part of the lake, where we all started to fish. After a while I felt a nibble. I jerked the line gently and it pulled back. I had hooked something big. Off in the distance a fish jumped. It was on my line. The man started giving me all sorts of instructions on how to reel it in. After what seemed to be a long battle, I finally got the fish next to the boat and the man netted it. It was a huge pike—about 14 inches long. The man congratulated me; it was one of the bigger ones caught in the lake. It was my first and only pike. It looked like a monster with very sharp teeth.

Mom told me to take it to the hotel chef and ask if he would cook it for my dinner. I did so immediately after landing. I pulled the fish out of the bag, gave it to the chef and he laid it out on the cutting board. Suddenly, it jumped.

"Not dead!" shouted the chef. He took a huge wooden mallet and hit it on the head. THUMP!

"Now dead," he said in his French accent.

His whole staff laughed, as did I.

They served it beautifully that evening for me, with all the trimmings of a full three-course meal and we were not charged a cent! Mom always thought that was great. The next day was Sunday and the hotel had its usual brunch set up on a long buffet table. About every six feet or so was a huge ice sculpture. There was a lobster. Another largemouth bass. Then a swan. Then a trout. Like everything else in the hotel, they were truly impressive. I had never seen ice sculptures before and thought this was great.

After the brunch it was time to catch the ferry back to the States. Looking back on this little trip, it was the happiest few days Mom and I ever spent together. The fun at the Lakeside Inn and its memory helped through the many rough years that would be coming in the future.

Love,
Papa

T,

Back in Lakeville, one of the first problems I faced was who lived near me that I could play with. There were no children on my street, except some toddlers at the end of the block. Across and next to me were several homes with elderly people. Some likely retired. I remember I never even saw some of the people who lived on the block, which consisted of about eight or nine houses. They left their houses early in the morning and returned late at night. However, across the brook on the next block, on Walton Street, lived Big and Billy.

Big was the older kid, about the same age as I, and more aggressive. Billy was a little younger but very friendly and a really nice kid. He was one grade lower than I. Big was in my grade but a different class. Like me he had stayed back in an earlier grade.

Their father was a laborer in one of the plants towards Canaan. He was tall, muscular and thin. Their mother was also thin, had reddish hair and looked a little like she might have been Irish. They were Catholic. Their house was a ranch-style home with the bedrooms in the back for the boys. Eventually I became friends with Big and Billy. We played together almost daily. It was easy to get to their house. All I had to do was cross Bostwick Street, go through the unkempt yard between the houses and find a way across Burton Brook.

Mom referred to them as B & B, always accompanied with a little internal laugh. Later I discovered from her that "B & B" was a drink of Bénédictine and brandy. Not sure who was Bénédictine and who was brandy in her mind.

It is strange to me now but I rarely got to go into their home, though there was little objection to them coming over to my house. It was as if the inside of their house was sacred: no one outside of the family was permitted in. I thought it unusual then but shook it off. Looking back, it was not a normal way for parents to behave towards their children's playmates. The excuse was their mother wanted to keep the house as clean as possible. She was afraid us boys would track dirt through the house. The only exception was if nature called and required urgent relief.

So when we played it was over at my house, usually in the field and on the balcony that ran from the front of the house to the northwest side. Our favorite game was war. What else would you expect? This was the 1950s. Though my "buddies" were a thing of the past, the memory of WWII was fresh in the cultural memory of the times and it was fresh in mind, as you know from earlier letters.

The balcony which ran around the front and side of my house was perfect to add to the adventures. The balcony's side faced the vacant lot and field going uphill. The hill was about 50 yards away, out of sight of the neighboring house due to the trees growing from the foot of the hill and beyond.

You could pretend you were in a bunker looking down on troops from the hill and when on the balcony it was a perfect ambush location. One could envision being in a bunker pretending to attack across the field and up the hill. Big, Billy and I would take turns on who would take the high ground. Sometimes, we were on the same side attacking invisible forces. They loved to "shoot" me and for me to do a summersault over the railing dropping the 4 fett to the ground below in a dramatic death scene.

Sometimes we would use a depression in the field as a machine gun nest. We would pile up extra brush around the hole and then place sticks in a way that would represent a machine gun pointing in the direction from which the charge would come. Big usually liked to take position in the "nest". He would sometimes ask Billy and me to go to the other side of the house to allow time to cover the machine gun nest with additional brush and would create another nest where Billy and I least expected. As Billy and I would cross the field, suddenly Big would start imitating a machine gun sound, followed by the shout: I got you! Drop dead!" which I would.

Other times we were charging machine gun nests that lay hidden in the forest at the back of the field. Here the pretend enemy was somewhere up the slope. We never charged up the hill, because the property belonged to those living on Lakeview Avenue. If the enemy was in the forest, looking down at us, all three of us would never complete the charge. We would all be cut down before reaching the treeline.

If all of this sounds familiar, well it is. I was the one initiating these games. My enthusiasm was so strong, I pulled Big and Billy into the game with as much excitement as you could imagine. My descriptions and complex planning made it seem real to them as it was to me. I would plot how we would attack, who would take up which positions, both us and the "unseen" enemy. when to call in for support, who would attempt to flank the enemy, and when the charge would take place.

It made the whole scene come alive in the minds of a group of second-graders. Though no longer in my daily consciousness, my past life experience was being played out over and over again in the casual play with my friends. Every time we "charged" it was I who would take the lead. I would be killed first in a dramatic fashion, hitting the ground and flinging myself in a contorted manner as I fell. Then after a pause, get up and renew the charge.

We would play actual games, ball and other things, but this was the most reoccurring activity. Looking back on it and considering Billy's age, he may have come back quickly, like me. He seemed very absorbed in the war games. Big just went along and loved to run quickly towards the invisible targets. This may have been the early development of what became his athletic prowess that proved to be beneficial in high school where he was a star running back; he became one of the chief sprinters on the track team.

I remember the woman who lived on the first floor, I think her name was Mrs. Little. She owned the house and on nice days would sit on the balcony and enjoy the good weather. She was concerned I might hurt myself for real in my dramatic falls. I never did.

For a birthday gift I received a toy shotgun from Mom. It was a small version of the real thing. The three of us would often use it in our play—better than our usual sticks and branches. Mrs. Little thought it was real and was very concerned. I had to let her handle it to show her it was plastic toy gun. She warned me to be careful because a policeman may not realize it was a toy and I could get into trouble. Good advice, especially now when toy guns look like their real counterparts.

We found an interesting cut in the brook that separated our streets. There was an undercut where rushing flood water had hollowed out a section of the bank which made for a narrow passageway. We could travel down the stream, without stepping in the shallow water, unseen by anyone looking in our direction. This was a great way to avoid being noticed by parents and neighbors. When B and B were not around, I would crawl through the tree roots and under the ground overhanging the brook. To a young boy this was an adventure of traveling unseen. If there was nothing else to do, this took up hours of time. The brook itself was seldom more than a foot deep and mostly only a few inches, so there was little or no danger. The real danger was slipping on moss-covered rocks. But no such accidents occurred and it continued to be a great place to play. It was also a good place to look for unusual rocks and a variety of small water bugs and tiny fish.

By traveling along the brook, it was a way to get down the block towards the ball field without notice which we did sometimes.

Love,
Papa

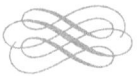

Hi,

You might call this "boys will be boys" and get in trouble. Well, I did. Here are the two episodes that stand out in my mind. They were months apart but mentally, as a child, they are grouped together simply because I got in trouble for both. It is certainly something a lot of boys, even today, will be able to identify with.

After a few months in the new apartment Mom decided my room needed a new color. I think I had been away with my Dad for the weekend and upon coming back the room had been painted in "A color that is perfect for a boy's room", according to the painter who did the job.

Well, it was a dull light brownish with an orange-red tint. I referred to it as throw-up brown. To me it was hideous and I quickly put my foot down in objection:

I hated the color! I cried, yelled and stamped my feet. "Why didn't you ask me first?"

I do not remember the previous color, which may have been a light pastel, or a plain old white, totally inappropriate for boys of the 1950s, but whatever it was, I preferred the old color.

Another factor in the equation was there may have been just too many major changes occurring over the past few months. This was just too much to handle. I went to bed that night in a room I absolutely hated and sometime during the middle of the night, I woke up. The idea came to me that black would be better. I started using the broad side of a pencil and shading the walls. I didn't get very far before I fell asleep again. Well, you can imagine what happened.

When Mom saw my modification to the wall she blew a gasket. She told Dad. She said Dad would be "talking" to me about what I had done. What was interesting was the area I had worked on was actually quite small, maybe just a little over a square foot of wall, but it was enough.

Of course, I was terrified of what Dad might do. I tried to erase part of it with a school eraser but that just smudged the area. Dad was mad but in control, thank goodness. I was given a long lecture about how much Mom was trying to give me a good home with a nice room and how I was ruining it. He did put in a plug for my old room which had been left behind and said that it was Mom's fault in the first place that I had such a small room in comparison. This last comment became the beginning of a verbal war between my parents over me.

Dad: "Mom took you away from your real home."

Mom: "Dad made it impossible for us to live with him."

Dad: "Is your mom still drinking too much? Wouldn't you rather be with a sober parent?" Mom: "Aren't you afraid that Dad will lose his temper again?"

Dad's criticism ceased only when he died. However, Mom's criticism of Dad would last until Mom died years later!

During the summer months, I got my first baseball glove and ball. That week Mom worked in the office in town. B and B were not around and I was home alone. I wanted to practice catch with myself. There was a big winged armchair in my room; the back and seat had good hard cushions and I started to throw the ball against the back of the chair, catching it as it bounced back to me. It worked perfectly. I started to throw harder. Well, the accuracy of a seven-year-old who is just learning to throw and catch a real baseball is not the greatest.

Sure enough, I missed the back cushion and hit the right wing of the chair. The ball bounced, not towards me, but right through the window. Crash! I knew I was in trouble again! Still remembering the trouble with the wall, I had to think of something that would deflect some of the blame. Then, it came to me. If I said that Big and Billy were playing catch with me in the hall and it slipped out of our hands maybe it would not be as bad for me.

When Mom saw the broken window, she was mad.

"How did it happen?"

I made up the story that the three of us were playing catch and that it slipped. Again, she said my Dad would speak to all three of us. The next weekend when B and B were over, Dad showed up. He gave all three of us a lecture about being careful and not playing with a baseball in the house. I remember B and B's quizzical expressions, not understanding a word of what he was saying or why he was addressing them. I mouthed that I would explain later. I felt sorry for dragging them into the blame for something they had no knowledge of.

After the "lecture" I told them that I threw the ball that had broken my window. Dad had assumed they were playing with me at the time it happened. I told them it was my fault. I also told them I didn't tell Dad I was by myself because I feared his temper. "If he thought you were playing with me he might not get angry."

I know there were other times I got into trouble, but those two times stand out in my mind.

Love,
Papa

Hi T – this is about your grandmother's jobs.

It was shortly after the split that Mom realized the Lakeville Letter Shop was not enough to support us. She tried to find other work. The first new job, and one which she would return to in future years, was at *The Lakeville Journal*. The *Journal* was a small weekly newspaper under the control of a very snobby Ann Hoskins. Catering to the upper class in the Salisbury Township and immediate surrounding area, it was the only periodical for local audiences. It was rare that any news about the middle or lower-class events were included in its pages.

The closest item of middle or lower-class interest would be the announcement of the first senior from Housatonic Valley Regional High School (HVRHS) to be accepted into a college or university. And when absolutely necessary, they would have a mini sports page reporting the HVRHS sports team results.

Mom was a great typist, about 90-110 words a minute. The paper needed linotype operators. Most have forgotten what a linotype is. It was a huge machine with a large keyboard, totally open, with a larger set of gears. To the side was a container of liquid lead—think of the toxic fumes the linotype must have been spewing out, but management didn't care, or didn't know, about their long-term effects. As you typed the words, the machine would spit out little lead bars about four inches wide (column width) and two inches tall. On the bar's edge were the words that you had just typed. These would be stacked on a tray. When completed, the typist had to proof the typeset then turn the tray over to the printers, who would place it in the larger printers where the actual paper would be produced. This would have produced a lot of noise!

There were three or four linotype operators. Mom was the first female to be given the job. She was also the best. But despite all the work she had done for Ann and others over the years in the Letter Shop, she was considered a blue-collar worker and treated like shit! The linotype room was crowded with the machines and operators. Of course, it was hot with all the hot lead around. I was surprised more people didn't get lead poisoning from all the lead oxide that must have been in the room. On summer days, they would leave the windows open and maybe put a fan in one, but the room got to well over 100o. There was no air conditioning—that was reserved for the front office and the reporters.

While at the *Journal*, Mom became close friends with Betsy and even closer to Ruth. Betsy was a reporter with a college education and tried to pretend to be an intellect. She never made it. Ruth was the principal photographer, actually most of the years there she was the only one, and was quite outlandish. She was very short—under five feet—wore a buckskin jacket and drove little sports cars very fast from place to place, claiming journalistic privileges whenever she was pulled over by the police. These two women, both divorced, became Mom's drinking pals. You've already heard a little about Ruth.

As you can imagine, this job did not last long due to the bad work environment, the attitudes of management and lack of benefits. When Mom started talking to the workers about joining the union, she got worse treatment. In the eyes of management these were men and woman who didn't deserve any more than what they were receiving. Certainly, not worthy of an income that might let them pay for college for their children. After all, if you are a blue-collar worker, your children should do no better. Most of the employees in the back room and in the print room downstairs were Black, reinforcing management attitudes. Of course, the management would refer to them as "n…s".

Mom started looking for work elsewhere. Hotchkiss School outside of Lakeville, on the road towards Sharon, and was founded in 1891. Back then it was a boy's prep school and the ultimate preppie environment. After all, JFK and his son John went there. Jackie O use to eat at Woodlands Café, the one we stopped in after it had become a restaurant for snobs (we left before eating). Other Hotchkiss graduates include most of the Ford family boys, as well as sons of other famous and infamous people from rich families. I believe Ike was the headmaster in the late 1940s before he decided to run for the White House after he retired as a 5 Star General.

Hotchkiss' medical clinic needed a secretary who could understand the medical terms and could transcribe the doctor's and nurse's notes into medical records, which would then be sent to labs and the students' home physicians, etc. Mom got the job and was there for several years.

One advantage for me was that I could go the school's indoor swimming pool a little more often and wander around the campus. I think Mom liked the job; she certainly got better pay than at the *Journal*. But the head MD of the clinic and she would get into disagreements, and after about three years, off she went again.

You can see, Mom's job situation was never very stable. She, like Dad, had a temper and would not be shy about showing it, especially towards any male who now could be called sexist. Back then, there were a lot of them. But, back then, if a woman complained she was either fired or treated worse. The former usually happened to your grandmother.

Love,
Papa

T:

When we were living in Lakeville, and in between the Letter Shop and the *Journal*, Mom was hired as a personal secretary to a Mrs. Spear. This was not full time but was needed. It lasted for a few years until Mrs. Spear died. Mrs. Spear was a very elderly woman, possibly in her late 80s or early 90s. She always wore very conservative white dresses. Typical of something you might have found in the 1890s, not the 1950s!

She lived in a beautiful house above Lakeville on the road towards Millerton, New York. What was most unusual about the house was she had an elevator installed. It was the first time I ever saw an elevator inside a house. Even to this day, I have seen this less than a handful of times. As Mrs. Spear got older, she could no longer negotiate the stairs. Later she had to use a wheelchair on most days, hence the need for an elevator. It does give you the idea of the money she had.

Mom would usually go to the house once a week when not working on a regular job. I think most of the work was on Saturdays. I must have been about seven and Mom didn't want to leave me alone at the house in Lakeville. If Mrs. Little was unable to look after me I would come along. Mrs. Spear put up with a child coming along but did not like it. Most of the time I was told to sit in a sitting room and look at the pictures in magazines. I was not to bother them in the study where they worked. I don't even remember what the magazines were. Probably *Life* and *Look*, which were popular, with plenty of pictures. There were many antiques and valuables around the house and I was constantly warned not to touch anything.

Mom told me that Mrs. Spear and her late husband had been major players in the YMCA/ YWCA (Young Men's/Woman's Christian Association). Mrs. Spear was pulling together some of her memoirs and other personal papers. Through the work Mom became more familiar with the early work of the Y and became very dubious of its original cause. According to Mrs. Spear and her husband, the goal of both Ys was to convert the "heathen" Catholics to good, recognized Protestant churches. Yes, the very conservative branches of Protestants considered Catholics heathen. Jews were considered subhuman and not worthy of such efforts. The Jews were not welcomed into the Ys Mrs. Spear was fond of. Black people were not even discussed.

This of course has totally changed today, but this is how Mrs. Spear described the work of the Y when she was active at the turn of the 20th century through the 1920s. She met her husband there. And they worked together, he for the YMCA and she for the YWCA.

Mrs. Spear was attempting to convince Mom that she was incapable of raising a child by herself. Since she was separated from Dad, I would not have any male role model or discipline. I would grow up to be wild in the streets and just headed for jail. I should be sent away to a reform school now and not cause society the trouble of being arrested and going through the courts. Only in a reformatory would I have the discipline and guidance necessary for a boy growing up in the 1950s, according to Mrs. Spear.

Mom told me about Mrs. Spear's attitudes a few years later, when I was better able to understand. It was this type of attitude that soured me to Connecticut, especially Litchfield County and Salisbury township.

Mrs. Spear was part of the Lakeville / Salisbury upper class. They cared little for the lower-middle or working classes, who were only needed as servants or hired for personal services—neither worthy of any major concern or deserving of help or assistance. To them, Mom and I were just insects to be used and then discarded when they got what they needed. The lower classes were nothing more than indentured servants. They were unworthy of college education. Their value was to tend lawns, do manual labor. They should not be considered for white collar employment, unless it was something like a bank teller. The middle classes were necessary for teaching in schools and the running of basic services, like managing grocery stores. They deserved a little more consideration. But not much more.

This attitude was typical in Lakeville. A woman who did not have a husband was incapable of raising a child. Likewise, if a family needed help, then it was a man who would receive it, not a single woman. Later on, I will describe another example of this attitude, which would lead to Mom and I being involved with the first black family moving to Falls Village.

This attitude was typical of Sharon too, if not worse. After all, it was home to the Buckley family. What else would you expect from the town that was the home to William F. Buckley! I will write about the caste neighborhoods of Sharon when I discuss Mom working for another elderly couple many years later.

Love,
Papa

Chapter 9

Floridian Parental Visits and Challenges

October 10 (day late, on my way to Paris, will mail it there)

Hi T:

While we were in Lakeville, shortly after the first year there, Dad lost his job. You know I repress my temper as much as possible. Well, it's Dad's temper I repress, although Mom's was equal to his at times.

According to the story I heard (never confirmed), Dad was a rug salesman in a major department store in Hartford. He had an hour commute each way. It was a tough daily routine, especially when most of the salary was based upon commissions. There was only so much bullshit he was willing take. I learned from a former co-worker that a notoriously bad customer came into the rug department one day. Dad started to wait upon the gentleman. First, the customer wanted to see one kind of rug.

"That was the wrong color! Show me another color…No, that was no good! Does it come in more colors? What about an oriental carpet? I don't like this design…!"

This went on for some time. The customer was not being shown what he wanted and started to get a little hostile towards Dad. But rather than defining his requirements, the customer continue to fulminate about Dad's poor service.

"What, are you stupid? Don't you understand English?"

The man had succeeded in pushing the one button that put Dad over the top. For Dad, who didn't have an accent nor would permit anything but English to be spoken in the house, to be told he "didn't understand English" was too much.

"Can't you do your job!" The man yelled.

The explosion happened. Dad would not be spoken to in that manner. His mercurial nature took over. He physically turned the man around and picked him up off of the ground by his belt and collar. Dad, a semi-pro ex-wrestler, had no problem picking him up. He literally carried him to the elevator, to the applause of the workers. This squirming screaming little malcontent was held off the floor al the way to the first floor. Word got out that Dad was "escorting" someone out of the store. By the time they arrived, the first-floor corridor was lined with store employees and each and every one of them was cheering this nonpareil co-worker as he carried the man, still kicking and yelling, but unable to touch the floor, out the door. Once the man was left on the street, Dad marched back to his manager. He was fired on the spot.

Dad knew what the result of his action would be. Unemployed and not likely to find a job in Connecticut, he started to look for greener pastures. Florida was an option. Shortly after this incident, Dad drove to Lakeville to see me. His old Oldsmobile was fully loaded—the trunk with his suitcases, the back seat with boxes and various odds and ends. He announced he was moving to Florida. Part of the reason was not being unable to find work in Connecticut. The other reason was to get away and start over.

I remember the only thing I asked him about was his promise to take me to a movie. I took any promise very seriously. Well, there was to be no movie! After a few parting remarks between Mom and Dad, he was off. I didn't hear from him for some months. Mom eventually got a letter. He was renting a small house in the suburbs of St. Petersburg.

After he was settled in, Mom thought it would be good for me to visit him. The next summer break it was agreed that I would fly down to be with him for a week. Mom drove me to Bradley Field, outside Hartford. Off I went. This was the first time I had flown in an airplane by myself and I remember the stewardess was very nice. She served me a great meal (oh, for the old days when airplanes had good service!). At restaurants I learned it was polite to give a waitress a tip, so I left some money on the tray for the stewardess. She tried to return it to me, explaining they didn't take tips, but I still tried to hide it under a plate when she came back. She didn't return it. I realized later she didn't get it. The tip likely ended up in the trash. But at that time, I was pleased in the thought she had kept it. I suppose those few coins are slowly decomposing in a landfill wherever they were tossed with the trash, to be found by some archeologist in the far distant future.

Dad picked me up at the Tampa/St. Petersburg airport. He was trying to be extra nice but immediately started digging at Mom. It was evident from the first few minutes he was trying to get me to side with him:

"Is she drinking too much?

"Don't you miss The Hill?

"Wouldn't you prefer to live down in Florida?"

On it went, not for just the drive but for the full week.

I found the house in St. Petersburg small, but I had a little room with a bed to myself. What was really neat was the oranges in trees in the backyard. The tree was in someone else's yard, but the branches reached over the fence. We helped ourselves and would have fresh oranges every morning. A little beyond the fence in back there was a swampy area. Dad warned me not to wander there because there were alligators. I very much wanted to see one but was told that another child had been badly bitten very recently in the same swap.

This was a small development with equally small houses build in and around the swamp. Unlike New England homes, none had basements or second floors. They seemed to be close to the ground. Was this a way to be ready for the next hurricane? Looking back at it I doubt any would have survived anything above a Category 2.

The one thing I found strange was that Dad was overly concerned about me doing "number 2." Apparently it was because I was at a different altitude and therefore should be sure to have a BM at least once a day, "if not more".

The Hill is less than a thousand feet above sea level and he was living at about 10 feet above sea level. I could never understand why that little change would make much of a difference. Even to this day, his preoccupation about me going to the bathroom seems strange. Well, that was Dad.

He took me on a special day trip on an old river paddlewheel steamboat, called the *River Queen*. According to Dad it was the same boat that Clark Gable used in one of his movies (*Gone with the Wind*?). I was never a fan of *Gone with the Wind* but loved him and Claudette Colbert in *It*

Happened One Night where they both won Oscars. It took the honor of being voted best film of the year of 1934, one of the few comedies that won best picture.

Dad was excited about standing on the same spot where Gable once stood but being about nine years old, this didn't make much of an impression on me. It was fun seeing the rear wheel splashing through the water pushing the boat along. Most of the paddle boats were side wheelers. The *River Queen* was one of, if not the only, rear wheel boat still operating since its launch back in the 1800s. That was a fun day trip with Dad.

Love,
Papa

More about Florida, sent from France:

Dad and I did do other fun things. He took me to a long pier in Tampa where we fished. I think I caught some moderate size fish, but nothing special comes to my mind. Still, it was my first experience fishing in the ocean and I enjoyed it. Dad did tell me that one boy, about 13 years old, had caught a huge shark there. He battled it for hours. When he landed a record size shark for light tackle (non-deep sea fishing gear), something like 8 foot and 600+ lbs, maybe more.

Suddenly two huge "fish" jumped out of the water. When they appeared, troops of kids dove into the water from the pier. Dad told me to watch. It was a pair of dolphins—the first I had ever seen. It was their daily patrol of the ocean near the shore. This pair were famous. They would follow the same route every day about the same time. Dad told me they would chase any sharks away. When the dolphins appeared, the kids knew it was safe to jump in for a swim. But only as long as the dolphins were in the area. The dolphins circled the kids and actually jumped among the boys as if playing with them. All those in and out of the water—dolphins, kids, fishermen and sightseers—were enjoying the playful scene. After about 20 minutes the dolphins made their cry and off they went to a nearby beach. There, the same routine of playing the other kids started a half mile down the shoreline. On the pier, the kids scrambled back up the ladders to safety, away from any sharks that might be returning.

I learned a pair of dolphins were likely to be brothers. Large pods were usually females with offspring. This was the beginning of a love and concern for dolphins. It was clear evidence of their intelligence, an intelligence far superior than even I could have imagined at the time. It amazes me how intelligent other species can be and most likely are. Dolphins are a magnificent example. Later I would learn about the exceptional intelligence of octopus from a first-hand experience.

A few years later, in a sports diver magazine, a diver wrote an article describing a dive he had taken on Earth Day. As he was diving not far from the Florida Keys, a female dolphin swam up to him with her relatively young offspring next to her. She came up to the diver and allowed him to scratch her belly. The diver thought: "This is Earth Day. If you knew what it meant what would you want to tell humans?"

The second those thoughts came to his mind, the pair swam off. A few minutes later she came back with a large piece of what looked like seaweed. The diver didn't think such seaweed was found in this section of the ocean. The dolphin came even closer, right up to him, and released into his hand a black plastic garbage bag. It was evident she had read his thoughts. She wanted humans to clean up their act by stopping plastics and other trash being thrown into the ocean. It appears humans have yet to learn that lesson.

Our day on the ocean, my first experience of the Gulf of Mexico, was coming to an end. I was enjoying the ride back to the house as the road ran alongside the ocean. Just before we were about to get on the bridge/causeway crossing over to St. Pete again, I stretched out and laid my hand behind Dad's seat. I felt something hot! I looked. There was a hole in the back floor and flames from the overheated muffler were rising up, burning the back of Dad's seat along with much of the rear seats.

I screamed: "FIRE!"

Dad swerved the car into a parking area, just feet before the bridge, where no stopping would have been possible. We both jumped out of the car. He grabbed a mini fire extinguisher from the glove compartment and quickly put out the flames. It appears this was not the first time the back seat had caught on fire. Nice little excitement for the end of a day.

A few days later, we went to Bush Gardens, Tampa. Back then it had just opened up the safari area. No amusement park yet, just the monorail through the "African plains". It was great seeing all the animals roaming freely around the park. Afterward, we toured the beer bottling plant. Dad loved this part because, back then, at the end of the tour you could get all the free beer you could drink. A few years later, they stopped the practice for two reasons: first, it was expensive and second because there appeared to be a high rate of car accidents on the road back to Tampa. Dad like the more expensive new brew to the Budweiser Company, Michelob! I think he had about three glasses before we left. They had free soda for the kids along with a few snacks on the tables. You could order meals there too, but all Dad wanted was the free beer.

When he took me to see the downtown area of St. Pete, I remember a little bridge off the main roadway. It went across a little bay to a rundown area. I him where the road went to.

Hi response was simple: "The niggers live on the other side. They may work over here but then return to their homes over there. We keep to ourselves and they stay in their own area."

That was the first time I had ever heard Dad referring to Black people in this way. I expected it from Mom's family, but it was a shock to me hearing it from Dad. It seemed moving south had released his, perhaps previously internalized, racism. Later, he explained it was because Black people moved into our section of Brooklyn that we had left New York. This was something new to me. But looking back on it, those boys who were picking on me that day on Lafayette were mostly Blacks and Hispanics.

A little further down the road Dad spotted a sign for All You Can Eat Shrimp. We looking at each other and nodded. Off we pulled. About halfway through our first serving, a family of four came in. Dad thought it would be good fun to challenge the father and his son to an eating contest. They accepted, thinking it would be easy since we had started. I don't remember how many serving of shrimp salad, the primary shrimp dish of choice, we had. After about 90 minutes, the other Dad gave up. Dad and I had won! We waddled out of the restaurant with extended bellies full of shrimp. The owner was smiling and waving goodbye, but with curses under his breath. Between the two families, we finished off at least three of the huge buffet serving bowls of shrimp salad. I bet that was the last All You Can Eat the owner wanted to host for some time!

It is funny and a little sad, but that was the only week I spent with Dad where I remember actually enjoying him. He was never so fun to be with before. Never again would we enjoy each other's company like this. The next time I would visit him, he would not be alone.

Love,
Papa

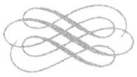

More of the Florida story:

Upon returning from Florida, I was telling Mom all that Dad had said about her. Most of it was criticism of her. The way she was raising me. Her excessive drinking. I don't remember exactly what I was saying but it upset Mom terribly. She kept quiet and just let me rant on about what Dad had said. I think she didn't want to counter because she realized it was the first time Dad and I had had fun. She had very mixed feelings about the trip. Happy I enjoyed my Dad. Miserable because of all the criticism I brought back.

The result was to be expected. Mom started drinking more heavily. A bottle of wine or bourbon was usually under the sink. Sometimes a cheap Scotch whiskey, or on rare occasions gin could be found there. Wine for guests. Bourbon for herself on other nights. She would come home, fix a drink and we'd have dinner together—often frozen TV dinners, which appeared with greater regularity. We would eat in almost complete silence. By the time dinner was over, I would go watch the TV and do homework.

Mom would wash dishes and have another bourbon on the rocks. By 9 p.m. either I was in bed or she was. If it was the latter, it was usually because she had stumbled into her bedroom and passed out. In the morning I would have cereal, get dressed and walk to school, about three quarters of a mile away; rarely would I see her. During the school year, I often left before she woke up—she seldom woke me up, but I was just happy to get out of the house and away from her drinking. Dad was right, but it was still better to deal with the drinking than his temper.

Adding to the drinking problem was Betsy, whom she invited over regularly. This likely was while Mom was working at *The Lakeville Journal*. Betsy, being a single Mom, would stop over to have a few drinks before going home. This only lasted until the next school year because apparently Betsy's ex-husband objected to her drinking and came up with the money for their son to be put in a boys' prep school. As a result, Betsy had no one but herself to go home to, except a dog. She would have a drink or two or three with Mom. I don't know how the two survived driving, but they did, as drunk as they both tended to become.

Betsy had a small house in Limerock and a summer home on Mt. Raga—the little mountain you got to off the main street in Salisbury, next to the county building. The road led up the mountain. As you approached the top, there were remains of an old iron foundry. According to local history, the chain which spanned the Hudson River during the Revolutionary War was made there. The chain prevented British ships from navigating the Hudson. Near the top was Betsy's summer home—a nice cottage with a large porch, where a dining table was set up. You could see the fields and stream a short distance away.

I would eat on the porch and play with Pinocchio, her dachshund. The house had outdoor plumbing, an outhouse, a hand pump for water in the kitchen, and no electricity. I remember hearing and sometimes watching quail families making their calls in the early evening. More than once a whole flock of them crossed the grass-covered driveway. There was also a great horned owl that would make an occasional appearance and foxes, both grey and red, every now and then. It was a pleasant place to visit and just a short ride back to our house.

When visiting during the day I would pick wild blueberries but had to watch for timber rattle snakes. Surviving the ride home was always a challenge. You can imagine by the time we left, after dark, the state Mom was in and she would drive down that narrow mountain road, which was sometimes paved and sometimes gravel. She was barely able to see the road little less drive straight. I remember more than once grabbing the steering wheel and "adjusting" our directions as we drove back to Salisbury.

It was shortly after the start of these episodes that Ruth joined in the after-work, mostly in our second-floor apartment in Lakeville and on rare occasions in either Ruth or Betsy's house. The three would get together, complain about work, former husbands, *The Lakeville Journal*, the town and men in general. All these sessions were with glasses of wine or something stronger. When the booze was finished or it was very late, Ruth and Betsy would stumble down the flight of stairs from our apartment and pour themselves into their respective cars. I would watch them weaving back and forth between invisible course obstacles only they could see.

One day Betsy really did have an accident on the way to Limerock. It almost totaled her car. She appeared to have passed out on the seat, avoiding serious injury as she was below the broken glass and windshield. Quite a trio. I was just glad that in the fall and winter the drinking occurred in our apartment so Mom would not have to drive.

As for me, this was the start of my avid TV watching. We had a small set. I sat really close, with the volume turned up. It could drown out the conversations in the kitchen and I would lose myself in whatever show was on. Comedy and variety shows were the best to lose my thoughts and escape what was happening. There was enough real drama in my own life, so the dramatic shows were skipped. TV was my evening companion. By my middle school years, Mom and I would start playing canasta. But not yet. That usually occurred with the TV on and Mom still drinking, just not as much.

I was very depressed about the separation. As with many children of parents that split, they blame themselves. I was no different. Being the cause of the hostile breakup made me feel I was the source of all the misery. It would be best if I didn't cause any more. The solution was to remove myself from this life. After all, I might be able to re-join my "buddies", even though they were no longer a part of my current life.

I tied a rope around a door handle, looped it around the top of the door and fashioned a noose on the other end. I brought a chair from the kitchen, climbed on the chair and placed the noose around my neck. I didn't want the sudden jerk a jump from the chair would cause. So, very carefully, I stepped off the chair. The noose tightened. I was really suspended above the floor. But I was not really choking. My neck muscles were too strong to stop the air flow. I hung there about

"Well, this isn't doing anything," was the thought that ran through my mind.

I raised my foot and dragged the chair under my feet. Then I climbed back on the seat and released myself from the noose. One failed suicide attempt. There would be another and thoughts of more later.

Love,
Papa

Hello, want a little excitement for a letter?

I brought the bike Dad had given me the last Christmas to Lakeville. Now, I had a whole town to ride in. The section where we lived was mostly flat, level with the ball field and park. Turning left on Main Street there is a little hill past the grocery store headed up to the street. Once on top of the hill where the old Lakeside Inn once stood the road continued towards New York. But the turn left went down towards the lake, past *The Lakeville Journal*. If you turned from my street towards Salisbury, there was a big hill I had to walk every morning to get to school. Still, overall it was a good place for a bike. Kids mostly rode on the sidewalks in town and outside the center of the town on the roads. There was no such thing as bike lanes back then.

Being a new bike, the breaks were not well adjusted—they were hand breaks. I was always fearful of squeezing the front brake too hard and flipping over the handlebars. The fear was real, because the front brake was the stronger of the two. The rear brake could slow the bike down, but did not grip enough to bring about a quick stop. I didn't know how to tighten them and had no one to help. This resulted in a long time/distance to stop. Not good in an emergency.

One day, I was coming back from the lake with Big and Billy behind me. We all loved traveling at a good speed down the hill on the sidewalk; I loved to go fast to feel the wind in my hair. I still do. Helmets at that time were a rarity, if nonexistent. I never saw anyone wearing one. So, I was barreling down the sidewalk from the grocery store at a fairly good speed—15 to 20 mph. Suddenly a car pulls out of a back-parking lot in front of me. My mind took over at great speed. This would not be the first time exceptionally clear and rapid analysis popped into my mind and it ultimately saved my life.

I looked to the left. Usually there would be a yard. But here surrounding this yard was a black iron fence with sharp spikes on the top, each pointing straight up. I would have been skewered for sure. No escape in that direction! Unless I wanted to become part of a human kabob for the family's evening meal. I looked to the right. It was packed with parked cars on the street.

If I made it between the parked cars, the oncoming traffic would have to be avoided. A car would have hit me unless I could squeeze between the parked cars and those on the road. Since I was on the left, if hit by a car it would have been a head-on collision with my head going first. I saw at least three cars coming towards me down the street. That option would have required a sharp turn between the cars and an equally sharp turn to avoid the cars coming towards me. At my speed, the narrowness of the cars on the parking lane made the chances of making those maneuvers next to impossible.

One option left: hit the car's side! I let out a great yell—"Look out!"—and aimed right behind the passenger-side front tire. If hit there I could roll over the hood of the car and possibly land on the other side. The most damage to the bike would be the front tire. If I timed it right the only damage would be few scrapes when landing on the sidewalk on the other side. That was the best choice.

Bang! I went flying exactly as I had thought I would. I actually launched higher than expected, ending up halfway across the front hood. I then hit the ground and rolled to a stop. A few scrapes, no blood, no serious injuries.

The driver got out. I thought it was an older man and he would be angry. A crowd gathered. I got up. My basic fear had come true—the front wheel of the bike was bent at a good 30-degree angle. I tried to assure everyone I was OK. Many thought I should go to the hospital in Sharon. Someone recognized me and got my mother. Although only a few blocks from home, Mom picked me up and drove me back. I told her all that went through my mind and why I hit the car. All those thoughts must have occurred in less than a second, but each and every part of the analysis was crystal clear. That is when she told me the driver was a teen who had just got his license. According to Mom, he was more scared than I.

It was a while before I replaced the wheel on my bike. We just couldn't afford a replacement immediately. When we could, you can be sure both the front and rear brakes were fixed and ended up in much better operating condition. I know! They were tested the same day the bike was fixed.

Lot of fun?

Love,
Papa

Hi T:

Have to tell you about my first visit to Texas. sister, and it was shortly after we moved to Lakeville that we took a flight to Texas to visit her. She lived outside Houston downwind of the oil refineries. Not having much money and in between marriages, Sun lived in a little house with no air conditioning. The smell from the refineries was constant. I referred to them as the "stink factories." They really did stink.

Mom was always close to Sug, her younger Sug's son, Gerry, was off with his father; her daughter Nikki, like her, had married young. Nikki and her husband Hershel lived on the opposite side of Houston. I don't remember seeing either of my cousins on that visit. Despite it being a small house, there was more than enough room for us to stay with Sug.

It was summer. and hot, even for Houston standards. Sug said it was hot enough to fry an egg on the pavement. I went into the kitchen, got an egg and broke it on the driveway. It took longer than a frying pan, but within 20 minutes I did have a fried egg. Sug said it a good experiment for a young boy to try out. She was a warm and caring individual and also very attractive. I remember years later, when Mom got me a birthday subscription to Playboy, one of the centerfolds reminded me of Sug. I carefully took that one out of the magazine and put it on the door to my closet up at The Hill.

We did visit your great grandmother. She was in a poorer section of Houston, where she ran a small boarding house. Behind her were another couple; I don't remember which, either the wife or husband, were her first cousin. Grandma was her usual Texas self. I did get a chance to see the old six-gun Mom learned to shoot with. It was a Colt 44 given to her by a great uncle. He used it when in the Texas Rangers, or that is what I was told. Years later when Mom asked for it, Grandma "couldn't find it." More likely she sold it as an antique.

Sug gave me a Texas joke book. After that visit one joke stood out in my mind. "If the Devil owned Texas and Hell, he'd would rent out Texas and still live in Hell." After that very hot summer visit, it seemed to be an appropriate joke. Years later we would be back for more visits. Once for my other cousin's (Mom's brother Forest's daughter's) marriage. When I saw her in the wedding dress, I said she was the most beautiful girl I had ever seen.

A few years later we went back for my uncle Lavern' funeral. Lavern was Mom's older brother. But that is worth a letter of its own later. At the funeral it became very clear why Mom hated Texas and her mother. The only family she cared for was Sug and Forest. She had taken care of them during The Depression in while living in Los Angles. Your grandmother was more of a mother to both her siblings than their real mother.

Love,
Papa

Animal time:

I am writing this letter on Halloween because Frankie, our blind Welsh Terrier, loves to go out trick or treating. I plan to take him out tonight and that reminded me of another dog in my life (I mentioned him briefly before).

Betsy's son, John, was going off to private school and Betsy did not want to take care of their Dachshund, Pinocchio. Pinocols, as he was called, was a short-haired black and brown Dachshund. He loved people and attention. I loved him.

I used to play with him when we visited Betsy's Mt. Raga and Limerock houses. When her son went to school, Betsy asked if I would take care of him for her. Of course, I wanted to take on Pinocchio! Even if it meant Mom would do most of the work, feeding and being sure he was let outside in the morning and before bed. As a typical seven-year-old, it was my duty to play with the dog. Pinocols came to live with us on the second floor.

B and B loved to play and visit with us as they like Pinocols too. When I went over to their house, their Mom would find a treat. But most of the time, I was with him alone.

I would take him to the big park where the ball field was and walked him on a leash down the sidewalks of Lakeville. But if we were not walking near Main Street, I would play with him in the vacant lot next to the house. In the apartment, when watching TV, he was in my lap. Mom knew she had a drinking problem and must have felt that having Pinocols would take my mind off of her problems. Instead of watching her get drunk every night, Pinocols would keep me company.

Three incidents stand out in my mind while I had Pinocols.

The first was when we were in the big town park. We had walked down the street, then cut across the brook to the park. Just as we entered the back side of the part a group of three larger "bully" dogs spotted Pinocols. I call them bullies because these three were often seen as a mini pack. They were very territorial attacking any dog entering the park if they were already there. Their owners were nowhere in sight. One, which could be considered the alpha dog, was a mixed shepherd, the other two were a little smaller, and likely mixed breeds. All three were much bigger than Pinocols. Since we were in the park, Pinocols was off the leash. I was over by the gazebo while Pinocols was taking care of his biological necessities past the Little League baseball field. The three dogs spotted Pinocols and took off after him. Pinocchio ran to the bushes. I was terrified the other dogs would tear him apart and started to run towards the bushes. I must have been twenty-five to fifty yards away.

There were a series of barks and growls, a huge amount of what sounded like snapping of teeth. I was still 20 yards from the bushes. Tears welling up in my eyes, envisioning Pinocols being torn to bits. Suddenly one dog let out a loud yelp and started to run back towards me. Then another. Finally, the shepherd appeared with his tail between his legs, running as if the devil himself was in hot pursuit. Sure enough, a second later came Pinocols, running as fast as his little legs could carry him, growling and barking after the three running away from him.

Everyone in the park who saw this laughed. I grabbed Pinocols and gave him a big hug. He was unhurt. I looked in the bushes where he had gone. He found a berry patch where he must have crawled under the thorns. Then he got on his back. If one of the dogs tried to bite him, he would grab their nose or neck as hard as possible with his teeth. When they tried to get his stomach, he would use his hind feet to scratch their eyes, mouth, or throat. Then the berry thorns did the rest. I know this because it happened again with a single dog later. I watched his strategy. Soon no dog in Lakeville would take on Pinocols. It was as if the dogs spread the word. When Pinocols came around, all the other dogs left him alone, no matter how aggressive or how large they were. Pinocols was the canine Napoleon of Lakeville.

The second incident was when I was riding back on my bike with B and B from the lake. It was raining and my bike slipped in the mud. I scraped my knee very badly and it hurt like hell! I got up and slowly walked back home, telling B and B to go on without me between painful tears. When I got home, Mom started to clean the area. Pinocols was right there; he seemed more concerned than Mom. He would try to lick the wound, carefully watching every move she made. She explained the licking was how dogs take care of their wounds. He was clearly worried about me and even through the tears and pain from cleaning the mud-soaked wound, I realized Pinocols was a very caring dog. I loved him all the more for it. Mom accepted the idea that dog saliva had anti-bacterial properties, so she only lightly pushed him aside as she put Bactine spray on the wound. She carefully bandaged up the rather large area of the knee that had been scraped. Every morning until the area was complete healed Pinocols would check it, giving the bandage a lick or two, just to be sure it was healing correctly—at least a dog's view of healing.

The third incident impacted all of Lakeville. Mom and I were out for the day. Somehow Pinocols got out of the apartment. He wanted attention! He walked to the end of the street and onto the narrow stone bridge that crossed Burton Brook. The same small stream that flowed between my street and where B and B lived. Once on the bridge's sidewalk, and seeing there were no cars in the immediate vicinity, Pinocols marched into the middle of the street, perpendicular to the actual road. Here was a small dog but a fairly large dachshund, lengthways on a narrow bridge, on Main Street, sitting on the center line!

You must realize that this was a small bridge. Barely two cars could pass each other keeping within their respective lanes. Trucks and busses had to cross one at a time. The way Pinocols had placed himself on the bridge, no car could get around him without running him over. Cars in both directions saw him in plenty of time to stop. If someone yelled or threatened him, he would snarl and bark back. Most who didn't know him thought he was a mad dog. Some locked themselves in their cars.

B and B's Mom was coming back from Salisbury and got caught in the tie up. At first she couldn't understand why there was a backup of twenty cars or more trying to cross the bridge into the town, so she got out. Walking towards the bridge she spotted what the problems was—Pinocle. Since Pinocols and I had visited their home many times, B and B's Mom knew him and he her. Mrs. P. called to him:

"Come here Pinocols! If you get into my car I'll give you a treat."

Pinocchio immediately came up to her. She picked him up and he gave her a flood of kisses. The she placed him on the front seat of the car and drove home. What was most important was that Pinocols got the attention he wanted. At her house he got some leftovers and was happy until Mom picked him up later.

The next edition of *The Lakeville Journal* had a front-page story about how Betsy's dog Pinocchio caused the only major traffic jam in Lakeville history, excluding construction delays. The *Journal* dubbed Pinocols "The Mayor of Lakeville." I only wish Ruth had been around to take a picture to run with the story in the paper.

Though not my dog, Pinocols was certainly one of my favorite pets; after Lily and Frankie he was my favorite dog.

Happy Halloween,
Papa

Sad partings but fun story:

The story of Pinocchio caught everyone's attention, especially Betsy who was embarrassed about the whole incident. She hated the fact her dog got more attention than her! It has to be remembered that Betsy was the stereotypically dumb blonde with education. It wasn't long before she was able to find a different solution for the care of Pinocols—if I was not able to keep him out of trouble and out of attention of others, then she would find another home for Pinocols.

Her son John had completed one year at his prep school, a very formal and regimented place with uniforms and a formal dining room. It was not one of the local schools, likely it was one in New York or Massachusetts. A vague memory is that it was one his father may have attended. His father was paying for it. Betsy certainly didn't earn enough at *The Journal*. It may have been one of the military academies for high school students who needed strong discipline.

John had gotten a little out of control after Betsy and her husband got the divorce. His grades had declined in the public school, and as with most teens, he was giving Betsy a lot of hard times. There was the "let's play the child against both parents" going on. When John visited his Dad, he got all the complaints about Betsy. Then when he came back home to Limerock, Betsy would have to put up with all the crap his father had filled into John's head. Sound familiar? As with Mom, this just led to more drinking and further justification for his father's complaints.

The way the story was told to me by Mom was that the school was looking for a mascot and John recommended Pinocols. The dean wanted to meet the dog in question. Pinocols loved people. The fact Pinocols would be surrounded by hundreds of boys all vying for his attention would be a dream come true. He would also be close to his real owner, who he also loved.

So, with tears in my eyes and a very heavy heart, I had to say goodbye to Pinocols.

Betsy would give us feedback as to what was happening with Pinocols as she was still a constant visitor to the apartment. She realized how attached I had become to him and was trying to cheer me up with stories about how he was doing at school. What was true and what was fable I cannot say, but this is one story that has come back to me.

Pinocchio was a favorite at the school. He became the mascot of the football team and would be at the center of all sporting activities. Every evening all the boys had a sit-down dinner with the teachers at a head table, much like what is done in Hogwart's, just not as large, only a fraction of the number of students, and without the special effects.

So, Pinocols would eat dinner with the rest of the school. According to Betsy, there was a huge fireplace with a giant stone mantle, extending six feet off the floor and some feet beyond the actual opening for the fire. All of this was behind the head table where the headmaster and a number of the faculty sit each evening.

Pinocols' place was on the mantle slightly behind the headmaster, where his bowl of food would be put. He would be lifted up onto a little cushion, which was secured in place. This allowed him to eat his dinner while everyone else was eating theirs. When he was finished he would lay down and watch until dinner was over. When people started to get up, he would give one short bark and would be lifted down to join the rest of the school in the egress from the dining hall.

One night a couple of boys were fooling around—this was something strictly forbidden during dinner! It appeared that the two were off on one of the side tables and had started a mini food fight by flinging food at each other using their spoons. Since peas were the vegetable for the evening, they were the perfect ammunition. One of the peas flew a little out of control, away from the table of origin towards the headmaster's table. It hit him—or at least somewhere near him. He got up and looked around for the instigator. He could tell which side of the room it came from but was unable to determine which one of the boys was the troublemaker.

"Who threw this pea?"

No response.

"I demand to know who threw this pea immediately."

Still no response. The boys who operated the pea catapult were attempting to remain as undiscovered as possible. Suddenly there was a single bark. Pinocols had been watching the whole incident. The headmaster turned to Pinocols and asked:

"Pinocchio, do you know who threw the pea?"

Pinocols wagged his tail. The headmaster carefully lifted Pinocols down from his bird's eye perch and placed him on the floor. Pinocchio immediately went to the table that started the trouble.

The headmaster followed. Pinocols marched straight over to one of the boys. He looked up at the boy and gave a single bark. The headmaster asked the rest of the table who else was involved. Now terrified, they identified the other culprit and confirmed that Pinocols had identified the chief suspect. The two lead troublemakers were put detention for a few days, due to the testimony of a small but very observant dachshund named Pinocchio.

Just another story about this remarkable dog.

Unfortunately, this was the last tale I was ever told about Pinocols. The next summer, when he and John were visiting Betsy, I was able to spend more time with this remarkable Dachshund. When I did visit Mt. Raga, Pinocols was excited to see me, jumping into my lap and giving me a good face washing. That may have been the only visit I had. Dachshunds, especially short haired, brown-black combinations. Pinocols.

Love,
Papa

Hi again:

I still have a soft spot for Any that remind me of

As I finished second grade, the teachers informed Mom that I would be held back. My reading skills were not sufficient to pass me to the third grade. This put Mom into a tizzy. She blamed the schools for not properly teaching and was mad the teachers had told her not to teach me herself. After all they "had the latest and most effective teaching methods." From that point on, Mom would doubt any advice given to her by teachers!

At this time, the Lakeville Lettershop had died and her job with *The Lakeville Journal* was not going well. Not enough money was coming inland Dad was not providing any child support, despite the court order.

If I was not to repeat a grade, I would have to change schools. Suicidal thoughts entered my mind again. Bactine was the popular first aid spray back then and there was a warning on the label, although I couldn't really read all the meaning on it. The idea came into my head that I could eliminate myself if I drank the bottle of spray. I climbed on the toilet seat to get to the sink. Once on the sink, the medicine cabinet was accessible. I removed the Bactine and climbed down. Carefully untwisting the top, I opened the bottle. I smelled it. No unpleasant odor. I then brought the lip of the bottle to my mouth. Up went the bottle. Down poured the antiseptic. All at once I dropped the bottle, my head jerked forward and I spat out all that was in my mouth. It was some of the most horrible tasting shit I had ever experienced. I quickly rinsed my mouth with handfuls of water. Thus ended the second suicide attempt.

Mom's short time with *The Lakeville Journal* was not very happy. She had been working in the print shop on the line-o-type. Of course, *The Lakeville Journal* was not willing to pay a decent wage, especially for one of "our class" (read lower middle class, especially a single Mom). So she found a new job. It was also around this time that we moved back to The Hill.

Remember Hotchkiss (this is the description from their website): "A 545-acre campus with academic and residential buildings, playing fields and green lawns, the deepest freshwater lake in Connecticut (Lakeville Lake), and lovely vistas of the Berkshire mountains."

They claim to offer scholarships to help deserving students, but back then, only if you came from the right families! It was the ultimate snob school. Graduates included Henry Luce (*Time / Sports Illustrated* magazines founder), Archibald MacLeish, Peter Matthiessen, and way in the future when it became co-ed, Elizabeth Chandler (*Sisterhood of the Traveling Pants*), and many other famous individuals on their way to Harvard, Princeton or Yale, and fame.

As mentioned before, Mom's job was in the health clinic as a personal / medical secretary to the physician. This job picked up her spirits, at least for a little while. Here she came up with a plan that would hopefully prevent me from repeating second grade. Nearby, on the hill below Hotchkiss and across the football field, was a small private elementary school called Town Hill. The setting of the school was picturesque. It was down the road from Mom's office and surrounded by trees; it was comforting to know she was nearby. Looking back on this part of my life it is safe to say I really enjoyed my year there. The classes were small and the teachers better than in the public school—they tended to be younger and better educated!

I loved Town Hill school. It was small, no long corridors to walk down. The classrooms were large and less formal than Salisbury Central. I liked the teachers and most of the students. They had a lot of hands-on activities. We put on plays. I remember a play we put included costumes, which I thought was great. One slightly overweight boy was dressed in Elizabethan tights and collar, which I thought a bit funny. So began was my first interest in theatre; I worked on the set and helped with the costumes. Though I am unable to remember his name, this boy was the closest person that could be called a friend at the Town Hill.

Most of the girls just ignored me completely and the other boys paid little attention to me as they were more into sports than I. Two teachers tried to help me, without much success. Like the boy, their names escape me after so many years. Despite their efforts, they had little lasting influence or impression.

There were a lot of craft projects I actually took pride in doing. Mini science experiments would fascinate me. Science and history became more alive. After reviewing a part of history, the teachers would encourage the students to develop mini plays where we would act out the parts of historic characters, which was a fun way to learn—much better than reading and reviewing boring books.

I remember a little of the special help from a teacher. The problem was that most of the students had been in this private school from kindergarten and they were much better readers. I was not able to catch up with my reading. At the end of the year, Town Hill told my mother I would have to repeat the third grade if I stayed there. So much for private school. If they couldn't bring me up where I needed to be, back to public school!

While at Town Hill I could walk around Hotchkiss, its beautiful grounds and old buildings. Sometimes I would walk from Town Hill up to Mom's office in the infirmary. Occasionally, the summer before Town Hill, I would be at Hotchkiss with Mom just have an excuse to get away from the boredom of house. I always watched the Hotchkiss students, who appeared to be exceptionally well dressed. They paid no attention to a young kid wandering around the campus.

It was around this time that Mom thought I should learn a little about golf. I was given a putter and told to try to hit a ball in the hole. I practiced on the practice green of the Hotchkiss golf course. I would hit the ball towards the hole, usually missing. After multiple shots the ball may have gone in. The basic problem was I had no coaching and no prior experience so had no real idea of what I was doing.

One day at the 18th green, someone hit a ball into the sand trap next to the practice green. At first the individual who hit the ball could not be seen due to a hill which was between the tee and the putting green. Not knowing that you do not touch hit balls, I went into the sand to retrieve it. As they approached the green, I walked up to them—a polite little boy—and said:

"Here is the ball you lost," giving it to the adult couple coming up the fairway. They were pissed! "Where was the ball when you picked it up?" one of them asked angrily.

I pointed to the sand trap. You could see my footprints. But the woman, whose ball it was, insisted she was better than that—it could not have possibly been hit into the trap. I was lying. No matter how much my attempt was to show where the ball had rolled in the sand and my footprints going into the moist sand and out again, she refused to accept that she had hit it into the trap. She dropped it just off the green, which gave her a much better lie. That day I learned not to touch golf balls and to stay away from golfers!

I was sorry to leave Town Hill but understood we didn't have enough money to pay for private school. Besides, I would be back with B and B and actually be in the same grade with Big since he had stayed back. Billy was still a year behind us. So, Big and I entered third grade together while Billy was in second.

Love,
Papa

Turkey Day

Happy Thanksgiving—a little late since you have now returned to college:

There was an additional advantage of my being close to Mom. While in third grade at Town Hill, Mom noted Hotchkiss had a good music department. She asked if I wanted to take music lessons again, having failed piano years before. I told her I would love to take violin lessons.

The violin instructor at Hotchkiss was a member of the New York Philharmonic. Mom asked him to take me as a private student. She rented a half-size violin and I began lessons. I took great pride in learning the different strings and being able to play them clearly after the first lesson, though no fingering at that point. I was much like you when you started. I remember the small little music studio where the lessons took place. The instructor was always seated and watched me closely. If fingers, arm, hands or anything else was out of position, he would interrupt and put me in the correct position.

At first, I would practice some of the drill you did during your first year of violin. I would carefully watch the positioning of the bow and the finger board. Then I started to learn where the basic finger positions were and would practice those. The instructor said I had perfect hands for a violinist as my fingers were long for my age, and strong. For practice, I would set up in front of the living room window, just to the side of the TV and in front of the secretariat.

Things were going well for the first few months. I remember the difficulty I had in putting my third finger in the correct position on the finger board when I started to learn fingering. The instructor was always picking up my finger and firmly placing it where it should be. I started violin before Dad took off to Florida. I told him about the lessons and showed him what I had learned about the violin. He acknowledged the lessons but did not encourage me.

As time progressed, I didn't practice as much as I should. Mom rarely asked me to practice; she would never made me or insist. She wanted me to take the lessons but she was never very encouraging. This is so unlike today's middle and upper-class children being raised by their parents. Mom was always a self-starter and mostly self-taught. She felt I should be the same way.

The fact Mom never encouraged the violin was a great detriment to my learning the instrument at the pace expected. She just never drove me to my potential. Her blasé attitude towards practice, as well as homework and projects or anything didn't help. She just left me alone. She would acknowledge accomplishments but she rarely helped, except for editorial assistance later. After Dad had left, I was in a single parent home. No male guidance, good or bad. Then only half a mother, considering the drinking.

One day something got into me. I wanted to do something different. Being around Mom, I noticed her "clear" nail polish. I decided to put some on my nails. Here I was, a third-grader who put nail polish on. I didn't think about it being for women. I just did it because Mom was my only role model. I didn't think about what others would say or how they might react.

When I got to Hotchkiss that week for my violin lessons, the teacher asked:

"What the hell is that on your nails? Is it nail polish? Don't you know only girls wear fingernail polish? What are you, some kind of sissy?!"

I was so embarrassed I could have folded up and died on the spot. Then he started talking about the problem of boys not having a father around. I was headed down a path to becoming a "fag" if such behavior continued. Although we continued with the lesson, I just wanted to crawl into a hole.

The long-term impact of this episode destroyed my desire to continue the lessons. I didn't want to be around the teacher anymore and I practiced less and less. I fell behind in what the instructor wanted me to learn. Soon he told Mom I was not making sufficient progress to continue and so ended my music career. This is something I have regretted all my life. It is also why I take such pride in your violin accomplishments.

What is interesting is that as I wrote this letter the "sissy" and "only girls" comments came back into my mind. It has been years since I even thought of the incident. Then as I was writing this, all sorts of memories of came back. One memory triggering another. Then a small avalanche starts. A snowball of a memory leading to a bigger and bigger avalanche of things long past cascading down the mountain into my conscious memory.

Love,
Papa

Happy Birthday T.

I realize the order of incidents are not falling into place. Mom's working at the *Journal* and then Hotchkiss occurred while still with Dad on The Hill. I remember Dad listening to my early violin practice before the separation occurred. The move to Lakeville, I think, occurred during the third grade at Town Hill.

Anyway, after my failing third grade at Town Hill, it was back to Salisbury Central. I was back with my old friends now living in Lakeville. I started walking up the hill from the apartment to the school every day. Third grade was an interesting year. I can't remember anything about the classes themselves. It didn't matter to me that I stayed back. What was most interesting in the year was the rampant infection of mumps. Our teacher came down with them one side of of her face in October. In came a substitute. Then in December she came down with them on the opposite side of the face. Out again. In the spring, she came down with full blown mumps on both sides of the face (at least this was what was being told the class). I never knew it was possible for one person to come down with mumps on one side then the other and have a repeated attack on both. To this day I wonder if the school was telling us something that was not completely accurate. Can you believe that was the only thing that stood out in my mind? For the whole year! However, there was another interesting episode.

I loved snowball fights. The upper school was at the top of a large hill. The path to the lower school was off the back parking lot and had a little level area 10 feet below. When it snowed, the parking lot was cleared and the snow piled up at the edge of the hill, which was the edge of the parking lot. It was a perfect fort from which to engage in a snowball fight, but this posed a problem for those on the lower ledge. They had little or no cover and would have to throw uphill about 12 feet to hit those behind the snow mounds. That rarely stopped two groups forming with a major snowball fight ensuing during recess.

I always liked to support the underlings—in this case, those on the lower level throwing up. We would use little trees for limited cover. Being small, slender trees they were never very much protection. The advantage for those on the upper walls is they had an almost endless supply of snow from which to make the snowballs. Those below were scrambling around in the grass and bushes to gather the snow. There was another potential problem. Sometimes the snow on the upper level was already packed into almost ice by the snowplow. Bits of gravel and pebbles would be mixed in.

You can see what is coming. I was on the lower level throwing up to those behind the bank of snow. Most of the time, I could see a snowball coming and dodge it—you have seen how I did that with you in winter when you were younger. It was the same way then. But when there are anywhere from 10 to 20 boys (girls never participated in these fights) on the upper level. You had more than one snowball coming at you simultaneously. You could neither see nor dodge them all. I was hit in the eye by one of the ice balls that had a stone in it.

I went down yelling and started to cry loudly. It is bad enough to get hit but to cry was worse. But it hurt! When my yells were heard by a teacher, they came down and took me to the school nurse. Yep, one hell of a black eye was forming. It swelled up to the point it was hard to see out of it. The nurse called Mom, and she picked me up since I had only one eye to watch for more ice and cross the streets. Her major comment when she heard the whole story was:

"You have to learn how to duck better!"

Good point. Typical Texan. She told me to be more careful in choosing sides next time. Later I overheard one of the Black kids, likely Eddie C., claim to have thrown the snowball deliberately packed with a stone.

Two things to learn from this letter.

First, I always liked to choose the losing side, or at least disadvantaged. Second, I sometimes forget to duck, especially if being attacked by more than one side. But I do watch for ice balls with stones inside. You will hear more about snowball fights once the letters hit the college years. After all, the two undergraduate colleges that were attended in northern climates with plenty of snow. Especially in New Hampshire. When you hear about another snowball fight, it will be a lot more amusing.

Love,
Papa
And I hope you had a very Happy Birthday!

Hello T:

I passed my second try at third grade.my mind. I remember neither the subjects, nor the teacher—a clear indication neither were impressive. There was little incentive for me to work hard. An image of an overweight teacher in her late 40s or early 50s popped into my mind as I write this letter. She was likely the teacher, but I have no memory of her name or what she was teaching that year.

I was still having problems with reading and English in general. My grades were doing well in science and math (Cs and Bs) but anything requiring extensive reading; history, English and social sciences, was a struggle (Cs mostly with, one Ds). Mom's only help was in reviewing some of my papers.

It is important to provide a little more about the "tracking system" in Salisbury Central during this period. Hopefully it has changed, but knowing Salisbury, I doubt it. Basically, there were two or three classes for each grade. There was a class for the upper-class kids. From the very beginning they were considered college bound. The class I was stuck in was the class referred to as the "dummies" class. We were usually given inferior teachers. If we were not dummies, we were taught down to least expectations. The results were predictable.

We came out of the class not expecting to produce. Not having self-esteem. Rarely receiving encouragement. All the minorities—lower income kids, kids in single parent households, and working-class kids like B and B—attended these "dummies" classes. It didn't matter whether they could do the work or not. In Salisbury Central if you were not of the proper class, you were assigned to this section.

I do remember in fourth grade, they were looking for student patrol to supervise the halls and the busses. I didn't understand how you got it. I put my name into the mix for possible

Fourth grade was a non-event; nothing stands out in selection. Of course, with the poor grades, in the "dummies" track I had no chance. I just didn't realize it. I thought it would be perfect for me to govern the corner at Main Street since I walked that way every day. Since when did logic ever prevail? When the selection was announced. Only the students from the "upper" classes were selected. So much for student patrol. A minor disappointment, but a disappointment, nonetheless.

What was interesting is there was a friend of Mom's who was interested in esoteric studies and Mom's work with Alice Bailey. She lived on the hill up from the street where I lived, about halfway from the school and my house. Looking at the map, it must have been Lakeview Avenue (strange name as it had no view of the lake). Being on the hill towards the school, the quality and size of the home were considerably larger and more expansive than those at the bottom of the hill, especially like those where B and B lived on Walton Street.

Mom would visit her in some of the evenings or sometimes after work and if while walking home I spotted her car, I would stop by the house. But I never felt welcome. This woman had no children. She did not like one coming into her house. Whenever I came into her house she was on top of me in a second: "Wipe your feet. Don't touch anything! Don't put anything on the tables. If you must sit down, then sit in this chair…"

It was the least expensive chair in the house. This woman thought she was in tune with the "other side." She hired a psychic to contact the other worlds. Mom would listen to her and her adventure with a psychic.

One day Mom brought home a tape the psychic had done for this woman. The psychic's usual voice had a slight British accent. My immediate impression, he was a fake. Mom thought so too. Then the psychic went into a trance voice. We heard a higher voice—he was in contact with the woman's long departed mother. He described how much she missed her daughter and described her concerns for her child. There was nothing indicating anything other than the usual type of thing you have gotten from Professor Marvel's crystal ball in *The Wizard of Oz*. Remember how he told Dorothy to close her eyes as he went through her purse and pulled out a picture of Auntie Mem?

After "communicating" with her mother, the psychic's voice shifted into a high falsetto:

"I am your little butterfly. Oh, how wonderful to visit you again."

He then proceeded to talk to her as a small child. When Mom and I heard that, we both broke out into uncontrollable laughter. It was unbelievable that anyone would be so gullible as to believe this nonsense. Mom kept visiting this woman, on and off, for several years. I never took her seriously after that tape.

There was one series of incidents that did occur. Mom and I went to a fair and won a parakeet at a contest. She was a beautiful little blue and green bird, with just a slight trace of yellow on her tail. In the park that summer there was a series of contests for kids. I entered the parakeet. She won most beautiful pet ribbon. There was also a joke-telling contest. Most of the kids entering were a year or two younger than me and I didn't want to compete with them, but the woman who was running the contest asked me to tell the best story I knew. So out came one of the Texas jokes learned from Aunt Sug:

There was once a man driving across Texas. He saw a sign saying you are entering The King Ranch. After hours and hours of driving he was still on King Ranch territory. When he finally reached a town, he stopped at a coffee shop next to a hotel. He ordered a small piece of coffee cake. The waitress came back with a huge slice of coffee cake.

"I thought I ordered a small piece of coffee cake?"

"You did," said the waitress. "But you're in Texas now and that **is** small."

He asked for a cup of coffee. She came back with a huge 36 oz mug.

"I only asked for a regular cup of coffee, not anything this big."

"You did, sir. That is our regular size," said the waitress. "You're in Texas now and that is the smallest cup we have."

After drinking the coffee he really needed to go to the bathroom. He asked: "Excuse me but where is the restroom?"

"Well you go down the hall over there, take the second hall on the left and it is the first door on the right."

He finished his coffee and then started down the hall. He took the first hall on the right and went through the second door on the left. Not watching where he was going, he walked right into the swimming pool. When someone started to reach in to help him out he screamed: 'Don't flush it! Don't flush it!"

I was awarded "best tall tale teller." I went off with some of my friends leaving the parakeet on the gazebo. After a few minutes I came back. The bird cage door was open and the parakeet was nowhere to be seen. I looked around. The only suspect was Eddie C, now walking a long distance away. Never knew for sure if he opened the cage or not. But he and his friend were the only ones mean-spirited enough to do such a thing. Eddie was the same who put the stone in the snowball and he and his younger brother were acknowledged as the bullies in town. We would have another confrontation some years later.

Mom put a notice in *The Lakeville Journal* with a small reward for the return of the parakeet. About a week later, someone from Sharon called. A parakeet fitting the description had landed in their back yard the evening before. They took it in and tried to feed it. But it was too exhausted to eat and died during the night. A sad loss.

Love,
Papa

Happy Holidays!

Shortly after the summer with Dad in Florida, we moved back to The Hill. The exact time is a little vague but was definitely by the beginning of the fifth grade. There was little cul-de-sac named Puddler's Lane. Where it intersected with Sugar Hill Road was the bus stop for the kids going to Salisbury Central. On Puddler's Lane a family consisting of a recently divorced mother with three of her five children moved into a house a little way up the hill from the stop. What is interesting it was the house next to Barnie's old home, now deserted and falling apart.

Mrs. M was recently divorce from her husband, Art, after 30 years of marriage producing five kids: three boys, two girls. Each of the kids was spaced five years apart so that by the time the youngest was born, her older sister was married and had a boy a few days before: mother and daughter were in the hospital at the same time delivering the children. The aunt, Susie, was younger than her nephew by a few days. This provided them with a good joke since they both went to Salisbury Central at the same time. They would hang out together and the boy would introduce his "Aunt Susie" to the teachers and other kids. Most at first would not believe them. It was good for a laugh when meeting strangers.

The oldest boy had graduated from high school and moved away. I do not remember ever meeting him. There was seldom any mention of him in the family. He may have joined the military. The important point was he got as far away from Falls Village and Amesville as humanly possible.

The middle male was Robbie. He was a tall skinny kid who would became a school dropout and then became an old fashioned milkman. Interesting!?! In current times, unless one watches movies from the 1930s almost no one has a concept of what a milkman was, or even that it was a career. The milkman would leave a couple of quarts of glass milk bottles on doorsteps in the morning for families to have fresh milk. At the same time, families would leave the "empties" on the same door step in the evening for the milk man to pick up in the morning. Isn't this what bottled water companies do now? Gee, some things do come back into existence, just different products.

In large cities, like Detroit, there was often a little door with a latch with a little shelf. It opened to the outside. These were usually placed on the driveway, towards the back. Their position gave an indication of where the kitchen or pantry was located. The family would put their empties on the shelf, and close and lock the inner door to keep it secure. The milkman was then able to leave the required number of bottles after picking up the empties. That way he would know how many quarts were needed. If you needed more, you would leave a note in the bottle asking for more. That was Robbie's job. As a drop-out there was little else available to him.

The most important part was that Robbie had his license. This made him the principal driver when his younger brother Peter needed a ride. Peter was the youngest boy, sightly less than a year younger than me, but we were in the same grade and class. As important was Cindy, their Norwegian Elkhound, who would come down to the bus stop every morning with Peter and see him off. Naturally she became very friendly with me. It was only natural that Peter and I would become close friends.

Peter's house was built over a very small running stream which moved to an underground flow just after passing the house. The house itself had no running water but had a hand pump in the kitchen and bathroom. There was also no toilet in the house—about 30 feet behind the house was an old-fashioned outhouse with a single seat. Interesting in winter. The outhouse even had the classic crescent moon on the door. The main source of heating in the house was a kerosene heater, along with the kitchen stove. A very dangerous combination but it worked. If you are around a kerosene heater all the time, you learn to be very careful.

There were bedrooms on the second floor but it was so cold up there most of the family slept on the first floor in winter. The electricity in the house was very sparse and usually consisted of a bare light bulb suspended from a wire in the center of a room. No TV, no radio, nor much of anything else. To say they were poor would be an understatement.

Bertha, Peter's mother, worked in a flower shop and made floral arrangement for customers, at a very low salary. The amount of child support she received from Art, her ex, was minimal. As a carpenter, Art rarely had a full-time job. He did contribute when forced, but that was seldom. The other problem was after the divorce he and Bertha both began to drink heavily.

While Bertha was at work, Susie stayed with her older sister. After school Peter and Cindy would come up to my house. When Mom and I moved back to The Hill, the old coal-burning furnace in the basement had been converted to oil. If nothing else, Peter and I could enjoy the heat of my house along with electricity and TV. But with the dearth of channels, TV did not offer much of interest. What we liked the most was going off in the woods to shoot our guns at various targets. The other option was to grab our fishing poles and trek down to the Housatonic River.

Of course this was the preteen age where curiosity about the opposite sex increased. You already read about B&Bs experiments in Lakeville earlier. But now Peter would often bring Susie his little sister along with him when visiting. One day he asked if I would like to see Susie naked. Of course I would. He convinced Susie to take off her clothes and show her little vulva. This resulted in an erection on my part. Susie wanted to see it as she thought it would be fun to look at. I soon stripped off my clothes and showed stiff cock in front of her. I asked Peter is she could have sex at this early of an age. He said it would be like a bull humping a young heifer and likely kill her in the process. Susie was simply too small and too young. But she still like the feeling of it rubbing against her, which was done until a spurting mess had to be cleaned off of her belly.

This was rural Connecticut, so a lot of kids had 22 rifles; Peter and I were no exceptions (remember, I got my 22 for my seventh birthday). Occasionally I would get out the 16-gauge shotgun and shoot it. Most of time we would shoot at a target set up next to the barn, on a branch of a tree, or some other target in the woods. We were fairly good shots and it would be a most unusual day of target practice when we did not get a bull's eye, if not two or three. We always said we were going hunting, but seldom did we shoot at an animal.

There was one time when Peter asked to shoot the 16-gauge shot gun. I pulled it out and loaded both barrels. We set up a tin can in the field. Peter hit it first shot but missed on the second. I reloaded the gun. Then in the distance, perhaps over a hundred yards or more, we spotted two crows flying away from the shots fired. I aimed at the crows. Bam. We watched for what seemed like minutes. Suddenly the crow in the back fell from the sky.

"Damn, that is the most remarkable shot I have ever seen!" shouted Peter.

I never had the heart to tell him I was aiming at the crow in front. It just happened that the crow in front was the perfect lead for the other following in the same flight path. Fatal for him.

The funniest hunting expedition was early winter. New snow had covered the ground and we decided it would be easy to track animals in the snow. Off we went to the back fields and wood past the Clark's field next to the driveway. Shortly after entering the wood we found a bobcat's paw prints in the snow. A perfect hunt! The tracks were clear. They were fresh. Even better, they were easy to follow. We followed the tracks for a good mile. We thought we were getting closer because the prints were fresher. The tracks kept turning ever so slightly to the right. It seemed logical. Older deer tracks following the same route through the woods.

Slowly we were turning in a great circle. After about two hours of tracking the bobcat we realized we were back where we started. We were now following the original tracks we first started to follow. The bobcat had led us in a huge circle. He likely started walking in his original tracks. Once he realized we were dumb enough to follow the tracks he carefully set for the two of us, he likely jumped into a tree. We were probably passing right under him. If a bobcat could laugh, I'm sure he would have. That was a typical "hunt" for Peter and myself.

Hope you had a Merry Christmas—I enjoyed having you around.

Love,
Papa

December 31

Hi T. Happy New Year.

You have to remember there was not much to do in Connecticut. Occasionally Robbie would drive us to Canaan and the movie theater there. Other times Mom would drive us to Canaan and promise to pick us up later. But she was hit and miss.

An example was when she dropped us off on Saturday afternoon. We would usually go to a movie, see which ever was playing in the single screen. I'm not sure if they still had the

Occasionally we would Saturday afternoon children's features there. The old Lakeville movie house once did, but that theater was history now, so we were stuck with whatever movie was showing in Canaan. The advantage was there were much fewer releases.

Off Peter and I went to Canaan. Mom told us to meet her at the little restaurant down the street after the movie, which was fine as it was half a block away. Easy to get to. Especially on this cold, drizzly day.

When we left the movie, we walked to the diner. It was a small—a few booths and a long counter with the old-fashioned round seats kids would love to spin on until their parents would stop them. The food was simple American fair. No foreign dishes there. Not much quality either. There was another restaurant in Canaan, but it was further away and cost a little more. This was the place where the working class would have a dinner or snack. Hang on to your hat, but there was no MacDonald's, Burger King, or any other fast-food places within miles of Canaan back then. Of course, if you went to Salisbury, there was The Inn, which was where the upper classes went for better dinners. Too far and too expensive for Peter and me, also we would not have been welcomed—we were not the accepted class of people.

So, on that cold winter day, getting inside felt good, as did the warmth of the booth we sat down in. We ordered hot chocolate. Peter had no money but I had a little to pay for both. We drank slowly. It was now 30 minutes past the time Mom was to pick us up; we had finished the hot chocolate and were waiting, and waiting, and waiting. No sign of Mom. Remember, these were the years before cell phones or any other means of communication other than rotary dial phones. Yes, I said rotary dial—push button phones were still a decade away!

After about an hour we were both getting a little restless. Also thirsty! The hot chocolate had been consumed. Not having enough money for any food, it was our thirst which began to be the focus of our mostly empty stomachs. I pulled out all the money I had. There was not enough for another hot chocolate. But I did have just enough for two Cokes. Yes, I did drink Coke back then. But this may well have been the last time. The Cokes were ordered and brought to the table and we started to drink them. After a few minutes our stomachs started to feel a little funny. Then the "little funny" turned into distinct pain for both of us. We were getting severe cramps. Mom eventually showed up over an hour late and by then the stomach pain was so bad, it was hard to walk the 20 feet to the car without buckling over.

As we drove home, Peter and I were doubled over in pain. We dropped off Peter at his house. When I got home I went straight to bed with one hell of a stomach ache. Lesson learned: never drink Coke on top of hot chocolate. They do not mix.

If we didn't go to the movies in Canaan or walk in the woods, we would watch very boring TV or go fishing. On nice days Peter and I loved to go fishing. Cindy would always to come along with us. Like most other dogs she would take in all the smells, looking for anyone or anything demanding her attention. Usually she would walk near us but if a rabbit or squirrel appeared, off she'd run until the little critter was safe out of the grasps of her jaws.

Most often the three of us would walk down to the Housatonic River and try various fishing holes. The river was seldom flowing very fast. We would start up by the dam and work our way down towards the falls. The flume was usually only a trickle of water. Not much of a flume. There were the numerous pools with fish trapped in them and if we were lucky a fish or two could be caught.

We never had any real luck in the large pool at the base of the falls. Some said it went down a hundred feet or more. The water was dark, with no view of the bottom, and colder than elsewhere. Shaded by the cliff, the falls and the trees it almost never got the sun. This protected it from the radiant heat, except in early mornings. Most of the other smaller pools had blue gill, suckers and occasionally some perch. Once in a great while you could spot a trout, both rainbow and speckled, in the faster-moving currents.

Cindy would follow us down the rocks. Where she couldn't climb down, she knew the area so well she would trot off to a place where she could easily get down. She watched the fish and got very excited when she saw one. Her curved tail would be wagging like crazy and her little whines of excitement sounded as if she was in pain. Occasionally after all this physical and verbal whining she would try to catch a fish. If she saw a fish swimming back and forth she would get on an overhanging rock and wait until the fish approached her. Then she would jump in and swim under water a few strokes to catch it. Sometimes she would catch a sucker, which is slow moving and not very smart. Once she caught a catfish. Usually she missed, but she had great fun trying. It was also an idea way for a dog to cool off on a hot summer day. Especially a dog bred for colder weather.

A funny incident happened on a hot summer day. This day was almost cloudless and certainly a bit hot for northwestern Connecticut—in the upper 80ss. We didn't start until shortly after lunch. Almost all the usual pools where dry or didn't have any fish. The remaining pools we were not providing any nibbles, little less an actual catch. Finally, we moved way down stream to a pool which was quite large. It almost always had a variety of small fish. But there were two problems. It was hot and the fish seem to not eat in the heat of the day. The second problem was how to approach the pool. You had to walk over a large ledge, easily 30 feet x 50 feet, carved out of the riverbed during the ice age. The fish can see you just as well as you can see them and if they spotted you, you could forget about trying to catch them!

On that day Peter and I saw about six fairly large perch in the pool. They saw us too. We tried to keep behind the ledge and cast our lines into the pool. The cast was fine but the fish were too smart to bite. No luck. The perch knew not to be tempted by worms on hooks if they saw a human. Then we approached the pool from the side and dropped our lines right in front of their noses, upon which they swam away from the wiggly worm! We kept trying to catch them for an hour. No luck. Finally, we climbed on top of the ledge. Being hot from the sun beating down upon us, the fact the fish were not going to bite, and being out for so long with no luck whatsoever, out of frustration we started to throw large rocks at them. Of course, we missed the fish. They could see the rocks coming and just swim away to their hiding places in the crevasses and little side holes in the river stream. The holes were small enough to hide in but with the lack of flowing water the fish were unable to swim to another part of the river. The only benefit was that two discontented teenage fishermen were able to take out their vexation by hurling stones into the water. The splash was the most exciting thing to happen so far that day.

We decided it was time to leave. But Cindy was nowhere to be found. Peter and I called and called. No response. Usually she was very good—she would give us a bark and start coming over the rocks. This time all was silent. Peter decided to stay. If Cindy was alright she could tell where we were calling from and would try to come to the sound of our voices. She likely knew which pool we were at. She often would join us there watching us fish. If she got bored, she would wander over the rocks to other pools and do her thing, whatever it was. This day was no exception.

We waited about 10 minutes. Being a little concerned, but only a little, since Cindy was such a hearty dog, we started to stand up to see if we could see her coming over the rocks. After close to 20 minutes since the initial calls, we could hear a muffled whimper. It was not one of pain or distress, but rather an excited one. We called again. Another whimper followed. This was closer. We knew she was coming and that she was alright. Then we spotted her. Over the rocks Cindy came with a foot-long trout in her mouth. She came right up to us and dropped the still-flopping fish at our feet. She was really excited. Her tail was whipping back and forth faster than a sperm cell trying to impregnate an egg. Peter and I laughed. Cindy was the best fisher for the day. We took the fish to Peter's house. I understood it became his dinner, which he shared with Cindy who loved fish too. But he was careful to be sure she didn't get any bones.

Love,
Papa

Hi T – I'm a little late:

First, so glad Obama is our new president. He is so superior to McCain as shown in his picks for the Cabinet. I have friends who work as staffers on Capitol Hill. They often told me McCain was too dumb to be a senator, little less a president. Guess his choice for vice president confirmed their opinion of McCain.

Back to Connecticut. Peter's father Mort, his nickname when not called Art, was a carpenter, as mentioned. When sober (which was rare) he was very talented. After the divorce he first lived with a friend, then bought a small piece of land on the Appalachian Trail. It was on the other side of Falls Village, about four or five miles away. The property was at the base of a large rock formation by a small road going up a hill toward a camp site. It was not far from Music Mountain music center. Mort decided to build a small shack there for himself. It was to be a retreat off the beaten track, where he and his friends would be able to hang out, get drunk and complain about their lives and all their lost opportunities.

Peter and I would sometimes go over to see the progress. The biggest problem was the property had a southern exposure and was in a very rocky area. As a result, a lot of timber rattle snakes would sun themselves every morning. Mort, after laying the foundation, put up a sign calling the cabin Rattlesnake Rest because of all the rattlesnakes he had to kill to build the house. He was always happy when Peter brought Cindy around. Cindy would find the hidden snakes thereby preventing any of us from being bitten. Mort would have a 22 pistol around to shoot a rattler if it was too close to the house or in the small yard. Too bad no one thought of eating the slain snakes, but back then it not considered.

After several months, Rattlesnake Rest was finished, well almost—at least the main room and kitchen area. As you entered the front door, you would first see a counter which extended from the opposite wall to about three-quarters the width of the room. There was a small dining table near the counter, a sofa and several cheap chairs scattered around the room. Then at the opposite end of the room was an elevated open fireplace. It was about two feet above the level of the floor. The fire generated most of the heat for the room. There was no fireplace safety door across the four-foot opening, not even a steel curtain. Keeping the logs on the fire were the andirons.

Behind the left side of the fireplace was Mort's bedroom, on the other side the bathroom. I don't remember it being completely finished. It did have a toilet, a shower stall and a sink, but the walls were never painted. A left door in the bathroom led to the bedroom. There were two beds in place, one for Mort, one for any of his kids who might stay over. Most would bring sleeping bags and camp on the main room floor. It was much warmer in the main room. Peter and I would love to go hiking in the area or try to climb the rocks behind The Rest but were careful of the rattlers who would be hiding in the cracks of the rocks.

Behind the counter was a small kitchen with a stove, mini refrigerator and sink. Of course, the refrigerator was well stocked with beer. A cabinet contained a good variety of cheap whisky, gin, vodka and other hard liquor. There were always sodas for Peter and me.

Mom liked taking us over so she could get free beer. If others were there, bourbon and soda on the rocks was her favorite. Mort developed a crush on your grandmother. She did not reject his advances but I never found out if it was any more than a flirtation. I think she just liked the ability to obtain free drinks.

I remember one evening, Ruth and Mom both came over, joining two of Mort's co-workers. Pete and I had been dropped off earlier. There was a large fire burning in the fireplace and the room was toasty on a cold late-autumn evening. Suddenly there was a large "pop" from the fireplace and two logs rolled out into the room. Mom, who was sitting on the bar stool let out a gasp. I was the one closest to the logs, which were now in the middle of the floor, so I ran over picked up one with my bare hands and carried it back to the fireplace. Then I turned around and picked up the smaller one and placed it on the larger in a way the andirons would now keep them in place. Nothing caught on fire. Peter and Mort couldn't believe their eyes.

You must be badly burned! Come over and put cold water on your hands," Mort said.

"I'm OK," I said as I went over to show them.

Nowhere on my hands was there any indication of a burn. Without knowing it, I had used the mental protection of fire walkers who walk over hot coals. From then on, Mort and even Peter looked at me a little differently—as someone with abilities beyond normal people, a little like a member of the X-Men. Mom just smiled; she remembered the marshmallow and my initiation of fire when I was four or five years old.

Peter and I would play poker, war and other card games, sometimes checkers, which I never liked very much. If Mort had other board games we would play whatever was available. We always enjoyed our days at "The Rest", but they were too few. As for Mort, since Mom was often at The Rest, he would often show up unannounced at our house for a beer or just to sleep off a hangover on the living room sofa. Later Mort got a dog, a black lab, which was a puppy when he got it, but who probably lived more at Peter's house than at The Rest. We called him Jumper. That's what he did—jump from one place to another. In deep grass in the fields, all you would see Jumper's black head bobbing up and down as he bounded across the field with Cindy, trying in vain to follow Jumper's trampled grass.

Love,
Papa

Hi T:

The last letter explained how Peter and I would play poker, sometimes with Mort but mostly alone. The basics of the game were learned, but not the percentages nor much of the strategy. Still, it was something to pass the time of day. After all The Rest had no TV, as the signals were blocked by being surrounded on three sides by rock cliffs. The only exposure was towards the south and there was no source for a TV station there until you reached New Haven, much too far from that section of Falls Village to allow any reception.

Peter's brother, a more advanced poker player, introduced me to the game. One day I visited Peter, when Robbie had been told to watch his brother. We were about 11 years old.

Susie, Peter's younger sister was with us. She was almost 7. The had to come along but sat in a chair and fell asleep. There was a poker game going on with other high schoolers in a neighboring house. Robbie wanted to play. Since he had been instructed to watch us, he simply told us to join him at the other house. Funny, I can recall none of the older boys' names nor where they lived. I suspect one was likely Joel M., the music teacher's son, who lived down the lane and across the street.

I had just learned to play. I had about 50 cents in my pocket. I was invited into the game. Robbie and the others thought they could easily take my money leaving me with none, in quick order. I entered the house. The game was in the kitchen. Typical of a 1960s poker game, smoke filled room, junk food and beer for all those underage high schoolers. Peter warned me they just wanted to take my money, but I wanted to find out more about poker in a real competitive game. The ante was a nickel. Raises would usually limited to a nickel or dime. The game was five-card draw. Texas hold 'em was unheard of at that time, at least outside of Texas.

I have to admit, being one of the youngest there, I really didn't know what to expect. I was a little afraid the older boys might cheat me. But Peter and Robbie protected me from those who wanted to cheat; I know because the others were trying to be sly, talking about dealing winning hands to each other until I was out of cash. Robbie interceded, not allowing the other boys to cheat.

I don't remember exactly what hands I got. I do know Peter was helping a little. He would whisper into my ear: "Raise", "Drop out", "Call" depending on the hand. I would win one and lose one. But the winners began numbering the losing hands. Slowly I was gaining money. Soon I had well over a dollar and was still going strong. Remember, this is the late 1950s, so a dollar was a lot to a kid like me.

We must have played for over an hour. It was now dark outside. Peter wanted to go back to his house and asked me to stop. The other boys didn't want me to leave. I was well over $5 ahead. I got up, despite all the complaints, left the game. I don't remember when I had that much money. Money I had got by myself. Peter told me I was lucky. It was good to leave.

When I got home I showed Mom the money. She was curious how I had obtained that much. "The Poker Game Robbie invited me to join."

Mom was very amused. Remember, she was from Texas. She knew poker and could play it, though we never did—our game was canasta. There was more than one poker game in her history, even one where she was the stake, but that is another tale. I told her the details of the game and how I kept winning. She said it was good Peter dragged me out of the game while I was ahead. The key to any gambling is to leave while you are ahead, she said. That is a lesson I have always remembered, but unfortunately seldom followed, be it gambling or the stock market.

That was my first experience in of poker; never my favorite game, but one I know. The next gambling lesson would be craps, my greatest weakness! When the concept of probability was grasped, roulette became a favorite, usually betting just, red or black, odd or even. Once, we were on a cruise ship, your mother had gone to bed, and I wanted to play in the casino. Playing roulette and betting on probabilities, I was soon over $250 ahead, almost the cost of the cruise. I walked away. But, not wanting to go to bed or disturb your mother, I went back to the table.

Mistake! I lost it all. I was betting black, but that night 13 reds came up. Years later I tried again, different casino, different location. But the cruise ship experience was telling me I would never gain any fortune from gambling. From that day forward, it cured me of any desire to return to a casino. Our brief visit when traveling across the country was one of the only other visit. Then you played the slots and lost all of $5. I didn't play any game. We both walked away.

Love,
Papa

Let me tell you about Music Mountain:

It was around this time Mom continued to find secretarial work in various places, one of which was Music Mountain. I'll give you some of the spiel from their webpage:

"Music Mountain is the home of the oldest continuing summer chamber music festival in this country. Founded in 1930 as the permanent home for the Gordon String Quartet, one of the leading string quartets of its time, Music Mountain is celebrating its 79th anniversary in 2008 and looking forward to its 80th anniversary season in 2009. Each season we offer a Chamber Music Series of 16 concerts, mainly on Sunday afternoons, a popular Saturday evening series of Jazz and Choral concerts, and a number of special events. As in years past, all of this concert activity offers many opportunities for visits to Music Mountain.... Gordon Hall and the Music Mountain residences were built by Sears Roebuck during the summer of 1930. The property and the buildings are listed in the National Register of Historic Places.

"Music Mountain was founded by Jacques Gordon, founder and first violinist of the Gordon String Quartet, in 1930 with the primary mission of education through the performance of the chamber music literature, specifically, the music for the string quartet. This mission is realized by bringing together professionals, amateurs, adults and children, by developing new audiences and by providing access to the experience of live music."

The job Mom got was publishing the programs for Music Mountain concerts. We would run them off on the A B Dick mimeograph machine, usually on Friday night or early Saturday, then drive them up the Music Mountain Sunday morning. Of course we stayed for the concert. One very funny item on the web page is that Music Mountain uses a Lakeville post office box when in reality it is in Falls Village. Lakeville just has more status than poor little Falls Village.

When I was still young (younger than 10), she would join Betsy, if Betsy was there as a reporter for *The Lakeville Journal*. Sometimes Mom would sit with Ann Hoskins, the *Journal's* chief editor, even though she thought Ann was a snob (she was). On those days, I would play outside, quietly, in the yard. There was no air conditioning so the windows were almost always open. One could hear quite well from the yard. Freebies were perfect. Baseball too loud because of the ball hitting a bat or the glove. They were afraid it would get loose and go through a window or in other ways disturb the concert. Football if just throwing / catching, no game. This was my first exposure to live classical music. It was amazing some of the artists who would play there.

Benny Goodman was a regular. He played almost every summer while still able to play, which was long after I graduated from college. For those who don't know about Benny Goodman, he was one of the jazz greats from the 1930s through the 1950s. Many of his band members would spin off and form their own bands. Glenn Miller was with Benny in the early days. Gene Krupa, the great drummer, played with Benny. So, did Lionel Hampton the wonderful vibraphonist. Benny was the first to have an integrated band. Fletcher Henderson, the great black musician would write and arrange scores for some of the black bands in Harlem. He joined Benny. Benny invited Lionel to join Gene and Teddy Wilson turning the The Benny Goodman Trio into a quartet. Benny Goodman earned his title of "The King of Swing". He was loved by your grandparents, and your father.

Benny lived in Connecticut and supported Music Mountain. He often played the Mozart clarinet concerto—he was famous for it. When coming into the world of popular music, he was invited to play Mozart in NYC. He made a name for himself as a jazz musician but one who could play classical. I heard him playing. What a thrill! But I did not connect the concert with the jazz musician's records I was hearing at the time. As a result, I was not fully aware of the guest artist, even though I had listened to his jazz recordings for years. It would be many years before I would hear him again and that would be another very memorable and historic occasion.

Music Mountain opened the classical music to my mind. It showed that jazz musicians could be very talented in a variety of venues. The Juilliard Quartet was there one year. There were many other famous names back then, most of which I have long forgotten.

Yehudi Menuhin may have been there one summer. I may have only gone half a dozen times each summer. The visits made a significant subconscious impression. It would be years before the impact was really materialized. As I got older, I started to come inside to listen. I remember there was a Baroque woodwind quartet that really caught my attention. I have loved woodwind chamber music ever since. The biggest problem with moving inside was the seats, which were hard wooden benches and not very comfortable. Still, you were right on top of the musicians in this very small auditorium. It was great seeing the artists perform so close.

Love,
Papa

Hi T:

Since this is the end of the winter season I thought a winter story would be appropriate. This will give you a little picture of why I created the tiny sled run for your second birthday when we had the mini blizzard—it was to give you a since of winter fun.

It was this time of year in Connecticut where the only two things to do outside. One was to go hiking through the snow, which was nice, especially in the mountains. The woods and hills when covered with newly fallen six sided crystals of frozen water, creating some of the most beautiful scenes in nature. The foothills of the Berkshires were perfect examples of this. You could follow the trails walking for miles just looking at the pure white snow, unpolluted by soot or exhaust from cars and trucks.

Sugar Hill, with the lack of traffic, certainly afforded the availability of the most beautiful winter pictures. That is, if anyone with a camera wanted to take the pictures. Mom and I did. Occasionally taking shots, especially after we created a little darkroom in one of the closets in the bathroom. All the photos were taken with her old 2 1/4 format Rolliflex camera she used during WWII.

The second option was taking your Flexible Flyer sled to one of the many large hills for a thrilling ride down. One of a good sled run was on the other side of The Hill. The crest of The Hill was a steep slope on two sides. One side ended up in the Clark's back yard. The other side, with no fences, went down to near Roger's. There was one small problem: how to get there. I could go completely around The Hill, down the driveway, down the road then turning into the road where the Roger lived, which was about a mile. The alternative was to cut across a thin stretch at the top of the hill. Being about fifty yards from the corner of our property to the top of the sled run. This would be easier saving a lot of time. It was the logical choice except for one small item.

The problem was it was the Clark's for fifty yards, or at least part of the property they leased, that had to be crossed. As said our property was an L-shaped property surrounded by the Clarks on three sides. Mrs. Clark hated us. We avoided walking on the fields where the Clarks might be able to spot us. Peter and I would often cross the fields adjacent the driveway but over the knoll of a hill which was not visible by the Clark's who lived at the middle level of Sugar Hill. Our house was on the upper level. Roger and his family were on the lower level of Amesville.

One crisp winter day I decided to take a chance on the short cut. This was visible from the Clark's house while traversing part of the hill. As I started across, I heard a door slam down towards the Clark's house some 150 yards downhill. Then, all of a sudden, I heard a "pop". I looked down the slope. There was old lady Clark with a rifle shooting at me. Another "pop" occurred. A rock about 10 yards away from me had a chip fly off. I ducked down and started running to the right to get away from high point of the ridge and get out of her view. She shouted something I couldn't hear. Safe. I was no longer in the sights of the rifle. Little did I know this was perfect preparation for working in the South Bronx years later.

Within a few minutes I crossed the barbwire fence and joined the Peter, and the other children of the neighbors. All sledding on the side of in the Clapp's field where we could not be seen. Someone asked who was shooting. I said old lady Clark missed me as I was crossing the field. That was the end of it.

We spent a good part of the day sledding down the back side of the hill and climbing back up. It was a good run, about 100 yards down a steep slope with some rocks to be negotiated around, just an added challenge. Roger's mother had hot chocolate for us when we got tired. When going back, I went with Peter to his house first, then returned home by the main road, avoiding the field I had crossed earlier, but I still had to go past the "B@#*$'s" house. She didn't dare shoot me on a public road.

Another sled run ran behind Peter's house up a hill and more towards the Housatonic River. This was a run that was close to three quarters of a mile and ended with a three foot drop off the top of a stone wall into a lower small pasture and small farm with a few cows there. The fun part of this sled run was it was winding and very narrow in parts. It would take close to an hour to get to the top of the run. The easiest way was to walk down to the Falls Road, turn left and walk another half mile then climb up a hill to the start of the run. This was another 30-minute, fairly steep, climb. Most of the time, when one got to the starting point, you just sat down for a while to catch your breath. You can see why this was a once-a-day run—and only when there was a lot of snow to cushion mistaken judgments on the sledding trail.

We would start down a very steep slope picking up considerable speed. After a few turns around small fir trees, we would be on the side of the hill facing the river. A sharp turn to the right next to a mini cliff, avoiding a 10-foot drop, then over a narrow patch. If you did not negotiate the turn carefully, you would either hit a tree or go over the cliff. Every now and then someone would miss the turn and drop the ten feet. The saving grace was that at the base of the rock ledge was usually a deep snow drift, which would be five feet deep when there was a good snowfall. The only time anyone would have tried to negotiate this run was after a large storm. We all knew the dangers. Going in between the trees required a good amount of snow to cover the possible brown dirt patches under the trees, especially in the early part of the run.

If you passed those obstacles you were heading back towards Sugar Hill and Peter's house. It was on the side of this slope where we would pick up more speed. It was hard staying on the sled since it listed down to the left while you were going around the hillside, but that was part of the fun. Then a little knoll up. Another turn to the left. Then a straight run down towards the road. The key was to get up enough speed to fly off the top of the rock wall and into the pasture. If you were lucky you would be in the air for three yards. There were little bumps on the slope just before the three-foot drop. The one saving grace for this last drop it was into a slightly swampy area. Yes, it was covered with snow and often frozen, but when you hit, it would be like sledding into a covered haystack giving way enough so to prevent painful landings.

It was always a competition to see who would go the farthest into the field. I did win once. Almost made it to the corner of the field, near the school bus stop. You just wanted to avoid the tiny creek which was at the edge of the field. I love sledding.

There was another similar run, but that was closer to Limerock and several miles away from the house. Peter and I went there only when Robbie was able to drive us. The farm where this run was, was owned by the Goodwins. Hezzie and Louie were twin brothers, and sons of the owner. There was no problem sledding on this property. It was also interesting that the local general practitioner, Dr. Miester, lived on the curve of the road just past a pond which was at the end of the sled run. His office was in his home. If anyone broke anything, we could easily get to Dr. Miester's office to get help quickly.

Dr. Miester brought many children into the world, maybe over a 100. Many had him as a godfather, including Hezzie and Louie. He was the official high school MD. As a typical old country doctor he likely deserves a letter all to himself. Not sure if that will happen, but worth consideration.

Love,
Papa

More Winter Fun—actually mailed on March 2nd, during the big snow storm:

Sledding was our main source of fun during the winter months. Mom had a winter job, running off the announcements and results for the Salisbury Winter Sports Association. The Association had only one main event, sky jumping. In Salisbury, against the small mountain (or large hill facing Amesville was an old-fashioned wooden ski jump. It was the mountain the Appalachian Trail passed over. If you followed the trail, it came out east of Salisbury. If took it southward over the mini mountain, you would eventually come to my driveway.

Salisbury had a ski jump to the right and behind the main street as you went through the town. By today's standards, the ski jump was pretty small. There was an even smaller training jump next to it. The training jump was never kept up and soon taken down. For the 1960 this was a modest ski jump, used for the Eastern US ski jumping championships. It was a 100-meter jump. In 1955 and 1956 it was used to determine which American jumpers would go to the Olympic 1956 games. It may have been continued used for Olympic trials through 1960.

There was a little shack near the entrance to the road which led to the jump hill where Mom would set up the A.B. Dick mimeograph and typewriter. The jump was a five-minute walk away. There was a woman, I think she was named Angie, who ran the Sports Association. I always thought she was strange looking. She was very masculine and walked in a very manly fashion. I would later learn the word "butch" which fit her.

I use to wonder about Angie until one day I was running the result from the judges to Mom. But Mom was not in the shack. Angie was. She was in a deep and passionate embrace with an attractive young woman, half her age. The younger woman's breasts were being kissed and caressed. I backed out quietly. Mom was headed back to the shack. I told her I had spotted Angie there with another woman. Mom made lots of noise as she stepped up the steps and onto the porch. Mom later explained some women like other women rather than men. This was my first introduction to any concept related to homosexuality and it was totally new for me, a lot for a youngster to digest.

Back to the ski jump. As part of Mom's crew, I would get into the jumping area for free. There would be thousands of people on and around the jump hill. It was truly the biggest event in Salisbury all year and for many years. The early crowd would surround the roped-off area of the landing zone. Others would be lining the incline to the base of the jump. From there you could look down the complete run to the landing areas. I used to try all the various views, especially if Mom didn't need me, which was often. She knew I loved watching the jumping. She would run off the stencils by herself, rather than getting me to do it. Some of the judges didn't trust me to carry the results. They would often run them down to the shack themselves.

My two favorite places where right next to the launch and the landing area with the bales of hay. This latter position was one of the two or three places where bond fires were blazing. They were the only warm places in the whole area. One day, it was windy and cold and keeping warm was a priority. The clouds threatened snow and a few flurries were flying. I had been up the slope, over the landing slope behind the roped-off area. After being there for over three hours, I couldn't feel my feet anymore. This was one of the bigger events. It may have been part of the trials for the 1956 Olympics. These could take all day from 9 a.m. to sundown around 4:30 p.m. I had a hotdog for lunch with some hot chocolate. But the warmth of the food and drink didn't reach my toes. Standing close to the ropes right next to the bonfire was a good option. The vision of the jump was partly cut off by the crowd. I literally put my toes into the coals of the fire, I was that cold.

I didn't pay much attention. My feet were getting warmer. I could see some of the action between the heads. One of the jumpers didn't stop in the usual place and skidded right next to the fence, straw and rope, scattering snow on me and the others standing there. Suddenly one of the men standing next to me tapped me on the shoulder:

"Son, your shoes are on fire."

I looked down. Sure enough, the leather soles of the shoes were smoldering and there was steam coming from my wet shoes. No wonder my toes felt warm. I pulled my feet out and pushed the shoes into the snow and the fire was quickly extinguished. Then I walked back un-phased.

Another time Peter came with us so I would have someone company. His brother Robbie knew one of the jumpers who was attempting to get a little glory for the locals. He would get the biggest cheers. He was a decent jumper, in the top 10, but he never made it to the Olympics. I only remember him slightly as a big teen with a round head and short hair. Perfect for the Marines.

By 1964 the Olympics were introducing the larger hills and bigger jumps. It didn't take long for the little Salisbury jump to fall into disrepair and disappear from all but a few fond memories. The road that led to the old jump was tuned into a facility for the snow removal equipment, with a few houses for the poor. Later one of my girlfriends' homes was there. I think the snobs of Salisbury were happy when the Winter Association died—after all, they would never bother with such activities.

Love,
Papa

Chapter 10

The Trio Plus and Remarkable Dogs

Ruth's Move:

As mentioned previously Ruth was Mom's closest friend during these years. She continued to have other friends, including Betsy, but Ruth continued to come out on top. Betsy was too unpredictable. In a lot of ways she was like the Kim Cattrall character Samantha on *Sex in the City*. She so desperately wanted to remarry, but never did. However, she would do anything to try! That included bedding down with any available man who approached her. All her latest adventures in the bedroom were related to Mom and Ruth when they were together. So were the heartaches. She would realize she was only used as a fuck machine by the horny middle-aged men in town, which drove her into a depression.

Ruth on the other hand celebrated her independence, much the same way as Mom did. She was more intelligent than Betsy (something Betsy would never have agreed with). That, and their similar backgrounds were other reasons for Mom befriending Ruth. Poor upbringings. Early marriages. Involvement with bootleg alcohol during Prohibition—it all just added spice to the relationship.

Ruth was about a decade older. She always drove a little sports car. She loved her buckskin jacket with fringe on the sleeves. I don't remember where Ruth lived when she and Mom first became friends. Ruth did have a son and a daughter, but neither came up to visit her very often. Neither provided any assistance. Both her children were married with their own children. Her daughter had her Ph.D. in fine arts and a teaching position in a lesser college. She considered herself a wonderful artist, but I never saw any of her work.

Ruth's son was an actor and playwright in NYC. He was constantly looking for parts in plays. Almost all plays were what is called Off Off (Off?) Broadway. Mostly down in Greenwich Village. Seldom paying much. He had a number of children. I only met Ruth's grandson once. He was also a teenage actor, following in his parents' footsteps.

There was one funny episode in his acting career he told me about. He had a kissing scene with another teen actress in a play rehearsal. He didn't like this girl, so he came up with a plan. He had a pet tarantula. During one rehearsal the spider was in his pocket. The spider was trained to crawl up to his shoulder upon a signal. While kissing his fellow actor, he gave the signal to his pet. The spider climbed up to his shoulder. When the girl opened her eyes during the kiss, there was a large tarantula staring back at her. She let out a terrifying scream. I'm not sure if she stayed in the cast—who knows, she may have even had a breakdown. From what I could gather the son likely got paid more than his father. I think Ruth's daughter-in-law had a regular job but was caught up in this totally impractical family of thespians.

I do remember the first time we helped Ruth move. It was from the little single-story house on the "Between the Lakes Road" described before. This was a very narrow dirt road between the Twin Lakes in the Canaan area (actually between Canaan and Salisbury). I remember several interesting things about the house. *The Addams Family* would have been very comfortable using this little cabin as a summer cottage. It was dark, ill-lit. No right-angles in the place. And plenty of creaks and groans anytime the wind kicked up. (Very funny, as I am writing this page. There is a Yankee baseball game playing on TV. Between innings they just played *The Addams Family* theme the second I finished this paragraph.)

Ruth's darkroom equipment had no place in this little house so was stored in a mini garage. The challenge was how do you set up a table, bed, sofa, etc. on an uneven floor so they don't rock back and forth when used? This was done for the sofa by staking a number of newspapers under the feet. The other problem was the bookshelves. They need to be fairly flat. Thank God for shingles—slanted wood pieces used as a type of siding on old houses. Where the newspapers were not leveling the furniture, the shingles were.

The cats, mentioned in an earlier letter, were there. The mother Siamese cat liked me and would sit in my lap, but the two daughters would hiss and scratch at me if I got close so I avoided them. They loved the uneven floor. They were constantly getting into trouble. One would run away if something broke leaving the other two get the blame. The older cat came with Ruth to the next house. I don't know what happen to the younger two. They seem to have disappeared from the house, never to be seen again. Maybe Ruth gave them away. Maybe they were captured by a fox when outside. I never found out. Never really cared. All I knew was the one cat I liked was still around.

The disadvantage of Ruth moving was the loss of the short walk, or drive, to various fishing spots around the two lakes. The main public entrance was on the opposite side of the lake. It had a beach, rowboats and canoes to rent. Mom and I would go to fishing one that side occasionally. If we were to take a boat out on the lake Ruth would come along, but otherwise she rarely joined us. Most of the time Mom and I would find a little cove where we could fish from shore in the smaller of the two lakes. The only fish caught were bluegill and occasionally a perch. If we went out in the boat we occasionally pulled in a large mouth bass, the favorite fish of the fishing channels. On rare occasions we did catch a lake trout. Mom liked to go fishing because that was our dinner and it would save money! If we caught enough fish we would share them with Ruth.

But with the move, all the fishing was lost. More about Ruth's new home later.

Love,
Papa

Hi T – this is about Lilly:

After Dad left for Florida, we moved back to The Hill. Mom thought it would be good for me to have a dog so we got a beautiful Irish setter, not a pure breed but very close. She was reddish but with a hint of brown. She was young and intelligent. We became very close, very fast. I called her Lilly.

When Peter and I often went out in the woods with Cindy, Lilly was a welcome addition. Lilly was someone Cindy could play with as Peter and I climbed over the Falls or sat and fished. One of the first times we took Lilly fishing, I was using a lure. We decided to try our luck at the base of the Housatonic Falls. It was a deep hole with a constant flow of water entering from the trickle coming from the Falls; it was rare for the falls to go over in full furry.

Figuring Cindy and Lilly were playing on the rocks, I was not paying much attention. I was using a fly rod, not my usual tackle. A fly rod is where you have to move the line back and forth to get it out in the pool. My favorite is a casting rod, where you have a single direct throw. Peter was using his usual casting rod and a worm. The lure was small and colorful. It would zigzag in the water to attract fish. Although I had tried it at Twin Lakes, I never caught a fish with it. If it attracted fish, there was no sign of its success. However, it attracted Lilly.

I didn't see her approaching me from behind. I cast backward and made the usual motion forward. I heard a yelp and the line did not follow the cast. I had caught a 45-pound furry fish that now howling as if she was about to die! The hook on the lure had caught Lilly in the lip and went all the way through. She was in terrible pain but also scared. SO WAS I.

I cut the string, but she was unwilling to walk with the hook in her. Picking her up I started to carry her back home, tears streaming down my cheeks. To this day it is a wonder how I was able to climb up the Falls with the dog in my arms, but somehow this feat was managed. With tears blurring my vision all the way the walk was a challenge—you must realize it was almost a mile. I was very thankful Peter and Cindy stayed with me. Peter was worried as he knew how much Lilly meant to me. Cindy was worried because of the whimpering coming from her new canine friend.

I called Mom. She raced home. We took Lilly to the vet. Lilly was almost in shock but still whining, just not as loudly. The vet took one look and said it was the biggest fish he had seen caught all year. He cut the barb off the hook, carefully remove the lure so neither of the other two hooks would catch her. Then pulled it out of her mouth. He put a little antibiotic cream on the hole and that was that. Once the hook was out Lilly was back to normal—playful and jumping for joy that the pain and strange object was no longer in her mouth. She never tried to catch a fishing line again!

Lilly was very well-behaved. Except for being near cows, she hated them! She showed exceptional intelligence. She slept with me in bed and waited until I came home, greeting me by running down between the maple tree lane. I finally had a companion when Peter wasn't around. Lilly was something to get me away from TV. That may have been part of Mom's strategy in getting a dog.

Remember Trudy and Morris, the Jewish couple from NYC? About ten months after Lilly became part of the family, they came for a visit with her two young boys. I remember this visit because Morris smoked cigars and occasionally a pipe. Dad smoked a pipe before I was born. But after his first heart attack around age 45 he stopped.

Dad's old pipe rack held about five pipes. It was still lying around the house. The pipe rack was a square black wooden box, with racks for four pipes on each side. In the center was a hinged lid, the humidor, in which to keep the tobacco. Two of the pipes were high quality, one was a corn cob. I remember the better-quality ones were beautifully carved and looked very attractive, as far as pipes go. Anyway, on this visit, Mom gave the whole thing to Morris. I didn't care at the time but now wish I had kept at least one of the pipes.

Lilly liked all the attention from the family. The two boys were not used to having a playful dog around and loved her attention. Morris said she was beautiful. A great dog. Trudy loved her long reddish-brown coat. By this time their two boys, Sam (?—I should know, as I went to his bar mitzvah years later) and Jeffery, were big enough to wander around. The oldest was around seven. Jeffery about three. Lilly liked having them play with her, especially if I was at school or off somewhere. One day Trudy and Mom were busy in the kitchen. The boys were playing in the front yard. I was not around, likely at school. This story came from Mom when I came home.

Sam found more than enough interesting things to do in the yard and barn. Like me he loved exploring all the old junk, wondering what most of it was. The scythe, the large wheelbarrow, with steel wheels about three feet in diameter, old unexplained tools all caught his attention. Typical for his age he had little interest in what Jeffery might be doing.

When Trudy came out looking for Jeffery, he was nowhere to be seen. She started running around the property, no Jeffery. She and Mom started calling out. No answer. Then Mom heard a muffled bark from Lilly. But it was way down the driveway, so she started to run down. Remember, it was close to a mile long, lined with trees and spanning a brook that led to the main road. Now she was calling Lilly's name. A muffled bark was the response each time called.

She got to Sugar Hill Road and there was Jeffery, walking down the main road. Lilly had his left hand in her mouth. She was keeping her body between Jeffery and the pavement. She was trying to turn Jeffery back to the house and was pulling gently on his hand. If he refused, which he did, she remained next to him, gently pushing him to the side of the road, not letting him on the pavement. Mom almost didn't believe her eyes. It took several minutes to catch up and by that time Jeffery was close to the Clark farmhouse.

When Lilly saw Mom, she released Jeffery quickly and barked loudly once, then took hold of his hand again. Mom said Lilly was the best babysitter anyone could have. Trudy came running down the lane with Sam in tow. By now Mom had Jeffery in hand and was leading him back to the house. You can imagine the relief that literally overcame Trudy once Jeffery was in her arms. The mixture of emotions, relief, joy, anger and every other feeling that might fit the occasion ran through her.

Looking back on this, Morris was not at the house, but upon hearing about the adventure he looked to Lilly as a hero. He likely snuck her some extra meat from the evening's meal.

Personally, I liked the family. Morris was always joking. He had a very kind heart. Trudy, being a friend of Mom who was no longer in Co-Masonry did not fit the usual picture of one of Mom's friends. But she too was friendly, warm and affectionate. We were always welcome to stay in their apartment in Brooklyn when we were there, though we seldom did as it was a small apartment. Mom would sleep on the sofa and I in the boys' room on a cot.

Love,
Papa

T, I bet you would like to hear more about Lilly:

Lilly and I were inseparable. As mentioned, she slept on the foot of my bed, not on the floor. She joined Peter and I on our fishing trips and hikes or just playing around the yard. The only problem was that she hated cows. Whenever the cows came close to our property, she would go crazy. She would run into the field and start to chase them away. The problem was they belonged to Mrs. Clark and were in her fields! I tried to break Lilly of this trait but couldn't. We tried to keep Lilly in the house when the cows were in the field next to the driveway. Mrs. Clark knew Lilly hated cows and would drive them right to the corner of the pasture next to our driveway. Lilly went nuts.

Somewhere during our travels, Lilly mated with at least two different males in the neighborhood. One must have been a boxer mix. We could tell she was pregnant. As the day for delivery came closer, she started to look for places to have the litter. One evening Lilly didn't come for dinner. Mom and I started calling for her all over. Mom went to where we kept the wood in the porch on the east side of the house. She heard a slight whining coming from under the porch. She called me. I took a flashlight. There was Lilly, under the porch, next to the foundation. I grabbed an axe and started to tear up the floor of the porch.

We created a large enough hole and found Lilly lying there with a group of small pups—twelve in all. Mom got a warm blanket and put it in a box. It was a cold late autumn evening so it is doubtful if the litter would have survived the night. Mom carefully lifted out each puppy and put it in the blanket. Lilly was watching carefully. During the process, Mom found one of the pups was dead. She told me to carry it away so Lilly would not see it. We could bury it later.

Eleven living puppies remained. Even after we had taken all the living puppies and put them in the box, Lilly got up and checked the box. They say dogs can't count, but don't believe it. Lilly gently nudged each of the pups in the blanket, as if counting them. Then she went back to the hole in the floor. She was looking to see if there were any left. Lilly kept looking back and forth, box to hole and back again. Mom realised she was looking for the dead one we had taken away earlier. We don't know for sure, but it was hard to get Lilly out of there until the rest of the puppies started to whine because they were hungry.

The new problem was that Lilly didn't have enough teats to feed them all. We tried to help, but after a few days, Lilly looked worn out. A friend of Mom's told her we had to get rid of at least three of the puppies, so Mom grabbed three of the smaller ones and turned them over to him. I don't know what he did, but I do know they were disposed of. Lilly didn't miss them. By now she must have been relieved not to have so many hungry mouths to feed.

As the puppies' eyes started to open they would run into my lap if they weren't not hungry. Within a few weeks when laying down on the ground I was surrounded by all eight of the remaining puppies. What FUN! They would lick me, crawl all over me, jump on my stomach and run all around me. They were a mix of the dark red color of Lilly but also some light brown, and one was black and dark brown. The smallest was mostly brown and adored his mother. You could call him the runt of the litter. Lilly didn't pay much attention to him, yet if she was sitting quietly in a particular position, he would always be next to her copying her every move. If she looked in one direction, he would too. If she drank some water, so would he. He quickly became my favorite.

When the pups reached eight weeks old, we started to look for homes for them. Lilly had housebroken all the puppies before they left! In theory it shouldn't be possible for such young puppies to be housebroken, but they were. They never chased cars. Seldom barked. Every one of them was perfectly behaved according to all their new owners. I wanted to keep the little one, but we couldn't afford another dog. This would be a decision which would have a disastrous impact soon after. After having puppies around for months, it was soon back to just Lilly.

Meanwhile, Mrs. Clark had come up with a plan. That bitch would deliberately drive her cows right next to the fence. If I was not there to control Lilly she would start to chase the cows and Mrs. Clark would call the game warden and complain I had a dangerous dog.

One day after I came home from school, Mom received a phone call. The game warden said that Mrs. Clark saw Lilly attack and almost kill one of her cows. She would have to be taken. I went crazy. I got so mad at Lilly I kicked her and spanked her, then in tears hugged her like I was about to die! Lilly didn't understand the schizoid behavior. The game warden came. I tried to hold on to Lilly. Tears and screams were coming out of me. Mom had to literally hold me back so the warden could take Lilly. I have never felt such sorrow before or since, except one Christmas many years in the future.

I had lost Lilly! To me she was the greatest dog in the world. I also hated Mrs. Clark! I knew she made up the story. Sure enough, two days later Mom saw the cow that was "almost killed" walking in the field with no apparent injuries. Mrs. Clark was the subject of my loathing for the rest of my years in Connecticut. It is a feeling that remains for what she did the day they took Lilly.

A year later, the game warden told Mom he didn't kill Lilly but because of the stories about her. He gave her to the Seeing Eye Dog Foundation. The last I heard was she was a great seeing eye dog, one of the best they ever had. Now you see why I regretted giving up the runt of the litter. If he only stayed with me for another four months, he would have been the only dog in the house. But then again, I'm sure the awful woman next door would have figured out a way to get rid of him too.

Love,
Papa

Hi T:

Learning Photography.

I think this is the right place for this episode. I don't remember my Dad being around when the darkroom was created. I got involved with photography shortly after the separation and the divorce after we moved back to The Hill. It would have been before the move to Massachusetts.

I remember very little about the divorce. The grounds for the divorce were physical abuse—of me. During the proceedings I was brought into the court. The judge asked me who would I prefer to be with, my mother or my father. There was a brief hesitation before my answer came out. I thought of Dad and his temper, but Mom's drinking and smoking came into my mind too. All these thoughts raced through my mind. Finally, I said:

"My mother."

The divorce was declared, and Dad was ordered to pay child support. The only problem was Florida's child support cooperation with Connecticut courts was anything but stellar and it was a struggle to get anything from Dad.

Mom had been an amateur photographer many years before and still had the equipment stored in the attic. After becoming acquainted with Ruth, she found a renewed interest in photography.

The bathroom had two closets. One was the linen and supply closet and the other contained all sorts of junk. All that was in the second could be readily stored elsewhere, particularly in the attic closets. Ruth told Mom the second closet would be perfect for setting up a darkroom and Mom agreed. We moved in a small table. Then positioned the supplies, the trays for developer, stop bath, hypo, paper on a shelf and Mom's old Bessel enlarger. Ruth came over to check to make sure that the "darkroom" was truly light proof. We had hung black curtains around the door and installed similar curtains on the bathroom windows. The water bath was on a makeshift shelf with a hose over the bathtub. For loading the film on the rollers, black cloth bags ensured light tight environment. Finally, the darkroom was ready.

I was curious about Mom's knowledge of photography. She had picked up the hobby when she was married to Bernard before the war (WWII). Bernard had been a photographer but lost interest. However, he taught Mom how to develop the film and print the photos.

She had her 2 1⁄4 - 2 1⁄4 format Rollie, which was given to your sister. It took great photos. Hidden away in various boxes were not only her award-winning photo, but many photos of Bernard, her favorite subject, especially with his pipes. Mom had really gotten into this hobby, and according to her, won first prize in an amateur photo contest in New York City around 1938. If you find one of people walking down Wall Street, that is the photo which won her the prize. Her winning photo now seems gray and bland by current standards. There are also many photos of post-war France in her collection.

Through her, my interest in photography was started. Mom taught me how to load and unload the camera. Ruth and Mom taught me how to take the film putting it on the spools for development. The Rollie had only 12 shots per roll. When 35mm cameras became popular, I would have to re-learn many of these skills. But that would be in high school and another darkroom. Here on The Hill, after the film was developed, I would put the film in the enlarger and printed the photos.

I can't say if I was any good or not. I don't even think any of my early photos are still around. Still, it was a fun and enjoyable new hobby. The one handicap was that Mom was never one for producing sharp contrast. As a result, I never had sharply contrasting photos during these years. This had a negative impact for years to come, both in jobs and at college. It is one of the hardest things to get right.

Not until I took a class with a teacher who had learned from Minor White, famous for the Zone System, did I begin to take better-contrasting photos. Most of the high-contrast photos are of the river and the snow in winter. There are odds and ends of photos of the house too. The small photos of me under the age of 10 were taken by Mom and most of them were sent in for development before the darkroom.

Sometimes Mom would set up a shot, then ask someone else to take it. Since there were no light meters built in the cameras back then, the light meter was critical for a good photo. Mom used a hand-held light meter, which is still useful; it's in a brown case. When I was in college, I pasted a Zone System, black to white grade-scale, on the meter. This increased the quality of photos taken.

At this time, I asked Mom why she never took photos of the UFO's landing tracks years before. She told me she was afraid of what Dad might have done and didn't want any more trouble with him. Too bad—that would have been one of the most important photos she ever took.

We did become active in the Aerial Phenomena Research Organization (APRO) in the mid 1960s. APRO was interested in UFO phenomena (it no longer exists). Members would interview individuals who had any encounters. A kid who was about 10 years old who lived about five miles from the Hill took a polaroid phone of a UFO that he reported was about 20 feet above the trees in his yard. The photo is very blurred but shows a series of lights on the underside of the craft. One member had been part of a team that interviewed Mrs. Hill. Betty Hill and her husband, by then deceased, were abducted by a UFO while driving on a country road. The APRO member felt she was not intelligent enough to make up such a detailed story. He believed her. A member of the group reported his car being followed one night when suddenly he blacked out. He woke up about 10 minutes later, approximately 20 miles from the last section of the road he was on and facing in the opposite direction. No other explanation was given. Though part of the group off and on for a year, we never disclosed what had happened behind the barn in our yard. Soon Mom felt that APRO was not adding to what she considered important, so we dropped out.

Even now, I occasionally go out to take photos. Remember the photos from France? The tour guild thought they were wonderful. This is where that interest started. All that is left of the darkroom is the old enlarger its lens and the paper holder. The Besslers' bellows cracked and broke making it useless. The old paper cutter we have was used for cutting the photos once printed, but everything else is gone.[1]

With current digital photography, those things are no longer important. Digital makes photography much cheaper now. Besides, a photographer would "burn up" rolls and rolls of film just to get a few perfect shots. With digital the expense of film is gone and the ability to enhance a digital photo using the digital tools eliminates the hours spent in the darkroom trying to get the perfectly developed shot on paper. Old darkroom skills are slowly dying.

Love,

Papa

Hi T:

I need to focus on your grandmother. So much has already been said about her, but this may be as good a place to pick it up again. I will start doing flashbacks covering her childhood in future letters.

This was about the time in my life that Mom started to tell me about her background. It was usually over dinner in the kitchen. Then in the last months of her life, she told me a great deal more as we were attempting to tape her life story. We never finished but I did get a good start. Unfortunately, the tapes have been lost—besides who has a cachet tape player anymore?

Upon moving back to The Hill, the dining room became The Lakeville Lettershop, as the little office in Lakeville had long since died. The dining room looked every bit like an office. In one corner of the room were her two large gray metal filing cabinets. A secretariat was covered with invoices and papers. Under the dining table in the center of the room, reams of paper, both regular and legal, were stored. At one end of the dining room table was paper stacked next to an A. B. Dick mimeograph machine. More boxes of different size and color paper, books and other junk were on the shelves and stacked in corners of the room. A mini typewriter table was just to the right of the dining room table. One of Mom's straight-back chairs was in front of the old Royal typewriter, which faced the window looking out to the south. This way Mom could put manuscripts on the table to her left and type with good light coming from both the south and west windows. It also gave her a view towards the south or west, where she could watch the trees and wildlife in the backyard.

To keep herself amused she started playing psychic games with the trees and other living plants outside the house. Pausing on a typing job would give her a chance to experiment. There is a fun story about her "interest" in plants. By focusing on one tree or a particular plant outside the window she wanted to see if it could pick up on her mental projection. In later years, when I was in high school, she and I read *The Secret Life of Plants*, which described plants as being able to telepathically receive human thought.

Before reading the book, she noticed a pair of related trees at the fence line, about fifty yards to the south. The trees were against the fence and about 15 feet apart. I don't remember what varieties of trees they were, but one had big leaves and the other smaller leaves. May have been two poplars. Both had the same name, but differed in terms of the actual species, judging by the leaf size. Mom felt sorry for the small-leaf tree that was about 12 feet high, while the large-leaf tree was about 20 feet tall. She started sending positive thoughts out to the small-leaf tree. She would mentally say: "You are lovely. You need to grow strong and tall like your cousin a few feet away."

---

[1]   By the time this book was completed nothing remained.

I didn't pay attention, but about two years later, I did notice that the small-leaf tree had caught up with the large-leaf tree. By the time I was in high school, the small-leaf tree was a good three feet higher than its cousin. Mom claimed her positive thoughts caused it to grow. I never doubted her. We never cleared the brush or fertilized it, so there was no other reason for this exceptional growth of the smaller tree. Here was clear evidence of the mental powers one could have on plants. But at that time, few would have believed it.

Back to the Letter Shop work. Since we were alone on The Hill, I took charge of the A. B. Dick mimeograph machine. From then on, if there was a rush job, or a large job, Mom would type the stencils and I would run them off on the mimeograph. This way we were able to get some jobs done quickly.

If I had a school project, or if there was no rush, Mom would do it all. If there was a crash job, I ran the A. B. Dick. We started getting in minor jobs and would team up whenever possible. Some of the jobs were just local club notices and boring stuff. Others that came in were more interesting—or at least more of a challenge. With her work with the Salisbury Recreation Association and knowing a lot of influential people in the area, jobs were fairly regular, seldom overwhelming. Just enough to put some food on the table and keep some clothes on our backs. But Mom was never happy.

A common meal we'd have in those days would involve Mum frying an onion, adding a couple of chopped apples to it, then a can of tuna fish. Mixing a teaspoon or more of curry powder in a cup of milk she would pour it over the simmering onion/apple/tuna fish. The frying pan would then be covered and placed on a low simmer while some white rice cooked. This was a cheap meal as a can of tuna fish back then was $0.35. Apples and onions were also cheap. We had this meal as many and three times a week. We couldn't afford meat, except occasionally some chicken or hamburger. Milk was also cheap as Mom purchased raw milk from a local dairy farmer for less than a dollar a gallon. That was fortunate as once I was in high school a gallon a day was commonly consumed.

Mom wanted more than this life just barely above the poverty line. Besides, it her work was very boring. No challenge. No mental effort besides proofreading, which was something considerably below her capabilities.

At this time, we got interested in civil rights. Discrimination was of the quiet type in Connecticut, but in many ways nastier than the South—not as violent, but just as effective. We both became very active, which resulted in quite a bit of trouble. More later.

Mom was also trying to pull together some of the old AUM Masonic group members who had been active after Alice Bailey's death. They started a correspondence course. This included papers of the members. All were of an esoteric nature and included glimpses members had obtained while in various states of meditation. Since she had been the unofficial secretary for the groups in the early years, she felt the timing was right to put in an effort to get started again.

Somewhere in the files are the old meditation papers and study group sessions she pulled together. It has always been an internal debate. Should they be made available or kept private? If the latter, I am likely the last person to know of their existence. I do not want them to pass into forgotten history but am fearful of making them public. Mom always warned me they were powerful tools and should not be played with. I know she was worried about some of the members of the group because they would not be able to continue the "work" due to a lack of proper psychic defenses. This would be graphically brought to life years later, actually about three years before you were born.

Life back on The Hill was active in the house but nothing exciting.

Love,
Papa

More on Grandma

As mentioned, with Dad in Florida, Mom tried to start up the old meditation groups again. Mary Bailey, Foster's new wife only reluctantly supported *The Spirit of Masonry*, which was published under Forster's name. Mom's old friend, and a member of the inner circle, Norman Artist, was the ghostwriter for Foster's book. He also had an interest in your grandmother, especially after the separation. But Mom was not interested in Norman. What most people don't know is that Foster did not really write the book; Norman and others pulled together the unpublished papers of Alice related to Masonry. The notes were put together in a somewhat logical order producing the book, since Foster was not a Co-Mason but a member of "regular" Masonry, the group I now belong to. It was thought the book would have greater credibility if published under his name hopefully to gain a wider readership. It is available in some Masonic supply stores such as Macoy's in Virginia.

I need to plug in an aside about Macoy's. It was one of the largest Masonic supply companies on the East Coast, originally located fairly near the Grand Lodge of New York's building near 20th Street in Manhattan. It was a large store with equipment and regalia for just about any kind of Masonic function you would find in the United States. They had, and still do, their own publishing branch. All of the New York Co-Masonic lodges would get their supplies from the New York Macoy's.

A story got to one of the owners that at one of the Co-M meetings a woman was carrying a sword as part of her duty in the ceremony. It was not Marie Deraismes Lodge, but Phoenix Lodge, which went belly up in the late 1950s. At that time there were three Co-Masonic lodges in New York City. As the woman passed the Senior Warden's pedestal, she saluted him sharply with the sword, but not having a strong grip to accompany the brisk salute, the sword slipped from her hand and flew across the room, embedding itself firmly in the wall. Imagine the sword swaying back and forth as the lodge members looked on. Somehow this story got to Macoy's. From that Moment on whenever one of the women, including your grandmother, went shopping in the NY Macoy's the owners would refer to them as the lady sword swallowers. Mom took no offense. After all, where else could she get her 32o ring to fit a lady's hand?

Back to the topic of the changes in the Arcane School. Many of Alice's inner circle did not like Foster's new wife, Mary. Almost all had separated from the Arcane School and formed a group called Meditation Group for the New Age. There is a more recent group that took on the same name, possibly the child or grandchild of one of the original members, but it is not the same group. A pair of members were Homer Carnegie and his wife.

Homer was a former WWI army officer. While in the army Homer was asked to come up with a training guide for the soldiers faced with daily combat that would improve performance and mental attitude and he came up with a series of mental exercises and disciplines that improved moral and performance. It became a course for army officers.

Dale Carnegie had tried to start up a little performance-based training retreat which later moved to Hauppauge, New York. Mom told me Homer's work in the army, shared with Dale, was used in the little management training company Dale had created. It was Dale that turned Homer's army efforts into a book *How to Win Friends and Influence People* in the 1930s. This book became the foundation of the Dale Carnegie Foundation and fortune.

Homer never shared in the fortune resulting from the book. To this day few, if any, know that Homer was the hidden genius behind Dale Carnegie's work. Mom showed me Homer's workbooks, which he had developed long before Dale wrote the book to prove the facts she told me.

I knew Homer as a child. He and his wife would come to The Hill to visit and talk about the work. The last time Homer and Mom met was at his house in New York. Mom later told me

Homer had turned to her and told her that if he was not married, he would have proposed to her. Mom was a little shocked but very much enamored of Homer and his work. His comment gave her an uplift lasting for several years.

Other members of the old Alice Bailey inner circle were my godparents, Marion and Rohe Walter. Marion had tried to take over Alice's work when Alice died and was active in Ancient Universal Mysteries (AUM), Alice's Masonic group. She was able to contact DK, who had dictated the books to Alice. However, in the early 1950s, Marion came under psychic attack. She was warned by DK to stop doing this advanced work immediately and even more importantly never to attempt to do it again!

Marion was not capable of defending herself against the dark side of the force, to borrow the phrase from *Star Wars (n*ot exactly what they would have called it, but it fits). The dark side can be seen in the grotesque visions of the saints in some of the medieval artwork. You see demons and monsters attacking the soon-to-be saint. The same can be said of the Buddha when tempted by Mara just before Enlightenment. Mom said those types of attacks are real and can be deadly unless you can defend yourself. Marion could not. Rohe, Marion's husband did not want to take up the work for fear it may impact Marion.

One younger member of the group was Marcia Moore, who I stayed with when we first moved to Concord. She was capable but was more into yoga and raising her young family and did not want to be involved. Lillian Pepper was no longer capable of working with the group as she was in the nursing home (see the letter dated November 23, 2007). Norman Artist had just married Marjorie and was not interest in leading the group. So, there was no leader. Homer was the figurehead. Mom did the correspondence and the workbooks—in many ways she kept it going. Other members were scattered around the world such as Wei Tat in Taiwan. The group tried to stay together but died in the late 1950s.

Later Mom was approached by DK to take up the work on Masonry. She turned him down. There were rumors that others in the group were approached, but none wanted the responsibility. Most were aware of the dangers, they all knew what had happened to Marion. A few years later DK came to Mom again but was again turned down. At this time your grandmother was smoking heavily and drinking too much. She felt that those vices would open her up to psychic attacks. Yet, she always said how important the work would be, in bringing Masonry to the position in the world it had meant to be—a universal spiritual school for all mankind.

The last time DK came to her was when I was in high school. The drinking was heavier. Her mental state in no condition to take on the work. DK was rejected a third time. At one point in my life I had wished he would approach me. But my training in meditation was never sufficient to advance me to that level. Mom was not teaching me directly, only hinting at what should be done. I did briefly join the Arcane School later, but it never lived up to what were the hopes and dreams of your grandmother, or myself to be honest. Soon, being active in Co-Masonry myself and having some disagreements with my "mentors" in The Arcane School. I dropped out. When that occurred, I realized I would never be capable of receiving DK's messages.

Such are the choices and turns from the path that can occur as we progress through this "mortal vale of tears". Ah well.

Love,
Papa

Hi T, another flashback:

This letter should have come a little earlier but I'll put it here as this incident took place when I was about nine years old. For some years Mom had been teaching me to drive, mostly in our driveway. In winter I would take the driver's seat once in the driveway and drive up to the last corner before the hill to the house. But more importantly, backing out. Managing the right-angle turn just before the brook required considerable skill. Then over the narrow bridge over the brook, negotiating another sharp turn and the little hill, which took a good deal of speed to manage if there were snow on the ground. Once on the main road, Mom would take over. By the time I was 11 I was already confident in my driving a manual transmission, at least in my driveway.

When Mom and I moved back to The Hill jobs were critical. One of the more interesting jobs was at the Limerock Racetrack. Limerock is a great little Le Mans type track, lots of curves and challenging areas. The starting area was the flat straightaway. At the end of the straightaway is a hairpin turn, followed by "the Ss" and then you circle around the back of a hill. The track includes one dip where you lose sight of the cars in front of you, hoping they didn't slow down as you hit that spot. Then a dip under a bridge. The bridge allowed the car trailers, pit teams and press access into the track's inner circle.

The actor Paul Newman loved this track. His first win was at Limerock, though it was years after the events in this letter took place. Tom Cruise was also taught by Paul how to race at Limerock, among other places. Later there was a movie filmed there.

No massive seating existed around the track, but a wonderful hill overlooking the straight section is where hundreds of fans could watch the races and have a picnic. The straightaway, hairpin and the "Ss" were all very visible from the hill. A driver could accelerate to over 200 mph in the straightaway, then put on the breaks, downshift to negotiate the hairpin at about 15 mph. The sharp "Ss" were accompanied by bales of straw lining the track for the cars spinning out. This occurred often. New drivers, not that familiar with the track, often hit the bales, at least until they mastered the S turns.

Interestingly, Limerock was very close to The Hill. It was actually behind the property, a little over a mile as the crow flies, and over a hill. But the geological shape of the hills and forest made the cars sound as if they were racing by the little brook at the back of the property. Every race day one could clearly hear the cars as if they were in the backyard.

Mom was hired to type and print the press releases after each race. She would load the old Royal typewriter and the A.B. Dick mimeograph into the car. As close as the cars sounded, the roads to Limerock were in the opposite direction. First, we had to go down Sugar Hill Road, then right at before the bridge at the river. Winding around the hill along the Housatonic, taking another right that would eventually get you to the racetrack. Once there she set up a little office at the foot of the press box. If it was a slow day with only a few races there was no problem and she would leave me at home. If there was an endurance race, a 300-mile, or multiple back-to-back races, hourly updates were demanded. The reports would give the standing of the cars in a race, if crashed the number of the car and the name of the driver, mechanical problems, etc. On those days there was only time for Mom to type the results on the stencils. She couldn't run them off on the A.B. Dick mimeograph. And it was on those days that I would be brought along.

There was very strict rule that no one under the age of 18 was to be allowed on the infield pit area where the press box and information center was located. The press box was elevated over and slightly behind the pit crews. The pit crews were stationed by the straightaway, the most logical place for pit crews to be placed. The Limerock management hated me coming there. But there was nothing they could do! I was there to run off the press releases. They had no one who knew the first thing about mimeograph machines. If they wanted timely press releases on busy race days, I had to be there! Between running off the releases I would distribute them to the actual press box. No problem, just strange looks. If there was still time before the next release, or Mom was still typing it up, I would wander the inner areas getting a closer look at the pit crews through the fence. I never got in the way, but there where many who didn't like me being anywhere in sight.

The next year, management found a way to get rid of me. They bought an electronic A.B. Dick which would "save time" and make it unnecessary for me to be there. Mom was told not to bring me in the pit area for the first race of the year. It was a busy day with a lot of races scheduled, so Mom typed up the first press release and handed it to management.

"Who do you have to run this off? I don't have time to do it."

They looked at each other with no answers. They naturally thought Mom would do it. She told them she only had time to type the stencils. Someone else had to produce the hard copies. No one could even knew how to put a stencil on the machine. It became apparent that Mom could not do the utensils and run the A.B. Dick in a timely fashion.

There was only one solution. Off Mom went in her car. Back home. Pick me up! On the way back she asked:

"Do you think you can work an electronic A.B. Dick?"

I said, "If it is a mimeograph, I'll figure it out."

We got there in less than 15 minutes, around Amesville by the Housatonic River and back. After looking over the new machine—no problem. There was the usual stencil catch. The inking brush was slightly different, but easy to figure out. The electric controls just turned the drum. The paper trays were almost identical to the old machine. It was just the hand crank that was missing. It took me less than five minutes to figure it out. The only real difference between it and the manual in the dining room was the little switch which would make the drum go around.

The only "automation" was I would no longer have to turn the red handle around a hundred of times for each run. I would just set the counter to the number of copies, hit the switch and watch the printouts to determine when more ink needed to be added. After the Limerock Racetrack management made such great efforts to get rid of me, there I was again! Not only for that year but for the next as well. Though that year was the last.

A little side note. My favorite races were not the really fast racers but the modified street cars. The car that kept winning the most in those races were the old box-shaped Volvo. At the time they were my favorite car—a lot of fun. I loved being at the races. Never had paid the money to sit on the hill overlooking the track like the public. After being in the infield for three years, I just couldn't see myself as part of the paying spectators.

The last summer we worked at the track, I must have been about 11. On our last job Mom asked if I wanted to take the car around the track. After the races were over those friends and family who worked in the infield were allowed to take a spin around the track. Mom sat in the passenger seat as I pulled out to the roadway. Since we started in pit row, it was only a short way to the hairpin turn. Then we followed the S turns. Around the back and up a hill. Then as you reached the top of the hill, there was a sudden drop. For just a moment I couldn't see if there were any cars in front of me. Then the car nosed downward, under the bridge between the infield and the main road. Another right turn and then the straightaway. I pushed the car close to 100 mph before the hard-braking for the hairpin. Only twice around, but what fun. It was the exact track where Paul Newman learned to race!

Love,
Papa

134

Chapter 11

Connecticut Racism

Hi T, Let me introduce you to The Wilsons:

It was around the time I was 10 or 11, a woman in her early 40s and her three daughters were in need of a home. She was slender, slightly taller than Mom, and soft-spoken. Exceptionally poor, as were many of the Blacks in Litchfield County. Falls Village being a working-class village, it was a likely place to find something affordable.

Mrs. Wilson was escaping a bad and violent marriage in the South. She felt this section of Connecticut would be the best place to hide from her estranged husband. Falls Village would be her retreat from danger, *if* she could find a house there! The problem was, hers would be the first Black family in town. Back then, Falls Village was a poor village with many run-down homes. The few middle class families lived away from the town center, which was where she was looking to find a house. Most townies were lower working class, undereducated Caucasians.

The problem was that Mrs. Wilson could not get a loan. She was *only* a cook. *Only* a servant! To the wealthy families in Salisbury and Sharon she was unworthy. No way was she going to obtain a loan from any of the lending institutions in the area. The banks didn't want to touch her and there were no credit unions in the area. Black males, just as impoverished, were able to obtain bank loans, she was not. The reason? Simple, she was Black, uneducated, poor, a single Mom AND A WOMAN! No bank would help her.

There were a number of local social organizations, such as the NAACP, the VFW and other groups who might have been able to help her. But she was neither a member nor known to any of them, having arrived only a few months before. The local "do-gooders", the wealthy Connecticut upper five percent, who claimed to want racial equality, refused to help her. The reason was simple and repeated more than once:

"There are so many needy men with families."

The prejudice against single Moms was evident. Even rich women would use this as an excuse. What most people don't know is that Connecticut, and much of New England at this time, was just as prejudiced as the South, just not open about it. To this day I seriously doubt if Salisbury or Sharon have changed much. New England prejudice was to stab people in the back. They would outwardly claim "equality for all", just as long as that equality conformed to what their vision of how a minority should be, how they should act.

If an individual did not fit the stereotypical "ideal" Black person—humble, obedient, subservient—forget help. A single Mom, obviously, was unworthy. They made sure the poor, Black people, (actually the term negro was used then in polite circles, and nigger everywhere else) and Hispanics would never get ahead. The minorities might get help to survive, but only to the extent that allowed them to feed and clothe their families, ensuring they were kept in low-income menial jobs. Today the term "under-employed" would be used.

In schools such as Salisbury Central, all were placed on the "dumb" student track. If they showed any intelligence or drive, it was carefully discouraged. In the South, they lynched them; in the North, they just prevented them from doing anything more than surviving. And then *only* if they were good lackeys and servants. This was the late 1950s.

Somehow Mom go word of Mrs. Wilson's plight. Mom didn't have money but through the Lakeville Lettershop, she knew most of the people who did. She went to the local chapter of the NAACP. Would they be willing to give this woman a loan for a house? No. After all, she was only a woman. If she were married then that would prove she was worthy of a loan.

Repeatedly she would hear: "Besides, there are men who were in need."

Mom went to the various civic groups. Same answers:

"A woman should be married if she has children."

"As a single Mom she is certainly not worthy of a loan Where's her husband? Where's the father of her children? She should have stayed with him and have him support the children."

Mom was furious! After all, she was a single Mom—the only difference was she had a job in the form of a letter shop.

I got caught up in all this. I remember one time when Mrs. Wilson and her daughters were visiting The Hill. The girls were playing outside. I was listening to the conversations going on in the kitchen. I ran upstairs and got my piggy bank. I took it downstairs and gave it to Mrs. Wilson:

"Maybe this will help. You can have it."

Mrs. Wilson opened it up. There was $12.32 in it. She gave me a big hug and thanked me for the offer. Tears welled up in her eyes.

Since all the places with funds had turned Mrs. Wilson down, Mom took out a second mortgage on our house to raise enough cash for a downpayment on the place Mrs. Wilson wanted. That killed the Lettershop business in Falls Village, even more in Canaan, a blue collar and racist town nearby.

Soon the Lakeville Letter Shop closed and the secretarial service ran out of our dining room at The Hill. I was called a "nigger lover" in school. We were threatened more than once by phone calls and in person around the town. Sometimes cars would start up the driveway. We could see them coming from the top of The Hill but by the last turn Mom and I would be standing on our front porch with guns in our hands facing them. Our reputation as crack shots was well known. When they saw guns in hand and us looking straight at them, the would-be intruders beat a hasty retreat. This is how the Wilsons were able to move in, becoming the first Black family in Falls Village, Connecticut.

That doesn't mean all was peaceful. The state police had to patrol Falls Village for months, every night. Never before had they paid any attention to the town, except when there was a bank robbery up on Route 7. But now they had to be sure no one would torch the Wilsons home in the middle of the night.

The local sheriff refused to lend a hand. The local judge likewise refused to issue restraining orders against those who were threatening the Wilsons. I suspected one who was on the opposing side was Peter's father, Mort, but because of his fondness towards Mom, he kept it to himself. Still

I would catch little comments about "the niggers" who moved into town every now and again when I was at Rattlesnake Rest.

Of course, if anyone torched the Wilsons, most of Falls Village would have burned to the ground. The buildings were all old wooden structures, built very close to each other. This threat continued for years but eventually the likelihood of it happening decreased slowly, as did the patrols.

It was this incident that got me involved in civil rights. From that day on, I became involved in racial debates and arguments. When the protests of the 1960s stated, I was in the middle of many in New England; I was part of marches in Connecticut and western Massachusetts and became a student member of the NAACP. But more of those tales in future letters.

I returned for my 35th High School Graduation Anniversary. I contacted Mrs. Wilson's oldest daughter, M, whom I always had a mini crush on. She had been married, divorced and was now single. I met her for lunch in a little restaurant in Lakeville. It was a delightful lunch together; I thought we really hit it off well. As we walked back to our cars in the parking lot, I gave her a kiss on the cheek. "Not here; my younger sister lives upstairs and I don't want to cause trouble for her," M said. Evidence of racism still surviving in Lakeville in the 1990s. Little had apparently changed, even after 30 years.

We got in our separate cars to drive to her mother's house in Falls Church. Mrs. Wilson was well, only looking older. She took one look at me and gave me a big hug. She reminded me of the piggy bank I offered some 40 years before, saying, "I always thought you were a good-looking boy."

She was delighted to hear that I had finished college and been accepted into graduate school. I was sorry to hear that M had married Bobby P., the only Black classmate from my high school, but had divorced him a few years later. Too bad, I always thought they would be a perfect couple. The good thing was that she had a decent job in Hartford and was doing OK. I never asked, but I knew that M's daughter was the product of a rape by her stepfather, a closely held secret at the time. When she married Bobby, the child born as a result of the rape was already several years old. I never asked when I saw Bobby what the cause of the divorce was, but wondered if that child may have caused conflicts in the home. I did learn there were no children from the marriage.

Love,
Papa

Do YOU know TOU?

With the Meditation Group for the New Age dying in the early 1950s, Mom had a new idea that needed a catalyst. Like me, Mom was an ideas person, but not a catalyst. She would pass on her ideas to people who knew the right people—people who could do something to get the ideas moving from a concept to an actual project.

Norman Artist had been interested in Mom romantically. But Mom didn't want to get involved for a number of reasons, one of which was that he was not financially stable. Eventually he married a woman named Marjorie. This marriage proved advantageous for Mom.

Marjorie had independent funds and contacts in higher circles; she was a connector, someone who knew a lot of people. This was just the kind of person Mom needed to pass her idea on to. Mom's idea was to create a central place where all the world's major religions could get together and find common grounds from which to work. This would become a major source of world religious learning and a place promoting peace, especially between the various faiths. Most of the wars in the history of mankind have been started due to the ignorance and narrow views caused by fundamentalism in religion. Even Buckminster Fuller, the architect and futurist, felt fundamentalism was second only to nuclear war as the main threat to the future of humanity. This center would allow for the free interchange of philosophies, ideas, theories and general theology, hopefully taking some of the wind out of the fundamentalists. The idea was to find the commonality among all the religions. Mom felt strongly that such a center would eventually lead to peace, especially in the Middle East.

The idea was first shared with Norman. He liked it. Mom suggested he talk to Marjorie about it. Norman agreed. Marjorie was convinced it was a brilliant idea. The next step would be to find the right person to promote it. The solution was to bring it to a Mrs. Juliet Hollister, who apparently had considered something similar, just not in the details Mom had developed. Mom fed the details of the plan to Marjorie and Marjorie then passed them on.

Mrs. Hollister proved to be the right catalyst for the concept. In 1960 the Temple for Understanding (TOU) was started. Mrs. Hollister knew the right people, who had the funds and the ability to promote a vision. Mom's goals were being carried out by people with the power, influence and money—just the right kind of people who could make it happen. Yet to this day, no one knows your grandmother was the individual who had the original idea way back in the early 1950s.

The TOU quickly gained traction. Some of the individuals who participated in the founding of the Temple for Understanding included the Dalai Lama, Anwar al-Sadat, Pope John XXIII, even Eleanor Roosevelt. There were a number of delegates to the United Nations who got on board and several very wealthy benefactors were contributing to the organization. It even was getting positive press. Mom was willing to take a quiet back seat; she did want to become active with the Temple of Understanding, but would help by doing mass mailings and anything else she could. This allowed her to keep dropping hints which expanded her original ideas. I met Mrs. Hollister and became the official "student representative" for the TOU; I believe I was the first to be formally recognized as such. I used to talk about it in my school and elsewhere, especially with other students.

Around 1962, the TOU had a special dinner at the United Nations. The guest of honor was the then-ambassador to the UN from Pakistan, Zulfikar Ali Bhutto, who would become the Foreign Minister on his return to Pakistan. I was the only teen in the dining room. Mom was in the main part of the dining room. But being the "official" teen representative, I was just three seats to the right of Bhutto on the raised platform at the head table. I remember the gift given to him by Mrs. Hollister. It was a world map with a clock and a moving shadow indicating where in the world it was day or night. I loved that clock. I would see exactly the same one over 40 years later in a special room in the Department of Homeland Security Mount Weather facility, deep within a classified area, called Area B. (In xxxx [year] *Newsweek* published an article with public information pulled from various sources that basically disclosed most of the "secrets" of "Area B", much to the consternation of the George W. Bush administration.)

Zulfikar Ali Bhutto became the leader of Pakistan and tried to make peace with India and allow the separation of East Pakistan from India, which became Bangladesh. He developed ties with China and Saudi Arabia, but he angered Muslim extremists in Pakistan. This led to his being deposed and killed. His death saddened me as I remember the dynamic, kind person behind the persona. His daughter, Benazir Bhutto, had a very similar fate as her father.

As for the Temple of Understanding, they raised a great deal of funds for the building of a temple. I remember the design. It had a central conference center with six wings. Each of the wings would be for a separate religion. They would have their own educational programs and classes. The major religions selected were Hinduism, Buddhism, Judaism, Confucianism/Daoism, Christianity and Islam.

What was interesting is Tom's (my college roommate years later) grandmother contributed thousands of dollars to TOU for the building in Maryland, not far from the Potomac. When I moved down to the Washington DC area, Mom came to visit. She had the address and wanted to see where the TOU property was. We drove out there and found the right neighborhood but no indication of the address. We later found out it was off the street. The woman who owned the street property refused to allow access to the land. The temple was never built and the property remained vacant.

By the way, a Maryland policeman started following us as we were looking. I was given a ticket for having an expired license plate tag (the little year stickies you put on your plates was out of date). I swore I would not want to live in Maryland. Boy, would that change after I retired.

Love,
Papa

Hi T:

Dad had moved from the small rental house in Florida where I had visited him the first time. He was now living in a trailer park. I had no idea what trailer living would be like, but would find out soon enough.

After a few years in Florida, Dad met a much younger woman named Liz. She was in her late 30s and Dad his early 50s. Dad was a horny old man and a real charmer when he needed to be. After a few months of dating, he married Liz. Do you remember meeting Liz when we went to Florida the last time? They had lunch with us. She was married to a Mr. White, her fourth marriage, I think, but Liz has since divorced him and is now by herself again. What is important is that she is your step-grandmother. Interestingly, Mr. White was Liz' only divorce. The other three husbands all died on her—Dad from a heart attack. I never asked how the other two died. Liz had not been married before she met my father. She was not very good looking, but was well endowed. Her looks actually improved when she got older. By the time you met her she was a pleasant-looking elderly woman. She was over-weight but very friendly and with a good personality. I didn't really feel one way or another about my father's remarriage. Unlike in romantic comedies, there was no illusion about Mom and Dad getting back together! Home was a lot quieter without him. Besides, I felt better.

The next summer I went back to Florida. The trailer had a hanging extension attachment, as did most of the trailers in the park. Most people used them as a covered porch. It was screened on three sides with the main trailer on the fourth. They had put in shades and a bed out there for me. What hit me the most was the close proximity to the other trailers. This extension was within 15 feet of the next trailer. What was even more interesting to a pre-pubescent boy was that there was a teenage girl's bedroom facing my bed. Naturally, being a young boy, I did keep a watch on her room when she was preparing to go to bed. This would have been well after my bedtime, but the possibility of seeing something often kept me from sleeping. I would lie there in the dark looking out to the next trailer. This was not a deliberate peeking tom type effort; it was just I had no other choice—after all, my bedroom was facing hers. Since our rooms were in close proximity, it was an "unavoidable" view. I think she suspected something because she carefully closed her blinds before undressing. Rats!

Down the street in another trailer was a girl by the name of Sharon. She was my age, about 12, and quite attractive. I would tell Sharon about how beautiful Sharon Connecticut was and compared it to her. While I was in Florida for those two weeks, Sharon and I were kind of going together. I would go by her trailer and we would walk to a movie or a park together.

Her mother and father would usually be sitting outside their trailer to cool off. Most of the trailers at that time did not have AC. Her father only wore a pair of shorts and her mother wore a pair of shorts and a bra, not a swimsuit but a bra, which was quite revealing. This shocked me a little, but it certainly did not upset me. Wandering around the park it became obvious this was common dress for many of the women when the heat of the summer day reached its peak. On such days few could remain inside, unless fans were placed in the doors to circulate some air. Many of the residents would sit outside in the extensions or under shade umbrellas with as little on as they felt they could get away with.

On Saturday nights Sharon and I went to a local community center in the trailer park. There were very large numbers of teenagers there. We danced to the music, no DJ, just a record player with speakers. There may have been an age limit, but owing to the fact I looked older and Sharon was friends with the boy who checked everyone at the door, we had no trouble getting into this "teen" dance. There were adult supervisors who ran the refreshments table and generally watched the proceedings at a distance. If they felt a couple was getting too sexually suggestive, they would tell them to cool it. But they were in the front of the hall and couldn't see what was happening in the rear due to the crowd.

Chubby Checker's *The Twist* was the favorite dance that summer of 1960. It was being played over and over again in the center for the dance. Slow dance music allowed Sharon and me to dance close together, which was the first time for me and most likely her. We just looked around the room and imitated what we saw others doing. Neither one of us knew any formal dance steps. Slow dancing involved minimal movement while holding your partner as close as possible. Most of the fast dances were either twist like or just random gyrations.

There was one boy who was a very good dancer; it was evident he had lessons at some time in his life. In many ways he was the 1960s version of John Travolta long before *Saturday Night Fever* came out in 1977. Like Travolta he danced solo. We all gathered around as his captivating moves were fun to watch. Slowly, a number of concentric human circles formed around him to see what the next step would be, all encouraging him to show his best moves.

Sharon and I were in the innermost circle. The others started gathering tightly around. I soon realized the reason. The adult supervisors who had seen the star dancing just thought it was his usual performance. They could not see what was happening in the center of the circle. This was a pre-planned strategy. The music was turned up. The crowd was cheering loudly and applauding with the rhythm of whatever the blaring tune came from the phonograph.

Suddenly, one of the boy's friends pushed an unsuspecting girl into the circle. She looked to be about 15. Looking around she realized she was to be his dancing partner. Not thinking much other than that it must be an honor to be selected, she smiled and accepted the dare to partner with this outstanding dancer. At first, she danced a little, trying in vain to keep up with his moves and rhythmic steps. Soon, a select group of boys positioned themselves within the inner most circle, a few feet apart from each other. She was surrounded. When she was near one of these boys they took one of her arms and begin to spin her around in one direction or another. Each time one of these boys touched her they "accidentally" unbuttoned part of her blouse. The main dancer was constantly taking her arms and twirling her around so much that, at first, she didn't realize what was happening to her. Once the buttons were fully opened they pulled at her blouse. She was unable to stop them. The cheers and music was so loud, her shouts for help were unheard by the chaperones.

Soon her blouse sleeves were pulled off. Only her bra remained above her waist. The next target was her shirt. Her dance partner gave her another swirl into one of the boys' arms. The catch above the zipper was half undone. The next move ended with her in someone else's arms. The zipper was totally down. She was flipped backwards in the air as a typical 1940s move which caused her shirt to fly off with just the slightest pull by one of the girls, who was now contributing the striptease. Another girl unhooked her bra, which was quickly removed. She was embarrassed, but when she tried to cover up, the boy who started the dance in the circle would grab her hands and do a very sensual twist around her partly naked body.

Soon the main dancer spun her around again and lifted her into the air. When in the air, someone grabbed her legs. Off came her panties. Now she was totally nude except for her shoes. The boy was forcing her to dance in ways that would expose all of her to the crowd. Everyone was cheering. The loud music prevented the chaperones from any awareness of what was happening.

Sharon said this boy was famous for doing this to girls who didn't expect it. The victim's arms were held apart to prevent her from covering her breasts. Every now and then someone would pick her up in a dance move. The twist music allowed lead dancer's legs to go between hers, while his holding her hands continue preventing any attempts to cover up.

Just about then the lights flashed. In another minute the music stopped. The adults were suspicious of what was happening. The crowd broke up. The evening dance was at an end. As Sharon and I left quickly, as the girl was trying to find her clothes and put them back on before the adults could see her. Sharon told me she had heard about these episodes. She was thankful she had someone to go with who looked older allowing her into the dance. It was usually the girls without a date who were selected for the treatment we had just witnessed. I always remember it as "the Florida Twist." Will send more letters when in Canada.

Love,
Papa

Hi T:

Special mailing from BALPEX the Baltimore Stamp show where the GWMSC (George Washington Masonic Stamp Club) holds their summer meeting.

The last letter mentioned Liz, your step-grandmother in Florida. Now to tell you a little more of the normal things about visiting Dad and Liz.

Dad did not have a TV; radio was the dominant form of entertainment in the trailer. I remember his favorite program, every morning it was the Arthur Godfrey radio show. I liked it too. Arthur Godfrey, the "Old Redhead," was a delightful character on CBS radio. He had a CBS TV show, which I do not remember seeing, but his daily radio show I remember. It remained on the air until the early 1970s. His two primary sponsors were Chesterfield cigarettes and Lipton Tea. His guests were from a wide circle of entertainers. It was interesting that Patsy Cline, Tony Bennett and Marilyn Horne, the great Met Opera singer, were promoted on the show. Established stars were also invited. Bing Crosby and Perry Como were two who seemed to enjoy being frequent guests. Godfrey would only occasionally sing while playing his ukulele. His favorite style of songs were Hawaiian. When seen in photos he is often wearing a Hawaiian shirt. He was also fond of polkas.

Godfrey was famous for his broadcast of the FDR's funeral where he began crying on the air. In the eyes of America, or should I say "ears" since it was radio, it made him human. America fell in love with him that day. I liked his humanity. So did Dad. When his show came on we would sit and play cards or dominoes, if Dad was willing to play. Other options were solitaire or just build little structures with the dominoes when Dad was not interested in a game. This visit with Dad, listening to Old Redhead, was my most enjoyable time with him. The main reason was that listening to the radio prevented him from bad-mouthing Mom or being critical of me.

Paul Harvey who died at around 90 was another person Dad liked. Harvey would pick a story in the news and elaborate on it with the words: "and now for the rest of the story." His conservative opinions were popular. The Paul Harvey News was broadcast on over a thousand radio stations. I understand he was a friend of J. Edgar Hoover and of Senator Joseph McCarthy. You can imagine why I did not like him. Even at 12 years of age I found him narrow-minded. He was very critical of anything he did not approve of. Most things were black or white, with nothing in between—a problem that has consumed our current citizens.

When not playing cards Dad would start an argument about Mom. He would ask pointed questions:

"Is she still drinking too much? Is she sober enough to feed you? Does she still hang around with her drunken friends?"

I would try to defend her but that would just get him mad. After a few days it would start to get to me.

I did have a very bad habit back then. I picked my nose. The problem was I didn't carry any tissue so I would deposit the findings under the armpit of my shirt like it was a handkerchief. Well, you can imagine it created a mess and my shirts would have to be washed. Liz, in doing the wash, gave me a strong reprimand. It broke the habit of me putting the boogers on my clothes! Still, Liz was kind to me. I liked her despite the scolding I received about bad habits. She would try to fix meals I liked and she acted as a good buffer between Dad and me. When she was around, Dad was nicer to me. This would significantly impact Mom and me later, more negative than positive, and for reasons I will explain.

Dad liked to go for fast walks and often wanted me to go with him. I'm not sure if it was the fact that I was not in good condition, with my flat feet, yet to be diagnosed, or the heat in Florida, but within a few blocks I would develop pain in my legs. This was followed by a stomach ache, like cramps. I would complain I couldn't go any further. He would become furious. I couldn't help it, it hurt to move! Dad and I would return to the trailer. He verbally brow-beat me for the rest of the day. I was a "fat weakling who couldn't even keep up with his father on a simple walk." Needless to say, any ego I had was totally destroyed by the time he was finished. Not fun.

Between his digs at Mom and his complaints about me, I did not have much fun in Florida, except for time with Sharon. Since Dad had married Liz, the separate trips to Bush Garden, going fishing, or just seeing other sights in Florida were greatly reduced. I don't blame Liz, just Dad for not waiting to take both of us anywhere other than the local beach.

Mom would tell me every time I returned from Florida that I would attack her just like Dad did. After this visit I was not encouraged to visit again. Frankly, I had little desire to visit. This was the last time I would see my father alive. It was too bad, because he could be nice when he wanted to. But his bellicose spewing turned him into an annoying gadfly. I will always be thankful his anger was never again expressed in a physical attack. The divorce must have taught him that lesson if nothing else.

Love,
Papa

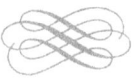

Hi T – ready to rewrite history or at least add to an ongoing story?

I'm going to describe your grandmother's life in flashbacks. These may not be frequent but will come every now and again. They fit here because it was during these years that Mom started to tell me more about herself. Later when we moved to Falls Church, VA, I tried to collect a verbal autobiography on tape but it was never completed. Her life was just as strange as mine so it will be fun.

Your grandmother was born on April 10, 1912, in the wilderness of New Mexico. She was the second child in the family. This was only months after New Mexico had become a state (in January 1911), becoming the 47th state. Mom said if she had been born before statehood, she might have had the choice to become a Mexican citizen. Rightly or wrongly, she thought prior to becoming a state, people born there would have the choice of citizenships. Well, no threat of that happening as there was no Spanish spoken in the household. Based upon what she found out later, she was born in a little dugout in the flatlands of New Mexico. The only help her mother had was from a woman down the road who acted as a midwife. There were no doctors or hospitals within days of the homestead.

I bet you don't know what a dugout is! My grandparents moved from Texas to New Mexico with the idea of homesteading a farm. This was when a family would be given or could purchase land cheaply for the purpose of turning it into a farm or ranch. Your great-grandfather was a farmer. The land settled on was very green for NM and had the potential for a good farm, but while your great-grandfather was trying to turn the land into a profitable crop-bearing venture, there was no money to purchase wood or supplies to build a house.

While clearing and plowing the land in hopes of bringing in a cash crop, they dug a long and wide trench in the ground on top of a hill and covered it with corrugated aluminum sheeting, curved to keep out the rain. This was where they lived. Your grandmother was born in a hole in the ground. No wonder she loved Tolkien. Mom liked the dugout. If you needed a new shelf or a place to keep things, you just dug a hole into the dirt wall! I know she continued to live in the dugout until she was at least three years old. I don't ever remember her mentioning a house ever being built. After many years of trying to make a go of the farm, and with the birth of a third child, Forest, they gave up on NM. After moving back to Texas, her sister Sug, real name Joan, was born.

Your grandmother's first clear memory was when Uncle Billy Tunstall's horse-drawn wagon pulled up one rainy evening in 1915. Your great-grandmother was part of the Tunstall family from Virginia where she was born. Her family had left Virginia in a covered wagon in the 1890s and moved to Texas. Mom was curious about Uncle Billy and the wagon. She snuck out of the dugout to look at it. In the buckboard section was a person lying down. His legs were moving. Mom sunk back inside.

When she got inside, her Mom was yelling at Uncle Billy. Mom had never seen her mother in such a fury. She treated that side of family as if they were holy. This is what she remembered her mother saying:

"Get him the hell off our property, Billy. I don't want that no good anywhere within 100 miles of this farm."

Mom didn't understand what was going on. She liked her Uncle Billy and wanted him to stay. Her mother continued:

"I don't care if he is hurt, you get back in your wagon and get out!"

Uncle Billy climbed out of the dugout and did as he was told. He drove away with whoever it was laying in the back of the wagon.

Your great-grandmother then turned to Vern, Mom's older brother, to explain what happened. Mom listened carefully and remember it like it happened yesterday for as long as she lived.

"Now Vern, don't you believe all those dime store novels and all that nonsense about Billy the Kid being killed by Pat Garrett. It is all a bunch of bull. Pat killed a boy named Billy that was set to look a little like Billy the Kid. Pat was the only one who knew the truth. He told everyone it was Billy the Kid. But the real Billy the Kid moved to Texas on the Tunstall ranch and still kept getting into trouble. I will not let Billy the Kid into my home! I don't care how shot up he is."

Think about this. Billy the Kid was theoretically killed in 1881. But this was around 1915. If it was Billy the Kid, he would have been in his 50s. The so-called history of Billy the Kid is an example of history being written by those who desire to control it. There was no one else who could identify Billy the Kid other than Pat. He had put Billy's name down on the death certificate.

This is not totally a new theory. There were several rumors of Billy's survival. It would have been easy for Billy the Kid to change his name and take a job on a ranch in Texas. After all, he had been known as Henry McCarty, William Bonney and possibly a number of other aliases. Also, the Tunstalls had a previous history of attempting to help Billy. John Tunstall was killed by a pair of Irishmen during the Lincoln County War for siding with Billy and Billy became one of the ranch hands who worked for Texas Tunstall. He reportedly was involved in an ensuing vengeful gun fight that killed a number of men. During the fight Billy was wounded in the leg. It would not be surprising if something similar happened on that rainy night in 1915. Billy was likely still hot-headed. Most likely he got into another fight and another Tunstall extricated him from danger. I don't know if this is true, it is just what your grandmother told me. It is up to you to decide.

Jumping forward now to an interesting trip to NYC...

It was around 1962. Mom was still very active in Marie Deraismes Lodge. We still went down to New York almost monthly. She may have been the Worshipful Master again(?). I was certainly too old to be babysat by Aunt Gladys. When we could afford it, we would arrive early, which would allow me to pick up a half-price ticket to one of the Broadway shows. After all, the Lodge was on West 52nd Street, only a few blocks from most of the major theaters. The timing was perfect. The matinees usually started between 1:30 and 2:00 p.m. and lasted about two and half hours. That would allow Mom to attend the meeting and talk Masonry with anyone who was staying after the formal meeting was over. Most knew I would come back once the show was over.

One of the most memorable shows that I saw was *Stop the World I Want to Get Off* starring Anthony Newley who wrote, directed and starred in the show. It was showing in the Shubert Theatre on 44th Street, about 10 blocks from the Lodge. It was easy to get a single ticket for half price. I got one in the orchestra seats—perfect! Just as I was about to go into the theatre I saw a sign posted outside:

"Mr. Newley is indisposed and will be replaced by his understudy for this performance."

Upon seeing this, many in line started to approach the box office for a refund. After all it was Newley who "made" the show. I didn't care. It was a show. I wanted to see it. The playbill had an insert. It said the roll of Littlechap was to be played by Joel Grey, who had become famous when he played the emcee in *Cabaret,* winning both the Tony and the Oscar for that roll. But that was in 1966. This was his second appearance as a main character in a Broadway show. At this time, he was still relatively unknown but that afternoon he became a major hit. Not sure if this got him noticed but the standing ovation for him lasted at least five minutes.

Another interesting point about the show: Sammy Davis, Jr. recorded three of the songs f: *Gonna Build a Mountain*, *Once in a Lifetime* and *What Kind of Fool Am I*. Each of them were major hits as singles by Sammy. I loved *Lumbered, Nag! Nag! Nag!*. The romantic closing song was

Someone Nice Like You—a sweet song. Later I got the record and must have played it to death. I still remember the routine from the *Nag!* song:

"God created woman some several years ago..."

Fun times! Might explain why I still love Broadway shows, even off Broadway and Off Off Broadway shows like *Avenue Q* and *The Toxic Avenger*, which we saw together.

Love,
Papa

Hi T:

We had moved back to The Hill by the beginning of the next school year. I got word that Billy—remember Big and Billy from Lakeville?—had been killed. His mother was not paying close attention while driving. A school bus stopped to let off kids and she slammed on the breaks. There were no seat belts back then. Billy was thrown head first through the front window. His head was crushed between the hood of his mother's car and the bus' rear bumper. This hit me very hard. I just didn't know what to say to Big.

Later that same week, one of the parents of another student died. Then, the next day, Mr. Nania the music teacher, who was about 42, died suddenly of a heart attack. His daughter was in the same grade as Peter and me, just not in the same classes. I heard about his death as I got off the bus and screamed:

"Let it stop NOW, or else God take me and no one else!"

My friend Peter was with me when I shouted this after learning about the music teacher. The whole school was in a state of shock. Many of my friends looked to me as the stable one. I think some actually thought I stopped the deaths by my declaration to God to take me rather than allow anyone else to die.

I was too upset to go to Billy's funeral. I have since regretted not going. His mother was in a severe depression, blaming herself for his death. Big's attitude in school began to change. He became withdrawn and even stopped talking to me. Mom went to visit the family after the funeral to try to console Billy's mother. The relationship I had with Big never recovered completely. His grades started to decline and he started to get into fights and hang out with the rougher crowd. Soon, he was no longer the Big of my earlier years. I don't think we ever did anything together again until high school.

Peter and I became closer. We would always ride the bus together in the mornings. We would talk about baseball cards. I loved to collect the Yankees. If I still had the cards I had back then in the late 1950s and early 1960s, they would be worth a small fortune. I had several Mickey Mantle, Elston Howard and most all of the team. My favorite was Yogi. I had the whole team for one of the years and a lot of other players of that era. When I went to college, Mom threw out all the old collection. Likely the current worth of that collection would be close to half a million or more. Not the last fortune that would escape me.

Peter and I would often talk about popular music. Johnny Cash was just becoming really popular. Elvis was on top, but never really my favorite at the time. I listened to Ricky Nelson, who I knew from the Ossie and Harriet TV show; Ossie and Harriet were his real parents. The boys David and Ricky played themselves on the family sitcom. It was a typical 1950s show where families were perfect and the Mom stayed at home to cook, clean and raise the kids. When Ricky became a singer, he had a huge following from TV, helping him to become a star. Most had followed him since he was about five or six on the TV show.

Peter loved Tennessee Ernie Ford's *Sixteen Tons* and would play it loud. That was possible on the bus since one of the last gifts Dad had given me was the very first Zenith transistor radio. It ran on batteries! It was black, with a gold handle. I would hang it on a nail or tree limb if I was outside. It was about 7" x 5". I kept it for years. I even had it when I drove a cab in Manhattan years later. When I went to Boston U for graduate work, the radio was returned to Connecticut. Years later, when visiting Ruth, I noticed that her boarder had it. Mom had given him the old Zenith. Still working after 20+ years.

With the Lakeville Letter shop closed and work being done out of the dining room as mentioned, Mom was getting restless. Soon there were to be some big changes in our lives.

Love,
Papa

Hi T:

More stories from Falls Village. The bus would pick up Peter and me at a stop by Barnie's house. Remember Barnie—the old recluse in the broken-down house? He was dead by then, but the house was still there. Peter lived two doors up. The "M"s lived down the opposite street.

Mr. M. was the music teacher for high school. I had taken piano lessons from him, but only for a few months. He had three kids. The oldest was Joel, who was in the high school, then Claudia a freshman. The youngest was still in grade school, behind Peter and me by a year or two. Joel was a bit of a bully; he liked to pick on me because I didn't have anyone to stand up to me. Peter had his older brother Robbie who had dropped out of school.

One day Peter and I were playing with something while waiting for the bus. Joel wanted to see it. Peter said, "don't give it to him". When Joel came over to me, I threw it to Peter. Joel punched me hard in the stomach. I felt I couldn't breathe. It was five minutes before I began to recover.

About three months later, the youngest M wanted to play with Peter and me after school. Neither Peter nor myself wanted any part of him. Peter and I walked to my house. As we turned into the driveway, we looked back and saw Joel and his younger brother following us. It was late autumn. We could see them through the trees. Peter and I thought Joel was going to pick on us for not letting his younger brother play with us. Out of fear of bellicose Joel's truculent behavior I went inside and got my 22 rifle. As they started up the maple lane, I came out with the gun telling them to get off my land. Joel speciously tried to convince us that they just wanted to play. Peter and I didn't believe him. He hadn't wanted to be with us before. We didn't believe his spurious plea now. They left.

That night Mom got a phone call. How dare I threaten their perfect son with a gun! We had a family meeting. The Ms refused to accept Joel had ever hit me. After all, his father was the music teacher and a model of the community. Needless to say, I was in trouble. Even Peter got lectured by his Mom.

The next school year, the bus stop moved further down the road. I now had to walk about a mile to get there. We were the first stop. The bus went by the river and over the steep hill to first pick up the Folkes' kids. The Folkes were a Black family at the foot of a hill on the Lakeville side. Mom was friends with the Folkes as they often worked for the same rich people, Grace as a cook (which I understand she was exceptionally good at) and Mom with her secretarial service.

After another 200 yards down the road, the bus would pick up the Galleo boys. One was about my age and two younger. The Galleos had moved into a beautiful house that was part of a large farm, next to the Belters' farm. I was never sure if the Galleo family owned, worked or leased the farm.

The next stop was to pick up John Belter who was in the same grade as Peter and me, along with his sister, his younger brother and cousins, I think there were about five Belters in total. John was my classmate all through elementary and high school. All the Belters lived in adjacent properties and the combined farm. What was interesting was the Belters boys played on the high school basketball team, usually as forwards. John was the tallest, around six foot two and his cousins were around six foot, all good players. There would be games when there would be three Belters playing at the same time, but that was years later.

Back to the bus. Robbie was Grace Folkes' granddaughter. You met Grace on our trip to Connecticut, she was the elderly Black woman we visited. Robbie was younger and was very pretty. She was shy but had a wonderful personality when given the chance to be herself. The problem was the Galleos were terribly racist, as were many Italians back then. The older Galleo boy would call Robbie a nigger and would pick on her, forcing her to move to the back of the bus. More than once I told him to lay off.

One day he was getting nastier, trying to pull up her dress. I grabbed his shirt:

"If you bother Robbie every again I'm going to personally knock your head through this bus window."

My advantage was I was bigger than him. Robbie was still scared of the Galleos but from then on she would sit in the seat in front or behind Peter and me. During that year she looked to me as her protector. As for the driver—he just smiled.

When Grace visited Mom, Robbie would come with her. I would tell her stories and play games with her while Grace and Mom talked. She looked up to me as a big brother. I didn't know it until we visited Grace years later that Robbie had a huge crush on me. One look at the photo of her ex-husband and daughter, an adult in the army, it dawned on me that she had married a white man. She must have been looking for someone like me who protected her. She was attracted to a man who resembled her guardian angel when she was a small, frightened ingenue.

I did see her one summer during college. She turned into a beautiful toothsome young woman. She and I talked for a while. I was dating JJ at college so I didn't dare thinking about asking her out—a regret, looking back. It would have been wonderful being with her for a few hours. I felt her attraction for me was still very strong. But where could I have taken her without getting those "looks" from the local rednecks?

The movie theater in Canaan had been closed for years. There were no fast food places like MacDonalds or Burger King anywhere around. The sit-down restaurants in Lakeville or Salisbury would not have welcomed us. The only option would be take her for a drive. The thought of taking into the fields near my house crossed my mind. But what then? Lay out a blanket, talk but most of all make love to her deep into the night. It was a beautiful thought, but I didn't want for her to carry an emotional burden that would result. I am sure she would not have resisted. Maybe that is another reason I didn't ask. I probably would have fallen for her in an instant. By the way she looked at me with her beautiful, longing eyes, she might have been having the same ideas. All those thoughts ran through my mind at once. Looking back on it, in many ways she reminds me of Charlene, your stepMom in my senior years.

Love,
Papa

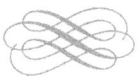

Flashback, T:

The other day when we were talking about cities I remembered something I should have written about last year, but can fit here.

While Mom and I were living in Lakeville we visited one of her friends in Atlanta, Georgia. Mom's friend was Dale Going. I think she must have been part of the Arcane School, but not a major participant. She married Commodore Going and moved to Atlanta. Mom and I flew down for a visit.

They picked us up in a nice car (Jaguar?) and took us to their ranch style house in the suburbs. The house was beautiful. A modest upper middle-class home, about 10 rooms and plenty of land on a hill with a great view of the valley below. In the distance the outskirts of the city could be seen. The large driveway led to a four-car garage. Next to the driveway was a stone wall three feet high separating the lower driveway from the main floor of the house and a field gently ascending from the wall for perhaps 70 feet or more.

When we got out of the car two boxers came bounding towards us. I immediately started to play with them. I noticed that one had gold teeth. When I asked about it, the Commodore told me the dog had a rare gum and tooth disease. "A dog without teeth will die," he explained, so they took him to a special dentist for dogs and had gold teeth implanted in his mouth. It was the only dog I ever saw with a $10,000 smile. This would have been before 1960! Shows the Goings had money!

That weekend one of the Goings' relatives was coming for a visit too. They were a family of three: father, mother, and son about eight or nine years old. I was about 10, maybe 11. Apparently, the boy's grandfather had died and left his grandson a 10-gauge, three-shot pump-action shotgun, which was at the Goings' home. It was a beautiful semi-antique gun; it may have been the first pump-action 10-gauge made. The boy's father and mother were pacifists and neither had ever handled a gun. They did not like the idea of their son getting one from his deceased grandfather, who specified that the grandson should have it. However, they did not want to appear unappreciative.

Mom suggested I could teach the boy how to shoot. We went out to the side of the driveway and stood on top of the stone wall with our backs to the pavement. It was the perfect spot for target shooting. The top of the stone wall was a good three to four feet wide and flat. The field was level starting at the top of the stone wall for about five yards, and then gently sloping upward. I placed three tin cans about 15 yards away, partly up the slope—in this way missed shots would just go into the ground. I showed the boy and his father how to load the gun and told them to space their feet apart and how important it was to hold the gun tight to the shoulder.

"Be prepared for a big kick that will force you backward if you are not ready."

The boy didn't to pay attention, he just wanted to shoot his gun. I handed it to him, then showed him how to take off the safety. He turned sideways and pointed the gun towards the cans. His feet were only a little distance apart and he was loosely holding it to his shoulder. Totally unprepared, he pulled the trigger. Bang! He went flying backward off the stone wall. Down he fell three feet landing on his butt in a puddle. I watched the gun go flying upward. Jumping over I grabbing it before it hit the stones; I felt it was more valuable than the kid! Of course, the shot hit about 10 feet wide and several feet short of any of the tin cans.

The boy, although soaked, got up and was crying slightly because he landed on his butt, rubbing his sore shoulder. Some of the tears may have been from his embarrassment. The father watched his son's epic failure and decided he wanted to try. At least he held the gun tightly, with the feet apart. Bang! He was closer but still off. I explained the gun sight again. He tried again. Boom! Still he missed, though it was a little closer. I was about to give more advice when he turned to me:

"Well, do you think you can do any better?"

I reloaded, stacked the three cans on top of each other. Bang! All three went were hit, but the one on top flew up. As it was still flying upward, I quickly pumped the gun. Bang! I hit the can in the air, making it fly higher. I pumped again. Bang! Perfect hit. Higher still! The third shot made it fly about fifteen feet in the air. I smiled to myself then turned back towards the kid and his dad.

I handed the boy the gun and walked back into the house. The father and the boy couldn't look me in the face for the rest of the weekend. I didn't say a word, but Commodore got the picture of what had happened. He was very nice to me the rest of our stay, as was Dale. I got the impression they were not very fond of the visiting relatives.

When we moved back to The Hill, Mom asked who I would want to take care of me if something happened to her. Reflecting on the house, the boxers and the respect I received from them after the gun lessons I felt the Goings in Atlanta would be the best of all Mom's friends. Likely the most stable. She wrote to them to see if they agreed with the arrangement. Mom told me they were delighted with the idea. The plans were put into place, but never needed. We exchanged Christmas cards and an occasional letter for a year or two. Sorry to say I never saw them again.

Love,
Papa

Chapter 12

Off to the Bay State

Change in locale, T:

The dining room Lettershop was not going well and the odd jobs at *The Lakeville Journal* or the private school failed to satisfy Mom. She wanted something different; she needed a challenge.

Mom had some very unique talents that were not being used. She had moved from LA to NYC with her second husband, Bernard, who was working for Alice A. Bailey. This was in the late 1930s. Bernard not wanting children and her desire to be a mother led to multiple arguments. By the early 1940s she broke up with Bernard. Being single, she needed a job.

She knew a little about the oil business from her first husband, Sarsfield, and she used that knowledge to get a job at brokerage house. It was Merrill Lynch (ML), one of the foremost brokerages a decade or two later. As with most women, she was hired as part of the secretarial pool but she wanted to become one of the analysts. In case you don't know, that is someone who determines which securities / stocks would be good investments. She never had enough to invest herself but she read *The Wall Street Journal* and was familiar with *Value Line*, the stock analysis publication. She also had enough intuition to pick good stocks for other people.

When WWII broke out, many of the security analysts who had been working for ML were drafted into military service. Mind you that was WAY before ML added "Pierce Fenner and Smith" to their name. ML had no choice. They needed individuals who could take on the vacancies being left by those men going overseas. This resulted in your grandmother being given a position and taking over numerous accounts. According to her, she was making a fortune for her clients. By 1944, she had proven herself many times over but still she earned less than half the salary of the remaining males, who due to age and being exempt from the draft, remained in the firm, doing the same job. She walked into the boss' office and demanded she be paid the same her counterparts. Her portfolio of clients stocks were as good and even superior compared with other analysts. She deserved equal pay. The next day she got her answer. She was fired!

Fast forward to the 1960s. She always remembered the fun she had investing. She contacted her old friend, Marcia Moore in Concord, Massachusetts. Marcia had been the youngest member of Alice Bailey's inner circle and part of the Meditation Group for the New Age. Marcia's father was Robert Moore, who with Earnest Henderson, founded Sheraton Hotels. Mom knew Robert. She convinced him and Marcia to introduce her to Ernie.

Ernie had a significant influence in an investment firm. Mom persuaded Ernie she would be perfect for managing accounts. This was during the summer, when I was off from school. She made several trips to Concord. We would stay with Marcia, Simons, her husband and their kids—Loulie, 11, Chris, nine, and Johnnie, seven. I didn't fully understand what was going on, but was fine meeting new people.

It was shortly after I started the sixth grade that Mom announced she had gotten the job with the Investment Trust of Boston. We would be moving to Concord the next month. I think it was October. After a few weeks of pure panic and packing we moved to Concord. Mom would commute into Boston on the train whose tracks were right behind the duplex we moved into. She could walk to the train station, less than a mile in town, or take a bus.

Mom was excited. She had the chance to really succeed in life at a job that was both a challenge and used her intelligence. More importantly, it was something she really liked to do. The other bonus was I would be going to much better public schools and I might be able to improve my grades and abilities. I was tired of the old teachers and lack of inspiration at Salisbury Central. This was a move I was looking forward to. It was going to be a new life for both of us.

Love,
Papa

Hi—interesting: the Concord letters are almost to the month Mom and I moved there!

My first day at school was one I will always remember. I remember back at Salisbury Central Elementary most of the teachers had been there for years. The rare teachers under 50 were married and their husbands worked in the few middle class jobs in Canaan. Some were professionals in the Lakeville / Salisbury area: lawyers, store owners, dentists, MDs, etc. There were very few young or inspiring educators.

I walked into this new school and was introduced to the counselor. He showed me to a class of sixth graders. The school had about four or five sixth-grade classes, which were ranked based upon the students' abilities. The best students were in the "best" classes, and the "dummies" were in a class that would have had the lowest income and most challenging students. Mom told them of the reading problems but that I was decent in math. I was placed in the middle class with a decent mix of good students. It was hoped the reading skills would improve in this section.

In the classroom there were round tables, four students seated at each. I was introduced to the class and shown a seat at a back table next to a kid named Skip. There were two girls sitting at the table with us. Back then, and at that age, boys and girls rarely talked to each other unless they were a "thing." I shook Skip's hand and noticed his clothes was a little like mine, not YUPPIE but more of what you would find in working-class families, jeans and a dark jacket. Black was all the rage for "cool" kids. I looked around the class. There were a large variety of posters and interesting all sorts of object on the shelves. Most related to science. The room was well lit and very bright. Very different environment than Salisbury Central. It looked like a fun classroom.

Then I looked at the toothsome teacher, Miss Madden. She was not very tall, blue-eyed and blonde, perhaps about 22 years old. A relatively recent graduate with a degree in education. This was her chance to prove herself as a good teacher. She loved it; she was full of energy and her eyes were always bright. She was also gorgeous. My eyes must have looked like the wolf in the old Warner Brothers cartoon, when he sees an exquisite woman (remember Jim Carey in *The Mask*). I turned to Skip and said in a rather loud voice:

"Back where I come from we don't have teachers like that!"

I was becoming a dirty old man in the sixth grade already. The whole class heard me. The boys snickered. Skip laughed. The girls looked shocked. Miss Madden turned bright red.

After class I told her where I came from we had mostly old and unattractive hags who were boring as anything. I apologized for the loudness of my comment, but did not apologize for the comment itself. I told her she really was the most beautiful teacher I had ever had. She blushed again. But we became friends. I really respected her as a teacher. She proved to me over the course of the academic year that she was an exceptional teacher.

Love,
Papa

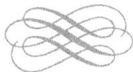

Hi T:

This is mailed earlier because of a new post office cancellation (giving a talk in MD).

The first day in school continued and it is a horror story. The duplex we were going to move into was not ready for a few months. Our furniture had not been moved. We were staying with Marcia. I knew the street she lived on and how to get to the bus stop and which bus to catch to get to school. The problem was on the way back from school the bus took a different street. Unbeknownst to me it ran parallel to the one I thought the driver was going to take and there I was waiting for my stop. We went through the main section of Concord. The road I was expecting to be on was Musketaquid Road. But we were traveling on Elm Street, a main road—not one I knew. I kept looking for the intersection of the street with Simon Willard Road. I didn't see it. I felt it should not have been more than a 10-minute trip from school. But no street sign labeled Simon Willard Road.

I stayed on the bus. Fifteen minutes went by. Soon we were in West Concord. Then further out of town and over 30 minutes from the school. Still no Simon Willard Road. The bus was slowly becoming empty. When the last kid got off, I was desperately trying to hold back tears. The bus driver turned to me asking why I didn't get off. By this time, I couldn't hold the tears back any longer. I didn't know where I was and I told him I didn't recognize any of the streets we were traveling on from the school. I told him I had just moved to Concord and was living with friends of my mother's in the last house on Simon Willard Road.

What I didn't know was that Simon Willard didn't intersect Elm Street. I should have gotten off at either the intersection of Musketaquid Road or Wood Street and Elm, but I didn't know either as the return stop. The problem was Wood Street changes on the north side of the intersection to Simon Willard. I failed to see it because I was looking the wrong way.

I should literally have gotten off at the third stop. Now I was way out of town. The bus driver was a little upset, but seeing me in tears, at my age, and realizing how embarrassed I was, and evidently close to panicking, he started to feel sorry for me. He looked up Simon Willard, turned the bus around, and started back to town.

He pointed out the corner where I should have gotten off. After thanking him profusely, I walked to Marcia's house but much later than expected. I guarantee you when I got off at Musketaquid and Elm, I looked at every house, landmark and even where a there was little upslope in the road. I was never going to forget that spot again! Marcia and the kids were wondering where

I had been. I told them I missed the stop and traveled to the end of the bus route. At least I arrived home, almost two hours later than expected.

When we did move into the new house, the bus was a different bus, going out Main Street, yet it was so close to Elm. I could have stayed on the same bus and just gotten off one stop early and walked to my new home. When spring came, I often walked to school, a little less than a mile. Gave me a good excuse to stop by some of the shops in a little strip mall on the way home and buy some Fruitloop gum.

Love,
Papa

Dear T: Happy Halloween!!!

Concord was Mom's dream of becoming successful in terms of professional fulfillment. More importantly, financially and psychologically it was a life changer. As mentioned before, she knew both Robert Moore and Ernie Henderson, who had significant interest in the Investment Trust of Boston, where she began to work.

The origin of her connections came from Mom's close relationship with Robert's daughter, Marcia. Marcia had been the youngest member of the inner circle of the Arcane School. Robert was interested in esoteric studies, encouraging Marcia to explore the world of meditation, yoga and comparative religion. Though never a member of the Arcane School himself, he was interested in their work and studies. Marcia had become an expert in astrology and incorporated the concept of esoteric astrology as found in the Alice Bailey books. It was through Marcia and their common interests and training that Mom met Robert. He got Ernie to "convince" them to hire Mom as a security analyst. As I began attending a new school, Mom was beginning a new career. She hoped it would turn our lives around and lead to a rewarding career with the money, influence, associations and resulting power, which would help us to a better future.

While living with Marcia's family I got to know her extended family. Marcia lived within walking distance from her father's home, down the street, up and over a hill, a right turn and then the last house on the right, before the next intersection. It was also the most beautiful house. Chris and Johnnie were constantly going over to their grandparent's home and I would often go along. The house was magnificent. It was not anything like a "McMansion", but a split-level ranch-like, and far more beautiful. The driveway had a six-car garage and was separated from the house by a covered walkway to the kitchen.

The main door opened into a foyer. The first thing I noticed was a large wooden panel directly in front of the door. When opened, it had the controls for all the lights in the house. Each could be turned on or off from this control panel. You could even dim each fixture to whatever level was desired.

Next, I noticed a huge living room just to the right of the panel and the open dining room further back. Both had large picture windows facing the backyard. The dining table, once extended, had over 12 of us seated together for a Thanksgiving meal. The kitchen to the right from the entrance was down a walkway next to the exterior wall towards the driveway, a good 30 feet away. As far as a kitchen, it had the best stove money could buy, a large island and lots of storage space. The freezer and refrigerator were new. In other words, it was a dream kitchen.

The stairs to the lower level were between the control panel and the living room. Downstairs there was a ping pong table. This is where I learned to play. There was a host of other items such as a TV, lounge, chairs and a very large recreation area. In the back was a glass-enclosed area where Mr. Moore indulged his geology hobby. He had a variety of saws for cutting all varieties of rocks, as well as polishers and all sorts of other equipment where he could cut and finish the rocks or minerals for gifts or for his own amusement. This was my first introduction to geology and fossils.

Behind the ping pong table and near the "rock room" were a set of sliding doors that led out to the patio and the large yard going down to the corner where two roads met. There were extra rooms there used as guest rooms on the lower level and a beautiful bathroom.

Back upstairs, left of the entrance, a hall led to the master and other bedrooms. I don't remember how many there were but I would guess at least four. Quite a house, one I remember fondly. It was far ahead of its time when built in the 1950s. Even when I visited again 50 years later, it was still a wonder, still beautiful.

Take care,
Papa

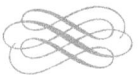

Dear T:

We only stayed a few weeks with Marcia, but would often get invited back for different occasions. By that time our apartment became available, we had become a regular fixture in Marcia's home. We moved into the house on Main Street. A duplex with the family/owners on the other half. This move was filled with the expectations that finally we were going to have a great life ahead.

The house was great—three and a half levels, if you counted the large cellar which was unfinished with a dirt floor, and an attic that was accessible via a pull-down ladder. There was a large kitchen and a nice-size dining room in the middle of the duplex. The living room was a good size with a circular bay window and seat overlooking Main Street.

The living room is where we had the TV and Mom would conduct her Co-Masonic meetings there later. A large fireplace at one end of the living room would be helpful in winter. On one wall hung a magnificent floor-to-ceiling mirror in a gilt frame. You could tell the original room took up both halves of the building. Since it was converted to a duplex, the original living room was divided in two. I suspect this was true for the dining room. The kitchen must have been added when the second apartment was created.

Upstairs, Mom took the bedroom facing Main Street. I had a room in the middle of the floor with easy access to the back stairs going down to the kitchen. There was a back room beyond mine which wasn't used. Mom had a mini letter shop set up there but I don't remember her doing any work in it unless it was for the meditation group. It was the smallest of the rooms with windows looking out on the backyard and a fence separating the property from the railroad tracks.

The "yard" was tiny. Since the house was a duplex, the entrances were on either side, rather than in front. As a result, the yard was really only a walkway to the "front" door. In reality these front doors must have been created when the house was split for two families. I could tell where the original door must have been and was actually part of the other half of the duplex, now the other family's living room. It gave you the impression the house was once one of the grand Victorian-style upper-class residences for those who wanted to live near the center of the town when it was built, likely around 1900.

There was a high wooden fence in the backyard only a few feet away from the back of the house. From the upstairs windows you could look over the fence and see the train tracks that led towards Boston.

Concord was a major commuter stop outside Boston. Many of the middle and upper middle Concordians commuted to work. You could not see the Concord station, but you could tell it was nearby—likely it was less than 300 yards away from the house. Mom would take the train into Boston for her new job. This was still the heyday of commuting by rail, which extended far beyond the subways/metros. Grand Central Station in NYC was still busy with over a million commuters a week passing through. But no longer! This is unfortunate for the environment.

The owners of the house lived in the other section. They were a typical couple with twin boys, younger than me, and a girl about two or three years older than me. We got along but never became friendly. I did have a mini crush on the girl, but only briefly. Let's face it, a pre-teen boy who is just becoming aware of the opposite sex will have a crush on any female he is in regular contact with!

The location was ideal. It was on the western side of town and within walking distance of the shopping area of downtown Concord. Another advantage was that it was away from the tourist area. I could ride my bike to the downtown activities in just a few minutes. I liked to hang around the old fashioned drug store where there was a soda fountain counter. I could have an ice cream soda, float, malt, etc., purchase chewing gum and read the latest *Superman*, *Batman* or *Justice League* comics. The variety of stores in this section of town were more interesting than the tourist trap in the town center. The establishments mostly smaller than on the main drag with a little convenience mart, gas station and the town's undertaker. The larger stores in the town center including clothing, jewelry, antique shops and numerous others were blocks away from this mini shopping area.

Just a little further was my school. I didn't usually ride my bike to school; the bus was easier. The corner where I caught it was one of the last stops before it reached the school. The ride was short. Sometimes on nice days I wouldn't bother with taking the bus home, but would walk home and then I could stop by the store to see what new comics had come in or buy a new pack of Beechnut Gum. Actually I preferred it to the more popular Juicy Fruit. I loved the color strips and different flavors of Beechnut. Occasionally, I would get a pack of Top's baseball cards with the usual large piece of bubblegum inside. I traded Boston players for Yankees—this was perfect as I was still a Yankee fan. It was 1960 and I had most of the Yankee cards.

Once I got to know some of the kids from my school this was an ideal place to live, play and have adventures. The biggest problem was it was all too brief.

Love,
Papa

Dear T:

The rest of the Moore family was very interesting.

Marcia had three brothers, a mother who was always most ladylike and kindly, and her famous dad. Marcia was known for her knowledge of yoga and astrology; she learned much of her yoga in India and had made several trips there to study. She held multiple outdoor yoga classes at her house every week. If the weather was bad, the living room furniture was pushed aside and turned into a studio; a little tight but doable. Most were held in the back/side yard which was flat and surrounded by trees. Would you believe, when Marcia forgot about a class or was late, your grandmother would take over and conduct the class?!? When she wasn't doing yoga, Marcia would do horoscopes for people for a fee. She had her own study to work on the charts, long before computers.

Marcia's husband was Simons. Simons considered himself a great intellectual and world traveler. He had written one book about his travels, which qualified him for the authors club he wanted to join. The other members I met never considered him very highly. I often thought Marcia most likely wrote the book for him. Simons considered himself very spiritually advanced and a perfect match for Marcia. The problem was he was insanely jealous and very domineering, not only with Marcia but the kids as well. He was a very poor example of spirituality, taking into consideration the way he treated others.

After Mom and I moved, our visits to the Moores were frequent, as I've said. I remember one New Year's Eve, we were all sitting around the TV watching the celebrations at Times Square. Johnny, who was only seven, wanted to stay up with the rest of us but Simons thought he should go to bed around his usual time, about 9 p.m. on weekends. Marcia and the rest said New Years was an exception, let him stay up. Simons finally consented. Mom and the others thought he would drop off before the ball dropped in Times Square.

At about 11 p.m. Johnny was exceptionally tired. Sure enough he started to drop off to sleep on the sofa. Marcia was going to carry him to bed but Simons stopped her. He picked Johnny and placed him in his lap. Johnny was very drowsy. While in Simons' lap he occasionally nodded off. Simons would shake him awake. Simons told him he had asked to stay up until midnight and he would make sure Johnny would stay awake. Every time it looked like Johnny would begin to fall asleep, Simons started shaking him. Johnny was so tired, he couldn't keep his eyes open. If he started to nod, Simons would shake him harder in his lap, forcing him awake again. Soon, it was apparent Johnny was in a great deal of distress.

Mom looked disgusted but didn't dare to interfere. Marcia started to plead with Simons to let her put Johnny to bed. He was unrelenting! Chris and Loulie just slipped further back in the room and tried to hide. I was next to the fireplace and had the most direct view of both Johnny and Simons. I did not like what I was seeing! Johnny began to cry.

Simons declared: "You wanted to stay up with us and now you are going to stay up whether you want to or not."

Johnny cried even more. As he fell to one side or another Simons would violently pull the opposite arm to get him upright again. This continued until midnight. It was one of the most uncomfortable evenings I have ever spent with another family. I was concerned about Johnny. When the ball dropped at Times Square, Marcia and my Mom said:

"Enough, now let's put him to bed."

Simons was proud of his accomplishment. He had taught Johnny a lesson. The rest of us were appalled by what we had witnessed. Johnny had endured both mental and physical abuse. It was the most obvious case of child abuse I had witnessed in a family up to that time. It was the first time I had seen a so-called "spiritual" individual show his real colors. It became an important lesson for me. Since then I have been very doubtful whenever I meet a "guru" or other self-proclaimed spiritual being.

Guess what, most of the gurus I have come across during my life followed Simons' mold. Few have been genuine.

Love,
Papa

Dear T – more on the Robert Moore:

Marcia's father Robert was the head of the clan. He was tall, thin and an impressive individual. I always liked him. Later he would teach me cribbage and some other card games.

Robert L. Moore based upon speculation, repeated by himself, was a former member of the Lafayette Escadrille, though I could never confirm this claim. Now for a little Wikipedia information:

"The Lafayette Escadrille (from the French Escadrille de Lafayette), was a squadron of the French Air Service, the Aéronautique militaire, during World War I composed largely of American volunteer pilots flying fighters. The squadron was formed in April 1916. The first major action was at the Battle of Verdun, May 1916. The squadron suffered heavy losses but its core group of 38 was rapidly replenished by other Americans arriving from overseas. So many volunteered that the Lafayette Flying Corps was formed, many Americans thereafter serving with other French air units. Altogether 265 American volunteers served in the Corps."

I love the movie *Flyboys* because it was about the Lafayette Escadrille. As far as I know, Robert was part of the replenished Escadrille. I have not been able to find his name on the original roster. According to him he volunteered early in WWI and loved flying, though he was shot down three times. He may have been shot down first at during the Battle of Verdun but recovered quickly. The next time he was shot down he was able to land the plane in a field and survived. No major injuries, just multiple smaller wounds, enough for a Purple Heart if he had been part of the American forces. The last time he was shot down grounded him for the remainder of the war.

At Thanksgiving Robert would pull out his old flight suit. The WWI flight suit was a neck to ankle fur-lined leather one-piece jump suit. It was a challenge just to climb into it. After placing your feet through the legs, the arms had to be extended through the sleeves. Then with considerable effort, as the suit was both bulky and tight, you would pull it up your back and shoulders. Then you buttoned it up. There may have been a zipper, I doubt it. Next would be thick gloves to keep hands warm during the flight. The last item was a strange leather helmet; it looked a little like the old football helmets from the 1920s but was also fur lined, at least partly.

The suit had the Lafayette Escadrille emblems on the front. Robert would tell the story of his flying while proudly displaying the suit. Then as he was telling about the last time he was shot down, he turned the uniform around for everyone at the table to see. On the back was a diagonal strip of machine gun bullet holes from near one shoulder down to his hip. I think the count was seven bullet holes. Most ended up in Robert.

As he pointed to the ones which must have penetrated into his back he would declare:

"This almost killed me. How I landed I'll never know, but somehow I did."

Two of the bullets were so close to his spinal column, located in the lower third of his spine, that they were never removed—the doctors were very reluctant to operate so close to the spinal column for fear of paralyzing the patient, so it was decided to leave them where they were. Though it is doubtful if such a decision would be made today, it worked. He lived well into his 90s. That whole episode and the way he told it put him on my list of true heroes.

Here is where his story takes in interesting turn. The last time he was shot down was after the United States had entered the war. According to Robert, while recovering in the hospital in France, a young officer who was part of the American dough boys ended up in the bed next to him. Ernest Henderson was part of the American Expeditionary Force. Being part of the infantry, he ended up wounded on the frontline. He happened to be carried back ending up in the hospital bed next to Bob. Little did anyone know what impact that would have on both of them in the future.

With nothing but time to waste, Bob and Ernie would spend hours talking over their ideas for after the war. First priority would be to get out of their respective hospital beds and into the beds of every good-looking woman in France and Germany. From the smiles on Robert's face while we would be playing cribbage and talking about his post war escapades, there was a strong feeling he was very successful at finding a lot of young, toothsome women. Remember, at the end of the war many of the women had but one choice to earn money. Based upon the smirk on Robert's face when reminiscing gave the impression there were many a young woman who earned their pay, much to his delight.

What will follow in the next letter will be the unofficial history, one that was only shared inside the families. It was never mentioned in the books about Bob or Ernie.

Love,
Papa

Dear T:

Part Two – Bob and Ernie

Here is the unofficial origin of a famous company. My mother told me this story. She asked me not to repeat it as it might destroy the image of Robert and Ernie. But since they are all deceased, I feel I can share it now.

She and Robert were drinking pals at various times. I assumed this tale was a result of Robert's defenses being lowered by a considerable consumption of alcohol. There is no way to verify if there was any truth to this tale. So, look at this letter as a marvelous example of quasi-historical mythology, if not fact.

As I mentioned in the previous letter, while traveling around France and Germany, screwing every pretty skirt they could get, Bob and Ernie came across a Germany paper company. The company was trying to rebuild a business after the war. It had a most unusual product: paper clothes. Bob had never seen this before. Both thought it rather unique. The items that really caught the attention of these comrades were the paper tuxedoes; they were perfect for a special night out and they could then be thrown away the next day. The paper tuxes were certainly much less expensive than purchasing a real tux, even less than a rental. If one was careful, it would be perfect for a single night at the opera or concert hall, where you could mix with the upper classes— as long as no one touched the suit! According to Bob they looked decent enough to be able to pass, as long as you were not exposed to direct sun light or a close inspection.

When the Bob and Ernie came back to the States, they tried a variety of schemes to make money. Nothing took hold. Then, as the Depression broke out, they got together and remembered the paper company back in Germany. Could they make use of the product to raise funds for other business adventures?

They contacted a variety of undertakers around Massachusetts, asking how much they would charge a customer if the corpse was buried in a tux. Well, the price was very high. What if they might be able to get a tux for under $2, would they be interested? Most said they would.

Bob and Ernie went back to the same paper company they discovered after the war. They asked how much the paper tuxes were. I don't know the exact amounts, but each tux was about a nickel in US currency yet as much as a thousand of the inflated reichsmarks, the German currency. Remember this was during the early years of the Depression. They put in an order to the company to make thousands. All were shipped to the USA.

Once they arrived, the paper tuxes were sold to the undertakers for $1 or more per tux. Not bad—over 2,000 percent profit for each one. The undertakers would put them on the bodies, and charge double or more what they paid Bob and Ernie. The The Weimar Republic was on the verge of collapse at this time, in 1930. Hitler's Nazi party began to win seats in the Reichstag. The few businesses that survived were thankful for any business deals that could be made. According to the story the Germany company was saved due to the orders.

Soon there was enough money for the purchase of the old Stonehaven Hotel in Springfield, Massachusetts. Once purchased, they made major renovations. But that was just the beginning.

With additional funds they bought another hotel, remodeled it, and then a third, and so on. The snowball started rolling until it became an international giant. They named the first hotel Sheraton and as they say, "the rest is history."

The official records of what happened is[2]:

"Sheraton began in 1937 when two entrepreneurs, Ernest Henderson and Robert Moore acquired the Stonehaven Hotel in Springfield, Massachusetts. They soon expanded their holdings to include properties from across the United States. In 1945, it was the first hotel chain to be listed on the New York Stock Exchange. Sheraton expanded internationally in 1949 with the purchase of two Canadian hotel chains. The 1960s saw the first Sheraton hotels in Latin America and the Middle East. In 1965, Sheraton opened its 100th hotel. The multinational conglomerate ITT purchased the chain in 1968, after which it was known as ITT Sheraton."

What is missing is the question: where did the money come from to purchase that first hotel? Now you know the answer. What I can't figure out is what happened between 1930/1932, when they raised the cash and the purchase of the first hotel in 1937.

The Sheraton hotel chain was taken over by ITT, but Bob remained as the source of institutional knowledge. At the time I was babysitting his two grandsons he was one of the richest men in America, but on first impressions, you would never have known it. That is why I liked him.

Now you can see how Bob Moore could afford the house he had.

Love,
Papa

December (late sent due to illnesses)

Dear T – more on the Moores:

Robert (Bob) Moore and his wife (I cannot remember her name) had four children, three boys and one girl: Billy, Robin, Marcia and Johnny. The latter was the godfather of Marcia's son, Johnny. The siblings were an interesting collection of personalities. This will provide a brief introduction to the Robert Moore offspring.

As mentioned before Robert Moore lived within walking distance of Marcia. I was over at his house often, for dinner parties, ping pong and a lot of other things. In the process I met Marcia's three brothers. I never saw them all together at the same place and time, but over the next few years, all would drop by their parents' home when I happened to be there.

---

[2]   From: The World of "Mr. Sheraton" There are variations of this history on wikipedia and elsewhere.

The oldest was Billy Moore. He was married with children at this time and was constantly trying to create an innovative way to make his own fortune, usually without success—at least as far as the rumors told it. I was told he had a number of failed adventures, many out of the country. One was rumored to be a gold mine in South America. Another was a hotel in the Caribbean and any number of other "investments." Billy was associated with a series of lost fortunes, much like Donald Trump, when examined closely. I only met Billy once at one of the major family dinners, it may have been Thanksgiving. I never saw him at Cuttyhunk, the summer retreat, or other family gatherings. I got the sense he was considered the black sheep of the family. I had heard "Daddy" bailed him out of many of misadventures.

Johnny, the youngest, was the more studious. I first met him when he had just graduated from law school. Then he passed the bar exam. With the help of his father, he got a job with Sheraton. I understand he did quite well. When ITT bought Sheraton some years later, Johnny was retained as one of their attorneys. I always liked Johnny. He was intelligent, always considerate of me and others, and never looked down upon anyone, a trait he learned from his father. Johnny, for me, represented the stable member of the family. I do not think he ever got married.

Many years later, I was at a convention in Boston. I drove to Concord, first to Marcia's old house. It was still there at the end of the lane, almost unchanged from 40 years earlier. Then I drove over the hill and into Bob Moore's driveway. I knocked on the door. Johnny answered the door. I greeted him by his name and he looked shocked. When I told him he knew me, a doubtful expression was displayed on his face. I told him go back in his memory 30-plus years.

"I used to babysit Johnny and Chris," I said.

Then I mentioned my mother's name!

"Oh, my goodness, you must be Walter!"

I was immediately invited into the old house. We sat down and had a long conversation about families and all sorts of other things that had passed during the intervening years. Joining us was his other brother, Robin.

Robin Moore was the most outrageous of all the siblings but very successful. He was most known for his books *The Green Berets*, *The French Connection* and *The Happy Hooker*. At the time I met him (1959), he was running back and forth between the states and his hotel / mini resort called The Blue Lagoon, which was located on the southern side of Haiti.

There were many stories about Robin. I have to think most were intended to promote his reputation. Here are some. At the time it was *rumored* that he earned extra money from the Haitian government by being a bounty hunter. Whenever a dangerous criminal escaped from their prison, the police would hire Robin to get the escapee "dead or alive" (the former being more profitable!). Again it may be another family legend but I was told by one of the kids that Robin would go into the Haitian jungles with plenty of weapons and a carpet bag. He would return to the police to get his reward after delivering the carpet bag, which would contain the head of the escaped prisoner. It appeared he got a bonus if only the head was returned rather than a live individual—after all, live prisoners cost more money than dead ones.

Remember, I do not know if this is story is true, but it was one of the myths circulating about Robin. More to come about Robin and the rest of the family! His summer visit to Cuttyhunk was certainly memorable and perhaps one of the most outrageous true stories about him. I witnessed it!

Love,
Papa

Dear T:

I was still living with Marcia and the kids in April. What was happening was we had a day off from school which I did not expect. Being new to Massachusetts, I didn't know about Patriot's Day. Nor was I familiar with the huge Concord / Lexington celebration. I had ridden my bike to the Concord's Minuteman Bridge but still didn't know any more than what was on the memorial plaque on the stone where a bunch of British were killed and buried. There was the famous Minute Man statue on the other side of the bridge towards the swampy area. I never paid much attention to it.

This was my first Patriot's Day. Since it was a day off the night before I watched Jack Parr's The Tonight Show. I loved The Tonight Show when Jack was host. I stayed up the night before thinking I could sleep late the next morning—after all, I was sleeping in the guest room. It looked out on the marsh and further down, the brook running through the woods. It never occurred to me that the brook continued flowing towards the Minuteman Bridge. As the crow flies, the bridge was probably less than 300 yards away. If I followed the standard streets it was a long way away, perhaps a mile and a half. By road, one had to go into town, around the Concord center, turn left, then continue towards the battle field. That was the only way to the bridge I was aware of. It never occurred to me this was just one giant circle which ended up close to Marcia's house.

I was sound asleep in bed when at 9 a.m. BOOM! I jumped up from a deep sleep to sitting up wide awake in an instant and shaking like a leaf. What the HELL was going on? Then over and over again BOOM! BOOM! BOOM! A whole series of shots happened. I could tell it was not a hunter. The boom sounded like a cannon. I thought something or someone was starting the Revolution all over again.

"Damn, someone is shooting at the house!" was my only thought. I looked out the window to see if there was any damage; nothing visible. I looked to see if any of the treetops were hit— nothing! Dressing as quickly as possible then running to the kitchen to see if anyone else was a scared as I. Everyone was calm as cucumbers!

"What's going on?"

I think it was Chris who answered: "Oh, that's the Patriot's Day celebration by the old bridge; you know, it is just the other side of the woods. We just can't walk there directly because of the swamp. It is a big deal and lots of things will be going on."

That was enough for me. I grabbed a quick breakfast and jumped on my bike. I rode as fast as I could to the other side of town. Going through the woods it was a short distance but would have to wear hip waders. Off to town, around the circle, then quickly to the battle grounds; I was there as quickly as I could peddle the bike.

Sure enough, there were all sorts of people, some dressed in period costumes. Others in military garb carrying muskets. There were red coats representing the British and militia minute men in period garb. There were women and kids dressed up too. One of the old houses there was open for free, usually there was a fee to get in. Vendors lined the main road, with all sorts of memorabilia to sell. There were lots of food stands. Lots of people. I didn't have more than a few dollars, so couldn't buying anything except maybe a hotdog or some candy.

By the bridge was a line of cannons—all facing my bedroom window! I did run into a few of my new friends from school and hung around with them for the rest of the day. It was a fun day except for the part of being shot at while sleeping. It gives you a good idea of what Concord was like on Patriot's Day. Later while at Boston University (BU), I would be able to see the finish of the Boston Marathon that happens on Patriot's Day. The finish line was a block away from the graduate dorm where I was living at the time.

If you ever plan a trip to Boston, start in Concord, move to Lexington, and try to get to the Marathon finish line before the end of the race, or better still, RUN IT! I now know the history of Patriot's Day, and why it is a state wide holiday in the Bay State! Remember to quote a famous from a Freemason: "The British are coming!"

Love,
Papa

Dear T:

Thanks to Bob and Mr. Henderson, Mom landed the perfect job. She was back doing what she loved—working the stock market as a security analyst for the Investment Trust of Boston. She had a large office and staff **working for her**. Her job was just like at Merrill Lynch: researching stocks and determine which had the best potential for returning a profit for the company and the clients. When she started it was the most upbeat and optimistic ever. She started to wear nice clothes. She drank less. We actually had a good time together. We were going to achieve our dreams, modest prosperity, considering the near poverty we had been experiencing, a solid home environment, and no more worries about money or where to live. The Hill was being rented providing a little additional income.

That was the plan. But, as with most dreams, it did not last long. The office manager, a Mr. Mickeljohn, hated the fact he had to hire a woman—worse, a woman who was so well connected and held in such high regard by important individuals. Mickeljohn was a short little man with an inferiority complex. While Mom was working there, the fortunes of the Investment Trust of Boston were beginning to turn around. By the third month, the investments were paying off handsomely. Mom had her old touch back. What was apparent was that Mom was more successful than Mickeljohn had been without her and this made him hate her all the more. I met him early in the job and did not have a very good impression of him. As the book *Blink* says, first impressions are usually correct.

After a few months Mickeljohn started to cause trouble. He would question every decision Mom would make. He accused her of not taking advantage of opportunities and overestimating the ones being invested in. Still, her track record was superior to his. What became apparent was that the whole office hated Mickeljohn. He fit the description of the worse kind of boss you can have—the same type described in the book *The No Assholes Rule*. Mom told me how much she hated this "son of a bitch." She constantly told me he hated intelligent women, especially a woman who could do a better job than him.

What may have added fuel to the fire between them was the whole office sided with Mom most of the time. If she needed something done—papers completed, forms filled out—the staff would help her as much as time would allow. If Mickeljohn needed the same it would take the same individuals twice as long to complete the same tasks they just completed for Mom.

It was sometime in late spring, I think, when Mickeljohn and Mom had a major face to face. I don't know exactly what caused it, but he started to swear at Mom. He called her incompetent, worthless, said that if she was not so well connected he would fire her on the spot. All this was happening out in the main office in front of all the workers. Mom could only take so much. He pushed her too far! She clenched her fist and hit him squarely on the face. According to the description that came to me, she hit him so hard that he flew backward in the air and slid on the shiny waxed floor about three feet.

Mom knew she was fired. She grabbed her things and marched out of the office, to a standing applause from all the office employees who had seen what happened. In many ways she imitated

Dad's last day in Hartford. There was never any suit or arrest. Apparently the office workers witnessed the verbal battery Mom had endured prior to the punch. All that came of it was the loss of the job. But this was the job she had wanted all her life. Now it was gone.

This was the beginning of the end of her hopes and dreams. It was the beginning of a long and consistent slide into excessive drinking and smoking. This was a major event in our lives. We would lose almost everything.

Love,
Papa

Dear T:

We tried to continue to live in the duplex as long as we could. I had a lot of adventures there during that time, and in Concord before we could no longer afford the rent. I'm going to back up a little to cover more of what was happening in my life, mostly at school. It is also important to realize the year was 1960.

I have mentioned my sixth-grade teacher and how beautiful she was. After getting over the fact Miss Madden was so attractive, I really did like her as a teacher, too. She loved teaching. You could tell it by the way she presented topics. When we studied the weather, she brought in a complete mini weather station. We had a rain tube/gauge to collect water to measure the amount of rain, therMometer, barometer and a host of other equipment for the two weeks spent on the topic.

Then, when we were studying dinosaurs and fossils in general, she brought in a whole collection of fossils. We were allowed to handle them. It was fun handling something 100 million years old (might have been the spark in my interest years later). I don't remember which ones she brought in but I'll bet one was a trilobite! She told us we could touch, but to be careful not to break anything.

It wasn't until about a year later that I found out something. If we were studying a topic and she knew of a graduate student or young professor at Harvard, MIT or elsewhere, majoring or teaching in the same area, she would convince them to let her have the equipment, samples, illustrations, etc. for the period her class was on the that topic. The class had a mini museum exhibit almost every week. It was a great learning environment.

I can just imagine she must have had a rather full "little black book" of men from the colleges in the area with comments on their majors. Depending on the stage of the school year she would just "renew" her interest in the contact that was able to lend her the teaching tools she wanted. That's what I call a dedicated teacher!

My most fond memory was when we were covering Ancient Greece. The class was to be divided into two camps representing Sparta and Athens. Each of the students could choose which side they wanted to be on. We had a week to prepare for a class debate on the advantages of each city-state. Skip and I, wanting to be seen as macho men (at least macho men in the making), chose Sparta. All the girls and many of the other boys chose Athens. The Athenians outnumbered the Spartans about two to one.

When it came time for the debate, the teams were so lopsided that Miss Madden joined the Spartans. I beamed with pleasure. Little else of the details remain; they were not really important. What was important was the enthusiasm and support Skip and I received from Miss Madden. We won the debate, mostly because of her help. When it was over, she said:

"Should I really tell which side I would choose?"

Everyone yelled: "Yeah!"

So she picked up her papers and moved to Athens. She taught me the importance of being able to argue both sides of an issue. Not only did we learn about Greece but we also learned the importance of how you handle yourself in a debate. Great class! Miss Madden, I'm forever indebted to you for what you taught me.

Love,
Papa

Dear T:

The first week in school went well. I enjoyed the classes. The teachers more enthusiastic about their profession than any previously experienced. I made a number of male friends, some smaller than me. I wondered if it was my personality or some other reason. It wasn't long before I found out.

Jackie P. was a boy from West Concord. It is important to know that West Concord, at the time, was a lower working class town. It was just down the Main Street a few miles. Most of the kids from West Concord were placed in the "lower" sixth-grade sections.

Jackie was the school's rapacious bully! Based upon all that I learned later, he had been that way for years. In many ways he was a typical (yes, this is stereotyping but it fit) bully, from a lower-class family, likely beaten by his father (an assumption), and doing poorly in school. His malice was towards anyone who might threaten his dominance on the playgrounds. My guess is there may have been a major inferiority complex underneath the acting out.

Jackie would try to beat up anyone who might challenge him on the playground or in the corridors. He had a few "gang" members who would often back him up if it appeared he may be challenged by any new student. I was a new student. And about to be challenged by this middle school malcontent.

It was a bright sunny day, likely in late October. I don't remember how it got started but before I knew it, I was being challenged by Jackie and two others. The name of the taller boy totally escapes me, but he was thin, about my height. The smaller one was named Richard. Jackie was about three inches shorter than me, but a lot heavier (let's call him just short of fat). He said he didn't like me and that he was going to teach me who was boss in the school. I tried to walk away, then I realized the other two were closing in behind me to cut me off. Jackie rushed forward, trying to push me off balance. I just turned slightly using his Momentum against him and pushed him aside. Then I noticed the shadow of the taller boy coming at me from behind. I quickly stepped aside, leaving out my leg. He tripped over the leg and with a little helpful push, ended up on the ground.

Being a sunny day my strategy was to keep the sun to my back as much as possible. Their shadows could be seen before any of these three could touch me. This worked remarkably well. If any of them tried to get me from behind, their shadow gave them away in time for me to make a counter move. Time and again, if they came at me from behind, a side step with an encouraging push would temporarily take care of the threat. Attempting to keep at least two in front of me, I would maneuver myself to a place where I could use the sun to my advantage. Any attack from the front I was able to parry. The three tried to grab me, but none were able to hold me for more than a second before I would counter with a move of my own, usually sending them flying to the ground.

Soon most of the kids and some of the teachers in the playground were beginning to gather round. There was a large circle of observers. I turned to one of the male teachers watching and said, "Stop this."

He looked at me with a smile and said, "We have wanted someone to teach Jackie a lesson, looks like you might be able to."

He just continued to watch with three other teachers joining in as spectators, all observing the fight. The whole of the audience seemed to be enjoying what they were witnessing.

This went on for ten minutes or more, no real punches, just poor attempts to throw me to the ground, or failed rushes to get a hold on me. One charge by the taller boy ended up with his head becoming bloodied when I pushed him face down into the dirt. He was now out of the fight and crying. Jackie became furious upon seeing his ally retreating from the scene. He tried to head butt me in the stomach, but I was prepared. I let his head hit my tensed stomach. Using his Momentum, I got my arms under him and with one step backward, threw him over my left shoulder right into little Richard behind me. Both landed on the ground with a huge thump. Richard's breath was knocked out of him. He couldn't move. Jackie was totally disoriented from being thrown head over heels into Richard. He had trouble getting up. I just started to walk back to the school. As I passed the teacher I said sarcastically:

"Thanks for the help!"

The response: "We have been waiting for years to teach that bully a lesson. You did it. Thank you."

As I walked through the crowd. A girl, slightly taller than me walked up to me and said, "Nice job. My name is Gail."

I told her mine.

Soon she was known as W's girl. Now my adventures had a girlfriend in many of them. Gail became my first real girlfriend.

Love,
Papa

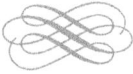

Dear T:

A little about my new girlfriend. Gail G was a good two inches taller than me. She was modestly thin, but strong (a little like you during your last years in TJ). She was attractive, but not beautiful. She had short brown hair and brown eyes. She had a wonderful smile and a good sense of humor. She lived on the opposite side of Concord. We had to ride our bikes to see the other. Mostly she came to my place after school.

Her home, I was there once, was in an upscale section of town, not the super-rich section where Robert Moore lived, but in the section with a lot of what are now called McMansions. I don't know what her father did, but whatever it was, he was successful at it in Boston.

Soon Gail and I would be seen together in the lunchroom at school every day. She loved my teasing and jokes. She would tease me in a half dozen ways. We made a good pair. She was not in the same classes as I was—she was in the "upper" classes for the smarter than average. But we became a steady pair in the school and rode our bikes around town. It was Gail who actually showed me around the Concord battlefield. On the next Patriot's Day celebration we rode all over on our bikes to see all the activities joining some of my other friends.

It is important to note here a little more on the "playground" for our school. This was HUGE!!! In the spring and especially the fall, during recess, the Boston (now New England) Patriots football team used to practice in the same playground / park (this was when they were part of the American Football League). At that time this was a small and struggling league compared to the NFL which was old and established. They were not seen on any national network only on local channels.

It was fun to watch them practice. Occasionally one of us would race out on the field and try to intercept a pass, and then run like hell as half a dozen players would chase after us. That was the far end of the playground. The playground had a separate soccer field, a baseball field and two fields for softball. It served as the playground for two schools, our fifth and sixth grade school and the junior high school (or commonly known as middle school). At any given time there could be a hundred kids scattered around the whole area from the different schools. Add the Patriots and there was potential for a lot of chaos, especially if the Patriot fans wanted to watch the practice, which was seldom. Usually there would be no more than a dozen or so spectators.

In the spring, Gail and I were in a corner (no exit near) of the playground surrounded by a eight-foot tall wire fence (where the football field was). I had my back to the playground facing Gail. Suddenly Gail said:

"W, quick—turn around."

There was Jackie with two new friends.

"I'm going to teach you a real lesson this time."

As he said this he pulled out a knife and started towards me.

Gail had slipped aside. Luckily for both of us her move had gone unnoticed, much to their surprise and downfall. Suddenly Gail shouted:

"W—catch!" She threw two glass bottles, one at a time, which I caught. Turning quickly with the bottles in my hand, I broke the bottom ends on the horizontal fence pipes.

"OK Jackie, now we're even."

Jackie was in shock. He clearly didn't expect me to have a weapon to counter his knife. Again, his emotions took over and he charged. I was able to sweep aside his attack with the knife straight-on by using one hand blocking the knife while making a sweeping move across his stomach with the other. The broken bottle sliced open his coat and shirt. I don't think it actually touched his skin, but there was enough impact that he lost some of his breath. He began to cry about the ripped clothes.

Simultaneously Gail had slipped behind the other two boys who were standing together watching the encounter between Jackie and me. Shocked by what they saw, they didn't see Gail sneaking up behind them. With a swift move downwards, her hands reaching from behind and through their legs, she grabbed both by the balls. She lifted them off the ground tossed them face first on the dirt. Both were in unbelievable pain! Within 30 seconds of the initial attack all three were on the ground. No one else noticed what occurred, but Jackie never bothered me again; he finally learned his lesson.

Gail and I walked casually back to the school. I was both proud and thankful she had came to the rescue! The incident sure united us for the time we were together.

Love,
Papa

(new return address after separation from your mother)

Dear T:

Admittedly I was a bit of a wise guy. While riding my bike in town one day in the spring the traffic was going very slow. This forced riding in the middle of the street because there were people getting in and out of their cars on the passenger side, making it unsafe for bike riders. Rarely did drivers look for kids on a bike. After purchasing gum or comics, I had to turn left once I hit Main

Street on the ride home. It was usually difficult with the traffic. Cars would be turning both left and right, largely ignoring a young boy on a bike. Logic would be to cross in a crosswalk, but at that time I don't remember one being there. It was slightly out of the strip mall area. The roads had been designed for cars with little or no consideration for bike riders. Wow, have things changed!

I was beginning to ride towards home the traffic almost at a standstill. I noticed a car with the sign on top with "Student Driver" prominently displayed. The driver's window was rolled down. As I passed I leaned down pointing to his wheel and said to him, "**Look** your wheels are moving!" in an excited voice. Then I quickly sped up to avoid any consequences.

Sure enough, the student driver leaned his head out of the window to look at his wheel and swerved out of his lane. I heard the teacher begin to yell at him, but I didn't stay around to see any further reaction.

It was at this time that I would buy comics and Mad Magazines whenever I had the money to do so. I was a Dell comic fan, as opposed to Marvel, which at the time was the start-up challenger. I preferred *Superman* and *Green Lantern* and I loved the *Justice League of America*. When Marvel came out with the *Dr. Strange* comics years later I collected the first series of 13 comics, all of them. As for *Mad*, I loved the Don Martin cartoons and *Spy vs. Spy*. Actually they began to help with reading. My love of *Mad* and other comics helped my reading ability and brought up some of my grades to solid Bs.

In school they started new special lessons using an experimental way to teach math and I volunteered for the new classes. It involved new textbooks and a totally new approach to the way math was taught. I loved it and caught on quickly. My math grades started to rise.

Remember Miss Madden? Back in my regular class with her, we started to study various kinds of science. I remember the areas we covered during the year included astronomy. True to her style, Miss Madden brought in star charts, a telescope and a host of other teaching materials which made it fun. She did the same for meteorology, paleontology, biology, etc. These were the advantages of having a teacher who thought highly of her classes.

She always made us learn, not only by the book, but how to use the actual tools we were reading about. It was fun. I even dreamed of turning the basement at The Hill, if we moved back, into different mini science rooms, one for astronomy, one for weather, one for fossils, one for chemistry, etc. My appreciation of Miss Madden was shown in my being willing to help in any way I could. If she needed something, I would get it for her. If she asked for a volunteer, I was the first with my hand in the air and was picked more than anyone else.

Skip once asked me if Miss Madden and I were secretly dating. Alas, I had to say no. But that would be my fantasy for years to come. It was the sixth grade that totally changed my attitude towards school and learning. I enjoyed school for the first time. I had a great girlfriend and other girls interested in me. I didn't have any more trouble with the school bully—actually he avoided me after the coke bottle. I had one of the best teachers a young boy could ask for, beautiful, intelligent and willing to go the extra mile to both help. She made every lesson as entertaining as possible. The special math classes were fun and exciting. They even had Saturday sessions which I signed up for. My grades were beginning to turn around. I felt good about my life.

It was truly a life changing year for me.

Love,
Papa

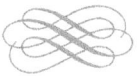

Dear T:

Of course this was 1960 when a Catholic became elected President of the United States, something most WASP Americans never thought would happen (sound familiar?). Being in Concord, most of the locals I was in contact with were Republicans (wealthy WASPs). They just couldn't imagine John Kennedy could win the election, even though he was from Massachusetts.

Of course he won and was inaugurated as President. It was after his election that he discovered the previous administration had promised support for a group of ex-patriots from Cuba to invade the island. The promise from Eisenhower's advisors was that attacking forces would receive air support from the United States and possibly additional military support to overthrow the Castro government which had taken power in 1959.

On [give full date], about 1,300 exiles armed with U.S. weapons landed at the Bahía de Cochinos on the southern coast of Cuba. Hoping to find support from the local population, they intended to cross the island to Havana. But the local support never manifested. The largest problem was that most Americans, including those in government, didn't realize how hated President Batista was and didn't consider the level of corruption in his administration. This is clearly shown in *The Godfather Part II* movie and was fairly accurate. What was interesting was that Batista's son was in a private school not far from The Hill in Connecticut. Never met the boy, but after being deposed I'm not sure if the younger Batista continued in the school.

As for the invasion it was a disaster. It was evident within the first few hours of fighting that the exiles who were attempting to retake the country likely were going to lose. President Kennedy had the option of using the U.S. Air Force against the Castro Cubans but decided against it. This allowed for the mobilization of the Cuban Army to proceed without interference. Remember, they were still fresh from a victory just a few years earlier. Many expected a counter invasion from the Batista supporters, but this failed to materialize. Consequently, the incursion was stopped by Castro's army who routed the invaders. By the time the fighting ended on April 19th, 90 exiles had been killed and the rest had been taken as prisoners. The major result was a deeper divide between the exiled Cubans who hated Fidel and the Cuban population that supported the revolution. So began the tensions between the USA and Cuba, which continue today.

About a year after the Bay of Pigs, Castro was looking for a way to defend his island nation from an attack by the U.S. He felt a second attack was inevitable. Consequently, he approved of Khrushchev's plan to place missiles on the island. In the summer of 1962 the Soviet Union worked quickly and secretly to build its missile installations in Cuba.

For the United States, the crisis began on October 15, 1962 when U2 reconnaissance photos revealed Soviet missile sites under construction in Cuba. Early the next day, President Kennedy was informed of the installations. After seven days of guarded and intense debate within the upper echelons of government, Kennedy decided to impose a naval quarantine around Cuba, hoping to prevent the arrival of more Soviet weapons on the island.

On October 22, JFK announced the discovery of the missile installations to the public and that action had been taken to blockade the island. He proclaimed that any nuclear missile launched from Cuba would be regarded as an attack on the United States by the Soviet Union. JFK demanded the Soviets remove all of their offensive weapons from Cuba.

I remember on Thursday, October 25 when U.S. Ambassador to the United Nations, Adlai Stevenson, confronted the Soviets. They refuse to respond. Stevenson made a masterful presentation, to the dismay of the Soviet delegation. It made me wonder what would have happened if he had been elected in 1952 or 1956. Adlai was defeated in both elections, mostly due to the popularity of Eisenhower, the five star general who led the US to victory over the Nazis in Europe. Adlai's defeat to Eisenhower was a classic example of hero worship defeating intellect. But had either election gone the other way it is interesting to imagine how the world might have been different. Eisenhower had missed so many opportunities to make the world safer and create a long lasting peace. But anti-communist fever, fueled by the House Un-American Activities Committee prevented any peace resolution and promoted the Cold War.

Back to the Cuban Missile Crisis. With the blockade around Cuba, it looked like we were on the verge of an actual nuclear war. How did all this affect me? How did it affect all the kids around me? We were all impacted by these events we had no control over. I remember riding my bike around Concord when I ran into a bunch of girls. We started to talk about the possibility of nuclear war within hours. Then we all discussed whether to have sex before we all died or not. I regret not pushing it a little more (I failed to lose my virginity at the time).

When not watching the news (can you imagine 11 and 12 year olds glued to the TV news?) we were practicing the "duck and cover" under our desks. Whoever thought of this as a real defense from a nuclear strike must have been off his rocker. Of course we knew that. It was a worthless exercise. The standard saying was:

"Duck with your head between your legs and cover so you can kiss you sweet ass good-bye."

We all agreed that the drills were stupid. For days we were expecting a blinding flash any minute. Most likely the flash would be coming from Boston. There was an overwhelming sense of hopelessness and helplessness. This was also true for many of the adults. They tried not to show it, but they were as pessimistic as the kids. It was a short period of mass depression, though no one wanted to admit it.

The Cuban Missile Crisis was perhaps the time when the Doomsday Clock got closer to Midnight than ever before. This is not evident by the yearly averages shown on the charts since the crisis was resolved. This clock was created in 1947 in response to the combined nuclear power of the US and USSR (Soviet Union). The closer the clock gets to 12 midnight the closer we are to nuclear war. Those were the tense days. I understood later that Kennedy called up Soviet Premier Nikita Khrushchev and reportedly said:

"Pull out the missile or it's nuclear war—your choice."

They were pulled out. The nation went into party mode.

I love the following quote y Soviet General and Army Chief of Operations, Anatoly Gribkov:

"Nuclear catastrophe was hanging by a thread…and we weren't counting days or hours, but minutes."

There are a lot of good books and several movies that have been made on the subject. Each has a slightly different perspective. *Thirteen Days,* released in 2000, was one of the most popular of the Cuban Missile Crisis movies, though not completely accurate. An older one is *The Missiles of October,* made in 1974, which is a little less dramatic and slightly more accurate.

What most people don't remember is how it impacted those who lived through those days. Looking back all I can say is that it was an interesting time that had a lasting impact on most who lived through it. It prepare many of us to protest the Vietnam War, which was already beginning to rage.

Love,
Papa

Dear T:

While living on Main Street in Concord, Mom and I would watch TV in the front room in the evenings. On Friday nights I loved to continue watching Jack Parr, host of The Tonight Show (later replaced by Johnny Carson).

The Dick Van Dyke Show was fun. Route 66 was a favorite of boys my age, as was 77 Sunset Strip (several boys had a version of the theme song which should go unrepeated). Sea Hunt with Lloyd Bridges (Jeff's father) was in its last year, but made scuba diving popular. It inspired me to get my license years later. Car 54 Where Are You? starred Fred Gwen, who became Fred Munster a few years later, was good for laughs.

Popular back then were a host of westerns. Mom and I would make time to watch Wagon Train, Cheyenne (my favorite), Bonanza (which had just started) and Have Gun Will Travel (the best 30 minute western EVER—great stories and wonderful acting by Richard Boone). Maverick suffered with the loss of James Garner who left the show after a few years, but we still watched.

One Friday evening (I think because I don't remember going to school the next day), we were watching one of the westerns or a detective show with shooting and loud noises. After the show we went to bed; it was just a normal evening.

I woke up early because of a noise outside. I thought it was my alarm clock, but it wasn't. I turned on the radio to hear the news. They started talking about the major train derailment that had occurred the night before in Concord. Suddenly I put two and two together. Getting up, I looked out the window. There in the backyard was part of a box car. I ran to the rear of the house and looked out. There were work crews with cranes and big machinery attempting to right all the box cars stacked up like matchsticks. The wooden fence separating my yard from the train tracks had several box cars against it. Only one, the one I first saw, was actually in the yard. There were several others on top of the crumbled fence.

I ran into Mom's bedroom:

"Mom there is a train wreck in our backyard!"

I quickly got dressed and raced outside. It was pure chaos. There were box cars, flat cars and tank cars piled all over the area. The commuter lines were blocked. No trains would be moving for days to come.

I walked through the large opening that had been torn in the fence and wandered around the wreckage, being careful not to interfere with the work crews. The size of the derailment was so large no one spotted me. If they did, they didn't seem to care since there was so much damage. I saw a piece of twisted iron and picked it up. It looked like part of the train wheel, the part that holds the wheel to the track. It had been sheared off. Although it weighed about five pounds, I took it home and wondered if this was what had caused the derailment. I also took some of the RR spikes that were thrown all over the area where the tracks were dislodged.

I believe some investigators came by days later. The main question was "did you hear anything?" Surprisingly, we had not. We had been watching TV and as a result we did not hear the huge train crash happening less than 20 yards away. All of our attention was focused on the TV. Also, we were facing the front of the house. Since the train tracks usually were a source of noise those living there had learned to ignore the noise in the back, even a major derailment. It was not until I was awakened by the repair crews that I realized what had happen around 10 p.m. the night before.

Later I learned all the cars in the derailment were empty except one. In total there were about 100 empty cars, most scattered all over the tracks. The noteworthy exception was the car immediately behind the engine It was the only car that had anything in it. The rumor was that it was filled with explosives (dynamite?!). It was never confirmed, but the story spread all around

Concord. The engine and that car were the only part of the train not impacted by the derailment. It appeared that the next car jumped the tracks, decoupling from the loaded car.

At school someone told me if the first car had derailed it would have exploded. It would have left a crater covering a 100 yards in all directions—including my house. In other words, your father would not have been around for you.

Lots of fun. More later.

Love,
Papa

Dear T:

This letter will border on what you don't really want to hear but it is what was happening with my life. Remember my girlfriend Gail? She was still an active part of my life. We were both going through a growing spurt. She was already super tall, but her breasts and pubic hair were just starting to grow. Naturally she wanted to show off her 'development.' Who better than her boyfriend? I was constantly shown how she was 'filling' out. She wanted to show how her breasts were just beginning to swell up as a sign of her growing maturity. She also wanted to show off her new pubic hair. Of course, she wanted to see me as well. No problem. There was a lot of personal show and tell between us.

I always told her that as much as I wanted she must not let me penetrate her for fear of her getting pregnant. She agreed. Being rather puerile we were limited to canoodling. Not knowing about oral sex, if we were I am very sure we would have engaged in it. Being ignorant of what could have been the rapture of lotus-eating, we had as much fun as within limitations. Mind you, that was a still lot of fun.

My advantage was living in a house with a mother who was working all day. In Gail's house such activities would have been impossible. Her mother was always around, especially if there was a boy in the house, although we could have found a privacy other than her bedroom. Still the fact that her mother would be looking for us every 5 minutes prevented any such adventures from taking place.

One of Gail's good friends was a rather homely girl named Betty (I think). Betty was a very sheltered girl from a very protective family. She didn't have any brothers and no experience with boys of any kind except in class. Her major attribute was some very large breasts for her age. I'm sure they were at least 36' at that time and growing. Remember this was a 6th grader.

One day Gail came over to my house with Betty. We played some board games and had snacks. Gail turned to me casually mentioning that Betty had never seen a penis. Gail told Betty:

"I bet W would be willing to show you his. Would you like to see it?"

Betty turned red in the face but nodded OK. I suggested we go up to my room, rather than stay in the living room. As we went up the stairs, I tried to make a deal with Betty: she show me her breasts and I would show her my cock. In my room Betty was afraid someone from next door would be able to see her from their 2nd floor.

I took her to the back room but it was still too open. My next suggestion was the basement, dirt floor and no windows. The three of us went down to the basement. We went to the best lit area. A few naked light bulbs were hanging from the rafters. Remember this was a duplex. The basement was not as sound insulated as the rest of the house, even if it was underground. There were small gaps between our section of the basement and the owners.

"Is this alright?" I asked.

She nodded. I again asked if she would undress if I did. No promise. Gail thought the whole thing funny. There were little snickers and a mischievous smile on her face the whole time. She was teasing us both. She tried to unbutton Betty's blouse. Betty always twisted away. Still a few buttons were undone showing a voluptuously overflowing bra with soft delectable flesh!

I started to unbuckle my belt. Then I opened my zipper. Betty was watching closely while pushing Gail away. I pulled my pants down. Betty was breathing fast in anticipation. I put my fingers in my underwear and started to remove them. I didn't even expose myself yet when there was a tremendous scream!

My immediate reaction was to grab my pants and become fully dresses instantaneously. Gail grabbed Betty and turned her face to face:

"What did you do that for? Don't you know there might be other people in the other side of the house!"

Betty turned red. Then said to Gail:

"But I thought you were supposed to scream when you saw a man."

Gail: "But you didn't even see him yet!"

We raced out of the basement and out of the house. I don't think anyone was home next door. The scream had not draw attention except our ears where still ringing. Betty was scared, nervous, as well as embarrassed.

Gail told her: "Don't scream like that ever again over seeing a boy. You missed an opportunity to see what you wanted to. We could have had some fun too."

Later Gail told me she thought if I had exposed myself, Betty would have been more willing to expose herself. She had a whole plan in her head. Her idea was while Betty was playing with me, Gail was sure Betty would not have paid any attention to Gail taking off her blouse. Then Gail wanted to persuade her to take off the bra. After she would take off her blouse and bra. Once naked, she wanted to slip behind Betty. Her vision was to sandwich Betty in between us rubbing her to a state of excitement. Gail's ultimate plan was to have us all naked on my bed and enjoy a threesome playing with each other.

It never happened. Betty never dared to return. Gail and I always wished the plan had succeeded. It would have been fun. I think that Gail wanted to play with Betty as an experiment of what it would be like to caress another girl, especially with a boy present.

Thus ended a show-me-yours-if-I-show-you-mine episode.

Hope this was not too much, but you must admit it's funny.

Love,
Papa

Dear T:

Cuttyhunk is an island near the Cape Cod chain off New Bedford, Massachusetts.

The Moores had a summer "house" in Cuttyhunk. Actually it was originally the Cuttyhunk Yacht Club! In other words, it was a former private club for guests to stay and fish from the cliff overlooking the Atlantic. Robert had purchased it after making a fortune in Sheraton. By that time the Country Club had ceased to exist and the place was beginning to get run down. It must have been a really great place in its heyday.

I could describe the place, which would take a series of letters. Suffice it to say it was huge with about 25 private guest rooms, maybe more. All of Marcia's kids would go there for the summer. There was more than enough room for the rest of the family, Robin, Johnny and Billy, including the latter's kids, but that summer only Robin joined us while Marcia was there. I was invited to join them our first summer in Concord and Mom would come out on the weekends. This was before her leaving the Investment Trust of Boston. Even getting there was an adventure.

After driving to New Bedford, you must take a private boat to Cuttyhunk. Then there is only one taxi on the island, and only available part time. The best way was to call in advance saying when you were arriving. We had to tell the driver we needed to get to the former Country Club.

There was a nice harbor, which could be entered through a long channel, so it was well protected, something needed in winter and when seas were rough. There was a small fishing fleet that harbored there (at least there was in the 1960s). Every morning the fleet would come in from fishing through the night. Many would clean and fillet the fish for market in New Bedford. One ship would take the prepared fish to the mainland for sale usually leaving before 8 a.m. The fishermen would then rest before going out in the evening for another night of fishing.

There were a number of lobster men, too. All around the islands in the area were lobster traps; you could spot them by the buoys attached. Each buoy had slightly different markings to identify which boat would pull it up and who it was owned by. Once a day, the lobsters would be pulled into the boats. The catch would come into shore, either at the island or the mainland.

Back then lobsters where considerably larger than the ones you see now, as they are overfished. No one knew it took over seven years for a lobster to mature and reproduce. We now have regulations protecting undersized lobsters, but they are grossly inadequate. I see lobsters that are much too young in Red Lobster and grocery stores all the time. Every lobster someone eats means a generation of offspring has been lost. At the rate we are going I would think the New England lobster will be extinct before the end of your lifetime. Anyway, back to that summer.

There was one church in Cuttyhunk. That summer it was where most of the people in town would all go on Sunday mornings. This was the only place I ever saw the very wealthy (e.g. the Moores and a few other families with exclusive homes away from the harbor), commoners, fishermen and poor people all in the same place, and all on friendly terms with one another. Cuttyhunk being small, almost everyone knew everyone else. I remember the fishermen would come up the hill from docks after preparing the previous night's catch for sale. They would still be wearing their boots and their shirts covered with fish scales.

Teens would come to the church in swimsuits or bikinis, often without a bathrobe. The elderly and wealthy, like Mrs. Moore, would wear fine summer dresses and hats. Their spouses most wore light summer suits, while others would dress in nice slacks and an open shirt.

The one service I remember the most. It was on a hot summer day. The temperature was getting close to 90 degrees when the service started. The minister came out with his usual white robe and vestments. He was in his late 30s or early 40s and full of energy. As the sermon started he began to sweat. After the appropriate number of hymns, prayers and his sermon, at about 11:45, he paused. Service usually ran from 11 to 12. But today it was HOT! Especially inside a non-air conditioned church. So, suddenly the minister said something like:

"So I think the best way to end this service is to see who can make it down to the beach for a swim the fastest."

With that, he jumped out of his robe with nothing but his swim trunks underneath. He raced out the side door, followed by all the teens, many of the adults who were similarly attired concealing swimsuits hidden under Sunday clothes. With the exception of the older parishioners, almost everyone raced down to the swimming area with shouts and screams of joy. Now that was a good church service!

More on Cuttyhunk in the next letters too.

Likely that is where we will stop for your college career.

Love,
Papa

Dear T:

More Cuttyhunk! The Yacht Club was a great place to explore by itself. There was a large dining table with seating for 20 if necessary. It was next to a large kitchen with a huge industrial stove and ovens. Mrs. Moore had a favorite maid/cook who would come to the Club to take care of chores in the summer; more on her later.

The common room was huge, at least 40 feet long and maybe 30 feet wide. There were sofas and chairs scattered around tables, most of which were the in the shape and style of old fashioned poker tables. Mr. Moore loved cribbage. It was during this summer when he taught me how to play. I had a great deal of fun with him learning the game while hearing about his adventures, especially when he was in the Lafayette Escadrille. This was where I learned a little about the real source of the first Sheraton Hotel and his partnership with Ernie Henderson. He basically confirmed most of the stories Mom had told me.

At the far end of the common room was a giant fireplace with an equally large mantel. Over the mantel was a very large stuffed sea bass, the favorite catch from shore near the Club in the old days. Below the stuff bass resting on the mantel was an enormous New England lobster claw. The claw must have been three feet in length and two feet wide. That claw alone, when caught with the lobster attached, must have weighed at least 20 lbs. I have never seen anything close to that claw before or since. Just goes to show how big lobsters can get if left to grow.

Across from the dining room was a smaller sitting room where the original registration desk once was. There were smaller card tables and more formal chairs around them. This was where the ladies would play bridge and other "polite" card games. Poker, cribbage and the games of chance would have been reserved for the men in the common room. Remember this was a "Club" that was popular in the 1800s but was shut down during the Depression.

One day Mrs. Moore showed me the registration book, where each guest was required to register. There were a number of spaces after each name. The extra spaces were used to record the fish caught. If caught from the shore of the Club or from a boat. The length and weight of the fish were recorded. The names you on the registry were unbelievable. William Howard Taft, Grover Cleveland (I think) and William McKinley were listed. Theodore Roosevelt was there and, of course, he had some of the largest catches both from shore and a boat, including a huge bass and a swordfish, bigger than anything you would find today. Quite an impressive guest list! There were other famous people of the era, but it was the presidents that made an impression on me.

I was allowed to stay in a room on the second floor. There were only a few rooms off the main building on the second floor. My room was a treasure for a young boy to explore. There was part of an old hard-hat diving outfit. I used to put on the glove to see how it could be used. It only had three fingers. Hard-hat diving would be used before Jacques Cousteau created the regulator and aqua-lung design which gave birth to new scuba technology the 1940s, which is what is still used today. Now you know how Cousteau got his money for his research.

There were old nets and other fishing gear. In one corner, I found a spear gun. It worked. I asked Mr. Moore (Mrs. Moore would never have approved) if I could use it. He said sure.

I started taking sailing lessons and made friends with two of the instructors (both older teens) but remember by now I was 5' 8' and 175 lbs. with a size 12 shoe! So few knew how old I really was. They would join the group of us at the Club and we would set up a softball field off the back porch. There is an old photo of me with a bat taken that summer.

Mr. Moore loved to do his own photography along with rock cutting and polishing, and a host of other hobbies. If you find the photo, it is one of the best of me ever taken. But when you look at it closely, you will notice I am batting left handed. I am a righty! Mr. Moore put the negative in the enlarger upside down. Later I took a photo of the photo since it was digital the contrast was improved and the photo flipped to show a right handed hitter. Thus, Mr. Moore did to me what the movie studios did to Gary Cooper when he played Lou Gehrig. They turned the film around because Cooper was not the same handed hitter as Gehrig! All of the batting scenes in the movie about Gehrig were filmed with him running to third base pretending it was first (little known movie trivia).

The softball games involved Marcia's children and some of the kids from town. Johnny Moore (the adult) played with us more than once, as well as any other adults who liked softball. The games were always fun. You just had to be careful not to hit the ball too far foul down the first base line as it would likely go off the cliff and end up in the ocean some 20 plus feet below. I don't remember if we ever lost a ball over the cliff and into the ocean, but it was a constant concern.

Horseshoes and volley ball were options, but softball seemed to attract the most interest. It certainly had the greatest number of participants.

Love,
Papa

Dear T, how about some sailing lessons:

Remember the last letter discussed sailing lessons at Cuttyhunk. Here is some more detail and a little adventure. The sailing lessons were a great deal of fun. We all started out in little sailfish boats. These are tiny sailboats holding only two people, one instructor or instructor's assistant and one student. We would sail them out of the harbor and around to the north side of the island. It was the most protected side as it faced the mainland and was away from the open ocean. This way we would learn how to tack (shift directions to take advantage of the wind while changing course to a new heading) and move with the wind. The importance of heading the bow first into large waves was taught. When sailing into the wind, the ability to maneuver back and forth (tack) at a slight angle to the headwind is a critical skill whenever you had a strong head wind in a sailboat. This way all the basics were covered.

After a week or so of lessons in the sailfish boats, we graduated to larger sailboats. These had both a sail and a jib (the little sail on the same mast as the main sail, but in front). These boats could hold four or five individuals, more if really squeezed together. Classes combined the preteens with the teens, the teens in the larger boats. I was one of the latter, though only 12 years old. We would take turns practicing how to come about, jibbing in a head wind and basic sight navigation.

I took to it fast. Now you understand why I enjoyed the few trips we took with Tio Chris in his boat. They brought back memories of Cuttyhunk.

On one of the trips, we completely circled the island—a good long trip with plenty of challenges due to the headwinds. At the northwest side of the island, you could see Martha's Vineyard in the distance.

As the summer was coming to a close, an end of class party was planned. We all piled into three of the largest boats owned by the yacht club. These sailboats could hold seven people if most of the individuals were small. This was the case because most of the classes were with young children (7 to 10 years old). The boat was crowded but manageable. The whole class with instructors went on a picnic to a neighboring island. The trip to the far side of the next island went very smoothly. We wanted the far side since it was a wonderful hideaway, out of the boat traffic lanes used by fishermen and others. Large sand dunes met the shore on the east side of the island. It was a great place to play, swim and eat our picnic lunch. No one wanted to go back home, including Chris and Johnny (Mr. Moore's grandsons) who were part of the younger class on the trip. As a result, everyone was reluctant to leave this quintessential beach and we stayed longer than expected. Everyone forgot the time due to having so much fun.

Suddenly one of the instructors noticed the time was late, then another instructor climbed one of the taller dunes and came running back shouting:

"We have to leave now! There is a storm approaching. We didn't see it because of the dunes. It's about to hit us."

We were on the northeast side of the island and the storm was coming from the southwest!

We quickly packed up all the gear and the kids in the boats. I was with the advanced instructor who I had taken lessons with. We pushed off. The sky was still blue overhead—until we turned the northeast corner of the island. Then we saw it. A major thunderstorm was striking Cuttyhunk, about a mile away, and heading straight for us. What was worse, the storm was coming from the direction we had to go in. The headwinds must have been 40 mph or more. There was no way we could get back in the anticipated half-hour it took us in the morning to get to the picnic area.

By the time all of this hit our minds, so did the storm. Within minutes we were being pounded with rain and wind. We told the smaller kids to keep under the bows of the boats as much as possible. The older pupils were helping as much as we could to control the sails, tacking back and forth into the headwinds. Tacking, the small zigzags, maneuvering against the headwinds involves a lot of "coming about", where the boom swings from one side of the boat to another.

Tacking right moved the boats slowly toward the mainland and the darkness of the storm would no longer be visible. Coming about, back towards the direction of the eastern shore of Cuttyhunk, the lightning and black clouds appeared to be bearing down upon us. The progress was painstakingly slow and the young kids were getting scared—frankly, so was everyone. The storm was more than these boats were designed to handle. Worse, the boats were full. All the kids had life jackets on, but now the waves were approaching four feet and higher. We were being tossed about like matchsticks. My boat was in the middle of the three. The first boat was barely visible in the storm. The last was closer to us.

Suddenly we heard a yell from the first boat. One of the younger kids had stood up just as they were coming about and was thrown into the ocean. It was impossible for the first boat to retrieve him. My instructor jumped into the ocean, telling me to take over. He grabbed the kid, but was unable to come back to my boat. The third boat saw what happened and picked the instructor and the boy up. My kids started to cry; they were close to a full panic. The third boat came close to us. The kids in that boat were scared shitless.

My instructor, now in the other boat, got an idea. The popular song of the summer was *Ahab the Arab*. He told everyone in both boats to start singing it:

"Let me tell you about Ahab the Arab

"The sheik of the burning sand

"He had emeralds and rubies just drippin' off 'a him

"And a ring on every finger of his hand

"He wore a big ol' turban wrapped around his head

"And a scimitar by his side

"And, every evenin', about midnight

"He'd jump on his camel named Clyde, and ride."

The kids actually got into the song. We sang it for a good hour as those in charge of the boats zigzagged our way back to Cuttyhunk. I'd like to think that the song saved a dozen lives that day.

By the time we got into the channel it was getting dark. We arrived hours later than planned and many of the parents were panicked. Most were on the docks. The Coast Guard had been called in for help but they had gone to the wrong island looking for us. The Coast Guard station on Cuttyhunk could have helped if they had known where to go.

By the time we got into the safety of the channel, the storm had subsided and when we docked it was close to sunset. We were drenched, cold and hungry. The kids were all shaken, but all relatively in good health. Even the kid who was knocked overboard was okay because the boom had hit his life jacket. It only knocked a little wind out of him and gave him a small bruise on one arm.

We got out and climbed on the docks, happy to have made it back.

The next week, two of the older kids and I went on another adventure. Mr. Moore had two fishing boats. One was a Boston Whaler a nice boat with a strong engine which could cut through the water and moderate waves. The other, an old fashioned row boat, was outfitted with a regular motor.

There were some fishermen who would take out paying customers to fish from their boats. They complained about a great white shark eating their catch of swordfish before getting them in the boat. Several swordfish in the last stages of being hauled in were attacked by sharks that would go after a good free meal at the cost of the fishermen.

I joined two other teens in an adventure, informing Mr. Moore they were part of the sailing instructors. Being teens we decided to go after the great white. First step catch a bunch of flounders and cut them up. The older teens were in the Boston Whaler were trailing the cut flounders behind their boat. Each had a spear gun. I trailed behind with the spear gun I had found in my bedroom. Watching the flounders, we waited for the shark to appear with the motor tied with a rope in the boat I was in. We were going in a straight line at a slow speed. The ocean was calm on that day. I could stand up and shoot the spear gun if the shark approached—at least that was the plan.

I watched the boat in front of me and the flounders. Suddenly one of the others pointed to my right.

"Shark! Huge!"

I was standing facing slightly to the left, still watching where the flounders were. I quickly turned right but the problem was I was standing the bow of the boat. DUMB! My sudden movement turned the boat to the left. I looked to my right. There was the great white, almost next to my boat; he had come up beside me without my knowing it. Me turning to the right and the bow turning to the left caused a loss of balance. I fell overboard.

I don't remember what happen next, but the boys in the Whaler said it was like watching a cartoon. They could have sworn that I jumped out of the water as fast as I fell in. It was like watching the film in reverse, I got into my boat so fast. They said I looked like Bugs Bunny or Daffy Duck trying to escape a shark.

I landed within inches of the shark's face—I think I scared him every bit as much as he scared me. I literally must have hit him with the spear gun—not the spear but the actual gun in my hand. likely on his nose. After I fell in, he turned and got the hell out of there. The free meal flounders had too many strings attached. Besides, there were larger catches in the ocean. Two flounders would barely have made an appetizer for him.

Once I was back in my boat, we all had a good laugh. It was really one of the funniest and stupidest things I have ever done in my life. But, those are the very things that if you survive, you laugh about years later.

So, two adventures in one letter. Hope you enjoyed them.

Love,
Papa

Dear T:

I'm sure you remember the letter about your grandmother hitting her boss to the applause of all the others in the office! Well, it did have an impact as Mom lost her job, of course. For a while we lived on unemployment insurance while she looked for other jobs but after a few months of looking with insufficient money coming in, we had to do something. By summer we had to find some solution. We moved out of the duplex. I don't know what happened to all the furniture, but I never saw most of it again. I was sorry about losing a huge gold-framed mirror that was beautiful, not my style, but beautiful. This letter will be about other impacts and some new people.

There had been a Boston Co-Masonic Lodge which had been dormant for years until Mom reactivated it. When we moved into the house we had a large enough living room to turn it into a small Lodge once a month. That's what Mom did. Marcia joined but it never kept her interest. I don't think she ever got her 3rd Degree. There was a couple from Holland, the Van Hulsts. Both had been Co-Masons in Holland and were interested in joining a Lodge again. I don't remember how Mom got their name, but she contacted them and another old member. Together with Marcia, that made five, enough to try to get a Lodge active. I believe they actually got some new members too. But since I was not invited to be in the house during Lodge meetings I didn't pay much attention.

The Lodge equipment, jewels, staves, Bible, tools, etc. was originally from AUM and stayed with us until Mom moved to Crystal City many years later. Most of the supplies (forms, rituals, robes, various signs for the degrees, etc.) that survived were in the wooden trunk. At first they were stored in the storage area in her Crystal City apartment in Arlington, VA. Shortly after Mom moved in there she started to worry about the trunk. There were two complete sets of Officer Jewels in silver, on nice blue cords. The appropriate stave toppings for the Deacons and Stewards (officers who move around the Lodge) were there too with the altar jewels, square and compasses. Mom finally had me retrieve the trunk. All the jewels and valuables had been stolen. This happened in the secure storage area in Crystal Towers 2. So it had to have been one of the staff or another tenant. Most likely one of the staff since each storage area was restricted. Mom was devastated. All that was left were the clothes for the principal officers and the top pieces for the Deacons' staves. The paper and cardboard signs used in the Degrees survived. The sets of beautiful silver jewels were gone. It was reported to the police, but nothing ever came of it.

What did survive were three candlesticks, each about 5 feet tall, because they had been placed in the apartment closet, not in the storage facility. Eventually all those Masonic supplies were given to a newly formed Co-Masonic Lodge in the Washington, D.C. area, with one notable exception. The three large candlesticks can now be seen in the George Washington Masonic Memorial's Alexandria Washington Lodge #22 room. They were the last of her possessions that Mom lent out.

The Master of the Lodge wanted to meet Mom when she was living in Falls Church, VA. He asked to borrow them. She thought it would be better if they were used rather than sitting around a basement. What is interesting is they were given on "permanent" loan until such time as she or one of her descendants desired to retrieve them for the purpose of forming a new Lodge. Since you and your sister are her only descendants who might form a Lodge, they are yours should you decide to have them. This was recorded in the minutes of the meeting that occurred immediately after her death.

Back to Concord. The Van Hulsts had two children around my age: a boy, slightly overweight, who was about a year older than I. The girl was closer to my age, and like her brother, very tall. Both were blonde and stereotypically Dutch in appearance. I would have expected them to have some wooden shoes in the closet waiting for the right occasion.

I remember going to a lake for a summer swim once. Both went into a spare room to change into their bathing suits and I was a little shocked they both went in together. Their mother saw my expression and said:

"They change in same room. No difference. They are brother and sister, what difference does it make?" I would have agreed if they were younger, but with both being tall and more developed than most their age, this surprised me a bit.

The place where we swam became an important location in the near future.

Mom's friend in Connecticut, Ruth the photographer, had a friend in the Concord area. Sandy (her nickname) was an attractive early 40s blonde who had a delightful house by a lake outside of Concord. Ruth told Mom to contact Sandy. They hit it off and quickly became friends. Since we lost the apartment, Mom asked if I could stay in her house for the summer. Sandy said it would be perfect. I could stay in the little guest room, and swim all I wanted in the lake. This sounded great. I moved in.

But life with Sandy was not what you would expect for a 12 year old.

Love,
Papa

Dear T:

Hope you had a happy 4th and got the tire fixed on your car.

So, life with Sandy was not what you would expect for someone my age. We would have a great time together, swimming, going to movies (when we could afford it), but then there were the "parties" Sandy would have in her home. She would entertain a host of mostly men, some behind the confines of her closed door, while I cooked the steaks on the grill and fixed the drinks. The drink of the season was a screwdriver (vodka and OJ). Beer was always plentiful. I became the unofficial bar tender and cook.

The chief orchestrator of these parties was a dentist who was referred to as TJ. He would invite his friends. Some evenings there would be as many as twenty men. Some brought their wives, only rarely their children, who came when it was to be an early party and everyone could go for a swim in the lake. Sandy was expected to entertain TJ's close friends. In the evening Sandy would disappear for 20 or 30 minutes with one of the men. Then come on down, take a gulp of her drink, talk to TJ for a minute, and retreat to her room again with another man. I do not know if Sandy charged for her services (she should have) or if TJ forced her to accommodate his friends for free. By the end of the party, Sandy was well used, drunk and very depressed. If she had a shower late in the evening TJ would stay over and take advantage of her. TJ was her sugar daddy and paid for most of her expenses.

Sandy did not like her life. More than once, after the party was over and the men had left, she would take a large dose of sleeping pills with another drink. On those nights I had to keep her walking and talking until the effects wore off. It often took hours and I did not get to sleep until early morning. Thank goodness it was during the summer when I didn't have school.

Other friends would come over, including a family that had an adopted daughter named Sophia. Sophia was in HS. She was slightly overweight, with huge breasts, black hair and glasses. Since I was about 5′9′ she assumed I was about her age (16 or so). We hit it off quickly, but more on her later.

So I had a great summer; steaks on the grill regularly, learning how to make a screwdriver, swimming whenever I wanted. I even bet Sophia I could eat a lunch underwater. I won the bet and the sandwich was not even wet. The key was I could hold my breath back then for close to two minutes. Great times! Naturally they didn't last.

Love,
Papa

Dear T:

Talking to a friend the other day I remembered something that should have been written earlier. It is important due to the impact it had. This occurred after Mom and I had returned to The Hill after Lakeville. Peter and I were back together as best friends and would often go out hiking with our 22 rifles. We weren't really hunting. More than likely we took shots at dead tree limbs, twigs, etc. for practice. This occupied most weekends and some afternoons. Back then it was easier and cheaper to get a box of .22 shells than a pair of movie tickets. So Peter's dad and Mom would supply enough shells for both our rifles, most of the time. When not, we would resort to fishing.

You likely realize by now that Mom had a drinking problem. This was evident while living in Lakeville and certainly when we moved back to Sugar Hill. She loved her bourbon, occasionally Scotch, sometime vodka, gin … there was a variety of bottles under the sink. The gin and other alcohol were mostly for Betsy and Ruth who would often come over. Those afternoons and evenings would quickly become a drinking party. For dinner or other occasions, Mom would have some cheap wine.

By the time they rolled into their cars, their blood alcohol levels would have exceeded any chance of passing a sobriety test. How they drove home, I cannot imagine. Betsy only had a few miles to travel to Limerock. Ruth was still living at the Twin Lakes house. Luckily neither took roads where the police would be present. A few times when Ruth tried to go down between the maple trees she would scrape the bottom of her sports car, but never any serious damage. She hated that driveway. Why she didn't turn around and go out the gravel outer lane with no center hump

I'll never figure out. I can only guess that by the time she was ready to go home, she was too drunk to turn around in the yard. The point was there was no lack of cheap booze in the house.

With all the adults drinking I thought it would be fun to see what I could come up with. If all the empties had a few last little drops, I collected those drops into an "empty" bottle, like a small pint bottle. I collected all the last drops out of several bottles into my little pint container for weeks. When I had accumulated about 3 oz. of booze in the pint (mind you, all mixed up), I put it in my book bag to take to the school bus.

On the bus I showed it to Peter. Since Bertha, Peter's mother, was also a heavy drinker, he quickly identified with what I had. He thought it was great. Wanting to take a sip, he asked for the bottle and I gave it to him.

Since we were behaving suspiciously, the bus driver took notice. Mind you, we were less than half way to school with only six kids on the bus. The driver literally stopped the bus and came back. Remember, these were country roads, so there was no traffic and it was common to stop for raccoons, possums, and other wildlife. Peter and I took no notice. We were near the Belter's farm, so the thought was there may be a stray cow on the road.

Being a narrow road with just enough room for two cars to pass, a stopped vehicle seldom presented a problem for cars going in opposite direction. You could stop on this road from Falls Village to Lakeville for 20 minutes and never see another car. What you would have likely seen was Tom Belter's father driving the tractor in the fields or crossing the road from one field to another.

Peter and I were only a few seats behind the driver. He spotted the bottle before we could hide it. Of course he asked us to hand it over. I didn't know this, but he knew my mother—not surprising considering how small these towns were. He opened the bottle and smelled it.

"Where did you get this?"

I told him I had drained all the empties from my mother's finished bottles to make it. He told Peter and me to never do this again; I could be in big trouble if it had been discovered in school. He pulled the bus up a few feet, stopping on one of the narrow bridges over a small stream. The topless bottle went flying into the stream. Later I pictured some of the trout in the stream likely getting drunk that day. I don't know if fish are affected by alcohol but it was an amusing thought.

The driver called my mother and told her about the incident. Mom scolded me and told me I could have been expelled from school. Between Mom and the driver, I realized the drinking example Mom was presenting was negative. Before, I just accepted it as adult behavior. Now for the first time drinking was presented as a negative, even from those who were drinkers.

Later, I would tell people it was my religious beliefs that prevented me from drinking. In reality is was this episode which had a significant impact on that decision.

The amount of hard liquor in the house decreased, but your grandmother's drinking problem shifted to cheap wine and beer. This lasted for the rest of her life, as you might remember. She usually had a can of beer on her little table whenever you visited her in the in-law apartment downstairs. You and she would read a book together or draw pictures, but in between each phase of the activity, she likely took a sip of beer. Even while in the hospital she convinced the MD to allow her a couple of cans of beer a day as "personal medicine."

I must admit she really loved you very much and just as surely would have loved your sister every bit as much had she lived long enough. The accomplishments both of you have made would have pleased her to no end—you as a teacher (and later as an MD) and your sister as a fashion designer.

Love,
Papa

Hello again:

While still in Connecticut before moving to Concord there was a significant increase in the rattlesnake population. They were all over the place, even in the back field. Since my early experience with one, I never was scared of them, just respected their territory. Most of the time if I ran into one it was among the berry bushes which had grown over the place the UFO had landed. If a rattler was there I would just stay out of striking distances. Sometimes I would sit down and just talk to them. In theory they don't have ears or can't hear, but I would talk to them as a way to calm them. I've always thought that all animals have a degree of telepathy; somehow they understand us in a very primitive way. When I talked they almost always relaxed and either went their own way or would just continue to sun themselves in the opening of the brush.

That particular year John Belter was sitting near Peter and me in class. Since he was aware of Rattlesnake Rest, John turned around and started telling us about all the rattlesnakes in the pastures and corn fields on the farm. A group of farmers were organizing a rattlesnake hunt. They planned to go through the field shooting as many as possible. Too bad no one thought of using them for dinner. Waste of good meat.

I told John the idea of a rattlesnake hunt was not a good one.

"But they might bite one of our cows. We have to get rid of them." he said.

"John, I wouldn't do that. The only reason they are increasing is because there is an increase in their food. If you kill them off you will have new problems."

John didn't take this seriously. The Belters and several other farmers had their rattlesnake hunt and the farmers were very happy the snake population was significantly reduced. The rest of the spring and summer went fine. Autumn came. Within a few weeks John was telling Peter and me about all the mice and rats that were eating the corn that had been put away for the cows during the upcoming winter.

I smiled: "John, why is there such an increase in mice and rats?'

His response was: "I don't know, I guess they just found good nesting places."

"Did you ever consider their increase is a direct result of you killing off most of the rattlesnakes? When the snake population increases it is because their food supply is large enough to support their numbers. When you killed the snakes you invited the mice and rats to come back."

John had to admit that was a valid point. I don't know if that sunk in with his father or the other farmers, but that winter some lost as much as a quarter of their stored corn to rodents.

No, I hadn't studied environmental science; to me it was just common sense. Much like the cause of global warming today comes from man. It is interesting how many people refuse to use common sense and ignore science when it does not fit their personally beliefs.

Love,
Papa

Hey T:

Back to Cuttyhunk. My letters about the summer with Sandy cover the summer after Cuttyhunk. Some including the flashbacks to Connecticut are a little out of sequence, but the stories hopefully are interesting. However, this would be an X-rated letter—but since it is not about me, here it is.

I loved my summer at Cuttyhunk. When Mr. Moore was there, he loved teaching me cribbage as mentioned. He loved the game but his grandchildren didn't want to learn it. As a result he was very happy I was willing to spend hours with him learning to play. It was very seldom, if ever, that I would win. But the fact that a young person was playing with him was exciting. I think he really liked me; at least he seemed to enjoy my company. I loved to listen to his stories.

One weekend, his other son, Robin came to spend the weekend. Robin had already been successful with one book *The French Connection*. He was thinking about his next, which would be *The Green Berets*. Later to become a movie starring John Wayne. That weekend Robin brought with him a little extra entertainment. It was not his wife, but two bimbos. Sorry to all the females who may be reading this but there was just no other way to describe them. They were mid-30s, stacked, blonde, sexy, and not very intelligent—or at least not showing any signs of intelligence. Of course, Robin brought a full case of vodka for his weekend stay.

That evening, the whole family, Marcia with her children Loulie, Johnny and Chris, Mr. and Mrs. Moore, Mom and myself, and Robin flanked by his two female "friends" all sat down at the huge dining table in the main room. The maid served the dinner. Johnny noticed his uncle Robin was already acting funny (read drunk as a skunk). Robin had his vodka on the rocks, finishing his second at the dinner table. The girls on either side were drinking heavily matching him glass for glass.

Suddenly one of them turned to Robin and said in a normal voice something like:

"Robin honey, when we finish here I'm going to give you the best cock sucking you have ever had."

The girl on the other side responded:

"It is my turn to give him a blow job then the best fuck he ever had"

Suddenly the two girls started shouting. Soon it graduated to a donnybrook. Both truculent females started physically fighting over whose turn it was to suck Robbin's cock. Up from their seats an all-out cat fight started, each pulling hair, and throwing wild punches at the other. All this took place in front of the whole family. Mr. Moore thought it was funny. Marcia and her mother were shocked. Robin loved being the object of the cat fight, snickering at every scream caused by a scratch or a bunch of hair being pulled out.

Mrs. Moore stood up in a most bellicose tone shouted, "Get out of my house now! Both of you!"

We were all surprised at both the volume and tone of her voice. None of us had ever seen her mad. She literally came over to the girls, grabbed both by the hair and dragged them out of the house. I was surprised by the strength she displayed. Her grip on the girls' hair was so strong if either resisted they would have lost a lot more hair than the few strains lost in the fight.

Once the girls were outside and the front door locked she got on the phone. Within minutes the only policeman on the island showed up. He put the two women in cuffs and took them away. The dinner continued in silence. Mr. Moore kept quite seeing his wife's reaction. The kids were trying to understand what had just occurred. It was very doubtful that any of them knew what a blow job was. My Mom sat quietly just watching the others, as did I. Meanwhile, Marcia was in a near state of shock, She couldn't think of anything to say or do that would have eased the tension in the atmosphere.

I think Mrs. Moore arranged with the Coast Guard to have the two women taken to the mainland that night. How, I have no idea. Possibly Mrs. Moore "donated" extra to them for this non-governmental duty. That island wasn't big enough for those women and Mrs. Moore!!!

As for Robin, he was devastated. He gave up eating food, downed a couple more vodkas, grabbed the bottle and disappeared into his room. He drank until he passed out. He was not seen until the next afternoon, with a huge hangover. This was my first major interaction with the famous Robin Moore—more next letter.

Love,
Papa

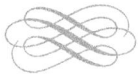

Dear T:

The day after the cat fight I think was a Saturday, maybe Sunday. The island was to have a big lobster fest; this was just up the hill from the docks and harbor. There were huge numbers of tables all filled with a variety of people. There was a tent was near the docks where the lobsters were being cooked with a number of exceptionally large pots on caste iron stands set over a roaring fire. Each were filled with water for the crustaceans to be submerged in. In another tent fish were being prepared, mostly flounders being filleted and cooked over an ope flame for those who wanted fish.

Fishermen were coming up the hill with baskets of freshly caught lobsters. Most lobsters were twice or three times the size of what you see today in Red Lobster or at the markets. This was before the over-fishing of lobsters occurred. The one pound creatures in stores and restaurants today are just not old enough to have reproduced their replacements. As much as I love them, I no longer eat lobster.

The Moores paid for all of us to go. I don't think the fees were that great, likely $15 per adult and $5 for those under 13. The whole town was there. There were those who were well off and dressed in "appropriate" casuals—in other words, even their casual clothes were expensive. Then, there were the town's folk in jeans and overalls. Teenagers wore bathing suits or shorts and t-shirts. Many who were the families of the fishermen got in free. After all, they were suppling the food. I think the whole fest was a fund raiser for the Cuttyhunk services (volunteer fire department, the policeman, road care, etc.).

I never had such a meal! Really fresh lobster, corn, cornbread, salad—and all you could eat. I must have finished off at least three lobsters, each well over two lbs. My extended stomach was making me waddle back up the hill as if I had been consuming beer as well as the lobsters. One of the main claws of a lobster at my table was almost as large as the whole lobster found in stores today. Of course all the lobsters were accompanied with hot melted butter—a cholesterol disaster, but boy was it good!

I'm not sure if it was the next day or the next weekend, but we had a family BBQ at the Club House. We set up a softball field and had a game. Johnny Moore, the Moore's youngest son was there playing with us. The rest of the family (except Billy) were either participating or cheering for one side or another.

This was when Robert Moore took the photo of me batting. After the softball game we had the BBQ, then a volleyball game. It was fun seeing little Johnny, Chris and Loulie all participating in the games. I enjoyed the softball since that was the sport I excelled at during those years.

As the evening rolled in, we lit a large fire, listened to a phonograph player and danced. Someone suggested doing the limbo. So we found a pole and had a contest.

Robin joined the family. Since he still owned his club in Jamaica, everyone felt he would be good at the limbo. At first he resisted. Someone suggested the only way he could get to go under the limbo bar was to tempt him with a vodka. I grabbed his glass and poured fresh vodka on the rocks. The drink was then dangled on the opposite side of the bar. It worked. Robin joined in and went under. He was actually very good and flexible. Not sure it was the result of good conditioning or enough alcohol in the blood stream to loosen up the body and bones. Still, he succeeded. He actually beat many of the others attempting to go under the bar, including myself. Downing a glass after each pass under the bar, he was about half way through on one of the turns when he fell backward on the grass. He was just barely conscious. We got him up, which was a challenge. He was placed in his chair, whereupon he passed out quicker than The Fat Boy in *The Pickwick Papers* when plopping himself amongst the cod fish and oyster barrels.

The games and feasting continued for another hour or so. Robin didn't stir. Someone placed a blanket over him and left him there until morning. Waking up in the middle of the large yard facing the ocean must have been a bit of a surprise. He stumbled into the house for breakfast around 10:30.

More on Cuttyhunk once you find a new place in the Bay Area (so a few weeks away).

Love,
Papa

Hi T:

There were lots of lazy days when we would spend the day at one of the beaches. Looking back on it I was surprised I did not spend more time fishing considering how much Mom loved to fish

There was one particular beach which was away from the direct ocean and therefore less chance for a large shark to be swimming by. It was in the Cuttyhunk channel. The channel was a decent length, a couple hundred yards, and there was a nice sandy beach at the elbow of the channel where you could sit there watching the boats come in and out of the island. Or, if you kept near the shore, you could swim. The challenge was the changing of the tides.

I loved to walk towards the opening of the channel near the ocean at high tide or near the docks at low tide and try to swim back to the beach. Most thought I was crazy. With the inlet being as large as it was, there was a lot of water moving through the channel. No one else dared to join me. Most simply played in the elbow where the current was not as strong. But if the tide was coming in, I would swim up channel towards the ocean. If the tide was going out I would try to swim down the channel towards the beach and docks.

The total distance would be between 50 and 100 yards. The effect was like swimming in a lap pool with the jet currents. Rarely did it take me less than an hour to swim that short distance. To me, it was a huge challenge, me vs. the current! By the time I was finished some days, I would barley have enough energy to walk back up to the Yacht Club. If you see the photo of me playing softball at Cuttyhunk, you now understand why I was in such good shape that summer. It was those swimming challenges!

Remember Marcia's daughter? She was into tarot cards and dabbled in the occult (more on that later). She was also interested in something the maid had. The cook/maid had her own ouija board. This was not like the ouija boards you would find in the local stores. This one was a solid block, an inch thick, in oak or walnut. The words and letters looked as though they had been burned into the board. The surface carefully varnished so it was perfectly smooth. I have never seen anything like it since. It was the length and width like most common commercial ones, just thicker and much heavier.

It had a pointer to go with it. The pointer looked like the usual plastic pointers but was made of white marble with a glass window in the center. Etched into the glass was a set of crosshairs to help people see the letter or number it was pointing to when moved. This was my first exposure to a ouija board and I was impressed with the craftsmanship that went into making this board. The maid told us it was well over 100 years old. That was when she told us kids she was really a witch. Of course none of the adults took her seriously, but to a bunch of impressionable kids under 13, that was a bit scary. To all except Loulie who was fascinated by witchcraft, already studying tarot, Voodoo, and other so-called "black arts."

The first time we used the board we were in the main room or the Club House and sat in a circle. I think it was the maid, Marcia's three kids and myself. The board rested on the edge of our knees, not on a table. The session was done in the usual way, by asking silly questions and putting our hands on the pointer. I questioned if the pointer was being controlled by anyone because I didn't believe it was moving without someone's hands on it; the maid assured me it was not. To prove it, on the next question we were to all concentrate on the question and not touch the pointer.

One of us thought of a question and shared it with the group. We were told to concentrate on it. Suddenly and very slowly the pointer started to move. After the first two letters it began to pick up speed. Soon it was traveling around the board as if it was trying to out-race a typewriter. Unfortunately the question and answer were not recorded. At the time the answer did seem to make sense and was directly related to the question. I was amazed and convinced it was for real.

About two years later, I heard the maid was using it to ask some taboo questions. She told us she knew it was not a proper use for the board. I'm not sure if it was related to getting money or perhaps to generate a negative spell towards someone she didn't care for, but according to the story the board burst into flames. Spontaneous combustion—it self-destructed. She showed a photo of the largely charred board with a burned hole in the center. Too bad, it was a beautiful board, and I was sorry that it no longer existed.

I was never able to get a pointer to move by itself with boards purchased in toy store. Nor have I found any board comparable to the old ones seen in antiques stores or occult shops since then. Actually, I have never seen any answers coming out of modern boards that were as fast and accurate as the old one. I soon lost interest in them.

As for tarot cards, they still hold my interest. Even now, if an interesting new deck comes out, it somehow tends to end up on a bookcase somewhere around. More on that later.

Love,
Papa

Hi T:

Towards the end of the summer, the Moores wanted to go out for a family picnic. Mr. Moore assigned everyone to one boat or another. I thought since my adventures with the shark (which he did not know about) and the sailboats in the storm, I would be one of the individuals piloting one of the boats. However, Mr. Moore was not aware of all my adventures and felt I was too young to handle a boat filled with people. When I complained he remained firm. In some ways he was right. After all, I was only a preteen at the time, but still was tell and very strong. If no one knew my age, they would have guessed at least 14 or more.

I was very upset. I felt I had proven myself and deserved to be something more than a passenger. I stormed off to my room and didn't participate in the picnic. Mr. Moore, I found out later, was saddened by my being upset and didn't understand the cause. I now regret my actions that day. He was such a good friend to me and my Mom and I had slighted him. However, that is long past now.

It was getting close to September. The days were getting shorter and the weather was cooling off slightly. There seemed to be more clouds associated with rain and storms rather than just an occasional afternoon thunderstorm common in summer. I knew we would all be leaving for school soon.

Sure enough, on a day late in August, Chris, Johnny (little), Loulie and I joined Marcia and my Mom on the ferry back to the mainland. I don't remember anything about the voyage back, except

I believe it was a cloudy day. Nor do I remember anything about the drive from New Bedford back to Concord, with the possible exception of stopping by a farmer's roadside stand.

There, fruit and cider were for sale. One of the gallon jugs was filled with cherry cider, not apple. I wanted to try it. We bought a gallon. I opened it up. Most of the others didn't care for it, which was just as well. More for me! What I didn't realize was that it was fermented. By the time we got home, I was really soused. Mom smelled the cider and realized it must have been 12 percent alcohol. I had finished off a large part of it. So I was poured into bed and slept it off until the next day. That was the only time in my life I ever got drunk or drank alcohol. Is it one hundred percent true? Really, just a guess.

Looking back, I can say that my summer in Cuttyhunk was the most delightful and most fun summer I have ever experienced. I learned a great deal, from filleting cod fish to sailing a small boat. I almost got eaten by a great white shark and swam against fierce currents. I sailed a boat in a storm using a silly song to save myself and my young passengers.

But it was also the beauty of the island that made a lasting impression on me. There we were in the Cape Cod chain of islands, but closer to New Bedford. We could see Martha's Vineyard in the distance (the summer home of the Kennedys). If you stood on the top of the highest hill, with a possible elevation of close to a hundred feet, you could see the mainland, the chain of islands and all of Cuttyhunk (almost) in one dramatic panorama.

It was serene and beautiful.

Years later, another 'Lakeshore Inn', this one in Lakeville was closing. Mom and I went up to the closing sale to see if there were any bargains to be had. It was there I spotted the large (and partly unfinished) watercolor painting. I took one look at the painting and realized it was a scene from the NW corner of Cuttyhunk looking toward Martha's Vineyard. If not, it sure looked exactly like the view of the island from that position with one slight difference. I didn't remember the large rock emerging from the ocean in the center of the painting, but you have to allow artists poetic license; it makes for a better scene. (However, as your sister is quick to point out, the hole in the rock is where the artist didn't complete his painting.)

I told Mom: "That's Cuttyhunk."

She asked if I really wanted it. Of course I did. We waited until the auction came around to the painting. It was one of the last items and all the valuable pieces of the Inn had been sold. Few people were interested in the few remaining paintings and other knickknacks that remained. The bid for the picture started at $35 (remember this was the late 1960s). Mom raised her hand. There were no other bids. We got it!

This is the story behind the watercolor and why I am so fond of it. It is the only visible memory of Cuttyhunk I have. We have had it hanging in various places from time to time. It was the first painting in my art collection, something that has continued growing for all my life. Even now, I can't seem to resist adding a new painting or a graphic to the collection every now and then.

No wonder Charlene convinced me to open an art gallery. It was not a money maker, but it is a place to find new homes for all those works that can't fit on the walls our house. The only problem is the art gallery, populated with art, just encourages one to buy more. It's a bad habit; but a beautiful one—better than cigarettes or booze! The old watercolor is now in the BenGate Gallery. (Unfortunately a year after this letter the gallery was shut down and all items sold in an auction house.)

Love,
Papa

August 31 a little late so you have a BALPEX cancelation

Dear T:

Back to Concord. It was still summer, but I was thinking about school. I was living back with Marcia in the little study that Simons used to use. Simons and Marcia were divorced by now and Marcia, as one of the heirs to the Sheraton fortune, was quickly surrounded by a number of suitors. But that's another story to be picked up later.

For now it would be important to know that Marcia was still teaching yoga and lecturing on the values of astrology when properly done by serious astrologers. She was becoming well known in a lot of circles. It was interesting to be in the house because there were a lot of international visitors. I loved listening to them discuss philosophy and religion. There were many guests from India and elsewhere around the world. Many were studying at Harvard or one of the many other academic institutions in the Boston area.

When given the opportunity I joined in the conversations, and was always complemented on the way I could carry on a conversation. I don't remember the people's names, but there were a lot of personalities that came to visit. What helped was the insistence that Mom made of me becoming familiar with other religious texts. I had read the Gita, the Torah, the Bahai prayer book, and several other texts. This impressed many of the guests, who thought very highly of me.

Many from India visited Marcia while she was still married to Simons, as they had spent months in India. The tanka paintings of Buddha and the small Vishnu the latter of which was in your bedroom for a while, the larger one in the hall, were gifts to Mom and me when she returned, years before we moved to Concord. At the side of the house, in a flat area, Marcia held her yoga classes, everyone standing on little mats doing various stances with my mother sometimes leading the group when Marcia was off somewhere else. I never attended any of the classes, but should have. It would have been good discipline.

I remember there was man who was interested in Marcia. He was a very thin and likely in his 50s. His claim to fame was being a health nut and he "knew" more about the holistic body than most in the world.

"I've never had any aches or pains in my body in my life." was his proclamation.

Right! That was one of his many claims, which came with food supplements he tried to sell. They remind me now of the Atkins Diet powder-drink mixes, but his were likely all dried and pulverized vegetables. I think he was looking for Marcia's endorsement to boost his sales. He was also interested in her romantically.

He promoted one exercise that would make your hand and wrist strong if practiced regularly. Start by holding a full folded sheet of a newspaper in one corner. Then using just one hand, wad it up into a ball so that you could cover it with your whole hand. I took a *Boston Globe* page and started doing exactly what he described as the exercise.

"Oh, don't be surprised if you are unsuccessful. Very few can do it. I'm sure a boy your age will not succeed, but give it a good try."

I tried. Slowly more and more of the paper was being wadded up in my hand. He was looking more and more amazed. Soon the whole paper was in a tight enough ball that my whole hand was able to fit completely around it. He couldn't believe it. Never had anyone as young as I been able to complete that exercise. I just smiled and handed him the wadded-up paper. Not only was he a prosaic individual but displayed a supercilious attitude towards the kids.

Loulie, Chris and Johnny agreed—he was a phony! We all agreed this character had to go. Loulie's interest in the occult, beyond the ouija board, now came into play. She had started working with tarot cards and actually got me interested. She was into fortunes. I was more interested in the symbols on the cards, but dabbled in fortune layouts (years later). She had a good collection of books on everything from astrology, palmistry, voodoo and witchcraft.

Loulie read up on how to create a voodoo doll. She listed all the things we needed. Johnny (I think, though it may have been Chris) took some scissors and cut a small piece of cloth from the coat lining of this man so it would not be noticed. I found some of his hairs on the sofa he had been sitting on. Loulie carefully constructed the doll. It was about six inches tall. She dressed it like this character and with pen and ink, she drew a face that looked a little like him. Then under the little clothes Loulie had made, we lined it with the cloth from his coat. On top of the voodoo doll's head, she glued the hair I had found.

I really didn't think anything would happen, but it was fun to watch all this. Loulie's fervent desire to get rid of this man from the house and from her mother's life was a show in itself.

The doll was placed inside a "magic circle" with candles around it. Then she took some long hat pins and stuck three or four into the doll's back in ritual format. We all went to bed.

In the morning the man was outside walking back and forth on the patio. He was groaning with pain. In particular, his mid and lower back were making him suffer terribly. I asked what was wrong. He turned to me with great effort and in a bold lie he responded:

"Nothing…!"

Needless to say he received an "urgent message" and had to leave—for good! The four of us all cheered. We thought it a great victory.

Love,
Papa

Chapter 13

Would You Believe Deutschland Bound?

Dear T:

A bit of a flashback before we can move forward.

I'm not sure if I told you about one of Mom's friends from NYC.

Marie B was someone who knew us in Brooklyn. She was about Mom's height. Her black hair was accentuated by black-rimmed glasses. Her smile was inviting and was able to carry on a good conversation on a number of topics, though never in detail. I don't believe she was ever involved in the more esoteric work grandmother was involved in. I was never sure what brought the two of them together.

Marie was a woman with several kids. She ended up moving to Connecticut not too far from where we lived—actually very close, by Salisbury standards. She and her kids moved into a little upstairs apartment after her divorce. She was hoping Mom could help her find work and start a new life, but northwest Connecticut was not a good place to start over.

She had a couple of boys who were older than I. The youngest was called Terry. The oldest child's name escapes me. But her youngest daughter Susan was just about my age, which at the time was around six or seven. I think Mom and Dad were still together but I'm not sure since this would have been close to the split.

Susan was a very pretty little girl. She was shy and soft spoken, just the type that was attractive to me. Naturally, I had a huge crush on her. We visited several times. Each time I would devote most of my attention to Susan and ignore the boys.

On one of those visits, we met an army sergeant named Roy. He was courting Marie. Roy was a strange man—short and pudgy and very military, a WWII veteran who had seen a lot of action. His bald head stood out, as did his oddly shaped nose. He really was quite ugly, but being a career army sergeant, he had a steady source of income and stable employment; he also had a very domineering personality. In all matters, everything had to be one way only: his way! Shortly after Roy and Marie started seeing each other, Marie moved. Mom told me they got married and moved to the military housing.

I didn't really have any more contact at least not for a number of years. Mom, however, kept in touch with Marie. Roy and Marie had a girl together, born shortly after Marie had moved away.

In the meantime, Roy was rotated to Germany. This would have been around 1958. They were stationed in Heidelberg, which is in Baden-Württemberg. This was around the same time that we moved to Concord.

When bad times hit us after Mom lost her job, she asked friends to take me in and then came up with an idea. She could send me to Germany to live with Roy and Marie. I would have some overseas living experience and maybe see a little of the world at the same time. I would also have a room and meals for a year. This was when we were facing being homeless. Marcia didn't want us as permanent guests. Mom didn't have a job. Sandy was too far away from anything considered stable for me to live with her.

Unknown to me, Mom sent a letter to Marie asking if they would take me for a year. I think the real objective was for me to have a roof over my head. Since the oldest boy in the family was leaving for the States, there was a spare room. I would be no trouble. The expenses would be minimal. Feeding seven instead of six would hardly make a difference in the budget or other expenses. If I came over that would leave Terry (17), Gail, who was around 15 had been adopted by Roy and Marie, Susan, and the youngest, Jenna a product of Roy and Marie's marriage.

Mom finally came to me and asked if I would be interested in living in Germany for a year. I didn't know what to say. Then she reminded me of Susan. "Of course, I would love to go to Germany!"

It was hard leaving Concord. I would really miss Gail and some of my other friends. Still, new experience could be fun. So the plan was laid out. I was to be in Germany for a full school year and return after summer break. This would give me the experience of living in Germany and exposure to other cultures in Europe. The only problem we didn't consider was Roy's personality. His lack of education would be reflected in his treatment of me and the other children but that was not taken into consideration; it should have been.

So a new phase in my life was about to unfold in many interesting ways. More next time.

Love,
Papa

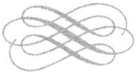

Dear T:

Now the first episode in a very strange part of my life. GERMANY! It has been hard for me to start these letters. Much of these episodes are not positive, actually they are quite negative.

It is funny. Sometimes the gods try to give you a warning, but at 12 years of age, who listens? Come to think of it, how many really pay attention to their intuition? There may be little warnings and doubts that come to someone who is making a decision. Our subconscious often knows what may not be best. But once a decision is made, few want to change their directions. They tend to ignore any warning that crosses their paths.

Plans were made to have me fly over in early September to begin 7th grade at the military-based American school.

In late August Walter Ulbricht, the First Secretary of the Socialist Unity Party of East Germany, didn't like how so many of his citizens were escaping to West Berlin. It is important to realize that Berlin was divided into four sectors at this time—the result of the peace treaty agreed to with the Allies after WWII. Each part was controlled by one of the WWII Allies: USA, England, France and the USSR (the Soviet Union, not Russia as it is today). Being an open city, people could fairly easily cross over, despite the tight security at the divisions.

In late August 1961 the Berlin Wall started to go up almost overnight. East-West tensions were very high. Remember, this occurred shortly after the Cuban Missile Crisis, so NATO-Soviet tensions were already strained. As the Wall went up, more and more East Germans tried to get through. Many were shot dead. I remember the TV news showing a young couple, just married, who were shot and allowed to slowly bleed to death at the foot of the Wall. Many thought military action was imminent. There were hawks (though not known as such back then) who wanted NATO to knock down the wall. The justification would have been similar to what led to the Berlin Air Lift in the 1950s, which busted the East German blockade of supplies getting into parts of Berlin under Allied control. But such an action would have been a violation of the peace agreement. Most military advisors felt it would have started WWIII.

Mom began to question the wisdom of having me go so near this hot-spot, but Roy assured her the 400,000-plus troops in West Germany would make it as safe as anywhere, especially if nuclear war broke out. If the USSR launched missiles, no one would be safe, especially those in the USA or around major cities; NATO was preventing any possibility of the Warsaw Pact hostilities by provided protection. Any invasion would be defended by the strong presence of the Allied troops stationed where he was: West Germany.

Mom and I had several long talks. I reminded her how just a few months ago, we were all practicing duck and cover drills in school, anticipating a Russian attack. I reasoned it made little difference if I was in a US city under attack or in Germany. At least in Germany there was slightly less of a chance of a nuclear attack. The winds carrying the radioactive fallout would kill as many in Eastern Europe and the Soviet Union as those in Germany. You were less likely to be killed by a nuclear blast there than in Concord. Besides, all the major cities in the eastern regions of the USA were major targets. New York City, Albany, Hartford, Boston, Worcester, and all the capitals of all the Eastern United States were targets, along with major industrial centers. If there was an attack, Boston would be hit and Concord would receive lethal radiation no matter which direction the winds blew. Radiation poisoning would not be a pleasant way to die—better to be killed by a shell or shot coming from the Russian troops. All this was part of our discussions.

In Germany, tensions increased. NATO-reinforced forced West Germany with tank and troop deployments near the boarders with the so-called Eastern Bloc (those within the Soviet sphere of influence). Soon there were more troops on active duty on both sides than had been since the final push on Berlin during the last stages of WWII. Mom was having second thoughts about the whole trip. She wanted to cancel. I just repeated the arguments I'd already given.

September approached and a decision had to be made. It is strange sometimes how world events influence personal directions. Though the German experience was more negative than positive, a few things came out of it that would change my life. I did not pay attention to signs that the trip may not be the best idea, despite the ominous world situation and personal doubts. The only favorable thing on my mind was my puppy infatuation with Susan and the possible relationship we might have.

A decision was made: I would go after all. So, I began to pack for my first trip to Europe. Flights were reserved. The whole itinerary was planned: I would leave from Boston, fly to London change flights to Frankfurt, Germany, where Roy and Marie would pick me up. Then we would drive me to Heidelberg and the Patrick Henry Army Base where the family lived.

Since the oldest boy was gone, I would even have a room to myself. Everything looked like it may work out. If nothing went wrong, it would be an easy trip. But Murphy's Law had other plans.

Love,
Papa

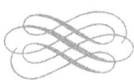

Hi T:

The fateful day arrived, my flight to Germany! For some reason the departure location was changed. I had to leave from Idlewild Airport in NYC (later renamed JFK) rather than Boston. The was a flight leaving in the afternoon, which was to arrive in London mid-morning on the next day. From there I was booked on a Lufthansa flight to Germany, after a brief layover. With enough lead time to make the connection should the flight be slightly delayed.

I was excited. I had been on several flights by myself to and from Florida to visit my dad. This would just be another long flight and was likely to be very boring—there were no movies back then, no radio or music channels, either. I was flying on a DC7, the old four-engine jet, which was very noisy. One difference was there were better meals and bigger seats than on current flights. The main cabin of a DC7would be considered economy class now.

I remember the flight taking off and heading east. We were several hours into the flight when one of the engines started to sputter. Eventually it conked out completely. The pilot got on the public address system:

"Ladies and gentlemen, this is your pilot speaking. We have lost our number four engine, but there is more than enough power in the remaining three to get us safely to Heathrow Airport in England on time. Please relax and enjoy the flight."

About 30 minutes later the engine on the opposite side of the plane started to sputter like the first. But this time, it caught on fire. The pilot cut the fuel off and the fire soon went out without the fuel to feed it.

"Ladies and gentlemen. You have noticed that our number one engine is malfunctioning. Don't worry, we can still safely make it to England. It may delay us slightly but we should have no more trouble."

Remember, this is when there were no phones on planes—impossible for people to reschedule flights if we were delayed. I didn't even think about the connection flight I had to make to get from England to Germany. They served extra drinks and food to those who wanted. Back then food and drinks were free and good quality.

About 15 minutes later number one caught on fire again and spread to the number two engine. Now people were beginning to panic. Some women were screaming when they spotted the flames. I just observed the whole thing with amusement. Mom had told me about so many of her close calls while flying, I was not worried (well maybe a little).

"Ladies and gentlemen, this is your captain again. We have almost reached the point of no return, but are still a few minutes short of that point. I will be cutting off the fuel to the engine on fire. That should extinguish the fire. In the meantime, I am turning the flight around to head back to the States. Hopefully we will be able to safely fly back to Boston. Sorry for the inconvenience. I will keep you informed."

There were then a series of back fires on the engines that were on fire. After several attempts, the fires were put out. The main problem was we were headed westward back to the States.

By 3:30 a.m. we were approaching Boston. No circling the airport on this approach, we were coming straight in towards the runway! Besides, flights rarely took off or landed after midnight.

I remember the approach. We were flying on one good engine. The others had been shut down. As we were near the airport we could see what awaited us: there were fire trucks and emergency vehicles on both sides of the runway. As we approached the runway some sparks started coming out of the troubled number one and two engines.

We started our approach. We could see the water in the bay. Soon our wheels touched down. There was a collective cheer. But as we went down the runway, all the emergency vehicles pulled off the grass and followed, full speed, after our aircraft. One fire truck put out the sparks almost before we stopped. All immediate danger muted. Passengers were quickly asked to leave the plane by the usual exits in the front and rear of the plane. The old style of exit stairs were in place as quickly as the crew could open the doors.

All were very grateful the second feet hit the ground. So, some 6-plus hours after leaving New York I was safely in BOSTON!?! The problem was there was no way to contact Mom. But I did have a way to call Roy and Marie to tell them what had happened? NO! The thought of needing to change the connecting flight didn't even occur to me. It should have. The connecting flight would have been taking off just about the time we hit the runway in Boston. None of the staff at the airline offered any help. Can't fully blame them. Everyone was so happy just being on the ground and few thought of the implications for those waiting for our arrivals in London and elsewhere.

Now what?

Looking back on it, this flight must have been the most exciting one I have ever been on. The next best, if you can call it that, was when our plane was struck by lightning when flying into Tampa to visit Dad. Another would be the puddle hoppers to Mayagüez from San Juan. Puerto Rico was still years away.

Love,
Papa

Hello:

So there I was in Boston at 5 a.m. in the morning, trying to catch a little sleep on the airport chairs. The airline was trying to find a new jet to take the passengers to England. Most were trying to telephone the various airline to reschedule their connecting flights, something I was blissfully ignorant of. That bliss would soon change, especially once I got to England.

Mom didn't know about the flight problems. Roy was just getting ready to meet me at the airport in Frankfurt. Word did not travel very fast back then: there was no internet, no cell phones and very few news channels that carried non disaster stories. No one on the ground fully realized what had happened. The airline was not communicating very much to the outside world, at least as far as I ever found out. The most anyone knew was there had been an emergency landing in Boston during the middle of the night and all passengers were safe. No mention of which flight it was or what had happened.

Meanwhile, around 6 a.m. we all boarded a new DC7 and took off from Boston headed to England. It was a smooth flight with no incidents and we all landed safely in England—18 hours late!

I got off and asked where the flight to Frankfurt was.

"Oh, that flight took off hours ago!"

Of course I didn't have a way to call Roy nor Mom. NOW I was beginning to panic. What could I do? How could I get in touch with anyone? Did anyone know what happened to me?

Later I learned that Roy found out about the problems once he arrived at Frankfurt Airport. Being US Army he was putting a great deal of pressure on Lufthansa Airlines to find me a seat on the next flight out of England. Of course all flights were filled up due to the usual passengers and the additional ones from my flight who had missed their connections. The airport staff was sympathetic but not very helpful.

"All flights are filled. There is no seat for you anywhere."

About an hour later I was told to go to a Lufthansa gate. I had a seat on the next flight! When we started boarding I was directed to first class! What a surprise (first and only time I've flown first class). We took off on time. I had a great meal. Being a German airline I was offered beer, along with a variety of other refreshments, including an assortment of fine German pastries. There was a very nice German gentleman sitting next to me who had been on the same flight as me from NYC. He was very sympathetic and said if he had only known I was traveling alone, he would have been happy to help me.

I landed in Frankfurt about 20 hours later than anticipated. Roy and Marie were there, as back then it was not a problem for people to meet friends and family at the gates! Even on international flights. Thank goodness!

We got through customs real fast (Roy had his uniform on, so no real questions or delays). I told them about the flaming engines and the emergency landing in Boston. All they knew was that the flight had to turn back due to engine trouble. They had not heard the details. Now that I had landed where I needed to be, it was easy to relate all that had happened on the original flight. Telling the story was very cathartic. It helped relieve the tension over the past 36 hours. It also helped Roy and Marie to fully understand all the problems that occurred.

When the flight to London did not land on time it was evident the original schedule was failing. Roy told me they had called the airports and the various airlines to put pressure on them to get me to Frankfurt on the next available flight, once they learned I had reached London. It worked.

We picked up my bags from the baggage claim and then I climbed into the back seat of their car and we were off to Heidelberg. They lived in an apartment building at the Army Base. It was a typical non-com (non-commissioned officer) apartment complex: a long brick building with no evaluator and several entrances. I do remember it was the building on the left as we entered the road between the two apartment buildings. Later, I would meet a friend of Roy's and the family who lived in the building on the right. They were Italian-American. The father was also a sergeant, like Roy. Both worked in telecommunications, which back then involved old-fashioned radios.

Once I arrived in the apartment the whole family seemed to be happy that I was coming to stay with them. That impression would quickly fade. Later, I learned my presence helped justify their large apartment of five or six bedrooms. With the oldest moving to the States they would have had to move into a smaller apartment, but with me staying with them it justified a bedroom for the youngest girl and one for Terry the older boy, Susan and Gail shared a room, Marie and Roy were in the master bedroom, there was an extra room for an 'office' (more on that later), and then a separate one for me. I had a good night's sleep that night.

Love,
Papa

Hello there:

(Years from now I will tell you about that greeting and my meeting your Mom.)

I was happy to have arrived safely in Heidelberg.

The apartment was long and narrow. The living room was open on the immediate right as you entered with the dining area in the same space, just placed a little further into the room. The kitchen was on the left. It was a decent size, with a small island and good stove. Next to the kitchen was the only bathroom in the apartment. You can imagine with the number of people in the apartment a single bathroom would cause fights. Eventually a schedule for the mornings was set up as to who would use it when. Beyond the dining area and the bathroom, the hall led to the bedrooms. The exception was the immediate room on the right—Roy's "playroom".

My room was the middle room down the hall on the left. It was a decent size and certainly larger than the little study I stayed in while living with Marcia and the kids in Concord (even though it was much classier).

Susan and Gail shared the largest "guest" bedroom, the first door on the left down the hall, next to mine. Jena, the youngest girl was on the other side of the hall from me, next to her parents room. Terry's was the last one on the left and across from Roy and Marie's master bedroom, the largest bedroom. After Terry, left Jena moved into that room as it was a little bigger, big enough to allow sleep overs with her friend Pearl.

The first room on the right was Roy's playroom. When I looked in I was shocked. It was a complete radio station! There were high powered transmitters and banks of other equipment I had no idea what the hell it was for. There was also a telegraph key! When looking in, I was told immediately that Roy was a radio ham operator with his own call letters. Most of his extra time was spent in this crowded room communicating with army buddies around the world. Looking in the room it was amazing how much equipment was stacked in there. Banks and banks of communications equipment were on shelf after shelf. There was every kind of transmitter and receiver one could imagine. Some of the latest transmitters and almost all of the equipment looked new. I really had no idea what most of it was for other than part of the overall communications set up. Later Roy told me his dream was to retire from the army and establish an independent radio station with all this "excess" cast-off equipment that would make it possible.

How could a sergeant afford all this? I would eventually find out.

As for the family, it was quite diverse. Terry was tall and thin. He wore glasses, much like my father's dark-rim glasses, but Terry's rims where thinner. He ultimately became my only friend in the family. Terry was just about to finish high school and had been applying to colleges. He was planning to go to college in the beginning of January midterm. Due to the crazy schedules of military schools, he had missed about half a year of studies due to all the moving around. I later found out he had been accepted. I don't remember where. He would be leaving just after the New Year. My only ally was with me all too briefly. Still there were things about our brief friendship that were a little upsetting.

The older brother had already left for college about a year before. I was in his room. It soon became apparent that Roy didn't care for this older boy. It might be due to this boy being part of Marie's family before she married Roy. It might have been due to Roy's personality. One day Roy turned to me and said:

> "If Terry becomes like his brother and never writes, I will dismiss him as part of the family. Right now I don't think his brother is worth the dirt under my fingernails. To me he is a piece of garbage. He doesn't exist."

This was the beginning of a realization about Roy's true personality. I soon realized Terry couldn't wait to get out of the home. Roy would soon say the same things about Terry as he did about his brother. But Terry would be better off.

Gail was an adopted daughter. She was heavy set (modestly fat), had a very round face and wore glasses. Jena was the baby of the family the only product of their marriage. She had asthma and was spoiled rotten.

Everyone had jobs to do in the apartment, except Jena—a fact she flaunted! She was about 9 or 10, short and thin but with a lot of strength hidden in that small frame somewhere.

I've saved Susan for last. She was the one I had desired to see by coming to Germany. She was as gorgeous as I remembered when I first developed a crush on her years before. She was tall, almost my height, and had long light brown hair and, I believe, blue eyes. I could be wrong about the eyes—it has been a long time. I immediately gave her a big hug upon arrival. I expressed my puppy love for her.

"It was the anticipation of seeing you again. That's what brought me to Germany."

Mind you it was about four or five years earlier, but it was still my fondness for her that made me want to come. She hugged me back and we spent some time talking. Later I heard her and Gail talking. She said I was: "A mushy lovey dovey boy." A type she hated.

My prime reason for coming to Germany was instantly shattered less than 48 hours. Susan's comments influenced my relationships with girls and later women for most of the rest of my life. I took it for granted that all women didn't want exceptionally affectionate men or emotional love. In almost all my relationships until college, I would be fond of my steady girlfriends but stopped short of 'love.' Certainly the word 'love' was eliminated from any conversations with any of the dates for the next six years. From that day forward, it became very hard for me to have strong emotional attachments to any female.

Looking back on my life, this could apply to your mother. Marisol was wonderful in a lot of ways. I certainly liked her. But contemplating our marriage, I really don't think there was ever much "romantic love" for her. In some ways what I felt towards her was the type of love a brother and sister may have for each other, just not the romantic passion that should be part of a marriage.

There was another impact. Overhearing that conversation set up what was to be a confrontational relationship between myself, Susan and Gail. Both began to make life difficult for me whenever possible. Eventually even Roy and Marie realized it, which didn't help the atmosphere in the home. It just made it worse. All this was reflected in my letters home, which I sent weekly. Roy insisted and supplied the envelopes. He would post them on the base for me. One prime example of the difficulties that were mounting up was when Marie became ill with what was likely the cold or possibility the flu. One of the girls once complained that I didn't use enough soap when doing dishes while on kitchen duty. That gave Roy an opening. He stormed into the kitchen while I was doing the dishes for the evening and held a dinner plate in front of me. There was a grease mark, likely butter, on it.

"You see this!" he shouted. "This is a plate which is not clean which I got from the cupboard. Your bad washing has caused Marie to get sick."

I was castigated for a full 10 minutes. The malediction made everyone assume I was the cause of Marie's illness. I was very upset, but didn't stop to analyze the situation. Marie could not have become sick instantly from one dirty plate that day. Later I realized it was a setup. The plate only had a smear of clean grease in one straight line as if applied by a large finger. There was no indication that any food/dirt was ever on the plate. All other plates were clean. Based upon the size of the finger mark, it was Roy who had set me up. However, I was forced to re-wash all the plates in the cabinets, which took an extra hour or more. From that day on I never trusted Roy again and realized they would always try to use me as a scapegoat.

I apologized and put more soap on the scrub brush. Yet inside I knew the plate was a plant. There was no way a plate could have been that clean everywhere except where the grease mark was. Roy must have taken some butter, smeared it on the plate in order to use me as a scapegoat for Marie's illness. Eventually the tensions would bleed over to all the family. This was especially true once Terry left in January. By February, it was becoming unbearable.

Love,
Papa

Hello:

A quick diversion for this letter, which is being sent around Halloween. I thought a letter about current activities would be a fun. Xsports had their membership appreciation night on the 28th. It was costume night, but I forgot to wear one. When I realized, I raced home and put on my Harry Potter Death Eater's outfit. I didn't use the cheap old skull mask I had worn previously, as I'd brought one great mask the day before, which was closer to the movie. With its black veil it worked well! I then had my usual black robe and the purple cape from the playroom closet. Of course I had my wand—the one made out of a cedar branch. What made it great was how the wood of the cedar had three colors. The outer was white. The middle layer was a brown/black. The inner section and the point were the dark red wood of the inner tree. When I got back to the club, the costume drew a lot of attention—it was a hit.

I had bought a modest size pumpkin and had it in the condo for a number of days. I decided to draw a rough sketch of the scene on the pumpkin for one of my typical carvings. Here is a description from the largest figure and going around to the right.

A witch was flying with a pair of bats. Below the witch was a small typical jack-o-lantern in typical 'fashion—eyes, nose and toothy grin. Then in the background and slightly to the right of the witch was a haunted castle on a hill. A horse drawn hearse/carriage was going up a hill to the castle. This never came out as much as I would have liked in the final product, but it was visible.

Then at the base of a hill was a graveyard with about six graves. One had a ghost rising above it. Another had an arm coming from the ground as the zombie within was attempting to crawl out. At the base of the hill behind the hearse was a dead tree with a werewolf standing in front of it. Professor Lupin would have been proud! I had a full moon above the tree with a few clouds drifting by. To the right of the tree was a village in the hills. This was in the background, perspective wise, and was meant to be seen at a distance from the tree.

In the forefront of the village was a guillotine, which for its size came out remarkably well. Then slightly behind it was a church. To the right what I tried to carve was a typical Eastern European set of simple buildings/homes. None really stood out, being more suggestive than well-defined. Behind the village was an outline of a mountain range with the clouds above it. This led to a slight space before we reached the witch again. Of course I carved out the drawing and scraped out the insides, not cutting through allowing for an eerie glow, and it worked GREAT!

Charlene, my new love after the divorcing your mother, had no idea how such a drawing was going to be realized. Her family, mostly due to having a conservative religious upbringing, never celebrated Halloween. A great loss for her family, in my opinion, and a source of a little disappointment in our relationship. So this was a new experience for her.

That Saturday her family came over. I brought out the pumpkin. It was a hit with her grand-nieces and nephew. Then later, when talking about the costume, I decided to put it on and came back into the house. The white husband of her nice who is Black saw me coming and thought it was great. But his wife just about had a heart attack. Charlene's daughter was ready to get a baseball bat and beat me to death.

On Halloween, Charlene and I went to Tyson's, where there was an afternoon concert which had one of her former bosses playing second violin. We walked around and to see all the kids in costume and trick or treating in the stores. Charlene wanted to go out for ribs. I called Sweet Water restaurant and asked if there were anything special going on. Not really but they encouraged my wearing a costume. Charlene was embarrassed at the idea, but she realized I love Halloween, so she put up with it!

When we got to Sweet Water the gal at the door thought the costume was great. After the initial shock she started to laugh. When she asked one of the hostesses to seat us, the first one took one look at me, shouted:

"No!" and ran away, trying to hide behind a male cashier.

The next one laughed and seated us across from elderly couple. When I took off my mask, they started a conversation with us about how happy they were to see that "people of our age" could have fun on Halloween too. On the other side of the partition was a young Black family. The mother was in a minor costume, and it was also her birthday. Her four-year-old was in costume too. We started a conversation with them. I asked her son if my costume was scary? "Yes," he answered, but with a big smile.

The hostess who I had scared before came over to talk to us and admitted she was terrified of the mask. Being an immigrant Halloween was new to her. At the end of the dinner, Charlene admitted it was fun. Maybe next year she will at least wear a mask. Good time!

Love,
Papa

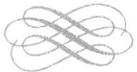

Hi:

Back to Germany.

Remember mentioning "jobs" in the apartment? There were household duties assigned to each of the children residing in the home, except Jena. Susan, Gail, Terry and me were assigned one of the chores each week. The duties were kitchen, floors, laundry and bathroom. The chores such as the bathroom included cleaning—sink, tub, bowl, etc., almost daily. With five duties and only four to be assigned, one of us had a week's break.

Floors included sweeping, dusting, vacuuming as needed and mopping weekly. This included all rooms, except if the person who's room it was objected. They would take care of it themselves. Gail and Susan never let me in their room. Jena's room had to be done daily due to her asthma.

The worst duty was the kitchen. This included preparing ALL family meals, cleaning up after the meals, washing the dishes daily. The meals had to be planned for the week. Marie would usually sit down with whoever had kitchen duty and plan the meals for the week. This allowed her to plan the shopping at the commissary during the week, knowing exactly what was needed for the meal.

Each Saturday morning the assigned duty would transfer to the next person, but only after an army-style inspection. If I was to take over the bathroom from Terry, I would inspect the tub, bowl, floors, fixtures, etc. If a spot or water mark existed, the transfer would be refused. Terry would have to redo the specific area noted until it was clean enough to pass.

If anyone found anything dirty, they could refuse the transfer. No one was permitted to leave the apartment on Saturday until their previous week's duty passed inspection. Only then was the duty officially passed on to the next person. The easiest was floors. I always looked forward to having that duty. A quick sweeping and a little vacuuming was all that was needed, except for Jena's room.

Passing the kitchen to the next person was hard, especially for me. Susan, who usually followed me, would make the inspection harder for me than anyone else. All the kitchen shelves, counter tops, etc. had to be spotless. The person inspecting could check individual plates on the shelves, pots, pans, floor…

One Saturday when the kitchen duty was to pass from me to Susan, she had left early with Gail while I was still cleaning the kitchen so Roy was going to do the inspection. Everything was going fine until he got on a stool and looked at the top of the cabinets. No one had cleaned those since I had arrived. He noted the dust and grease. I protested, explaining those were never part of the inspection previously because no one used the stool or ladder to get up there. When he looked at the accumulation of dirt, this was evident. Surprise—he let me pass. This might have been the only time he was considerate of me regarding the household duties. The next time I had the kitchen, a wipe on the top of the cabinets was made so they were not as bad.

Now for a bit of truth.

I have often said I learned to cook at home. This is not entirely true. It was while in Germany that I learned to cook many of the basics as a result of kitchen duty. These would not be complex meals. I don't clearly remember, but I think there was a choice of about a dozen menus we were expected to be able to prepare for the family. Spaghetti and meatballs, or some other variety of Italian dish was once a week, same with meatloaf. There was usually a casserole during the week. Wurst and sauerkraut was another option—after all, this was Germany. Chicken in a variety of recipes was a regular meal. It could be roasted, fried or cooked in a sauce.

Marie would help me with the basics if needed, but after the first two kitchen duties and with a little help from Terry, that was the last of the requested help. Whoever had kitchen duty could select what to fix on any particular day. This is where I learned to prepare Italian sauces and a lot of other usual items for the first time. Yes, I learned more at home, once I got back, but it was in Germany where I really started to cook.

Once Terry left, there was no free week. It was interesting that Gail and Susan would conspire to make it hard for me to pass initial inspection just to keep me from going out on Saturdays. Of course, not having transportation, there weren't many places to go, but it was still nice to get out and walk around Patrick Henry Village, where we lived.

Love,
Papa

Dear T:

Remember Roy's workshop/office with its complete radio station? It was quite an impressive room. There were tens of thousands of dollars of equipment, maybe more. I wondered how an army sergeant second class could afford all that equipment. I would soon find out.

I asked Roy where all the equipment come from. He said it was excess from old parts and supplies. I doubted this because some of it looked very new. All pieces were in typical army-green color, the same you often find on trucks and field equipment. I knew it was not from private sources. Then, one evening something happened that made it all very clear.

Roy and Marie used to invite his superior officers over for a family meal, especially if they were living alone and away from their families, which was not unusual. These were usually lt. colonels or "full bird" colonels. It is at this level they would have signature authority for requisitions. It has to be remembered that, in the Washington, DC area, lt. colonels are a dime a dozen; for that matter, so are one-star generals. However, in a place like Heidelberg, Germany, they can carry considerable weigh.

One evening Gail was on kitchen duty and was asked to fix something special. I stayed out of the way, much like Harry Potter during his aunt's visit, but without any magic. A full bird colonel was coming for dinner.

Marie immediately offered him an apéritif, one she knew he liked. The second the glass was drained, she refilled it again. Then, dinner was served. Wine came with the main course. A nice dessert—rum cake or if near Christmas a rum pot was the favorite. This was followed with an after-dinner shot of an appropriately strong drink. By this time the colonel was drunk, as you can imagine. Suddenly Roy pulled out a folder with papers in it.

"Colonel, you know I wanted this additional radio equipment to upgrade the older pieces we have at the base. Would you please sign these purchase requisitions for me?"

By now the colonel had been wined and dined to the max. He was both full and very intoxicated. "Of course Roy, I would be happy to sign this for you." He leaned over the coffee table and sign the requisitions without even reading what he was signing. I remember Marie had to even guide his hand to the proper place for his signature.

A few weeks later some new radio equipment came into the apartment. Roy happily spent several nights installing it. I knew it was not "used" equipment because it was being unpacked from the original cartons. Now I understood how Roy could obtain $100,000 (maybe more) worth of radio equipment for his own use. Roy was a master crook. He had first rate radio equipment sent directly to his apartment and as a communications sergeant he would sign for the shipments. His explanation was he wanted to inspect the items previous to taking them to where it was expected they would be used for the theoretically use. The only problem was they were never meant for military use, only Roy's private radio station.

I came to a new realization. The Army could be easily corrupted by unscrupulous lower-level soldiers or employees. When I got to the Pentagon years later, this lesson proved valuable in my dealings with other offices and people. I didn't see the outright theft of equipment, mostly due to being too high up in the chain, but there were a number of illegal requisitions that I did catch and tried to stop. One, which you will learn about much later, involved a shipment of new computers that instead of going to the office that had illegally requisitioned them, went to the incoming secretary of defense himself. But that is for some future book.

Love,
Papa

Hello again—ready for some bathroom stories?

I must admit there were many interesting stories coming from Roy's and Marie's household. One of the more interesting was Marie's story about a bet with a group of men when she was pregnant with Jena. She wagered she could have the baby faster than it took them to take a crap in the morning.

Many men do take a long time when seated on the "throne." I knew it would take Roy a long time to do his thing when in the only bathroom in the apartment and I was subject to his being in a hurry one afternoon.

I was at the apartment after school when Roy came storming home.

"Who in the hell is in the bathroom? I have to take a crap." Then, when it was discovered that it was me: "Get the hell off the seat, I have to go now!"

So in a rush I cleaned myself and no sooner had I got halfway out the door, when Roy rushed in and stayed in there for a good 20 minutes. Of course his shouting was loud enough so the whole household could hear, making the whole incident a major embarrassment.

Marie slightly scolded me for taking too much time in the bathroom, not letting Roy have first priority when he came home from work. I never figured out the exact time he would get home, but just tried to stay away in the afternoons from then on.

Getting back to Marie's bet. She told me most men take a long time in the bathroom (as I get older, I must agree). She figured that most of the men she knew would take anywhere from 15 to 30 minutes each morning to "take care of their business." When she was in her ninth month with Jena, she bet that group of men that she could go into the hospital and have the baby in less time than it took for them to go to the bathroom that morning. This was her fourth child.

She had a history of fast deliveries. According to her, she went into labor in the early afternoon with Jena. She took her time but entered the hospital a while later. 15 minutes after she entered the hospital, Jena was born.

Most of the men that day (all were to keep track of their times for the bet, and have them confirmed by their spouses) took more than 15 minutes. Marie told me she collected a huge amount of money from the bets she had made.

I need to tell you a little about the school in Germany. I lived in Patrick Henry Village, but the school, both "middle" (called junior high back then) and the high school were in another part of the city. I think it was called Mark Twain Village, but not sure.

These were schools on US military bases. We would catch a bus outside the apartment building, ride about 30 minutes to school and return at the end of the school day. There were a number of buses leaving at about five-minute intervals for about half an hour in the morning. The first was the one I tried to catch every morning for several reasons.

First, the driver was funny. His favorite phrase was: "I had fun yesterday last night" implying that he had sex the prior evening.

Most on the bus thought it was funny to hear him talk like that. The "braver" girls would tease him, occasionally flash him.

Although I was a few years younger than most, I was large for my age and not rejected, even if not totally accepted. So I liked to hear the older kids talk. I also tried to escape the apartment as early as possible every morning. I must admit it was on these bus rides that I first learned about oral sex and a lot of other things you would not learn about in a normal household. It was an education all by itself. So I enjoyed my rides on this bus, watching the kids make out in the back, talk about their adventures in the front, moderate fun and crude jokes told every morning.

I might add, although the first to leave, we were one of the last to arrive. The driver got a kick out of the stories too (adding his own to the conversations) so he would take a way that took longer to reach the school. It was an hour of entertainment, all unofficial and mostly "R" rated. But most important, I was not with any of the other family members I lived with, as they preferred the later buses which would allow them an extra 15 minutes of sleep.

Love,
Papa

Greetings,

Happy Thanksgiving—hopefully sent from NYC a little early, just to get the NYC postmark.

Continuing where I left off in my last letter: We arrived at school and would proceed to our homerooms. I don't remember much about my homeroom or any of my classes, other than they were pretty routine. I was not a very good student back then—I was average or below average. The classes were not exciting.

Before going to Germany, Mom had told Marie I had problems with some aspects of school, mostly related to reading, spelling and comprehension. As often as possible all my homework would be checked by Marie. This helped a little. Roy made the rule that all homework had to be checked by Marie or him before I would be allowed to do anything. This was a regular routine. Now, math and science were not a problem. As a matter of fact, Marie soon realized I was a snap at math and would rarely check it. She concentrated on the English related work. I would do the English, history and social studies homework, then Marie would check it and I would make the necessary corrections. Now, it is important to realize that Marie had more education than Roy and she was a great deal more help than he could ever be.

Despite not remembering most of the classes, there was one class that likely changed my life. It was at this time I started to take a music class in the middle school. This is the only class that stands out in my memory, mostly because of its influence.

In this particular school, music appreciation was a requirement for all middle school students. Most of the students in the class didn't care for the mandatory classes and this was especially true for music appreciation, but I had a different view. I thought the enthusiasm of the teacher and his love of classical music came through so strongly he made me want to listen. We were to memorize certain pieces and then be tested on our ability to recognize some pieces by the beat / rhythm. He would tap out a beat with a pencil and we were to say what piece it was. At first I was not very good. But slowly I got better. I was also beginning to learn about classical music. Beethoven's Fifth was easy. J. S. Bach was a little harder, but the regular rhythm of the Baroque could be detected. It helped there was a limited number of pieces we had to select from. Some of Mendelssohn was easy, especially his *Wedding March* from *A Midsummer Night's Dream*. Wagner was new to me, and difficult. He has since become one of my favorite composers.

Most of the kids in the class hated music. The exceptions were those who had some kind of outside musical training. Most of them were the children of officers and were taking instrument lessons on the side. I began to love the class. Except for my brief disastrous violin lessons years before, most of the exposure was new and difficult. I liked the teacher. When he described what was in the piece, he showed us how to listen to what the music was meant to portray, as well as the message. I started to get interested. Soon, I could hear the differences between the music of the major periods—Baroque, Classical, Modern—and the some of composers within each period.

The teacher was most animated about Mozart and Beethoven. It was he who told us the story about Beethoven, who on his death bed, heard a loud thunderclap. Beethoven raised himself up, shook his fist at God for making him deaf and fell back dead. I don't know if this is real or not, but it made for good story. The teacher's stories about the composers made me more interested in their compositions. He drummed into us that music is a blending of melody, harmony and rhythm. Because we were in Germany emphasis was on the "three Bs": Bach, Beethoven and Brahms. By the end of the class, the three Bs were some of my favorite composers and they remain so today. I'm still thrilled when I hear a Beethoven piece for the first time—mostly his chamber music pieces as all the symphonies and large orchestral works are well known.

About a year later, Mom got me a subscription to the Columbia Record Club with focus on classical music. One of the first bonus pieces was George Szell's recording with the Cleveland Orchestra of the four Brahms Symphonies. It was one of my favorite in my record collection—you know those flat black plastic disks with groves in them? Brahms' First became one I liked the most. I've even used it as a seduction piece in high school a few years later. Mom pulled out some of my dad's recordings that he loved. I started to amass a small collection of classical music.

When I got back to the States, and especially to Connecticut, my radio station became WQXR, the radio station of *The NY Times*, the principle source of classical music. Classical music was becoming my number one choice for listening from then on. My friend Peter noticed the change in me and accepted it. But it never sunk in why my view of music had changed so much. I just couldn't get him to understand the superior emotions and skill that went into composing a great classical work.

Soon the rock stations no longer held any interest, especially after The Beatles came to the US. Classical was 90 percent of my choice for music listening.

Love,
Papa

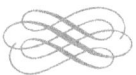

Still more adventures in Germany.

I don't remember whose dog it was—I believe it belonged to another family—but I was walking it for a few weeks every evening. Roy agreed to take care of it while the family was on vacation. The dog was a Weimaraner, named Tammy.

I remember Tammy did not have her tail bobbed (cut short) like most Weimaraners. She would get very excited when meeting people and the tail would be wagging like crazy. She would wag it so fast, the tail would literally wag the dog. The s-shaped dog was twisting back and forth like a sidewinder moving quickly through the sand. At those times the tail could have been considered a deadly weapon. Not only that, if the tail hit something or someone, it could do considerable damage.

One not very sturdy table leg was broken in half by her tail. Some people would end up with bruises on their legs if they were not careful. Of course, like other Weimaraners, she would get very excited whenever she met someone new—even more excited when it was someone she already knew and considered a friend. It was wonderful to see her excited, even though she couldn't control her movements. But that was not the most interesting thing about Tammy.

The funniest thing about Tammy was she would sit and listen to people talk. She would watch people in a conversation very closely, then try to talk herself, opening her mouth and trying to make human sounds. This was frustrating for her because all that came out was a series of funny whining noises. This would make her mad. She would try harder and harder to talk until she would hang her head in shame and tuck it in a friendly lap. It was both funny and pitiful to watch her efforts. Most watching her would laugh when this happened but I felt a little sad for her. She could see how our mouths moved, but she couldn't control her mouth like a human. Yet she tried so hard.

Naturally, Tammy and I became close friends and I would volunteer to walk her in the evenings. There were several bullies in the neighborhood that, for the most part, left me alone. Occasionally they would try to start something, but usually I avoided problems. One evening when walking

Tammy, I decided to take her for a run across a park. This was a late October or early November evening. It was getting dark; the only lights were the scattered street lights around the post.

I saw a group of the trouble makers at the side of the park. One of guys who didn't like me shouted something which I didn't quite hear, other than to detect it was likely an insult or derogatory comment. Then, out of the corner of my eye, I saw something coming toward me. It had been thrown by the boy making comments. Because it was dark, I didn't see it coming until it was too late to dodge it. Either it was the angle of impact or the coat I was wearing, but a rock about the size of a baseball hit me in the chest and bounced off. Since I was running with Tammy, I felt it hit. Yes, it did hurt, but not that much. I kept running as if nothing happened. I did notice the group had seen me get hit and appear unaffected. This amazed them. From that time on, the bullies in the area left me totally alone.

Another time I was taking Tammy for a walk, and I had a new pencil in my pants pocket. The point was facing upward, or it would poke a hole in the pocket. I didn't think about how long it was, nor how sharp the point. Naturally Tammy and I started a run. As we started running up a hill, my leg action became more elevated. The point was so sharp it went through my shirt and undershirt, stabbing me in the lower left side. When I got home, I took off my shirt and saw it had bled for a while. I cleaned the area as best I could, but it felt as if part of the pencil lead was in the wound. I went to the bathroom and looked. Sure enough the stab wound was blackened. I squeezed the area and the lead came out. I was a little scared of lead poisoning, but didn't want to tell Marie what had happened. It healed, but a mark stays with me to this day. It looks like an exaggerated ageing mark, but it is really the old stab wound. I've told some of my doctors what caused it. Most don't believe the story. They all believe it is a natural mark. It couldn't have been caused by a pencil wound so long ago. If that is the case, how come it has been with me since I was 12 years old? None of them can explain that! Funny how many doctors, if not a major issue, don't pay much attention to what patients say. This is something for you to remember as you pursue your MD.

As for Tammy, after her couple of weeks stay with us, her owners returned and reclaimed their dog. I never saw her again.

Love,
Papa

Hello:

At the school Germany there was this VERY large kid who was known for being a major bully. He was in the high school and some felt he was mildly disturbed, mentally.

I had gotten a copy of an erotic classic novel. I think it was *The Adventures of Tom Jones*. Remember I had problems reading. I was not up to snuff when it came to reading out loud. I wanted to share the more suggestive passages with two of my friends, but I was unable to read it with the proper inflection and fluidity. So I saw this kid near us. I told my friends I would ask him to read it. They were shocked.

"He is a bully and we shouldn't go near him."

My response was: "What better way to get him to be a friend and be on our side?"

The three of us walked up to this kid. I told him I had problems reading a passage out loud and asked could he help. He looked at the title of the book and his face lit up. He took the book from my hands and started reading the passage. When it got to the spicy parts, he added wonderful vocal inflections that were much better than what I could have done. After about two pages, the bell rang and we all had to go inside. I thought the attempt to make friends was a success. A few months later I would find out otherwise.

On some of the weekends most of us would pile into Roy's car and go for a little tour of the area. Terry and Gail, being older, would often be with their own friends and not join us. So it would be Marie and Roy in the front seat, me, Jena and Susan in the back. We would sometimes travel to see some of the country side outside of Heidelberg. Other times we would take a look at different parts of the city. I remember seeing a castle from a distance, but do not remember ever seeing it up close. Too bad, it was one of the most outstanding landmarks in that part of Germany.

One day we were traveling on some of the back streets of either Heidelberg or possibly Frankfurt. We were looking for a German family who were friends with Roy and Marie. Apparently, Roy had met them on his previous tour in Germany. Marie told me they gave the couple a king size bed for their wedding present; a king size bed was not very common in Germany at that time, so this was a special present.

After traveling up and down a series of back streets and becoming hopelessly lost. Roy saw a German unloading the back of his car and decided to ask him for directions. We rolled down the window. Roy asked in the best German he could:

"Wo est ein Kinderstrausser?" (or something like that—in other words: Where is Kinder Street?).

The German started to turn towards us and said in a very strong Texas accent:

"Well, you go on down yonder about five blocks, and then hang a right. It should be just a short piece down that there street."

Without looking at us, he knew we were Americans. But it was even funnier that his accent was so Southern Texas! Roy asked him about his English. He had been in a German military unit assigned to Texas for several years. He took some courses at one of the universities down there and loved the Texas dialect, he adopted it as part of his learning English.

What I learned from that encounter, and others that followed, was that most Germans know English. Those that don't will still try their best to answer your questions.

I'm sure we found the family we were looking for. Yet, I have no memory of that visit, other than it was a middle aged couple. Marie and Roy talked with them for some time. I think I was watching German TV and paid little attention to what was going on around me. I have a faint memory of having a good lunch with them with lots or wursts and sauerkraut and likely red cabbage too. Potatoes would have been the main starch. We returned home late in the afternoon or early evening.

HAPPY BIRTHDAY!!!! See the date this would normally be sent.

Love,
Papa

Happy New Year & Hello:

I don't remember the details of how I got into this situation, but I sure remember the solution.

Jena's closest friend was a girl her age that lived in the next building over. She came from a large Italian family with at least five children. Her father was another sergeant of about the same rank as Roy.

Roy and he got along well. They were kind of drinking buddies and the families would visit each other regularly. I thought he was a typical everyday man with a large family. I was to find out he had other interests besides his wife and children.

Jena's friend Pearl would occasionally sleep over with Jena. I was used to seeing her coming in and out of the apartment. They were constant companions. I mostly ignored them and they ignored me. However, the families were constantly getting together, more informally than for formal occasions. I don't remember the other children—likely they were older. They would have had no interest in visits to the Roy's home.

One day I was staying late at school due to asking for assistance from one of my teachers. There was a late bus to take me back to Patrick Henry Village, but somehow I missed it. I didn't have the faintest idea of how to get back. I started walking to the post exit and was thinking about walking the several miles to the apartment. I wasn't sure even which way to go. Lacking any identification, I was not sure if I could have even gotten through the gate. As I got close to the post gate where the school was, our neighbor drove by in a big army truck. He asked me if I needed a ride. Well, that was obvious.

"Yes, thanks. I missed the bus." I got in.

We were driving through town carrying on small talk. I was not paying much attention to him, but I was happy when I saw the entrance to Patrick Henry village. After we entered the gate, he started to take a long way around to the apartment buildings. At first I thought this a little strange. Out of the blue he asked me if I liked to jerk off. I was put off by the question, but tried to ignore it.

Suddenly, he started to reach over and unzip my pants. He reached inside and tried to pull out my penis. I really don't remember if he actually got it out, but I do remember his large fingers touching me. He told me how good it is to cum and he would love to make me have an orgasm. The truck was slowing down. Somehow I think he was trying to pull out his own cock at the same time as trying to get my pants open.

Since he was bigger and much stronger, I felt helpless. He succeeded in reaching inside my pants. I was really getting very uncomfortable but too scared to do anything. I did move as close to the opposite door as possible. Yet he had a long reach. He almost had my cock in hand, trying to pull it out.

By now with all the activity or attempted activity going on, the truck was traveling at a snail's pace. He had his cock out and wanted me to jerk him off. This whole episode was clearly exciting him. He tried to pull my closest hand over to stroke his Don Johnson (as some of the old Victorian porn called a cock stand). We had made a circuit around the back side of the village. The truck made a turn towards the housing apartments.

As he was driving around a corner I seized my chance. Grabbing the door handle and giving a quick push, the door flung open. Wasting no time, I took a huge leap out of the moving truck as it was making the turn. Thank goodness it was going no more than about 10 miles per hour so I was able to stay on my feet as I landed.

I started running in the opposite direction, across the lawns and gardens, mostly so he couldn't follow me in the truck. I was only a few blocks from the apartment and ran as fast as possible. Out of breath, I reached the building and ran up to the apartment. No one paid any attention. Thank goodness I was not on kitchen duty that week, or else dinner would have been late. I would have been in the dog house.

Shaking with fear and anger, I went to my room. My mind was racing. Was he a homosexual or just a pervert? Could I tell Marie or Roy about what had happened? Would they believe me over their longtime friend? All the answers to my internal questions kept leading to one conclusion: it was obvious that I could never tell anyone about this, until now.

It was my first case of attempted child molestation but back then, no one would have paid any attention; I would have been considered a trouble maker. Besides who would ever believe a preteen against a decorated career soldier? You are the first one to hear this tale. Not even my mother was told about this incident. I was just too ashamed. In many ways I felt like a lot of women who are molested by someone known in the family. But, because the molester was well known and liked many, like me, felt they would not be believed. So victims keep silent.

Love,
Papa

Hello again:

Quick catchup on what's current. My post-retirement was interrupted by a short stint as a contractor. There has been a bit of a gap due to the job I took on and then lost it three weeks later—I just couldn't get my head back into the work mode. It was good to get a little extra money, but not worth the stress and tension, to say nothing of the trips that I would have had to take to Parkersburg, WV (six hours each way). Ah well.

Back to Germany: Since Christmas was coming, the family planned a trip to Berchtesgaden in the German Alps. Berchtesgaden was famous as the location of Hitler's Eagle Nest retreat. It was a beautiful mountain retreat where he used to take Eva. The plan was to have a weekend skiing vacation. We packed into the car and drove south east. We stayed in a beautiful area with lots of lodges for families.

Roy told me I was not to do any skiing until he decided how good I was, but I objected, saying I had been skiing in Connecticut for years (true) and could handle the modest slopes in Germany with no problems.

Once we got to the slopes I put on some skis and took a small rope tow up a slight hill. Then, when the rest of the family got out, I skied down to where they were. Roy was furious; I had violated his rule. I pointed up at the gentle slope I had just come down—it was just a practice run, not a serious slope—but it didn't matter. I was ordered to take off my skis and go back to the lodge.

I was in tears. This was supposed to be a weekend on the slopes, but it was clear the only skiing for me would be the hundred yards down a little slope. All chance of going further up the hills, still less the mountain slopes that I was fully capable of handling, were destroyed. I took off the skis and boots and put on my shoes and Roy gave me a key to the lodge room. I was to go back and stay in the room until the evening.

When they all returned to the room Roy was still furious. The family went out to eat, but I had to stay in the room. That evening Marie took me shopping in town. I think she felt sorry for me. Berchtesgaden was a beautiful city. There had been some recent snowfall and the streets were covered. Unlike in the USA where they try to plow all the snow to the side, in Berchtesgaden they appeared to just pack it down and drove on top of the packed snow. The town also used a sleigh as a bus. It was being pulled by large horses, likely Morgans or Clydesdales. People could get on and off as they liked and the sleigh was large enough to hold over a dozen people. This was to avoid buses getting stuck in the snow. It was as if I were in a town out of time—like the 1700s, not the 1960s.

I loved walking around, seeing everything decorated with Christmas lights and the many shops that had lovely decorations in the windows. I learned that we were near the church (just across the Austrian border) where *Silent Night* was composed. I was in love with Berchtesgaden.

As we were walking through the streets, a woman bumped into me as she came out of one of the shops. She said something in a dialect I didn't recognize. I turned to Marie and asked:

"What did she just call me?"

"She didn't call you anything. That was 'excuse me' in the local dialect."

It was nothing like the German I had been exposed to on the trip.

Our visit to Prague over Christmas reminded me of Berchtesgaden: the shops and the colorful decorations, the multitude of people carrying boxes and bags full of Christmas gifts. Being in the town gave me a few hours to help me forget what had happened on the slopes earlier that morning.

The next day Roy pulled out a math book and in his typical bellicose tone, he told me to do over 100 problems. I was not to go to the slopes. He thought the problems would keep me busy all day long, but I finished in a little over an hour. I laughed at the thought of him trying to do the same problems, which in all likelihood would have taken him the better part of the day. Here is where the "modern math" classes I'd taken in the sixth grade paid off. Most of the problems were answered in my head as fast as I read them.

I walked around the immediate area of the lodge community and the day passed with me just looking at the beautiful trees and the new snow. Roy was not happy I had spent so much time out of the room, but I had completed the homework he gave me, so he couldn't say anything. Validating my accomplishment was when Marie checked the answers and all were correct.

By the way, I did stay in the same room with Terry, who was to take off to the States the following month. That night, another strange encounter occurred with him. He wanted us to jerk each other off. Again I was very reluctant. He had pulled out his erection. Turning his back, he opened a small silver packet and applied it to some part of either his body or perhaps swallowed some form of a pill. Then he turned back to me constantly grabbing my hand to get me to jerk him off. The more I resisted, the more of a gadfly he was becoming. So rather than fight it, I started to move my hand up and down his cock. In just a few minutes he ejaculated what would be normal for a teenager. I thought he was finished. But he demanded I keep working him. This was easy now with the moisture from the first coating of sperm now soaking his cock. He began to buck his whole body. A massive ejaculation followed. It was equal to anything the porn star Peter North would ejaculated in his films years later and when he was in his prime. I had never imagined such an amount of sperm was possible in an organism. I was no longer reluctant but curious. It was something to do with the packet he kept hid. No matter how much I asked he never told me what it was.

The next day Roy pulled out a math book. In his typical bellicose tone, told me to do over 100 problems. I was not to go to the slopes. He thought the problems would keep me busy all day long. Unlike him, I finished in a little over an hour. I laughed at the thought of him trying to do the same problems which in all likelihood would have taken him the better part of the day. Here is where the 'modern math' classes I took in the 6th grade paid off. Most of the problems were answered in my head as fast as I read them.

I walked around the immediate area around the lodge community. The day passed with me just looking at the beautiful trees and the new snow. Roy was not happy I had spent so much time out of the room. But I had completed the homework he gave me. He couldn't say anything. Validating my accomplishment was when Marie checked the answers, all were correct.

By the way I did stay in the same room with Terry who was to take off to the states the next month. That night another strange encounter occurred with Terry. He wanted us to jerk each other off. Again I was very reluctant. He had pulled out his erection. Turning his back, he opened a small silver packet and applied it to some part of either his body or perhaps swallowed some form of a pill. Then he turned back to me constantly grabbing my hand to get me to jerk him off. The more I resisted, the more of a gadfly he was becoming. So rather than fight it, I started to move my hand up and down his cock. In just a few minutes he ejaculated what would be normal for a teenager. I thought he was finished. But he demanded I keep working him. This was easy now with the moisture from the first coating of sperm now soaking his cock. He began to buck his whole body. A massive ejaculation followed. It was equal to anything the porn star Peter North would ejaculated in his films years later and when he was in his prime. I had never imagined such an amount of sperm was possible in an organism. I was no longer reluctant but curious. It was something to do with the packet he kept hid. No matter how much I asked he never told me what it was.

The next day we returned to Heidelberg. So while staying in one of the premiere skiing resorts and locations in the Bavarian Alps, I only had a little run down a modest slope. That sucked! However, the town was beautiful.

Love,
Papa

Dear T:

Back at home Roy told us about Christmas in 1944. He was on the front lines in WWII. The US Army and the German Army were separated by a river. I don't think he was in Belgium, where the Battle of the Bulge was happening, but elsewhere.

On Christmas Eve, the US troops started singing Christmas carols. Then the German troops started singing their carols. Soon there was an informal truce. The two armies would take turns singing and dancing to the Christmas tunes. Both sides knew *Silent Night*, and each in their own language they sang together. It was as if the war had stopped for the night and the Christmas spirit everyone dreams of took hold, if only for a Moment. This kept up for several hours. It was a lull before the next storm. Roy said when the sun came up, they ended up shooting at the very men who were taking turns singing carols the night before. War is strange. What did occur to me was that I was not far away from where I was killed in my previous life but surrounded by the Germans. Life is strange.

I would listen to Roy's war stories but never had much respect for him. I knew math homework had to go past Marie because Roy was very poor in math. It was hard to get away from the family and out of the apartment, even on weekends. After weeks of being inside, stuck with the family, I was invited by one of my school friends to join him one Saturday afternoon. Roy wanted me to complete my homework first, especially the math, before I would be allowed out.

I did the homework quickly and double checked all the answers. No problem. Marie was out, so I asked Roy to check them so I could leave.

My friend knocked at the door and I let him in. Roy said I had to wait for Marie to return to check the homework. I was in a hurry to leave and didn't know when Marie might be back. I tried to convince him that they were alright, but he wouldn't listen. Then I remarked:

"I know you have less than an eighth grade education, but that is no reason for you to delay me from going out."

The second that came out of my mouth, I knew I was in trouble. Roy's malevolent expression was evident. I took one look and told my friend he had better leave. He asked if I would be OK. I told him it would pass. I better not try to go out today. He left but was very hesitant to go.

I knew Roy was boiling. He retreated to his radio room. I followed to apologize but before I could get a word out he hit me with a fist to the cheek. I went flying backward on to the floor. After the blow I said I was sorry to Roy, but knew it was too late and retreated to my room.

He yelled that just because he didn't get a chance to get a good education it didn't mean he was some kind of dumb idiot. He may have been smart, I couldn't tell, but it was evident he was devious, rapacious and willing to commit any amount of skulduggery to obtain what he wanted. All the radio equipment proved that. His knowledge of how to use it proved a level of intelligence. The fact he knew Morse Code was another sign of his learning capabilities. But in so many ways he was callow, ignorant, and in some ways a misanthrope. His prejudices would also be evident.

One evening we were listening to the Armed Forces Radio. There was no TV in the apartment. Judy Garland was singing. Roy turned to the family:

"Judy Garland was an addict and a whore." So much for his knowledge of alcoholism.

Another time, when asked why we went on the Christmas trip to Bavaria instead of Austria, he responded:

"I'm not going into any socialist county. They are no better than communists."

Again evidence of his total lack of understanding of socialism, economics and the political realities of the world. Only a prosaic view of his little world.

It seems today in the United States we suffer from the same misconceptions. Socialism and communism are NOT the same. Yet too many rightwing Americans interchange the two as if they were. But then again, I have felt for most of my life that the overall population in the United States is woefully undereducated and exceptionally ignorant about most political, economic, and scientific facts.

We refuse to learn from others. We don't take history into account. We tend to repeat our mistakes over and over again. Hopefully that will change before it is too late, but it's not likely in my lifetime and perhaps not even in time for many of the next two generations who I fear will fall prey to the greed of the agricultural businesses (including GMOs) and the military-industrial complex. There is a deep feeling within me that possibly as much as a third of the world's population will cease to exist over the next hundred years due to war, global warming, coastal flooding, famine, pandemics and just plain stupidity. But you will be better able to tell if I'm right about that. Just save these comments for when you are 50 years old or more and see if your father may have been right way back then.

By the way, Marie did check the homework, and it was 100 percent OK.

Love,
Papa

T – I wasn't sure whether send this or not but changed my mind, so an unusual story.

It was sometime in early February. Susan and I were the only ones in the apartment. Roy and Marie were out for some function. Gail was out with her friends and Jena was staying over a Pearl's.

It was getting to be late. I think we had school in the morning. I had been getting ready for bed and had just my bathrobe on. Susan was in pajamas and a bathrobe. She came to the door and started a nice conversation with me. I thought she had begun to see me more favorably. I might add she was very attractive, so I was wishing and hoping for a more positive relationship.

We were talking about school and other small stuff. I was astounded—she was actually being very pleasant—the first time since I'd arrived. We talked for quite a few minutes when she heard the front door being opened. She said good night and started to her room, which was next to mine. I didn't realize it, but she had disarranged her robe to make it look like she had just put it back on.

Roy came in and saw her going to her room from mine. He was in a rage.

I had already slipped off my robe and was in bed. He ran to my door and screamed, "What the hell were you two doing?"

I said we were talking. The exchange continued. My tranquil demeanor was the exact opposite of his hostility and this just made the situation worse. He insisted I get out of bed and come over to him. Marie and Susan were at my door. I had nothing on as I sleep naked, so I refused. He insisted. This continued for a minute when Marie reminded him I likely didn't have anything on. I felt that he was so furious, if I got out of bed I would likely get another fist to the face. I was at a loss as to what was going on and couldn't understand why he was mad.

The accusatory questioning continued for what seemed like an age. Somehow I convinced him that all Susan and I were doing were having a nice conversation. NOTHING else. Marie was convinced and whispered something to him.

He was still mad, but no longer at me. He then pulled Susan into her room. I could hear the conversation through the wall. He accused her of deliberately making it look as if we had been in bed together when she was slipping back into her room. He caught on that she had been attempting to get me in trouble. Then I heard him slap her. She was crying and screaming back something unintelligible. The slaps continued. The crying only increased. Marie had to step in again to stop him from hurting Susan more than he had already.

I made a poem that night in my diary. I don't remember it exactly but it was something like this:

Roy E. M., hear me, for you will be judged.

Roy E. M., hear me, for you will be judged.

Roy E. M., just you misjudge us, but you will be judged justly.

Roy E. M., hear me, the gods will see that you receive your punishment.

Roy E. M., hear me, you will be judged.

Roy E. M., you will be condemned to a life without love of your children …

So Roy E. M., hear me, for you will be judged …

Of course, when he read the diary he would have seen the poem. I'm sure he would have been enraged by it. Looking back, I certainly hope so.

At first I didn't want to believe Susan had deliberately done this to get me in trouble, but as the days passed it was very evident she had. I couldn't trust anyone in the family anymore. Now most of my focus was to watch my back at all times.

Household duties were scrupulously done with extra care. There was a constant checking and rechecking for possible sabotaging of any work done. It was a very uncomfortable existence. At the time there was no light to be seen at the end of this nightmare.

Don't worry, it did get worse.

Love,
Papa

(Happy Valentine's Day, a day late)

Hello again:

After the "homework fist" to the cheek, things in the house really started to deteriorate beyond what Susan had done. Susan and Gail both had come up to me and told me not to insult their father and they were now plotting even more against me than previously.

As for Roy, the punch took out his anger but I knew he didn't forget or forgive.

I never was able to go out with that friend and was told he was not welcome in the apartment, so I was stuck. For some months I had been writing Mom. She was aware I was unhappy and wanted to come home. Everything I said or did was criticized. I was playing chess one afternoon with someone, I don't remember who, and mentioned that my father had started teaching me chess when I was six years old. I was not very good. The whole family laughed. I wrote Mom to tell them when Dad had started to teach me chess. She did state in her reply that she remembered Dad beginning teach me chess when I was around six or seven, but since I had no one to play with, I didn't really improve my skills.

I also mentioned that Mom was a Mason and again I was laughed at.

"Women can't become Masons; they join the Eastern Star," Roy insisted.

Another letter went out. Mom wrote back how Co-Masonry was formed and she was a "MASON", not an Eastern Star.

Of course each one of these exchanges increased the tensions in the home, but I refused to back down if I knew I was right.

School was my only retreat. I loved most of my classes, except German, at which I was hopeless. I learned to count, but that was the extent of my German, with the exception of "good morning", and other very basic greetings. I was still doing very well in math. The only drawback was where reading was involved: English and social studies. My reading skills were improving, SLOWLY, but my comprehension was still poor for my age. I still loved the music class and was really getting hooked on classics.

Mom wrote she was trying to find a way to bring me home but didn't have the funds to fly me back to the States, so I would have to wait. January went by and nothing. Then in February something happened in school that would change the picture of the school and my life.

Remember the bully I thought I had made friends with? I was walking across the playground one day when I came face to face with him. He started to push me backward. I thought he was joking with me. By the time it dawned on me that he was seriously mad, it was too late. Attempts to ask him what the matter was were totally ignored. Didn't he remember the book I had asked him to read? Again, no change in the bellicose attitude or response; he seemed to be totally crazy. It was as if he was bi-polar and this was one of his negative days. Nothing was getting through to him.

His "buddies" opened the boy's room door and I was pushed in. Now out of view of most the of the teachers or staff, he started to pound me with his fists. Since I was much smaller than he, I crouched down in a ball by one of the sinks and tried to protect my head.

He was flaying around like crazy with his fists. I knew some of his blows hit the sink and he was actually being hurt more than me. It seemed like this lasted for an hour. More likely it was less than five minutes but when you are the target of a deranged psychopath, seconds seem like hours. Eventually, between the cheers of his buddies and the commotion outside, some teacher or administrator heard the noise and stopped the "fight", if you could call it that.

I only had a slightly swollen lip. His knuckles were bloody. I was taken to the nurse who check me over. Nothing serious. Then back to class. I caught the usual bus home. By that time, phone calls must have come into Marie. She likely told Roy about what had happened.

You can imagine this was NOT the end of it.

Love,
Papa

T, now for "The Fight Follow-up":

It is funny but the date of this letter almost corresponds to the incidents of 50 years ago.

After the fight, I was lead to the principal's office. The bully was there also. The principal asked me what had happened. I basically told him. The incident was unexpected since a few months before, he had read a passage of a book that was hard for me to read and I thought we had become friends. I was totally surprised by the attack and taken back his violence towards me. There was no justification for it, that I could see.

At home, I got into more trouble. Roy yelled at me that when you are attacked, you don't crawl into a ball and duck behind cover: "YOU FIGHT BACK!"

I tried to tell him that the kid was a full foot taller than me and much heavier. He wanted no excuses. I should have fought back. I was an insult to the family and a coward. This didn't make me feel any better. Now the whole family ignored me except to criticize me.

The next day, Friday, a letter came from Mom. She had found a way to get me back to the States. I was to go to Holland THAT WEEKEND and meet with a family friend of the Van Hulst's, Mom's Dutch Masonic friends in Concord. There I was to spend the weekend with a family and afterwards meet up with Babs Freesmann, Mrs. Van Hulst's sister, who was traveling to the States.

It didn't occur to me, but I am sure that Roy and Marie had withheld the letter from me for at least a week or more. There was no way Mom would have given them just 48 hours or less notice. After reading Mom's letter, Marie said:

"Be careful what you ask for—you might get it. You will be leaving an excellent opportunity to experience another country."

Funny, I remembered Berchtesgaden, but there was not much opportunity to learn about other places and I didn't really picture this changing. With Roy's and Marie's preoccupation with their own lives and their children, there would have been little chances for me to explore anything that may have caught my attention. Her comment also confirmed a feeling I had that they were reading my letters. No privacy in that home! Of course at this stage, I couldn't have cared less.

When I got home to the States, I found that all my letters had been opened and resealed. Roy and Marie had been reading everything I had been writing and everything Mom had been sending to me.

When I read the letter I was excited. I went into the my room to begin to pack but noticed that Roy and Marie had packed everything already while I was at school!

I should not have trusted them, but I was too excited to care. Once I got home, I discovered they had not packed my diary, in an attempt to find something they could hold over my head or put my friends in a bad light. I was glad I had never put anything incriminating into the diary.

I'm sure Roy was furious there was nothing there. If anything, he would have realized how much I hated him and how unhappy I had been.

That afternoon my friend called me:

"The bully has been expelled and has sworn vengeance. He's planning to bring a gun to school on Monday to kill you."

I told him I was leaving; it didn't matter. The attack on me was the last straw for the school. This kid had caused a lot of trouble over the years. He was likely psychologically unstable. The problem was this was a military service school for dependents and just like the military, it rarely recognized kids with psychological problems. However, being on a military base, guns were easy to get AND there were no metal detectors! I was glad to be leaving. Perfect timing!

The next day with all my bags packed into the car, Roy and Marie drove me to Holland. This was the end of my German adventure. My Holland journey, though short, was the most enjoyable time I spent in Europe during that visit.

Love,
Papa

Hi T:

A fun letter for a change. I don't remember much of the drive to Holland, except seeing the Heidelberg castle in the distance as we left the city. I was always sad I didn't get a chance to see more of the city or the country side. But if I had to wait for Roy and Marie to take me anywhere it wasn't worth the stress and close to truculent behavior inflicted by Roy.

The drive was several hours, but they went by quickly. Roy had no problem finding the home. I could tell immediately that the family was upper middle class and **educated**. Roy and Marie quickly removed my bags, greeted the family, and introduced me. Then they got in the car and took off—never to be seen nor heard from again! The transition must have been less than three minutes.

The Dutch family was exceptionally friendly and welcoming. I enjoyed being with them at once. The husband was a businessman, by all appearances very successful and I would estimate he was in his late 40s. His wife was fairly attractive and very warm. A bunch of kids were gathered around—I think some were part of the family and others friends of the family wanting to meet the American.

The older boy, who was around 16 or 17, was friendly. He had a younger brother my age, but he was shy and introverted. There were two, maybe more, girls there; I think one was a daughter and the other a friend of hers. They quickly took my bag to the older boy's room where I would spend the next two nights.

My roommate and I started to talk and I was making jokes with risqué overtones. He enjoyed my conversations and laughed at my slightly dirty jokes. Later he told me that if his younger brother who was my age, acted like me, he might consider him human.

Then there was a light dinner, as the larger meal for the family was usually either in the morning or at noon. I don't remember what we had, but it was a nice change from the M.'s run of the mill food I had been living on for months. What is more important, I was relaxed. That night I would sleep better than I had for months. Even though I was in a strange home with people I had just met, I knew I was safe and in good hands.

The next morning I was introduced to a "Dutch" breakfast! There was bread, cheese and fruit; they must have had 20 expensive cheeses and 10 breads. They insisted I try each kind of cheese and I settled on two I really liked. I ate much more than I should, BUT IT WAS SO GOOD! This was my first introduction to really great cheese. I liked most of the breads too. Even the butters (more than one kind) were great.

Most of the family had plans already in place for the day and disappeared one at a time. The older boy put me on the back of his motor scooter and off we went for a quick tour of Amsterdam. We went all over—the historical area, the red-light district (not as well defined back then), and the canals. It was a great time. We stopped for lunch at a little cafe and talked more. I don't remember any of the details of what I saw, nor the conversation, all I remember is that IT WAS FUN! We told each other "dirty" stories and jokes, looked at all the "girls" in the red-light district (not as obvious as today), and commented on their breasts, legs, etc.

When we got home I think we played a short game of chess. I lost. There was a late dessert with the family and then off to bed. This is what I had envisioned my trip to Europe to be like.

The next day was Monday. I said goodbye to everyone and got into the father's car. He drove me down to the port, where I was greeted by a VERY tall, woman in her late 50s. This was Babs! She was immigrating to America to join her sister's family. Later I discovered her sister was Mrs. Van Hulst from Boston.

She was to be my chaperone on board the *Rotterdam* (not the same as the current cruise ship with the same name, but an earlier version by the Holland-American line). Babs welcomed me. She was a full-figured woman—would have been a perfect Brunnhilde or one of the other Valkyries, if she sang opera, but she was pure Dutch, not German. In some ways she was so outgoing that it was a little intimidating. Still she seemed nice—besides, anything (well almost) would have been better than Roy, Susan, Gail, and Marie.

Turning to the Dutch father I thanked himfor the great weekend and boarded the ship with Babs.

I regret losing the name and address of that family as I never heard from them again. Mom also lost their names and addresses. Roy, of course, had kept the letter from Mom which had the information about the family. But any chance of getting it back from him would have been a waste of time.

Still they were great people. WHAT A CHANGE FROM WHAT I HAD BEEN LIVING WITH! Thus ended my first European adventure. But the fun getting back was just beginning.

Love,
Papa

Hi T:

Have you ever heard stories about crossing the North Atlantic during winter? Besides the *Titanic*! Well, they proved to be true. Most talk about huge storms and turbulent seas, not the clam icebergs of *Titanic* legend. This is what I experienced.

Babs and I were to share a small room in the economy section (bunk beds). She was an extreme extrovert, salubrious, and nice. I was still a little overwhelmed by her. We settled in. I must admit I was a little embarrassed by sharing a room with a strange older woman, but I adjusted. We soon set sail, as they say.

I started to explore the ship. It was a "three-stacker" (three smoke stacks), with multiple decks. The top was restricted to first class. During my travels around the ship, I met a boy of around 15 or 16. We played shuffleboard and some board games. Dinners were great: there was a buffet to choose from with all sorts of great dishes. I was in heaven.

Babs was pleasant. Once I got used to her Dutch accent, she was fun to talk with (although at that age I would never had admitted it to anyone). Her sister wanted her to join the American branch of the family. Funny how I can remember Babs' name but not the first name of her sister or her two children. I actually knew Mrs. Van Hulst longer, but not in such a concentrated way as my association with Babs. After all, we were together daily for a week crossing the Atlantic. My Mom was her sponsor. To become a legal immigrant, you needed a sponsor, so Mom stepped in.

When I was not with Babs I had fun just walking and exploring the ship with my new acquaintance. We even tried to get to the boiler room and the places off limits to passengers, just to see what was happening where the work was being done. I know we were chased out of several sections—politely—but still asked to remove ourselves.

Then, on about the third day out, the weather changed. The breakfast table was bolted down. The plates fit into grooves to prevent them from sliding around the table. But with the constant rolling back and forth, WHO COULD EAT? I retreated to my room and threw up everything, not only from breakfast, but from what seemed like the whole trip. I was green, sick as a dog. Babs let me alone for that day. She seemed to be enjoying the rolling of the ship.

Then the next day, with me still unable to keep even water down, Babs said:

"This is enough!"

She insisted I get dressed:

"Get out and breathe the fresh air, you will feel better."

I didn't believe her, but she literally dragged me out of the cabin. Then got me outside in the COLD air, rain and sea mist. Every wave that hit the bow was like a splash in the face. Babs pushed me right to the edge of the ship.

"Now breathe the fresh air."

I did, and began to feel better. Within in the hour I was ready to eat. Slowly getting my "sea legs" under me.

My new friend met me and we started to walk around. Toward the stern of the ship, it was too exposed for passengers to go to without safety lines, so we got two safety lines around our waists and went to the lower deck. We also grabbed two ponchos, which were for passengers who went outside and were indistinguishable from most of the crew who might be outside too.

It may have been off limits, but in this storm, none of the crew checked on passengers who were outside on the decks. We would lean over a LITTLE bit to see the waves hitting the bow of the ship. It seemed like the ship was shifting as much as 90o or more with each wave and 45o up when crashing into the next wave mountain. Then as we went down the other side, 45o down, with the stern sharply higher. The description of being tossed around like a matchstick was true. Thank goodness we were going head into the waves. I am sure if the side of the ship had been struck by one of these waves, it would have gone over.

There was one large wave that hit the bow before the ship had recovered from the previous one and we watched as it passed over almost the entire ship to come crashing down on the lowest deck near the stern. I had never seen so much water passing over such a huge ship in my life. I loved it. It was scary! It was exciting. One of the crew members on the deck below was hit by either that or the next wave. The safety line provided little help when hit with so much water and he slid across the deck and was almost at the edge of the ship when the safety line around his waist stopped his further slide to a watery doom.

The storm lasted for about two days, then all was quiet. The sea after the storm the next night it looked like a sheet of glass it was so smooth. You could not believe it was the same ocean. When the moon came out, you could see a perfect reflection in the water. Just as the storm had been almost unbelievable, so was the calm.

Love,
Papa

Chapter 14

Home Again, Home Again, Jiggity Jig

Hi T:

I don't remember my arrival back in the USA from Germany. I do know I moved in with Marcia and the kids again. Back in the little study upstairs. I don't know where Mom was living, but I suspect that she was staying with Sandy whenever possible. Remember, we had lost the apartment on Main Street.

I was now in junior high and in the seventh grade. They immediately put me in the middle track again, until they saw my scores from the previous year in math and science. As a result I was put in higher classes for those subjects. For the same reason put in a lower level for reading and social studies.

I remember the first day I was back. The principal took me to one of the classes and said this is where I would be placed. He asked if I recognized anyone. I responded yes and said, "Hi Jimmy! I'm back" to one of the boys I was friendly with the previous year.

I apparently must have shouted it too loud and the principal quickly pulled me back into the hall and scolded me for shouting and disrupting the class. I was then put into another class and told to keep quiet.

We rotated between teachers for each subject, like high school and college. The one blessing was I had a really great math teacher. He was ex-army and tall—about 6′4″. Although in his 50s, he was in very good physical condition. I deliberately took a seat in the front row and slightly to his left. He really pushed me all year. By the time I finished his class, I was confident in math.

He demanded your full attention in class. I remember one day a boy towards the back was talking to his friend sitting behind him. His back was to the teacher who was presenting the lesson for the day. The teacher tried to get his attention twice. The kid ignored him. Big mistake. The teacher picked up one of those old classic six-inch-thick dictionaries that was on the corner of his desk and threw it 25 feet, hitting the kid squarely on the back with the flat of the binder. The kid was thrown off his chair and slid to the wall. The desk he was next to was broken. No parent threatened to sue the school and no action was taken by the school. Back then teachers' "rough" treatment of those misbehaving was accepted. By the way, the boy never spoke out of turn or turned his back to the teacher again.

Science class was not as advanced, and although I was still a poor reader, I enjoyed it. For the same reasons, my social science and English grades suffered. I would get As in math, Cs or Bs in science and C- to D+ in English and social studies. The latter would pick up, but not until high school.

My other strong suit was sports. During gym class everyone wanted me on their team. I was good in most things. This was before I started to gain weight. I looked good. I was always good in football and surprisingly good at hurdles. I was introduced to the shot put and did well in that, too. I just didn't have the speed of a sprinter. I was a good outside shooter in basketball, something that would serve me well in the South Bronx years later.

Softball was my strength. I even had a small following of the kids who wanted to see me bat. Most games were slow-pitch softballs that were easy to hit. The distance of the hit would depend on timing and strength. My timing was perfect back then. I would usually take a stride forward with my left foot, then put all the shifting weight into the swing. My wrist action helped, just letting my arms do the rest.

I remember playing a game during gym class. I was at bat. The field was on the west end of a huge playground. This was a section of the same playground used when in the sixth grade. Beyond this ball diamond was the corner of another baseball field and then a regular football field. Remember it was where Boston Patriots practiced during the summer and off season?

I was up to bat. A friend of mine was playing center field and looking at me coming up to bat, he automatically backed up 25 feet or more. He was actually standing in the next field's right center field, even though they had a game going on at the same time. The pitch came in. It was in the perfect place. I stepped into the pitch, my swing and wrist movement were all perfectly timed. The ball went flying from the bat. The hit went farther than anyone would have thought possible. It was easily 20 feet OVER my friend's head and still rising (remember he was actually in the next ball field). He watched it come towards him and as it flew over, he continued to move his head backward, then deliberately continued his head movement following the ball way over his head until he fell backward. Luckily it was soft ground. We all laughed.

That ball hit a good 400 feet from home plate and where the second bounce hit the fence I would estimate to be around 500 feet from where it was launched. No one believed a seventh-grader could hit it so far. The gym teacher said he had never seen anything like it outside of Yaz (Carl Yastrzemski) or Ted (Williams) at Fenway (two of the greatest Red Sox hitters of all times). It was one of the best hits I ever made (P.S. we won the game).

I had a few hits in Connecticut which were not as good, but still remarkable. In one adult softball field, not only did I clear the right center field fence, but the ball bounced on the paved road 30 feet beyond. Easily a 400-foot home run.

Papa

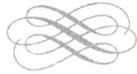

This is too interesting of a letter to wait 20 years for me to write it. I want to relate a real incident that occurred on Friday, April 1, 2011. Charlene and I had been planning to see a movie at the East Wing of the National Gallery of Art, here in Washington. The movie was *Gauguin in Tahiti* and was shown at 2:30. So, on a cold April Fools Day we treated ourselves to a free movie and art exhibit.

Charlene had gone in to work early so she could walk down from her office to meet me at the theatre on the lower floor of the National Gallery; I Metro'd into DC. She met me on the bench just above the stairs to the lower gallery and we entered just as the lights were dimming. I was impressed by the number of paintings Gauguin had done while in Tahiti and the other islands. There was a second movie about the latter years of Matisse, which was also good.

We decided to see the Gauguin exhibit after the movie. We started up the stairs to the second floor and entered the first room of the exhibit about 4:30. We finished the exhibit in the first room and went into the second. I noted that the circular stairs leading up to the rest of the exhibit had rarely been open before at this end of the museum. We usually took the stairs on the east end of the mezzanine.

Charlene and I were admiring the very famous, perhaps the most famous, of Gauguin's Tahiti painting on the south wall, *Two Tahitian Women*, which he painted in 1899. Charlene moved to the painting on the west wall while I was taking a look at the sculptural images and a sketchbook in a case in the center of the room. Suddenly at about 4:45 p.m., several things happened simultaneously.

I heard a loud pounding and shouting, looked to my left and saw a woman pounding the front of *Two Tahitian Women* with her fists. Based upon the sound of the fists landing on the painting, I immediately realized it was covered with plastic or plexiglass, not glass. She was shouting something I could not make out. Charlene let out a loud scream. Later she told me the woman was shouting "Evil!" repeatedly.

When she couldn't break the covering, she grabbed the bottom of the frame and began to pull the painting away from the wall. She pulled it to about 45° but the hook held it to the wall. By this time her shouts of "Evil!" were audible to me.

A large guard had grabbed her and was trying to pull her away from perhaps the one of the greatest post-impressionist painting of the 19th-century, but the woman had an ironclad grip. She was short but heavy, with a great deal of strength. She held on.

I raced over to her, grabbed her with my left arm around her back and began to pull her left arm. Her left hand, which the guard had a hold of, let go of the frame, but the right was still holding firm.

I raised up my right arm and brought it down hard across her right arm to break her grip. It was too much for her and she released the frame. With my left arm around her left side, the release of her right hand caused her to twisted to the left, right where my left leg was positioned. She fell over my leg. This enabled the guard and me to wrestle her to the floor, face down. The guard held her down on one side of her back and I was on the other. The painting fell back into perfect position.

The guard was trying to get the supervisors on his walkie talkie. No success. There was a young guard who had just come into the gallery and was staring at all that was happening, frozen, with a blank stare on his face. "Our" guard yelled at this young guy to get the supervisors. We both continued to hold her down for a minute or two when suddenly one of the supervisors appeared. The guard got up and the second he did, the woman rolled on her right side and tried to get up. I was on her left side and quickly pushed her shoulder back towards the floor. Since she had not gotten a good look at me, I knew she didn't know who I was—I could have been a guard or police officer. With my left hand on her shoulder, I placed the first finger of my right hand in the middle of her back. A single finger in the back through multiple layers of clothing would give the suggestion of a gun.

"Don't even try to move," I said, then added, "The only one here who is evil is you."

Then a gallery officer with a real gun and cuffs finally came in. He put her in cuffs. She was worried about her purse, so I picked it up and give it to another officer. Other guards started to clear the gallery, except for Charlene and I, who were identified as witnesses, along with one other woman.

We were told to fill out statements downstairs. We started out of the gallery and I turned towards the elevator. But the woman who had attacked the painting, along with about four officers, was in it and there was not enough room for the rest of us. People who had gathered outside were told they could return to the exhibit.

One of the supervisory guards told us to take the stairs. He led us back down to the movie theatre but through the door in the back. There was an underground tunnel to the west wing of the gallery. As we reached the end of the tunnel we went through the second door. I could see the woman in cuffs flanked by two guards about 30 feet in front of us. We eventually came to a number of offices. The woman was in a conference room in a chair. I made the comment, rather loudly, that she was a terrorist and should be put away permanently.

Charlene and I were given an office to fill out some witness reports. Charlene quickly completed hers, I took more time. Replaying all that had happened, much the same way these letters have been completed, I wrote down all the details. The report included which painting she was attacking, how it took two of us, the guard and me, to get her to the floor, but only after I had hit her right arm with a downward strike. After signing the statements, we were led up a series of stairs.

But we had to stop as a gang of guards and officers came charging down the stairs toward the door we had just gone through. After letting what seemed like a dozen of them pass, we proceeded up these back stairs. I shouted after the last few: "The action is over. You are not needed anymore."

It was after 6 p.m. by the time we left, so we walked to Chinatown and had dinner. Neither of us were hungry due to all the excitement. I was still on heightened alert. Charlene said that it was exciting being with me, but she didn't expect that kind of excitement. After dinner we walked to a hotel which had elevators to the parking garage where her car was parked. So what did you do for April Fools?

>*(Excerpt from the April 4, 2011 Washington Post:*
>
>*The woman who allegedly attacked the painting was "immediately restrained and detained" by the museum's federal protection services officers, who charged her with destruction of property and attempted theft, Ziska said in a statement.*
>
>*The painting's alleged attacker was "tackled by a guy who was visiting the gallery," Degotardi [witness interviewed] said. She described him as a social worker from the Bronx [me!].*
>
>*Ellen Goldstein of Washington, who was visiting the exhibit with Degotardi, said she was in an adjacent room at the time and heard "screaming and shouting.")*

I didn't pull any tricks but sure did have to deal with a fool by the name of Nancy Barnes! the one who attacked the painting.

Love,
Papa

Hi:

April 22, (sorry, I missed a few weeks)

How about a grandmother flashback? We haven't had one in a long while.

Your great-grandfather was still trying to make a living on farms. He had abandoned New Mexico; it just was unsuitable for the crops he was trying to grow. So after a few years the whole family moved to Texas. This meant abandoning the dug-out where your grandmother was born.

A very likely reason for the move was your great-grandmother had friends and family in Texas and wanted to be near them. Also, there was still some problems with the Native Americans in New Mexico. In theory all Native Americans were under various peace treaties by 1916 but there were still considerable tensions. It was not unusual for an occasional Indian being found dead. This would result in a white person found dead a few days later. It was never determined who started what, but such killings were not uncommon even in the pre-WWI years.

Carrie, your great-grandmother, told me of a family not far from where their farm had been, were killed in an Indian raid. This was around 1911. Likely one of the last raids of the Apaches, since I doubt if the Comanches were so far southwest. As a result, she hated Indians.

After moving to Texas, your great-granddad tried farming in rural Texas, but Carrie wanted to be closer to the city so the family split into two homes. Carrie and the kids, Lavern (born around 1909), Grandma (your grandmother, born 1912 in New Mexico, just after it became a state), Forrest (born in Texas around 1914), and Sug (born around 1918), all lived in a house in Houston.

I think it is interesting how the children alternated boy, girl. Carrie only cared for the boys. Boys grow up and get good jobs or can work on the farm, so they were worth the effort and attention. Girls were a waste of time and energy. If she thought she could have gotten away with it, Mom was certain her mother would have been quite happy if she and Sug were "accidentally" killed. If their father hadn't cared for Grandma and Sug, Mom felt there would have been a pair of infanticides in the family. From an early age Mom was always leery of Carrie. The oldest, Lavern, was the blessing to the family—Grandma nothing special! Sug was an accident, an unwanted burden.

Grandma started to raise herself more than being raised after she turned five. Lavern and Grandma were in school. Sug and Forrest still too young. Grandma started reading everything she could. First it was the Bible, then there was a series of books called McGuffery Readers which she loved. Written by a teacher born around 1800, they were intended to help young readers in primary school. Each book was a collection of stories, an occasional speech, essays and poems. As a child advanced in the books, their vocabulary would increase.

When you were small, Grandma bought you a copy of them. Don't know what happened to them. Most likely your mother, Marisol, donated them to the library. Grandma's father got them for her as either a birthday or Christmas gift. He encouraged Grandma to read; the problem was he was not around enough to really help.

Carrie just gave your grandmother orders in Houston. Grandma was to cook and clean the house all the time. After learning basic reading and "ciphering" (math) Carrie felt a girl need not go to any more school. She should get a job and help contribute to the home.

While caring for baby Sug after school and cooking, your grandmother developed a theory that all things were animate. This included rocks, stoves, all things. Later in life she used the argument that since all things are made of atoms and the atoms are in constant movement, all things must be animate. She would put food on the stove (back then it would have been a wood stove) and take care of Forrest and Sug outside or elsewhere in the house. She always knew when food had to be attended to. The stove would tell her by making a noise with the pots or a loud pop with the wood that was burning. She would run in, stir the food and everything would come out OK. She would thank the stove and go back out with the younger siblings.

She loved school, but had little time for homework, being so busy with Forrest, Sug and chores. You have to realize her mother, Carrie was barely literate and could not read above a third-grade level.

Whenever possible the family would join their father in the farm. Grandma loved the farm, but not the work. It was there she learned all the basics of farming and life. This would be the only time she and her dad could be close: when he would tell her stories and read to her. She loved him a lot. I think this attachment to her dad caused more friction with her mother. Most importantly, she learned how to handle a gun on the farm, first a rifle, then a six gun (revolver). It was on the farm that she would learn to shoot and compete with her older brother, but that will be in the next letter.

Love,
Papa

Grandmama continued:

April 22, (sorry, I missed a few weeks)

Hi:

How about a grandmother flashback? We haven't had one in a long while.

Your great-grandfather was still trying to make a living on farms. He had abandoned New Mexico; it just was unsuitable for the crops he was trying to grow. So after a few years the whole family moved to Texas. This meant abandoning the dug-out where your grandmother was born.

A very likely reason for the move was your great-grandmother had friends and family in Texas and wanted to be near them. Also, there was still some problems with the Native Americans in New Mexico. In theory all Native Americans were under various peace treaties by 1916 but there were still considerable tensions. It was not unusual for an occasional Indian being found dead. This would result in a white person found dead a few days later. It was never determined who started what, but such killings were not uncommon even in the pre-WWI years.

Carrie, your great-grandmother, told me of a family not far from where their farm had been, were killed in an Indian raid. This was around 1911. Likely one of the last raids of the Apaches, since I doubt if the Comanches were so far southwest. As a result, she hated Indians.

After moving to Texas, your great-granddad tried farming in rural Texas, but Carrie wanted to be closer to the city so the family split into two homes. Carrie and the kids, Lavern (born around 1909), Grandma (your grandmother, born 1912 in New Mexico, just after it became a state), Forrest (born in Texas around 1914), and Sug (born around 1918), all lived in a house in Houston.

I think it is interesting how the children alternated boy, girl. Carrie only cared for the boys. Boys grow up and get good jobs or can work on the farm, so they were worth the effort and attention. Girls were a waste of time and energy. If she thought she could have gotten away with it, Mom was certain her mother would have been quite happy if she and Sug were "accidentally" killed. If their father hadn't cared for Grandma and Sug, Mom felt there would have been a pair of infanticides in the family. From an early age Mom was always leery of Carrie. The oldest, Lavern, was the blessing to the family—Grandma nothing special! Sug was an accident, an unwanted burden.

Grandma started to raise herself more than being raised after she turned five. Lavern and Grandma were in school. Sug and Forrest still too young. Grandma started reading everything she could. First it was the Bible, then there was a series of books called McGuffery Readers which she loved. Written by a teacher born around 1800, they were intended to help young readers in primary school. Each book was a collection of stories, an occasional speech, essays and poems. As a child advanced in the books, their vocabulary would increase.

When you were small, Grandma bought you a copy of them. Don't know what happened to them. Most likely your mother, Marisol, donated them to the library. Grandma's father got them for her as either a birthday or Christmas gift. He encouraged Grandma to read; the problem was he was not around enough to really help.

Carrie just gave your grandmother orders in Houston. Grandma was to cook and clean the house all the time. After learning basic reading and "ciphering" (math) Carrie felt a girl need not go to any more school. She should get a job and help contribute to the home.

While caring for baby Sug after school and cooking, your grandmother developed a theory that all things were animate. This included rocks, stoves, all things. Later in life she used the argument that since all things are made of atoms and the atoms are in constant movement, all things must be animate. She would put food on the stove (back then it would have been a wood stove) and take care of Forrest and Sug outside or elsewhere in the house. She always knew when food had to be attended to. The stove would tell her by making a noise with the pots or a loud pop with the wood that was burning. She would run in, stir the food and everything would come out OK. She would thank the stove and go back out with the younger siblings.

She loved school, but had little time for homework, being so busy with Forrest, Sug and chores. You have to realize her mother, Carrie was barely literate and could not read above a third-grade level.

Whenever possible the family would join their father in the farm. Grandma loved the farm, but not the work. It was there she learned all the basics of farming and life. This would be the only time she and her dad could be close: when he would tell her stories and read to her. She loved him a lot. I think this attachment to her dad caused more friction with her mother. Most importantly, she learned how to handle a gun on the farm, first a rifle, then a six gun (revolver). It was on the farm that she would learn to shoot and compete with her older brother, but that will be in the next letter.

Hi:

How about a grandmother flashback? We haven't had one in a long while.

Your great-grandfather was still trying to make a living on farms. He had abandoned New Mexico; it just was unsuitable for the crops he was trying to grow. So after a few years the whole family moved to Texas. This meant abandoning the dug-out where your grandmother was born.

A very likely reason for the move was your great-grandmother had friends and family in Texas and wanted to be near them. Also, there was still some problems with the "Indians" in New Mexico. In theory all Native Americans were under various peace treaties by 1916 but there were still considerable tensions. It was not unusual for an occasional Indian being found dead. This would result in a white person found dead a few days later. It was never determined who started what, but such killings were not uncommon even in the pre-WWI years.

Carrie, your great-grandmother, told me of a family not far from where their farm had been, were killed in an Indian raid. This was around 1911. Likely one of the last raids of the Apaches, since I doubt if the Comanches were so far southwest. As a result, she hated Indians.

After moving to Texas, your great-granddad tried farming in rural Texas, but Carrie wanted to be closer to the city so the family split into two homes. Carrie and the kids, Lavern (born around 1909), Grandma (your grandmother, born 1912 in New Mexico, just after it became a state), Forrest (born in Texas around 1914), and Sug (born around 1918), all lived in a house in Houston.

I think it is interesting how the children alternated boy, girl. Carrie only cared for the boys. Boys grow up and get good jobs or can work on the farm, so they were worth the effort and attention. Girls were a waste of time and energy. If she thought she could have gotten away with it, Mom was certain her mother would have been quite happy if she and Sug were "accidentally" killed. If their father hadn't cared for Grandma and Sug, Mom felt there would have been a pair of infanticides in the family. From an early age Mom was always leery of Carrie. The oldest, Lavern, was the blessing to the family—Grandma nothing special! Sug was an accident, an unwanted burden.

Grandma started to raise herself more than being raised after she turned five. Lavern and Grandma were in school. Sug and Forrest still too young. Grandma started reading everything she could. First it was the Bible, then there was a series of books called McGuffery Readers which she loved. Written by a teacher born around 1800, they were intended to help young readers in primary school. Each book was a collection of stories, an occasional speech, essays and poems. As a child advanced in the books, their vocabulary would increase.

When you were small, Grandma bought you a copy of them. Don't know what happened to them. Most likely your mother, Marisol, donated them to the library. Grandma's father got them for her as either a birthday or Christmas gift. He encouraged Grandma to read; the problem was he was not around enough to really help.

Carrie just gave your grandmother orders in Houston. Grandma was to cook and clean the house all the time. After learning basic reading and "ciphering" (math) Carrie felt a girl need not go to any more school. She should get a job and help contribute to the home.

While caring for baby Sug after school and cooking, your grandmother developed a theory that all things were animate. This included rocks, stoves, all things. Later in life she used the argument that since all things are made of atoms and the atoms are in constant movement, all things must be animate. She would put food on the stove (back then it would have been a wood stove) and take care of Forrest and Sug outside or elsewhere in the house. She always knew when food had to be attended to. The stove would tell her by making a noise with the pots or a loud pop with the wood that was burning. She would run in, stir the food and everything would come out OK. She would thank the stove and go back out with the younger siblings.

She loved school, but had little time for homework, being so busy with Forrest, Sug and chores. You have to realize her mother, Carrie was barely literate and could not read above a third-grade level.

Whenever possible the family would join their father in the farm. Grandma loved the farm, but not the work. It was there she learned all the basics of farming and life. This would be the only time she and her dad could be close: when he would tell her stories and read to her. She loved him a lot. I think this attachment to her dad caused more friction with her mother. Most importantly, she learned how to handle a gun on the farm, first a rifle, then a six gun (revolver). It was on the farm that she would learn to shoot and compete with her older brother, but that will be in the next letter.

Love,
Papa

Grandmama continued:

When the family was on the farm, Lavern and Grandma learned to plant crops, pick cotton, and take care of farm animals. Your great-granddad bought a Model T Ford—the great, low-priced, mass-produced car created by Henry Ford; the car that made him a fortune. The car had a buckboard on the outside. This was a step running by the front to rear doors on both sides, which allowed people to step up on the buckboard and easily get into the car. Cars were elevated a more than they are now, which is one reason for the buckboard's popularity. The cars had to have higher clearance because the roads were very poor and rarely, if ever, paved. Most were made of dirt, and after a rain, MUD! Your great-grandfather had his farm in Texas where roads would be few and far between.

One of the things Grandma and Lavern enjoyed to do was shoot. Being brother and sister, they loved to compete and shooting was a favorite competition. Your grandmother thought rifles a little too boring. Her brother always aspired to shoot like the great gun fighters, the legends of the Old West. Pistols were their favorite choice. After all, this was where the Wild West really existed just a few years before. The classic six-gun was used in many of the shootouts. It was the favorite of law men and gun fighters alike. At least one if not two of their great uncles were a part of the Texas Rangers. It was the six-gun both Grandma and Lavern used. Lavern was a southpaw (left handed). Grandma right.

Their father taught them both to shoot a rifle first. Then the colt revolver. At first they were given second-hand guns with holsters. Grandma soon developed a technique of pulling the trigger with her middle finger. This freed her first finger to be aligned parallel with the barrel. In this position she would "point" at the target shooting without sighting the gun.

Your grandma and Lavern's favorite pastime was a rather unique shooting contest. But this was a shooting contest that would not even be considered possible with today's indoor, stationary targets. It would be shooting moving targets out of the sky while moving themselves. The competition consisted of standing on the buckboard of the Model T. Lavern, being a lefty on the driver's side and Grandma on the passenger's. They would loop their arms around the door frame of the car and your great-grandfather would drive through the corn and cotton fields. The game was to shoot the crows as they flew up while driving on the unevenly plowed rows in the field.

Now, realize: they would be traveling through bumpy fields at about 5 to 10 miles an hour. Their arms were wrapped around the window frame of the car. In this position they would draw their guns out of the holsters. Once drawn, both would attempt to shoot at crows as they took off from the ground. THIS IS A FEAT MOST PEOPLE CAN'T IMAGINE BEING POSSIBLE NOW.

Grandma, with her pointing method, consistently won. This frustrated Lavern so much he would go crying to his mother. Carrie would then scold Grandma for showing up her brother. Mom told me after a while she would rarely miss. She got so good all the men in the family thought she was another Annie Oakley (the woman shooter in Buffalo Bill's Wild West Show) in the making. There were other uncles who were part of the Wild West Show and had actually seen Annie Oakley. Mom had a good idea of who she was from relatives who had seen Annie first hand. Grandma became so good at this one of her great-uncles who, according to the stories was an original Texas Ranger, gave her his old six gun. I saw it once. It was a classic. Be worth a fortune now. But it disappeared. When your grandma asked for it in 1955 no one knew where it was. She suspected Carrie had hocked it for the money. The story that accompanied the gun was the uncle was called out of retirement to join the shoot-out with the Dalton Gang in 1918. He was credited with one kill (according to the family). That was the shootout that brought the official end to the old Wild West! Mom tried and failed to teach me how to shoot that way. Her logic was great: if you learn to point the your finger accurately, the bullet will follow where you point—an alternative to a laser pointer before laser sights.

I could never do it. But when she was teaching me to shoot in Connecticut, she would simply point the pistol at the target and pull the trigger. She never missed. I would see her squeeze off all six or seven shots from the hip and keep them clustered inside a three-inch circle. She showed this capability to me more than once.

Back to Texas. Grandma would get into trouble for beating up her bigger brother if Lavern bothered her or Sug. Although smaller in size, Grandma was always a fighter who could usually generate enough "chi" energy to overpower anyone who challenged her. By the way, she also learned to use a whip, plus could play the harmonica and skin an animal for dinner! She hadn't lost any of her technique.

I got the whip in San Antonio, Texas when I went there for a convention. When I took the whip home, Grandma said to just think of it as an extension of your arm. Though she had not used one for easily 50 years, she took it out side her little apartment downstairs and immediately showed me how to knock off individual leaves from the maple tree outside her door. I had heard about her skills, but had never taken them seriously. Once again your grandmother surprised me. After all these years, still hitting her targets MOST of the time (she did miss a few) was remarkable, be it with a whip or gun.

Love,
Papa

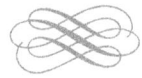

T:

An out of sequence letter. As a teacher out there with young kids (second graders), what is coming should be a treat.

As I told you I am sending you a box of fossils and rocks I found on a personal trip a week ago. I talked to you on the phone about them but here is a little more detail about what I found in Gore, VA. I was looking for trilobites but didn't find any. There may be a trace of part of one in some of the rocks I am sending. If one of your class finds one, give him or her a bonus but let me know. I did find a lot of brachiopods and a few crinoids. There is one rock held together with a rubber band when separated you can see a faint crinoid formation, small and thin, but there. I do not know the exact age of these fossils but would estimate between 100,000,000 to 300,000,000 years old. I do plan to go back to that site in the future. MOST OF THESE ARE VERY FRAGILE, SO BE CAREFUL!

I have also included shark teeth from Calvert Cliffs, MD. Most of these are about 50 to 65 million years old. It is evident these were the smaller members of the shark family.

Between the brachiopods and the shark teeth, there should be enough for every member of your class to have a real fossil for keeps. There is one large piece (about 7″ x 2″), curved with a lots of brachiopods clustered together. Would be good for the class collection. Please keep it and eventually get it back home as it is a great specimen. Be careful of the edges as they are sharp.

I am including a rock or two as examples of conglomerate formations. You can see the mineral crystals trying to form in some of the areas, while the rock shows multiple kinds of materials.

Thought it would be part of your display. I found that at the base of Mt. Weather which happened to be on the way to an outcropping.

Hope you are having fun. Give your kids my best wishes.

Love,
Papa

Intro to Sandy:

I remember that year I excelled in math. Social studies and English were still hurting. Sports were fun. Whenever the chance came up I would go over to Sandy's house on the lake to hang out. Mom would often take me there. I had met Sandy before going to Germany; she was Ruth's friend. She had the lake house where I was the bartender. I took care of her when I spent the weekends there. It was always a lot of fun being there even if there were mostly adults getting drunk.

Sandy felt I needed someone who was more my age to be with during the parties and get togethers. Sandy and one of her boyfriends, TJ, used to play golf as a foursome—at least three plus one because Sandy was too embarrassed to play where a stranger could see her. One of the couples she knew and played with had an adopted daughter named Sophia, who I've mentioned previously. Here is a little more about Sophia: She was born in Greece but adopted when a small child. Her American parents were a typical middle-to upper-middle-class family. Although she and Sandy seemed to get along, I later questioned it based on what I learned from Sophia.

At this time, Sophia was about 15 or 16 years old. I was still 12 (she didn't know that) but I looked and acted much older and was already my current height. She naturally thought I was about her age and took to me quickly. She quite short, wore glasses, and was EXCEPTIONALLY well developed, so the attraction was mutual.

I remember traveling in her family car one afternoon. Her dad was driving and my mother was in the front seat, Sophia and I in the back. I was very fearful of her showing any affection with her father driving, knowing he could see in the rearview mirror. But she was cuddling up next to me and wanted me to kiss her. I was hesitant. Finally I relented and gave her a kiss. Her father saw it and shouted:

"Don't give up your kisses to anyone. I don't want to see you kiss him again!"

So we just continued to hold hands.

To get away from her father, Sandy arranged for Sophia to come over to the lake house as often as possible. Whenever Sophia came over I would be conveniently working in the kitchen or somewhere out of sight. Sometimes I would already be down in the lake, which was a good 30 feet lower than the house. The lake was surrounded by dense woods blocked any view of shore. The immediate beach area and little raft anchored in the lake likewise not visible unless one started the decent down the steps to the lake. This is something we knew her father would not do. As a result, her father often thought Sophia just wanted to be with an older woman. Her father didn't know I would be there. This was true when I moved into the house later that summer.

Sophia and I ended up seeing a lot of each other. We used to swim in the lake and out to the little raft about 40 feet off shore. She was a good swimmer. As a result, we would spend the afternoon on the raft, swimming in the lake or just lounging on the shore. They were very pleasant days that summer. We would have make-out sessions in the little changing shack near the water. I only wish I had knowledge about sex, it would have been very beneficial for both of us.

I do remember a dare one day. Sophia bet me I couldn't eat a whole lunch underwater. I could hold my breath for about two minutes, which came from my constant practicing of swimming long distances under water. There were plastic sandwich bags even back then, so eating lunch under water was easy. So, I took the sandwich in the bag under water. Then, with the bag above my head and me swimming on my back, under water the bag would be opened a little. Thus a small bite could be taken, chewed and swallowed. Then I'd come up for air and repeat.

To prevent water from entering my nose, nose plugs were used. I even ate the piece of cake and drank a bottle of soda. The expression on Sophia's face was comical. She couldn't believe I was actually doing it. I won the bet!

Love,
Papa

Hello again:

Going from Marcia's to Sandy's was culturally and socially night and day.

Marcia, now divorced, constantly had a string of guests and suiters who were mostly well educated and great intellects. She would have international students, professors and lecturers from Harvard, MIT, and many of the other schools in Boston. Most hanging around the house on weekends. Occasionally there would be a gathering of many of her friends, including couples. For some reason, there were few American couples. Most were from India, which made sense, as Marcia had spent some time in India and loved the culture and customs.

Whenever possible I would join in the conversations, especially if they included discussions around reincarnation and spiritual existences. Several were genuinely impressed by this middle schooler having such a broad view of the spiritual. Sometimes I didn't even know where the ideas were coming form. Later I learned it was old memories from another life, in India which would creep into the conversations.

Some guests like Mr. and Mrs. Brewer were friends of her father, a wealthy businessman. Other authors would show up on her doorstep. On weekends the house resembled the line of suitors outside Penelope's door when Odysseus was fighting the Trojan War.

Isaac Asimov was one of the men who sought out Marcia attentions during these times. He was a visiting professor at Boston University (where I would meet your mama years later). He was one of the big three in science fiction. He was famous for his *Foundation* series of books and for the *Robot* books. The problem was he was still married to Gertrude and was Jewish. Yet he used every excuse to come over, be it yoga lessons, or ask for Marcia to work on an astrology chart for him. I think eventually his wife put a stop to his coming over, because suddenly his visits ceased.

Loulie's interest in the tarot, and the other occult / esoteric philosophies were attracting my interest. I remember how we drove one of Marcia's suitors away with a voodoo doll. I didn't readily dismiss the occult. Tarot later became one of my favorite tools for awakening the unconscious, in myself and in others. The symbols and images on the Tarot cards, in the various decks, can tap into the Jungian concepts of archetypes and unleash unconscious thoughts held deep within one's self. This would eventually lead to a bit of study in the Kabbalah, more of the Christian side than Jewish. To go further into the Jewish side would have required greater knowledge of the Hebrew language. I always had difficultly grasping languages. Learning Hebrew was not considered an option.

There was another funny incident while staying at Marcia's. A family down the street wanted a babysitter for their two boys. Because they were boys, they wanted an older boy who could take care of them when they went out. One day while walking to Marcia's from the bus stop they asked if I could sit for them. Since I wanted the money it was a no brainer. When I saw Mom, I asked her if it was OK. She smiled and said sure. I became a regular babysitter for this family. What was funny was the kids knew me from school—I was only a year ahead of the oldest in the same school. The parents never asked me my age, and I certainly didn't tell them that a 12-year-old was babysitting their 10-and 9-year-old boys. The kids didn't like the usual babysitters, so they never let on. We always had a good time playing games. Never had any problems.

Love,
Papa

Hi T:

During the summer I was at Sandy's, a number of talents developed.

Sandy loved to have parties. There would be a lot of men and only a few women at these parties. Sophia's parents were one of the very few couples invited. Mom would occasionally show up.

Sandy wanted me to learn how to cook on the grill. With all the macho men around, I constantly got pointers. Some were good, others not so much. With steaks I would baste them with butter and grill them close to the flame or coals. This would be for medium-rare steaks, partly charred on the outside and red in the middle. Still my favorite! The steaks were usually thick and the best cuts. Most were brought over by the men coming to the parties. Soon I became famous for grilling them perfectly. Along with the steaks came a host of other items I cooked to perfection, corn, potatoes, chicken, hot dogs, etc.

I later mastered mixing basic drinks and the grill as I mentioned before. As the evening parties wore on fewer and fewer were able to make their own drinks. Some of the men took a fancy to me and wanted to teach me golf. They would take me out to their favorite club and teach me golf. I remember they taught me how to swing a golf club. Soon I became good with my drives and chip shots. However, I could never putt.

There was one time when there were three men and myself going to their club. Each wanted to put in a bet for the last hole. I wanted to be part of the bet, however, they didn't let me. They had been drinking during the round so by the time we got to the last hole none were hitting as straight as when they started. On the last hole they were all over the place. It was a par 5 and I was on the green in 4. I then three putted for a seven. Each of them had been hitting in the ruff and sand traps. All three of them scored an eight. I would have won the bet and could have made $30 or more, especially if they allowed me a handicapped.

Love,
Papa

Dear T:

As the time with Sandy progressed, it became apparent that she was not happy. TJ continued to be an asshole. He treated her like a whore. No matter what Sandy did for TJ it didn't matter. Either way TJ being in a querulous mood would castigate her in the most truculent manner.

By the end of the summer Sandy wanted to break up with TJ. She had met a nice young Japanese-American architect. He was far more intellectual than TJ, despite the 'DDS' after TJ's name. I felt this new Promethean acquaintance was better educated, at least he was much more rounded. The other fact in his favor, he treated Sandy as the toothsome, intelligent woman she was.

I remember as my birthday came around he gave me a record of Hector Berlioz's *Harold in Italy*. What was interesting was this was one of my father's favorite pieces. I still wasn't quite sure if I was into Berlioz yet, but Germany had certainly began to turn me in that direction. This record helped push me further in the classical direction. It helped that he gave Sandy a new record player (what is now called a turntable). Soon he had brought over a number of other classical records. We would play them and then discuss the work.

That was not the only extent of our listening. Sandy and I would listen to LPs for hours. We would alternate between classical and easy listening. She really loved the theme to the movie *Exodus* played on two pianos by Ferrante and Teicher. That record she wore out she loved it so much. While listening to the records Sandy and I would discuss philosophy, religion and touch on the esoteric side of what I had come across. She soon look at me like the son she aways wanted and also the confidant she needed.

During this time there was a competition for a design for the new Prudential Plaza in Boston. Many of the large architectural firms were bidding for the project. This would have been a major project worth millions. Some of the best and most famous architects were submitting proposals. What surprised everyone, including us, was that Sandy's new friend submitted a proposal. He was considered too young for the competition, but he won it! After he was notified he called Sandy to tell her he won and was on his way over. He was going to have a big surprise for her. I was there. She thought he would ask her to marry him and was excited. At last she wouldn't be under the yolk of TJ. She wouldn't have to put up with his demands. She was going to start a new life.

However, he never made it. His car slipped on some payment on his way from Boston. He was killed instantly. Sandy was devastated. All her hope for happiness seemed to end in that car crash, which killed two people. As you will find out later, it really was.

Love,
Papa

Hello again:

As mentioned, it was during my time in Concord that I excelled in math and started to improve my science abilities. Gail and I were still friends but some how not as close as before Germany. She gave me the record *Traveling Man* by Ricky Nelson, my favorite male singer. After all I, like most of America had watched Ricky growing up on his parents' TV show The Adventures of Ozzie and Harriet. Many people forgot Ozzie had been a band leader, so it was only natural that Ricky would go into the music business.

I had a few other girl friends, with the exception of Sophia, none stand out in my mind. I remember having quite a reputation, both for protecting the little guys and for being attracted to the girls. I remember several girls made out with me, but there was one who was attractive to me. She lived close to the school. I would walk with her but she refused to let me in as it was against her mother's orders. But she really wanted me to make out with her. After several days, she invited me in. She led me to the sofa in the living room. After a very brief conversation I kissed her. It was her first romantic kiss. One kiss led to another, each more passionate than the previous. I then started to unbutton her blouse. She didn't resist. I slipped her blouse completely off. Her was a pair of totally undeveloped breasts. No adolescence grow! In other words, she was flat as a pancake. Still she was thrilled at being half naked with a boy. I kissed her breasts, but when I tried to removed her skirt, she drew the line. One more passionate kiss then I told her:

"Give me a call when you begin to grow." Flicking her nipple.

She watched me as I went out the door, never covering up. She was actually proud of the courage of exposing herself to one of the most infamous boys in the school.

There was a birthday party for one of the girls and her friends. It was to be at her father's house which was attached to his place of business, a funeral parlor. I remember the party was mostly unchaperoned. Gail accompanied me.

As a dare we moved into the parlor. Then the dare was for different couples to make out in the empty coffins. Most of them did. The coffins were a bit kinky, but usually lined with soft silk, or other fine fabric. Gail and I made out in one. Later I heard that once couple did it after the party without clothes. The girl later said it was a real turn on. Not sure if it was a felt or silk lined coffin or just the boy she was with. More likely a combination.

At the end of summer Sandy was planning something special for me. Gail would not be invited as her parents never let her go out unless they knew the family and all who may be in attendance. This likely was one of the reasons Gail and I were not seeing each other as much as before. I wanted all my friends from school. Yet at my birthday party none of my schoolmates were invited. Partly because most were not permitted that far from town without their parents and partly due to the fact no one knew Sandy, my mother or any of the adults that might be present.

Most were men. Sophia and her parents attended, and a several other of my friends from the neighborhood came. We were having a great time, swimming down at the lake, then going up to the house for food and dancing (kind of). Sandy brought out a beautiful cake. On the cake was the words: 'Happy 13th birthday W.' Sophia took one look at the cake and said in an astonished voice:

"You mean I have been in love with a god damn 12 year old!"

Remember she was about 16, but due to my size, she never expected I was younger than her. She swore that she would have noting to do me anymore (that didn't last long) but I still had a wonderful time.

I was in Marcia's home during the school week. Mom was still living out of the car when not at Sandy's. I think Marcia was a little uncomfortable me being the house and constantly making little passes at Loulie. I remember one weekend when she invited a friend over for a sleepover. This girl was in the same grade as Loulie a grade ahead of me and my age. She knew my reputation. Loulie suggested she visit me in the study if she wanted to make out with me. She was tickled with the prospect of having a session with me, away from the adults in the far end of the house.

It being a Friday night I was watching The Late Show with Jack Parr, a show I loved to watch. In the middle of the show there was a slight knock at my door.

"Come in!"

In walked this unexpected guest. She had a bathrobe on that covered her whole body. I was still laying down on my bed. She smiled, walked over and sat on the edge. By now you must realize I sleep in the nude. Thus had no clothes on when she entered the room, but covered with the sheets. She was mildly attractive, blond, developing breasts, slightly overweight but nicely shaped in a Rubinesque way. After a few Moments of talk, she leaned over and kissed me. Not objecting, the kiss was returned.

Encouraged by this, she stood up and dropped her robe, revealing her naked form. I raised the sheet as to invite her to join me. She readily accepted. Once on her back, I began to climb on top of this really beautiful feminine form but instead laying on top, I maneuvered myself so that one foot was next to her buttock. Suddenly I shifted my body next to the wall, pushed with the foot, landing her plop on the floor.

"Thanks for the offer but I like to decide when and where!"

She was shocked, embarrassed and humiliated. She grabbed her robe and went crying out of my room. Jack Parr had Jonathan Winters on that night, which was far more entertaining than a romp with the uninvited guest who left crying. Oh how young and foolish this seems to the adult me who would have likely taken full advantage of the invitation.

As the eighth grade progressed, Mom's efforts in finding new work were not going well. She did pass her insurance license exam. After a while decided it would be just as easy to sell insurance in Connecticut as in Massachusetts. Besides, we had not been together for quite some time.

By late October it was decided we would move back to The Hill. We couldn't afford any movers so all the books were loaded in the car with some of our clothes as we headed back to Connecticut. The remainder of our possessions were moved one trip at a time. The furniture was abandoned. Lamps and other smaller items were either put in the back seat or tied on the roof of the car for the three hour drive to Falls Village.

The move would actually take several trips, sometimes two in one weekend. The years in Concord, mixed in with my months in Germany had come to an end. A new part of my life was beginning. Would years in Concord make a difference? How about Germany? Would Roy and Marie M. try to get involved again, since we were moving back into their old territory? I hoped not, had enough of them. Also wasn't sure if my old friend Peter would still be close. How about Susie his sister now she was a few years older. All these questions and others were running through my mind.

One funny incident did occur. When Mom was part of the Arcane School, she became good friends with one of their mentors. Linda was a little woman, likely in her late 50s or early 60s. She was in Boston, but wanted to visit Grandma at The Hill to discuss the status of The Meditation Group for the New Age, a spin off group from the Arcane School. These were advanced students who were asked to volunteer to mentor new students. I was still attending school while Mom was getting The Hill ready for my permanent return. Linda told Mom she would drive me to Connecticut.

Having said goodbye to my Concord schoolmates, I piled the last of my books and clothes into her back seat. There was not much left to move. We started out. Soon we were on the Massachusetts Turnpike. About 90 minutes out, a police car came up behind her. She felt she must be going too fast. The speed limit was 55 mph. She was going almost exactly that, but she slowed down after spotting the police car behind her. Now the policeman was following more closely.

"I must be going too fast. I've got to slow down even more."

Now we were traveling at less than 45 mph. The police car put on his lights and pulled us over. He told her the Mass Pike had a minimum speed limit and proceeded to give her a ticket **for going too slow**. Later Linda became a mentor to one of my adult girlfriends. She laughed when she heard this story. It was exactly like the picture Linda had painted in her head from the correspondence they had exchanged.

Love,
Papa

Hello again:

I'm going in different directions for the next few letters. First to catch you up with what's happening this weekend. Warning: these next few letters are not proofed.

This weekend is Charlene's birthday, the woman I began dating after the divorce from your mother. She will be a year older than me for 22 days, and as a result we will be spending a long weekend together. Starting tomorrow, the 11th, and continuing until the 16th, when we will be returning to my Condo.

This should be fun. I originally planned to go to Williamsburg, mostly to go to The Old Country, but that would have been for me not her. So, in thinking what would she enjoy, knowing she loves gardens, new experiences and adventures, I decided to take a trip to Lancaster County, Pennsylvania. On the last day we hit Longwood Garden for fireworks on Saturday after a walking/driving tour of Lancaster and Intercourse, PA. Then a full day of gardens on Monday, after visiting Hershey Park, and the York Red Lion. There was a fair after breakfast at the Red Lion B&B, which was a new experience for Charlene.

Her birthday is Sunday, and her favorite color is purple, so we stayed that night in the Pheasant Run Farm, a really nice B&B in the country, in a room called The Violet. The thought was to have a nice quiet room to close out what I hoped would be a perfect day. It actually worked perfectly. She loved the Pheasant Run Farm B&B. The rooms were on a second floor in what was once a large totally renovated barn. The main room has a 30-foot ceiling. It could be considered the games room as there were some cards and games available, as well as a huge fireplace. Downstairs was a big room for a major receptions. There was NO TV, only a nice Bose radio/CD player. I found some wonderful classical CDs, which we put on. The sound bounced off the stone walls, and was easily heard upstairs.

The second floor covered only half of barn, the other half opened to the games room below. The space above the main room had wonderful furniture which made it a nice reading room and presented a great view of the open area below. There are four bedrooms down the hall. The Violet Room was the first on the left. The most luxurious room was next to it.

Under the bedrooms was the kitchen and dining room. Again, both spacious and very comfortable; it was a delightful place. This trip was Charlene's first experience with B&Bs and though she liked the Red Lion, she was not excited about it. But the Pheasant Run Farm impressed her so much, as we were leaving she said she would go there for her next birthday.

I have been ignoring these letters because I have been concentrating on the Nim book. I have completed the first draft now, but am currently taking a course on writing better sentences, from The Teaching Company. I want to finish it before going back to the book and completing the second draft. (Actually the advice in the course was a disaster! I have to rewrite the book again.)

A woman you know, Mischa, is suggesting I put the Nim book on line. To see if it drums up interest before I try to get a publisher. Now, speaking of Mischa, she got a job at The Teaching Company to help them improve their websites. Meanwhile, Matt her husband applied to Teracore, where Charlene works. She is getting credit for the referral. Just a few months ago Charlene got a little bonus for making the most referrals to Teracore.

Charlene has told me she has planned a special mini vacation over Labor Day Weekend, for my birthday. This will be after BALPEX (Baltimore Philatelic Exposition), where the George Washington Masonic Stamp Club will have its meeting on Saturday. So we will leaving BALPEX around 4 p.m. From there will head out to her special planned getaway for my birthday, on Labor Day. Don't know the details, but know it will include a day in Delaware. Where??? Not sure. But she told me we will have to take a ferry to get to our destination.

More REAL SOON. I want to bring several letters to me this coming weekend to get different post marks, including Intercourse, PA.

Love,
Papa

P.S. Charlene later change her mind later after experiences in other B&sBs. But we did return to the Pheasant Run Farm the next year. On our return visit, were given the larger bedroom, even though we reserved The Violet. We thought it was to be at no additional cost, but then the owners charged us full price. Was a little surprised. We paid it but they lost us as a repeat customer. After all, we were the only ones there those nights.

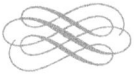

Dear T:

Back to Concord and post move. Sandy wanted to get away from TJ but the hopes of finding new happiness, plus the death of the architect, deflated all possibilities of her pulling out of this hopeless relationships. Let's be frank, TJ and many of the other men treated her like their personal whore. When your grandma tried to defend Sandy to TJ, he accused her of being in love with Sandy and having a lesbian relationship with her (remember this was in the 1960s where homosexuality was not acceptable). The suggestion got TJ a huge slap in the face.

What was worrying me is the fact Mom was returning to Connecticut. Without me nearby as I was in school, I didn't know how Sandy would react. At that time Mom and I were her only safety lines. She could talk to us and would feel more secure when we were around.

I stayed in the Concord schools off and on, for the next two years. What I didn't know was that the math was preparing me for the next challenge in my life once I returned to The Hill. I remember spending the early autumn weekends and some evenings over at Robert Moore's beautiful home. There were often exchange students staying there. If a Japanese or Chinese student, or anyone else who played pingpong was there, I would be there in the basement playing as often as possible.

Now this was a basement unlike most others. It had a beautiful set of glass doors, that exited the house to the lower section of the hill it was built upon, which allowed in sunlight. The natural light would illuminate the whole basement to the maximum extent possible.

Off in the far corner was Robert's workshop previously mentioned. It was enclosed in scratch resistant glass and illuminated by specialized lamps, most focused from above on the rock saw. Here is where Robert would sit and cut various samples of rock, to expose all sorts of beautiful minerals. The resulting pieces' flat bottoms placed on felt and given away as presents, either as paperweights or bookends.

There was a bathroom and an emergency guest room on the section under the main floor, where the other bedrooms were located. I call this an emergency guest room, as most guest stayed up stairs. Calling it an emergency guest room ignores the separate full bath, gorgeous decor and spaciousness of the room, which had a closet for clothes, most middle class families would be envious to have in their homes.

I remember Marcia telling me one day, I need you to keep track of Johnnie on Thursday. However, it being Monday, I didn't remember and she forgot to remind me.

Thursday came. Johnnie was riding his bike over to the Moore's house. After ascending the steep hill on foot Johnnie was coasting down the other side. He was pretending to be preparing for a race, down the very steep hill, resembling a mini mountain descent. He hit a bump and was thrown off his bike, into the gravel ditch, only a few yards from the Moores. He was badly banged up.

I was inside and didn't hear his yell. Mrs. Moore did. She carried the bloodied, crying youth into the house and the maid called a local doctor, who came over as fast as he could. Get that, it was a HOUSE CALL! This being a time when house calls, especially for IMPORTANT patients were still common.

When Marcia arrived, the stitches were in place and Johnnie's face resembled one of the monsters from a Frankenstein movie. He did recover, with some minor scares. Marcia told me she was sorry she forgot to remind me to watch Johnnie. His horoscope predicted the strong possibility of an accident on this day. That was the first time I learned that Marcia had completed detailed horoscopes on all the kids, guiding their activities in the directions indicated by the stars (actually planets, moon and sun). I learned Marcia swore by astrology. She became one of its leading lecturers and even wrote a book or two on the subject, along with her book *Reincarnation*, which I have.

A few years later there was a biography on Marcia called *Yoga Youth and Reincarnation*. The author stayed with the family for a month as part of his research. Marcia was very pleased with the book, but Mom thought it was a very sly mockery of her and her philosophy. She said Marcia's head was so far in the clouds she didn't see it. Never did find out what Marcia's father thought of it—I don't think he would have been pleased. Robert was too smart for anyone to pull the wool over his eyes; I'm not sure about her mother. Marcia inherited her mother's almost guileless perspective on life—a rose-tinted glasses approach (a phrase that was very appropriate during this period).

Love,
Papa

Greetings!

That was Salavdor Dali's favorite greeting. Now you know where I got it from. I saw a TV interview of Dali back in the '50s. He advised people should not bore others with a simple "Hello" but with an enthusiastic "Greetings!" when you meeting someone for the first time. Have no idea why, but have adopted it ever since.

Now for a flashback to Grandma's early life.

The farm in New Mexico was a failure. The Powers family decided to move back to Texas. I am unsure if they moved to Houston at this time or to Cement City, outside Dallas. Much of her life between the move and her early middle school and high school years I know next to nothing about. I do know that by the time she was in eighth grade, she excelled in English and spelling. I wish I had inherited those genes.

Based on what was told, gives the impression wherever they moved it was the first of several moves. She like school. Her favorite part was sports. She excelled at the high jump and claimed she could clear almost her height, 5′2″. If true, that height in the 1920 Olympics would have won her a medal. But where would a poor girl ever learn about the Olympics? She also got involved with swimming and diving, winning the city's championships for her age group. But her mother couldn't care less. Your grandmother soon had to give those activities up to care of Sug and Forest, her younger siblings.

It was at this time she became friend with a girl named Bonnie Parker. This is why I think she may have lived in Cement City, which is where biographers put Bonnie at that time. Like your grandmother, Bonnie was also excellent in spelling and English in high school. According to your grandmother, Bonnie lived just a few houses down from the Powers' home, allowing them both to walk together to school.

Mom became close with Bonnie, even though she was her senior by a number of years. Bonnie got involved with an older boy. One day while walking to school, she burst into tears and told Grandma she was pregnant. She was scared of what her parents would say and found someone to give her a back alley abortion. You grandma was traumatized. Not knowing anything about sex, she nightly prayed:

"Lord don't let me get pregnant. Please don't let me get pregnant."

Ignorance of sex and where babies came from was common. She thought it was because Bonnie kissed Roy, who Bonnie married the next year, when both dropped out of school.

Bonnie and Grandma kept in touch as best they could. Bonnie did occasionally return to stay at her old home. It was at these times that she would come over to Grandma's and catch her up with what had been happening. She soon she told Grandma she divorced Roy. There may have never been a legal divorce. Roy was a precursor to Clyde. The first impression Clyde made on Mom was that he was no good, less so than Roy. Mom didn't like either.

Clyde Barrow was a small-time thief. Mom regretted that Clyde took Bonnie away. Not only away from her as a friend, but also from an education. Mom thought Bonnie should have stayed in school because she was a good student. Bonnie's her family, like grandma's, did not put much into educating girls.

The last time your grandmother saw Bonnie was when she and the other kids were playing in the road. There was a series of sirens coming from down the road. Carrie, your great-grandmother, quickly called the kids into the yard proper, out of the road. Just in time. Down the road roared a car. In the back seat was Bonnie, waving and yelling to your grandmother from the open car window:

"**Hi Louise!**" She shouted, waving frantically.

The police were in fast pursuit. Several police cars followed, but loosing ground. That was the last time your grandmother saw Bonnie until she moved to Houston. They may have seen each other one more time, but I'm not sure.

When she heard of Bonnie's death in a hale of gunfire, your grandmother cried. She said that Bonnie was one of the nicest people she ever knew and never believed Bonnie took part in the reported killings attributed to her by the press and the police. To her dying day, she refused to watch the movie *Bonnie and Clyde,* not wanting to bring up the old memories of her childhood friend. Even more true was not wanting to see the way Bonnie's life was ended even if on film.

Interesting thought: Faye Dunaway would be perfect to play your grandmother should her life ever come on film. They looked a lot alike at similar ages

Fun?

Papa

Hi T – the last of the weekend letters mailed from PA.

Want to tell you a little more about Johnnie, the kid who fell off his bike. His older brother, Chris and sister were very verbal and intelligent individuals. But neither cared for math or anything indicating talent in engineering or mechanics.

Johnnie was different. Johnnie would take scraps from around the house and build little figures or models of different items. On his birthdays, possibly Christmas, someone gave Johnnie an air plane model. Johnnie was excited. He loved planes, and that was a natural consequence of his grandfather's tales of his WWI exploits, in his French bi-plane, and being shot down three times.

Every time Johnnie showed his newest creation to his mother, Marcia's spurious praise was: "That's nice" But rarely any genuine acknowledgement of his new creation. Then quickly turning her attention elsewhere.

This pissed off your grandma. Chris and Loulie were being given all the encouragement for their skills, reading writing, studying other subjects. Johnnie was receiving next to no encouragement where his real talents lied. I felt sorry for him. Mom and I supported his love of models. I would sit with Johnnie and help with the first few models. Soon he was able to put together the models without any help. When grandma saw the possible engineering aptitude, she started to give Johnnie air plane models to build whenever possible. I would help with the stickers. Sometimes I made suggesting about painting the finished product.

In no time Johnnie's room was filled with models hanging from the ceiling, on the shelves, and everywhere. I was impressed by the details in the paint job and the stickers applied to the models. It was very evident where Johnnie, with just a little encouragement and guidance, could become an engineer or mechanic. But Marcia refused to hear of it. These professions were too low, undistinguished. She asked Mom to stop buying the models. I just felt this was the loss of a possible great talent.

After we moved back to Connecticut, I don't remember ever seeing the kids again. Marcia and Mom would occasionally get together, but this became more and more seldom as time went by, until her death. Her death was one of the most gruesome murders I have ever read about. But that will be in another letter, when I am writing about my college years.

Love,
Papa

Chapter 15

Back to The Hill

Hi T – back to Connecticut:

I'm sure to have a few flashbacks to Concord in the future, but for now it is time to be back to The Hill in Falls Village (Amesville). When we moved back, I was in the eighth grade. It was around October or November. Once again I was placed in the classes Salisbury school system felt was appropriate. In other words, if you were poor or from a broken family, you were put in the "slow" classes. I admit, there was still problems associated with reading. But for math, Salisbury Central had just switched to a new set of books, which were considered the "new math" methods for teaching. What was funny, it was the same books I had when in the sixth grade advanced class and the seventh grade regular math class in Concord. I knew those books SOLID.

The science teacher was kind of cool. She was the youngest teacher and this may have been her first or second year. She didn't realize the "caste" system that existed in the school. We got along well. I was always full of challenging questions like:

"Is sexual arousal part of one automatic biological systems, since we rarely control when an erection occurs?"

This was asked when we're covering biology. The class was attempting to determine what was part of the automatic and non automatic systems in the body. She couldn't answer my question. She said it would be a good topic to research, but she never did and the class never found out. But she thought the question was really good and that it was asked in all sincerity. The previous science teacher would have likely considered it inappropriate and thrown me out of the class. It was a positive change, at least in science class.

In the English class was taught by a dumpy old woman who mentally was still in the Depression and had NOT kept up with any times, little less the 1960s. One of my first assignments to read an autobiography or biography. For me it was an easy choice. As a fan of Jack Paar's The Tonight Show (yes, the same show that Johnny Carson and Jay Leno hosted), the obvious book was *My Saber is Bent*, the autobiography by my hero Jack Paar. I didn't even ask permission, I just started reading it.

The teacher went through the roof.

"It is not an appropriate book for your age. I don't approve of you reading this book; if you want to get credit you have to select one of the books I approve of."

These consisted of the usual boring books written for "young audiences." None of which appealed to me. All written at an intellectual level which I felt was insulting. I refused to read any of her selected books. I tried to argue, so I got an F for that assignment. The year was off to a great start! But if you think that was bad, let me tell you about the math class.

The math class was taught by one of the oldest teachers, even older than the English teacher. This woman made no bones about the fact she didn't like the new text book. But she was forced to teach this "new" math! The problem was, she didn't know how to handle the book. She didn't understand the logic of the book. The problems were too abstract for her. She failed to understand how the of the lessons progressed, how each built upon the previous and how they were mutually dependent. Halfway through the class, she would say something that didn't make sense. Or was just out right WRONG! My hand would rise up. When called upon, I would correct her mistake. She would become furious!:

"How dare you tell me I'm wrong. I'm the teacher, learn your place,…blah, blah, blah…"

Usually I persisted, carefully point out the error. This would continue even when she was telling me to keep quiet. I would tell the class how the problem should be done. Then how to derive the correct answer. By the time I was finished, I was sent to the Principal's Office.

This became a weekly routine. I would show up and he would take one look at me:

"You corrected Mrs. Minor again?"

"Yep, she had it wrong again."

"Well sit there until class is over and go to your next class."

Big difference from Concord, where if a student was smart enough to correct a teacher, they were usually praised. At Salisbury Central you were punished.

My eighth grade social studies and English class grades were rarely above a C or D. Science was a solid B. In math by scoring a perfect 100 on the final and solid As on all the other tests Mrs. Minor had to give me a A but out of spite added "—" after the A. She really hated to do it. But by this time there had been such a ruckus raised about her inability to teach the class she had no choice By the end of the year she was a little scared of me. The reason of which will be made clear in the next letter.

Love,
Papa

More of Salisbury Central:

The arguments with Mrs. Minor continued all year long. I was in the principal's office so much, he gave me a suggestion. I carried it out. He had suggested I complain to my mother asking her to take the complaint to the PTA. It was easy to give her examples of what was going on in the class. On many a piece of homework, problems would be marked wrong for process, not the answers which were almost always correct. Mrs. Minor's reaction to me were evident in the manner in which she "corrected" the homework and the oversized red marks.

Mom brought up the complains to the PTA. Other mothers who had the more intelligent students suddenly got up the courage to complain as well. The end result was that Mrs. Minor was forced to retire at the end of the year, but that did little for me. The hell I was in while attending her class continued if not intensified due to the complaints now coming from the PTA. She suspected that I was the originator of what was becoming real problem for her.

What was funny was that all the brightest kids were coming to me in the playground, or in study periods. They were asking me for help with the problems and for an explanation of the problems in the book that eluded Mrs. Minor. I remember one kid by the name Donny came to me almost once a week. I was his personal tutor. Of course Minor didn't dare mark me down in grades since all my work was perfect. All my tests were in the high 90s. I continued to ace the class, despite her hating giving me the high grades.

By the end of the year, I had tutored ever decent student in the class, including the "genius" girl, who last I heard had become an officer in the Air Force. She was working in the Pentagon, when I retired from Department of Homeland Security—who would have guessed that we would have been so close in our careers! She an officer, me a civilian working for the Office of the Secretary of Defense.

At the graduation ceremony there were prizes for the best student in each class. I knew as Mrs. Minor hated me there was little chance of being recognized for an award in math. Yet there was little doubt I was the best in math class. When they announced for the best male math student "Donny" was asked to come to the stage and receive his award. He got up and received the prize, a brand new plastic slide rule (his was the old tool used before the electronic calculators were invented). It was something I REALLY wanted and could have used. I was totally pissed. Donny told me in private, he could not have won it if it had not been for my help. But he kept the slide rule!

English and Social Studies were not much better. My poor grades were justified, except for the autobiography assignments. My reading problems were still evident in both classes. The teachers were not helping much. With boring assignments, little or no encouragement, nor really caring about me as a student it was a case of my living up to their low expectations. It was a daily struggle for me. I don't remember anything else about the classes—not what we studied, nor how well I didn't do. Just that all my grades were Cs or Ds.

I do remember some of the obscene jokes and the occasional loud fart that would interrupt the classes, causing everyone to burst into laughter. There was one small boy who was the usual culprit. That and the comments about "dewberries" hanging from the hairs of one's ass were the favorite jokes. Dewberries were the little pieces of turd which would stick to the hairs on one's anus. When one of the girls said to a boy he was no better than a dewberry on her ass his response cracked up the class.

"You don't even have any hairs on your ass. No tits either!"

The class broke up.

One interesting class was music. As part of junior high we had music class. It was far short of what was experienced in Germany. It was purely an introduction to music instruments, and then still very limited. There were vocal sessions and if you wanted we could take an instrument. Violin was a failure way back. So I asked Mom what I could study. The answer was whatever didn't cost anything. The only thing we could afford was a set of drum sticks (as an aside they are still around some where; I think your sister found them and used them when she was dating her high school beau David).

I started to take drum lessons, which like the violin, didn't lead to anything. But at least I can claim I had a few months of how to hold the sticks. Back then they taught to hold them so it forms an almost 90-degree angle where the tips would meet. This was the formal method of playing the drums. It is a grip which is seldom used today, but one I still watch for. The better drummers, be it in jazz, classical, or rock, can be spotted using that grip indicating the drummers was taught the old-school manner of holding them. Usually they prove to be superior, though there are exceptions, just not many.

Science was still fun and I was getting good grades (Bs mostly). I remember one experiment where we were using a gallon milk container filled with water. It would be placed up side down in a tank of water. The object of the experiment was to see who had the greatest lung capacity. Each student would blow into a tube which had one end in the bottle. Most of the girls emptied between 1/3 and 1/2 of the gallon jug. The boys were getting close to emptying it, but were always a little short.

With my years in Concord, with all the swimming, the advantage was in my corner. I took a deep breath, then slowly exhaled. All the kids were crowded around the tank. It impossible for me to see how well I was doing. Suddenly the teach and the kids all gasped. I was blowing bubbles. The gallon bottle was emptied of all of its water and I was still going strong. No doubt I was the best in the class for lung capacity. Wish it was still so.

Love,
Papa

September 5

T – this is my birthday letter and I might add a thanks for your gift of the extended director's cut of *The Lord of the Rings*. It arrived just after I found out about the Detroit disaster (riots). So I just relaxed and watched *The Fellowship of the Ring*—what a relief after the disappointment. THANK YOU!!!! IT WAS THE PERFECT GIFT AT THE PERFECT TIME.

During the eight grade other things were happening outside of the class.

There was my old friend "Big", who had grown up quite a bit and was one of the more dominant of male students. I gave him a head swipe in line one day, while waiting in line, to return to the JHS building after lunch. It landed a little harder than I wanted. He almost slugged me, but didn't. He just said:

"Watch it, B …"

I did say: "Sorry, that was harder than I expected" and the incident ended.

Remember Big and his younger brother Billy, who was the kid killed in the car bus collision? They were my best friends when I lived in Lakeville. But now I had been away too long and Big had changed. I was not in Lakeville except for school; I was hanging out with Peter and the others around Amesville.

There was another kid in the school who was known as a trouble maker. Apparently he and Big had fought and no longer bother each other. Eddie Clark wanted to prove to everyone he was the number one fighter in the eighth grade. But unlike Concord, there would be no support from any teacher in stopping a fight. Nor was there anyone else to prevent him from picking on me, or providing support to anyone but Eddie. The best place for a fight would be the steep footpath on the hill to and from lunch which was in the upper building.

The old building, down the hill. for the Junior HS, did not have any lunch facilities. As a result the seventh and eighth grades had to walk up the hill, on the small paved path, to the elementary school's lunch room each day, and back again. No problem most times, but in winter it could be covered with snow or ice, making it a challenge.

It was late November when Eddie wanted to pick a fight. I don't remember why I took a little longer than usual at lunch, but I was one of the last to return to the other building down the hill. I approached the path at the end of the elementary school parking lot and found Eddie with two of his "friends" waiting for me. Eddie had a slender, flexible, stick in his hand that he had cut from the bushes that were on either side of the trail. As I approached instinctively I knew there was going to be trouble.

I watched the three of these kids, all from the poorer section of Lakeville. I determined it would be impossible to pull another Jackie stunt, as the two hanger ones were just going to watch a fist fight with Eddie. This was the appropriate setting, all to Eddie's advantage. Instead of being an open flat area this was a narrow path and a slanted hill. There was no place nor room to maneuver. Also, it being late autumn and cloudy, there was no sun to keep behind me.

I was a logical fighter, not a boxer. I knew there was little chance of beating Eddie and didn't want to even try. As I approached Eddie hit me with the stick.

"I just hit you, what are you going to do about it?" he growled.

"Nothing Eddie, you are just trying to start a fight and I have no intension of fighting you."

He hit again. "You still not going to do anything about me hitting you?"

"Eddie, you are just trying to provoke a fight to prove you are a better fighter than I. I am willing right here and now to acknowledge you are a better fist fighter than me. OK, now excuse me, I'm going back to the school."

With that, I passed Eddie and his friends as they looked on not knowing how to react. I never had any problems with Eddie ever again.

There was another story that circulated about a very attractive girl in my class. She was a bit of a prude, but her younger sister, who had developed breasts much faster than her found out how to make extra money. At first she would expose herself to Eddie and some of boys in town. Then she learned to get more money, just go a little further. In no time she learned how to make a LOT of cash by letting the boys do a circle jerk around her naked body. I heard Eddie wanted more and either raped her or payed her enough to let him fuck her. Thus she was the youngest whore in town, only 13.

Eddie dropped out of school, never went past the second year in HS. I totally lost all knowledge of Eddie. During our 35th reunion of the HS class, I asked about Eddie and several remembered him (as he was the only the second black in the class), but no one knew what happen to him.

Eddie's younger brother was even worse. Though neither as large nor as strong as Eddie, he was his class' bully. There were a lot or rumors about him. The tales of the trouble he would get into were numerous. He was drafted. Remember this was the middle of the Vietnam war we never should have been in. I learned that Eddie's brother ended up being killed in Nam. Strange fate. His death likely prevented worse karma should he had survived. I just expected him to be one of those out of control adults who would eventually kill someone. Years later I did find his name on the Vietnam Memorial in Washington.

Love,
Papa

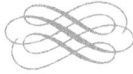

More on JHS:

During the eighth grade, my best friend was Peter. We had renewed our friendship and now I was hanging out with him and his brother Robbie. Whenever we needed a ride anywhere Robbie was our source. What is interesting is Robbie dropped out of school and was barely literate. The only job he could get was being a milkman!

The only memory that exists today of the milkman can be found in popular TV ads or in the old movies. As a reminder, a milkman delivered quarts of milk, in glass bottles, to subscribers. EVERY morning, during the weekdays, usually between 6 and 10 a.m. Because this was a rural area, Robbie's route was fairly large, including Falls Village, Amesville, parts of Canaan, and extending down towards Cornwall, which was south as you follow the Housatonic (the river that caused massive damage during Hurricane Irene—not as bad as in 1955 (in a letter from years ago), but cutting off several towns and a great deal of damage in VT).

At school Peter and I hung out together a lot, usually in the playground, rarely playing but talking about anything that came to our minds. Coming back to Connecticut I was looking for a girlfriend. Being new to many, there was one girl that was attracted to me. Her name was Linda. She was cute and very lively. She started hanging out with me and really seemed to be interested in me. I asked her out for a date. Peter warned me that she was trouble. She had a string of boys she'd flirt with, then dumped for no apparent reason, except to prove that she could attract them.

I didn't want to listen, so invited her out to a double date one Saturday night at some event happening down by Lakeville Lake. Mom to drop us off. She was to pick us up at 10 p.m. Peter, with his date, Linda with me. We had fun. While waiting for Mom we decided to walk towards the old railway station, long closed, but still at the entrance to the park area that included the lake. It would be easy for us to spot Mom's car and she would be able to easily see us.

We were playing around, and running all over the parking lot. I asked Linda if she would go steady with me and she quickly agreed. We kissed. I thought I had a regular girlfriend. We continue to wait—thank goodness it was a warm night for late autumn. It was long past 10 by now, and still no sign of Mom. At around 11 Mom finally pulled into the parking lot. When we got into the car, I realized she was about as drunk as you could imagine. So much so I didn't think she could drive safely. I sat in the front, ready to grab the wheel if necessary. Going less than 10 mph on the roads, Mom zig zagging back and forth between one side of the road to another, I was totally embarrassed. How we dropped off the dates and made it to Amesville. I have NO idea.

On Monday when I saw Linda, she returned the commitment ring I had given her. She saying she wanted to date other boys:

"I don't want to stick with any one individual," she told me.

I tried to keep her, but looking back I wonder if my mother's condition may have contributed to her decision. Peter came up to me afterwards and simply said:

"Told you so."

I had to admit he was correct. That has to have been my shortest relationship ever.

Back to bowling.

When we could get Robbie to join us, we'd drive to Pittsfield, Massachusetts, where there was the nearest automated bowling ally. There had been a bowling alley in Canaan; if I remember correctly there were only two or three lanes and all were manual. In other words, every time you rolled the ball down, someone would climb into the alley, remove the dead wood, and roll the ball back. As you can tell by the description each game would take an hour or more. Pittsfield's bowling alley was automated. Robbie would take Peter and I when we had enough money. Often Peter and I would sit in the back when Robbie's date joined him in the front of the car. He rarely stayed with Peter and me, preferring to go elsewhere with his date. Then later he would pick us up on the way back home, usually dropping us off first and then disappearing with his girlfriend until MUCH later at night. That was the era when the classic joke was:

"People in the front seats cause accidents, accidents in the back seat cause people."

I'm sure Robbie was "playing" in the backseat with his dates whenever possible. The only positive thing was that his father, Mort, had taught his sons, even Peter at the age of 12, the use of condoms, accompanied with STRONG lectures not to get anyone pregnant. I never had such instruction. The first time I saw a condom, shortly after this, I didn't even know how to use it.

Love,
Papa

T:

There were a couple of girls that were attracted to Peter and me. We would go to the movies as often as possible. My new girl friend was Cindy, a slightly overweight girl with an aggressive personality that reminded me a little of Gail in Concord, just not as attractive. Peter was going with Nancy, a shy, tall girl with glasses, who I thought was attractive. Later she married right out of HS, what I thought was a big mistake.

This was the time of Elvis Presley, the beginning of Johnny Cash and a period where dressing in black pants and a dark shirt was the style—kind of like the slightly Goth period that your sister was going through. Funny but she was following her father's behavior at exactly the same age period, even in things she was totally unaware of.

There was another couple, I can't remember their names, who occasionally hung out with us too. I was the undoubtedly the leader. As a result I got the nick name "Pops." Cindy liked being called, believe it or not: "Poppoleto," close to Papagano in the Mozart opera. Funny coincident looking back on it now. Peter was "Daddio" and Nancy was "Daddio's Chick." As a foursome (sometimes the sextet) we would go to the movies in Canaan together.

All of us almost always sit in the four to six front seats on the left side of the theatre. We appropriated this as our private viewing area. There was sufficient room to stretch out and pretty much do what we wanted without people seeing. The movie screen was not a giant one but off to the right from our seats. If anyone in the theater was concentrating on the movie screen it would have taken our seats almost out of their preferable vision, at angle from where we were most our of antics would not be noticed, as long was they were quiet. Making out and sometimes lying on the floor was common.

Our group did not conform to the expected norms. The teachers, especially the English teacher, who I was already in trouble with, and the social studies teacher, who we had home room with, did not care for any of us. Whenever there was any trouble, Peter was usually blamed, the teachers not daring to blame me. For one, because I rarely did anything overtly wrong, but also because my reputation and fight with Mrs. Minor, the math teacher, all the way to the PTA was known.

One nice day, while at recess, Peter and I were in the front of the school. Some of the kids in our home room class opened the window, jumped onto the roof of a basement entrance and skipped the afternoon sessions. The home room teacher saw the window open and immediately accused Peter of opening it to let his other friends out when she was not in the room. Peter was shocked; I was pissed. She knew both of us were in the front of the school when it happened. She told Peter to go to the Principal's Office. Still not fully comprehending what for, nor aware of what had happened, I couldn't stay quiet anymore and stood up:

"You know full well that Peter and I were in the front of the school when this happened. He had nothing to do with it. If he goes to the office, I will too and tell the principal what happened."

I then sat down, signaling to Peter to do the same. The teach was too stunned to do anything. We simply resumed class. Needless to say, my negative reputation among the teachers fell even lower, but my status with the students in the class rose to heroic levels. The aftermath of this was that a lot of others wanted to be part of our group whenever possible, especially when one of us would have parties, usually at one of their houses, since Peter and I were too poor to host a party. Of course this only applied to the lower-class kids.

I was still considered poor white trash to most of the upper-class kids. But since they were in the "advanced" classes, both for regular classes and for different home room assignments, there was little interaction between our two groups. Just another manifestation of the caste system that existed in Northwestern Connecticut.

Love,
Papa

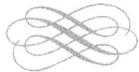

T: Detroit trip mailings #1

I tried to renew my interest with Susan B, whose mother had remarried, to a farmer not far from Amesville. Peter told me to stay away from her too. But she was attractive and I still remembered when I had a crush on her from years before. However, she wanted nothing from me but a casual friendship.

I found out why Peter warned me. Her older brother had raped her. Now she was having sex with both stepbrothers and her real brother, along with a number of other boys, for a slight fee—or so I was told.

Peter and I would go over to the farm to visit the brothers. Susan and her younger stepbrother Jimmy, who was about 11 years old, always welcomed us. This youngest brother had an old wreck of a car that his father let him drive in the field. Peter and I would ride in the car as Jimmy would practice his driving skills, what little there were of them. One of these was practicing shifting the gears on the steering column gear shift, something I haven't seen in 40 years.

The car's shift was a standard "H" with reverse on the part of the lower H away from the driver. Second gear was on the lower part of the H, closer to the driver. It is necessary to tell you the H was near the steering wheel at a slight angle (about 20 degrees) making an upper and lower branches of the H. You would start shifting by starting in first as you stepped on the clutch. As you picked up a little speed you would shift to second, the lower part of the H away nearest you. Eventually shift to third which was on the only part of the H left, up and away. Neutral was the crossbar of the H. This is not too different from your Mazda, except the shift was only three forward gears and reverse with the shift bar on the right of the steering column.

Jimmy had trouble getting the car into reverse. Reverse was close to second gear. Jimmy would drive at varying speed around the field, avoiding any cows that may be there. Then usually slam on the brakes just before we would hit a tree, the old barn, or a haystack. If he had hit the barn it might actually have improved the structure from a good hit from the car. It would have likely taken down the whole dilapidated building.

The problem was Jimmy would then have to back up the car to get it out of trouble. Time and time again, he would push in the clutch, pull on the gear shift and gun the gas. Time and time again the car would lunge forward instead of backward. Jimmy put the car in second, not reverse. This would demand an instant slamming on the breaks, throwing all of us forward. There were not seat belts yet!

Peter and I were better drivers, even at the age of 12 and 13. We would laugh our heads off. Jimmy became know as "Second Gear Jimmy" among us and later his classmates when they heard the stories. The car ended up rusting away in that field. One day, when Peter and I were not there, Jimmy stopped the car just short of a tree with a double trunk branching out from the surface of the ground very dramatically. Sure enough, Jimmy stopped the car just short of the "V". Putting the car into reverse, he popped out the clutch. As you have likely guessed, the car was in second gear. Believe it or not it lurched forward so fast, that before Jimmy could put on the brake, the car was firmly wedged between the V part of the tree, making any kind of egress impossible. Jimmy had to get out of the car by rolling down the back window and climbing through it to extricate himself from the local version of the "whomping willow" from Harry Potter. The car could be seen between the branches of the tree for 10 or more years, slowly rusting apart, and definitely replenishing the iron content of the soil.

Love,
Papa

T: Detroit trip mailings #2

Her older brother was in my class. Through him I met her. Her brother was not very bright. When I met the family I discovered why. She was a family of 10 children. When I met her mother I was shocked to learn she was only in her mid-30s yet she looked as if she was in her 50s due to too many children, too little education, bad diet and a very poor environment. Their father was a physical laborer and usually worked on road and sewage construction. You can imagine the smell in house when he arrived home in the evening.

There was one incident when her mother, not knowing much about garbage disposals, put her hand in the sink while it was running. Sure enough, it tore two fingers apart. I was there. We got in the car, her fingers wrapped in cloth, and drove to Sharon Hospital's emergency ward. I sat close to her in the front seat, shifting the gears for her and offering to drive if she felt faint. Luckily, we made it. After her fingers were stitched up and she downed several painkillers, we drove back to Salisbury and her home.

What was interesting was in Massachusetts Sophia was still very interested in me and wanted to visit me in Connecticut. How she got her father's permission I'll never know, but she showed up for a weekend visit. She wanted me to go to bed with her, but I was dating Myra and was very loyal. I invited my friend Peter over to meet Sophia instead.

He was to sleep in my room. Mom had her room next to mine, but with the walk-in closet in between her room and the guest room little noise passed between the rooms. Sophia was staying in my old room I had as a small child. Peter went to "visit" Sophia after my Mom went to bed. Mom usually fell to sleep quickly (the quantity of alcohol consumed helped). I figured Sophia and Peter would likely end up having sex. Well, within a few minutes, I heard Peter's footsteps going down the stairs and out the front door. I looked out my window and there was Peter smoking a cigarette. He was shaking like a leaf.

"Peter, what the hell happened? Come upstairs and tell me."

When he came into the room he was still shaking. He had NEVER experienced a girl as sexually aggressive as Sophia. It scared the shit out of him. He gave a detailed description of what happened, then opened his wallet and dumped out a bunch of condoms.

"Here take them all, I swear I'll never need them again until I'm married."

Well you can imagine how long that promise lasted, but it was funny. After that weekend I never saw Sophia again. I continued to date Myra for a few more months until her parents told her she had to break up with me.

I need to fill you in about my Aunt Sug. At about this time, Sug was going through her fifth divorce. The grounds were abuse. Not the first time. She loved picking the wrong men. She had already lined up her next husband; I never found out if she hooked up with him right after the divorce or before. By the end of March she was married again. By September he had beaten her at least twice. Time for another divorce. By October she had started dating. Nelson, the new prospect, was an oil geologist.

Unlike her previous men, her geologist was a gentleman, well-educated and one of the most successful wildcatters in Texas. In case you don't know what a wildcatter is, it is a geologist who finds oil in areas not previously explored. Nelson was an independent and would be hired out to whichever company wanted to pay his hefty fee.

By December Sug married Nelson. Three husbands in one year! But this one proved to be different. Not only was he a nice individual, he was fairly wealthy. They lived in one of the nicest areas of Houston, in a typical single-story ranch-style house. We visited them the next year just before Christmas.

Nelson was having one of his wells coming in over the next few days. It was about a two hour drive from Houston. And he was called on Christmas Eve as they expected the well to come in that night. I was invited to go with him to the site. If they hit oil, it would likely produce a classic gusher, as seen in the movies. The gusher would be quickly capped and the regular pump put in place (much faster than seen in the movies).

On that night, it was unusually cold for Texas. I only had a light jacket with a sweater underneath. That was fine. But when we got to the area of the drill site it was near freezing. Add to the fact it was a swampy area with high humidity, and IT FELT COLD. Wishing I had gloves, I kept hands in my pockets most of the time. What was amusing was that the Texas crew were in heavy coats complaining about how cold it was.

Nelson was watching core samples (cylindrical rock formations pulled from the drill) to see how close they were from the oil he suspected was down there. About 11 p.m. one of the samples came up. Nelson pointed out to me all the various layers. When it got down to the bottom of the sample he stood up, shaking his head.

"We missed it. Pack it up. We'll try again."

On the drive home he explained to me the core told him there was oil near by but not where the drill had sunk into the ground. He felt if they drilled 50 yards in either north or south, or both, of the current site they would find the oil. It appeared they had hit a fault line that divided the pools deep under the ground. Such is the life of a wildcatter—hit and miss. That night was a miss, but it did lead to two additional wells both produced oil. Without a doubt it was one of the most interesting Christmas Eves I ever experienced, though not very much in the Christmas spirit. By the time we arrived back to the house, I was wet, cold and miserable, Nelson even more so. Sug fixed me hot chocolate and a late dinner about 3 a.m., more likely an early breakfast. The rest of the stay was delightful.

Sug looked to me as the son she wished she had. Her first marriage had produced two children. Nicky, her oldest, was born when Sug was 18 years old. Don't know for sure, but it may have been a shotgun wedding. Gary came a few years later. During that week Gary took me fishing. He was a typical chauvinist Texan. Being older than me, he had already been married and divorced. Like his mother, Gary was a very good-looking man and had no trouble finding women. But once they realized what was under that exterior, few wanted to put up with him. His wife accused him of physical and mental abuse.

On the way home from fishing he was drinking a beer. When he finished the can he asked me to roll down the window. He threw the can into the swampy area on the side of the road. I was shocked. Never would I consider throwing trash out of the window. Gary lost a lot of respect on that trip. The next time I saw him he was married to his third wife. I was in the back seat of his car and his wife had forgotten her purse. Gary was in the doorway.

"Gary, could you bring me my purse, I forgot it, it's on the table by the door."

Gary grabbed it and tossed it to his wife. Then came a diatribe:

"Men don't carry purses. Don't you ever ask me to do that again or I will beat you to within an inch of your life."

Again I was shocked at his reaction. Less than a year later, this wife filed for a divorce based on physical cruelty.

As for Sug's daughter Nicky, like her mother, she got pregnant and married in that order. Her husband, Hershel, was a nice, quiet man—the opposite to her mother's husbands prior to Nelson. Nicky only had the one daughter. Though not an exceptionally happy marriage, it was good. As Nicky told me, she had to love Hershel with all the shit she had given him over the years. Nicky was the only cousin that I ever felt close to. Years later, I got a call from Hershel. Nicky had died of cancer. He never informed me she was sick and I didn't even get notified of the funeral, which I would have certainly attended.

Love,
Papa

Hi T:

Myra and I were really attracted to each other. Though only about 12, her breasts had already formed. She loved to wear a t-shirt with no bra just to get me excited. More than once she would flash me. They were beautiful for a girl of her age. She was slightly overweight, but that just added to some sexually attractive curves. She was the oldest girl in the family. With nine brothers and sisters it was next to impossible for us to be alone. A few times we would find an empty room to make out in. I loved playing with her breasts. Once when in the movies I put my coat over my lap. She was giving me a handjob in the theater. Suddenly my mother came over to see where we wanted to go after the movie. Her sudden appearance scared the hell out of me. Mind you, Myra and I rarely worked each other to organism. One Fourth of July, Myra and I were in Lakeville, making out on a blanket. A family was behind us. The father told us we shouldn't be doing that in front of his children. My flippant response:

"What, you don't get any from your wife? You better teach your children the facts of life."

I could never even take Myra for a walk alone in the neighborhood. Her mother suspected me of wanting to screw Myra. She was right. One day we were found her parents were out. Being a summer day, all the kids were playing in the yard. We went into her parents bedroom. Not daring to strip naked, she raised her shirt and blouse. I lowered my pants. She didn't have panties on. I started rubbing my erection against her. She liked the feeling. Then I tried to get into her. The tip of the head got in. She was wet. Then when I tried to go further. She gave a suppressed cry of pain. I pulled out.

"It hurt, please stop."

Kissing her I said: "I'm sorry, I thought it would go right in."

When we raised ourselves, I must have partly taken her virginity. There on the sheets was some blood. We dressed and she washed out the blood with a wash cloth. From then on when we had a chance, we would dry hump. Every time with my cock against her bare pubic area. But not wanting to hurt her again, penetration was never again attempted.

A few days later Myra told me I couldn't see her again. I took the long walk to where Mom was visiting a rather friend near the old Salisbury Central Elementary school. Her claims towards spiritual consciousness were callow. It was about a two-mile walk. I suddenly appeared at the door. My eyes had been filled with tears all the way. When her friend saw me at the door, she almost refused to let me in. She hated children. The rule was none were permitted in her home. But Mom took one look at me and knew something was wrong. I sat quietly while the visit was cut a little short.

Mom's friend had a psychic contact who had just sent her a tape recording, MOM HAD TO HEAR! He went into a trace calling up "a little butterfly" in his reading. On the way home, I told Mom that Myra's mother had forced a breakup. I was devastated. That stayed with me for a long time. But then Mom asked what I thought of the psychic. My impression was that he was an insidious fraud wheedling funds out of this silly woman with his claptrap. Once the conversation shifted to the tape, Mom actually was able to get laugh out of me by the time we reached our driveway.

Love,
Papa

T: Detroit trip mailings #3 (any more will be hand-written notes)

Sandy came to visit.

She had just experienced the death of the architect she loved and was very depressed. She didn't want to go back to her life with TJ. She didn't know what to do so Mom invited her to come up for a week and relax.

She drove from Concord to Falls Village, but didn't arrive until after dark. She missed our driveway and drove up to the neighbor's driveway where she tried to turn around. Of course at this time of night, she was intoxicated.

The neighbor was an artist and his wife—the Chiminos. They called to tell us that Sandy's station wagon was hung up on the large rock at the beginning of their driveway. She had tried to turn around, but had no way of realizing she couldn't back into the road without going completely into the property. Not seeing the large rock at the corner of the entrance she backed right onto it. When I walked down to the car, the front was facing towards the road, but the rear of the station wagon, fully loaded with all sorts of junk, was solidly lodged on the rock with BOTH rear wheels off the ground. She must have accidentally gunned it in reverse.

There was never much traffic up and down Sugar Hill Road, but Sandy's front end of the car was in the center of the narrow road just past a sharp turn. I had to get it off the rock ASAP just in case one of the other dozen residents further up the hill came and around the corner. If they were going more than the speed limit, they would have either swerved down into the embankment, or collided with the front of the car.

I looked at the rock and the car. The rear bumper was only a few feet away from more solid rock leading further up to the hill where the Chiminos' house was. If I could place my back flat against the back of the trunk of the station wagon, my hands under the bumper, and my feet planted on the rocks, I just may be able to pick up the rear up enough to get it off the rock.

Sandy felt it would be impossible. Mom thought I was crazy. But it might be worth a try. Mom got into the driver's seat. Mom had related to me stories of when she needed extra strength, it would come to her unexpectedly. So anything was possible.

I got behind the car. My hands were placed under the bumper. My back flat against the old Ford's back end. My feet at about 110 degree angle on the rocks around 18 inches behind the car. I gripped tightly. Then with a great focus of visualizing my legs straightening out, I just pushed against the rock bed. Slowly the car began to lift. Sandy didn't believe her eyes. Mom, feeling the car move, started to ease up the clutch; still no traction. I pushed further. Suddenly the car moved, my legs straightened and I was now sitting on the rock! The car moved off into the pavement. I let go and tumbled backwards over the rock into some bushes.

Mom drove the car back down the hill and into our driveway which was only about 20 yards away. Sandy said I pushed a whole fully loaded back end in the air by about 6 feet. She estimated I lifted over 2,000 lbs. that night. I probably did—it was an old fashioned station wagon and they were built like mini tanks back then.

More on the visit when I get a chance.

Love,
Papa

T:

In the effort to pull together the Nim book, I have been neglecting your letters. Although already working on my next book, I hope to resume the letters with a little more consistency (so of course this and the next few are weeks late).

The last letter I sent was about Sandy's visit to The Hill. She would come into my room and we would talk for an hour or more. The subjects included reincarnation, religion and various esoteric subjects. She looked to me as her spiritual guide. But Mom thought Sandy and I were having sex. Whenever we left my room, there was Mom with a drink in her hands, no matter what time of day.

It was a brief visit, as Sandy soon returned to Concord. She phoned me and promised to send me the sextant she gave me as a b-day gift as soon as she could pull herself together. It was a great antique sextant. I loved it. Being patient with Sandy, I waited. In the meantime, having lost the love of her life, TJ tried to start up his relationship with her again. But by this time Sandy had enough of his bullshit and wanted nothing to do with him. She didn't want to slip back into his clutches and be forced to "entertain" his friends.

It is important to realize that TJ was a very successful dentist. I believe his practice was not in Concord but near by. As a dentist he had access to all sorts of medicines and sedatives, everything from sleeping gas to a variety of drugs that would easily knock out anyone. If not carefully administered, any combination could produce very serious reactions. Same with an overdose.

Mom suggested she change all the locks on the doors since TJ had keys. He likely made copies rather than returning them when Sandy demanded. Mom suggested she come back to Connecticut to get away, but Sandy wanted to stay in Concord because of a possible job she was lining up. Later Mom told me it was because she didn't want me to see the bruises on her face and arms TJ had given her when he beat her.

Mom was very worried for Sandy's safety. About a week later we received a phone call. It was Sandy's brother, who we knew but seldom were in contact with. I watched Mom's face grow more and more grave. She was near tears when she hung up the phone. Sandy was dead. After a few more phone calls with Sandy's brother and sister-in-law this is what we discovered:

Multiple calls to Sandy from her brother over two days were not returned. He called the police to investigate. A police officer went out to the house and knocked on the door. There was no answer. He saw a car in the driveway but when he called in the license plate, it did not match the car registered in Sandy's name even though it was the same make and model of her station wagon. The police concluded she was not home. Later it was discovered TJ had transposed two of the letters on the plate. In fact it *was* Sandy's car.

We will never know if that was an accident or deliberate. Yet when the police first arrived it would have been in time to save her as she was likely in a drug-induced coma. After more calls to the police asking them to break into the house, when they entered they discovered Sandy's body in her bed.

The bed was perfectly made. The sheets and blanket carefully tucked in and smoothed. She was lying on her back <u>with the neck brace on</u>, her arms crossed over her chest. The autopsy said she had died in her sleep of an overdose of medicines, which were not disclosed. Result—suicide. RIGHT!!!

Sandy was cremated and buried in a family plot. I don't know where. After the funeral all valuable possessions she had were gathered by her brother. I talked to him and asked him to send me the sextant. After convincing him it really was mine, that Sandy had given it to me as a present, he said he would send it. The next month we got another phone call, his house had burned down and everything was destroyed, including the sextant.

So I have nothing but a fond memory of Sandy. A sweet woman who's life was cut short. By the way, there was a rumor that a police chief received a sudden increase in his bank account of $10,000, provided the investigation concluded that suicide was the cause of death.

Love,
Papa

Chapter 16

High School, More Protests and the Admiral

Hello,

I graduated from eighth grade and entered Housatonic Valley Regional High School (HVRHS), about three miles from The Hill.

My best friend Peter had been accepted into a trade school in Torrington to major in auto-mechanics. It took him 30 minutes each way to attend, and so we seldom saw each other again, as his commute had him leaving early and coming home late.

At HVRHS, it was rather boring most of the time. But some key events did happen that impacted me. Being from a "broken" home and not having the best grades in English, I was put in the "general" track, not the college bound one. I was taking Earth Science, which I loved, but found it very hard the first few months. When I asked the teach, Mr. K (remember him?) for extra help. He told me I was just not trying hard enough, but if I went out for the football team, he may be able to find time to help me. I refused. So I passed with a low C grade.

I have to describe our principal to you. Dr. Stoddard was well over 6'3' and at least 300 lbs, so he walked with the assistance of a cane. He had a distinctly huge lower lip, caused by a habit of constantly pulling on it. He was an imposing figure to anyone who met him.

I knew he and Mom were friends as she had done small jobs for the school when they couldn't do it for themselves. Whenever a girl came into his office she was told to take a seat. The leather of the chairs would grab the bottom of her dress (remember this is back in the 1960s and girls wore skirts and dresses, and boys pants, not jeans). Since the sofas were oversized, when a girl sat down she would naturally slip forward exposing more of her thighs than normal. Now I don't know if that was by design but it was well known among the girls and it resulted in him gaining a reputation of being a dirty old man. I

Being only a freshman there were many events that I could not take part in. One afternoon in early spring there was an announcement over the speaker system:

"Will 'W' please report to the Principal's Office immediately."

My natural response was "What the hell did I do?"

On this day the senior class was going on their class trip to The Globe Theatre in Milford (?), Connecticut to see *Hamlet*. Dr. Stoddard knew I was placed in the "lower" section of the English classes and he had an idea. Since many of the seniors knew me from the Young Thespians' Club I belonged to, most didn't really know what year I was in—they just assumed I was a transfer Junior or Senior and accepted me as such.

I went into Dr. Stoddard's office. He stood up, towering over me.

"How would you like to see Hamlet today? One of the seniors is sick and we have one seat open for the production. Do you want to go? I have already called your mother and it is OK with her."

"Sure, I would love to!" was my response.

"Well then get ready the bus leaves in five minutes."

I was hardly dressed for a theatre trip, but did have a dark shirt on and at least had some decent pants on. I grabbed my coat and jumped on the bus. This was a fantastic adventure. I didn't talk to many of the Seniors on the bus, but when we got to the theatre, I became enraptured by Shakespeare—my first exposure to The Bard.

The next day I ran into Dr. Stoddard's office and thanked him over and over. He stood there with a stern expression, only when I turned to leave, while looking over my shoulder did I see a huge grin spread over his face and a twinkle in his eye. Deep inside me I realized he would be an ally in the school. This proved to be true throughout my first three years.

To this day, I feel he introduced me to the classics and especially theatre but most importantly Shakespeare. I will be forever thankful to him, holding in the fondest of memories from my high school years.

Love,
Papa

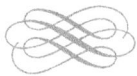

Hello again,

Freshman year was interesting. I was in the "dummy" classes for social studies and English because of my poor history in middle school with those classes, but in the regular algebra class being taught by Mr. Just. I liked him. I heard that he was a WWII hero, though exactly what he had done never came to me.

Mom liked him so he may have been a flyer. He had a habit of pointing to formulas on the blackboard by tapping his middle knuckle on them. He would tap so often that by the end of the year he would have a large calcium growth on a knuckle of one of his fingers and every summer had to have it surgically removed before the next school year. But he never stopped tapping the board with the same knuckle. Thus every summer, back to surgery, and every September a big bandaid would be on his finger.

I sat by the windows behind a small skinny kid by the name of Richard. Richard was exceptionally smart (later got a PhD in math). When the class was going slow, especially on a warm day with the sun shining into the classroom, Richard and I were diverting our attention to these tiny little (yes a double adjective describing the same thing as they were no more than 1/32 of an inch across) red bugs crawling along the black window sill. Mind you this was the new wing of the school with better classrooms than Pappberg's. When we both understood what Mr. Just was explaining we would line up two or more of the bugs and try to race them in one direction by prodding them with our pens. A penny bet on which would win. I have no memory of who won the most pennies.

That was the year *Batman*, the campy TV series, was on. I use to go swimming at the Hotchkiss school pool when it was open to the community (remember Grandma used to work for them years before). I would often meet another friend there, Tom W, and we would then hang out afterwards. I remember Tom telling me how his older female cousin spend a weekend at his house one weekend. She was a senior in HS. I actually met her. She was not very attractive and a little strange. Tom told me how when the parents were out after he went to bed, she came into his room and asked if he had ever had sex.

He said: "No."

Her response was that it was about time, whereupon she took off his robe, and began by going down on him. Disrobing herself she then humped him by climbing on top the more than once that night before the adults returned. Tom was the second of my friends who have an active sex life (after Peter) by the end of freshman year in high school.

Mind you this was my freshman year in high school and most other freshmen were a year younger than me. To think sexting and current sexual activities in the same age group is unacceptable. Adults need to get their collective heads out of the sand and realize sexual exploration, be it exchanging nude photos or actually having sex is normal at this age. If our culture was more accepting of the fact, the age of consent would be reduced to 16 at least between teenagers. Sex between those of that age would be considered sexual experimentation, not a federal offense. This country is just not realistic in its attitude towards youthful sexual experimentation. But it is willing to accept the most violent acts in movies and on TV. Somewhere we have lost our senses.

One day when Tom and I were taking showers after a swim, he commented that I would physically make a better Batman than Adam West, the star. Although slightly overweight by then, I was in decent physical shape and strong. Tom thought West looked far too puny for the roll and that I would be better. Good for the ego.

One afternoon a year later, Tom was over for a sleepover. We started playing with Tarot readings. I read his cards and was remarkably accurate. He then asked me to do a reading for something else. Like what? He suggested why not the country? So I shuffled the cards and began to lay them out. Suddenly my arm froze just before turning over the next card. I got an instant blinding headache. I couldn't move. After bearing the unbelievable pain for a minute, the arm would only move in one direction—by putting the card I had in my hand back on the deck. Then the rest of my body unfroze and the headache disappeared as quickly as it occurred. I thought the whole thing very strange and decided it was some kind of psychic warning not to do that reading.

The next week I was taking my English class on the second floor of the old wing of the HS. Suddenly there was an announcement over the loud speakers from Dr. Stoddard:

"The president has been shot in Dallas. We will tell you more as it comes over the news."

We all sat totally stunned in the class. The teacher couldn't teach and sat down. Some of the girls started to cry. No one spoke a word. We just sat there.

I just remembered the Tarot event the weekend before and realized what the card were about to tell me. Then about 20 minutes later the familiar voice came over the PA system again. He announced:

"President Kennedy is dead!"

I swore I would never do another Tarot divination again. From that time on I have used them for meditation or have done lay outs for other reasons. But I stopped trying to tell fortunes for people and countries.

I never believed the Warren Commission Report on the assassination. In 1973 a conspiracy movie questioning the Report called *Executive Action* came out, starring Robert Ryan and Burt Lancaster. At the end of the film there was a list of individuals who died "natural" deaths, or were killed in traffic accidents, etc. Most were witnesses who pointed towards the "grassy knoll" where they heard a least one shot fired. They were not pointing to the Book Depository where Lee Harvey Oswald was. The odds of those witnesses all dying within two years all potential witnesses was, as one mortuary statistician put it, a trillion to one. Also ignored, or should I say suppressed, was the sound analysis done by a reputable company in Boston that did an analyzed the tape of the assassination. They found there were actually four shots, not three as reported in the Warren Commission. I also discovered that several of the individuals involved the Watergate scandal during the Nixon administration had been in Dallas the day before. Was there a connection? We will never know. But I continue to feel the JFK assassination has never been resolved. What was interesting, one of the script writers was Dalton Tumbo, one of the "Hollywood Ten" who refused to testify before the House UnAmerican Activities Committee and as a result became a victim of the Black List of the 1950s.

Love,
Papa

Hello T,

As far as mischief is concerned, I did get into a little.

My freshman homeroom, was Mr. Pappberg's in the back of the school. I never had any classes with him—I heard he was not an inspiring teacher. Mr. Pappberg was rather short had a bit of a belly. I think he could have played Mr. Pickwick in a theater production with very little padding or makeup. He like to have complete control. Quiet was demanded in his room and he was intolerant of any kind of mischief. He had a special hatred for paper airplanes. If he caught you throwing one or even folding one, you were in big trouble.

Every evening, he would carefully lock all the windows in the class and secure the door. This way no one would disturb his classroom which was always neat and clean. He also was one teacher who came in just a minute or two before the first bell. I used to "help" lock the windows, at least to the eye.

Occasionally I would position one of the locks in the locked position short of the actual catch. Early the next morning I would slip into the classroom through the window and put a paper airplane in his desk drawer or on his chalkboard. I would then lock the window properly, slip out the door, which could be exited and closed into its locked position. He would come in as usual, then you could see his face redden went the paper airplane was discovered. This would be repeated about once a week. The rest of the homeroom thought it was hilarious. Almost all of them knew I was behind it. Pappberg began to suspect me, but could never prove it. I was very careful to come in extra early on the paper airplane mornings, do the dirty work, get out and have both window and door relocked. Then I'd slip out the side doors of the school and reenter through the front door when the later busses began to arrive. This gave me the excuse that I arrived after some of the other students were waiting outside the homeroom door.

What was funny was that he suspected I was not securing the windows; I was able to detect his thoughts. Every time he checked to see if I was not locking the windows all were in perfectly locked position. I would have intuition when he was to check the windows and at those times I'd lock each tightly. The class knew what I was doing and were amazed at my timing.

One day my homeroom mates all made dozens of paper airplanes for a special occasion. I slipped in through the window and let in the class. We put paper airplanes EVERYWHERE! One the chalk trays, in the lights, stuck on the ceiling, in his desk. Any place where one could be put in an exposed position. Then I locked up everything, slipping out of the class and quietly sat in the hall.

Pappberg was late that morning and opened the door quickly when he arrived. Looking in the room he turned RED instantly! His expression was priceless. No sooner than we had hung up our coats, the bell rang. We all ran to our first classes before he could say anything. It was hard to contain the laughter as everyone proceeded to their first class.

Later that day during study hall I was sitting in homeroom. All the evidence had been removed. Someone had left a copy of the *New York Times* on my desk. I took it and started to fold it into a giant paper airplane. Pappberg was watching me closely. He had a habit of leaning back in his chair as he would read a book or magazine when in his classroom was a study hall. I proceeded to fold a double sheet paper airplane and held it up:

"Mr. Pappberg isn't this the biggest paper airplane you have ever seen?"

He just stared at me. Finally, with his red face he said:

"Throw it away NOW!"

"OK but you're closer to the trash, can you do it for me?" Whereupon I threw it towards him.

Just then two things happened. The bell rang so I grabbed my books and ran out, and simultaneously the paper plane hit him in the chest sending him off balance and backward into the chalkboard, out of his chair. I can tell you I was three corridors down the school by the time he got up.

Yes, I was sent to Dr. Stoddard the next day, but he just looked seriously at me and told me to stay there for a period, that was all. By the way, even if the windows were locked, a narrow metal ruler could pop them. This allowed me into the school any time day or night, something very few other students realized, but which I would often take advantage of, as you will read later.

As far as my love life went, I was still attracted to Myra, even after her parents made her break up with me. This resulted in my having little to do with any other girl for most of my freshman year. The memory of the breakup still had a significant impact. In the next year Myra entered HS, but after her freshman year she dropped out. At 15 she married another dropout who lived a few doors down from her home and had two kids fairly quickly. But after the second child she became sterile. Thank goodness! Or else she would have ended up like her mother—old before her time, with more children than she could afford or handle.

Your grandma ran into her mother some time later. They talked briefly, which is how I learned of Myra's children and her inability to have more. Then Mom told me her mother said:

"It was the lucky for her that she couldn't become pregnant any more. Likely will save her life."

Love,
Papa

Hi T:

I will devote a letter leading up to my trip to the March on Washington in my next letter. That was an exciting episode. A year or two after I became active in the Civil Rights movement, Mom made a suggestion in a totally different direction. If I volunteered to work three or four days a week at the local summer stock theatre, The Sharon Playhouse, maybe I would be able to get free tickets to all their shows. I thought it was a great idea.

We went to the director, who needed help with building the sets. I suggested to him that if I worked three days a week, I could get two free tickets for each production. It was a deal. The play list for the summer started off with *Once Upon a Mattress*, the musical that made Carol Bernett famous. The season ended with *Our Town*, with a host of really good plays in between. Each play ran for six days— Tuesday through the Sunday matinee. Back then there was a different play each week. Rehearsals for the next play would be done in the backyard or driveway, while the current play was being performed on stage. During the week we would build and paint the flats for the next production and plan the lighting. Then Sunday nights the stage crew would strike the set and rebuild the new one for dress rehearsal Monday afternoon. It was an all-night effort. This was when they needed the most help.

It must be remembered that at the age, I was already 5′10″ but looked like I was over 16 years old. No one knew how old I really was, so management treated me like the rest of the crew. My first week I worked mostly on building the sets. What was interesting was the actors often got involved in the sets if not needed on stage for rehearsal.

I expressed an interest in lighting. There was only one lighting director and he NEEDED help, especially as we prepared for Tuesday night premieres. I learned the names of all the lights, the different plugs, and how to work the dimmer control board. Light controls are now done on a little laptop but back then there were huge switches and on a control device four feet wide, four feet tall and three feet thick; I mean, we are talking BIG! I learned to use the spot and I filled in for one of the productions when the usual person working the spot was sick. It was a blast.

Remember my fear of heights? What could be a worse job for me than working on tall step ladders and catwalks above the theatre. I remember adjusting the lights stage left in the front. The director told me to do adjustments on the lights of stage right. Rather than allowing me to get down this 15 foot step ladder where I was **sitting** on the top step, he just grabbed the ladder and dragged it across the stage. I thought I was going to have a heart attack. If I lost balance I would kill myself on the front row of seats twenty feet below or fall onto the set and break half the bones in my body. Let's face it, there was no such thing as following safety rules in summer stock!

One very funny incident has to be told. A young woman named Sandy (interesting, same as my friend who was murdered) —mildly attractive, a little overweight, but with nice blonde hair and a big ego—used to walk around saying how much more beautiful women are than men. Finally the crew had enough of her talk and challenged her to a contest. She and one of the male apprentices would walk on stage in front of all the crew and actors and we would vote for who we felt was the most beautiful. Naturally this was to be a parade across the stage in the nude.

The male representative was a short but VERY good looking dancer named Jim S. Although small, he had the build of a perfect dancer, well-toned muscles and a perfect overall physique. He was the obvious choice to represent the male of the species. The crew, which included most of the actors, sat in the audience. Sandy and Jim came out. Sandy was really quite attractive, with well developed and full breasts and a slight belly which only added to her curves in a slightly Rubenesque way (Peter Paul Rubens, famous for what would now be called overweight female figures, especially his young 16-year-old second wife). Jim was never outspoken; friendly towards everyone. The crew all had enough of Sandy's boasting about the superior beauty of women over men. The results were unanimous. Jim got every vote!

Sandy was so depressed she went crying from the stage and ran naked across the playhouse property to the director's trailer in the back. She poured out her tears on his shoulder. Of course she never did get dressed. He comforted her throughout the night. I was told the trailer was rocking back and forth most of the evening. More on Sandy later. What was worse was the director's wife showed up the next morning to surprise him. She sure DID! I had left but I understand the fireworks that morning were much more exciting than the 4th of July.

I missed the last play of the season. Funny, but I have not seen a stage production of *Our Town* to this day. But I had something else to do that last week in the summer of 1963.

Love,
Papa

Dear T, here is a little historical incident:

OK, so I left working PT for the Sharon Playhouse for another event. Gee, when was this??? Oh yes, it was August 1963. A group from the NAACP (where I was a youth member) were organizing a group from Connecticut to take a train down to Washington, DC in the latter part of August. I was asked to join because of my previous activities. It was to be a march for jobs and equality.

The local NAACP wanted a contingent from Connecticut to attend. I asked Mom and she signed me up. Mom warned me that DC was VERY hot in the summer and that I should take an extra few gallons of water in case some forgot to take any. The result was I had a huge back pack with mostly water and snacks in it. As I boarded the train in Hartford very early on the 28th of August the backpack must have been over twenty pounds.

We arrived at Washington's Union Station. There were a lot of trains, many specials, arriving all for this "little march." Hundreds were all moving from the platforms towards the exit. As we got off the train, I noticed we were directed through this double line of National Guard troops. Each guardsman had fixed bayonets, through which we had to pass. One of them was talking to his buddy saying something like:

"…can you believe all these idiots."

I turned to him and said: "Today will change the course of US history."

They laughed and said something like no one cares about a bunch of niggers. I shook my head, turned and caught up with my group to get on the bus to the Mall. The bus dropped us off around 21st and Constitution. We walked toward the Lincoln Memorial.

The crowds were overwhelming. Our group stopped under the second tree on the northwest side of the reflecting pond. I looked around, people were coming from all directions. It was the biggest crowd EVER. As far as I could see there were people standing shoulder to shoulder, up the hill to the Washington Monument, way into the trees on the other side of the reflecting pond. Every open spot visible was quickly occupied. Yet busses kept dropping more and more people every minute.

Some of us sat down. Others stood to see as well as hear the speakers up on the steps of the Memorial. There was a long list of Civil Rights activists; James Farmer helped organize it, couldn't be there because he was in jail. John Lewis of SNCC (Student Nonviolent Coordinating Committee) gave a speech that I loved. Roy Wilkins, Whitney Young talked, Harry Belafonte, Paul Newman, Marlon Brando, Sidney Poitier, Ossie Davis, Sammy Davis, Jr., even Charlton Heston were visible on the Memorial.

I looked up and saw a woman speaking. She introduced Rosa Parks and many of the other women. I had not heard her name and didn't realize who she was. Years later I came to realize it was Josephine Baker, my hero without any stage makeup or fancy clothes. I didn't even recognize her. Nor did I fully realize all that she had done, *yet*. I had only heard bits from Mom about her WWII exploits, how she helped the Allies in North Africa. To this day I am so happy that I at least saw her this one time in person, even from a distance.

We tried to sit, even though the crowd was so great it was hard to find a spot so most stood for hours. Many of the Civil Rights songs were sung, *We Shall Overcome*, more than once. *If I Had a Hammer* was led by Peter Paul and Mary, who I loved. A bunch of spirituals many led by Mahalia Jackson. Dylan and Joan Baez sang, along with Marian Anderson. The spirits of the people there were up lifted. It was an exciting event.

A subgroup of SNCC members were holding a counter protest not far away advocating a more revolutionary solution rather than waiting for Congress. I think this group became or were part of what was to be called the Black Panthers.

Word was coming that if we were to catch the bus back to the train we would have to be leaving soon. Just as we got that word, someone got up to the microphone. I have to admit I was impressed with his speech, the constant refrain of "I have a Dream!" was very catchy and emphasized the points why we were all there that day. I asked one of the leaders who was speaking.

"Oh, that is Martin Luther King. He is one of the organizers of this march."

Just as we reached the bus MLK finished his speech. We caught the train arriving back late that night. Mom picked me up.

"I think we did something important today," I told her.

Of course that was the March on Washington. Newspapers and the Park Service, which did not do official estimates, reported that maybe 250,000 people were there. Yet as the bus went back to Union Station, I could see the whole mall was packed all the way back to the Washington Monument hill and from Constitution to Independence Ave.

To this day I refuse to believe less than a million people were there. I have never seen such a crowd on the mall since, not even the March for Sanity in 2011. Of course this little March on Washington for Jobs and Freedom led to the Civil Rights Act signed by L.B.J. later, after Kennedy's assassination. As we know now this march really did change the course of US history. But there was a lot of violence we all faced later after King was assassinated, creating catalyst for the riots of 1966-7.

Love,
Papa

HELLO

When the Senior play Arthur Miller's *The Crucible* was being planned. I would watch the rehearsals, then work on the lights after the cast left. Some evenings I would be there until after midnight when I would spend a dime and call Mom to pick me up.

One night I was focusing some of the lights on different parts of the set, standing on a tall step ladder. I was placing a light to be focused on the stage's sofa used in the first act. Sandy from the Playhouse came on stage wearing a white robe. I was a little surprised as I thought everyone else had left. She laid down on couch.

I said: "Oh, hi Sandy, I didn't notice you came in."

I was glad she was there—it helped me with the light. She looked up into the light and asked if the flesh tones came out with that filter.

"I think so."

"Maybe this will help," she said, as she took off the robe from her naked body. She spread her legs wide as she started to masturbate.

"W, I'm so horny, please come down and fuck me!"

"Thanks for the view Sandy but I'm too busy, I have to have all the lights set for tomorrow's dress rehearsal," was my immediate response.

So I passed up a very delectable senior ingenue to work on lights—talk about being naïve! I did the lighting for 22 productions on that stage, many not associated with the HS, but private groups as well. On the wall behind curtain, I listed each production on the bricks.

Later when the Sharon Playhouse was installing a new lighting system. I got them to donate to the HS their old lighting control board. Thus HVRHS had one of the most advanced lighting systems of the rural HS in Connecticut for its time. The problem was although the board was free and delivered by the Playhouse, it took months to get the money together to get the damn thing installed, which cost thousands of dollars.

You have to realize Mom would have me drive forward and backwards in our long driveway since I was 13. Then when I was 15 she would let me drive on the local roads. Being a country high school, Drivers' Ed was a requirement, as close to one's 16th birthday as possible, but I had been driving unofficially with Mom already. By the time I was ready to taker Drivers' Ed, the instructor, Mr. Gregory, knew my mother and was well aware of my driving skills. Classes usually had four students—three in the back seat with one being instructed behind the wheel. Each student would take the wheel for 15 minutes before passing it on to the next.

With me Mr. Gregory would say: "Wake me up when your turn is over" and immediately close his eyes with his head resting on the passenger window.

One time, when driving on the back streets in Falls Village, there was a dump truck parked at an angle with a high rear bed extending into the road. There was a car parked opposite and slightly in front. As I approached the truck, Mr. Gregory, noticing the slowing of the car, looked up and said: "I don't think you can get through. Stop and turn around."

"Don't worry, I know how I can fit."

As I approached the truck, having cleared the car by an inch, I turned the front bumper under the flat section of the truck and squeezed by with no more than an inch or two between the truck and car, on both sides.

"I didn't think that was possible" was Mr. Gregory's response. He never questioned my judgement again.

Another fun incident was when Mr. Gregory had us practice parking. The perfect place to practice was behind the school, next to the Future Farmers of America building. There was a twenty-foot gap between the school's pavement and the steep downward slope to the football field, a slope I would race up the only year on the football team. The pavement ended about eight feet before the downward grade. There were three girls in the back seat. As I approached the end of the pavement, they started to say

"Stop."

"Stop…"

"STOP!!!"

Mr Gregory said: "You still have room, go up a little."

Now the front wheels were off the pavement. The girls didn't know how far the flat of the grounds went before the 40-degree descent—being in the back seat they were unable to judge the distance. I continued forward on the grass. The screams from the backseat were so loud some of the FFA class took notice. I suddenly stopped just inches before the drop. Mr. Gregory and I laughed at the panic coming from the back seat. He always loved to play tricks on the students when possible.

Another driving lesson came from Mom. Having received my license shortly after my September birthday, winter was post driving test lessons. Whenever the school was closed due to snow, which was rare for this section of Connecticut, Mom would say after breakfast:

"Let's go to Torrington," which was a good 30 minutes away on a nice day.

On snowy days, it was a major challenge, especially the large hill before you reached Torrington. Repeatedly on bad weather days, she would have me get into the driver's seat and drive all the way. The lessons were invaluable: I learned to drive in the worse possible conditions. One time ascending the infamous hill, we passed a police car which had slid off the road into the ditch. We waved as we passed him. Mom thought this was great fun.

One time we made it up the hill, but going down the light at the bottom of the hill turned red. The traction was such that stopping in time was next to impossible. Mom pointing to the right said:

"Turn towards the snow bank."

Thud!

We stopped just before the light in the large snow pile before the intersection. It took 20 minutes to dig out, but the lesson was, snow banks are softer than other vehicles, so hit the snow bank if that is the only option.

Most cars back then were rear-wheel drive. If you slightly turn the steering wheel and gun the engine on a slick road it would spin the back wheels whipping the car around the turn. I love rear-wheel drive for that reason, used that tactic often on the back roads of northwestern Connecticut in winter time.

Many years later you and your sister were sledding with a friend on a hill behind a local school. You called on a cell phone asking if I could pick you up as all of you were cold, wet and tired. The school was less than half a mile away, but I jumped into the Honda and headed towards the school's parking lot, which led to the sledding hill. There had been no plowing of the parking lot which had about eight inches of snow. I plowed forcibly into the parking lot front-end first. You spotted me and everyone piled the sled and saucers in the back of the car then climbed in.

"How are you going to get out?" you asked.

"Drive out forward."

Your puzzled look was matched your sister and her friend in the back seat. The car was put in reverse, the turning the wheel slightly, and, gunning the engine, the car did a perfect 180 heading directly back out to the main street. You all thought that was an amazing stunt. I looked you and said:

"That was fun, let's do it again."

Turning the wheel and gunning the engine again, the spin took over, only stopping when a perfect 360 was completed. We then drove home. That's how to become a hero in the eyes of your children.

Later, when I had my license, I would drive down to the HS and work on the stage lights if I couldn't sleep. Of course the school was locked up tight. Naturally I knew how to pop some of the windows (remember the freshman year incident?) to get in. As I drove into the school, I would often see the principal's office light on—a clear indication Dr. Stoddard was working late into the night. This was a VERY common occurrence as he was the first and only principal of the school and dedicated his whole life to it.

One night I dragged out the tall step ladder to work on the front row of lights above the stage. This put me at about 15 feet above the floor of the auditorium. If I fell it would have been a BIG fall. It was about 1:30 a.m. I had hoped Dr. Stoddard had not heard me pulling the ladder across the stage nor the lights being arranged on the stage floor prior to being placed where they were needed above the stage. His office was directly across from the theater entrance.

Suddenly I heard a very creepy squeak of the auditorium door being opened. Then came a very distinctive sound, CLUMP CLUMP CLICK, CLUMP CLUMP CLICK, CLUMP CLUMP CLICK, CLUMP CLUMP CLICK, it could be no-one other than Dr. Stoddard with his cane. Then came the familiar booming voice:

"And just what do you think you are doing here this time of night?"

The response: "Fixing the lights for tomorrow, what else?"

"And just how did you get into the school?' he asked.

"Now Dr. Stoddard, you wouldn't want me to give away my trade secrets would you?"

"Well no, but only because you are an honest burglar."

He then sat down on the front row and continued working with his files and folders he had carried in. From then on, if I was working lights late at night, I would still sneak in, but would pop my head into Dr. Stoddard's office to let him know and if working on the step ladder and on those nights he would join me in the auditorium. I really loved that old man, even if we never said a word on those nights. I liked him being around to "watch over me." I'm sure he was happy to have human companionship on the nights I did show up. We really became good friends.

Another funny note about Dr. Stoddard. He taught senior psychology class in the auditorium. It was appropriate since I believe his Ph.D. was in psychology or academic/child psychology. One day the same back door that squeaked was left open during class. There was a lot noise in the hall while the psychology class was going on. He saw one of the girls named Bonnie who had a "loose" reputation sitting in the back.

"Miss X would you please shut the door."

She got up and tried to shut it but couldn't.

"Dr. Stoddard, it won't go all the way."

"Not like some people I know," was his instant response to the laughter of the whole class and a bright red blush from the girl.

Love,
Papa

HI T:

Remember the minister Charles R who came over to mediate Dad and Mom's confrontation after we moved to Lakeville? Charles left Sharon. He divorced his wife, who I always felt wanted a more glamorous lifestyle. Eventually Charles moved to NYC or New Jersey. Mom had kept in touch. It was during these years that Charles asked Mom to marry him. I would have been happy with him as a stepfather, but Mom couldn't picture herself as a minister's wife, so she turned him down. I often wonder how all three of our worlds many have changed if she accepted. I think all three of us would have been better off. But it was during those years she had a dream / vision she was to find a new husband by the name of Roswell Hart. Strange name.

Years later she ran into a Roswell Hart. He was was Admiral Thomas C. Hart's oldest son, whom she would work for years later. But Roswell was married and Mom thought he had a repulsive personality.

One Saturday when she was Worshipful Master of Marie Deraismes Lodge, Charles agreed to take me for the afternoon around downtown. We stopped in a number of stores. We walked over to 5th Avenue And into the old flagship store for FAO Schwarz. As we walked back towards 7th Avenue, there was a bar / club which had a sign outside: Gene Krupa Live: Shows 2, 8 and 10 P.M. It was shortly after 2. Remember I always loved Benny Goodman and Gene Krupa, so I asked Charles if we could go in. He told me that bars like that usually didn't allow children. As a compromise we just stood outside for 10 minutes so I could hear my drummer hero.

I found out later that Charles had applied to Columbia University for their Ph.D. program in theology. He wanted to specialize in a very narrow area of early Christian theology. His application noted the seven languages he spoke and/or read (think Latin and Greek for the research, but also Spanish, Portuguese, German and French, maybe Hebrew). His graduate work was mostly completed but he was still not an official doctoral candidate. He was short of a dissertation and he needed a sponsor. Mom told me Columbia rather than accepting him as a Ph.D. candidate, they offer him a job to teach the very area he wanted to concentrate on. They told him there were no faculty members who could advise him in the area he wanted to study. He was the most qualified person for that particular field they knew, but he didn't want to teach so he turned it down.

Fast forward 10 years. When I was at HVRHS Charles was remarried with two teen stepchildren. His wife was a quiet, shy woman who seldom spoke—the opposite of his first wife. He had been given a church in Winsted, Connecticut 25 minutes from The Hill and the same town where the 1955 flood hit so bad. While there, Timothy Leary was invited to speak at the local junior college. Leary was the famous proponent for the use of LSD back in the 1960s. There were protests against Leary from coming to Winsted. Charles came to his defense. He cited the concept of freedom of speech. He said what Leary was promoting was the same spiritual experiences the Christian mystics had undergone throughout history. Leary was just offering a dangerous short cut. Leary did speak. Charles said when he finished Leary walked off the stage with his arms in a crucifix position. Charles told me Leary acknowledge what LSD did was what early Christian fathers had experienced when overshadowed by the Holy Spirit. He was impressed by Leary's presentation.

Charles' church was a Congregational / Methodist (I think). It allowed him considerable freedom in his sermons. I used to drive over to hear his sermons about every other month. I liked his special service where all the young children who were in the child center came in to sit in the front two rows. He would then come down from the podium and sit on the step in front of the kids, then present a short sermon to them in a way which almost all, no matter what the age, could understand.

As for older children, it was more of a challenge. Charles' stepson was a particular handful, never wanting any direction and constantly getting in trouble in school and elsewhere. The stepson wanted nothing to do with church nor anything Charles was pitching. The daughter was just a few years younger and was beginning to behave in ways that emulated her older brother. When Charles was at a lost for what to do with these kids I would get a Friday night phone call: "W could you come to the service on Sunday? I need someone to talk to about my stepchildren."

I never turned him down. After the service, I would stay long after the parishioners left. Services were 11 to noon. By the time we talked it was often after 1 p.m. We just would sit in the side room and talk about the troubles he was having. I acted more as a sounding board than a counselor. The boy was the opposite of my personality. Still if it helped Charles just to get it off his chest, the sessions were worthwhile. I usually didn't get home until 3 p.m. or later. Charles, being a poor minister, never offered me lunch, so by the time I got home I was starving.

Interesting, a minister asking help from a teen. No wonder I ended up becoming a social worker. Shows the respect Charles had for me, and my love for him.

Love,
Papa

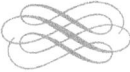

Hey T,

I've been tardy since my last letter!

During my sophomore year I joined the football team and met a crazy girl. More on her later. The football team proved interesting. Due to my size the coach wanted me to play an interior lineman. Offensive, though I would have preferred defense. The practice started in August. We would weigh in before and after practice. One hot summer day, practice was held in full pads. I got on the scales after the practice and saw I had lost 17 pounds. The coach didn't care. Only now do I know how dangerous this was. It was lucky I didn't pass out or even have heart failure.

The practice was on the flood plane of the Housatonic. The building was on top of he hill which was at about a 40 degree decline you might remember the description from the Drivers' Ed class. During all practices when running sprints I was one of the slowest. Big (of B & B) was the fullback for the team and fast. At the end of practice we would race up the hill to the building, four at a time. The first two hit the showers. The last two had to race up the hill again. What seemed unbelievable was that I would finish in the top two no matter who I raced against.

One time Big was next to me. We raced up the hill. I was watching him on my right. We were neck and neck, but in the last two yards, I pulled inches ahead. He looked at me in disbelief. Up the hill I was the fastest on the team. The assistant coach asked how it was possible for me to be so slow on the field but so fast on the hill. The answer was simple. The pads added five to eight pounds. To someone my size it made no difference when going up the hill, but for those smaller, without the leg strength (and size) the weight of the uniform slowed them down.

There was one memorable game. We were opposed by one of our hardest competitors. As the right tackle I came face to face with their top interior lineman. He was well over six feet and easily 50 pounds heavier than me. What was worse, he was fast. He was making mince meat out of me. I tried going low, but he just pushed me to the ground and went over. If I tried to block him high, he would literally brush me aside like a twig. He made several tackles in a row. The coach was furious, yelling at me all the time. Then an idea came to me. I couldn't beat this monster playing it straight. The next play, I started to go high and he followed. Then I ducked down as if to take him out at the knees. He started to adjust by going low again. That was when I raised up as fast and hard as I could. My shoulder and helmet landed right on his chin strap. He went down like a rock. Out cold.

His replacement lined up against me: "Please don't hit me hard. You just knocked out our best player."

"OK, just put up a little hit and let me block you out of the play and I'll be gentle."

It worked. He never got through to tackle our quarterback while at the same time we put on a show as if we were going at it much harder than we were.

Over the season the hits started to take a toll. About three quarters through the season I started getting headaches. Could it have been from concussions? Might have been. We constantly practiced full contact. The games would be more helmet to helmet hits. One day while riding the scooter to school, a violent headache hit me. I couldn't keep myself awake. On a turn up a slight hill approaching the road to the high school, I blacked out and woke up a few minutes later in a pile of bushes. The doctor told me I had to drop out of football. I did, but for the rest of my high school career, those on the team would refer me as a pussy. NOT to my face, but behind my back.

The same year there was a freshman who I became attracted to because of her wacky personality. What I didn't realize was she was actually several years younger than me, having skipped two grades. Like me, she looked older than her years. When I asked what her name was she said: "Sam."

I thought that strange and asked where it came from.

"Oh that's easy, the 'S' is last letter of my last name. The middle letter of my middle name is 'A.' The first letter of my first name 'M.' Together they spell SAM."

Sam was exceptionally intelligent. I think she thought I was unusual having been involved with the protest marches and not the usual jock. We soon began joining what could best be called the hippy crowd in the school, thereby being rejected by all the "in" students. Over the next few years there were a lot of adventures with Sam, even after we split as boyfriend and girlfriend. In many ways this set a pattern of my attempt to keep a "friendly" relationship with former female friends, and continues today (I hope) with your mother after our divorce.

I was taking middle level of English with a teacher we called Drack. He got this nickname due to his slicked back black hair that made him resembled Dracula. This teacher was famous for his knowledge and love of 18th-and 19th-century American literature. He had the ability to make it interesting, even fun. I remember one class when, rather than his usual greeting, he immediately began to read from a book. We all hastily open our notebooks and started taking notes, then we started to realize something was funny.

"New England was call that because like England it was rocky and hilly, except where it was hilly and rocky."

We stopped taking notes. Sure enough he had been reading from *It All Started with Columbus*, which was a funny satire on American history. When we realized he had pulled a joke on us, he just couldn't hold back anymore and laughed until he was red. All this as we pulled out the pages of the notes we had been taking and threw the crumpled paper at him. His favorite book was *Moby Dick*, which he would love to talk about, even when we were not reading it for class.

Back in those days, it was not uncommon for a teacher to invite some of his favorite students to a party at their house. So Drack invited Sam, myself, and a few other students to his house for a spring party. He and his wife had plates of finger food all around the table. Deserts and drinks were on the dining table enabling everyone would grab a plate and help themselves. Since it was in their home both Drack and his wife were drinking a considerable amount of wine. It was then we realized just how crazy he was about Moby Dick. His dog was called Ahab (the crazed captain), the cats (I think) were called Starbuck (1st mate) and Pequod (the name of the ship), some other pet I think was called Queequeg (the Indian harpooner), His eighteen-month-old baby boy was Ishmael, named after the main character.

All around the house was scrimshaw, mostly of whale teeth (some bone), with the carved scenes of whaling ships. Etchings of 18th-and 19th-century whaling were all over the walls. A chess and cribbage sets made of scrimshaw (likely worth many thousands of dollars today but also illegal to sell) were sitting on a table The house was a Melville museum! First editions, biographies, pictures and other materials were everywhere you looked.

Drack's wife, now well relaxed from the wine, told me I had to see their bed. The bed was the bow of a whaling skiff, the boat that was lowered from the main ship to harpoon the whales. She told me that was where she got pregnant with Ishmael. She giggled and said that when Drack was having sex, he was pretending he was stabbing a whale when he achieved organism and shouted "There she blows" as he came.

She said that was a night of great sex and it resulted in their first child.

Drack's English class had a class trip up towards Pittsfield, Massachusetts stopping at a host of famous sites. Many were where Melville, Hawthorn, Thoreau, and the elderly Emerson enjoyed over a hundred years before. It appeared all these famous authors had their summer vacations and get away homes in the area.

We stopped by a small mountain. Drack told the class that was where Melville, Hawthorn, Thoreau and Emerson were all picnicking when a thunderstorm came up suddenly. They and their wives all retreated to a cave. After finishing all the wine soon they all were quite drunk. The picnic turned into an orgy where all the men were changing places with the others' wives while the elderly Emerson cheering them on.

I loved Drack's knowledge of American literature! Especially the unwritten parts. I can imagine the trouble a teacher would get into now a days for telling this version of history. But then maybe that is why American schools are in such a sorry state.

It was about this time we got a call from Uncle Nelson. Sug was dying of cancer. Of all the family members she was the only one who didn't smoke. Mom and I had known for a number of years Sug was battling the disease. We flew down and I visited Sug in the hospital. She was a shadow of her former self. I took her hand and told her what to experience on the other side. She knew both Mom and I were firm reincarnationists. Mom had often told her about my earlier experiences. I told her not to be afraid. Then came the kiss goodbye, mixed with tears. She had been in remission a few months before. They put her on chemo to kill off the rest of the cancer that may have been still there, but then she got seriously ill again. I always felt that it was the chemo that actually killed Sug. Cancer was just the catalyst.

A month later Sug died. We flew down again. Since Sug had been ill for over two years, Nelson seemed relieved. He actually got married a short time later. It appeared he had a mistress on the side while Sug was sick. Can't totally blame him. As for a funeral, I have no memory of the actual service. My cousin Nicky and her husband Hershel were there. Sug had given Mom one of her rose paintings, a theme of paintings she had started when the diagnosis came. It helped her relax. She was good.

Nicky asked for the rose painting. She wanted to have all of Sug's rose paintings. Mom felt it was the only thing she had from her sister. So Nicky made me promise to give it to her when Mom died. Unfortunately Nicky, who smoked worse than Mom, died of cancer like her mother before the painting was returned. Later I found one additional panel painting by Sug. Both are part of my collection.

Love,
Papa

(more or less sent from Europe)

Hi T:

Hope you remembered Sam, my casual girlfriend, from the last letter. Sam lived with her Mom, dad and little brother in the largest state park in Connecticut. Her father was the park Ranger. The whole family lived in the park ranger's residence, a quaint but nice log cabin style home. It was miles from the town of Kent. What most did not know was that the park road, the main entrance of which was through Kent had a narrow dirt road that led to the southern section of Sharon Connecticut, where your grandma worked.

I remember when driving back around 3 a.m. one night, the brakes were slammed to avoid a group of deer. Most ran off to the right. One doe tried to jump up the embankment on the right but fell back. She tried again and again. Each time getting closer to the car until I was right next to the open passenger window. No longer terrorized by the headlights I was now stopped. She started looking around. Suddenly put her head inside the window. I stroked her nose and said:

"Hi there."

She was totally shocked and pulled back her head and ran off to the rear of the car.

Sam was trying to teach herself guitar, painting, and a variety of other hobbies, all of which she was remarkably good at, but great at none. As said I didn't know Sam was that she was 3 years younger than me. I was 16 and driving. Remember I had repeated 3rd grade, while Sam skipped 2 grades and was in HS right after turning 13. She didn't look 13. Her long hippy style hair and a very adult outlook on politics, life and being very well read contributed to the deception. Another interesting point was her refusal to concentrate in class nor try hard on any homework assignments. When the final exams came around she would consistently score 98, 99 or even 100% without any bonus questions! She would have to be given A's by the teachers though they hated her lack of doing homework..

We actually took Latin together, but that is another story. Some of us 'hippy' types in the HS were all into Tolkien and the whole *Hobbit/Lord of the Ring* books. Just as much, if not more than the Harry Potter books when you were in Middle and High School. It was Sam that first turned on your grandmother to Tolkien. They both got me into the books.

What was interesting is that Mom was a former Theosophists. She would talk about the 7 ages of man, of which we were in the 4th and moving into the 5th. She strongly felt that Tolkien was writing about the 3rd Age which ended with the beginning of the rule of man. In many ways it fit the books very closely. I wished she would have lived to hear about the Hobbit hominid (Homo floresiensis) discovered a few years back. She would have claimed Tolkien was right. A section of Indonesia would have been the perfect place for Middle Earth. It would be interesting to discuss this with Sam. I'm sorry I have not been in touch with her since college. Someone told me she was unmarried (or divorced) and still living in Kent—what a waist! She had so much talent that would have exploded away from those small town attitudes.

In sophomore year, the HS offered the option of taking geometry and algebra 2 at the same time. This was open to only a handful students. The idea was to take differential equations and advanced algebra in your junior year then 'Advanced Math' a pre-cal course in your senior year. The key was everyone said calculus would make or break you once you reached college. Sure enough it broke me, but more on that in the college years. Still I finished Freshman year as a solid A student in algebra 1, I was permitted to do the double math option. It worked out well. It also got me out of the stereotype of NOT being college bound.

The whole stage lighting for ALL productions on the HS stage ended up under my charge. No matter what school production was being done, what outside group was going to use the stage, I was in charge of lighting, ALL FOUR YEARS. Sam and some of the other hippy types joined the Young Thespians (drama club) mostly because I was so active. Some worked sets and costumes, but none on stage, more latter.

In the meantime, although Mom did have a job, the problem with drinking, especially in the evenings and weekends continued. It was as if I didn't have a mother during the evenings, unless we played canasta. Even then there was a bottle near-by and by the end of the game, she was ready to nod off.

One Saturday afternoon there was something I wanted to do and needed the car. Mom had been drinking since morning. She objected to either what I wanted to do or something I had done the previous evening. My response was how could a drunk like you dare to reprimand me! She became mad. I was sitting on the edge of the bed in my old bedroom. Mom was so mad she picked up a shoe and started hitting me as hard as she could. Fortunately it was on the shoulders and chest, not the face. I just laughed at her. This just made the blows become more and more furious. Finally when she realized she was not hurting me, she just collapsed on the floor crying. I got up and left.

There was another interesting incident involving Mom's drinking. One summer afternoon I was watching TV. It was a program I was looking forward to watching, possibly a Yankee game. Mom was drunk as anything. She complained I was watching too much TV. As she told me, she was stumbling around the room. I told her she was drunk and go to bed to sleep it off. At the same time a thunderstorm was brewing outside.

Instead of going upstairs, Mom went out to the breezeway. She stood in the doorway vocalizing some kind of chant. I couldn't quite hear it, but saw her looking up into the sky. Suddenly a bolt of lightening struck near by. Out went the lights. I was frustrated as hell. The TV was dead. Mom was giggling slightly and went up to bed. I walked down the driveway to see where the power outage originated. Reaching the road you could see all the other houses on Sugar Hill Road had lights. Then turning around in my own driveway, there next to the brook, was a downed power line. We were the ONLY house without power.

The next day I accused Mom of doing black magic to cut off the power. She denied it and said I was crazy. Yet there was a chant. There was a lightning strike just as she was chanting. But the thunder storm was building. You be the judge. Was it nature or was it magic?

Love,
Papa

(more or less #2 from Europe)

Bonjour T,

Remember my activities related to the stage? Not all was in the auditorium. My sophomore year the senior class wanted to do a play which was part of the theater of the absurd, Eugene Ionesco's *The Bald Soprano*. It was to be performed in the senior class' new large classroom in the recently completed extension to the old HS. The room was perfect for theater in the round, or almost, having seats on 300 degrees around the center of the room, with just a desk and blackboard on the remaining wall. The room was in the shape of an octagon (I think) and the stage was to be in the center.

My challenge was to arrange lights in a room not designed for a theater production. No overheads except for the standard classroom lights. The solution was to run wires under the front row. We had to prevent anyone from sitting on those seats where the spots and fenels were placed. Most of the lighting then would be from below, just adding to the absurd atmosphere of the play. Things were going fairly well, but the wires in use were VERY old, definitely not good. All the front row had wires taped to the base of either the tables or the seats behind the tables. It was surprising how well everything was going, even moving the dimmer board into use.

Then in dress rehearsal on the afternoon before the evening performance, one of the kids went to sit to rest in the front row. This is where the lights were. He got a mild shock from the rather old, frayed wire. But there was no time to replace the yards and yards of wire—replace them with what???? There was no money for new wire. I told my assistants to put the current on low and proceeded to grasp every inch of the wires. Whenever they saw my hand raised they would bring electrical tape to cover the raw wire. Thus started voluntary electrocutions. Every bit of wire was squeezed to determine if there was any exposed wire that could lead to a shock. By the evening's performance I had been electrocuted over twenty times. All mild shocks. None as bad as one I would get the following year.

The show went very well. It was a satire of the most absurd kind. As all the actors shout at the end of the play:

"It's not that way it's over here. It's not that way it's over here. It's not that way it's over here."

Yes, I was happy it was over—here! The book version of the play is somewhere around, hopefully. I've kept it all these years as a memento of the electrifying production.

1966 senior year started. The Young Thespians had to elect a new president for the year. All the faculty advisors wanted me to be elected, as did all the serious members. But suddenly a new member decided to run against me. She was loud and popular among the "inner" circles, and she won hands down! The faculty, including Drack, were furious and their fears that she was the wrong choice proved right.

The Club had to select a play. No one could agree. Finally after major pushing by the faculty advisors it was to be *JB* by Archibald MacLeish, which is based on the book of Job in the Bible. Satan and God have a debate over the God loving and very loyal JB debating questions of JB's loyalty if everything is taken from him. Will he still be loyal to God? First Job's business is destroyed, then his children killed, then his house burned down, but still he is loyal. God wins the bet and that is the end of the play, basically. In the Bible everything is eventually restored, new wife and children, even more successful business etc., but not in the play.

Lights and staging were enough. Yet the faculty advisor (Drack, who else) asked me to read for the lead.

"No thanks!" I was a backstage kind of person.

"We need you to read with this girl who wants to try for the role of the wife."

"OK I'll read with her."

Lee was a young sophomore, skinny but very smart. Later I discovered Sam knew her and liked her. She got the lead. The only problem was so did I, despite my objection. So began the long task of learning the part. I hate memorizing!!!!

As the months progressed we had many rehearsals. Lee and I were doing well as were my friends who were playing God and Satan. Yet NONE of the lesser parts were learning their lines. The president of the Club was no where to be found and didn't help in any way.

The dress rehearsal was held a week before the play was scheduled to open. During the scene where I come out of my burning business, it occurred to me that just being in rags was not enough. So I set my shirt on fire. Then I walked on stage slowly patting the flames out with my hands. Great effect but it scared everyone half to death. Still, the secondary roles weren't there! Not even for the dress rehearsal. The play was cancelled.

Is it true leading men and women form an attraction for each other? Yes. Lee and I became VERY close. I wanted to date her, but her mother objected since, again, there was a three-year difference in age. Still, we met when could and spend long hours just talking in the park where she lived. Lee had a lot of psychological problems and a troubled home life, but I was attracted to her intelligence. She was a wonderful and very kind person. To this day she is very high in my thoughts.

"Would you only consider marrying a virgin?" she asked with a blush on her face during one of our walks.

"Lee, once I would have answered yes. But now I feel that if boys are having sex before marriage, there is no reason for a girl not to have the same pleasures. So it no longer matters to me."

She looked deep into my eyes and squeezed my arm in the most loving way. It was evident she was very interested in me but was fearful that she might not be accepted due to the fact she had already had sex. None of this was said verbally, but her physical and facial expressions voiced a thousand words. In the same way, I felt the sex she may have had was not consensual.

She and her mother were at odds, even the few times I saw them together. But she did not want to talk about her dad. There was a strange feeling there, and not a positive. Years later when studying social work in graduate school, covering the chapter on the emotional harm to a family with incest is involved, Lee popped into my mind. I wondered if it was her father that may have caused the ultimate family harm. Lee may have been raped by her father. By this time there was no contact between us but I would have liked to try to help her in any way I could.

That same year I was elected VP of the Chess Club, even though I was not a very good player. We would follow the world competitions and would replay many of the famous games, but I never could learn the various openings nor the basic text book defenses. I enjoy the game, even today, but I am only a beginner when it comes to chess.

Latin was the language choice, as you only had to read and translate, not be fluent. I was in Latin Club. Sam and most of my friends from the Drama Club were in it too. All felt the Drama Club's rejection of me was unfair, so as a favor they elected me president of the Latin Club, must to the dismay of the teacher. She told me I was the worse student in Latin to ever be elected president. But we got along well. It was a good year for the Club. The best thing to do was to delegate roles and responsibilities, something I was able to do. We would have readings, historical papers and generally a good time. Even the teacher had to admit I did a good job, considering my limitations.

Since I was a senior it was my turn to take the famous psychology class. But Dr. Stoddard was no longer at HVRHS! As a matter of fact, he was no longer alive. At the end of my junior year he was "removed" from his job the only one he had for ninety percent of his adult life. He tried to get a job at Marvelwood School for boys. This was the prep school Mom had worked at for a few years and where I met Johnnie, the gay cook, and had a summer job. But Dr. Stoddard showed up to the interview wearing a food-stained tie. Mom saw him before the interview. She knew there was no chance he would get a job. Here was an obese, elderly Ph.D, with a strong personality and a superiority complex. But at Marvelwood he was trying to get a regular teaching job. His resume would have shown he was clearly over qualified. Needless to say, his application was rejected. He died a short time after.

A new psychology teacher was teaching Stoddard's old course. He was good. For most in the class it was a boring. I was doing OK but nothing outstanding, a solid B. One of the best seasons was when he asked our foreign exchange student, who was a star on the soccer team, to give an introduction to meditation and Buddhist practices. Ti and I were good friends. He explained advanced meditation techniques and how to achieve an out of body experience. In such a state one could visit another on that plane, communicating to the other person as if together physically. He then asked the class to remain quiet for a few minutes as he did the traditional chant. I was doing a meditation.

At the close he smiled while looking up at me, then said: "You see, W and I had a strong connection during the meditation. If we practice I'm sure we could stay in contact even when I return home to my country without the use of physical letters."

We didn't, but it was a good class.

To give us greater understanding of what was included in the field of psychology, the teacher organized two field trips. One to a "home" for mentally and physically disabled children. Another to a psychiatric hospital in New York.

It should be mentioned that at this time I was dating a nice innocent Italian American girl, Terry Z. She was quiet and rather shy. A little chunky but not fat. She can be seen in my senior year book with me in at least one photo. Terry and I did a lot of things together. This included the psychology field trips since they were for the entire senior class taking the class. Terry knew my belief in reincarnation. She even got me a little Masonic pin when I joined Co-M in February of my senior year. She told me the jeweler who sold it to her looked at her strangely—he was also an Italian Catholic. She told him it was for a friend. But one trip was to the institution for the what was then called "retarded" children. We were going through the wards. We entered one small room, where there was a child with a hugely swollen skull—the advanced stages of encephalitis—lying in bed.

The doctor conducting the tour informed the class it was surprising this child had lived to be three years old. His skull was enlarged to the point he could neither turn or raise his head without assistance. To prevent bed sores a nurse would come in and turn him over every few hours. We were informed he was not expected to live much longer, a few months at most.

Most of the class moved on, but Terry and I stood there staring at the child. His eyes turned towards us. There was such a look of sorrow and self pity in them. Looking at the child, I asked: "Oh God, why does this child have to suffer so?"

I held my hands together, as if waiting for a divine answer. Suddenly the child started to mumble something that sounded like German. It was unintelligible but the sounds reminded me of the German language. Terry heard it and agreed it sounded a little like German. Then an intuitive answer came to me. He was suffering for his own sins. It was karma—a most explicit example. A vision came to me that he had been an SS officer for the Nazis in WWII. He was one of those who helped the extermination of the prisoners in a death camp. This would be the first of many lives of suffering he would have to endure to work off his karma. I told Terry the vision. She felt it made sense.

The second field trip is in the next letter.

Love,
Papa

(maybe from the center of Alchemy in 16th Century France—Sarlat)

Bonjour again T,

Remember the psychology class? Terry and I both went on the field trip to the residential psychiatric hospital in New York. I was familiar with the hospital as Mom and I would sometimes take that route to NYC for the meetings. On the bus trip we were told to interview some of the less dangerous patients and do a brief psychological writeup.

I was assigned a woman in her late fifties or early sixties. She was an alcoholic, depressed and self institutionalized. After a short interview based upon her language, description of her life and why she was in the hospital my write up basically described her as a lower middle or lower class individual. I guessed she was at most a high school graduate, but likely a drop out, and suggested she was divorced but no longer had any ties to family or children, if there had been any. This was just a part of the write up. The teacher who had reviewed the files of those being interviewed said I was 100 percent on target (this was long before HIPA and the securing of personal information for patients). He was exceptionally impressed with the analysis.

After completing the interview, the class entered into the more dangerous wards with an escort. There was a large number of male patients. Some were considered bellicose and dangerous. All around the room were paintings. They most depicted African American scenes of the inner city. Some appeared to have been of Harlem. The guide told us all the paintings were by one of the patients. He pointed at one Black man in the corner who was painting on a small canvas. Terry and I went over to see what he was painting. The painting was of an Egyptian. Obviously royalty, possibly a pharaoh. The painting was much smaller than those on the walls which were as much as

4 to 6-feet tall and/or wide. This painting was only about 18x24 inches. It was mostly finished—the artist was putting on the final touches to an ornamental headdress. Looking at the face I noticed that the eyes were not even. One was distinctly lower on the face than the other.

"Why did you paint the eyes unevenly?" I asked.

"That's the way I remember seeing him," was the man's response.

I looked quizzically at him.

"Yeah. That was when I lived in Egypt," he explained.

I nodded and thanked him for the explanation. I looked at Terry. "Another case of reincarnation." She smiled and nodded.

Turning to the artist I said, "That has to be one of the most beautiful portraits of an Egyptian I've seen. You are doing an outstanding job."

Later the guide told us that his art was not for sale, that the artist would only permit his paintings to be displayed in the hospital. Offers had come in for thousands of dollars for some of his larger works, but the institution respected the wishes of its patients. All his art was hanging around the different buildings. When and if he died the hospital would have had a fortune worth of his art. I was told we were lucky that he spoke to us. The guards were closely watching. He was querulous and considered one of the most truculent patients in the ward.

One more psychology class incident. Sam and I had another friend we called Fred. She was very much a hippy from a single parent home. Her father, who had immigrated from Hungary, was a classic nonconformist. I don't know what he did, but he looked like an ageing Bohemian-Gypsy in the classic sense of the word. Fred told me she had been sexually active since she was 12 years old. Her father would often tell her about all the women he screwed in Hungary before migrating to the United States. And in turn Fred would tell him about her sexual adventures. He seemed to like to hear about them. She told me that he loved her promiscuous activities because it reminded him of the whores he knew in Budapest during his youth.

One day in the same psychology class I was sitting next to Fred. She was in terrible pain. I offered her an aspirin. She took several. I asked her what was the problem. She told me she had an illegal abortion the day before and didn't dare to go to a regular doctor because the cause would be evident. This was before Roe vs. Wade, so abortions were against the law and if she had gone to a regular MD he may have reported her. She might have ended up in jail. I held her hand. She squeezed hard when the pain got worse. This went on for the whole class.

From that day on, and knowing my mother's experiences which almost cost me my life, I became a pro choice advocate. I never wanted another woman to go through the pain Fred was experiencing. I'm sure it was not as bad as some of the incidents Mom had experienced in Texas.

Most of the adventures that year were associated with the stage; more in a minute.

I was on the Track Team, shot putt and part of the flying elephants. The "flying elephants" were the shot putters who weighed over 200 lbs. After practicing our sport, and a little discus and maybe javelin, we would go over to the high jump pit to practice jumping over a low bar.

You must know two things about our practice field. First it was right next to the Housatonic River, therefore on the flood plain, where the water table was just inches below the ground. Second, the old jumping pits were not the nice inflated balloon you jump on now. They were hard sawdust, often packed down by rain. What was neat about the flying elephants was when we landed in the high jump pit the whole field would shake, sometimes all the way over to the baseball field, where Kirby and the physical education teacher, Mr. T were coaching their prized baseball team. They would wonder why the earth was shaking under their feet.

274

Quick note about the baseball team: Steve Blass was from our HS and a star player. He later pitched for the Pittsburg Pirates joining the team in 1964 when I was at Housatonic. He was credited with winning the 1971 World Series for them by pitching a winning COMPLETE GAME in game one and game seven. He was then selected as the pitcher of the year. The next year he couldn't take the pressure and dropped out of baseball altogether. His record was one of the worst in baseball history.

When asked what happened by some of the locals, Steve told them he had succeeded in achieving everything he dreamed of, a World Series victory (including the ring), being voted the Cy Young awardee, and the acclaim that came with it, and there was nothing else he wanted. So he just seemed to give up as a player. His younger brother joined Peter and I a few times to go shooting. The kid was a remarkably good shot with his 22 rifle.

Back to the stage. There was one new arrangement of lights being completed while rehearsals were going on. The stage had huge rectangular plugs that went into the floor sockets. They were usually attached to the side lighting poles with multiple spots, lekos and fernels.

On this night all the lights were finally in place with appropriate color gels. I walked over to plug in the lights into the female connection, when BAMB! I was hit with what may have been thousands of volts of an electric spark. It threw me backward (remember *Jurassic Park* the movie and the kid on the fence?) all the way across the stage, about 15 feet. Drack and the others came running up to me to see if I was alive. All said there was a tremendous spark that hit me and threw me backward. When they saw me move and try to get up, everyone was relieved. What they couldn't believe was that the second I got up, I walked over to the plug and finished plugging it in.

Then I turned to everyone: "Lights are ready!"

In another play, likely in junior year, we were setting up the same kinds of lights. The name of the play escapes me, but I do remember that my friend Gail S. was singing *Try to Remember* in it. She was a very near-sighted girl, the type you could say she couldn't see her friends until they were right on top of her, as the old joke went. But that is another story between us, which you don't want to hear about. What was strange is the song was added for Gail. It didn't belong in the play that was being done. They wanted all seniors who wanted to participate to be part of the production in it even if it didn't quite fit. It was the first production in November of 1965. The rehearsal was running late, it being a little after 5 P.M. and we all wanted to get out by six.

I had just finished setting up the whole light configuration. The lights on the poles over the stage were in place. The overheads were ready. The side polls were loaded with the spots, ready to be plugged in. But this time when I plugged in the plug into the floor, all the lights on the stage and the whole auditorium went out.

"What did you do?" everyone repeated over and over.

Flash lights and a few lighters were lit so we could see in the dark. After about 90 seconds the lights came back on. I checked all the circuits and breakers, all was in order. When we left the school and Falls Village, we soon discovered all of New York (including NYC), New England and parts of Canada, including Ontario, were dark. It was the great black out of 1965. Now, they may want to tell you it was caused by some character incorrectly setting a protective relay on a transmission line at the Niagara generating station outside Ontario. But the real secret is it was set off by my stage lighting!

We came on in 90 seconds for another seldom known reason. Remember the power plant on the Housatonic River? Well that was only a half mile away. They were able to cut themselves off from the grid. Using their own hydro-electric generators were able to bring on the Falls Church area lights almost immediately. This was fortunate for Bradley Field, the airport outside Hartford.

When all the air ports from Boston, Maine, NYC, NJ, etc. went dark, it was the little Falls Village power plant that got power to Bradley Field. All planes in the air had somewhere to land. Most were rerouted to Bradley. That was the ONLY northeast coast airport open for a long time, at least a long time if you are flying around in the dark. I bet those lights were a sight to behold as pilots were rerouted to Bradley to land before they ran out of fuel. Of course, there would be more blackouts later in my life.

It was after this blackout that Mom and I made another trip to NYC, as again she was needed for one of the meetings at Marie Deraismes Lodge. I was to keep busy by seeing a show while she was in the Lodge. It turned out the ticket for the matinee showing of a little show called *Cabaret*! It was a chance to see Joel Grey again, the first time since *Stop the World* years before. It was my lucky day, no substitutes for the performance. Lottee Lenya played Fraulein Schneider opposite Jack Gilford. Lenya was the widow of the composer Kurt Weill. A letter could be devoted to their relationship alone. But you can look up that strange marriage by yourself some day. Her last roll was Rosa Klebb in *From Russia With Love*, the second James Bond movie. She and Gilford played the perfect romanic older couple broken up when the Nazis rose to power in Germany. Joel Grey was the Emcee! His performance was unbelievable outstanding: risqué and funny. I think the only shortcoming was Jill Haworth who played Sally. She was OK but not a stand out. Still overall the production was one of the greats! After all, it won eight Tonys!

This was likely the last time I did not attend the Lodge. In February of 1967, shortly after my 18th birthday, I petitioned the Lodge as a "Lewis." According to Le Droit Humain rules, no one under the age of 21 could be admitted. The exception was the son or daughter of a Mason could join at the age of 18. We followed the usual traditions of having an investigating committee appointed to interview me. It was hard to find three members who didn't know me. The head of the committee was Harry H. He had a strong egotistical personality. Of all the members of 352, he knew me the least. He had been a member of one of the lodges that closed in the 1950s. The vote was taken in January and I was told that I would be admitted on February 4th. Girli Karll was the Worshipful Master of the Lodge. It was a wonderful ceremony with Myron Kitaif as my conductor. Myron and Jane were two of the old members of the lodge and both wonderful people. Myron the intellect, Jane the intuitive straight shooter.

After my initiation we had a celebratory dinner and started home. A long day, one that would impact me the rest of my life. It may have been this trip or another when we were driving back to Connecticut one evening. It was later than usual and Mom and I were both tired. Mom asked me to drive. We got on the Saw Mill Parkway headed home. I was a bit drowsy. Mom was awake but tired. Suddenly I exited the Parkway and slammed on the breaks for a stop sign at the bottom of a hill. Mom snapped to with a start.

"Why did you get off here?" she asked.

"Well the sign told me to EXIT, so I did."

We both laughed until we had tears in our eyes. It was probably a good thing. The laugh kept us awake until we got back to The Hill.

About a week later I had a dream. It was obviously stimulated by the Entered Apprentice Degree just received. It is long but worth describing.

I was standing in a bar in Alaska. There were a number of men and some women drinking all talking loudly. It appears I had just finished a dinner and was paying for the meal when some men came into the saloon.

"A bear just attacked a bunch of men over the ridge. We have to get it before it attacks anyone else."

A large group of us immediately grabbed guns and went off into the snow. There was a terrible blizzard outside making progress difficult. It was hard to see. Even harder to walk through the drifting snow. About a mile out, we found the bear tracks. It was a huge animal. By the size of the tracks it must have been at least eight feet tall. A group of us followed the tracks to a steep valley. A river flowed at the bottom. It was a narrow trail down the slope. That was the direction the tracks led us. Down we went,

At the river's edge the tracks went into the water. Three canoes were found nearby. As many as possible slipped into the canoes. I was among them. As we were paddling down the river, the bear could be seen in the distance. He turned on us as if to charge. But suddenly he changed into a phoenix and flew away and as he did, the walls of the canyon opened up.

A large tributary appeared, flowing into the river we were on. As we watched this stream, the rock walls separated and a golden boat appeared. It looked a lot like the royal barge of Thailand, just as beautiful but a little larger with more decks. As it approached I saw a Tibetan looking individual standing in the prow. Somehow I knew it was DK.

As the barge pulled alongside our canoes, four of us were told to climb aboard. I quickly jumped over. The other three were very reluctant, but joined me mostly out embarrassment at being less brave than a teenager. One was the sherif of the village where we came from. Another was a priest, dressed in black and had the traditional collar of a member of the clergy. The third was a lawyer. When the last boarded the barge, it turned back towards the cliffs whence it came.

As we passed into the narrow fjord, the weather immediately changed; it was no longer cold. It became warm and pleasant. Green fields could be seen on either bank. The four of us in the golden vessel took off our heavy coats and boots. The boat was approaching a giant temple. It looked something like that pictured in Cole's painting Youth in his "Ages of Man" series of paintings in the National Gallery of Art in Washington, DC.

The barge pulled up to the dock near the temple. Ropes secured the vessel and we were instructed to get off. The Tibetan led us into the temple. The walls were a translucent white marble, the floors of zebra marble. Each door was huge and crafted from hardwood. Once inside we were told to take off our shoes as the temple was holy ground. We took off our shoes and then put on special robes.

We were led into a preparation room. One could equate it to a Chamber of Reflection once used in Masonry, but it wasn't a dark, underground room; this was a bright room, lit by the glow that came from the walls themselves. No visible source of light could be seen. The temple itself was the source of all light.

We were then commanded to kneel at a narrow altar, where there were four small glasses with a clear liquid in each. A monk approached:

"Before proceeding further each of you must drink from the vial in front of you."

The sheriff started shaking:

"You can't make me force me to drink when I don't know if it is poison or not. How do I know you are not trying to kill me? I'll have you all arrested."

The clergy suddenly said: "This must be an unholy drink from Satin. I refuse. I am a man of God and will not drink."

The lawyer shaking more than any of the others said: "You are holding me illegally. I've been kidnapped. How do I know if you are not trying to drug me? You'll be sued!"

I looked at each of them. All were terrified. Each was looking for a way to escape, but there was no obvious way out.

DK came me and asked me to drink. I did without hesitation. It was bitter.

"This is the drink representing life, its hardships and challenges. Do you understand?"

I nodded yes. But that nod was not entirely truthful as I didn't fully know the meaning he was attempting to convey. When I finished the drink, only I was permitted to rise and follow the Tibetan into the inner courts of the temple. The others were escorted out. I never saw them again.

Inside the temple, it resembled a Masonic Lodge. I was seated at the southern end, where a junior warden would usually be placed. I could see the tessellated pavement on the checkered floor; the walls and floors were of white marble and there were benches made of beautiful polished wood, with gold gild on the backs and arms for the principal officers.

Three trumpet cords sounded reminding me of the opening notes to the overture in Mozart's The Magic Flute. A procession started into the lodge room, but those on the sides were not permitted to watch it directly. All of us had our eyes cast downward towards the floor. As the procession passed. I felt the great energy coming from these exceptionally holy beings. I was not even sure if they were in physical form. The most powerful sat in the east, the second was in the west. A faint idea came to me that it was Jesus and Buddha were in the east and west.

Just as they knocked the lodge to order, I was conducted out.

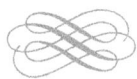

Bongiorno T:

During my last years in HS Mom gave me a motor scooter to get to and from school. Actually it was when I turned 16 but I used it throughout the rest of High School. This saved on gas and would allow me to get there whenever needed to work on the stage. But that was no longer easy. In my senior year Dr. Stoddard was dismissed and the bane of my existence, Mr. K, was taking over. This is the same man who taught Earth Science and implied if I joined the football team I might get extra help. That was held against me, especially by him. So, the midnight stage jobs had to be extra secret and only when the office lights were out and K's car not around. Fortunately that was often as he was no where as devoted, time wise, as Dr. Stoddard who I sincerely missed.

Remember Latin Club (yours truly was president)? Sam and I were in the same advanced Latin class. We were no longer dating but still good friends. One late spring day the sun was shining on the center court of the school, the windows were open, and a fly came in, buzzing around the room. Sam sat right in front of me next to wall opposite the windows. In an attempt not to disturb the class as the fly came near me. I gentle waved my hand tried to get it away. No success. So a waved a paper. No luck.

By this time all focus had turned from the class to the pesky fly still buzzing around my head and desk. Suddenly it landed right in front of me, but repeated slaps missed it. It flew up and came right back to the edge of my desk. I had a strange thought that maybe sound waves would stun it enough for me to kill it. So with a big gulp of air in my lungs I let out a loud:

"Barf!"

Poor Sam. The sound not only knocked the fly to the ground where he was quickly stepped on. But Sam had been so shaken up she too was on the floor. The rest of the class in pure shock. The poor one legged teacher looked like she had just came back from the battle front of WWII.

It dawned on me what had happened. Apologizing to the class and the teacher, I tried to explain it was a fly I was after, pointing to the dead fly on the floor. As for poor Sam, she was shaking and needed help to get up, which I quickly provided. So if I ever yell Barf! you know where it came from.

There were other lesser adventures, like the kids putting my scooter in the girls bathroom. Once discovered I had friends hold open the doors to the bathroom and the back door to the parking lot and rode the scooter through the halls back to where it belonged.

Another time when I was riding the scooter to Lakeville. There was an attractive girl walking on the side of the road just as I was going around a curve. Suddenly my attention was redirected to the road—immediately in front of me was a backup of cars next to a construction site. All traffic had stopped. But I was going too fast to stop behind the car. The breaks of the scooter was applied, but it began to spin out of control. I did all I could to keep it upright, but the scooter swerved from one side to another and finally stopped right in front of the flag man. I just shrugged and smiled. He shook his head at me.

During senior year there was one non academic test required. It was a funny aptitude test required of all seniors by the guidance counselor to help steer you towards a career. Not taking it seriously, the answers were just jotted down quickly—any answer that popped into my head was marked. The optimal score for any career was 100. I scored 99 on politician and 98 on minister or priest. This caught the guidance councilor's attention and puzzled her.

"How can you explain how you scored so close to a politician and a priest?"

"Simple" I said "One thinks he speaks for God and the other thinks he is God, no real difference."

She didn't accept that. The analogy evidently upset her. The only other profession that scored above 80 was librarian. Much to Mom's dismay, business was actually a negative score. The counselor noted she had never seen a negative score before in all her years of giving that tests.

In September Mom took me to a college fair. There were a LOT of colleges represented there, many smaller colleges from the mid-west. In reviewing some of the college it seemed unusual that a college with only 680 students would have a campus over 1,200 acres. The representative was asked what they did with all that extra land.

His response was: "We give half an acre to each student and let them decide."

Of course it was a joke, but the humor made me think maybe I should apply there. Thus, in late September, off went an application to Rockford College, in Rockford Illinois.

Looking back on the college fair in Hartford, it was a good drive away from Falls Village. The colleges represented where widely dispersed around the country. Of the 200 schools represented, it was very strange I selected Rockford out of the whole group. Yet that's what happened. Since the application had been sent for early acceptance, the response was fast. By early October I had been accepted by a college!

By the way *The Lakeville Journal* had ALWAYS had an article about the first Housatonic Valley Regional HS student to be accepted to a college each year. I was accepted by the second week in October. That was the first year in the memory of the *Journal* they did not run that article. God forbid that a poor student on scholarship would beat out all those upper-class snobs to being accepted in college. Yet that's what happened. So the *Journal* refused to run the article in 1966. That was typical of that part of Connecticut. If you were not part of the upper crust, you were not worth of the ink of a story, except on the crime page!

Graduation was mostly uneventful. Adm. Thomas Hart was our keynote speaker. He also handed out many of the diplomas. Afterward I asked Mom if he might have noticed by Masonic pin in the lapel of my jacket. She felt he most likely had. As the class exited the auditorium we all sang:

"We got to get out of this place if it is the last thing we ever do..."

Maybe there might be another story or two about the HS years, but I want to move to college, where it gets strange again.

Love,
Papa

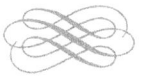

Chapter 17

College(s)?!?

(last letter sent from Europe)

Ciao T:

Rockford College, and a very strange freshman year. During the summer incoming freshmen were notified as to who would be their roommates. They liked to room freshmen together. All dorms were arranged with suits of three rooms, two bedrooms for two students each, a common room, with the bathroom off of it.

Soon after the assignments were announced I got a phone call from a Tom who said he would be my roommate. A little strange, but a nice gesture. Wasn't quite sure what to make of this overly friendly character. He was really that nice, outgoing, and for real??? As it turned out, Tom was and continues to this day considered as one of my best friends though we rarely talk or exchange letters any more.

Rockford was too long of a drive for Mom's old car so off from Bradley Field in Hartford, Connecticut I went. This would become a familiar trip, to and from the air port over the next three years. Only in August of 1970 did Mom drive out and we drove back together.

The first month at Rockford was relatively quiet. I was busy registering for classes, getting use to the rules, location of the various classes, and introducing myself to the teachers. For language I registered for German, as did Tom. Calculus was a priority since I had a "math concentration" in high school. After less than a month German was dropped. I was hopeless! Tom stuck it out, but regretted doing so and took up another language. As for calculus, I would read the book and thought I understood it. Then the professor would explain the lessons. Was he reading the same materials as I? He would totally throw off all understanding of the book. I escaped with a D-. They always said calculus would make or break you. Well, it broke me!!

In early October there was a college dance. The school had few blacks, less than 10 percent. Yet there on the side was a thin attractive Black girl. I walked up to her and asked if she would like to dance. She accepted. When the next dance was a slow dance, she actually started to hold me tighter. This was the start of my relationship with JJ. There is NO doubt that she was my first great love! Soon we were inseparable.

We played ping pong together (won mixed doubles competition in the school in our junior year), loved the same shows and movies and soon became very much in love. Two problems. The first was that she was a party girl (the first semester she got mostly Ds!). The other problem was she smoked. I attacked both problems, one at a time.

Using the argument that after cigs her breath smelled bad and it was bad for her health, I tried to get her to give them up. Finally I told her every time she had the urge to smoke, she should kiss me instead. It worked. She quit.

Now the next problem—the grades. Her parents saw the first semester's grades they hit the roof. Her mother threaten to pull her out of Rockford. You must realize her mother was a professor at a college. She was listed in the Who's Who of academic women. While her father was the chief chef and caterer for a major DC hotel. JJ's problem was she wanted to play hearts rather than study. I started to pull her out of games. If homework was not done, NO GAMES. Slowly her grades picked up. Spring mid-semester grades were all As and Bs. Her parents wanted to know why. She told them her boyfriend forced her to study. In a letter they expressed an appreciation towards this unknown boyfriend. They wanted to know: Why didn't she let him talk to them? What was he like? Where did he come from?

She didn't want to tell them I was white! After a few months I threatened that if she didn't tell them I would write a letter to them. I did, not telling them much other than I convinced her to quit smoking and got her to study. I would ask if the homework and studying was finished before she could play cards with friends or party in the dorms. By the way, the dorms were separate, boys not allowed in the girls' dorm and visa versa except for two hours one night a month.

Her mother called right after they got the letter. My last name was the give away:

"IS HE WHITE?????"

JJ had to admit I was. Her mother was very unsure about this, but her father said:

"W has gotten her to give up that horrid habit and has JJ back to getting good grades, what more could you hope for?"

Reluctantly her mother came around. In the summer I went down to DC and met them. Her father immediately greeted me with a huge hug, he was a fun, and like teddy bear, a genuine man who became very fond of me. Her mother was always a little standoffish, but as the years progressed she accepted me.

As for JJ and I, we were walking down a DC street one day, she telling me which stores didn't allow Blacks just a few years before and which did. A Black man came up to her and told her to dump the whitey. I forget what she said, but it put him in his place. He looked at us and then said: "You must have a good thing going. Good for you."

What was amusing is that some 45 years later, Charlene, my wife after the divorce with your mother, and I were walking arm in arm down one of the streets in DC. A female graduate student came up and asked if she could take a picture of us. Unlike myself, Charlene is anything but camera shy.

She said: "Sure."

Then we asked why?

"I'm working on a graduate paper describing how the culture of Washington has changed since the 1970s. I would have been next to impossible for a Black woman and a white man to be seen together back then."

Charlene nodded. We continued walking. I turned to Charlene. "Should I have busted her bubble by telling here that in 1968 I was walking down these same streets with another beautiful Black woman?"

Charlene's reply was, "No, let her keep thinking it has changed. For most people it has. You're just different."

Love,
Papa

Dear T,

Have to have a flashback in this letter and the next. I knew there would be stories from the HS years to recall. This a little of a downer but VERY important—the death of WAB, your grandfather. It was in my sophomore year, before I had a driver's license, so must have been that year. If remembered correctly it was early Saturday morning. The phone rang in Mom's room. She picked it up and after an exchange of words, came into my room where I was just waking up.

She told me: "Your stepMom is on the phone, your dad died."

Getting on the phone Liz' voice came over the line. She told me Dad had died the night before of a heart attack. She asked if I would be coming down for the funeral. Knowing the difficult position we were in financially, at first Liz was told I couldn't come down. It was a brief call leaving a very complex of emotions, sadness, frustration, a bit of emptiness.

Turning to Mom, I said, "Going for a walk, I'll be back."

I walked down the driveway without thought or any real emotion. As I reached the main road, I turned automatically towards the school bus stop and continued walking. It was here I had the realization I would never see my Dad again, that he was really dead! It began to hit me. The regrets of not seeing him for the past three years, not getting along when we were together, of the fighting between him and Mom all came flooding into my mind. Now negative emotions were beginning to overwhelm me.

Walking to the break of the hill, where the road begins to decent I spotted the action of two squirrels. It was a pair chasing each other around the tree. Soon it became evident that it was a male and female. Every so often they stopped, had fast and furious sex, then off for another run around the branches. When suddenly the female would stop, present herself and he would mount her to have sex again. At first the though went through my mind, "Don't know my dad just died? How can you do that?" But then the truth that life goes on hit me. Turning around I headed back to the house.

"Mom, I want to go down for the funeral can we do it?"

"We'll manage. I'll call Liz and tell her your are coming down."

Liz and all the friends of dad's down there were very consolatory towards me upon arriving. My mind was mostly blank. The next day was the funeral. All though the ceremony my mind was mostly a void of emotion or thought.

Dad was there in front of the chapel. A nice simple beautiful white flower arrangement had been sent by his fraternity in NYC. Those were the only flowers, but it seemed appropriate. Then when the funeral ceremony came to a close, we were to pass the open casket. IT HIT ME! There was the man who was my father. Dead! About to be buried! I would never see, speak, or write to him again. A sudden feeling of loss overcame me. What chances were missed to talk together! Opportunities would never be manifested. He would never see me graduate from HS, college, never see me driving, never talk to me again. There at the casket I froze.

Liz tried to help me away. I couldn't let go of the casket. All the years of built up emotions suddenly flooded out. Breaking down hysterically my knees collapsed, tears flooding down my cheeks. Screams of pain came out of my mouth. Some of the men there picked me up and literally carried me out of the funeral home. My screams and cries could surely be heard throughout the building. Carried to the car we drove off, Liz trying to console me as best she could but to no avail, for 20 minutes.

By the time we arrived at the reception, breathing was back to normal. My tears were dried. It was over. For the rest of the evening I was back to my normal self. After apologizing for the breakdown, people were amazed that after such a breakdown at the funeral I could be so normal. But the breakdown got all the emotions out of my system.

The next day I flew back home. Liz and I always exchanged Christmas cards and an occasional letter. She remarried, was widowed, remarried, widowed and then remarried to Mr. White, who you met in Florida (later she divorced him).

Dad's insurance, according to the divorce decree, was to come to Mom and me. But he had assigned all of it to Liz. Mom wanted to fight it. I asked her not to as Liz was a nice person. So Liz got the money at a time Mom really needed it. How we survived the next two years was a mystery. We were as poor as you can imagine of anyone who still had a roof over their head. Then Mom started working for the Harts in Sharon with Adm. Hart and his wife Missy.

Love,
Papa

I've lost track of what has been sent and what has not so there may be some duplicates here. That's OK since I have so many envelopes for you!

Hello there—ready for another flashback?:

The year after Dad died, Mom tried to start up the Lakeville Letter Shop, with a minimum of success but with a notable story. There was one famous personality who lived on the shore of Lakeville Lake. Artie Shaw was the second most famous clarinetist next to Benny Goodman during the jazz era of the '30s and '40s. Remember, I use to hear Benny at Music Mountain in Falls Village as he was just as comfortable with classical as jazz. Shaw didn't have the talent to cross over to other kinds of music so he never played there, at least to my knowledge.

Somehow Artie Shaw and some of his friends had come up with the next great movie script: *Hope is a Thing with Feathers*. It was terrible! He had to have 110 copies of the script to get out to all contacts in Hollywood. He called the Lakeville Letter Shop.

"Can you put together 110 scripts within a week?"

Mom needed the money so she said she could. This was before word processors, copiers, or any of the modern methods of producing books, stories, or scripts. It was all to be done in a typewriter, stencils, run off on a mimeograph machine as described before.

The dining room was for typing and mimeographing. Bridge tables were set up on the living room to assemble the pages as they came off the A.B. Dick hand-crank mimeograph. Mom would type the stencils and proof each. If corrections were needed, out came the correction fluid, then reinsert the stencil into the typewrite, line up the line and column perfectly and type over the corrected mistake. Then the finished stencil was handed over to me.

The stencil was then put on the mimeograph machine. 115 copies were run off. All by hand cranking the machine barrel around and around, stopping only to add ink and swish it around to be sure all the ink would be evenly spread over the stencil. Once the number of copies was reached, piles of the individual pages was placed on the card tables in the living room. I would then grab two sheets, one in each hand. Then moving down the tables, would pick up the next two and the next etc.. Then cross thatch those collected at the end of the tables. This would continue through the first set of pages. The same process would occur with the next set and the next. Usually about 25 pages per set.

When we had about 1/3 of the manuscript completed, which took several days, I would put them together in order and place them on the floor before starting on the next third of the script.

We busted our balls to get it done in the timeframe Shaw wanted, but we did it. Boxes of paper purchased for the job were now carrying the finished scripts. The stencils were carefully placed between sheets of newspapers and placed in other boxed in case additional copies would be needed. Mom spent a small fortune on paper, ink and stencils for this job, then adding the time and labor costs she delivered both the scripts and the bill to Shaw.

THE BASTARD REFUSED TO PAY!!!!

He said the charges were way too high. Mom explained she was unable to produce the products at the lower rates he would find in NYC because she was a small shop with higher overhead costs. He was charged the same costs with a little discount that was charged to anyone coming to the Letter Shop. He didn't care. He wouldn't pay.

Mom had to take the case to small claims court where he was instructed to pay to the fee. She got a little less than the cost of the supplies for the job, and NO PROFIT! She gave up the Letter Shop after this experience. To this day I love the '40s music but refuse to listen to Artie Shaw recordings, thinking that bastard lived to be in his 90s. He died owing Mom over a thousand dollars, but unfortunately by then she was already dead too.

After the Letter Shop ceased to exist, she had jobs at *The Lakeville Journal* as a typesetter which didn't last long. She hated the place. She felt the major writers and Annie Hoskins (?) the editor, were a bunch of snobs and frankly not too smart. Their only claim to fame was their money and contacts. The key was the job was regular income plus she was working with her friends Ruth and some of the blacks who worked in the print shot. These were the same people who were members of the VFW she joined.

There was a funny incident during that time. There was a headline story about Sharon Hospital, possibly related to an expansion and fund raiser, not sure. There on the front page was the headline: "Sharon Horpital." The paper hit the street with the incorrect spelling. Mom asked the guys in the basement of the building if they had seen the error. Of course they had, but proof reading was not their job. They were just the "dumb niggers" working in the print shop (their words, not mine).

If you treat people badly, guess what? You only get the minimum. Remember NW Connecticut was (is?) a hotbed of racism. More subtle and not as overt as you would find in the South, but there nonetheless.

Love,
Papa

Hello there—here we go with a series of Hart episodes:

It may have been Mom's doctor, Dr. Joe, who got her in contact with the Harts. More about Dr. Joe later, as she was a most remarkable individual.

The Harts were the family living in King House in Sharon. Missy (Mrs. Caroline Hart) needed some secretarial help. Dr. Joe suggested my Mom could fit her needs. Missy came from a Naval family. Her husband "The Admiral" (retired, 4-star) was the only officer in US Navy history to see fighting in the Spanish American War (on a gun boat), WWI (sub commander) and WWII, where he got in trouble trying to warn Washington in early 1941 that the Japanese were preparing to attack US territory. Later he was appointed as a senator from Connecticut upon the death of a sitting senator. Thus Mom started to work for Admiral Thomas C. Hart and his wife Missy. By the way, the Admiral was only about five-foot and Missy less than 5 foot.

At first she was just the secretary for Mrs. Hart. Soon Missy realized Mom's capabilities. She decided she wanted to have a biography written about her father, Admiral Brownson. Partly because she really cared for her father, but Mom felt Missy also wanted to put down her husband while elevating the memory of her father.

Adm. Thomas C. Hart was famous in many areas, as you can see, but Missy's father, Admiral Brownson, was part of the second US fleet to enter Japan. This was after Adm. Perry had opened up the previously closed country. Admiral Brownson was active throughout Asia, later taking charge of the Naval Academy, all the while rising through the ranks. Mom started doing the research on what became *From Frigate to Dreadnought,* many copies of which are in the storage units along with copies of the notes and journals, and some of the original letters. Some of the items given by Missy to your grandmother include letters from the White House signed by President Teddy Roosevelt and much more.

Mom thought the book boring and tried to have more of the exciting materials included, but Missy really wanted a family memoir. As a result, all the exciting parts of Brownson's career are absent. Instead it focused on the family and friends.

Missy was an interesting character. She was born in Asia (China?). The servants called her "little Missy." So for the rest of her life she like to be called Missy to elevate her status before others. Mom noted one time at lunch with the Admiral and Missy they had gone over some of Brownson's notes.

There was an entry: "Visited (name of a woman????)"

Missy was shaking her head:

"I don't remember having an aunt there."

But the Admiral burst into snicker that almost caused him to loose the food in his mouth. Very quietly said to himself, but loud enough for Mom to hear:

"So that moral bastard got his nuts off there too."

Mom found out that "Aunt whatever" was a code name for one of the most famous whore houses in China. Hart certainly knew of it. Now, much to his delight, he knew his father-in-law who always tried to portray himself as morally superior, visited the very brothel, which represented the depths of immorality. As an Admiral, Brownson likely would have been entertained by three young girls at the same time, if not more. Mom always wanted to do another more interesting biography of Brownson. All the notes were copied but she never got back to it. The materials are still in my possession. As for Brownson vs. Hart—I would have chosen Hart any time.

On days when I had the car I would come over to pick up Mom. This was during the Vietnam War. The second I entered the house the Admiral, who was a staunch Republican, would call me into his office and ask me to sit down.

"What the hell do you think about *XYZ?*" It might be about the war, a political debate in the press, or anything he could think of.

Naturally I would take a left of center view. He the opposite. We would sit there and argue for 30 minutes or more about the issues. While in college the Admiral learned I took ceramics and during one spring break he called me into his office.

"I hear you are taking ceramics? Do you use one of those new electric wheels, or are you learning the REAL way, with a kick wheel?"

What followed was a 30 minute argument over whether electric wheels produced "real" ceramics. I naturally took the defense of the electric. He argued about how the old fashioned kick or stick wheels were the real tools of a skilled potter.

Mom finally called me saying we had to go. As I was leaving his office I turned to the Admiral and said: "Admiral, I have a secret. I prefer the old kick wheels."

Mom found out that "Aunt whatever" was a code name for one of the most famous whore houses in China. Hart certainly knew of it. Now, much to his delight, he knew his father-in-law who always tried to portray himself as morally superior, visited the very brothel, which represented the depths of immorality. As an Admiral, Brownson likely would have been entertained by three young girls at the same time, if not more. Mom always wanted to do another more interesting biography of Brownson. All the notes were copied but she never got back to it. The materials are still in my possession. As for Brownson vs. Hart—I would have chosen Hart any time.

On days when I had the car I would come over to pick up Mom. This was during the Vietnam War. The second I entered the house the Admiral, who was a staunch Republican, would call me into his office and ask me to sit down.

"What the hell do you think about *XYZ*?" It might be about the war, a political debate in the press, or anything he could think of.

Naturally I would take a left of center view. He the opposite. We would sit there and argue for 30 minutes or more about the issues. While in college the Admiral learned I took ceramics and during one spring break he called me into his office.

"I hear you are taking ceramics? Do you use one of those new electric wheels, or are you learning the REAL way, with a kick wheel?"

What followed was a 30 minute argument over whether electric wheels produced "real" ceramics. I naturally took the defense of the electric. He argued about how the old fashioned kick or stick wheels were the real tools of a skilled potter.

Mom finally called me saying we had to go. As I was leaving his office I turned to the Admiral and said: "Admiral, I have a secret. I prefer the old kick wheels."

He laughed out loud. The Admiral loved a good intellectual argument. All family, friends, and relatives feared him (and wanted to be included in his will). Years later Mom told me he once said he wished he could have recommended me to the Naval Academy:

"He (me) would either have become one of the youngest Admirals or kicked out before he could graduate. I bet he would have made admiral!"

Mom said our arguments where some of the most fun he had in his senior years (he died at 98). I was the only one who would take him on. He loved me for our exchanges.

Love,
Papa

Hi T – more about the Harts:

After Mom finished the Brownson biography she continued to work as Missy's secretary. Mom kept pushing Missy for raises. She used the want ads from *The New York Times* to show Missy how much secretaries were making, not telling her that locally it was about half as much. So by the time she left she was making a very good salary for the position she was in. There were a number of other interesting ties to the Harts; it was as if the fates deemed Mom to work for them.

Years before, in a meditation, Mom asked if she would ever find another husband and the response was a clear name: "Roswell Hart." That was the name of one of Missy's sons. He was married, but later divorced. By that time Mom learned that he could be a real SOB, so no romance there. But Mom always wondered why that name had come to her during a meditation.

Mom's second husband was Bernard Morrow. Bernard was a WWI veteran who served on subs (very dangerous in WWI, more so than WWII which was also dangerous). As part of the North Atlantic sub fleet Bernard was stationed on the commander's sub. Guess who was the commanding officer? Terrible Tommy Hart (the Admiral's nickname).

Mom told the Admiral how much Bernard admired Hart. She related one episode where Bernard was on night watch. During the night and as often as possible, the sub would cruise on the surface. On one night the fleet of seven subs was cruising on the surface somewhere in the North Atlantic during a storm. Bernard and the other subs signal officers would use lights to signal Morse Code to each other and keep in touch. Bernard would be counting which subs where on either side of Harts. So he would count three on one side and three on the other.

Suddenly he counted three on one side and four on the other. He called for confirmation. The subs started signaling each other. As they were counting, there was only three on each side again. The seventh sub had disappeared. Conclusion: a German sub accidentally joined the fleet thinking it was German. The Admiral asked Mom:

"Why in the hell didn't he wake me up?"

Mom said that Bernard felt by the time they could take action it would be too late. Why wake up the commanding officer when nothing could be done. The Admiral thought for a Moment and responded: "Damn good seaman, I should have promoted him."

Between the wars he became the Commandant of the Naval Academy in Annapolis. At that time he was a two-star admiral. Again following the footsteps of his father-in-law who also served as commandant many years before.

Another incident from WWI that came up again in the beginning of WWII was the failure of torpedos to detonate when striking the hull of ships. There was a major design flaw in the detonation cap in the front of the torpedos: the subs would go out and fire blanks, which would reveal the presents of the sub allowing a counter attack. Several subs were lost due to these torpedo failures.

Hart was well aware of the problem. He would write Washington telling them not only of the failures, but how to fix them. Eventually during WWI, he would personally inspect all his torpedos and those placed on his convoys to be sure they were not the ones with the flaws. When WWII broke out, there were shipments of the old style torpedos and the same problems occurred. Tommy raised bloody hell over it. This time the problems were fixed quickly.

During the early days of WWII (long before we entered the war) he pulled all naval personnel out of the Philippines, warning MacArthur to do the same. According to Hart, MacArthur was an arrogant bastard. MacArthur refused to believe Japan would attack. The only attack he could imagine would have been a landing from the sea, which would be quickly defeated. He couldn't imagine an attack over land, coming down the islands from the north. Instead of using landing craft, the Japanese used bicycles to move southward. When the Japanese attack proved successful, massive numbers of Army soldiers and personnel were captured. They were put through the famous death March. Most Naval personnel were safe in Sidney, Australia, thanks to Adm. Hart.

Hart felt MacArthur was a very poor warrior and should not have been a four-star (later awarded a fifth), little less put in charge of the Army on the Asian front. He used to tell me how they would have shouting matches. MacArthur hated anyone taller than him and would try to brow beat anyone smaller (Hart). The problem was that Tommy wouldn't put up with it.

I remember during Christmas break the Admiral invited me into his office. It was shortly after December 7th, the anniversary of Pearl Harbor. The conversation was close to this:

"You know W, that SOB of a President (FDR) knew full well the Japanese were about to attack us. My spies learned in April the Japs were planning an attack. I personally sent telegraph after telegraph that they would attack. By November 1st I figured out that it was going to be either Guam or Pearl, possibly Midway, but I lost track of their fleet. We knew the attack would be on a Sunday. I thought it was going to be November 30th, but that December 7th was possible. By this time I just thought Guam was more likely. He (FDR) allowed the attack to take place so we would go to war. The least he could have done was scatter the fleet at Pearl as I had done with the fleet in the south Asia. He (FDR) caused thousands of deaths needlessly."

The Admiral died while I was in college. Mom was a close friend with the nurse who cared for him in his last months. She told Mom that just before he died he turned to her and said, "What a terrible life I've had."

A bad marriage, a career focused on wars and a retirement of minimal (in his mind) importance. He was accepted to the Academy at the age of 15, without a HS graduation—a boy genius. His life was devoted to the military. His wife, Missy, was to help him gain influence and wealth. There was little or no love, certainly none towards the end. When I think of this, I feel great sadness. It will never be known what he would have liked to do. The world may have lost a great man if he followed a different path. Still, he did have a lasting impact in many ways.

Love,
Papa

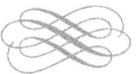

Hello there,

After a few months in college, something was becoming evident: there was an abnormal number of students who had psychic abilities or were trained in meditation and occult studies. JJ and I were becoming friends of a lot of different students. This was in the late 1960s and the occult and New Age philosophies were on the rise. Yet it was rare to have more than a few individuals with these interests together. Here at Rockford there was an unbelievable number of exceptionally talented students, not just academically, but psychically. Some were even unaware of their talents until they became exposed to the right catalyst.

By November JJ and I had found several people who remembered past lives. Some could see elemental beings—elves, gnomes, fairies, etc. There were others who could travel on the astral planes. Some could communicate with other worlds and the dead. Others could see what no one else could, not while in a trance or meditative state but while awake and walking around. I became aware of several upper-class students who were involved in various forms of pagan practices, rituals, and witchcraft.

One of the latter came up to me. She felt I had unusual abilities. We talked. She was a practicing witch but felt that she and all the others with the psychic abilities were drawn to Rockford for one purpose. I listened with great curiosity. I had to admit never seeing so many in such a small concentrated area. Then while thinking about how Rockford was selected, it was through a series of unlikely events and responses. The Questions she raised could not be logically answered. Why were there so many students with these abilities in Rockford? Could there be a reason why they were choosing Rockford? Did I think someone was behind bringing so many with these talents to the college? Was there a hidden motive?

For weeks these questions were racing through my mind. In meditations and just through observation, there appeared to be one professor who kept coming into mind. Dr. L. had a following of female students. She would usually dress in flowing robes and dresses with large pieces of jewelry, mostly containing a lot of precious and semi-precious stones. Her close followers were often dressed similarly but with less jewelry.

Looking at her bio I discovered she had studied in India and was interested in pagan religions and philosophy. What was not written was the possibility of her practicing what she learned. Was it her influence and psychic ability that was pulling in students into her web with all these unusual abilities? Slowly she was trying to meet with most of the students whom she may have attracted. Being a new freshman I was not high on the list, but shortly after meeting with Dr. L., students said they felt a depletion of energy. It was as if something was draining them. Some actually felt they were being attacked by the professor (psychically not physically).

Meeting again with our newfound witch, JJ and I sat down to talk. Was Dr. L. pulling all these people together to drain their energies? Yes! Was she gaining power by draining the power of others? Likely! Was she a danger to students? Yes! What could we do?

Our student witch said she was going to challenge Dr. L. on the astral plane. Over the next few weeks she described how she was starting to probe Dr L.'s powers. Soon the professor felt the impact of these measures. Students who had not fallen under her influence were becoming ill in her counter attacks.

Many came to me for protection or advice. A number were taught a "ring pass-not" for protection. Others started experiencing unusual visions. One night two women were walking towards the women's dorm. Suddenly they screamed and ran in fear into the dorm, slamming the door behind them. They had spotted a huge white wolf, which they described as a werewolf. They told this to JJ. Others without any abilities who were with them didn't see it. Yet the two who did swore it was a real wolf.

Others started seeing ghosts and little demon-like creatures were spotted outside their windows. One girl was attacked by a giant bat that only she could see. At first I dismissed her account, then she showed me her ankle. There was two puncture marks that looked as if something had bitten her.

I too felt as if someone was attempting to attack me. I had to keep up my defenses. Almost daily after waking up, I would perform the same ring pass-not exercise that had been taught. Mom was called a couple of times. Each time she provided me with an additional exercise for protection.

I met with my witch friend on Sunday evening. JJ was with me. Things were coming to a head. She was determined to break Dr. L.'s powers tonight but needed my help. In case she failed she gave me her power ring. I was told me to focus my energy through the ring to her. The ring was not to be returned unless she won.

That night was long. I placed the ring on my desk in my room. Thank goodness Tom, my roommate, was sound asleep. Only one small reading lamp was lit. Most of the night I stared at the stone in the ring. The ring's stone was untouched, but it kept changing colors—almost glowing at times. JJ and I met her for breakfast. My friend was exhausted, but I felt she was victorious.

The next day Dr. L. called in sick. Never before had she reported being ill. A week later she returned to campus. She looked 10 years older. No longer was she wearing any of her jewelry or her robes. It was over. The energy in the college totally changed for good. Soon Dr. L. left and many of her students left too. Just as there was a wave of students attracted to the college, now a wave transferred out. Rockford was back to being a normal college.

Love,
Papa

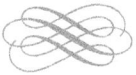

How about a flashback?

The letters about my college years missed many of my summer jobs, but they should be included as part of an unusual life. First because they are fun and second, after seeing the movie Selma, I have to report my encounter with Georgia Governor George Wallace. So that is where we will start.

The most interesting summer job I had was in 1968. Mom was working for a character who owned a string of small newspapers. And she asked if one of the papers might be willing to hire me for the summer. So I got a summer job with the *Pawtucket Times* in Rhode Island. Mostly as a cub reporter taking the obits and small news items on the candlestick phones. There were some nights when went I took the graveyard shift, taking calls late into the night and listening for police and other items to come over the Associated Press and other syndicated sources the paper subscribed to, looking for anything that may have a local connection.

Since I had a camera and was interested in photography I asked if I could do some photo shoots. I tagged along with "Flash," the lead photographer on some jobs. This way many of the other photographers got to know me (*Boston Globe, Providence Journal*, etc.). We covered mostly disasters but other stories as well. What was really interesting about Flash was that he not allowed by the union to type any of the captions or other news items associated with his photos. That was for the reporters, most of whom were hunt-and-peck typists (about 20 words per minute).

One night Flash wanted to leave a lot of information to a reporter about some photos he had taken. Since most reporters were out of the newsroom, he put a sheet of paper in a typewriter and typed up the report. Himself His fingers flew over the keys, even faster than Mom's speed (which was about 75+ words per minute). I asked how fast he was. He told me he had been timed at around 100 WPM once. Always thought it funny that the best typist on the paper was NOT allowed to type!

One of the first jobs we went on was to a glass factory which had a fire. Flash and the rest of the journalists were being given a tour of the factory. The tour guide was careful to show where there was minimal damage, avoiding the central source of the fire. When he asked everyone to follow him, Flash pulled my arm back, and signaled me to be quiet. The others proceeded on the tour and Flash told me the factory owners were attempting to hide what really happened. We proceeded to a lower level, where there was glass was all over the floor. The heat it was giving off showed that it was a very recent spill. Later I learned one employee had molten glass totally encasing one of his legs, and most likely it would have to amputated. Flash took a few photos of the glass on the floor. We couldn't get any closer to the source as the floor was too hot to walk on. The *Pawtucket Times* was the only paper which showed some of the real damage to the factory. On the way back to the paper Flash told me not to follow instructions from "official" tours of a disaster sites they often would avoid the press from getting to the facts, especially if they would implicate them in some way.

Another photographer told me about covering traffic accidents. He showed photos of a car which had wrapped itself around a telephone pole.

"I was taking pictures of the scene when my foot hit a bag on the ground near the pole. A fireman came running up to me telling me I shouldn't kick the bag. Why I asked why, he said "Because that's the kids' head. The car tried to climb up the pole. Made it almost half way."

It was apparent the kid was thrown through the broken windshield and sliced into pieces in the process.

About a week later I was asked to cover another accident scene but it was a day late and all the debris and evidence of the accident had been cleaned up. The best I could do was to photograph the place where it had happened. Four teens had stolen a car and thought it would be fun to see if they could jump the gap between the sides of a now-removed railroad bridge. No tracks remained as that line was terminated years before. The gap was about 15 feet and 12 feet above the country road which ran underneath. The photo showed where the car ALMOST made it. I asked some of the local firemen what they found. They said the speedometer showed the car hit the abutment close to ninety-five miles per hour. But the kids didn't have any type of ramp of means to propelling the car upward which was necessary to jump a gap. They just rammed into the opposing stone wall. The driver and the front seat passenger were killed instantly. It was difficult to get the body parts out of the engine. One of the kids in the back seat was alive when the first responders arrived. The problem was most of his intestines were in the gas tank. He died before they could extricate what was left of him from the wreckage.

Flash told me how various news sources tend to exaggerate stories to gain readership and make new items more exciting. An example he gave is the reason why he rarely accepts anything in the papers or on TV news. The previous year there was a teacher's strike in Pawtucket. According to Flash, there was a math teacher who did not like the vice principal. As the VP was crossing the picket line, the teacher called him a scab. The VP faced off with the teacher. Words escalated and turned into a fist fight between these two men. The police broke it up, taking both to the police station until they cooled off. The *Pawtucket Times* reported it close to what actually happened. The *Providence Journal* picked up the story and reported that a major fight broke out between several teachers and administrators who attempted to cross the picket lines. The *Boston Globe* carried the story of a major riot that occurred in Pawtucket between multiple teachers and numerous administrators which resulted in the arrest of at least 20 individuals. That is why Flash does not trust the news outlets. Just think, with FOX News and other radical cable "news" channels, this has only gotten much worse since then.

On one photo job I was on my own. The old racist governor George Wallace was running for president as an independent. He actually carried five states, all in the South. He was having a convention in either New Port or Providence and I was assigned to cover the event. I had the press credentials and badge. The convention was filled with Rhode Island rednecks. In the back of the hall there was a large group of Blacks and a few other demonstrators. The photographers' roped area was right in front of the speaker's podium.

I took some photos of Wallace, one of which was used on the front page. It showed him with one of his typically ugly sneers and his finger pointing down at an angle—a great photo showing him at his worst! Then I slipped out of the photographer's area towards the demonstrators. They were getting more vocal. As I approached, the Wallace goons locked their arms together, and along with the rent-a-cops they started marching in on the demonstrators, who had NOWHERE to go. As a result, they were being packed in like cows in a cattle car off to the packing plant.

Suddenly one of the Black women fainted. One of the goons behind the front line shouted: "Get her, she is trying to break the lines."

The "security officers" started hitting her with billy clubs and kicking her while she was down. I tried to take a photo of the incident (unfortunately it didn't come out due to the movement of the camera and being pushed) when a rent-a-cop shouted: "Get that kid and his camera!"

The next thing I saw a half dozen goons after me. I jumped on the tables and leaped from one table to another with the thugs right behind me pushing seated people to one side or another. As I approached the photographers roped-off area, they were within a few feet of me. I shouted out for help and made a huge leap towards the other photographers.

Two of them, who resembled interior linemen of a major league football team, caught me in mid air then quickly stood me on my feet and faced the goon squad.

"If you want this kid, you'll have to come through us!"

They were larger than the goons! Now the whole photo corps was looking at us. Wallace's men turned away, swearing. I thanked the guys and told them what happened. They continued to escort me safely to the company car.

The next week the rumor was that the *Pawtucket Times* photographer was to receive an award for the best photo coverage of the Wallace Convention. When they found out it was a summer part-timer, the award quietly disappeared into the stratosphere.

A few weeks later there was news about a local teenager who had turned a former funeral hearse into a hippy wagon. I was sent over to take a photo. Arriving at the address I was told the teen was out. I sat with his father waiting for the kid's return. As we started talking he suddenly opened up about his younger daughter who had joined us. She sat in my lap. He looked at me. She apparently never took to strangers like she did to me. He father then told me an interesting story about when she was younger.

When she was about four years old they were living in Maine. He had been working as a lumberjack. It was a Sunday morning and the girl came running in.

"Mommy can we go for a ride in our surrey?"

Her mother looked at her in total bewilderment.

"Honey, what's a surrey?"

The daughter looked up at the mother and said:

"I'm sorry Mommy, that was before I came to visit you and Daddy."

She then gave detailed description of a surrey and how much fun she used to have when going for a ride on Sunday mornings.

This was not a well-educated family. Neither parent knew about reincarnation nor what a surrey was. In the following months the girl related that she had been a boy in her past life and likely had lived out in the Mid-West. Her father then started reading about reincarnation and tried to learn as much as he could.

During this conversation the girl would nod when her father was describing some of the details. She would occasionally jump off my lap and start playing in the front yard, but she kept on listening to all that was said. I told the father how more than one child can be expected remember bits and pieces of past lives and she was not that unusual. The father was much relieved as a result of our conversation and his daughter never returned with the subject of the happy hippy hearse tale. But the trip was well worth the time, just not for the paper.

There was one pleasant job I had. Miss Pawtucket had been selected to go to the Miss Rhode Island pageant, which would decide who represent the state in the Miss America Pageant later in the year. I drove over to the address given, introduced myself and took shots around her yard. One on the porch steps. Another on a hammock. I didn't ask her to change into any other outfit as the photos taken showed both her beautiful figure and her nice smile. Her miniskirt and silky blouse were perfect for the photoshoot. She was an attractive blond with a nice personality.

After the photos I took were printed, the editor objected to one photo—the one on the hammock. It showed too much leg. The photographer who told me about the car accident was told to go back out, and get more photos of her in different clothes. He included one in a bathing suit. A combination of his and my photos were printed the next day, including the swimsuit one. Talk about leg showing! Mine was rejected for too much leg while the swimsuit showed the whole leg and then some. Ah well.

Love,
Papa

Back at Rockford.

Don't think you were told about me being in Rockford at the end of October of 1968. I occasionally worked on the college paper. I heard presidential candidate Herbert H. Humphrey was going to be Rockford for a campaign whistlestop. He was behind in the polls but was beginning to turn it around. What killed him was the violence and riots that occurred after the killing of RFK and Martin Luther King, Jr. The riots at the Chicago Conventions hurt even more. Ultimately it allowed old "Tricky Dicky" (Richard Nixon) to win. This rally was just two days before the election. On the podium Mohammad Ali was getting the crowd raved up. Humphrey was moving in my direction. When he got close I asked what would he most want.

"One more week," was the response.

This was logical. More and more of the old Richard Nixon was coming out, raising doubts about who he really was. Nixon had been a huge supporter of the House UnAmerican Activities Committee as Ike's vice president. He supported all the shit Joe McCarthy was pulling on that committee. He supported the blacklist, which destroyed the lives of so many individuals. The movie *The Front* will give you an idea of what was happening during that time. Many stars who were blacklisted appeared in the film. If you haven't see it, you also need to view the movie *Good Night and Good Luck*, which is about how Edward R. Murrow had the guts to take on McCarthy on TV—AND WIN. McCarthy ultimately became disgraced and drank himself to death.

I had some good photos of Humphrey, several of him shaking hands in the crowd. I was right next to where he was so they were close-ups. The Secret Service were not as tight on security as they are now, so it was easier to get close. I always wondered how things may have been different if he had won the election. But the anti-Vietnam War backlash, and Humphrey's association with LBJ prevented such a result. Later I was glad the Health and Human Services new building was named after him. I really felt he cared for the people.

JJ and I were not the only interracial couple on campus. A "D" (not his real initial) Black student started dating a white girl on campus. But the backlash was much worse than what JJ and I were experiencing. Having enough of the racial insults from the local students and social ostracism from most of the rest of the campus, they dropped out. He became more militant and joined the Black Panthers in Chicago. By December they were married and living in the Panther's group home on Chicago's West Side. On December 3rd they decided to come to Rockford Collage to say high to some of those few who they became friends with on campus. Then on the morning of the 4th we heard on the radio about the police raid on the Panther's house. Fred Hampton and Mark Clark, two of the leaders, were shot dead. When D heard what happened he came to me for help.

Could there be a way he and his wife could stay on campus until the situation cooled down and the police were no longer looking for him and other members of the Panthers? Since only I was aware of his association with the Panthers, I invited him to stay in our dorm. Several others in the dorm agreed to let him crash in the various common rooms. JJ invited D's wife to stay in the girl's dorm. We would get food from the cafeteria bring it back to them. After about a week D was told by contacts in Chicago not to come back but that he was no longer being hunted by the police. The next day they left Rockford. I never found out how they faired but wish them well.

Love,
Papa

One more on the Harts:

Mom continued to work for Missy after the Admiral died. The priority was to finish editing and publishing the Bronson biography. Of course it was published privately with Missy's money. I actually got a photo credit for one of the pictures, of a silver tea set given to Bronson by the Mexicans for chasing out of the coastal area some pirates during the Spanish-American War. I think—it has been a long time since I looked at one of the books. Mom said it was one of the most boring books she had ever read. Missy just wanted to glorify her father and ignored the really interesting parts of history, as well as the spicy stuff that her father could not have possibly had anything to do with, which I told you about before.

With that book out of the way, Missy liked the attention of being a published author. She hired a writer to do one on the Admiral Hart. The book eventually was called *A Different Kind of Victory*. This is one I actually read. Mom was not given any credit for it as the writer insisted, but she did gather most of the of the research and pulled together all the papers. She also looked up answers to any questions that came up. Just about the time that book was completed, a naval ship named *The Thomas C. Hart*. I don't remember what kind of ship it was, certainly not one of the big ones, but Missy was there for its launching. After that Mom continued to work as Missy's private secretary. But now Missy wanted to have some other kinds of excitement. She noted the gardener's wife was exceptionally jealous of almost anyone. The wife suspected her husband was having an affair with Mom, despite the fact that Mom was about 20 years his senior. Besides, Mom had absolutely no interest in him, but Missy thought it was great fun and stirred the pot whenever possible.

If the gardener's wife could find him, Missy would say she saw him going upstairs. Of course Mom would be coming down the stairs just as that was said. So the wife jumped to the conclusion they had just had sex. Mom would be wondering what the hell was going on, but soon caught on that Missy was deliberately causing trouble, just to watch the fun, if you can call it that. Mom was getting very fed up with this kind of nonsense and it would lead to her eventually quitting, but not immediately.

Another thing was that Missy always had had cooks for her and the family. Her treatment of the cooks and other staff was terrible. Unless they were really desperate for work, few stayed for more than a few months once the Admiral died. The gardener's wife tried, but she couldn't really cook. Besides, she was far more interested in watching her husband than cooking for Missy. I might add he never did fool around with anyone. Soon the wife was fired as a cook. Mom brought in Grace Folkes (remember the elderly Black woman we visited? That was Grace.) Grace was an excellent cook and had served in many important homes. But she couldn't take Missy beyond a few months, though she really needed the money.

Once, in between cooks, Missy wanted rhubarb for dessert. You have to cook rhubarb for a few minutes for it to soften and taste right. Missy insisted that she could make it herself. She cut up a couple of stalks, added sugar and strawberries (a usual combination) and served it with powdered sugar on top. She was delighted that she had fixed it herself. Mom took one bite and politely told Missy she was too full from the sandwiches she had fixed for the lunch. What she didn't tell Missy was she had not cooked the rhubarb. They were eating it raw. Missy was so wrapped up in the conviction she had fixed it just right, she didn't even notice it was a little extra crunchy! There was definitely an increase in fiber intake that lunch.

After a few years of post Admiral and a lot of Missy nonsense, Mom quit. By that time I was no longer in college and had moved to NYC, but more on that if there is a next book.

Love,
Papa

294

Hello T,

Can't believe it has been year-plus since the first of these letters? Recently at the shamanistic weekend one of the people there made an interesting comment: "Your life is like Forest Grump. It's true."

All that was experienced now on the verge of the 50th anniversary of the March on Washington time to start these up again. So... back to college.

After the witch situation at Rockford, things quieted down quickly. During the summer break of 1969, I was able to get my Fellow Craft Degree at Marie Deraismes Lodge. As a Lewis, the requirements were that at least two years had to have passed between the first and second degrees. Demetria Taylor was the Master of the Lodge for the ceremony. Myron was again my conductor. Mom was there as the second degree was always her favorite degree. Now I was eagerly anticipating the third degree but knew I couldn't get it until I was 21.

That year I did make a few trips to the Theosophical Society (TS) headquarters outside Chicago, not so much for the Theosophical Society meetings but to attend the Masonic lodge meeting there. They used what was then called The British Craft (BC) Ritual. It differed from Marie Deraismes, which was a traditional Scottish Rite working, referred to as The North American Ritual. I had seen the BC ritual before shortly after my EA Degree as the TS was having their international convention in NYC.

At the convention the TS rented out the Grand Lodge of New York's room. The rental agent was not part of Masonry. During the ceremony I was drafted to be the Junior Deacon, but the procession was totally different from that used in Marie Deraismes Lodge. Thank goodness to Norbert Orzula who was the Grand Senior Deacon helped guide me through the opening and closing. When the New York Grand Lodge found out the hall was rented to an un-recognized Masonic order THAT ADMITTED WOMEN, the rental agent was fired. Looking back on it, it was quite a ceremony with many 33 Degree Masons seated in the East. Most were women!

Back in Rockford. JJ and I were a major item on campus, especially noticeable in redneck Rockford. When going to the movies or dinner off campus, the looks we got were unbelievable! One time, when JJ and I walked into a pocket billiards bar with a group of other students. The looks at JJ and I got were as if they would lynch us both at any Moment. Well, chi energy came to my rescue. I walked to one of the pool tables not being used. I took a stick and a cue ball placing on the table about four inches from the edge in the middle of that side of the table. Taking the stick sharp downward spin stroke on the ball worked perfectly. The cue ball shot out and did a perfect U-turn and went right into a side pocket behind where it started, behind where I struck the ball. All of a sudden I looked up and the expression of the rednecks had totally changed.

I looked them in the eyes: "Anyone want to take me on?"

They all looked away and shook their heads, scared of taking on the pool shark who just walked in! Little did they know that was the luckiest shot I ever had in my life. Once we left JJ burst out laughing. She knew I couldn't play pool, but she loved the way the chi came through when needed.

There was another funny incident which involved one of the local rednecks at a dinner party. An exchange student from the Seychelles Islands wanted to cook a traditional meal for a group of students. JJ and I were asked, along with three other couples, one of which was a local boy and his girlfriend. I had seen them around on campus but not often. Every time the boy saw JJ and I together he would give us a look as if we shouldn't exist. We would have been killed instantly if looks could kill. But here we were in the same house on the same evening. Prior to sitting down for the dinner he avoided us like the plague. For dinner JJ and I sat across the long table from him and his girlfriend.

When we sat down the exchange student said: "I have prepared a traditional meal for you this evening. The most popular meal in my home on the Seychelles is curried chicken with rice. But I must warn you it may be a little spicy for some of you.

JJ and I were used to spicy food, especially curry. As I was growing up, during the leanest of years, Mom would cut up onions and an apple, fry them together, add a can of tunafish, which was very cheap back then, mix curry powder in milk pouring the mixture over the onions, apple and tunafish. It was all we could afford. Thanking back, it had to be a terrible curry dish. But when you can't afford anything else, it was a feast we had several times a week. JJ's father being a chef, certainly fixed curried dishes for the family on different occasions. But for this couple across from us, it was going to be an experience they likely didn't forget.

The funny thing about curry is that at first a hot curry isn't very noticeable. But then heat builds up in the mouth as an after-effect. The curry served that evening was no different. I took a bite. It was a HOT curry, but I loved it. JJ liked it but ate it with a fork of rice with each bite. As for the guy across from us, he took a large bite, didn't notice the build-up of heat until several more mouthfuls were wolfed down. Suddenly it caught up with him.

"Hot, it's hot, it's hot, it's hot, get me a glass of milk!" he shouted.

Very calmly I said, "You don't want to drink milk. Drink water instead."

With a face turning red from the build up of the curry's burning flavor in his mouth as well as his evident dislike of me he shouted, "Don't tell me what I should drink of not! Where can I get some milk?"

The hostess pointed to the kitchen and the adult who owned the house poured him a glass of milk.

I turned to the rest of the table and told them I grew up on curry.

"Milk only intensifies the heat. He needs to drink water or eat some peanut butter."

Then from the kitchen came a horrid cry: "**I'm dying in here!**"

JJ and I just laughed. I got up and helped myself to a second dish of the curry from the pot in the kitchen and came back to the dining room. I wanted to get a peek at his continued suffering. He was still in the kitchen, drinking and rinsing his mouth out with water.

When we had the chance, JJ and I would love to go to the movies. One movie we saw was Peter Sellers' *The Party*, who played an ignorant Indian extra on a movie set. There was a huge Indian palace the director wanted to blow up for the movie. However, Peter's character accidentally blew it up before the cameras were rolling. This caused a multi-million dollar set to be destroyed without it being caught on camera. In the movie after blowing up an expensive set BEFORE the filming started, the director put Peter's character's name on a blacklist to be sure he would never work in movies again. But the paper he scrawled the name on was the reverse side of invitees to a party he was throwing.

JJ and I saw this one on the big screen. I was laughing through much of the film. There was a scene where Sellers character was in the control room for the house's sound system. He noticed an oscilloscope moved when he coughed. Every time he coughed or made a sound the lines moved. Then moving around the room there was a parrot in a cage with a bowl for food with the "birdy numnum" printed on the rim of the bowl. He then said into the oscilloscope:"birdy numnum."

The wavelengths on the oscilloscope went crazy with the sound. He then did a dozen variations of "birdy numnum" into the speakers, each funnier than the last. What he didn't know was it was being broadcast throughout the house with all the guests wondering what the heck was coming over the sound system. That cracked me up. I was laughing so loud I actually fell out of my seat. JJ was now laughing not only at the movie but at me laughing so hard. For the rest of the year if anyone said: "birdy numnum" your father would break out in laughter. But more often when faced with a crazy situation my response is "birdy numnum."

Remember JJ's love for playing Hearts? We continued to play being a fantastic couple playing a number of friends, but ONLY after homework. Her behavior was modified. As a sophomore her grades were all Bs and As. The other thing we started doing together was playing ping pong. We both practiced whenever we had time. Remember, it was a Japanese exchange student who taught me so I was just picking up where I left off in Concord some years before, still using a pen grip.

The ping pong room was in the basement of the main building that included the dining room upstairs and snack bar downstairs. Ping pong room was next to the TV room. The room was a little tight so I would use the wall behind me as a springboard to get back to the table faster after returning a hard hit ball. One afternoon playing singles against a slam player, I was using the wall quite a bit. Then the opponent slammed a real hard one. I hit it back but instead of bouncing off the wall, I went straight through it. On my back, between the seats and the elevated TV I looked up at the astonished faces looking at me and asked: "What's on?"

It was a good laugh for all. Bill Cullen was hosting *The Price is Right* on the TV, a show I still watch regularly.

By the time we were juniors we were noted as one of the best pairs players. We entered the college's mixed doubles competition and WON!!!! It was great. But the college was so cheap because other than recognition on the sign-up sheet, we got no recognition. Always thought we deserved a small trophy or plaque. Ah wel

Remember JJ's love for playing Hearts? We continue to play being a fantastic couple playing a number of friends, but ONLY after the homework. Her behavior was modified. As a Sophomore her grades were all Bs and As. The other thing we started doing together was playing ping pong. We both practiced whenever we had time. Remember it was a Japanese exchange student that taught me so I was just picking up where I left off in Concord some years before, still using a pen grip.

The ping pong room was in the basement of the main building that included the dining room upstairs and snack bar down. Ping pong room was next to the TV room. The room was a little tight so I would use the wall behind me as a springboard to get back to the table faster after returning a hard hit ball. One afternoon playing singles against a slam player, I was using the wall quite a bit. Then the opponent slammed a real hard one. I hit it back but instead of bouncing off the wall, I went straight through it. On my back, between the seats and the elevated TV I looked up at the astonished faces looking at me and asked:

"What's on?"

It was a good laugh for all. Bill Cullen was hosting *The Price is Right* on the TV. A show I still watch it regularly.

By the time we were Juniors we were noted as one of the best pairs players. We entered the college's mixed doubles competition and WON!!!! It was great. But the college was so cheap other than recognition on the sign-up sheet, we got no recognition. Always thought we deserved a small trophy or plaque. Ah well!

Love,
Papa

T,

Got to give another flashback to the summer of 1968.

Towards the end of the summer, Mom stopped communicating. This made me worried. Later I found out she had lost her job. This led to her taking the job with the Harts, but for a few months, there was only unemployment benefits coming in.

What was worse was I got the job at the *Pawtucket Times* because her employer owned that paper. As the summer started to end, some of the younger workers at the paper were Baha'is. Mom had taken me to the temple outside Chicago so the Baha'i faith was known to me. I even had a few of the Baha'i books, including the small blue prayer book.

When the co-workers found out that I knew about Baha'i they invited me to a long weekend at the Newport Folk Festival. Of course I accepted. They picked up some others on the way. One was an elderly Black woman named Doris.

Doris had become a Baha'i mostly out of frustration from her traditional Baptist upbringing; her old church gave her absolutely no spiritual satisfaction. Doris and I were sitting in the back seat as we traveled towards Newport. As we talked the discussion turned to religion and spirituality. She was very spiritually inclined but had many unanswered questions. I looked deep into her eyes and asked: "You have memories of past lives don't you?"

Her whole expression was both serious and almost relieved at the same time. The conversation then turned to the process of reincarnation and how some people remember past lives. I told her about the Battle of the Bulge and my experiences. We discussed the transitions between lives. How an individual's karma would carry over from life to life until it was balanced out. Only then could you become one with the deity. All this and more was what she was looking for but didn't know where to find it.

Soon she totally opened up. Our conversations continued after we left the Folk Festival later that evening when we were crashing in a friends house. It was then that she asked me: "Are you HE who has come again?"

I It was evident that she thought I was the Christ reincarnated.

"Doris I'm so short of being divine," I said. "I still have my faults and failings. But if I have helped you resolve the conflicts you have had all your life, then my duty for this weekend was fulfilled."

She gave me a kiss on the cheek. When we got to the place where were staying and she retired for the evening. The next day she told me it was the most sound sleep she had in years. All of her self doubts and questions were answered. She told me if I was to start a church, she would be one of the first parishioners.

This encounter with Doris had a deep impact on me. To think someone could ask me if I was the reincarnation of Christ!!?? It was beyond my personal comprehension. Yet at the same time, it told me I should share my story with others, as so many out in the world are ignorant of their own spiritual selves and previous lives. Yet so many had memories, just like the girl I had visited as part of the job earlier that summer.

This was the same Folk Festival where I felt the spiritual aura of Pete Seeger (which I wrote about in a letter long before this one). It was a very interesting weekend. By the way, the Baha'is gave me a rose petal from the founder's rose garden in Jerusalem. It use to be in my little blue Baha'i prayer book, but when last checked, must have fallen out. Too bad, as it's precious to Baha'is.

Love,
Papa

Hi T so much more to tell you about college and beyond.

Winter breaks at Rockford College were all of January for three weeks allowing for independent or special studies. Our Sophomore year there was an opportunity to go to France.

Since scholarships paid for basic college, Mom scraped together enough funds to let me go. JJ spoke a little French, and signed up immediately. We would be traveling to France with the French professor, Guy R., leading the troupe of Rockford College students. We were very excited since this was to be our first trip to Europe. Even better, we would be together. Yet this was a study trip. The task was to look at what may have caused the 1967 riots in Paris that actually cost the life of at least one student.

Paris in winter is a whole different atmosphere than during tourist season and the Parisians were much more welcoming to Americans. When we arrived, little did we know the French Foreign Ministry had prepared a banquet for us on the night after our arrival. But Guy had not notified anyone in France where we were staying.

On the second night in Paris the Foreign Ministry contacted our group after contacting the college. We arrived at the palace where the banquet had been planned for the previous night. It must have rivaled the one in the *Beauty and the Beast* movie. The servants were dressed in 17th-century costumes and it all went totally to waste. We could just imagine the food that was laid out, as most was now thrown out. When we found out, many of us were VERY pissed off that Guy had not let the Government know our itinerary and where we were staying. Still, we feasted on the left overs from the previous night. Even if a day old, what was offered turned out to be some of the best food on the trip. The rest of the stay in Paris was delightful. We toured much of the city but the main purpose was to talk to the political leaders to determine what caused the riots.

We spoke with a personal representative of Georges Pompidou who was similar to the vice president here in the states. Pompidou became the Prime Minister after Charles de Gaulle died. We met members of several government departments—Parks, Education, etc.

The most unusual meeting was with Jacque Duclou, the the head of the Communist Party. His position was typical of the time: the proletariat were suppressed by the government. A capitalistic system failed to pay the people decent wages. As for the student riots, they were a direct result of the failures of the government to provide jobs upon graduation. Gee, sounds like what we are suffering from today.

The head of the French Socialist Party was little known outside of France at the time. Francois Mitterrand received us in his Paris apartment. The apartment overlooked one of the magnificent parks in the city. The ceilings were 12-feet tall. The furniture was elegant but not excessive. Mitterrand was gracious, welcoming all of us personally. This was a man who greatly impressed me. Intelligent, knowledgable on a host of issues; an enticing personality.

Mitterrand's chief complaint was the censorship of government-controlled TV. How could someone oppose the Gaullist-controlled media when it ran his political ads? The news stories about him were all slanted in such a way that made him look like an extreme socialist, not the progressive socialist that he really was—much like FOX News does today. Somewhere in the stack of photos in one of my many boxes, there is wonderful photo of Mitterrand standing by his fireplace which I took that evening.

Finally in 1980, ten years after the death of de Gaulle, Mitterrand won the presidential election. I was elated. When he died his widow and mistress stood arm in arm mourning the man they both loved. Even his death served as a lesson to Americans and all their false sense of morality.

During Freshman year, Tom and I supported our mutual interest in art. Thanks to Mr. Dedrick, the art teacher, art dealers were invited to campus. We were able to amass an interesting collection of etchings and Papuan "primitive" art. Tom had an outstanding copy of Titian's *Flora*, which was the center of the "suite's collection." By our second year the gallery had become famous.

That same academic year Tom, JJ and I started running for various student offices and committees. By the end of the year, the three of us were members of perhaps 75 percent of the student committees and bodies. Many we controlled. After seeing my effort in religious activities, and being the one who did the introductions for Lama Govinda and Joseph Campbell I was invited to sit on the facility's religious affairs committee. I was the first student to ever do so.

After his talk, Joe Campbell mentioned to President Howard that he wanted to see the famous art gallery. Not the college's but the one in our dorm room. Upon being escorted to Dorm B he sat to talk with Tom and me long after his scheduled departure. I think his wife may have been offering a special dance seminar at the same time. I gave him one of my etchings. When Joe returned a month later for a follow-up presentation, he presented me the first English edition of his *Masks of God: Primitive Mythology*, with some of his personal notes for what would become the American edition. Soon almost all the intellectual guests to the college wanted to visit the Dorm B art collection in our suite!

President Howard was livid! But we had many outside guests. I learned how to play Shogi from one of our Japanese guests; I shouldn't say learned, as I had a set but only knew how to play from the book. He showed me how much more I needed to learn before I could consider myself a true Shogi player. Still, we had fun, despite the language barrier.

There were a lot of Vietnam protests on and off campus at this time. The whole student body was polarized. The conservatives were mostly locals students. The increasing number of Eastern and Chicago students were way left of center. What was worse was the three of us, Tom, JJ and I, were pushing our liberal agenda in all the committees and school organizations we were involved with. By the next year, Tom, JJ or myself were the president and/or head of so many committees. It was difficult for President Howard, an ultra right winger, to address any committee without facing our pointed questions. We were willing to debate him on all his decisions. It would only get worse over the year.

During my summer break back in Connecticut, Sam, Fred, hippy girlfriend from high school, and I got together for a couple of events. We had a Summer Solstice party. A few weeks later Fred, Sam and I went to a large fund raising event in Kent, where Sam lived. We wandered around the various tents, full a lot of junk. I bought a balloon. Then I spotted a large painting. It depicted a large African mask with a beautiful blue sky background. The frame was white leather over wood. The tag had "600" on it. Since almost of the objects in the whole fair were seldom more than a few dollars, I asked one of the attendants:

"Is this $6.00?"

She looked at the tag. "That's what it says."

I handed her $6.00 in cash. The balloon we had collected earlier was tied to my front tooth. The three of us went to place the painting in my car. I was planning to paint over the original and use the canvas and frame for myself.

Now you must realize, all three of us were from the area. Sam was well known. Yet, the next week the weekly newspaper reported: "Two beatnik girls and one hippy boy, obviously from out of state, purchased a 600-dollar painting, donated to the fundraiser by the artist, for $6.00."

Mom read the story and laughed. What is interesting is that Kent was almost as snobbish as Sharon. They couldn't admit the three that purchased the painting were locals. By the way, my hair was down to my shoulder at the time and I had a mustache. What is sad is this was last time I would see Fred.

Love,
Papa

300

Hello T, trying to catch up a little about Rockford College.

The boys girls were literally locked into separate dorms (no inter-visitation except on specifically designated days). Dorm B, where your father resided, at Rockford offered four interesting suite-mates who came with the art gallery. Tom and I had most of the art. Kirk was a chemistry major with no funds. The fourth member during freshman year, was Wolfgang from Germany. After freshman year he dropped out due to mental problems. His father had been a Nazi. During the year he started dating an Egyptian Jew. It was a very strange relationship. Jasmine, his girlfriend, felt guilty that her family were not killed during Hitler's reign of terror. She felt she should not have been born. Then when born being surrounded by Muslims created another tense environment.

When she and Wolfgang were together they were very affectionate towards each other. But their love making sessions were exceedingly strange. Wolfgang was relatively small, around five foot two or three. Jasmine was just about the same height. The suite soon learned that they would go off into the woods for a love making session. But the foreplay was Wolfgang literally jumping on Jasmine. Then he would whip her ass until it was red. By this time he would have a full erection which she whipping with a belt of some other item. It was the first S&M relationship I was exposed to. As for the sex itself, there was anal, but possibly no vaginal. There was a lot of oral, but usually one at a time, not 69.

As the year progressed, Jasmine broke it off. Wolfgang began to behave in very erratic ways. Eventually he was committed. The word was he was put in a padded cell in a straight-jacket. As they closed the door on him, he laughed saying they couldn't keep him in the nut house.' The story goes that when they took breakfast to his cell in the morning, he was gone. No one from our suite ever saw or heard about him again.

During our sophomore year a local wanted to stay on campus He moved in our suite now on the opposite side of Dorm B. This gave us the advantage of having a window facing the main section of the campus. One walking between some of the nearer buildings would be able to see the art exhibited in the window. Our newest member of the suite contributed a few primitive art pieces. The key was Mr. Dedrick's friend, the first major art dealer who had gone into the interior of Papua. During his trips to the States, he would make a special trip to Rockford College to sell items to Mr. Dedrick's students. We may have been the only college he visited.

On the visit the next year he told us about him sending one of his employees into the Papua highlands. The man never returned. About 10 years later, he went up to the same area. The tradition of one of the tribes was to cut off the heads of enemies and tribal leaders. The heads would then be treated, covered with a clay, painted, and placed on a shelf in the men's hut. According to their tradition, the tribal leaders were to know which skull belonged to what individual. If they couldn't remember what tribe or the name of the person whose head was on display, it was disrespectful. Mr. Dedrick's friend went up to this tribe which had been "pacified" and made a deal with the tribal elder.

If certain tools and supplies were left on a certain place in the village, there might be some heads which accidentally fell off the shelves and under the walls of the men's hut. He would be able to pick them up, provided no one saw him. Thus he collected a few heads. Upon getting them back to Australia, he was examining one of the heads. It was an odd shape for this tribe. When taking a piece of clay out of the mouth, there on the tooth was a filling. Upon further examination it turned out to be his former employee's head who had disappeared ten years before.

Pets were not allowed on campus so naturally there were some in our dorm. Upstairs in the dorm a guy had a pet iguana named Pam. Funny how one remembers the name of animals but not their owners. Pam got to know quickly where she was welcomed and where not. So she would come down and visit us and we would have some vegetables for her. There was a pet crow down the hall from Pam. When outside the crow would swoop down and try to land on people's shoulders. Fine for his owner, scared the hell out of other people. Unfortunately both died—Pam from the cold, the crow likely killed by someone who didn't know he loved to fly and perch on your shoulder without warning.

One of the most interesting characters in the dorm was Crazy Ruby (aka: Super Jew). A small guy from Queens NYC but unbelievably strong. He would climb up the exterior brick walls of the girls dorm by hooking his fingernails into the bricks climbing up the two or three stories. Most of the girls whose window he would look in knew him. It was just accepted the peeking Tom was Crazy Ruby. When the chapel was being built the basic beams formed a three-sided pyramid. When the three massive I beams were put in place, one night it was reported someone was sitting on the top of the I beams some fifty feet or more above the foundation. It was Ruby.

Another night while chatting in the halls, the watchman came through the floor. They would patrol the dorms and punch in a time clock at specific places. One time clock was on the opposite side of Dorm B than where he came in. Like many "rent a cops" back then, this one was not the brightest. Ruby was next to ceiling, bracing his feet on one wall, an arm on the other. He would stay up there 30 minutes. When the watchman passed between Tom, Kirk and me, he never noticed Ruby above him. Ruby gently lifted up the guard's hat and put it on. The guard went to the end of the hall, clocked in and returned. When he came back, Ruby put it gently back on his head, but backward. This while Kirk and I were distracting him slightly with meaningless conversation. When the guard got out of the dorm, he tried to pick up the cap by but the visor but couldn't. Lifting it off he couldn't figure how on earth the hat got on his head backward.

In the main building a group of students decided to form a little night club/coffee house for Saturdays (after all, compared to going into Rockford city, the coffee house was exciting!). *Playboy* magazine had published Shel Silverstein's *Lafcadio: The Lion Who Shot Back*. This is LONG before it became a children's book. (People forget that Silverstein was a close friend of Hugh Hefner and many of his cartoons and short comic stories publish first in *Playboy*.) I used to love his Uncle Shelby's Scout's Handbook, which was a satirical article with his usual illustrations.

Back to the coffee house. I would drive Tom and Kirk nuts reading *Lafcadio* in the dorm. It was suggested that it be read in the coffee house. You can just imagine how the voice would be raised when the gun in the story went BOOM!!! My narration was a great success. The next week a woman read Molly's soliloquy from Joyce's *Ulysses* despite the administration claiming it was unfit for students (obscene). Eventually the coffee house was closed by the president because of the "inappropriate" forms of entertainment. Yet it was mild considering what was to occur in my next college. Naturally, the coffee house was for the left-leaning students whom the president considered undesirables.

There were a number of "house" sporting competitions—intramural is what most colleges call it. Our greatest opponent was Dorm C. It was Rockford's much smaller version of the Army-Navy competition. In touch football I was an interior lineman, usually defense, but offense too. I was infamous. Almost always double teamed. Most of those on the opposing team being smaller and not nearly as strong as I, were tossed aside with a madman coming out in me, then running at their quarterback. Eventually the other teams recognized that cutting me down at my knees would take me out. I would have trouble rising or walking and was often carried off the field. Three plays later I'd be back out there again. Now you know the source of my bad knees.

One game stands out in my mind. My Dorm B's A team was scheduled to play Dorm B's B team. Of course being in the same dorm and team, B usually cheering from the sidelines in the other games. This game I was tripled teamed by the offense. My most unforgettable play occurred in this game. The ball was hiked. Players on the right and left were just picked up with my arms and thrown aside. Then a straight body hit to the third knocking him out of the way. Now there was just one player between me and the quarterback. At full speed, shoulders lowered, he was hit hard. He was thrown off his feet and landed on his back, out cold. I raced another three paces towards the quarterback when the thought hit me: "Oh, my God, that was Tom."

Turning around, sure enough Tom, my roommate, was out cold on the ground.

"Tom, are you alive?"

Slowly he came to.

"Remind me never to try to block you again." He never did.

For basketball there were more teams. The worse players in Dorm B created a team called the "chicken men." Wino, a senior, known for his drinking, and I were co-captains. Tom was on the team. We were so bad, the first rated teams would play four on our five or actually help us make a few baskets. The A team from Dorm C had one of their players stay under our basket and shoot. He scored more points for us than our whole team. Tom's only basket came in a game where he tried to pass the ball to me. The other team's player jumped up deflecting upward. The ball rose up. It hit our backboard. Suddenly it bounced around the rim and through the net. That was Tom's only basket all season. The only chicken men who could score were Wino and myself. There was one game where I scored over 20, but then our total score was less than 30. The opposing team was well over 50.

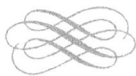

Hello T:

It is funny that we are still talking about college when there is so much more. I wanted to tell you how my suite-mate, Kirk. He and I "penny'd in" our chief rivals in Dorm C. This is done by putting in pennies in the door jam while pushing hard agains the door. It only took a dozen pennies, but by wedging them into the doors so tightly, when someone tried to exit, the door would not open. The pressure on the latch was too great for anyone to open the door from the inside. No one in the dorm could get out that morning. We were never found out. A friend who would regularly play Hearts with JJ and I had to jump out his window to get to class. He couldn't get out of the dorm any other way. When he saw the pennies, he was able to pry them out releasing the doors.

One of the other funny incidents was when Kirk changed the distributor connections on the campus police car. The cops were in their offices. Kirk asked me to come with him.

"What are you planning?"

"I'm going to mess with their car. But I need someone to be on lookout. Would you do that for me. Just signal me if they begin to move towards the door."

I agreed. So off we went to the other side of the campus.

I laid behind a mound where the campus cops could be observed from a distance. They couldn't see me in the dark through the building's window. Kirk slowly and quietly lifted up the hood of the campus police car. Then he reached inside and changed the distributor connections. When he completed this he retreated to the same mound where I was.

It wasn't long before campus police were scheduled to do their rounds. When one of them got into the car, the car when started sounded like it was having a heart attack. The bangs and pops coming out of the engine were hilarious. At least to us. The police lifted up the hood and just scratched their heads. Kirk and I retreated, holding in the laughter until we got back into the safety of our dorm.

Lot of other fun stuff, typically college pranks and adventures. Tom, Kirk, Wolfgang (Freshman year only) and others often got drunk out in the state park that was adjacent to the campus. I would have to retrieve them being the only sober one. There was one night when Wolfgang came in, more than a bit tipsy, and asked where Kirk was. I told him he took off to the park looking for him. So Wolfy took off. A few minutes later Tom came in looking for Wolfy. Same response. Off went Tom. Then Kirk came in claiming he had lost Wolfy and Tom. I told him they were out looking for him since he had most of the booze. Kirk grabbed his bag with the beer and took off again. No one returned after that. They apparently found each other somewhere in the woods and passed out. In the morning the three came dragging themselves back into the dorm with huge hangovers.

Quick note on classes. I pulled out of German class after the first week. It was headed towards a disaster. Tom stuck it out and ended up with a D", as did most of the class. He was sorry he didn't follow my example. I ended up taking Latin. Felt it was the best option since that was what I had in high school. The first day of the class I came in a minute or two late. Rather than at desks the class formed a large circle of chairs. The professor, a smartly dressed young man, took one look at me, pushed a girl aside who was seated next to him welcoming me with:

"Please take a seat here next to me."

Since there was a chair elsewhere in the circle I took it instead. Yes, he was gay. For the next two months he did everything he could to get my attention, out of class. Everything failed. Finally out of frustration he dated one of the girls in the class. She was aware of his preferences but wanted to see if she could alter his orientation. She later told me he couldn't even get it up.

Classes I enjoyed included ceramics and etching. I excelled in both. And later became the teaching assistant for the latter. Drawing class was amusing. We had to do the traditional skeleton (I got a B+), but for another class, figure painting, the school could only afford a model some of the time. When asked if any student would volunteer, I raised my hand. Then I found out it was to be a nude portrait. So there I was sitting on a stool in the front of the class, totally nude for a long thirty-minute pose. There was a very attractive blond in the front row who caught my attention.

Suddenly a friendly voice said: "W, stop moving!"

"I'm not moving, Lois."

"Yes you are."

I looked down. Yes I was. The blond in the front row, realizing she was the cause of that particular part of my anatomy standing at attention. She turned as red as you can imagine. I just smiled, shrugged and tried to focus elsewhere.

Another art class was sculpture. This included welding, which I was very good at. Lead-casting excited me. First you make a wax figure, then you put a plaster mold around it, then melt the wax out, replacing it with liquid lead. The problem was we had to use the torches for the welding to melt the lead in small pots. Not really enough ventilation, but at least it was done outside. The problem was I liked the smell of melting lead—and lead oxide is not good for anyone.

One time when melting a piece of lead cut off a lead bar; with the safety mask on I had limited vision. There was something to my left in my way. I picked it up and moved it a few inches. But as my hand sunk into the object I realized it was the other part of the lead bar, which was still hot. Funny, my hand was evenly singed but there was no lasting damage. Remember the kiss of the flames when I was small? I just feel the elementals of fire didn't want to hurt me.

Another interesting class was the comparative religion. The instructor was a blind, fundamentalist Baptist with a very nice seeing-eye dog. No matter what religion was being discussed, all were viewed either with contempt or having the same concepts of hellfire and damnation as his faith. At the end of the semester everyone had to write and read a paper in class. I chose the topic of reincarnation. Using the story of the blind man in the Bible, and the phrase "only he who is born again" as a reference to reincarnation NOT baptism, it was a well constructed argument. Though the professor sat still, I could tell underneath the calm exterior he was fuming. I got a C+ for the class. Some of the students praised me for the paper and for the chutzpah for using the blind man parable. A few saw me as a cleaver sophist.

One time one of the guys from the other dorm was making it with his girlfriend in the woods. This was in the large state park with lots of animals. You never could tell what creature you might run into. In this case, this guy got bit in the ass by a rabid fox while humping his girlfriend. I guess the bobbing up and down of a white ass was just too much for the fox to resist. The only problem is how do you explain that!?!

I ran into a raccoon with rabies. At first it just appeared to be a normal *friendly* raccoon. When bending down to pet him it was evident that he was in the last stages of rabies. I could see in his eyes. He was asking for help. With his paws on my pants, he tried real hard to resist biting me. But when he opened his mouth on my jeans, I jumped back and just said:

"I'm so sorry but I can't help you." Sad! I walked away with JJ almost crying.

There was the January trip to Paris already mentioned. JJ and I went and actually were allowed to room together for part of it. It was a very romantic time and we were very much in love. We saw other sections of France. I loved Carcassonne, an ancient city with a series of walls around the central castle. It is like walking back into the 10th century. JJ and I walked through the city and at one of the outer walls we saw a man herding a flock of goats. It was as if were thrown back 700 years instantly. The little woodcuts (3"x3") of men came from there. Also the four old Tarot cards that are framed.

JJ was largely rejected by the other Black kids at Rockford for dating a white boy. Racism runs in both directions. There was a Black History class we took together. One assignment was to take sides in a debate. I took the side of a black slave owner. She thought I did a great job and laughed about it. But the other more militant blacks thought those were my real feelings. Ah well, ignorance is so great (that's satire, my friend).

The fact that JJ, Tom and myself were active in a number of student committees irked the president to no end. Little did we really find out how much until the next year. Together we deliberately started to swing the student groups to the left, politically. The open voice bulletin board was one of our favorite means of communicating to the campus. I was posting comments almost weekly. Some would be removed by the next day. I suspected the president was keeping a collection of my comments.

When a Religious Policy Committee was formed, being the only semi-Buddhist and a friend of the chaplain, I was asked to be one of the two students on the committee. There was a lot of good work. This led to a lot of interesting guest speakers including Joseph Campbell who came to the Dorm B art gallery, which you read about before. Lama Govinda came to the campus twice. Once for an open discussion on Tibetan Buddhism., the second time to conduct a session on meditation. In the first session I was asked to lead an invocation. I used the Arcane School's Great Invocation, which I had to preface with the comment "Christ" in the invocation was the generic christ, the bringer of wisdom. It was not meant to be Jesus' return:

"From the point of light within the mind of God
Let light stream forth into the minds of men
Let Light descend on Earth.

From the point of love within the heart of God
Let love stream forth into the hearts of men
May Christ return to Earth.

From the Center where the will of God is know
Let the purpose guide the little wills of men
The Purpose the Masters know and serve.

From the Center which we call the race of man
Let Plan of love and light stream forth
May it seal the door where evil dwells

Let Love and Light and Power restore the Plan on Earth.

What was unusual was the audience was asked to remain seated, with their backs straight and feet flat on the floor. I was actually very nervous. The greatness of Lama Govinda was intimidating. You could feel that *here* was a holy man. When he came back his wife Li accompanied him. She was attempting to re-create the lost tankas of Tibet that had been destroyed by the Chinese when they invaded the ancient Kingdom of Tibet. Her memory was remarkable. She was in charge of a whole group of Tibetan nuns working on this project, before their memories failed or they died of old age.

Again I was able to introduce Lama Govinda, but this time to a smaller crowd. He and I had lunch together. Then both he and Li retreated to the Dorm B art gallery. In part of his lecture, he discussed the Buddhist theory that when one passes over to the other side, he or she drinks from the fountain of forgetfulness. It is done because each incarnation is to be an independent experience. What karma from previous lives is there and to be worked off, but not as a conscious effort. It is no good to remember past lives, as they often interfere with the current incarnation. I looked him into his eyes:

"What is if you didn't drink and have memories of past lives?"

He gave a big grin: "Some people can handle it, can't they?"

He squeezed my hand with a reassuring clasp. Later it was with great pleasure I read his *Way of the White Clouds*, an autobiography. His *Creative Meditation and Multi-Dimensional Consciousness* was for more advanced students and very instructive. His *Foundations of Tibetan Mysticism* was the most difficult as it requires a more in depth knowledge of Buddhism than I had at the time it was read. All are well worth the effort.

The work on the Religious Policy Committee led to an invite to sit on other committees—NOT student committees, but faculty committees as a student representative. This had been against the rules. It was without voting rights. My work on all the committees was valued by many of the faculty. I ended up on about five of the committees. At the end of the year they voted to have me as a voting representative for the students. Once again this violated all the rules and bureaucracy that had been set up by President Howard to ensure the students had minimal power.

Tom and JJ were getting into the other committees, both student and faculty as voting members. JJ and Tom headed several student groups themselves. By the end of our sophomore year we controlled most of the school groups, from the Photo Club (me), to the JCs (Tom), and Women's Issues (JJ) etc.

At the time there was the SDS (Students for a Democratic Society). This was created by activists in the Chicago area to promote a left leaning political and community action. During the 1968 Democratic Convention they were part of the group that was hanging out in Brian Park.

Major Daily of Chicago ordered them to be cleared out. SDS moved their informal gathering into a formal demonstration against Major. The police forcibly removed all the "hippies" from the park. This was not done nicely. They were pushed, clubbed and beaten by the police. They felt, and justifiably so, it was due to the Democratic Convention being held in Chicago. Many felt the heads of the Democratic Party that ordered the eviction of the students in the park. The students moved into the streets. The police, National Guard (brought up to protect the Convention), and other law enforcement agencies now tried to control the street demonstrations. The demonstration turned into a full scale protest and the law enforcement authorities moved in. This led to the 1968 Democratic Convention riots. It was most likely the scenes of the riots cost Humphrey the election.

By 1969 a group of students wanted a chapter of that SDS on campus. But the rules were no sororities or fraternities. The Dean declared that SDS fit into the category of a fraternity so therefore would not be permitted at the college. My solution was quick. I created the Students for a Liberal Society (SLS). There was little doubt it was a reflection of the SDS, but with a different name. It was to be a group allowed to discuss the political issues of the time. There could not be the objection since we were totally unaffiliated. I believe JJ was elected as president. I tried to work behind the scenes as I was active in so many other bodies. Yet my finger prints were all over this new organization.

You can just picture President Howard's reaction. When he realized we had created SLS modeled after the SDS, but within the rules of Rockford, he must have went through the roof. There was nothing he could do. At least within the rules that existed. Most of the East and West Coast students joined SLS. At least those from the left of center families. It became an overnight success! Our object was to present students who had ideas on how to improve the atmosphere on the campus. This was to really shift the focus from an extreme right to a more leftists slant. Support came in from many of the faculty as well. The fury came from the administration.

Even classes were getting interesting. There was a requirement of three semesters of a foreign language. I was taking Latin. Every class the gay teacher invited me to sit by him. Each time I found a "comfortable" spot elsewhere. After the class came over put his hand on my shoulder and ask if I needed any additional help. Again each advance was politely avoided. I was not a good Latin student. I couldn't just reject him outright. But he did become aware of my dating JJ. He was so frustrated when he couldn't get me interested in him. I told you about the first date with a girl. After the second with him, she told me:

"He couldn't even get it up unless he took me from behind and in the ass."

As for grades in the other classes, I switched from a math major (calculus broke me) to art and after Latin was finished, usually made the Dean's list. But the excitement was waiting for my junior year.

Love,
Papa

Hello T,

In the summer before my Junior year JJ and her mother had a trip to NYC and I was able to get down over the weekend. I stayed overnight at one of the Co-M houses, Demetria's I think. That way was able to have dinner with JJ and her mother Saturday evening.

Sunday morning we got together before I had to take the train home in the afternoon. Since her hotel was close to Central Park, we decided to go for a *Sunday in the Park* walk (to borrow from a play). For summer, it was an unusually cold and drizzly day and the park was almost empty. As we were walking another couple was approaching us. I immediately recognized the man and his *first* wife. As we got closer, the short, shy gentleman began to try to disappear behind his taller wife. As we passed he was almost on the opposite side of her, as far as could be from us. As we passed I politely said:

"Good morning Mr. Allen."

We continued to walk past the couple, not paying anymore attention. Suddenly he turned to us and said:

"You know me?"

"Yes, Mr. Woody Allen, the actor and writer of some fun films. I liked *What's New Pussycat?* Didn't care for *Tiger Lilly* that much."

"You're not going to ask for an autograph?"

"No."

A look of great relief came over him. He then looked carefully at JJ, and myself. Though only average height my strapping appearance was evident even under the jacket.

"Would you mind if we accompany you?"

Turning to him with a casual smile, and knowing his xenophobia reputation, the question was taken as a compliment. Without saying a word, JJ and I reversed our path and in total silence walked next to the Allens for some time. As we approached Columbus Circle, I turned to him and simply said:

"Good afternoon."

We parted without any other words. JJ was actually proud of my response. She learned celebs carried little weight on my emotions.

Junior year was very active. One both tragic and funny episode occurred when the college was planning an international night and wanted to invite the Japanese consul to the campus as part of a day of the celebration. I was known for being somewhat familiar with Eastern cultures, as there were NO Asian students at Rockford at that time! The head chef came to me to ask what the appropriate dinner would be for a Japanese dignitary. I told them the most common dish would be tempura. Raw fish would have been too dangerous for the kitchen to prepare. Pickled cucumbers and onions on the side with a miso soup would be a good meal. He thanked me.

A few days later he saw me in the dining room. He felt tempura would be too difficult to prepare. He decided on fried rice. I warned him that was NOT a Japanese dish. Not only that, I doubted if he knew how to fix it. The day came. The afternoon celebrations around campus went well. Then came the dinner. Rockford College's president, beaming with pride, and the Japanese guest were seated at a specially arranged head table in the main dining room. The fried rice was served. But the rice had been fried *before* it had been cooked—the chef had tried to fry the rice directly thinking it would become soft in the frying pans. The result made it totally inedible! The side dishes and desert were equally ill prepared. The Japanese consul took one look at the food and got up with the rest of his company and left the dining room. Knowing the Japanese traditions for restraint and politeness he must have considered the meal a major insult to walk out during the dinner. It was a disaster. Afterward the chef apologized to me for not taking my advice.

I was working on several facility committees at the time. The Curriculum Committee wanted to form a new chemistry class as a result of my suggestions. The problem was all the science classes were designed for science majors. There was no "easy" science class for non science scholars. The head of the Committee was the head of the Science Department, also the main chemistry professor. Working closely with him we came up with an idea. Why not create a chemistry class where the history of chemistry was reviewed—all the great discoveries would be re-created in the lab. The Committee loved it. The rest of the year we worked on the contents of the class, from early alchemical concepts to the latest developments in modern chemistry. I was really looking forward to taking this class in my senior year as I had yet to meet the science requirement.

Meanwhile, the Religious Policy Committee developed a very secular and open agenda allowing students from different religious backgrounds to deliver the services on Sundays. President Howard, being fundamentalist, went ballistic, but the attendance at the services went up. The newly opened chapel felt more inviting. Almost all the students were very happy with the changes the committee had made. But Howard had enough. He notified the chaplain that at the end of the year he would not be allowed back.

The faculty and students were mad as hell. The National Associations of College and University Chaplains did an investigation and came to a unique solution. Rockford College was under a notification of prohibition. NO respectable chaplain wanted to come to the college after that. At the end of my junior year, there was no replacement for the chaplain. By the beginning of my senior year, he and I both lamented what had happened to us both.

What happened to me? In April there were anti-Vietnam protests, some of which I participated in. Some of the conservative students wanted to take control of the committees away from JJ, Tom and myself. I suspected that Howard was behind this effort but couldn't prove it. Then when some possible students visited the campus, the three of us told them of the repressive attempts of the president to limit student voices. At the same time my posts to the student bulletin sounding board were getting more anti-establishment.

Some time in May I was directed to report to President Howard's office. Coming from ceramics class, I was covered with clay. Much to my surprise he asked how I was doing. I told him I was doing well and expected to be on the Dean's List. I left, suspecting nothing.

During the summer after my junior year, I was working with Tom in the college library. In the beginning of July I was notified that I was being "required to withdraw" from the college and was being fired from my job. According to the letter a newly formed "Dean's Committee" met in June and decided that I was to be kicked out for charge of "arrogance." I was joining the ranks of the college's most famous expelled alum, Jane Adams, who was expelled for smoking.

Because it was completely a private college, the ACLU and everyone else who would normally take my case didn't want to touch it. Yet the letter did say President Howard would assist in helping find an alternative college. Never believe it! All summer I was filling out college applications. Wherever transcripts were sent, I suspected Howard would call or write a letter to that college's president instructing him to reject my application. Naturally, all did.

By August it looked like I was not going to have a senior year. Then a friend called me. Mark had graduated from Rockford the year before. He was one of the radical students who was constantly protesting the Vietnam War. His most infamous student stunt occurred when the National Guard was called up in Rockford because of the anti-war protests and marches. Mark and others were usually at the lead of these protests. On this day a group of about a dozen of the anti-war group, pilled into a VW minivan and drove into the National Guard parking lot along with and a couple of old cars. The National Guardsmen, sitting down having lunch. The "hippies" slowly got out of the vehicles and walked near the Guardsmen. At Mark's command all pulled out water pistols and balloons. They tried to get as many of the uniformed guardsmen wet as possible. The initial water attack being over, the protesters started running back to the cars. The Guardsmen got up running to where their rifles were stacked and opened fire with live ammo! I saw how the minivan was shot more than once. Thank goodness no one was hit.

You can imagine Mark was a good friend. At the time he was considered a draft dodger. He was also wanted by the FBI for his anti war protesting and other federal law enforcement agencies for not responding to being called up in the draft. I called Mom, telling her of Mark's plight. Of course she was as anti-war as any of us. Mom helped him get to Canada to escape the draft. First by hiding him out at The Hill, where Mark had hitch-hiked to. Then driving him across the New York-Canadian border. While Mark was staying with Mom he found out what Rockford had done to me. He suggested Franconia College. Some of the other students who couldn't stand Rockford ended up going there. We kept the name of the college in the back of our minds.

I got home in July. All the college applications sent out were rejected. One afternoon Mom and I were completing other college applications. I was very stressed. Mom was concerned. Would we find a college for me to graduate from, hopefully on time?

As I was attempting to find something I needed for the application, I looked at the typewriter. The application was missing. Yet just a few minutes before it was there, ready to be completed. I freaked out. After a frantic look around the room Mom turned to me telling me to calm down. She felt it was the elemental creatures who were playing tricks on us to relieve the tensions. Together we sat down on the little kitchen table to have a cup of coffee for her and a cup of tea for myself. As we were relaxing, even joking, Mom suddenly said:

"Look," and pointed toward the dining room.

The application form was gently floating downward in mid air. It landed on the typewriter.

Mom said: "They are telling us not to worry and to relax."

I completed the application. Mailed it. And of course it was another rejection. The fairies or elves that lived with Mom were telling us not to be worried.

Franconia was the only option left. Few had ever heard of it. Since it was getting to be mid August and not wanting to miss a year of college I called the admissions office. After speaking with the head of admissions (later finding out he was the ONLY person in admissions) he sent an application in the mail. It arrived mid August. Once completed it was personally driven up to New Hampshire as the fall semester was quickly approaching. The head of admissions was in his office. I handed him the application, explaining to him what had happen at Rockford and that I was on the Dean's List in my last semester. He just shook his head saying:

"I've heard there were colleges like that. Of course you are accepted, I don't care about transcripts! Just get an advisor and you are in. But you need a senior advisor before it is official."

I told him sociology would likely be my new major. I had completed at least eight classes which would be considered part of a sociology major at Rockford. I had been working on a double major, sociology and fine arts, but sociology was the most logical choice. He told me where the sociology prof lived, and off I drove to the next town to get my advisor/professor's signature.

The timing was perfect. He and his family were just coming back from a day at the beach. I told him about my situation and he signed the form immediately. So, I was accepted into the most remarkable college in existence at the time.

It would take until December of the next year to complete all the requirements, but I did go to graduation in June the next summer. What happened during those next 12 months were some of the most fun ever!

A quick side note. After being thrown out I was staying with one of the Rockford faculty members. His wife loved horses. There was a spacious pasture behind their house and at one end was a barn which housed several horses including their own. They asked if I would like to go riding.

"Sure, I used to love riding when I was young."

"OK, I'll saddle up my horse and you can take him out for a ride. He needs the exercise."

She saddled up Dante, a beautiful black stallion, and warned me that he could be rather spirited. I should have backed out right there. Still, up in the saddle I got. Nudging him forward, instead of going into a trot, he jumped up as if he as Roy Roger's Trigger. I jumped out of the saddle, landing on my feet. There were two other girls who were riding buddies with the woman. They came up offering to ride on either side of Dante to keep him in check. Up I got again. We started out as a moderate walk. Each of them were on either side. I was about to turn to thank them for coming along when suddenly Dante bolted forward. He was off at a full gallop, as fast as one of the race cars at Limerock Track, or at least that was what it seemed at the time. From that Moment on all I remember was looking forward and wondering where I could jump off safely. Suddenly Dante made a sharp turn to the right, accompanied by a strong bucking action. I was thrown into the air.

I have no memory of landing. Then next thing I remember was walking over the field towards the house. The two girls took after Dante to bring him back to the barn. When I got to the house, Tom, the teacher and his wife all said I was as white as a corpse. I sat down, not even realizing how injured I was. Soon the pain came in. I must have landed on my hip and the pain started to overcome me. They gave me some over the counter painkillers, which did little. The wife suggest I sit in a cold bath to prevent swelling.

Her husband said: "No, you need to sit in a hot bath."

This argument went on for some time. He won! Wish he hadn't.

So I was put in a hot bathtub. It eased the pain but the swelling sure increased. That day I learned that for the first 48 hours after an accident, you should use cold not heat. By the way, the wife told me a few days later that when she took out Dante, he tried the same stunt on her. But she was an experienced horsewoman and wouldn't stand for it. Dante was punished. Don't know how, but that is what I was told.

Love,
Papa

Chapter 18

Franconia and An Unknown Future

Hello T,

What was not discussed in the last letter was the impact of being thrown out of Rockford.

Mom and I were both devastated. JJ was upset. We drove out there on the weekend scheduled for the students to return to the dorms. The resident assistant came up to me said he had instructions not to let me back into the dorm. He was greatly relieved when I told we were only there to pick up my things. I packed up to move out on the weekend most were moving in. The chaplain, JJ, Tom, Mom and I had dinner together at a local restaurant. Mom got drunk and kept asking why. The chaplain was at a loss. He just didn't understand why the two of us were thrown out for such trivial reasons. It was a very depressing dinner!

The drive back to Connecticut was long and silent! JJ and Tom were told that I had been accepted at Franconia but were instructed NOT to tell any one else at Rockford.

Once back home, there was only two days to get ready to move to Franconia College dorm. It was interesting from the start. The form for the dorm application asked for a choice of roommates: same sex; mixed (for rooms or suites with more than two); individual room, or didn't matter.

I checked the last. I ended up with a musically orientated New Yorker. He and his close friend became a core of a group of semi folk musicians. We were placed in a suite style set of rooms. Two of us in each with a bathroom in between. Down the hall was an interesting character who, like me, loved classical music, Earhart from Germany. He was a huge Beethoven fan. On Beethoven's birthday he would play all nine symphonies sitting on his bed, smoking pot, while tripping on LSD. I would come up to visit him several times that day and listen to what ever symphony was playing at the time. We rarely talked, but just absorbed ourselves in the music.

The first student meeting occurred around the third week. Leon Botstein had just been named president and introduced himself. He and his bride, Jill, had moved into the house across from the sports field. Leon was violinist and the youngest college president in the history of American colleges. He was less than two years older than I.

All committees had equal members of students and facility and one administrator. I introduced myself and how I came to Franconia. Noting work on Rockford's Curriculum Committee and had a desire to continue, I wanted to build on lessons learned. This led to the student body immediately nominating and electing me as their representative.

The other important duties in the main building was the appointment to the fire brigade. During fire drills, which were many, I would done on a fireman's coat and check all rooms were vacated. There was one girl, Ted (nickname), who loved sleeping in. When a fire alarm went off, she was often in bed not paying attention. So in I would rush in, pick Ted up and shoulder carry her down the stairs to the sports field where everyone was to assemble during the drills. It became accepted that I carried Ted during all the fire drills.

Classes were pass/fail and very informal. Expecting to go to graduate school, I had to request grades! Most classes were from 5 to 15 students, average around 8. Soon I realized the faculty were largely from major academic environments. Like me, many were kicked out for various reasons. Most were decidedly Marxist in their perspective and quite radical anti-capitalists. It was the exact opposite from Rockford. Now I was the conservative on campus (can you believe that?)!

Yes, there were two others from Rockford who had been friends with Mark. They were surprised seeing me at Franconia!

What was truly unique about the college was that you could have any major you wanted. If they didn't officially offer it, then you would work with your advisor, come up with a major. Next you had to determine how you would get enough credit for a degree beyond the regular classes, be it through independent study, developing and giving student seminars where at least two other students would attend for non-credit or apprenticing to a related company or professional.

The person (for the life of me I can't remember his name) who wanted to major in comic book science. His independent studies looked at the authors, the artists, the history of Marvel and Dell (the major comic companies) and even explored some of the underground comic which had popped up a few years before (ZAP, etc). I took two of his seminars on the art work and one on the history of Dell—I don't remember them now, but both impressed me. Those attending had to fill out an evaluation and give it to his advisor before he would get credit. We did and so did he.

Most of us wondered what the heck he would do with his degree when he graduated. But he had a plan. It was rumored (never got solid confirmation) that after graduation he took his Comic Book Science BA down to NYC. He got into the office of Stan Lee, President of Marvel. He walked up to Stan's desk and plopped down his degree and said:

"Who else has this qualification?"

According to one of my friends who was closer to this student, he was hired on the spot for $30+K a year—a remarkably huge salary for 1971. When I finally got a job in NYC it was only $8,000!

Love,
Papa

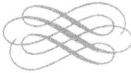

Hello T,

Shortly after moving in Franconia would have a movie night. Usually showing old films in the small studio which could sit about thirty, but with room on the floor for some to lay down closer to the screen. On one occasion it was to be a special treat. One of the students, with his father's permission, had brought his father's considerable collection of old eight mm pornography. These were a huge collection of films on little reels. Most only ran for 10 or 15 minutes. But there were a few on large reels which were feature porn movies lasting as long as 45 minutes. Many were classic porn films some silent movies dating from the early 1920s. There may have even been a few dating even earlier. A retrospective course on movies would have shown these classic early porn. Others were from the 50s.

Rumor got around the college this special movie night was coming. That night the movie room was filled. The kid whose father had lent him the movies started the projector in the projection booth. His girlfriend was up in the booth with him. A local farmer and his wife, both likely in their 50s watched for a while. I was seated behind them. After watching for a good 30 minutes maybe longer he turned to his wife:

"Have you ever seen anything like that?"

"No!" was her response.

"What do you think if we try it?"

She smiled and said: "Let's get home, I'm wet as anything and ready to try."

Unfortunately the scene that turned them on is long forgotten. I just hope they had a lot of fun trying to recreate the scene once they got home.

Leon and Jill (the president and his wife) were in one of the more comfortable seats towards the front, slightly to the left of the screen. They were watching intently! Soon her hand looked as though it was in his pants. If you watched closely you could swear she was stroking his erection. Though not evident from were I was sitting, Leon's hand did seem to be under her dress stroking her as they watched. After about 45 minutes of watching, they walked out between the changing of reels to their house across the soccer field in the front of the college. They didn't bother to return.

After about three hours of the films, the room was beginning to empty out. A few of us, like myself, who were not hooked up with any sexual partners, stayed. Suddenly the movie started to jump all over the screen. I stood up. Looking into the projection booth which was only slightly elevated from the floor the reason for the film gyrations was evident. The projection booth was not very concealed to anyone in the back of the theater, like myself. The student who was showing the films was getting a blow job from his girlfriend. This was while his hand was on the table where the old projector was placed. After he came, the projector was once again showing the films without the jumping effect, at least for a while. Then it started again. But this time not as radically as before.

What was wonderful about this age is a man can quickly regain an erection. Sure enough, after he came in his girlfriend's mouth twice, and watching a few of the films, he was stiff as before. But now she wanted some action. She bent over the bench in the projection room. He mounted her from behind. It was probably good they had switched from the silent films to early porn talkies of the 30s and 40s as her enjoyment was certainly vocal. One of her hands had hold of the projection table, thus the movement, until she let out a scream of pleasure. That resulted in a big jump on the screen showing the films resulting in almost everyone turning around and giving them a cheer. No one had any doubt as to what was going. After the cheer we all sat down again with big smiles of delight that they were enjoying more than just the movies.

Love,
Papa

Hi T, it's sports time at Franconia.

This was the most fun filled college year. Yes there were ups and downs. Moments of depression, but overall it was a great year. There was a touch football team. A black student named Muff was our quarterback. He had an exceptional strong passing arm. During one of the practices a pass hit my wrist so hard it broke a metal watchband. The team mostly played local men's town teams. During an early snow, I was wearing sneakers. The ground was slippery. No footholds could be found. To stop from being pushed back there had to be another solution. Frustrated by the lack of traction, the sneakers were removed. I played in the snow barefoot. The result was my toes would be able to grab the ground under the snow. Suddenly I became the great blocker and defensive lineman matching my reputation. The result was my resistance to infection was lowered.

Many of the kids at Franconia tended to be hypochondriacs. The local doctor who handled the college kids didn't want to see these students who were suffering from more mental illnesses than physical. I had strep throat several times during the winter months. Especially after this barefoot football game in the snow. Sure enough, about 3 days later, my throat was killing me. I called the doctor, he asked me to come in. One of the students drove me to his office. He recognized me immediately.

"It's OK nurse, if he's here he has something serious."

I went into his examination room.

"Open wide."

I did.

"Nurse Betty, you have to look at this! It is the most classic strep throat I've ever seen."

Everyone in the office took turns looking down my throat. I found a picture on the web which comes close. I had pale green gray and a little blue gray growth. It was worse than what you see in most posted photos. He did ask why I never had my tonsils removed. My response was we couldn't afford it if not absolutely needed. Never saw the need. Now looking back on it, glad they were not removed. The result was when I called him, he would see me without hesitation. This was not the same for other students.

The other great sport at Franconia was soccer. This was my first attempt to play "international football." But I played a defensive position, fullback. Where your were not expected to be a great runner. That was good since on a flat surface speed was not something that promoted my running ability. Muff was on the right side of our goal. I took the left. Our captain was Bottier, an older student from Mongolia. He was tall and thin, very fast and could really handle the ball. He would teach us how to hit the ball illegally with our fist. Key was to have the ref behind you then place the fist next to our chest or shoulder as we jumped as if we were heading the ball. He said if the ref was behind us, it would look like a header. The team also picked up some fancy kicks and other tricks from Bottier. Later in the season we learned he had been on the Mongolia profession soccer team before he came to the US. Needless to say he was our highest scorer.

There was one short student Stroll. He was perhaps 5' 2" at most and with a long black beard. He ran in the most unusual way. It was with his arms straight down his sides. Being short he looked like a dwarf out of Tolkien, running up and down the field.

We did have two girls on the team who had played soccer in high school. Both good in forward positions. The rest of the team was a pick up group of students and one of the faculty who pretended to be a student during the games. He was from the Philippines and missed playing, so he would join in when we played at home. He was also the team's faculty sponsor.

One game was at another small college in the southern part of New Hampshire. We arrived in several cars and vans. We had no uniforms but tried to wear the same color shirts. One of our wings was another bearded character called Power Trip Flip due to all the pot and LSD consumption. He constantly was high. During halftime of the game he dropped another tab of acid. In the second half when the ball came towards him he tried to stop it. Instead of stopping the bounce, he stepped on it giving it a backspin which ran it up his leg and hit his beard. He actually tried to kick it out of his beard. In the process twisted his knee badly. He was carted off the field. After the game we took him to a clinic where he got some pain killers. On top of all the other drugs the only thing anyone could get out of him for three days as a starry eyed OOOOH! expression, as if he was seeing another world.

The team had one girl who was the hero in the same game. She wore a velcro jersey. As one of the opposing team's men approached her with the ball, she pulled open her shirt showing her VERY attractive tits, steal the ball and made a great shot just out of the goalie's reach. GOAL! One of the greatest moves ever seen on a soccer field! She pulled that trick in several games she played. This was the only time where it resulting in a goal.

Up until the last game of the season, we were unscored upon. That last game was on our home field. A junior college challenged us. They were mostly ex-vets from Vietnam. All gung-ho! As they had a formal warm up with all the exercises like jumping jacks and a lap around the field. Our team mocked them by doing all their exercised backward or doing a silly run! They started shouting they were going to teach us hippy freaks a lesson in how to play soccer.

Steve one of our mid fielders had long curly black hair. He was not one of our best players. Their striker was bringing the ball down the field. Steve tried to stop him but fell as this ex-marine moved around him. The marine then put a back spin on the ball where it was next to Steve's head. He kicked the ball, but the follow through put a gash in Steve's head that would require a lot of stitches.

Muff and I looked at each other, "hamburger drill" he said in a low voice.

When the Marine came down the field again Muff and I hit him from two sides at the same time. He went down. Muff pivoted on his foot kicking the ball into the Marine's mid section. Then Muff tried to send the ball down the field. The follow through kicking the marine in the stomach. The ball didn't go far as one of their players tried to kick it back. Now it was next to the downed striker's head. I needed to get it further out of play. Of course the follow through of my kick hit his head and knocked him out cold. He had to be carried off the field. We won, 3-2 but it was a HARD FOUGHT bloody match!

Love,
Papa

Hello T,

There were academics in Franconia too. One of my favorite classes was taught by George. George had been a student of Minor White, a great photographer and one of the proponents of the "zone system" method of photography. George was just a few years older than myself. He would mix photography and philosophy in all his classes. One exercise required each of the students to sit in a meditative position with closed eyes. He would then place a color photograph in each of our laps. The class was then told to open our eyes and stare into the photo.

"See what you feel from the photo."

The picture in my lap was the front passenger side of a partly burned car. There was the red of the car's paint curled at the edges of the charred hood. The dented black scorched edges were evidence of intense burning. As a photo it was great, as were most of the photos of this exercise. The only problem was I could "feel" the flames and heat destroying the car. It was as if my body was being burned with the intense heat. The searing pain was terrible. A cry came out of my lips.

When asked to share our experiences, I had to chastise George for picking a photo that could be conceived as negative. I told the class of my experience. It was certainly the most intense session of the whole class.

George also taught a philosophy class in his log cabin in the forest. One evening his dog Ansel (named after Ansel Adams, the great photographer, of course) was there enjoying the attention for all the students. Ansel was very fond of me. I had played with him previously. During one of the classes Ansel was sleeping in my lap. The discussion was about Martin Heidegger, the German philosopher. Heidegger was widely seen as a seminal thinker in the Continental tradition, particularly within the fields of existential philosophy and psychology. Sorry, but Heidegger was boring!!!

Being a cold night but a warm cabin, with a dog sleeping in my lap, my attention began to wander. Suddenly I saw myself running through a field of tall grass. I was chasing a rabbit as it zigged and zagged through the field. It was such fun. It was Ansel's dream. I opened my eyes. His legs were moving in just the way it would take to turn one way or another that fit the dream. Suddenly an awareness of the class came back into consciousness. Realizing I had drifted off my head raised up and I apologized to the class for being distracted. The vision of Ansel's dream was related to the rest of the class and how I found myself a part of it. From that day on, my reputation for having exceptional psychic abilities quickly spread around the college.

The psychology class was taught by the professor who also taught statistics. This was way before calculators or computers, so NO "R" programming. Here is where the introduction to Carl Jung held most student's interest. Freud was largely dismissed. Wilhelm Reich was covered as an example of the suppression of our government of ideas that were considered radical. Reich's concept of "orgastic potency" was too dangerous to be discussed openly while he was alive. His theories resulted in him being thrown in jail. Though not part of the reading list, we were given the titles of his works. Later I would read his _The Mass Psychology of Fascism, The Function of the Orgasm_, and _The Sexual Revolution_. You father is definitely one of his fans.

We also covered R. D. Laing using his _Divided Self_ as our text. His _Knots_ was also read. It was a lot of fun. Laing treated schizophrenics; his philosophy was we live in a schizophrenic world so therefore the only really normal people were the schizophrenics. He ran Kingsley Hall in England which had such as successful record in "curing" his patients that the British psychological association became to threaten by his radical ideas. According to the professor the mainstream psychologists closed Laing's hospital and drummed him out of the business. Good class especially for those interested in radical psychology.

There was a history class by another young professor who was able to get his book on aggression published during the school year. His basic position was that USA is one of the most violent countries in the world. Our love of guns, glorification of the Old West, and current gang activities (remember in the later 1960s and 1970s) in the cities were all fodder for his position. AND THIS WAS **BEFORE** THE NATIONAL RIFLE ASSOCIATION HAD BOUGHT CONGRESS!!! All that has happen in the past decades are only confirmation of his position and argument made in 1970! His theory is evident in the constant mass killings around the country or the gangs running wild in Chicago's south side. As bad as the late 1960s were for violence, today is worse. America still refuses to take the necessary actions to restrict gun sales and use. I keep a gun available, mostly because there are so many others. After all there appears to be a concept that two wrongs do make a right in this crazy country.

Remember how I had been elected to the Curriculum Committee? I told you how at Franconia each committee consisted of a teacher, an administrator and a student. Majority ruled. Ed, my advisor, the sociology professor was the teacher rep. I was the student representatives on the

Curriculum Committee. Leon was the administrator. We were interviewing possible candidates for a poetry position. One of the interviewees came in. He had published a few small books of poetry. He sat down and told us interviews are stupid.

"What can I tell you? I knocked up my wife. She was sick as a dog with morning sickness for months. Then she shit our son out of her cunt. What else would you care to hear about?"

That was the extent of the interview. We had reviewed his resume. It was impressive. He was asked to leave the room while we deliberated. Leon jumped up:

"We got to have him!!!!"

Ed and I just looked at each other in total disbelief. But Leon was so animate we didn't want to go against him. Besides the other candidates were total bores.

At times Franconia was a strange college.

Love,
Papa

Hello T,

Ping pong was very popular at Franconia. There were a series of small study rooms and one large room in the basement where a ping pong table was located.

One geeky looking player no one could beat. This student was constantly smoking. He wore glasses, had long black hair, and a slightly stocky build. He would just stand right next to the table and return the ball the second it hit. No spins. No smashes. Just little returns. He could position his paddle so perfectly the ball would just clear the net and bounce harmlessly back on his opponent's side. Spins, slams, back spins were all returned with the same casual manner. He would drive all his opponents, including me, nuts. He simple waited until you got so frustrated by his returns that in your effort to get around his defense you would make a shot that would miss the table or go into the net. Looking back on it, his anticipation of where the ball would hit the table was uncanny. His reflexes were remarkable. Without a doubt one of the most boring defensive players one would ever meet. The trouble was NO ONE could beat him. Some came close, especially those with exceptional slams to the corners, but they would get maybe 15 points in a 21-point match. Don't think your father ever got more than 13 against this player.

One day it was decided that two of the small rooms should be converted into a single TV room. The maintenance crew told us if we could take down the wall, they would finish off the floor and adjourning walls to make it look decent. Someone told them the students would take care of the tearing down the wall. After all the separate beautiful wooden dorm in the woods had been built as a student project a few years before. For the next 20 minutes there was a joint effort of guys (including your father) who knocked down part of the wall in the most effective manner. Elbows, hands, feet were all used to knock down the dry walls. Then the one by two inch boards supporting the dry walls had to go. The only rule: NO tools. Fun and very effective. The next week the college had a nice large TV room where there was only a couple of storage closets before.

Another role I took on was as a teacher of meditation. I had completed several stages of the Arcane School's meditations and had additional forms taught by your grandmother. In an attempt to get the students away from drugs, I would teach meditative astral travel as an experience superior to drugs and a means to keep total control. Though unable to get "out there" myself, teaching others was a natural.

One night I was conduction a mediation class. One of the students was a local named William. One of my roommates joined in as did Taffy who shared with me some of the same classes. We were doing a very deep meditation. Little did I know but the student "witch" was doing a psychic reading in the room immediately below us. As I was guiding the participants in the meditation there was a little scream from down below. Thankfully it was not noticed by those being guided in the meditation. About 20 minutes later, after the meditation class was over, the girl doing the reading below knocked on my door.

"What were you doing?" Came the question from a slightly shaky voice.

Explaining the meditation class and the exercise that was being done satisfied her. She described that at the same time all the candles she was using in her tarot reading suddenly had flames that shot up three feet. It scared the hell out of herself and the other two girls in the room.

Soon several others wanted to try the meditations. Several of the heavier drug users joined the meditation group. The college's advisor encourage and even referred some of the student to the sessions. As for the gal who's candles went crazy we became good (not close) friends.

Love,
Papa

Hello T,

The main building was an old hotel. There were five floors, counting the "basement." Around the top floor was a ledge about 18 inches wide just below all the windows. During winter, the snow would accumulate on these ledges. Often the snow was well over a foot deep on these ledges.

William, who lived with his parents a few miles away went to the college and would often stay in a vacant bed on weekends. One snowy winter night two teams were formed for an indoor snowball fight. All we had to do is open a window and make snowballs. Most of us would hide a supply on the ledges just outside certain windows.

William was on the opposing side. I had stores of snowballs all over. I would charge down "enemy lines" with an arm full of snowballs clobbering all those on the other side. During one of these charges, William was waiting at the end of the hall where I least expected him. Out of snowballs and with all the floors and stairs wet from melting snow, upon seeing William with his arm full of snowballs, there was only one escape. Down the stairs. But I slipped and slid head first towards the stairs with William coming on fast. There was only way to escape the onslaught of snowballs. Head first down the stairs I dove, using the hands to pull myself down. Then making the U turn to get past the little landing to the floor below. I resembled a seal climbing down the rocks to the ocean. William was throwing snowballs all the time, but he was laughing at the sight so hard, he COULDN'T HIT ME!. Of course we got in trouble for all the water on the floors the next day. But it was a great snowball fight. The custodian was not happy about all the water that accumulated in the hall ways which he had to clean up the next morning.

Most everyone at Franconia slept in on Saturday, being hung over from Friday nights. What they were hung over from varied with the student. My roommates tended to get high on pot. Some on booze. Many on a combination. Some on harder drugs. Many drugs were tolerated, but not condoned. Heroin was the only absolutely forbidden. If a needle was detected, he or she would be turned into the administration for disciplinary action and counseling. Phone calls Saturday mornings were rare before 11 a.m.

There was a limited number of phones available for each of the floors. Most were the old fashioned coin operated public phones, the same found in old schools and highway rest stops. You must remember this is before there was such a thing as personal phones, smart or mobile communications. They were the old fashioned rotary dial pay phones. Students gave their parents and friend the number of the pay phone nearest their rooms. Being about three phones per floor, when a call came in, whoever happened to be nearest the phone was responsible for answering it and get the person being called.

One early Saturday morning, I received a call. Being Saturday and with the top floor 90 percent male, I went out in the usual way I slept—naked! It never occurred to me that anyone who didn't know it was the men's area would bring anyone up to that area without announcing their presence. Your grandma was calling about 9:30 a.m. It was a heavy conversation about her job and the possibility of her losing it. She was fired two weeks later.

During the conversation I had my back to the stairwell, which was about 15 feet away. What I didn't know was that Ted, the girl I carried during the fire drills, was showing parents around the school. Hearing a noise behind me, I turned around with a phone braced against my shoulder, with pen and paper in my hands. I was suddenly aware of being fully exposed to Ted and her parents. Not knowing what else to do I did a little bounce up and down to wave hello with the only appendage that was not holding anything. Besides it was a little erect from not having relieved myself before picking up the phone call. Ted turned red. Her mother looked totally shocked. Her father was stunned. Ted apologized later and explained to her parents that it was the men's floor. Maybe they should have announced themselves before coming up. Ted and I talked later. She actually thought my wave was funny, after the initial shock at seeing her first semi-erect penis.

On weekends William started to invite me over to his house in Sugar Hill, New Hampshire, about five miles away. We would play chess and backgammon. There was no TV or radio in the house, only a phonograph player and a small selection of records. William was really good at chess and would encourage mental chess. This is where you both stare at an empty board and announce your move: King's pawn to King four, etc. Or if you use the British system the rows are numbered and columns are associated with letters. We got up to 25 moves one time and I just gave up. He then replayed the whole game with real pieces and pointed out where one of my moves was illegal as the knight does not go over one and up one.

Our other favorite game was backgammon. In backgammon we were virtually equal. There was an added challenge that began to come into our games. Being a little on the psychic side, we would try to control the dice. If we needed a specific number to get out of trouble, William or I would focus on the particular needed throw. More times than not that number came up on the dice thrown. It became more of a contest of who had the most psychic abilities than of backgammon skills. Once that game was played I usually won a little more than William.

Later in life William would have more psychic fun in attempting to time his phone calls to me in NYC for the most inconvenient times. Of course it would be while I was making love to my companion at that time. It got so regular that one of my partners who had met William would shout:

"Hello William!" as I answered the phone if we were in the middled of sex.

The only time when she didn't shout to William was the time she just knocked over the phone when hearing it ring. That time all William could hear was her organismic screams of pleasure in the background. He laughed knowing his timing was perfect.

Love,
Papa

Hi T,

This is a letter which violates your rules about your father's extra curricula bedroom activities, but only because it is funny.

Taffy was a sophomore. Her father was an MD. She and I shared a number of classes and were study buddies. During the spring as we were studying she looked at me.

"Do you like me?"

Of course I did. She had a great personality and a very good sense of humor. Taffy always worried about her exanthema how it may impact any lover she may hook up with. But as friends, she felt less threatened by possible exposure of the rash.

She would talk about her family and how much they envied her. Partly for being in Franconia where the choices were so great and where a student could create their own programs. Also because their daughter was experiencing the sexual revolution. She told me how both her parents envied her with the invention of the birth control pill. They would have open discussions with her saying the open and casual sexual encounters were something they never experienced.

While having this conversation one day in my room while studying for an exam Taffy turned to me and asked why we never had sex. I responded:

"Because we were just friends."

She quoted the old Eydie Gorme song: "*It's the friendliness thing two people can do.*" With that she leaned over and gave me a passionate kiss.

So much for studying the rest of the afternoon. She quickly stripped off my clothes, taking my erection into her mouth as it was exposed. I then focused on her. As her blouse and bra were removed her ice cream cone breasts popped out. They were not very round but well formed, projecting from her body in a most inviting way. Her nipples were not very prominent but loved attention (gee just like your current stepMom). As I rolled down her jeans and panties, her public hairs were already wet with anticipation. No need to go down on her. I just picked her up and placed her on my bed.

There was a brief rubbling of my cock against her clit and wet lips. Then a sudden penetration was met with an equally vigorous upward thrust of her hips. I was engulfed in her instantaneously. Trying hard to not reach organism too quickly, the thrusts were varied. Some deep. Others shallow. She was loving every minute. Soon I could hold it off no longer. With a few rapid deep thrusts, I started to come. She wrapped her legs around my hips and tried to take even more of me into her. It was great. We both enjoyed it, though I was never sure if she had achieved an organism. But back then, only a few years after Masters and Johnson, few fully understood female organism at that time. I am certain looking back on my encounters there were many a partner who did achieve climaxes.

Needless to say there were other escapes between us, most of which are not going to be shared here. There is one exception.

One Spring night it was exceptionally warm for New Hampshire. My window was open. I was in bed. Taffy came by and said she was horny. Opening up the sheets in a clear invitation to join me, she quickly undressed and jumped in naked. Taffy told me to tell her all that I was feeling and experiencing during our love making. She wanted to know exactly what a man was going through physically and mentally during love making.

After about 30 minutes of foreplay and just enjoying our bodies there was a knock on the door. A high school senior who was visiting Franconia on the weekend designated as visitor's weekend said my roommate told her she could sleep in his bed. Seeing Taffy and I naked in bed together she was a little embarrassed, but undeterred. I told her she was welcome to stay here but that Taffy and I were still going to do what comes naturally. She said she didn't care. She got down to her underwear and climbed into the bed on the other side of the room. She turned her head towards the wall in an attempt to ignore what was going on our side of the room.

Taffy and I thought it was kind of funny. Frankly we didn't care if she was there or not. Besides Taffy wanted a stiff cock in her! Being such a close friend, I was not going to disappoint her. With the unexpected company out of our minds Taffy and I started our love making again. She was getting very excited. At first she got on top and rode me cowgirls style for several minutes. Then I rolled us both over so I could get on top as I was getting very excited. I didn't know how much longer I could hold back an organism. Remembering Taffy wanted me to be telling her all I was experiencing during the act. I was telling her how I was feeling, what I liked about her body. How much I liked being inside her. After a few minutes the climax was getting closer and closer.

Just then the college motor cycle group rode up to just below my open window. One of them noted his cycle was misfiring. He wanted to adjust it. Taffy and I paid no attention but continued with our own pleasures. Soon my climax was arriving. I felt the testicles tightening up and the sperm beginning to take its trip into the tunnel of delight. This was just as the cycle was being revered up by its owner. No longer able to hold back. In a rapid breathing breath Taffy was told:

"I'm coming, I'm coming."

This passionate announcement occurred almost at the same time as the peek of the noise from the cycles outside came in through the window. All of a sudden the high school girl in the bed on the other side of the room rolled over, sat up, and shouted:

"God damn those noisy motor cycles!"

Taffy and I buried our faces in the pillow we were laughing so hard, knowing full well it was NOT the motor cycle noise. It was obvious what really was bothering her.

Love,
Papa

Hi T,

One of the last scheduled social events in the college was a talent show. I was still very shy when it came to performing or presenting anything in public. But Taffy wanted us to do a routine based upon some comic characters. I suggested Groucho and Margaret Dumont the woman who was the foil for most of the Marx Brother's films. We came up with a short skit where she would sit on my lap and I would use a combination of Groucho and W. C. Fields jokes.

Although we were fairly well prepared as the day approached, I got cold feet. Taffy sat with me on the front lawn. We talked about it for some time. She noted we could run in and do the routine any time in the next hour or so. Some of the students were aware of us possibly doing it. I just froze. To this day although Taffy hugged me and said it was OK, I felt I let her down. I really regret it looking back over all these years.

During the holiday break from Franconia, I did make it down to Marie Deraismes to get my Master Mason Degree. It was February 13, 1971. I was very proud to finally achieve that goal. Harry H was the Worship Master for the ceremony which was slightly modified. There is a place in the ceremony where the candidate is to be carried around the Lodge room. Owing to the fact most members were women, rather than carrying me around the lodge I was laid low in the west where most would usually be carried. Interesting modification.

Myron and Jane Kitaif were very happy to see me finally receive my MM Degree. There was one old member Alma Olinde, originally from Estonia. She was a sweet, elderly person who was always soft-spoken and very kind. She came up to me after the ceremony telling my how happy she was that a young person was coming into the Lodge. Though I only knew her for a short time and only through the lodge, she made a lasting impression on me as a wonderful kind individual. She had migrated from Estonia after the Soviet Union took over. She joined Co-M while in England. Then she migrated to the US and became a member of Marie Deraismes sometime during the 1930s.

Afterwards rather than driving back to Connecticut immediately, some of us went out to dinner to celebrate. Demetria, Edris M who was brought into the Lodge by Demetria, and a few others joined us. I don't remember where we went, but it would have been one of the establishments close by. I don't remember if Alma joined us but you will hear more about her in the future.

Love,
Papa

It's still me.

June 1971 was coming fast. All those who were planning to graduate within the year were invited to ceremony. A whole 30 students were planning to graduate. Remember Franconia was a VERY small college.

I had a reputation of keeping a bottle of Major's Grey's Chutney in my pocket, not only at Franconia but in Rockford too. It would be applied to all the tasteless meats served in college.

Taffy, who often ate with me, gave me a special graduation gift. It was a very small cookbook on chutneys and pickles. She signed it with her name and advice: "Have a fucking good time." Love that cookbook. It allowed me to capture a couple blue ribbons in cooking contests years later.

Before the graduation the school was closing down the main building for a week. I was to stay with William. Just as we were all moving out, Taffy came up to me and said: "W, I had a terrible dream last night. That you were killed in a car accident just before graduation. Please be careful."

I listened but was not too concerned.

About three minutes later the Philippino teacher who was the sponsor of the soccer team came up to me with a scared expression.

"W!" he shouted. "Last night I had a dream the graduation was turned into a memorial service for you. You had been killed before the ceremony."

Now I was paying attention. One dream is interesting, but two! Then one of the other students who I didn't know that well, other than a few ping pong games, came up and said:

"W, please take care, I had a very bad feeling last night that you were going to be killed in an accident this coming week."

THAT'S IT! Three is just too many. William came to pick me up. Taffy who had heard the others related their feelings told William. Turning to William she said:

"Keep him locked up in your house until graduation."

William promised he would.

What followed was a week in William's house. Normally it would be ideal. Lots of books, classical music on vinyl, and a beautiful setting on Sugar Hill with view of the mountains. By Thursday I was going crazy.

"William, let's go to the rock shop in Littleton."

"No way are we going anywhere until graduation on Saturday!" was his immediate response.

It was a rock shop we had visited before to buy crystals and other geologic items. I begged and begged, but William was unmoved. Finally I said I was going to a walk down a small street not previously explored. Little did I know years later I would meet someone who had their summer house down that road.

I started walking down the little road. Suddenly I had a vision as if there was a double exposure in front of my eyes. William was driving in his car. I was in the passenger seat. All this vision came while actually walking. In the car suddenly as we turned down the street towards the rock shop a mother was driving a station wagon ran a stop sign. BAMB! Right into William's car and ME! I looked at my watch. It would have been the exact time it would have taken to get to that intersection if William and I had left when I was begging. The danger was over. By walking instead of driving in a car, my life was saved.

At graduation several people were very happy to see me, including the teacher who had the dream. I told him the vision I had and it's timing. He was relieved. My Mom arrived and heard some of the conversation. After the ceremony she had one too many drinks but still she insisted on driving because of all the dreams. I felt more of a threat from her drunk driving than anything that may have happened in the dreams. Still she drove. We reached home—somehow.

In reality I did not receive my diploma at graduation. My graduate thesis was not completed. That summer I did volunteer work at the East Side House Settlement. I was doing a paper comparing the Czech immigration of the 1890s with the Puerto Rican migration, which was a constant. Both populations were served by the East Side Settlement House, the country's second oldest, after Hull House founded by Jane Adams in Chicago.

I stayed on the top floor of their offices which was a little apartment with two bed rooms, two living rooms and one kitchen. Between researching the Czech immigration of the 1890s and the then present day influx of Puerto Ricans into the South Bronx, I was busy typing the thesis. Mom would proof read and helped retype parts of it. Remember this is before word processors so every little mistake was whited out with correction fluid and retyped.

The main theme was not good enough. Ed, my advisor, wanted it re-worked. It was submitted again. Still more was needed. This time Ed put in a huge amount of edits he felt necessary. So once more, AND with feeling, the thesis was totally reworked.

Love,
Papa

December

Happy Birthday. Hope you opened your present and this letter on your day!

While staying at the East Side House Settlement to earn my keep they suggested doing volunteer work at Mott Haven Community Center a block away. Mott Haven Center was a few blocks from Paterson Projects on 3rd Avenue and across the street from Mott Haven Projects. A fire house was next to the Community Center. A Pueblo grocery store and the Settlement House on Alexander Avenue dissected the two projects.

To save money I would buy turkey tails for 0.10/lb. I quickly learned how to cook them 20 different ways. Curried, broiled, in soup, in stew, cut up and fried with vegetables. The tails and turkey necks were the major source of meat during that summer. That's all I could afford. But the most interesting thing that happened was to take place at the Mott Haven Community Center.

Mott Haven Community Center was open from two in the afternoon until nine at night. The sessions were mostly to keep preteens in the afternoons, and the teens in the evening off the streets. This was a rough neighborhood. It was just on the edge of what was called Ft. Apache which was centered at police station at Fox and Simpson Streets a little over dozen blocks away.

The first afternoon at the Center the head of the center introduced me to the staff announcing I would be volunteering with the kids and would do tutoring and helping out any way possible. I suggested doing some art work with the kids, which was readily accepted. All the time there was an interesting young woman sitting across from me. I could not take my eyes off of her. Later it was learned she had a black/American Indian mother (50/50 I was told) and a Jewish Czech father who disappeared after her younger brother was born. The combination made her look Indian from India! As I was looking at her, my subconscious told me we had been together in a previous life. Closing my eyes and focusing on that thought, it came to me. She was my wife when we both lived in India. This was hundreds of years ago.

In the summer when I was thrown out of Rockford, during the Depression, I tried a mediation. I actually achieved an out of the body experience. I was up on The Hill, lying down on the breezeway. Sam and other friends were around to try to cheer me up. It didn't work. I asked to be alone for a little while and retreated to the breezeway to lay down.

I went into the meditation. Due to the depression and not really giving a damn about anything, an out of the body experience occurred which would change my life began. I raised above my body. There was an overlaying plane of existence. In a field was a red fox, much like the fox Mom had killed and nailed up on the corner of the same breezeway. In the dream/vision the fox stared at me. Then began to chase me. I ran. But strange, as I ran he was always chasing me, but somehow was in front of me. It was as if he was using his will to force me to follow him.

Every now and then the fox would stop commanding me to look at myself. When we stopped one time, I was dressed as a Hindu priest on the banks of the Gangues river. My whole life came into memory instantly. I had a wife with five children, two boys and three girls. My wife loved to wear an orange sari. Considering how poor we were, it was likely her only sari. Looking at that life, it came to me, as a poor priest I died early, maybe around age 27. My wife refused to commit sati (throwing herself on my funeral pyre). She realized someone had to stay behind to care for the kids. It was a wise decision but one which put her in bad light with the religious community.

That vision faded. The fox started to chase me from the front again. We stopped and I looked down. Still in India but now just a short life—likely as a dalit, an untouchable—appeared. Not wanting to see further about that life, I looked up. We ran again. Once more we stopped. I looked at myself. I was in a silk sari wearing beautiful jewelry and living in luxury. I was a high class courtesan, known for her beauty and sexual prowess. Somehow the thought came to me that I was sold into prostitution as a young child. I looked for the fox and shouted: "NO!"

He started to run again. Then suddenly he darted after a rabbit, leaving me alone. I looked down. I was above the breezeway of my house with my physical body below. Floating about 15 feet above the roof I realized that I had to re-enter the meditating body below. It took a long time to get back in the body but I did. It was like reversing the direction of smoke as it rises from the simmering fire. But this time I was the smoke needing to rejoin the slumbering embers.

All this came back to me while in the meeting with the Mott Haven staff. I realized this woman who would be my supervisor was my former wife from India. After the meeting I walked up to her and said:

"So happy to see you again. What's your name?"

"Carol," she answered while backing away in shock at what was said.

"See you tomorrow," was my response while turning to leave.

The next day Carol came in with one of the strangest expressions, both terror and curiosity. It was as if she wanted to run away but ask questions at the same time. I walked up to her and asked: "Carol is there something you want to ask me?"

Looking down and in a squeaky voice she said: "No…well maybe." There was a long pause. "Did we know each other in India?"

"Yes"

"Oh NO!!! Were we married?"

"Yes"

"OH MY GOD! Did we have children?"

"Yes, five."

Then in a squeakier and higher voice, "Three girls and two boys?"

I nodded. "Did you have a dream last night?" I asked.

"I don't want to talk about it!!!! What was my favorite color sari?"

"Orange."

"Oh no! I don't want to talk about it!!!!!!!"

Slowly I was able to pull out of her the previous night she had a dream. It was a total recall of our past life together. The karmic connection was obvious. We had something we needed to complete together.

Needless to say, we started going together. She who was brought up as a black Baptist and had no knowledge of reincarnation before our meeting. She had heard the terms but never considered it as something that could be real. This was a truly revolutionary change in her life.

Love,
Papa

Hello there,

Bit of a flashback since it is close to Christmas, but also a "Debby Downer" story about my worse Christmas. Taking you back to Rockford years and JJ.

As has been mentioned, Christmases were not the best of times in my life. Mom would try her best but being poor, gifts and celebrations were muted. Yet one Christmas was looking up to being one of my best, at least at first.

JJ and her mother were visiting friends in NYC during the Christmas break of our junior year. Mom invited them up for a pre-Christmas gathering. The plan was for them to drive up from NYC in a rental car and join us overnight. The guest room, my old child's room, with two beds was all prepared and the house cleaned up. Even the letter shop in the dining room was straightened out. We would have been actually able to eat on the dining table.

I had gone into the woods and found a nice pine. Cutting it down and dragging it to the house was no problem as there was little snow that year. I decorated it with great care. As I put on the traditional bubble lights all my thoughts were on JJ coming up. It was a mixture of feelings. She would see the old house and aged furniture, the poverty I grew up in was evident. Also, no matter how hard we cleaned, the stale cigarette smoke permeated many of the rooms. Still the joy I felt having my love be with me, even if only one evening, was overcoming any doubts.

A letter we had given them detailed instructions how to get to The Hill. Mom was looking forward to finally meeting JJ as she knew how much in love with her I was. She wanted to meet

JJ's mother in the hopes of developing a positive relationship, fully knowing that in the early days of our dating I had helped her focus on her classes, raising her grades. JJ's mother was not exactly positive about her daughter dating a white boy.

The day arrived when they were to drive up. I woke up to hear the forecast on the radio: snow! We called JJ and her mother at their hotel. They would wait to see how bad the snow was before driving up to the hills of northwestern Connecticut. The storm was getting worse. Two hours later they called. The snow was still coming down hard, even in NYC. As much as twelve inches, possibly more were predicted. I pleaded with her mother to make an effort, but coming from DC which rarely has as much snow, she was unsure of the driving conditions. They had to cancel. I talked to JJ telling her how much I loved her and would miss her. Then I hung up the phone with the realization the ideal Christmas was not to be.

Thus on the evening of December 23rd, with tears welling up in my eyes, I started to take off the bulbs and decorations of the tree which had been so carefully decorated just a few days before. To me that Christmas was over. Mom watched but said nothing, realizing the mental anguish I was experiencing. By the time I started to unscrew the bubble lights, the tears were blurring my sight. Constantly wiping both eyes and nose, the last of the lights were carefully stored away, while I sat in total despair. Not even my tradition of playing the recording of *Mr. Pickwick's Christmas Party* with Charles Laughton nor *A Christmas Carol* with Ronald Coleman on the other on the other side was heard. To me there would be no Christmas this year.

Mom watched the final parts of the celebration being taken down without a word. Looking back it was selfish of me to deprive her of a Christmas tree just two days short of the holiday. Yet she knew how much I was looking forward to JJ joining us, even for one night. After I was finished she quietly slipped into the kitchen to have dinner by herself.

No dinner for me. No joy that usually accompanied watching the snow come down. Just a long cry into my pillow until sleep overtook me.

Though cried out, the next few days were shrouded by my depression. JJ and her mother made it back to DC and her father. We called them briefly on Christmas Day. But when the call was completed, it just set the tears to rolling once again. This was undoubtedly my worse Christmas.

Sorry for a depressing letter so close to Christmas, but it was this season that brought back the memory and was a catalyst for this flashback.

Love,
Papa

Sent From Philadelphia (I have a talk up here).

Hello T,

A sad, amusing and funny mix—back-flash to before graduation:

At Mott Haven help was always needed with homework and supervising the kids. The former more in the afternoons and elementary students. The latter more in the evening with high school age teens.

I started elementary art classes, teaching color theory, basic elements of drawing, color wheels, and whatever else the kids wanted. A young Puerto Rican named Juan loved art. He was my prize student initially. He started hanging out with me as much as he could while in the center.

In July he went missing, along with his best friend George. We searched the neighborhood and asked around. No luck. After about a week, the police notified us that the bodies of two young boys were pulled out of the East River. They were identified as Juan and George. Both had been killed and thrown into the river, but by the time they were found their bodies were bloated and malformed. This was my real introduction to the South Bronx. We could only speculate. They must have witnesses a drug deal or pissed off one the gangs. Their murder was never solved and didn't even make the news. Just another day in the South Bronx.

This being the summer months, the thesis required for graduation was not finished. Ed wanted to discuss the latest draft with me so I planned to drive up in Mom's car. I asked Carol if she would like to see the college and New Hampshire. Of course she wanted to—any excuse to get out of the city.

One weekend we took the bus to Connecticut, then drove the car up to Franconia. I dropped off Carol at the college/hotel after introducing her to William who had first met her in NYC. Then Ed and I met for 90 minutes at his house. Carol was shown around the building by William. I caught up with them shortly after leaving Ed's house.

Since it was summer, I asked her if she would like to cool off in the swimming pool. She brought a swimsuit, and I think it was Ted who let her change in her girls dorm room. When she reappeared she asked if I'd brought a suit. I responded:

"How many swimsuits do you see in the pool?"

She looked. Her eyes widened. Everyone was naked, even the two girls. I took off my clothes and jumped in. She jumped in after. She confessed later that she was too busy looking at all the exposed cocks. She had only seen three before in her life. Seeing a dozen or more nude men fully exposed was a totally new experience. Of course all were shrunk due to the VERY cold water in the outdoor pool. She admitted enjoying the sight. I told her how after each soccer game the team would strip off their clothes and jump into the pool if it was still early tall or late spring. Other times it would be too cold.

The pool was never drained as it was the water source should a fire start in the building. It was always interesting to see visiting team's reaction. Some would join us, especially if the two girls on the team stripped and jumped in the pool. The only team that didn't even consider it was the very conservative team with the former Marine.

After we drove up to William's house to spend the night. Williams parents were in Florida so there was no problem with Carol spending the night. I don't remember anything specific, but we must have played backgammon and listened to classical music. Of course Carol and I made love, since we knew that William would not interrupt by making a phone call.

Something happened in June which had a significant impact on me later. A series of meetings sponsored by the Administration on Ageing (AoA) part of Health, Education, and Welfare (before Education was separated) were scheduled to discuss issues concerning the elderly. Littleton New Hampshire was looking for breakout group leaders and recorders for each group. Ed was to lead the Spiritual Needs discussion group, and he called me to ask me to be the recorder. He thought it would be a good opportunity, especially since I was very interested in geriatrics.

In early June we drove to Littleton North Country AoA sessions. Ed was right, it would prove valuable. We were introduced as coming from Franconia College. You must realize the college was referred to by the Manchester Union Leader, the major state newspaper, and the governor as "the little house of sin on the hill."

Ed being conservatively dressed for the occasion looked normal. As for me I wore nice clothes but my hair was still down to my shoulder blades. Most of the participants were elderly.

I diligently took notes and followed up on any motions or suggestions that had not be well formulated for a final submission. There was a Federal representative from Boston's AoA. He was quite interested in they way I would lead the discussion to conclusions that could be forwarded to AoA. He would come into my life a few years later when pursuing a degree at Boston University's School of Social Work.

There was one 30-year-old woman who looked at me in terror as if I was a bloodthirsty monster. I ignored her until the luncheon break. During one break the woman ventured up to me and asked: "Are you really from THAT college?"

"If you mean Franconia, yes."

She then asked: "Is it true that the keep sheep in the dorms to allow the men to satisfy themselves in the evenings?"

This was just so outlandish it deserved an appropriate reply: "Madam there are NO sheep in the dorms... but the pigs are delightful."

Needless to say she kept as far away from me as possible for the rest of the sessions. By the way one of the teachers did have a farm with sheep. NO they were not used in any other way than for wool.

Love,
Papa

Hi T,

Finally, after all the re-writes and bottles of white out, Ed accepted my undergraduate thesis. I was awarded my B.A. from Franconia College, Franconia, New Hampshire, something that in itself was a rarity as the college was not going to survive much longer. I drove up to the half year graduation ceremony. Though not formally mentioned, since I was listed as a graduate the previous June, I was able to see some of other of my friends receive their BAs. It was a very small ceremony. Carol was with me.

After the ceremony Leon and Ed formally presented me with my BA in sociology. Thus, my undergraduate work was completed. Now I was worried about getting into graduate school. Ed agreed he would recommend me. So would Leon if needed. I was thankful for requesting grades in all my classes. Must say I was close to a 3.8 GPA the last year in Franconia. I was proud of the courses completed, the committee membership, the fire drill team, the soccer team and almost all the other experiences in Franconia. It was a good experience, one sorely needed after the negative experiences at Rockford. What also pleased me was the outsmarting of Rockford's President Howard.

Of course all my classmates at Rockford had graduated. I tried to keep up with JJ but once I left she turned towards a different path. Within a few months of her senior year, I was mostly forgotten. However, she did tell me years later the other black women on campus treated her like she had leprosy. They refused to accept her because she had been dating a white boy for her first three years.

As for Tom, Kirk, they both graduated. Kirk went on to get his Ph.D. in organic chemistry. He had been dating another chemistry major at Rockford. She went on to get a Ph.D. in inorganic chemistry. They were married somewhere between their degrees. Kirk got a job doing research in the Mid West, I think. She at an Eastern university teaching (what else can you do with a degree in inorganic chemistry?). Their long-distance marriage worked as Kirk's wife got her pilot's license and would fly to Kirk every weekend.

Tom applied to various graduate library programs. He was accepted Case Western. The only problem was being 1A in the draft and a high number. Sure enough late in the summer he was drafted. When he was notified to show up to be inducted. He rushed to the Air Force recruiters. They were more than welcoming. He was an honor roll student. He had been accepted into graduate school. They accept him for possible officer's candidate training. His draft board was notified he was going into the Air Force so no further action was needed. He asked the Air Force if he could continue by starting his graduate work. They approved, telling him when they needed him, they would call him for induction. By the time Tom finished his MLS (Master's in Library Science) the Viet Nam war was over. The Air Force simply forgot to call him up. Thus he avoided military service all together.

As for me, I forgot to tell you that while in Rockford, I took a weekend off to become an official draft counselor. It was an excellent weekend. When I got back to Rockford, any of the men who wanted draft advice came to me. Of course this just pissed off the administration even more. Just another straw leading to my being kicked out. At Franconia, much of the same advice was freely handed out.

After taking the draft counseling course, one day while lying on my bed at Franconia, I was reviewing all the deferments. Knowing graduation was coming up soon, something had to be found to keep me out of the war. While reviewing all the categories I realized my extreme flat feet might be good for a 4F deferment. I was actually about to complete the letter to my draft board to ask for a 4F using my flat feet as the justification, when I reread the qualifications for 4A. This was a deferment for a veteran. But one of the clauses stated "and the sole surviving son of a deceased veteran, who died from war injuries." My father had died of a heart attack. He had been dismissed from the Army during WWII for hypertension.

I wrote my draft board requesting a 4A deferment. The argument was simple. My dad got hypertension while servicing in the Army. He died of a heart attack, which though happening years later was a direct result of that hypertension. It was a shot in the dark. I really didn't think it would work.

About a month later, I received in the mail a new draft card 4A. IT WAS ACCEPTED! My first reaction: I couldn't believe they had bought it. Yes my letter had been serious and logical, but it was still mostly bull shit. Hooray! Never was sure if it was due to my letter or the fact all on the draft board knew my mother. She had done work for most of them. She knew what I was attempting. She may have applied a little pressure of her own. Never was sure. Never asked. All that mattered was I would be out of the war and could pursue whatever life I wanted.

I asked East Side Settlement if I could continue to be housed in their top floor while volunteering at Mott Haven Community Center. They accepted. Since Carol and I were going steady and then some, they were more than accommodating since she spoke highly of my interactions with the kids at the center.

Now with a B.A. in hand and hopes for an independent life it was back to NYC. Now all I had to do was to find a job. In 1971 that was not easy. Still it would be the start of a new phase of my life. Being in the South Bronx was a major challenge. Carol would help. The volunteer work would keep be busy. Graduating from a non-traditional college would a graduate school accept me? How would I pay for it? What was missing was income. Jobs and New York were an adventure leading to a variety of experiences, a master's degree, and different vocations. All of which would come to a dramatic end as NYC would face bankruptcy five years later, forcing me to leave the city.

After NYC would be another lifetime of drama. But for now where could I find a job, and what would it be? Would the horoscope prediction of contributions to the Department of Defense come true? Certainly not in New York. Where else could I find a job? All these thoughts were racing through my mind as I packed up and got ready for a move. To my birth city. To the first phase of an adult life.

Love,
Papa

PHOTOS

Visions of Mom
In the 30's after the Divorce

In the 20's possibly at Sarsfield's mother's funeral

Mom & Sug in bathing suits
Sarsfield's shadow below

Mom on sunny day

The Texas siblings
Lavern, Sug Forest, Mom

Dad doting over infant son

Loving being in mother's arms

Uncle Bill & Aunt Margaret

Joint venture to
park with Uncle
Bill & Dad

My 1st Birthday cake
Dad holding it up for photo

Asleep in dad's arms

Mom & Dad on the Hill

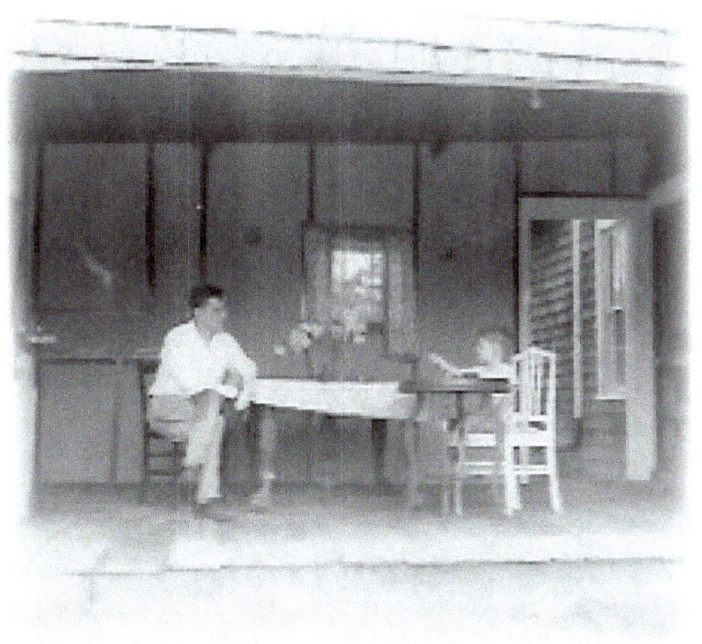

Dad & me on breezeway

At petting zoon
Catskill Game Farm

In snow on front yard

About to go down THE Hill

Age 12, taken by Robert Moore, co-founder of Sheraton Hotels

From the infield at Limerock Race Track

Phony cigarette ad for Ruth

Senior Prom with Terri

Huber H. Humprey the day before the election

Mohamed Ali (left) at Humprey rally

JJ at end of Freshman year
Worried about being separated over the summer

Acknowledgements

THANKS GOES OUT TO my oldest daughter "T" who suggested an autobiography in the form of letters be sent to her during her undergraduate experiences. She had heard of many experiences retold in It's Me The Early Years and encouraged the letters take the form of an autobiography. Included were biographical notes on her grandmother and her experiences growing up in Texas and New Mexico and her challenges.

To my mother, who during the last years of her life lived in an in-law apartment. We would go over most of the early life experiences and refresh my earliest memories, as well as her own, previous to her death. It was through these conversations where many of the incidents contained in this book were recollected and elaborated upon. Also to Mr. Schall who drew me when I was eight years old over several sessions and is the cover of the book.

To Marie Deraismes Lodge #352 Le Droit Humain, in NYC, where I was baptized, accepted, and learned the moral and spiritual lessons which have been retained all my life. Even after leaving Le Droit Humain to join what is considered regular Freemasonry, they continue as a guide.

Special thanks to initial editor, Tatiana Wilde who helped with the original manuscript and her encouragement.

Finally both my wives. My first for delivering two brilliant daughters who have grown up to be successful professionals. To my current wife for putting up with hours and hours of writing efforts.

www.ingramcontent.com/pod-product-compliance
Lightning Source LLC
Chambersburg PA
CBHW080946120626
46546CB00010B/2854